QuickBooks® Pro 2004

A Complete Course

JANET HORNE, M.S.
Los Angeles Pierce College

PEARSON

Prentice Hall

Upper Saddle River, NJ 07458

**To my husband and our sons
with thanks for their support, patience, and understanding**

Senior Managing Editor: Alana Bradley
Editor-in-Chief: Jeff Shelstad
Assistant Editor: Sam Goffinet
Senior Editorial Assistant: Jane Avery
Executive Marketing Manager: Beth Toland
Marketing Assistant: Melissa Owens
Managing Editor (Production): John Roberts
Manufacturing Buyer: Michelle Klein
Manufacturing Supervisor: Arnold Vila
Senior Media Project Manager: Nancy Welcher
Media Project Manager: Caroline Kasterine
Design Manager: Maria Lange
Cover Design: Kiwi Design
Cover Illustration/Photo: Victoria Pearson / Getty Images, Inc.
Printer/Binder: Courier–Westford

Microsoft® and Windows® are registered trademarks of the Microsoft Corporation in the U.S.A. and other countries. Screen shots and icons reprinted with permission from the Microsoft Corporation. This book is not sponsored or endorsed by or affiliated with the Microsoft Corporation.

Pearson Education LTD.
Pearson Education Singapore, Pte. Ltd
Pearson Education, Canada, Ltd
Pearson Education–Japan

Pearson Education Australia PTY, Limited
Pearson Education North Asia Ltd
Pearson Educación de Mexico, S.A. de C.V.
Pearson Education Malaysia, Pte. Ltd.

10 9 8 7 6 5 4 3 2
ISBN 0-13-147779-X

TABLE OF CONTENTS

Page

Preface..*xiii*

Chapter 1—Introduction to Computers and QuickBooks® Pro
Computers Have Become a Way of Life 1
Introduction to Computer Hardware 1
Introduction to Software 4
Manual Versus Computerized Accounting 5
System Requirements for QuickBooks® Pro 2004 6
Versions Of QuickBooks® 2004 6
How to Open QuickBooks® Pro 2004 7
How to Open a Company 7
Verify an Open Company 9
Introduction to QuickBooks® Pro Desktop Features 9
QuickBooks® Navigators 10
Menu Commands 12
Keyboard Shortcuts 14
Keyboard Conventions 16
Icon bar 18
On-Screen Help 18
QuickBooks® Pro Forms 20
QuickBooks® Pro Lists 23
QuickBooks® Pro Registers 25
QuickBooks® Pro Reports 26
QuickZoom 27
QuickBooks® Pro Graphs 27
QuickReport 29
How to Use QuickMath 30
How to Use Windows® Calculator 30
Access Windows® Calculator Through QuickBooks® Pro 31
How to Close a Company 31
How to Copy a File 32
How to Create a QuickBooks® Pro Backup File 32
Create a Duplicate Disk 35
How to Exit QuickBooks® Pro and End Your Work Session 35
End-of-Chapter Questions 36

Chapter 2—Sales and Receivables: Service Business
Accounting for Sales and Receivables 40
Training Tutorial 41
Training Procedures 41
Company Profile: Contempo Computer Consulting (CCC) 42
Begin Training in QuickBooks® Pro 42
How to Open QuickBooks® Pro 42
Open a Company—Contempo Computer Consulting (CCC) 43
Verifying an Open Company 44
Add Your Name to the Company Name 44
QuickBooks® Navigators 45
Beginning the Tutorial 46
Enter Sales on Account 47
Edit and Correct Errors 50
Print an Invoice 52
Enter Transactions Using Two Sales Items 53
Print an Invoice 54
Print A/R Reports 57

Use the QuickZoom Feature 59
Correct an Invoice and Print the Corrected Form 61
View a QuickReport 64
Void and Delete Sales Forms: 65
Prepare Credit Memos 71
View Customer Balance Detail Report 73
Add a New Account to the Chart of Accounts 74
Add New Items to List 76
Add a New Customer 77
Modify Customer Records 81
Record Cash Sales 82
Print Sales Receipt 84
Print Sales by Customer Detail Report 86
Correct a Sales Receipt and Print the Corrected Form 88
View a QuickReport 90
Analyze Sales 91
Record Customer Payments on Account 93
View Transactions by Customer 97
Deposit Checks Received for Cash Sales and Payments on Account 98
Print Journal 100
Print the Trial Balance 101
Graphs in QuickBooks® Pro 102
Prepare Accounts Receivable Graphs 102
Use QuickZoom Feature to Obtain Individual Customer Details 105
Prepare Sales Graphs 106
Use QuickZoom to View an Individual Item or Customer 107
Back Up and Close Company 108
End-of-Chapter Questions 111

Chapter 3—Payables and Purchases: Service Business

Accounting for Payables and Purchases 120
Enter a Bill 123
Edit and Correct Errors 125
Print Transaction by Vendor Report 129
Use the QuickZoom Feature 131
Enter a Bill Using the Accounts Payable Register 134
Edit a Transaction in the Accounts Payable Register 137
Preview and Print a QuickReport from the Accounts Payable Register 139
Prepare Unpaid Bills Detail Report 140
Delete a Bill 141
Add a New Vendor While Recording a Bill 143
Modify Vendor Records 146
Enter a Credit from a Vendor 146
View Credit in Accounts Payable Register 148
Paying Bills 149
Printing Checks for Bills 152
Review Bills That Have Been Paid 153
Petty Cash 154
Add Petty Cash Account to the Chart of Accounts 154
Establish Petty Cash Fund 155
Record Payment of an Expense Using Petty Cash 156
Pay Bills by Writing Checks 158
Edit Checks 161
Void Checks 162
Delete Checks 163
Print Checks 165

CONTENTS

Prepare Check Detail Report 167
View Missing Check Report 169
Purchase an Asset with a Company Check 170
Customize Report Format 172
Print Accounts Payable Aging Summary 174
Print Unpaid Bills Detail Report 175
Print Vendor Balance Summary 176
View a QuickReport for a Vendor 177
Create an Accounts Payable Graph by Aging Period 178
Use QuickZoom to View Graph Details 179
End-of-Chapter Questions 181

Chapter 4—General Accounting and End-of-Period Procedures: Service Business

General Accounting and End-of-Period Procedures 189
Change the Name of Existing Accounts in the Chart of Accounts 191
Effect of an Account Name Change on Subaccounts 193
Make an Account Inactive 194
Delete an Existing Account from the Chart of Accounts 195
Adjustments for Accrual-Basis Accounting 196
Adjusting Entries—Prepaid Expenses 197
Adjusting Entries—Depreciation 200
View General Journal 201
Owner Withdrawals 202
Additional Cash Investment by Owner 205
Noncash Investment by Owner 206
View Balance Sheet 207
Bank Reconciliation 208
Adjusting and Correcting Entries—Bank Reconciliation 213
Print a Reconciliation Report 218
View the Checking Account Register 218
Edit Cleared Transactions 219
View the Journal 220
Prepare Trial Balance 221
Use QuickZoom in Trial Balance 222
Print the Trial Balance 222
Select Accrual-Basis Reporting Preference 223
Prepare and Print Cash Flow Forecast 224
Statement of Cash Flows 225
Print Standard Profit and Loss Statement 227
Print Standard Balance Sheet 228
Adjustment to Transfer Net Income/Retained Earnings into Brian Colbert, Capital 229
Print Standard Balance Sheet 231
Print Journal 233
Exporting Reports to Excel 233
End-of-Period Backup 235
Passwords 236
Set the Closing Date for the Period 237
Access Transaction for Previous Period 237
Edit Transaction from Previous Period 238
Print Post-Closing Trial Balance 240
Print Post-Closing Profit and Loss Statement 241
Print Post-Closing Balance Sheet 242
End-of-Chapter Questions 246

Help 4 You Practice Set: Service Business

Help 4 You Practice Set: Service Business 255

Chapter 5—Sales and Receivables: Merchandising Business

Accounting for Sales and Receivables in a Merchandising Business 266
Company Profile: Year Round Sports 267
Open a Company—Year Round Sports 268
Add Your Name to the Company Name 265
Customize Report Format 270
Customize Business Forms 272
Enter Sales on Account 274
Edit and Correct Errors 276
Print an Invoice 277
Enter Transactions Using More Than One Sales Item and Sales Tax 278
E-Mail Invoices 280
Enter a Transaction Exceeding a Customer's Credit Limit and Add a Word to the Spelling Dictionary 283
Accounts Receivable Reports 284
Prepare Customer Balance Detail Report 285
Use the QuickZoom Feature 286
Correct an Invoice and Print the Corrected Form 286
Adding New Accounts to the Chart of Accounts 288
Add New Items to List 288
Correct an Invoice to Include Sales Discount 292
View a QuickReport 294
Add a New Customer 295
Record a Sale to a New Customer 297
Modify Customer Records 302
Void and Delete Sales Forms 303
Prepare Credit Memos 307
Print Open Invoices by Customer Report 309
Record Cash Sales with Sales Tax 311
Print Sales Receipt 313
Entering a Credit Card Sale 314
Record Sales Paid by Check 315
Print Summary Sales by Item Report 318
Correct a Sales Receipt and Print the Corrected Form 319
View a QuickReport 321
Analyze the QuickReport for Cash Customer 322
View Sales Tax Payable Register 323
Record Customer Payments on Account 324
Record Customer Payment on Account and Apply Credit 325
Record Payment on Account from a Customer Qualifying for an Early Payment Discount 327
View Transaction List by Customer 331
Print Customer Balance Summary 332
Deposit Checks and Credit Cards Receipts for Cash Sales and Payments on Account 332
Record the Return of a Check Because of Nonsufficient Funds 334
Issue a Credit Memo and a Refund Check 338
Print Journal 340
Print the Trial Balance 341
Customer Center 342
Customer Detail Center 343
Graphs in QuickBooks® Pro 344
Prepare Accounts Receivable Graphs 344
Prepare Sales Graphs 345
Back Up Year Round Sports Data 346
End-of-Chapter Questions 348

Chapter 6—Payables and Purchases: Merchandising Business

Accounting for Payables and Purchases 358
View the Reminders List to Determine Merchandise to Order 360
Print the Reminders List 362
Customize Purchase Orders 362
Purchase Orders 363
Verify Purchase Orders Active as a Company Preference 363
Prepare Purchase Orders to Order Merchandise 364
Prepare a Purchase Order for More Than One Item 365
View Purchase Orders List 368
Change Minimum Reorder Limits for an Item 369
View Effect of Reorder Point on Reminders List 370
View Stock Status by Item Inventory Report 371
Print a Purchase Order QuickReport 372
Receiving Items Ordered 373
Record Receipt of Items Not Accompanied by a Bill 373
Verify That Purchase Order Is Marked Received in Full 375
Enter Receipt of a Bill for Items Already Received 376
Record Receipt of Items and a Bill 378
Edit a Purchase Order 379
Record a Partial Receipt of Merchandise Ordered 380
Close Purchase Order Manually 381
Enter a Credit from a Vendor 382
Make a Purchase Using a Credit Card 384
Pay for Inventory Items on Order Using a Credit Card 386
Enter Bills 388
Change Existing Vendors' Terms 391
Enter a Bill Using the Accounts Payable Register 393
Edit a Transaction in the Accounts Payable Register 394
Preview and Print a QuickReport from the Accounts Payable Register 395
Prepare and Print Unpaid Bills Report 397
Paying Bills 398
Pay a Bill Qualifying for a Purchase Discount and Apply Credit as Part of Payment 400
Print Checks to Pay Bills 402
Pay Bills Using a Credit Card 404
Sales Tax 406
Print Sales Tax Liability Report 407
Paying Sales Tax 408
Voiding and Deleting Purchase Orders, Bills, Checks, and Credit Card Payments 409
Vendor Detail Center 409
Create an Accounts Payable Graph by Aging Period 411
End-of-Chapter Questions 413

Chapter 7—General Accounting and End-of-Period Procedures: Merchandising Business

General Accounting and End-of-Period Procedures 422
Change the Name of Existing Accounts in the Chart of Accounts 424
Make an Account Inactive 425
Delete an Existing Account from the Chart of Accounts 426
Fixed Asset Management 427
Adjustments for Accrual-Basis Accounting 429
View Profit and Loss Statement to Determine Need for an Adjustment to Purchases Discounts 434
Adjusting Entry to Transfer Purchases Discounts Income to Cost of Goods Sold 435
Prepare Profit and Loss Statement 436
View General Journal 437
Definition of a Partnership 438
Owner Withdrawals 439
Prepare Balance Sheet 441

Transfer Combined Capital into an Individual Capital Account for Each Owner 442
Distribute Capital to Each Owner 445
Bank Reconciliation 446
View the Checking Account Register 454
Credit Card Reconciliation 455
Record an Adjustment to a Reconciliation 457
Undo a Previous Reconciliation, Delete an Adjustment, and Redo a Reconciliation 459
View the Journal 463
Prepare Trial Balance 464
Use QuickZoom in Trial Balance 465
Print the Trial Balance 466
Select Accrual Basis Reporting Preference 466
Print Standard Profit and Loss Statement 467
Adjustment to Transfer Net Income/Retained Earnings into Eric Boyd, Capital, and Matthew Wayne, Capital 470
Print Standard Balance Sheet 472
Close Drawing and Transfer into Owners' Capital Accounts 473
Exporting Reports to Excel 475
Importing Data from Excel 476
Print Journal 477
End-of-Period Backup 477
Passwords 478
Access Transaction for Previous Period 479
Edit Transaction from Previous Period 480
Inventory Adjustments 482
Adjust the Journal Entry for Net Income/Retained Earnings 483
Print Post-Closing Trial Balance 484
Print Post-Closing Profit and Loss Statement 485
Print Post-Closing Balance Sheet 486
End-of-Chapter Questions 489

Desert Golf Shop Practice Set: Merchandising Business

Desert Golf Shop Practice Set: Merchandising Business 500

Chapter 8—Payroll

Payroll 514
Select a Payroll Option 516
Create Paychecks 516
Print Paychecks 523
Change Employee Information 524
Add a New Employee 525
View Checks, Make Corrections, and Print Checks Individually 531
Voiding and Deleting Checks 532
Payroll Summary Report 534
Prepare the Employee Earnings Summary Report 535
Payroll Liability Balances Report 535
Pay Taxes and Other Liabilities 536
File Payroll Tax Forms 538
Prepare and Print Form 941 and Schedule B 538
Prepare and Print Form 940 543
Prepare and Preview Employee's W-2 Forms 546
End-of-Chapter Questions 549

Chapter 9—Computerizing a Manual Accounting System

Computerizing a Manual System 560
Company Profile: Movies & More 561
Create a New Company 561
The EasyStep Interview 562

General Section of the Interview 563
Welcome Topic 563
Company Info Topic 565
Preferences Topic 575
Start Date 576
Income & Expenses Section 577
Income Accounts Topic 578
Expense Accounts Topic 579
Income Details Section 581
Introduction Topic 582
Items Topic 582
Inventory Topic 586
Opening Balances Section 589
Customers Topic 589
Vendors Topic 591
Accounts Topic 592
What's Next Section 599
Preferences 600
Chart of Accounts 604
Customer Information 606
Vendor Information 607
Employees 609
Complete The Payroll Setup Interview 609
Add Employees Using Employee Template 617
Add Year-to-Date Amounts 624
Adjusting Entries 629
Specifying a Company Logo 631
Customize Forms 635
Customizing Reports 637
End-of-Chapter Questions 640

Capital Books Practice Set: Comprehensive Problem

Capital Books Practice Set: Comprehensive Problem 652

Appendix A: Introduction to Windows®—Screens, Terminology, and Disk Duplication

Introduction to Windows® 672
How to Use a Mouse 677
Mouse Terminology 677
Duplicating a Disk 678
How To Create A QuickBooks® Pro Backup File 681
How To Restore A QuickBooks® Pro Backup File 683
How to Close or Shut Down Windows® 685

Appendix B: QuickBooks Integration with Microsoft® Word and Excel

QuickBooks Letters 687
Exporting Reports to Excel 693
Importing Data from Excel 695

Appendix C: QuickBooks® Features: Notes, Time Tracking, Job Costing and Tracking, and Price Levels

QuickBooks Notes 696
Tracking Time 700
Job Costing and Tracking 705
Sending Invoices Through QuickBooks' Mailing Service 710
Sending Merchandise Using QuickBooks' Shipping Manager 711
Price Levels 712

Appendix D: QuickBooks® Pro Online Features

Intuit and the Internet.. 716
Downloading a Trial Version of QuickBooks® Pro 716
QuickBooks® Pro Updates.. 717
Connecting to the Internet in QuickBooks® Pro 719
Access QuickBooks® Online Features.. 722
Online Banking and Payments.. 724
Personalized Web Site and Domain Name 732
QuickBooks Credit Check Services.. 733
QuickBooks Billing Solutions 734
QuickBooks Merchant Services.. 738
Online Backup Services.. 741
Direct Deposit... 742

Index... 743

PREFACE

QuickBooks® Pro 2004: A Complete Course is a comprehensive instructional learning resource. This text has been designed to respond to the growing trend toward adopting Windows applications and computerizing accounting systems. As a result of this trend, the text provides training using *Windows® XP* and the popular *QuickBooks® Pro 2004* accounting program. The text was written using Windows XP and QuickBooks® Pro 2004 but may be used with Windows 95/98/2000 and QuickBooks® Basic or Premier versions.

ORGANIZATIONAL FEATURES

QuickBooks® Pro 2004: A Complete Course is designed to present accounting concepts and their relationship to *QuickBooks® Pro 2004.* In addition to accounting concepts, students use a fictitious company and receive hands-on training in the use of *QuickBooks® Pro 2004* within each chapter. At the end of every chapter, the concepts and applications learned are reinforced by the completion of true/false, multiple-choice, fill-in, and essay questions plus an application problem using a different fictitious company. There are three practices sets in the text that utilize all the major concepts and transactions presented within an area of study. The third practice set is comprehensive and utilizes all the major concepts and transactions presented within the entire textbook.

The text introduces students to the computer, Windows, and QuickBooks accounting for a service business, a merchandising business, payroll, and company setup for QuickBooks. The appendices review Windows, disk duplication; back up files, and file restoration. QuickBooks Integration using Word and Excel; QuickBooks Features including QuickBooks Notes, Time Tracking, Job Costing, and Price Levels; and QuickBooks Online including online updates, Internet connection, payroll services, downloading a trial version of the software, online banking and payments, personalized web sites and domain names, credit check services, billing solutions, merchant services, online billing, online credit card billing, online backup services, and direct deposit.

DISTINGUISHING FEATURES

Throughout the text, emphasis has been placed on the use of QuickBooks' innovative approach to recording accounting transactions based on a business form rather than using the traditional journal format. This approach, however, has been correlated to traditional accounting through adjusting entries, end-of-period procedures, and use of the "behind the scenes" journal.

Unlike many other computerized accounting programs, QuickBooks is user-friendly when corrections and adjustments are required. The ease of corrections and the ramifications as a result of this ease are explored thoroughly.

Accounting concepts and the use of *QuickBooks® Pro 2004* are reinforced throughout the text with the use of graphics that show completed transactions, reports, and QuickBooks screens. The text helps students transition from textbook transaction analysis to "real-world" transaction analysis.

The text provides extensive assignment material in the form of tutorials; end-of-chapter questions (true/false, multiple-choice, fill-in, and essay); practice sets for a service business, a merchandising business, and a comprehensive practice set.

Students develop confidence in recording business transactions using an up-to-date commercial software program designed for small to mid-size businesses. With thorough exploration of the program in the text, students should be able to use *QuickBooks® Pro 2004* in a "real world situation" at the completion of the textbook training.

Students will explore and use many of the features of QuickBooks as it pertains to a service business and a merchandising business, including recording transactions, preparing a multitude of reports, closing an accounting period, compiling charts and graphs, creating a company, and preparing the payroll. The transactions entered by students become more complex as they progress through the text. Students also learn ways in which QuickBooks can be customized to fit the needs of an individual company.

COURSES
QuickBooks® Pro 2004: A Complete Course is designed for a one-term course in microcomputer accounting, but can be used for a short-term course. This text covers a service business, a merchandising business, a sole proprietorship, a partnership, payroll, and company setup to use QuickBooks. For a short course in microcomputer accounting or for use in any accounting course requiring introductory work on an integrated computerized accounting package *QuickBooks® Pro 2004: An Introduction* may be used. It focuses on using QuickBooks Pro in a service business and includes payroll and a practice set. When using either text, students should be familiar with the accounting cycle and how it is related to a business. No prior knowledge of or experience with computers, Windows, or QuickBooks is required; however, an understanding accounting is essential to successful completion of the coursework.

SUPPLEMENTS FOR THE INSTRUCTOR
Instructor's Manual and Teaching Guide with Tests is a comprehensive answer key to all the questions, the exercises, the exams, and the practice sets. All computer assignments are printed in full and included for use in grading or as a student answer key. In addition to answers to text assignments, the *Instructor's Manual and Teaching Guide with Tests* for *QuickBooks® Pro 2004: A Complete Course* contains master data files for all the companies in the text, backup company files for each chapter that may be restored to a QuickBooks company file, a sample syllabus/course outline, lectures for each chapter, written exams for each area of study, a written final exam, an exam for each practice set, and suggestions for grading. Instructor materials include a lecture outline for each chapter with a hands-on demonstration lecture, the answers to the end-of-chapter questions, transmittal sheets that include the totals of reports and documents, and excel files for all the reports prepared in the text.

ACKNOWLEDGMENTS

I wish to thank my colleagues for testing and reviewing the manuscript and my students for providing me with a special insight into problems encountered in training. Their comments and suggestions are greatly appreciated. A special thank you goes to Alana Bradley, Sandra Dubin, and Bill Todd for their help and assistance with the text.

INTRODUCTION TO COMPUTERS AND QUICKBOOKS® PRO 2004

LEARNING OBJECTIVES

At the completion of this chapter, you will be able to:

1. Turn on your computer, open and close Windows, and open and close QuickBooks Pro.
2. Recognize system requirements for using QuickBooks Pro and Windows.
3. Use a mouse.
4. Identify QuickBooks Pro desktop features and understand the QuickBooks Navigator.
5. Recognize menu commands and use some keyboard shortcuts.
6. Open, copy, back up, and close a company on disk.
7. Recognize QuickBooks Pro forms and understand the use of lists and registers in QuickBooks Pro.
8. Access QuickBooks Pro reports and be familiar with QuickZoom.
9. Prepare QuickBooks Pro graphs and use QuickReport within graphs.
10. Use QuickMath and the Windows Calculator.

COMPUTERS HAVE BECOME A WAY OF LIFE

In today's world, computers are appearing in many different places—from the desktop in the home or office to someone's lap on an airplane or at a sporting event. No longer is a computer simply a large, bulky piece of equipment used for "crunching numbers." Computers are used to process documents such as letters, memos, and reports; to perform financial planning and forecasting; to draw pictures, and design equipment; to store and print photographs, to play games and music; and, of course, to keep the financial records of a company. A computer system is actually a group of hardware components that work together with software to perform a specific task. The steps involved in the processing cycle are input, processing, output, and storage.

INTRODUCTION TO COMPUTER HARDWARE

"Computer hardware" refers to the equipment used as part of a computer system. While there are several computer classifications, this text will focus on the personal computer and its use in computerized accounting applications.

The hardware components used in today's computer system are as follows:

Input Devices

Input devices are used to enter data or commands into the computer. Essentially, during the input process the computer receives information coded in electrical pulses that indicate an on or an off state. The electrical pulses are called bits, which stands for binary digit, indicating either the on or off electrical pulse. The bits are grouped into a series of eight pulses to form a byte. In essence, one byte is equal to one character typed on the keyboard.

As information is input, it is temporarily stored in the random access memory (RAM) of the computer. Program instructions are also stored temporarily in RAM. Even though it is a temporary storage area, RAM storage is measured in bytes (remember, one byte is equal to one keyboard character). Because of the graphics used in today's software programs, RAM storage must also be quite large and is usually in the range of 128 to 768 megabytes (a megabyte equals 1 million bytes and is abbreviated MB) or greater.

The most common input devices are the keyboard, the mouse, and a scanner. Of all the input devices, the keyboard is used most frequently. The keyboard allows the user to key in text, numbers, and other characters for use by the computer to process the data and provide information. Many times software commands or instructions are given via the keyboard.

Another popular input device, primarily used to give software commands, is the mouse. Many program instructions are given by pointing to an icon (picture) and clicking the primary (usually left) mouse button.

To input entire documents at once, a scanner can be used to scan the document and insert an image of the document into the computer.

Processing Devices

The data that have been input into the computer and the necessary

program instructions are sent to the central processing unit (CPU) for processing by the computer. The control unit of the CPU directs the transfer of information from RAM into the ALU (Arithmetic/Logic Unit). Using program instructions, the ALU performs the necessary mathematical and logical computations on the data and formulae entered. The results of processing are sent to RAM, and the control unit of the computer sends these results to output or storage devices.

Output Devices

As indicated, the result of processing is output. Output can be shown on the monitor, it can be printed on paper, and/or it can be stored on disk or other media. The most common output device is a monitor.

Output is frequently in the form of a printed or "hard" copy. Several types of printers are available for printing output. The two most common types of printers used are ink jet, which spray small droplets of ink on paper to create characters; and laser, which use a combination of a laser beam, static electricity, and ink toner to produce high-quality text.

Storage Devices

The most common storage device is a disk. The most common disk is a removable floppy disk that is 3½ inches wide. The amount of storage space is measured in bytes. Remember, one byte is equal to one keyboard character. Storage space is calculated exponentially, so 1 kilobyte (abbreviated K) of memory is 1,024 bytes. For ease in calculations, the storage capacity is rounded to the nearest thousand. A double-density 3½-inch disk holds a little over 720K, and a high-density 3½-inch disk holds more than 1.44MB. New types of disks that hold 100MB or more are currently on the market and are becoming popular. One form of storage is called Zip disks. Another is portable USB storage and is often called a flash drive or a jump drive. In addition to floppy disks, Zip disks, or USB disks, most computers have CD-ROMs as installed drives in computers. These may either be used to access information; and, in some cases, to store information.

Most computers have internal storage on a hard disk. These permanent disks hold a great deal of information inside the computer. Most of the hard-disk space is used to store software programs; however, data may also be stored on the hard disk. In a classroom environment data may be stored on the removable floppy disks, in an assigned storage space on the hard drive, or in an assigned storage space on the network. Storage space on a hard disk is also measured in bytes. Because of the size of the programs residing on it, the hard disk is becoming larger and larger. Hard disks are usually measured in gigabytes. (A gigabyte is approximately 1 billion bytes. The abbreviation for gigabyte is GB.)

INTRODUCTION TO SOFTWARE

Data can be keyed on the keyboard and sent to RAM, but the central processing unit will not know what to do with the data unless it is given instructions via a computer program. The computer programs are called software and are divided into two different categories—operating system software and application software.

Operating System Software

System software gives the computer basic operating instructions and is required no matter what application software is used. The operating system software allows data to be input using a keyboard. The operating system software sends the data and program instructions to the central processing unit for processing, and it allows the results of processing to be shown on the monitor, sent to the printer, or stored on a disk. In addition to being the controlling program for the computer, the operating system software is used for disk and file management and organization.

The most common operating environment is Windows. It uses the principle of a graphical user interface (GUI) with pictures or icons representing software programs, hardware, and commands. Windows receives instructions or commands when the user points to and clicks on an icon with a mouse. There are several versions of the Windows operating system in use.

There are many other operating systems on the market today. Most of the time you are working, you will not have much direct contact with the operating system; however, it is always important to know which system you are using.

Application Software

Application software is task-specific software. In other words, if you want to keep the books for a company, you use a program such as QuickBooks Pro to enter information regarding your business transactions and to produce your financial reports. If you want to type a term paper, a word processing program will be the application program to use. To do financial forecasting and perform "what if" scenarios, a spreadsheet program will be used. If you want to play a game of pinball using the computer, a computer game will be the application. Each application program is designed to respond to the commands you give. The way you send a particular command can vary from application to application.

In the Windows operating system, program commands may be given by pointing to an icon and clicking the primary (usually left) mouse button. For example, no matter what Windows program or application software you use, clicking on the picture of a printer sends a copy of your document to the printer, or it may take you to another screen on which you can set printing options.

One of the exciting features of Windows is OLE (object linking and embedding). OLE allows you to work with a document in one application program and retrieve it and use it in another program.

MANUAL VERSUS COMPUTERIZED ACCOUNTING

The work to be performed to keep the books for a business is the same whether you use a manual or a computerized accounting system. Transactions need to be analyzed, recorded in a journal, and posted to a ledger. Business documents such as invoices, checks, bank deposits, and credit/debit memos need to be prepared and distributed. Reports to management and owners for information and decision-making purposes need to be prepared. Records for one business period need to be closed before one moves to the next business period.

In a manual system, each transaction that is analyzed must be entered by hand into the appropriate journal (the book of original entry where all transactions are recorded) and posted to the appropriate ledger (the book of final entry that contains records for all the accounts used in the business). A separate business document such as an invoice or a check must be prepared and distributed. In order to prepare a report, the accountant/bookkeeper must go through the journal or ledger and look for the appropriate amounts to include in the report. Closing the books must be done item by item via closing entries, which are recorded in the journal and posted to the appropriate ledger accounts. After the closing entries are recorded, the ledger accounts must be ruled and balance sheet accounts must be reopened with Brought Forward Balances being entered. All of this is extremely time consuming.

In a computerized system, the transactions must still be analyzed and recorded; however, posting is done automatically or by giving the command to post. Reports are generated based on an instruction given to the computer—for example, by clicking on a menu item: "Report—Trial Balance." Some computerized accounting systems require the accountant/bookkeeper to enter both the debit and credit portions of each transaction in a General Journal. Other programs allow the use of special journals such as Cash Disbursements or Cash Payments, Sales, and Purchases journals. QuickBooks Pro, however, operates from a business document point of view. As a transaction occurs, the necessary business document (an invoice or a check, for example) is prepared. Based on the information given on the business document, QuickBooks Pro records the necessary debits and credits behind the scenes in the Journal. If an error is made when entering a transaction, QuickBooks Pro allows the user to return to the business document and make the correction. QuickBooks Pro will automatically record the changes in the debits and credits in the Journal. If you want to see or make a correction using the actual debit/credit entries, QuickBooks Pro allows you to view the transaction register and make corrections directly in the register or use the traditional Journal. Reports and graphs are prepared by simply clicking "Report" on the menu bar.

SYSTEM REQUIREMENTS FOR QUICKBOOKS® PRO 2004

The hardware requirements are an IBM-compatible 200 MHz Pentium computer (350 MHz Pentium II or higher recommended); 64 MB RAM (96 MB recommended); 250 MB of hard-disk space available for QuickBooks Pro, an additional 70 MB of hard-disk space for Microsoft® Internet Explorer, 2x CD-ROM drive, 256-color SVGA monitor; Internet access with a connection speed of 56 Kbps or higher (for optional services), and a printer supported by Windows. The operating system must be Windows 98, Me, 2000, or XP. If you plan to use the integration features of QuickBooks Pro, you will also need: Microsoft® Word 97, 2000, 2002, or 2003; Microsoft® Excel 97, 2000, 2002, or 2003; Microsoft® Outlook 97, 98, 2000, 2002, or 2003; or Symantec® ACT! 3.08, 4.02, or 2000.

QuickBooks Pro may be networked if you have a Windows 2000 or 2003 Server. A peer-to-peer network using either Windows 98, 2000, Me, or XP may also be used.

VERSIONS OF QUICKBOOKS® 2004

While this text focuses on training using QuickBooks® Pro 2004, it may also be used with the Basic and Premier versions of the program. As the names imply, the Basic program will allow a company to keep basic records in QuickBooks and the Premier versions offers some additional enhancements not available in the Pro version. The Premier version of the program is also available in industry specific versions; such as, Accountant, Contractor, Healthcare, Manufacturing and Wholesale, Nonprofit, Professional Services, and Retail. There is also a Web version of QuickBooks that is available online for a monthly fee. However, the functions available are limited and many features of QuickBooks Pro cannot be utilized.

For a comparison of features available among the different versions of the QuickBooks programs, access Intuit's Web site at www.quickbooks.com.

BEGIN COMPUTER TRAINING

When using this text, you will be instructed to perform a computer task when you see a graphic of a button ▮ and the words **DO:**.

HOW TO OPEN QUICKBOOKS® PRO 2004

Once you are in Windows, opening QuickBooks Pro is as easy as point and click.

 DO: Click **Start**
Point to **Programs**

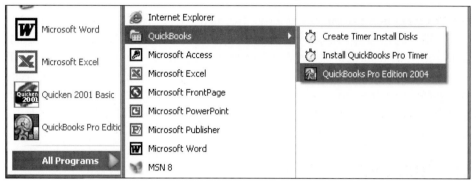

Point to **QuickBooks Pro** (or the program name given to you by your instructor)
Click **QuickBooks Pro**

HOW TO OPEN A COMPANY

To explore some of the features of QuickBooks Pro, you will work with a sample company that comes with the program. The company is Larry's Landscaping and is stored on the hard disk (C:) inside the computer.

 DO: Open the Sample Company
When you open QuickBooks you may get the following screen:

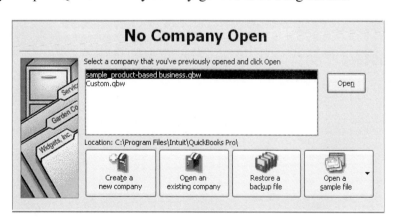

Click the **Open a sample file** button

Click **Sample service-based business**

- *Note:* You may or may not have the same names displayed in the "Select a company that you've previously opened and click Open" section of the screen above

   OR

If you do not get the No Company Open screen or would like to use the menus, click **File** on the menu bar

Click **Open Company**

On the Open a Company window, check **Look in** at the top of the screen

Make sure it indicates **Drive C:** or shows a folder named **QuickBooks Pro**

- To look in the C: drive, click the drop-down list arrow next to Drives and click **C:**
- Follow instructions provided by your instructor to locate the folder for QuickBooks Pro
- *Note:* If you are working in a laboratory environment, the folder names may not be the same as the folder names indicated here. Check with your instructor for specific information on accessing the sample company. You will note that the folder used in this text is QuickBooks Pro 2004.

Click the file named **sample_service-based business** in the center of the screen

File name text box should have **sample_service-based business**

Click **Open** button on the lower-right side of the dialog box

When using the sample company for training, a warning screen will appear. This is to remind you NOT to enter the transactions for your business in the sample company.

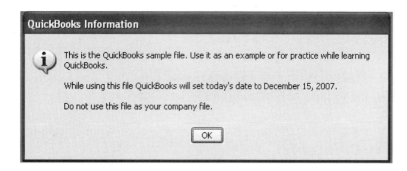

Click **OK** to accept the sample company data for use
- If you get a screen regarding Automatic Update, scroll to the bottom and click **Begin Using QuickBooks**.
- If you get a What's New screen, close it.

VERIFY AN OPEN COMPANY

It is important to make sure you have opened the data for the correct company. Always verify the company name in the title bar.

DO: Check the **title bar** to make sure it includes the company name.
The title bar should show:
Sample Larry's Landscaping & Garden Supply - QuickBooks Pro 2004

Sample Larry's Landscaping & Garden Supply - QuickBooks Pro 2004

INTRODUCTION TO QUICKBOOKS® PRO DESKTOP FEATURES

Once the computer has been turned on, Windows has been accessed, and QuickBooks Pro has been started, you will see QuickBooks Pro on the desktop. QuickBooks Pro displays a title bar. If a company is open, the title bar displays the **Company Name - QuickBooks Pro 2004**. The Windows minimize, maximize, close, and control buttons are available in QuickBooks Pro and appear on the screen. Beneath the title bar is the menu bar. By pointing and clicking on a menu item or using the keyboard shortcut of Alt+ the underlined letter in the menu item you will give QuickBooks Pro the command to display the drop-down menu. For example, the File menu is used to open and close a company and may also be used to exit QuickBooks Pro.

Below the menu bar, QuickBooks Pro 2004 may display an icon bar containing small pictures that may be used to give commands by pointing to an icon and clicking the primary mouse button. On the left of the screen is a list of QuickBooks Navigators available. While using QuickBooks Navigator is optional, it is a quick and easy way to give commands to QuickBooks Pro based on the type of transactions being entered. Beneath the list of navigators, QuickBooks displays the windows of the program that are open.

This text will use various methods of giving QuickBooks Pro commands, including use of QuickBooks Navigator, menu bar, icon bar, and keyboard shortcuts.

QUICKBOOKS® NAVIGATORS

QuickBooks Navigators allow you to give commands to QuickBooks Pro according to the type of transaction being entered. A list of QuickBooks Navigators will appear on the left side of the screen when you open the program.

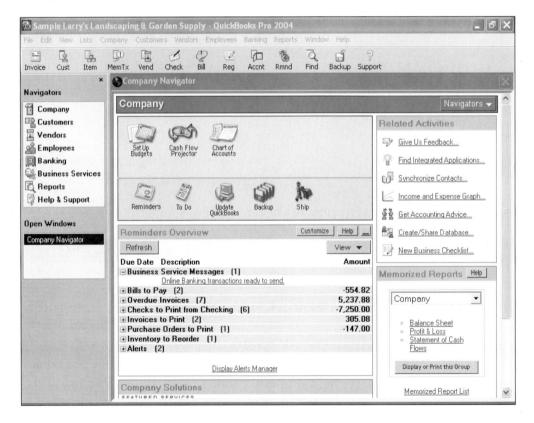

Each of the navigators accesses a different area of the program and is used to enter different types of transactions.

Company allows you to display information about your company. It allows you to set up budgets, use the cash flow projector, and access the chart of accounts. QuickBooks Pro update service may be accessed, a backup of company files can be made, To Do's and Reminders may be created, and the QuickBooks Shipping Manager may be accessed. In addition, the Company

Navigator contains areas with information regarding reminders, related activities, company solutions, and reports.

Customers allows transactions associated with cash sales, credit sales, cash receipts, and bank deposits to be entered. Customer accounts, sales item lists, customer manager, and customer registers may be accessed and updated. Letters may be written in Microsoft® Word using data available in QuickBooks. In addition, credit checks may be made on customers if you subscribe to this optional service. The Customer Navigator also provides quick, easy access to reports associated with sales activities and to related activities.

Vendors allows you to enter your bills and to record the payment of bills. Companies with inventory can create purchase orders and record receipt of items. Vendor accounts and lists may be accessed and updated. Quick, easy access to reports associated with accounts payable activities is provided, and 1099s may be printed.

Employees allows paychecks to be created, payroll tax liabilities to be paid, and Forms 940, 941, and W2 to be printed. Employee information, payroll items, liability adjustments, and tax tables may be accessed. Payroll reports may be prepared.

Banking allows you to write checks, transfer money between accounts, use online banking, make bank deposits, reconcile the bank statement, and record credit card transactions. The check register may be accessed. Traditional General Journal entries may be recorded. The Loan Manager may be used and certain supplies may be ordered. Bills may be paid online if the service has been activated. Reports associated with the checking account may be generated.

Business Services provides information regarding various items in QuickBooks Pro—either provided or optional—for managing your business, your employees, and your cash flow.

Reports accesses the Report Finder and allows all of the reports in QuickBooks Pro to be prepared. These include specific reports, such as, Profit and Loss, Balance Sheet, Tax Reports, Transaction Detail Reports, Journal, General Ledger, Trial Balance, Income Tax Summary, Income Tax Detail, Journal, and an Audit Trail. There is also a variety of reports specific to payroll, customers, vendors, inventory, purchases, banking, and taxes.

Help & Support provides information on Help, resources for your business, ways to contact Intuit, and product information and news.

The central area of the QuickBooks Navigator screen shows a flow chart with icons indicating the major activities performed in the area of focus. For the Customers, the center area of the screen shows a flow chart with icons indicating Invoices, Statements, Finance Charges, Refunds and Credit, Receive Payment, Sales Receipts, and Deposits. You'll notice that the icons are arranged in the order in which transactions usually occur. You would not record a refund prior to creating an invoice for a sale, so the icon for Invoices appears before the icon for Refunds and Credit. In addition, there are icons displayed to access lists that QuickBooks Pro uses for Customers and Items & Services. It will also show icons for Customer Manager, Customer Register, Write Letters, and Credit Check.

 DO: Click the **Customers** on the Navigator list on the left side of the screen
- View the lists and occasional activities, flow charts for main activities, and reports available.

Repeat for each of the other groups on the Navigation bar: **Company, Vendors, Employees, Banking, Business Services, Reports,** and **Help & Support**

MENU COMMANDS

Menu commands can be the starting point for issuing commands in QuickBooks Pro. The following menus are available for use in QuickBooks® Pro 2004:

File menu is used to access company files—new company, open company, close company, and switch from single to multi-user; begin the EasyStep interview to set up a company; back up and restore company files; import and export data, archive and condense data, utilities, make accountant's copy of company files; printer setup and printing; e-mail forms, and shipping, update QuickBooks Pro, and exit from the program.

Edit menu is used to make changes such as: Undo, Revert, Cut, Copy, Paste, Use Register, Use Calculator, Simple Find, Advanced Find, and Preferences.

View menu is used to select the use of an open window list, icon bar, shortcut list, or multiple windows, and to customize the desktop.

Lists menu is used to show lists used by QuickBooks Pro. These lists include: Chart of Accounts (the General Ledger), Items, Fixed Asset Items, Price Level Items, Sales Tax Code List, Payroll Items, Class List, Customers:Jobs (the Accounts Receivable Ledger), Vendors (the Accounts Payable Ledger), Employees, Other Names, Customer and Vendor Profiles, Templates, and Memorized Transactions.

Company menu is used to access the Company Navigator, Business Services Manager, Company Center, change company information, set up users, change passwords, modify service access, perform advanced services administration, set up budgets, access the To Do list, access the Reminders screen, use the Alerts Manager, enter vehicle mileage, and access the Chart of Accounts. It is also used to make journal entries, write letters, print mailing labels, synchronize contacts, access company services, and create a Web site.

Customers menu is used to enter transactions and prepare business documents such as invoices, sales receipts, credit memos/refunds, statements and statement charges, finance charges, receive payments, and accept credit card payments. It is also used to access the Customer Navigator, the Customer Center, the Customer Detail Center, the Customer Manager, the Customer:Job List, the Item List, and to change item prices. Additional choices for billing solutions, credit checks, and customer services are also provided.

Vendors menu is used to access the Vendor Navigator, the Vendor Detail Center, the Vendor List, the Item List, the Purchase Order List, and Vendor Services. In addition, this menu is used to enter transactions for recording bills, paying bills, paying sales tax, creating purchase orders, receiving items, inventory activities, and printing 1099s.

Employees menu is used to pay employees, edit/void paychecks, process payroll liabilities, process payroll forms, run payroll checkup, set up payroll services, add or change payroll services, get payroll upgrades, and access the Employees and Payroll Items Lists, and Employee Navigator.

Banking menu is used to write checks, use the check register, make deposits, transfer funds, enter credit card charges, use the loan manager, reconcile accounts, make journal entries, set up online financial services, create an online banking message, access online banking center, get the chart of accounts, access the Other Names and the Memorized Transactions Lists, and use QuickBooks' Banking Services, Banking Navigator.

Reports menu is used to access the Report Finder and to prepare reports in the following categories: Company and Financial; Customers and Receivables; Sales; Jobs, Time & Mileage; Vendors & Payables; Purchases; Inventory; Employees & Payroll; Banking; Accountant & Taxes; Budgets; List; Custom Report Summary; Custom Transaction Detail Report; Transaction History; Transaction Journal; and Memorized Reports.

Window menu is used to switch between documents that have been opened, to arrange icons.

Help menu is used to access Help. The Help menu includes topics such as: Help Index, Help on This Window, New Features, Buy QuickBooks Premier Edition, Help and Support, Internet Connection Setup, About Automatic Update, QuickBooks Privacy Statement, and About QuickBooks Pro 2004.

DO: Click on **Customers** menu and view the commands available
- Many commands will remind you of commands you can make using QuickBooks Navigator.
- Notice that available keyboard shortcuts are listed next to the menu item
Click outside the menu to close

KEYBOARD SHORTCUTS

Frequently, it is faster to use a keyboard shortcut to give QuickBooks Pro a command than it is to point and click the mouse through several layers of menus or Navigators. The following charts list common keyboard shortcuts available for use in QuickBooks Pro.

GENERAL	KEY
Start QB without a company file	Ctrl+double-click
Suppress desktop windows (at Open Company window)	Alt (while opening)
Display information about QuickBooks Pro	F2
Cancel	Esc
Record (when black border is around OK, Next, or Prev button)	Press Enter key
Record (always)	Ctrl+Enter

HELP WINDOW	KEY
Display Help in context	F1
Select next option or topic	Tab
Select previous option or topic	Shift+Tab
Display selected topic	Enter
Close pop up box	Esc
Close Help window	Esc

DATES	KEY
Next day	+ (plus key)
Previous day	- (minus key)
Today	**T**
First day of the **W**eek	**W**
Last day of the wee**K**	**K**
First day of the **M**onth	**M**
Last Day of the mont**H**	**H**
First day of the **Y**ear	**Y**
Last Day of the yea**R**	**R**
Date calendar	Alt+down arrow

EDITING	KEY
Edit transaction in selected register	Ctrl+E
Delete character to right of insertion point	Del
Delete character to left of insertion point	Backspace
Delete line from detail area	Ctrl+Del
Insert line in detail area	Ctrl+Ins
Cut selected characters	Ctrl+X
Copy selected characters	Ctrl+C
Paste cut or copied characters	Ctrl+V
Increase check or other form number by one	+ (plus key)
Decrease check or other form number by one	- (minus key)
Undo changes made in field	Ctrl+Z

MOVING AROUND A WINDOW	KEY
Next field	Tab
Previous field	Shift+Tab
Report column to the right	Right arrow
Report column to the left	Left arrow
Beginning of current field or report row	Home
End of current field or report row	End
Line below in detail area or on report	Down arrow
Line above in detail area or on report	Up arrow
Down one screen	Page Down
Up one screen	Page Up

Next word in field	Ctrl+Right Arrow
Previous word in field	Ctrl+Left Arrow
First item on list or previous month in register	Ctrl+Page Up
Last item on list or next month in register	Ctrl+Page Down
Close active window	Esc or Ctrl+F4

ACTIVITY	KEY
Account list, display	Ctrl+A
Check, write	Ctrl+W
Customer:Job list, display	Ctrl+J
Delete check, invoice, transaction, or item from list	Ctrl+D
Edit lists or registers	Ctrl+E
QuickFill and Recall (type first few letters of name and press Tab, name fills in)	abcxyz Tab
Find transaction	Ctrl+F
Go to register of transfer account	Ctrl+G
Help in context, display	F1
History of A/R or A/P Transaction	Ctrl+H
Invoice, create	Ctrl+I
List (for current field), display	Ctrl+L
Memorize transaction or report	Ctrl+M
Memorized transaction list, display	Ctrl+T
New invoice, bill, check, or list item	Ctrl+N
Paste copied transaction in register	Ctrl+V
Print	Ctrl+P
QuickZoom on report	Enter
QuickReport on transaction or list item	Ctrl+Q
Register, display	Ctrl+R
Use list item	Ctrl+U
Transaction journal, display	Ctrl+Y

KEYBOARD CONVENTIONS

When using Windows, there are some standard keyboard conventions for the use of certain keys. These keyboard conventions also apply to QuickBooks Pro and include the following.

Alt key is used to access the drop-down menus on the menu bar. Rather than click on a menu item, hold down the Alt key and type the underlined letter in the menu item name. Close the menu by simply pressing the Alt key. *Note*: Menu items do not have an underlined letter until you press the Alt key.

Tab key is used to move to the next field or, if a button is selected, to the next button.

Shift+Tab is used to move back to the previous field.

Esc key is used to cancel an active window without saving anything that has been entered. It is equivalent to clicking the Cancel button.

DO: Access the **File** menu: **Alt+F**, view the menu choices, close File menu: **Alt**
Access the **Edit** menu: **Alt+E**, view the menu choices, close Edit menu: **Alt**
Access the **View** menu: **Alt+V**, view the menu choices, close Edit menu: **Alt**
Access the **Lists** menu: **Alt+L**, view the menu choices, close Lists menu: **Alt**
Access the **Company** menu: **Alt+C**, view the menu choices, close Company menu: **Alt**
Access the **Customer** menu: **Alt+U**, view the menu choices, close Customer menu: **Alt**
Access the **Vendor** menu: **Alt+O**, view the menu choices, close Vendor menu: **Alt**
Access the **Employee** menu: **Alt+Y**, view the menu choices, close Employee menu: **Alt**
Access the **Banking** menu: **Alt+B**, view the menu choices, close Banking menu: **Alt**
Access the **Reports** menu: **Alt+R**, view the menu choices, close Reports menu: **Alt**
Access the **Window** menu: **Alt+W**, view the menu choices, close Window menu: **Alt**
Access the **Help** menu: **Alt+H**, view the menu choices, close Help menu: **Alt**

DO: Access **Customer** menu: **Alt+U**, access **Create Invoices**: type **I**
Press **Tab** key to move forward through the invoice
Press **Shift+Tab** to move back through the invoice
Press **Esc** to close the invoice

ICON BAR

Another way to give commands to QuickBooks Pro is to use the icon bar. If activated, the icon bar will be placed below the menu bar. The icon bar has a list of buttons that may be clicked in order to access activities, lists, or reports. For example, to see a list of customers and the balances they owe, click the Cust icon. An icon bar may be customized and may be toggled on or off via the View menu.

 DO: Access activities using the icon bar:
If the icon bar is not on the screen, click the **View** menu, and click **Icon Bar**
When the icon bar is on the screen, click the **Cust** icon
- You will see a list of customers and the balances they owe.
Press **Esc** to close the Customer List

ON-SCREEN HELP

QuickBooks Pro has on-screen help, which is similar to having the QuickBooks Pro reference manual available on the computer screen. Help can give you assistance with a particular function you are performing. QuickBooks Pro help also gives you information about the program using an on-screen index.

Help may be accessed to obtain information on a variety of topics, and it may be accessed in different ways:

To find out about the window in which you are working, press F1, type your question in the textbox for Ask a Help Question and click Ask , or click How Do I.

To learn about the new features available in QuickBooks Pro, click New Features on the Help menu.

To get additional information on how to use QuickBooks Pro or to enter a question and get immediate answers drawn from both the QuickBooks Help system and the technical support database, click the Help menu and click Help and Support.

To obtain information regarding specific items, click Help Index on the Help menu. QuickBooks Pro Help screen appears. There is a text box where you may type the first few letters of the name of the item with which you need help. As you key in the item name, QuickBooks Pro index displays items alphabetically. When the topic you need appears on the screen, double-click the topic to display it.

When the topic for help has been located, information about the topic is provided in the Help window. If there is more information than can be shown on the screen, scroll bars will appear on the right side of the help screen. A scroll bar is used to show or go through information. As you scroll through help, information at the top of the help screen disappears from view while new information appears at the bottom of the screen.

Sometimes words appear in blue and may be underlined in the QuickBooks Pro Help screen. Clicking on the blue word(s) will give you a pop-up definition of the word. Clicking on blue underlined words will take you to other topics.

Often, the onscreen help provides links to an external Web site. To visit these links, you must have an Internet connection and be online. Links to sites outside the QuickBooks help are indicated with a lightning bolt symbol.

If you want to see a different topic, you may type in a different key word at the top of the screen. Index will give you the information on the new topic.

If you want to print a copy of the QuickBooks Pro Help screen, click the Printer icon at the top of the green title bar for the Help topic.

You may close a QuickBooks Pro Help screen by clicking the Close button (X) in the upper right corner of the screen.

 DO: Click **Help** on the Menu bar
Click **Help Index**
If a Help & Support Help Search screen appears, click **OK** to close it

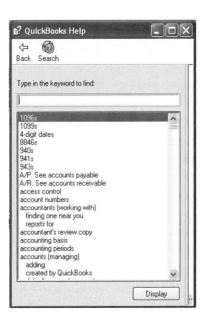

Key in **pr** in the textbox for "Type in keyword to find:"
Preferences will be highlighted
Click **General** in the listing displayed under preferences
Click **Display**
Click the blue words **QuickBooks Administrator**
Read the pop-up definition
Click in the **Help** window to close the pop-up definition
Close **Help** using one of the following methods:

    Alt+F4
    Click the **Control** menu icon (the icon to the left of QuickBooks Help on the title bar), click **Close**
    Click the **Close** button in the upper right corner of the Help screen

QUICKBOOKS® PRO FORMS

The premise of QuickBooks Pro is to allow you to focus on running the business, not deciding whether an account is debited or credited. Transactions are entered directly onto the business form that is prepared as a result of the transaction. For example, a sale on account is recorded by completing the invoice for the sale. Behind the scenes, QuickBooks Pro enters the debit and credit to the Journal and posts to the individual accounts.

QuickBooks Pro has several types of forms used to fill in your daily business transactions. They are divided into two categories: forms you want to send or give to people and forms you have received. Forms to send or give to people include invoices, sales receipts, credit memos, checks, deposit slips, and purchase orders. Forms you have received include payments from customers, bills, credits for a bill, and credit card charge receipts.

You may use the forms as they come with QuickBooks Pro, you may change or modify them, or you may create your own custom forms for use in the program.

When preparing a form, you move from one field to the next to enter the information needed. To move from one field to the next, press the Tab key or position the mouse pointer within a field and click the primary (left) mouse button. While each form does require different types of information, there are several common features within forms. Examine the invoice that follows.

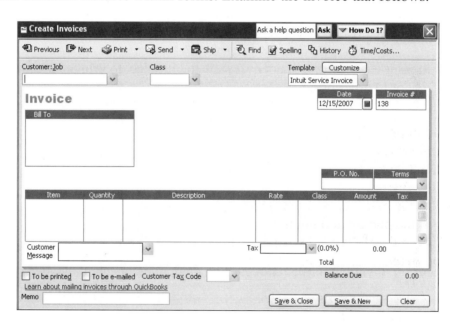

Field is an area on a form requiring information. Customer:Job is a field.

Text box is the area within a field where information may be typed or inserted. The area to be filled in to identify the Customer:Job is a text box.

Drop-down list arrow appears next to a field when there is a list of options available. On the invoice for Larry's Landscaping, clicking the drop-down list arrow for Customer:Job will display the names of all customers who have accounts with the company. Clicking a customer's name will insert the name into the text box for the field.

Title bar at the top of form indicates what you are completing. In this case, it says **Create Invoices**. The title bar also contains some buttons. They include:
> **Ask a help question** and an **Ask** button. To get assistance with a question, click in the Ask a help question text box and type in your question; then, click the **Ask** button.
> **How Do I button** that is clicked to obtain help.

Close button closes the current screen.

Toolbar at the top of the invoice has icons that are used to give commands to QuickBooks Pro or to get information regarding linked or related transactions.

Previous is clicked to go back to the previous invoice. This is used when you want to view, print, or correct the previous invoice. Each time the Previous icon is clicked, you go back one invoice. You may click the Previous icon until you go all the way back to Invoice No. 1.

Next is clicked to go to the next invoice after the one you entered. If the invoice on the screen has not been saved, this saves the invoice and goes to the next invoice. The next invoice may be one that has already been created and saved or it may be a blank invoice.

Print is used to print the invoice on paper, to view the invoice, to print a batch of invoices, to print postage, or to order business forms.

Send is used to fax or e-mail invoices.

Ship is used to ship merchandise.

Find is used to find invoices previously prepared.

Spelling is used to check the spelling in a business document.

History allows you to view information regarding any payments that have been made on the invoice.

Time/Costs icon opens the Choose Billable Time and Costs window where you can select which costs to include on the current invoice.

Buttons on the bottom of the invoice are used to give commands to QuickBooks Pro.

Save & Close button is clicked when all information has been entered for the invoice and you are ready for QuickBooks Pro to save the invoice and exit the Create Invoices screen.

Save & New button is clicked when all information has been entered for the invoice and you are ready to complete a new invoice.

Clear button is clicked if you want to clear the information entered on the current invoice.

  DO: Click **Invoice** on the icon bar
OR

Use QuickBooks Pro Navigator:
   Click **Customers** on the Navigator bar
   Click **Invoices**
Locate the invoice features described previously
Click the **Previous** icon to view invoices that have been completed
Click the **Close** button to close the Create Invoices screen
Look at some of the other forms used in QuickBooks Pro:
   Click **Check** on the icon bar to view checks, click **Close** to exit checks
   Click **Enter Bills** button on the Vendor Navigator to view Enter Bills screen,
      click **Close** to exit bills
   Click **Customers** on the menu bar**,** click **Enter Sales Receipts** to view a sales
      receipt, (If you get a Merchant Account Service Message, close it) click
      Close to exit sales receipts
   Click **Banking** in the list of Navigators**,** click **Deposits** to view a deposit slip,
      click **Close** to exit deposit slip

QUICKBOOKS® PRO LISTS

In order to expedite entering transactions, QuickBooks Pro uses lists as an integral part of the program. Customers, vendors, sales items, and accounts are organized as lists. In fact, the chart of accounts is considered to be a list in QuickBooks Pro. Frequently, information can be entered on a form by clicking on a list item. For example, a customer name can be entered on an invoice by clicking the drop-down list arrow next to the Customer:Job text box and clicking on the customer name from the Customer:Job List.

Most lists have a maximum. However, it's unlikely that you'll run out of room on your lists. This table shows the maximum number of entries each type of list can hold:

TYPE OF LIST	# OF ENTRIES
Chart of Accounts, Class, Terms, Payment Methods, Customer Type, Vendor Type, Job Type, Customer Message	10,000
Items, Names (Customers:Jobs, Vendor, Employee, and Other Names lists combined)	14,500
Memorized Transaction	14,500
Price Levels	100

With so many entries available, there is room to add list items as you work. In fact, QuickBooks Pro allows items to be added to lists "on the fly." This means, if you are preparing an invoice for a new customer, QuickBooks Pro allows you to add the new customer to the Customer:Job List while you are filling in the Customer:Job text box for the invoice. QuickBooks Pro allows you to do a "Quick Add" to add a customer name or to use "Set Up" to add complete customer information.

If you open the Customer:Job List, it will appear as follows:

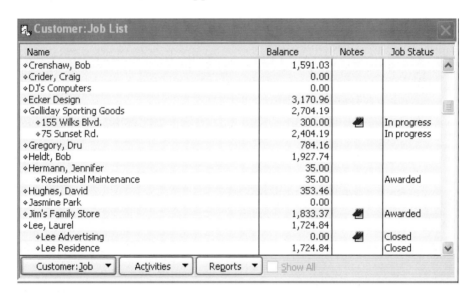

 DO: Use the **Lists** menu to examine several lists:

Click the **Lists** menu, click **Customer:Job List** to view the list of customers, click **Close** to exit

Click the **Lists** menu, click **Chart of Accounts** to view the Chart of Accounts, click **Close** to exit

Click the **Lists** menu, click **Vendor List** to view the list of vendors, **Ctrl+F4** to exit

Click the **Lists** menu, click **Item List** to view the list of sales items, click **Close** to exit

Click the **Lists** menu, click **Other Names** to see a list including names of owners, partners, and other miscellaneous names and descriptions used in transactions, double-click the **Control menu box or icon** next to Other Names List on the title bar of the list window to close

Use a QuickBooks Navigator to examine other lists:

Click the **Employees** Navigator, click the **Employees** icon to view a list of employees, **Ctrl+F4** to exit the list

With Employees Navigator screen showing, click the **Payroll Items** icon to view payroll items and categories, click the **Close** button

QUICKBOOKS® PRO REGISTERS

QuickBooks Pro prepares a register for every balance sheet account. An account register contains records of all activity for the account. Registers provide an excellent means of looking at transactions within an account. For example, the Accounts Receivable register maintains a record of every invoice, credit memo, and payment that has been recorded for credit customers.

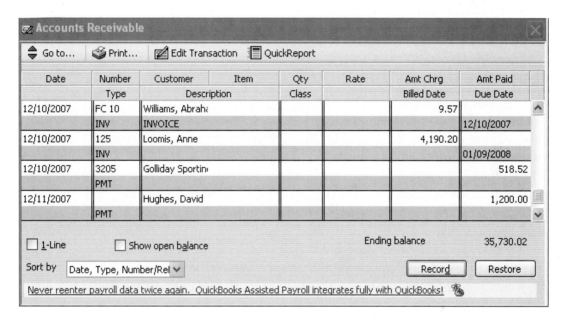

  DO: Click **Company** on the Navigator bar
Click **Chart of Accounts**
Click **Accounts Receivable**
Click the **Activities** button at the bottom of the screen
Click **Use Register**
Scroll through the register
Look at the **Number/Type** column
- Notice the types of transactions listed:
  INV is for an invoice
  PMT indicates a payment received from a customer
Click **Close** on the Register to exit
Click **Checking** account in the Chart of Accounts
Click **Activities**
Click **Use Register**
Scroll through the register
- Notice the types of transactions listed:
  CHK is for a check we wrote
  PAY CHK is a paycheck for an employee

PMT is a check received for accounts receivable
TAXPMT is a payment made for payroll taxes
RCPT is for a transaction entered on a sales receipt for a cash sale
BILLPMT records an accounts payable payment
DEP records a bank deposit
TRANSFR records a transfer of funds from one account to another
Close the **Register** using **Ctrl+F4**
Close the **Chart of Accounts List** using **Ctrl+F4**

QUICKBOOKS® PRO REPORTS

Reports are an integral part of a business. Reports enable owners and managers to determine how the business is doing and to make decisions affecting the future of the company. Reports can be prepared showing the profit and loss for the period, the status of the Balance Sheet (assets equal liabilities plus owner's equity), information regarding accounts receivable and accounts payable, and the amount of sales for each item. QuickBooks Pro has a wide range of reports and reporting options available. Reports may be customized to better reflect the information needs of a company. Reports may be generated in a variety of ways.

Reports menu includes a complete listing of the reports available in QuickBooks Pro and is used to prepare reports including: company and financial reports such as profit and loss (income statement), balance sheet; accounts receivable reports; sales reports; accounts payable reports; budget reports; transaction reports; transaction detail reports; payroll reports; list reports; custom reports; graphs showing graphical analysis of business operations; and several other classifications of reports.

Reports Navigator takes you to the Report Finder, which includes a complete listing of the reports available in QuickBooks Pro.

Report Finder in the Memorized Reports section of each QuickBooks Navigator takes you to the Report Finder.

DO: Prepare reports from the Reports menu:
Click **Reports** on the menu bar
Point to **Company & Financial**
Click **Profit & Loss Standard**
Scroll the Profit and Loss Statement for Larry's Landscaping
• Notice the Net Income for the period.
Click the **Close** button to exit the report
Prepare reports using the **Report Finder** in the Memorized Reports (lower-right) section of a QuickBooks Navigator:

Click **Company** on the Navigator bar

Click **Report Finder** in the Memorized Reports section of the Company Navigator

Make sure **Company & Financial** appears in the **Select Type of Report** text box

- If it does not, click the drop-down list arrow for the **Select Type of Report** text box and click **Company & Financial**.

Click **Balance Sheet Standard**

Click the **Display** button on the lower right side of the **Report Finder**

Scroll through the report

- Notice that assets equal liabilities plus equity.

Do not close the report

QUICKZOOM

QuickZoom allows you to view transactions that contribute to the data on reports or graphs. When viewing a report, place the mouse pointer over an amount. The pointer will turn into a magnifying glass with a Z inside. To see detailed information, double-click the mouse. For example, double-clicking on a fixed asset shown on the balance sheet will provide information regarding depreciation and the original cost of the asset.

DO: Scroll through the Balance Sheet on the screen until you see the fixed asset Truck

Position the mouse pointer over the amount for **Total Truck**

- The mouse pointer turns into a magnifying glass with a Z.

Double-click the mouse to see the transaction detail for the Truck

Click the **Close** button to close the **Transactions by Account** report

Click the **Close** button to close the **Balance Sheet**

QUICKBOOKS® PRO GRAPHS

Using bar charts and pie charts, QuickBooks Pro gives you an instant visual analysis of different elements of your business. You may obtain information in a graphical form for Income & Expenses, Sales, Accounts Receivable, Accounts Payable, Net Worth, and Budget vs. Actual. For example, clicking on the drop-down list arrow for the Report Finder menu for Select a Report when the Type of Report is Company & Financial, and clicking on Net Worth allows you to see an owner's net worth in relationship to assets and liabilities. This is displayed on a bar chart according to the month. To obtain information about liabilities for a given month, you may zoom in on the liabilities portion of the bar, double-click, and see the liabilities for the month displayed in a pie chart.

DO: Report Finder should be on the screen
Click the drop-down list arrow for **Select a Type of Report**
Click **Company & Financial**
Scroll through the choices for Select a Report
Click **Net Worth Graph**
Click the **Display** button or double-click the Net Worth Graph

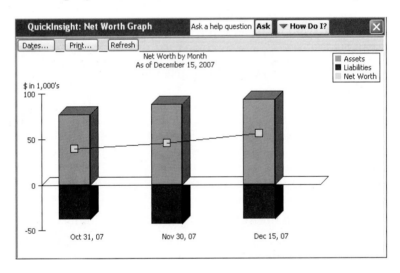

Zoom in on the Liabilities for October by pointing to the liabilities and double-
clicking
View the pie chart for October's liabilities

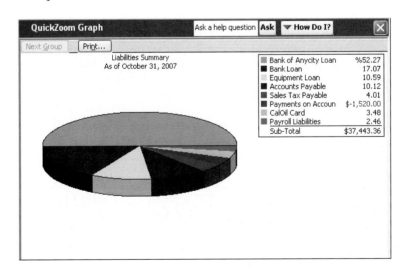

Click the **Close** button to close the pie chart
Zoom in on the Net Worth for December and double-click
View the pie chart for December's **Net Worth Summary**

Ctrl+F4 to close the pie chart
Click the Close button to close the **Net Worth** graph
Close **Report Finder**

QUICKREPORT

QuickReports are reports that give you detailed information about items you are viewing. They look just like standard reports that you prepare but are considered "quick" because you don't have to go through the Reports menu to create them. For example, when you are viewing the Employee List, you can obtain information about an individual employee simply by clicking the employee's name in the list, clicking the Reports button, and selecting QuickReports from the menu.

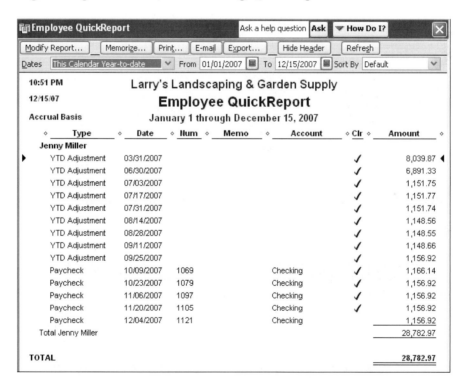

 DO: Click **Lists** on the menu bar
Click **Employee List**
Click **Jenny Miller**
Click **Reports** button at the bottom of the Employee List
Click **QuickReport: Jenny Miller**
Click **Close** to close the **QuickReport**
Click **Close** to close the **Employee List**

HOW TO USE QUICKMATH

QuickMath is available for use whenever you are in a field where a calculation is to be made. Frequently, QuickBooks Pro will make calculations for you automatically; however, there may be instances when you need to perform the calculation. For example, on an invoice, QuickBooks Pro will calculate an amount based on the quantity and the rate given for a sales item. If for some reason you do not have a rate for a sales item, you may use QuickMath to calculate the amount. To do this, you tab to the amount column, type an = or a number and the +. QuickBooks Pro will show a calculator tape on the screen. You may then add, subtract, multiply, or divide to obtain a total or a subtotal. Pressing the enter key inserts the amount into the column.

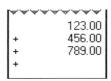

   DO: Click **Invoice** on the icon bar
Click in the **Amount** column on the Invoice
Press the =
When the adding machine tape appears, press the +
    Enter the numbers: **123+**
                                  456+
                                  789+
Press **Enter**
The total **1,368** is inserted into the Amount column
Click the **Clear** button to clear the Amount column
Click the **Close** button on the Invoice to close the invoice without saving

HOW TO USE WINDOWS® CALCULATOR

Windows includes accessory programs that may be used when working. One of these accessory programs is Calculator. Using this program gives you an on-screen calculator. To use the Calculator in Windows, click Start, point to Programs, point to Accessories, click Calculator. A calculator appears on your screen.

   DO: Open **Calculator**
Click **Start**
Point to **Programs**
Point to **Accessories**

Click **Calculator**

Change from a standard calculator to a scientific calculator, click **View** menu, click
Scientific

Change back to a standard calculator, click **View** menu, click **Standard**

Numbers may be entered by:

Clicking the number on the calculator

Keying the number using the numeric keypad

Typing the keyboard numbers

Enter the numbers: **123+**
                                       456+
                                       789+

The amount is added after each entry

After typing 789+, the answer 1368 appears automatically

- *Note:* Using the Windows Calculator does not insert the amount into a
  QuickBooks form.

To clear the answer, click the **C** button on the calculator

Enter: **55*6**

Press **Enter** or click = to get the answer 330

Click **Control menu icon**, click **Close** to close the **Calculator**

ACCESS WINDOWS® CALCULATOR THROUGH QUICKBOOKS® PRO

When you are working in QuickBooks Pro, you may access the Windows calculator by clicking the
Edit menu and clicking Use Calculator.

     DO: Access Windows Calculator through QuickBooks Pro

Click **Edit** on the menu bar

Click **Use Calculator**

Close the **Calculator** using the keyboard shortcut **Alt+F4**

HOW TO CLOSE A COMPANY

The sample company—Larry's Landscaping & Garden Supply—will appear as the open company
whenever you open QuickBooks Pro. In order to discontinue the use of the sample company, you
must close the company. In a classroom environment, you should always back up your work and
close the company you are using at the end of a work session. If you use different computers when
training, not closing a company at the end of each work session may cause your files to become
corrupt, your disk to fail, or leave unwanted .qbi (QuickBooks In Use) files on your data disk.

DO: Click **File** menu, click **Close Company**

HOW TO COPY A FILE

A copy of the company files should be kept as a master. A master file is never used. It is set aside in case something happens to the file you are using to do your work. Work within the text will always be performed on a duplicate copy of the company data.

  DO: Make a duplicate of Contempo Computer Consulting
                 Check with your instructor to make sure this is the procedure to be followed.
                 Insert the CD-ROM that comes with the text in the CD-ROM drive (usually labeled
                     D:)
                 Insert a formatted disk labeled **Contempo** in **A:**
                 Right-click the **Start** button
                 Click **Explore**
                 Scroll through the **All Folders** side on the left side of the Explorer screen
                 Click the icon for the CD-ROM (usually labeled D:)
                 On the right side of Explorer, double-click the Browse folder, then double-click the
                 Company Files folder, right-click **Contempo**
                 • *Note:* Depending on the setup of your computer, the file extension .qbw may
                     be displayed. A file with a .qbw extension means that it is a QuickBooks
                     working file and is used to record transactions.
                 Click **Send To** on the pop-up menu that appears
                 Click **3½ Floppy [A:]**

HOW TO CREATE A QUICKBOOKS® PRO BACKUP FILE

As you work with a company and record transactions, it is important to back up your work. This allows you to keep the information for a particular period separate from current information. A backup also allows you to restore information in case your data disk becomes damaged. There are two different ways in which you can make a backup of your data. If you use Windows Explorer you can make a duplicate disk. In Windows, this is called making a backup. If you use QuickBooks Pro to make a backup, you are actually asking QuickBooks Pro to create a condensed file that contains the essential transaction and account information. This file has a **.qbb** extension and is not usable unless it is restored to a working company file that has a **.qbw** extension. Before entering transactions for Contempo Computer Consulting (CCC) in Chapter 2, make a QuickBooks Pro backup of the company data from the Contempo disk created above.

  DO: Insert the **Contempo** disk in **A:**

Click **File**
Click **Open Company**
Click the drop-down list arrow for **Look in**
Click **3½ Floppy [A:]**
Click **Contempo** in the center of the dialog box
- *Note:* You may or may not have the file extension.qbw shown in the dialog box. Check the "Files of type:" text box at the bottom of the screen and make sure the file type is .qbw.

Click the **Open** button

Once Contempo Computer Consulting is open, click **File** on the menu bar
Click **Back Up...**
- QuickBooks Backup has two tabs: Back Up Company File and Schedule a Backup.

The **Back Up Company File** tab should be active

Verify the Current Company information
    Filename is Contempo.qbw
    Location is A:\
Backup Current Company should be to Disk
    The circle in front of Disk should have a black dot in it
    Filename should be Contempo.qbb
        If it is not, click in the text box and enter Contempo.qbb
    Location should be A:\
        If it is not, click in the text box and enter A:\
            OR
    Click the **Browse** button
    The **Back Up Company To...** dialog box appears
    Click the drop-down list arrow next to **Save in**, click **3½ Floppy [A:]**.
    Click **Save**
Click **OK**

- *Note:* If you store a backup file on the same disk as a company file, QuickBooks may not allow you to use the disk when you are working. QuickBooks needs a certain amount of disk space used for temporary storage in order to record a transaction. Check with your instructor regarding the storage location of your working file and your backup files.
- QuickBooks Pro will back up the information for Contempo Computer Consultants on the **Contempo** data disk in the A: drive.

QuickBooks Pro displays a dialog box stating that the backup was successful. Click
    OK
Click **File**
Click **Close Company**

CREATE A DUPLICATE DISK

In addition to making a backup of the company file, you should always have a duplicate of the disk you use for your work. Refer to Appendix A: Introduction to Windows–Screens, Terminology, and Disk Duplication for instructions on how to use Windows Explorer to make a duplicate copy of your disk.

HOW TO EXIT QUICKBOOKS® PRO AND END YOUR WORK SESSION

When you complete your work, you need to exit the QuickBooks Pro program. If you are saving work on a separate data disk (in A:), you must not remove your disk until you exit the program. Following the appropriate steps to close and exit a program is extremely important. There are program and data files that must be closed in order to leave the program and company data so that they are ready to be used again. It is common for a beginning computer user to turn off the computer without exiting a program. This can cause corrupt program and data files and can make a disk or program unusable. Always close the company as you did in the How to Close a Company section of this chapter before exiting QuickBooks Pro. Once QuickBooks Pro has been closed, remove your data disk from A: and shut down Windows in the manner you have been instructed to use by your instructor.

 DO: There are several ways to exit QuickBooks Pro properly.
Select the method of choice and close/exit QuickBooks Pro:
Click the **Control menu box** or **icon** in the upper left corner of title bar, click **Close**
Double-click the **Control menu box** or **icon** in the upper left corner of title bar
Click the **Close** button in upper right corner of title bar
Click **File** (or **Alt+F**), click **Exit** (or type **X**)
Alt+F4
Remove your Contempo data disk from A:\ and if instructed to do so shut down Windows

SUMMARY

Chapter 1 provides general information regarding QuickBooks Pro. In this chapter, the mouse was used, the computer was turned on, different menus were accessed, a company was opened and closed, reports and business forms were examined, a duplicate of a company file and a backup file were made.

END-OF-CHAPTER QUESTIONS

TRUE/FALSE

ANSWER THE FOLLOWING QUESTIONS IN THE SPACE PROVIDED BEFORE THE QUESTION NUMBER.

_____ 1. There are various methods of giving QuickBooks Pro commands, including use of QuickBooks Navigator, icon bar, menu bar, and keyboard shortcuts.

_____ 2. In QuickBooks Pro, the Window menu is used to switch between documents that have been opened, to arrange icons, and to show more than one open window.

_____ 3. RAM storage is measured in bytes.

_____ 4. If an error is made when entering a transaction, QuickBooks Pro will not allow the user to return to the business document and make the correction.

_____ 5. In a computerized accounting system, each transaction that is analyzed must be entered by hand into the appropriate journal and posted to the appropriate ledger.

_____ 6. QuickBooks Navigator appears beneath the title bar and has a list of drop-down menus.

_____ 7. If you use QuickBooks Pro to make a backup, you are actually asking QuickBooks Pro to create a condensed file that contains the essential transaction and account information.

_____ 8. The Alt key + a letter are used to access the drop-down menus on the menu bar.

_____ 9. When you have exited your application programs and are ready to close Windows, you need to follow proper exit/closing procedures.

_____ 10. Customers, vendors, sales items, and accounts may be added only after the end of the period has been closed.

MULTIPLE CHOICE

WRITE THE LETTER OF THE CORRECT ANSWER IN THE SPACE PROVIDED BEFORE
THE QUESTION NUMBER.

_____   1. QuickBooks Pro gives you an instant visual analysis of different elements of your
business using ___.
A. line graphs
B. pie charts
C. bar charts
D. both B and C

_____   2. QuickMath displays ___.
A. a calculator
B. an adding machine tape
C. a calculator with adding machine tape
D. none of the above

_____   3. QuickBooks Pro keyboard conventions ___.
A. are keyboard command shortcuts
B. use the mouse
C. use certain keys in a manner consistent with Windows
D. incorporate the use of QuickBooks Navigator

_____   4. Buttons on the toolbar and on the bottom of an invoice are used to ___.
A. give commands to QuickBooks Pro
B. exit QuickBooks Pro
C. prepare reports
D. show graphs of invoices prepared

_____   5. The Help Index provides ___.
A. step-by-step instructions for using Help
B. an on-screen index used for finding Help topics
C. a search of all occurrences of a word or a phrase
D. all of the above

_____   6. QuickBooks Navigators ___.
A. are frequently used windows that provide fast access to areas of QuickBooks Pro
B. are icons shown in a row beneath the menu bar
C. appears above the menu bar
D. appears at the bottom of the screen

_____ 7. An icon is ___.
   A. a document
   B. a picture
   C. a chart
   D. a type of software

_____ 8. The QuickBooks Pro program is a type of ___ software.
   A. operating system
   B. forecasting
   C. application
   D. word processing

_____ 9. There are ___ sections or categories available on the Navigator bar.
   A. 5
   B. 7
   C. 8
   D. 4

_____ 10. To verify the name of the open company, look at ___.
   A. the icon bar
   B. QuickBooks Navigator
   C. the menu bar
   D. the title bar

FILL-IN

IN THE SPACE PROVIDED, WRITE THE ANSWER THAT MOST APPROPRIATELY COMPLETES THE SENTENCE.

1. The most common input devices are _____, _____, and _____.

2. The information processing cycle comprises _____, _____, _____, and _____.

3. Two types of software used are _____ software and _____ software.

4. In QuickBooks you open a company, close a company, and backup a company by making selections on the _____ menu.

5. Lists used in QuickBooks Pro have a maximum of _____ to _____ items.

SHORT ESSAY

Describe the term "on the fly" and tell how it is used in QuickBooks Pro.

_____

_____

_____

_____

_____

SALES AND RECEIVABLES: SERVICE BUSINESS

LEARNING OBJECTIVES

At the completion of this chapter, you will be able to:

1. Create invoices and record sales transactions on account.
2. Create sales receipts to record cash sales.
3. Edit, void, and delete invoices/sales receipts.
4. Create credit memos/refunds.
5. Add new customers and modify customer records.
6. Record cash receipts.
7. Enter partial cash payments.
8. Display and print invoices, sales receipts, and credit memos.
9. Display and print Quick Reports, Customer Balance Summary Reports, Customer Balance Detail Reports, and Transaction Reports by Customer.
10. Display and print Summary Sales by Item Reports and Itemized Sales by Item Reports.
11. Display and print Deposit Summary, Journal Reports, and Trial Balance.
12. Display Accounts Receivable Graphs and Sales Graphs.

ACCOUNTING FOR SALES AND RECEIVABLES

Rather than use a traditional Sales Journal to record transactions using debits and credits and special columns, QuickBooks Pro uses an invoice to record sales transactions for accounts receivable in the Accounts Receivable Register. Because cash sales do not involve accounts receivable, QuickBooks Pro puts the money from a cash sale into the Undeposited Funds Register until you record a deposit to a bank account. Instead of being recorded within special journals, cash receipt transactions are entered as activities. However, all transactions, regardless of the activity, are placed in the General Journal behind the scenes. A new customer can be added on the fly as transactions are entered. Unlike many computerized accounting programs, in QuickBooks Pro, error correction is easy. A sales form may be edited, voided, or deleted in the same window where it was created. Customer information may be changed by editing the Customer List. A multitude of reports are available when using QuickBooks Pro. Accounts receivable reports include Customer Balance Summary and Balance Detail reports. Sales reports provide information regarding the amount of sales by item. Transaction Reports by Customer are available as well as the traditional accounting reports such as Trial Balance, Profit and Loss, and Balance Sheet. QuickBooks Pro also has graphing capabilities so you can see and evaluate your accounts receivable and sales at the click of a button.

TRAINING TUTORIAL

The following tutorial is a step-by-step guide to recording receivables (both cash and credit) and cash receipts for a fictitious company with fictitious employees. This company is called Contempo Computer Consulting (CCC) and is sometimes referred to as "CCC." In addition to recording transactions using QuickBooks Pro, we will prepare several reports and graphs for CCC. The tutorial for Contempo Computer Consulting will continue in Chapters 3 and 4, where accounting for payables, bank reconciliations, financial statement preparation, and closing an accounting period will be completed.

TRAINING PROCEDURES

To maximize the training benefits, you should:

1. Read the entire chapter *before* beginning the tutorial within the chapter.
2. Answer the end-of-chapter questions.
3. Be aware that transactions to be entered are given within a **MEMO**.
4. Complete all the steps listed for the Contempo Computer Consulting tutorial in the

   chapter. (Indicated by: **DO:**)
5. When you have completed a section, put an **X** on the button next to **DO:**.
6. If you do not complete a section, put the date in the margin next to the last step completed. This will make it easier to know where to begin when training is resumed.
7. As you complete your work, proofread carefully and check for accuracy. Double-check amounts of money.
8. If you find an error while preparing a transaction, correct it. If you find the error after the Invoice, Sales Form, Credit Memo, or Customer:Job List is complete, follow the steps indicated in this chapter to correct, void, or delete transactions.
9. Print as directed within the chapter.
10. You may not finish the entire chapter in one computer session. Always use QuickBooks Pro to back up your work at the end of your work session as described in Chapter 1 and make a duplicate disk as described in Appendix A.
11. When you complete your computer session, always close your company. If you try to use a computer for CCC and a previous student did not close the company, QuickBooks Pro may freeze when you put in your disk. In addition, if you do not close the company as you leave, you may have problems with your company file, your disk may be damaged, and you may have unwanted .qbi (QuickBooks In Use) files that cause your data disk to become full.

COMPANY PROFILE: CONTEMPO COMPUTER CONSULTING (CCC)

As the name indicates, Contempo Computer Consulting (CCC) is a company specializing in computer consulting. CCC provides program installation, training, and technical support for today's business software as well as getting clients online and giving instruction in the use of the Internet. In addition, Contempo Computer Consulting will set up computer systems for customers and will install basic computer components, such as memory, modems, sound cards, disk drives, and CD-ROM drives.

Contempo Computer Consulting is located in Southern California and is a sole proprietorship owned by Brian Colbert. Mr. Colbert is involved in all aspects of the business and has the responsibility of obtaining clients. CCC has three employees: Monique Wilson, who is responsible for software training; Jason Jung, who handles hardware installation and technical support; and Maria Garcia, whose duties include being office manager and bookkeeper and providing technical support.

CCC bills by the hour for training and hardware installation with a minimum charge of $95 for the first hour and $80 per hour thereafter. Clients with contracts for technical support are charged a monthly rate for service.

BEGIN TRAINING IN QUICKBOOKS® PRO

As you continue this chapter, you will be instructed to enter transactions for Contempo Computer Consulting. The first thing you must do in order to work is boot up or start your computer.

     DO: Turn on computer and monitor, if not already on
                  Allow the computer to boot up and show the Windows desktop

HOW TO OPEN QUICKBOOKS® PRO

As you learned in Chapter 1, once you are in Windows, opening QuickBooks Pro is as easy as pointing and clicking.

     DO: Insert **Contempo Data Disk** in **A:**
                  Click **Start**
                  Point to **Programs**
                  Point to **QuickBooks Pro**
                  Click **QuickBooks Pro**

- *Note:* Refer to Chapter 1 if you require more detailed instructions.
- Check with your instructor to see if there is a different method you should use to open the program.

OPEN A COMPANY—CONTEMPO COMPUTER CONSULTING (CCC)

In Chapter 1, Contempo Computer Consulting (CCC) was opened and a backup of the company file was made using QuickBooks Pro. CCC should have been closed in Chapter 1. To open the company for this work session you may click the Open an Existing Company button on the No Company Open screen or by clicking on File menu and Open Company. Verify this by checking the title bar.

DO: Open **Contempo Computer Consulting**
Click **Open an Existing Company** button at the bottom of the No Company
   Open screen
   OR
Click **File** on the Menu bar and click **Open Company**

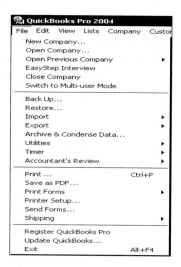

Click the drop-down list arrow for **Look in**
Click **3 ½ Floppy [A:]** or whatever drive your instructor wants you to use
Locate **Contempo.qbw** (under the **Look in** text box)
Double-click **Contempo.qbw** to open, or click **Contempo.qbw** and click **Open**

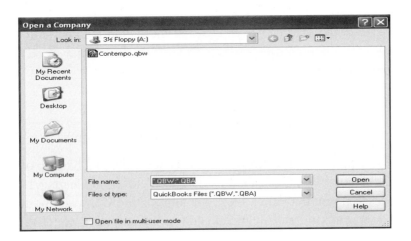

If you get a screen to Set Closing Date Password?, click **No**

VERIFYING AN OPEN COMPANY

    DO: Verify the title bar heading:

- *Note:* Unless you tell QuickBooks Pro to create a new company, open a different company, or close the company, Contempo Computer Consulting (CCC) will appear as the open company whenever you open QuickBooks Pro.
- If you do not close the company at the end of your computer session and another student tries to work for CCC using the Contempo disk he or she created in Chapter 1, QuickBooks Pro may freeze. Also, if you do not close the company as you leave, you may have problems with your company file, your disk may be damaged, and you may have unwanted .qbi (QuickBooks In Use) files that cause your data disk to become full.
- Always close your company at the end of the work session.

ADD YOUR NAME TO THE COMPANY NAME

Because each student in the course will be working for the same companies and printing the same documents, personalizing the company name to include your name will help identify many of the documents you print during your training.

    DO: Add your name to the company name

Click **Company** on the menu bar

Click **Company Information**

Click to the right of **Contempo Computer Consulting (CCC)**

Replace the words **Your Name** by holding down the left mouse button and dragging through the "Your Name" to highlight

Type your actual name, *not* the words *Your Name*. For example, Alex Story would type **Alex Story**

Repeat the steps to change the legal name Contempo Computing Consultants (CCC)—Your Name to Contempo Computing Consultants (CCC)—Student's Name

Click **OK**

- The title bar now shows Contempo Computing Consultants (CCC)—Student's Name

> Contempo Computer Consulting (CCC)--Student's Name - QuickBooks Pro 2004

QUICKBOOKS® NAVIGATORS

QuickBooks Navigators are graphic screens you may use to enter information/transactions in QuickBooks Pro. You may also choose to use the menu bar, the icon bar, or the keyboard to give commands to QuickBooks Pro. For more detailed information regarding QuickBooks Navigators, refer to Chapter 1. Instructions in this text will be given primarily for QuickBooks Navigators. However, the menu bar, the icon bar, and/or keyboard methods will be used as well.

When you first enter QuickBooks Pro, you will see the list of Navigators on the left side of your screen. As you click on the Navigator headings, you will open the QuickBooks Navigator for that area of transactions. For example, when you clicked Company on the Navigator list, you opened the QuickBooks Navigator for Company. You may open other QuickBooks Navigators by clicking the Navigator list (Customers for instance) or by clicking the Navigators button at the top of the current Navigator, Company.

Company

BEGINNING THE TUTORIAL

In this chapter you will be entering both accounts receivable transactions and cash sales transactions. Much of the organization of QuickBooks Pro is dependent on lists. The two primary types of lists you will use in the tutorial for receivables are a Customer:Job List and a Sales Item List.

The names, addresses, telephone numbers, credit terms, credit limits, and balances for all established credit customers are contained in the Customer:Job List. The Customer:Job List can also be referred to as the Accounts Receivable Ledger. QuickBooks Pro does not use this term; however, the Customer:Job List does function as the Accounts Receivable Ledger. A transaction entry for an individual customer is posted to the customer's account in the Customer:Job List just as it would be posted to the customer's individual account in an Accounts Receivable Ledger. The balance of the Customer:Job List will be equal to the balance of the Accounts Receivable account in the Chart of Accounts, which is also the General Ledger. Invoices and accounts receivable transactions can also be related to specific jobs you are completing for customers. You will be using the following Customer:Job List for established credit customers.

Customer:Job List	Ask a help question	Ask	How Do I?	
Name	Balance	Notes	Job Status	
Bailey, Eric Research Corp.	815.00			
Banks, Jones, and Monroe	1,915.00			
Childers, Timothy CPA	475.00			
Design Creations	3,230.00			
Earl, Raymond CPA	0.00			
Green, Bernstein, and Chung, CPA	0.00			
Jacobs, Young, Porter, and Wenzel	3,680.00			
Jimenez, Claire	0.00			
Morales, Juan	150.00			
Movie and Sound Innovations	1,295.00			
Nassar, Armagh Imports	300.00			
Roberts Illustrations	3,830.00			
Sanders, Omar, Kandar, and Hickam	0.00			
Wagner, Rose, and Brandeiss	3,685.00			
Waterson Productions	3,190.00			
White, Improta, and Valdez	0.00			

| Customer:Job ▼ | Activities ▼ | Reports ▼ | Show All |

Various types of income are considered to be sales. In CCC, there are several income accounts. In addition, there are categories within an income account. For example, CCC uses Training Income to represent revenues earned by providing on-site training. The sales items used for Training Income are Training 1 for the first or initial hour of on-site training and Training 2 for all additional hours of on-site training. As you look at the Item List, you will observe that the rates for the two items are different. Using lists for sales items allows for flexibility in billing and a more accurate representation of the way in which income is earned. The following Item List for the various types of sales will be used for CCC.

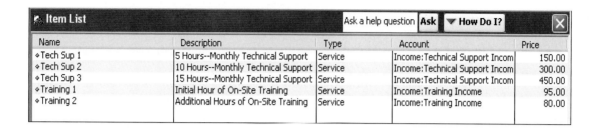

In the tutorial all transactions are listed on memos. The transaction date will be the same date as the memo date unless otherwise specified within the transaction. Always enter the date of the transaction as specified in the memo. By default, QuickBooks Pro automatically enters the current date or the last transaction date used. In many instances, this will not be the same date as the transaction. Customer names, when necessary, will be given in the transaction. All terms for customers on account are Net 30 days unless specified otherwise. If a memo contains more than one transaction, there will be a horizontal line or a blank line separating the transactions.

MEMO

DATE: The transaction date is listed here

Transaction details are given in the body of the memo. Customer names, the type of transaction, amounts of money, and any other details needed are listed here.

Even when you are instructed on how to enter a transaction step by step, you should always refer to the memo for transaction details. Once a specific type of transaction has been entered in a step-by-step manner, additional transactions will be made without having instructions provided. Of course, you may always refer to instructions given for previous transactions for ideas or for steps used to enter those transactions. Always double-check the date and the year used for the transaction. QuickBooks automatically inserts the computer's current date, which will probably be quite different from the date in the text. Using an incorrect date will cause reports to have different totals and transactions than those shown in the text.

ENTER SALES ON ACCOUNT

Because QuickBooks Pro operates on a business form premise, a sale on account is entered via an invoice. You prepare an invoice, and QuickBooks Pro records the transaction in the Journal and updates the customer's account automatically.

MEMO:

DATE: January 2, 2004

Bill the following: Invoice No. 1—Juan Morales has had several questions regarding his new computer system. He spoke with Brian Colbert about this and has signed up for 10 hours of technical support (Tech Sup 2) for January. Bill him for this and use <u>Thank you for your business.</u> as the message.

DO: Record the sale on account shown in the invoice above. This invoice is used to bill a customer for a sale using one sales item:

      Click **Navigators** button at the top of the Company Navigator, and click

          Customers

          OR

      Click **Customers** on the Navigators list

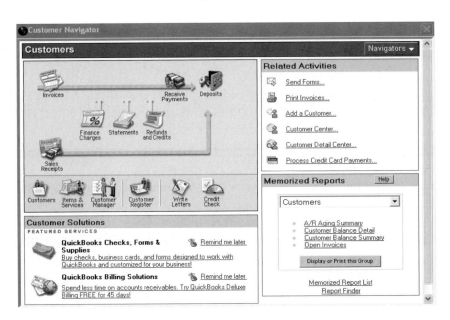

      Click **Invoices** icon
- A blank invoice will show on the screen.

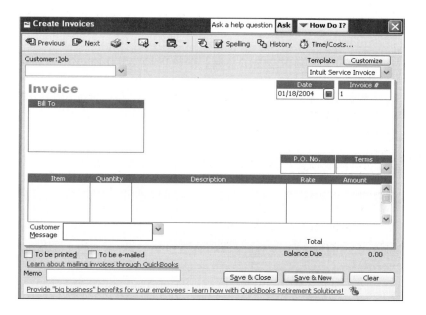

Click the drop-down list arrow next to **Customer:Job**

Click **Morales, Juan**

- His name is entered as Customer:Job, and Bill To information is completed automatically.
- *Note:* The invoice has an icon next to Customer:Job to check the credit of a customer. This is an optional subscription service.

Tab two times to highlight **Intuit Service Invoice**

- Intuit Service Invoice should be displayed in the text box beneath Template. If it is not, click the drop-down list arrow next to the Customize button, click **Intuit Service Invoice**.

Tab to **Date**

- When you tab to the date, it will be highlighted. When you type in the new date, the highlighted date will be deleted.

Type **01/02/04** as the date

Invoice No. 1 should be showing in the **Invoice No.** box

- The Invoice No. should not have to be changed.

There is no PO No. to record

Terms should be indicated as **Net 30**

- If not, click the drop-down list arrow next to **Terms** and click **Net 30**.

Tab to or click the first line beneath **Item**

Click the drop-down list arrow next to **Item**

- Refer to the memo above and the Item List for appropriate billing information.

Click **Tech Sup 2** to bill for 10 hours of technical support

- Tech Sup 2 is entered as the Item.

Tab to or click **Qty**

Type **1**

- The quantity is one because you are billing for 1 unit of Tech Sup 2. As you can see on the Item List, Tech Sup 2 is for 10 hours of support. The total for the item and for the invoice is automatically calculated when you tab to the next item or click in a new invoice area. If you forget to tell QuickBooks Pro to use a quantity, it will automatically calculate the quantity as 1.

Click in the textbox for **Customer Message**

Click the drop-down list arrow next to **Customer Message**

Click **Thank you for your business.**

- Message is inserted in the Customer Message box.

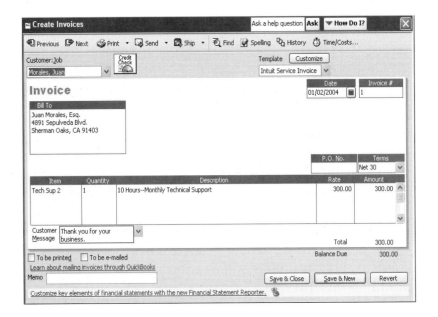

EDIT AND CORRECT ERRORS

If an error is discovered while entering invoice information, it may be corrected by positioning the cursor in the field containing the error. You may do this by clicking in the field containing the error, tabbing to move forward through each field, or pressing Shift+Tab to move back to the field containing the error. If the error is highlighted, type the correction. If the error is not highlighted, you can correct the error by pressing the backspace or the delete key as many times as necessary to remove the error, then typing the correction. (Alternate method: Point to the error, highlight by dragging the mouse through the error, then type the correction or press the Delete key to remove completely.)

DO: Practice editing and making corrections to Invoice No. 1:

Click the drop-down list arrow next to **Customer:Job**

Click **Childers, Timothy CPA**

- Name is changed in Customer:Job and Bill To information is also changed.

Click to the left of the first number in the **Date**—this is **0**

Hold down primary mouse button and drag through the date to highlight.

Type **10/24/04** as the date

- This removes the 01/02/2004 date originally entered.

Click to the right of the **1** in **Quantity**

Backspace and type a **2**

Press **Tab** to see how QuickBooks automatically calculates the new total

To eliminate the changes made to Invoice No. 1, click the drop-down list arrow
    next to **Customer:Job**

Click **Morales, Juan**

Click the cursor so it is in front of the **1** in the **Date**

Press the Delete key until the date is removed

Type **01/02/04**

Click to the right of the **2** in **Quantity**

Backspace and type a **1**

Press the Tab key

- This will cause QuickBooks Pro to calculate the amount and the total for the
  invoice and will move the cursor to the Description field.

- Invoice No. 1 has been returned to the correct customer, date, and quantity.
  Compare the information you entered with the information provided in the
  memo.

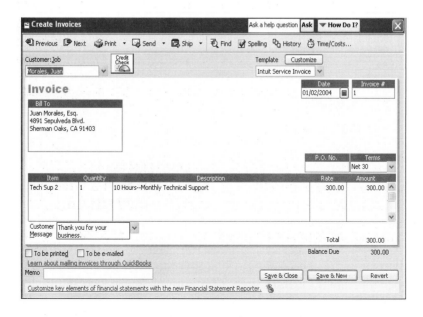

PRINT AN INVOICE

 DO: With Invoice No. 1 on the screen, print the invoice immediately after entering information

Click **Print** at the top of the **Create Invoices** screen
- If you click the drop-down list arrow for the Print button, you will get a list of printing options. Click the **Print** option.

Check the information on the **Print One Invoice Settings** tab:

Printer name (should identify the type of printer you are using):
- This may be different from the printer identified in this text.

Printer type: Page-oriented (Single sheets)

Print on: Blank paper
- The circle next to this should be filled. If it is not, click the circle to select.

Click the **Do not print lines around each field** check box to select.
- If there is a check in the box, lines will not print around each field.
- If a check is not in the box, lines will print around each field.

Number of copies should be 1
- If a number other than 1 shows:
  Click in the box
  Drag to highlight the number
  Type **1**

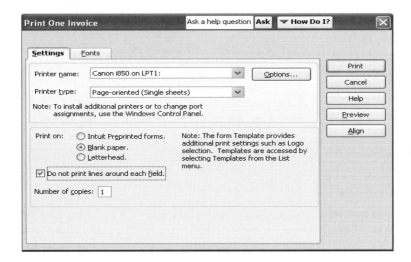

Click the **Print** button
- This initiates the printing of the invoice through QuickBooks Pro. However, because not all classroom configurations are the same, check with your instructor for specific printing instructions.
- If QuickBooks Pro prints your name on two lines, do not be concerned.

Click **Save & Close** button at the bottom of the **Create Invoices** screen to record and close the invoice

ENTER TRANSACTIONS USING TWO SALES ITEMS

MEMO:

Date: January 3, 2004

Bill the following: Invoice No. 2—Timothy Childers, CPA, spoke with Brian Colbert regarding the need for on-site training to help him get started using the Internet. Bill him for a 5-hour on-site training session with Monique McBride. Use <u>Thank you for your business.</u> as the message. (Remember to use Training 1 for the first hour of on-site training and Training 2 for all additional hours of training.)

DO: Record a transaction on account for a sale involving two sales items:
Click the **Invoices** icon on the QuickBooks Customers Navigator
Click the drop-down list arrow next to **Customer:Job**
Click **Childers, Timothy, CPA**
- Name is entered as Customer:Job. Bill To information is completed automatically.
Tab to or click **Date**
Delete the current date
- Refer to instructions for Invoice No. 1 or to editing practice if necessary.
Type **01/03/04** as the date
Make sure that Invoice No. 2 is showing in the **Invoice No.** box
- The Invoice No. should not have to be changed.
There is no PO No. to record
Terms should be indicated as **Net 30**
Tab to or click the first line beneath **Item**
- Refer to Memo and Item List for appropriate billing information.
- *Note:* Services are recorded based on sales items and are not related to the employee who provides the service.
Click the drop-down list arrow next to **Item**
Click **Training 1**
- Training 1 is entered as the Item.
Tab to or click **Quantity**
Type **1**

- Amount will be calculated automatically and entered into the Amount Column when you go to the next line. Notice the amount is $95.00.

Tab to or click the second line for **Item**

Click the drop-down list arrow next to **Item**

Click **Training 2**

Tab to or click **Quantity**

Type **4**

- The total amount of training time is five hours. Because the first hour is billed as Training 1, the remaining four hours are billed as Training 2 hours. The total amount due for the Training 2 hours and the total for the invoice are automatically calculated when you go to the Customer Message box.

Click **Customer Message**

Click the drop-down list arrow next to **Customer Message**

Click **Thank you for your business.**

- Message is inserted in the Customer Message box.

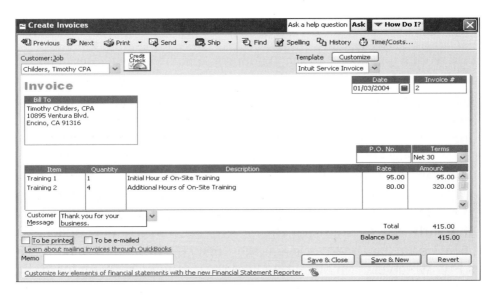

PRINT AN INVOICE

 DO: With Invoice No. 2 on the screen, print the invoice immediately after entering invoice information

Click **Print** button on the **Create Invoices** screen

- If you click the drop-down list arrow for the Print button, you will get a list of printing options. Click the **Print** option.

Check the information on the **Print One Invoice Settings** tab:

Printer name (should identify the type of printer you are using):

- This may be different from the printer identified in this text.

Printer type: Page-oriented (Single sheets)

Print on: Blank paper

- The circle next to this should be filled. If it is not, click the circle to select.

Do not Print lines around each field check box should have a check mark

- If it does not have a check mark, click the box to select.

Click the **Print** button

- This initiates the printing of the invoice through QuickBooks Pro.
- If QuickBooks Pro prints your name on two lines, do not be concerned.

Click **Save & Close** button at the bottom of the **Create Invoices** screen to record and close the invoice

PREPARE INVOICES WITHOUT STEP-BY-STEP INSTRUCTIONS

MEMO:

DATE: January 5, 2004

Bill the following: Invoice No. 3—Claire Jimenez needed to have telephone assistance to help her set up her Internet connection. Prepare an invoice as the bill for 10 hours of technical support for January. (Remember customers are listed by last name in the Customer List. Refer to Item List to select the correct Income account for billing.)

Invoice No. 4—Sanders, Omar, Kandar, and Hickam have several new employees that need to be trained in the use of the office computer system. Bill them for 40 hours of on-site training from Monique McBride. (CCC does not record a transaction based on the employee who performs the service. It simply bills according to the service provided.)

Invoice No. 5—Green, Bernstein, and Chung, CPA, need to learn the basic features of QuickBooks Pro, which is used by many of their customers. Bill them for 10 hours of on-site training and 15 hours of technical support for January so they may call and speak to Jason Jung regarding additional questions. (Note: You will use three sales items in this transaction.)

Invoice No. 6—White, Improta, and Valdez has a new assistant office manager. CCC is providing 40 hours of on-site training for Beverly Williams. To provide additional assistance, the company has signed up for 5 hours technical support for January.

 DO: Enter the four transactions in the memo above. Refer to instructions given for the two previous transactions entered.

- Remember, when billing for on-site training, the first hour is billed as Training 1, and the remaining hours are billed as Training 2.
- Always use the Item List to determine the appropriate sales items for billing.
- Use <u>Thank you for your business.</u> as the message for these invoices.
- If <u>you</u> make an error, correct it.
- Print each invoice immediately after you enter the information for it.
- To go from one invoice to the next, click the **Save & New** button.
- Click **Save & Close** after Invoice No. 6 has been entered and printed.

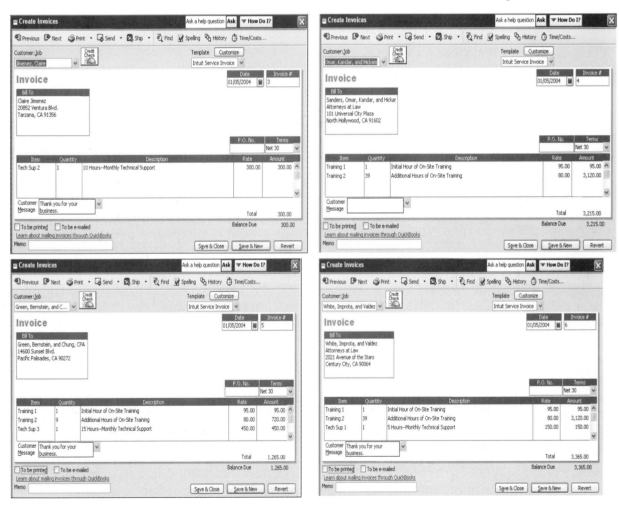

PRINT A/R REPORTS

QuickBooks Pro has several reports available for accounts receivable. One of the most useful is the Customer Balance Summary Report. It shows you the balances of all the customers on account.

DO: Click **Reports** on the menu bar
Point to **Customers & Receivables**
Click **Customer Balance Summary**
- The report should appear on the screen.
- The current date and time will appear on the report. Since the dates given in the text will not be the same date as the computer, it may be helpful to remove the date and time prepared from your report.

To remove the current date from the report:
Click **Modify Report**
Click the **Header/Footer** tab
Click the check box next to **Date Prepared** to deselect this option
Click the check box next to **Time Prepared** to deselect this option
- Note: Some reports will also have a Report Basis—Cash or Accrual. You may turn off the display of the report basis by clicking the check box for this option.

Click **OK** on the **Modify Report** screen
Change the Dates for the report:
Click in or tab to **From**
Enter **01/01/04**
Tab to **To**
Enter **01/05/04**
Press the Tab key
- After you enter the date, pressing the tab key will generate the report.
- This report lists the names of all customers with balances on account. The amount column shows the total balance for each customer. This includes opening balances as well as current invoices.

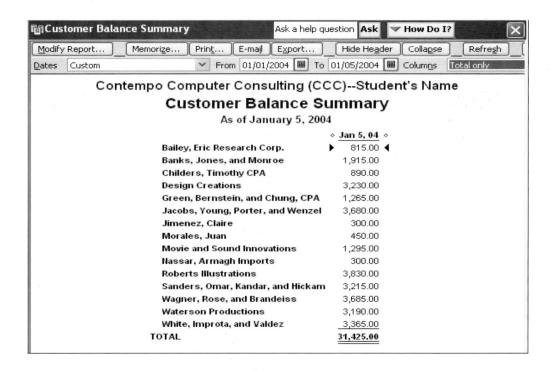

Click the **Print** button at the top of the Customer Balance Summary Report
- You may get the following dialog box. If you do, click **OK**.

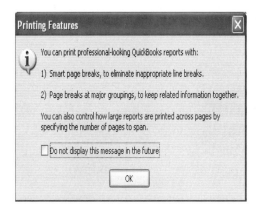

Complete the information on the **Print Reports Settings** tab:

Print To: The selected item should be **Printer**
- Printer name should appear in the printer text box. This may be different from the printer identified in this text.

If the printer name is not in the text box:

Click the drop-down list arrow

Click the correct printer

Orientation: Should be Portrait. If it is not, click **Portrait** to select Portrait orientation for this report

- Portrait orientation prints in the traditional 8 ½- by 11-inch paper size.

Page Range: **All** should be selected; if it is not, click **All**

Page Breaks: Smart page breaks (widow/orphan control) should be selected

Number of copies should be **1**

If necessary, click on **Fit report to one page wide** to deselect this item

- When selected, the printer will print the report using a smaller font so it will be one page in width.

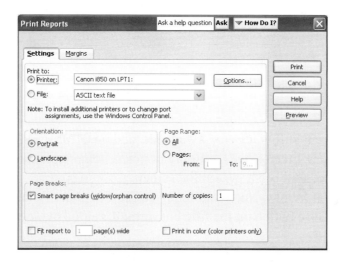

Click **Print** on the **Print Reports** screen

Do not close the **Customer Balance Summary Report**

USE THE QUICKZOOM FEATURE

Brian Colbert asks the office manager, Maria Garcia, to obtain information regarding the balance of the Sanders, Omar, Kandar, and Hickam account. To get detailed information regarding an individual customer's balance while in the Customer Balance Summary Report, use the Zoom feature. With the individual customer's information on the screen, you can print a report for that customer.

DO: Point to the balance for **Sanders, Omar, Kandar, and Hickam**

- Notice that the mouse pointer turns into a magnifying glass with a **Z** in it.

Click once to mark the balance **3,215.00**
- Notice the marks on either side of the amount.

Double-click to **Zoom** in to see the details

The report dates used should be from **01/01/04** to **01/05/04**

Remove the Date Prepared, Time Prepared, and Report Basis from the header
- Follow the instructions previously listed for removing the current date from the header for the Customer Balance Summary Report.

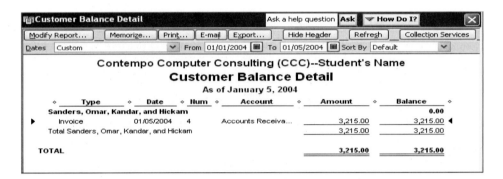

- Notice that Invoice No. 4 was recorded on 01/05/2004 for $3,215.
- To view Invoice No. 4, simply double-click on this transaction, and the invoice will be shown on the screen.
- To exit Invoice No. 4 and return to the Customer Balance Detail Report, click the **Close** button on the title bar of the **Create Invoices** screen for Invoice No. 4.

Print the **Customer Balance Detail Report** for Sanders, Omar, Kandar, and Hickam
- Follow the steps previously listed for printing the Customer Balance Summary Report.

Contempo Computer Consulting (CCC)--Student's Name

Customer Balance Detail

As of January 5, 2004

	Type		Date		Num		Account		Amount		Balance	
Sanders, Omar, Kandar, and Hickam											0.00	
	Invoice		01/05/2004		4		Accounts Receiva...		3,215.00		3,215.00	◀
Total Sanders, Omar, Kandar, and Hickam									3,215.00		3,215.00	
TOTAL									**3,215.00**		**3,215.00**	

Click **Close** to close **Customer Balance Detail Report**
- If you get a screen for Memorize Report, always click **No**

Click **Close** to close **Customer Balance Summary Report**

CORRECT AN INVOICE AND PRINT THE CORRECTED FORM

Errors may be corrected very easily with QuickBooks Pro. Because an invoice is prepared for sales on account, corrections will be made directly on the invoice. We will access the invoice via the register for the Accounts Receivable account.

MEMO:

DATE: January 7, 2004

The actual amount of time spent for on-site training increased from 10 hours to 12 hours. Change Invoice No. 5 to Green, Bernstein, and Chung, CPA, to correct the actual amount of training hours to show a total of 12 hours.

DO: Correct the error described in the above memo and print a corrected invoice:
Click **Company** on the Navigator list
Click **Chart of Accounts** on the QuickBooks Company Navigator
In the Chart of Accounts, click **Accounts Receivable**

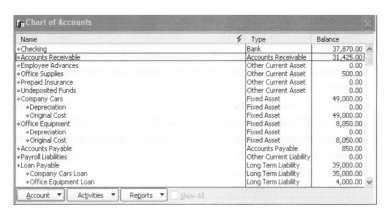

Click **Activities**

Click **Use Register**

    OR

Double-click **Accounts Receivable** in the Chart of Accounts

- The Accounts Receivable Register appears on the screen with information regarding each transaction entered into the account.
- *Note:* This is the same as the Accounts Receivable General Ledger Account

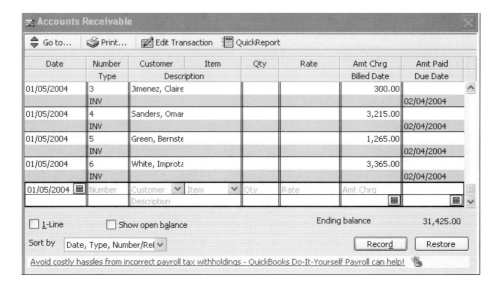

If necessary, scroll through the register until the transaction for **Invoice No. 5** is on the screen

- Look at the **Number/Type** column to identify the number of the invoice and the type of transaction.
- On the Number line you will see an invoice number or a check number.
- On the Type line, INV indicates a sale on account, and PMT indicates a payment received on account.

Click anywhere in the transaction for Invoice No. 5 to Green, Bernstein, and Chung, CPA

Click **Edit Transaction** at the top of the register

- Invoice No. 5 appears on the screen.

Click the line in the **Quantity** field that corresponds to the **Training 2** hours

Change the quantity from 9 hours to 11 hours

Position cursor in front of the 9

Press Delete

Type **11**

Press Tab to generate a new total

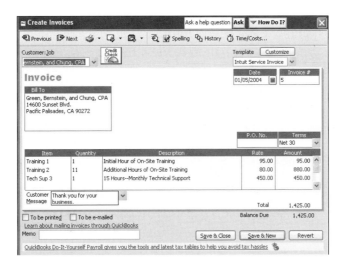

- Notice that the date remains 01/05/2004.

Click **Print** button on the **Create Invoices** screen to print a corrected invoice

Check the information on the **Print One Invoice Settings** tab:

Printer name (should identify the type of printer you are using):

- This may be different from the printer identified in this text.

Printer type: Page-oriented (Single sheets)

Print on: Blank paper

- The circle next to this should be filled. If it is not, click the circle to select.

Do not print lines around each field check box should have a check mark

- If it does not, click the box to select.

Click **Print**

Click **Save & Close** to record changes and close invoice

Click **Yes** on the Recording Transaction dialog box

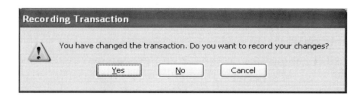

VIEW A QUICKREPORT

After editing the invoice and returning to the register, you may get a detailed report regarding the customer's transactions by clicking the QuickReport button.

DO: After closing the invoice, you return to the register.
Click the **QuickReport** button to view the **Green, Bernstein, and Chung** account

Verify the balance of the account. It should be **$1,425.00**
- *Note:* You will get the date prepared, time prepared, and the report basis in the heading of your QuickReport.

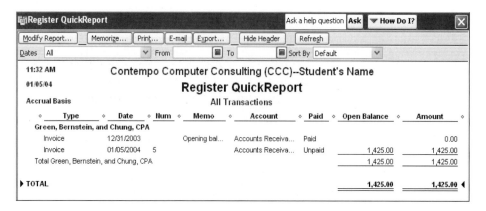

ANALYZE THE QUICKREPORT FOR GREEN, BERNSTEIN, AND CHUNG

DO: Notice that the total of Invoice No. 5 is $1,425.00
Close the **QuickReport** without printing
Close the **Accounts Receivable Register**
Close the **Chart of Accounts**

VOID AND DELETE SALES FORMS

Deleting an invoice or sales receipt permanently removes it from QuickBooks Pro without
leaving a trace. If you would like to correct your financial records for the invoice that you no
longer want, it is more appropriate to void the invoice. When an invoice is voided, it remains in
the QuickBooks Pro system, but QuickBooks Pro does not count it.

Void an Invoice

MEMO:

DATE: January 7, 2004

Claire Jimenez called on January 5 to cancel the 10 hours of technical support for
January. (This was the same day the invoice was recorded.) Because Invoice No. 3 to
Claire Jimenez was prepared in error, void the invoice.

DO: Void the invoice above by going directly to the original invoice:
Use the keyboard shortcut **Ctrl+I** to open the Create Invoices screen
Click the **Previous** button until you get to **Invoice No. 3**
With Invoice No. 3 on the screen, click **Edit** on the menu bar
Click **Void Invoice**
- Notice that the amount and total for the invoice shown above are no longer
  300. They are both **0.00**. Find the Memo text box at the bottom of the screen.
  Verify that the word VOID appears as the memo.

Click **Save & Close** on the **Create Invoices** screen
Click **Yes** on the Recording Transaction dialog box
Click **Reports Finder** on the Company QuickBooks Navigator
Click the drop-down list arrow for Select type of report
Click **Customers & Receivables**
Click **Transaction List by Customer** from Select a Report
- You will see a sample report displayed on the right side of the Report Finder.

Click in **From**
Enter **010104**
Tab to or click in **To**
Enter **010704**

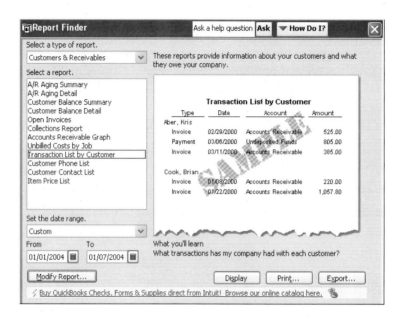

Click the **Display** button to display the report

To remove the date prepared and the time prepared from the report heading:

Click **Modify Report**

Click **Header/Footer** tab

Click the check box next to **Date Prepared** and **Time Prepared** to deselect these
    options

Click **OK**

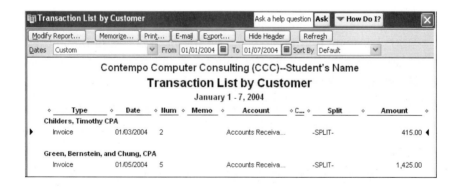

Print transactions for **January**:

Click the **Print** button at the top of the **Transactions List by Customer Report**

Complete the information on the **Print Reports Settings** tab:

Print to: The selected item should be **Printer**

•   Printer name should appear in the printer text box. This may be different from
    the printer identified in this text.

    If the printer name does not appear:

> Click the drop-down list arrow
> Click the correct printer

Orientation: Click **Portrait** to select Portrait orientation for this report

- Portrait orientation prints in the traditional 8½- by 11-inch paper size.

Page Range: **All** should be selected; if it is not, click **All**

Page Breaks: **Smart page breaks** should be selected

Fit report to one page wide should not be used. If it has been selected, click it to deselect

- If selected, the printer will print the report using a smaller font so it will be one page in width.
- Because you are not using the option to fit the report to one-page wide, this report may print on two pages.

Click **Print** on the **Print Reports** screen

- This report gives the amount for each transaction with the customer.
- Notice that Invoice No. 3 is marked VOID in the Memo column and has a √ in the **Clr** column.
- The SPLIT column tells you which account was used to record the income. If the word **-SPLIT-** appears in the column, this means the transaction amount was split or divided among two or more accounts.

Close the **Transaction List by Customer Report**

- If you get a screen for Memorize Report, always click **No**

Close the **Report Finder**

Delete an Invoice

MEMO:

DATE: January 7, 2004

Because of the upcoming tax season, Timothy Childers has had to reschedule his 5-hour training session with Monique McBride three times. Timothy Childers finally decided to cancel the training session and reschedule it after April 15. Delete Invoice No. 2 to Timothy Childers.

DO: Delete the above transaction, using Find to locate the invoice:

- Find is useful when you have a large number of invoices and want to locate an invoice for a particular customer.
- Using Find will locate the invoice without requiring you to scroll through all the invoices for the company. For example, if customer Jiminez's transaction was on Invoice No. 3 and the invoice on the screen was Invoice No. 1,084,

you would not have to scroll through 1,081 invoices because Find would locate Invoice No. 3 instantly.

- QuickBooks Pro 2004 has two methods for finding transactions: simple find and advanced find.
- Simple Find allows you to do a quick search using the most common transaction types. Transaction Types include Invoice, Sales Receipt, Credit Memo, Check, and others. The search results are displayed in the lower portion of the window. You can view an individual transaction by highlighting it and clicking Go To, or you can view a report by clicking Report.
- Advanced Find is used to do a more detailed search for transactions than you can do using Simple Find. Advanced Find allows you to apply filters to your search criteria. When you apply a filter, you choose how you want QuickBooks to restrict the search results to certain customers, for example. QuickBooks then excludes from results any transactions that don't meet your criteria. You can apply filters either one at a time or in combination with each other. Each additional filter you apply further restricts the content of the search. The search results are displayed in the lower portion of the window. You can view an individual transaction by highlighting it and clicking Go To, or you can view a report by clicking Report.

To use Simple Find:

- Click **Edit** on the menu bar

Click **Simple Find**

The Transaction Type should be **Invoice**.

- If it is not, click the drop-down list arrow for Transaction Type and click Invoice.

Click the drop-down list arrow for **Customer/Job:**

Click **Childers, Timothy CPA**

- This allows QuickBooks Pro to find any invoices recorded for Timothy Childers. This is sufficient for now.

Click the **Find** button on the Find dialog box

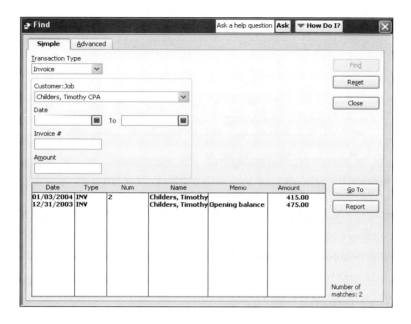

Click the line for **Invoice No. 2**

Make sure you have selected Invoice No. 2 and not the invoice containing the opening balance.

Click **Go To**

- Invoice No. 2 appears on the screen.

With the invoice on the screen, click **Edit** on the menu bar

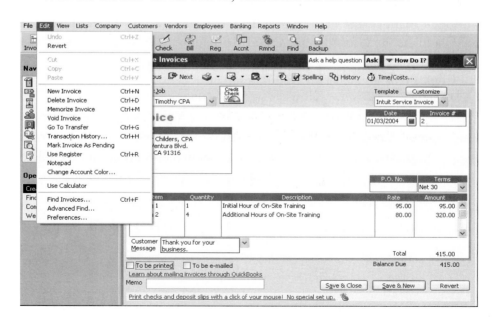

Click **Delete Invoice**

Click **OK** in the **Delete Transaction** dialog box

- Notice that the cursor is now positioned on Invoice No. 3 and that the voided invoice is marked Paid.

Click **Save & Close** button on the **Create Invoices** screen to close the invoice

- Notice that Invoice No. 2 no longer shows on Find.

Click **Close** button to close **Find**

Click **Reports**

Point to **Customers & Receivables**

Click **Customer Balance Detail**

To remove the current date, time, and report basis from the report:

Click the **Modify Report** button, then click the **Header/Footer** button

Click the check box next to **Date Prepared**, **Time Prepared**, and **Report Basis** to deselect these options

Click **OK**

Dates should be **All**

Click **Print** to print report

Click **Print** button at the top of the **Customer Balance Detail Report**

Complete the information on the **Print Reports Settings** tab as previously instructed.

Click **Print** on the **Print Reports** screen

- Look at the account for Timothy Childers.
- Notice that Invoice No. 2 does not show up in the account listing. When an invoice is deleted, there is no record of it anywhere in the report.
- Notice that the Customer Balance Detail Report does not include the information telling you which amounts are opening balances.

- The report does give information regarding the amount owed on each transaction plus the total amount owed by each customer.

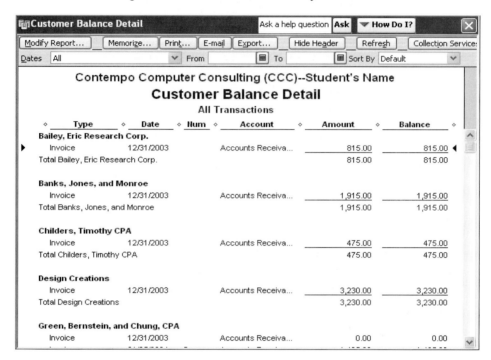

Close the **Customer Balance Detail Report**

PREPARE CREDIT MEMOS

Credit memos are prepared to show a reduction to a transaction. If the invoice has already been sent to the customer, it is more appropriate and less confusing to make a change to a transaction by issuing a credit memo rather than void the invoice and issue a new one. A credit memo notifies a customer that a change has been made to a transaction.

MEMO:

DATE: January 8, 2004

Prepare the following: Credit Memo No. 7—Sanders, Omar, Kandar, and Hickam did not need 5 hours of the training billed on Invoice No. 4. Issue a Credit Memo to reduce Training 2 by 5 hours.

DO: Prepare the Credit Memo shown above:
Click **Customers** on the Navigator bar
Click **Refunds and Credits** on the Customers QuickBooks Navigator

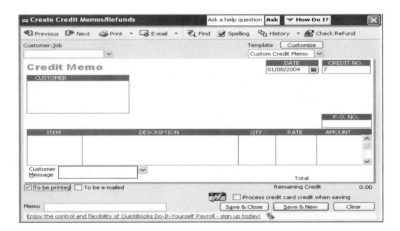

Click the down arrow for the drop-down list box next to **Customer:Job**
Click **Sanders, Omar, Kandar, and Hickam**
Tab twice to **Template** textbox
• It should say **Custom Credit Memo**.
• If not, click the drop-down list arrow and click **Custom Credit Memo**.
Tab to or click **Date**
Type in the date of the credit memo: **01/08/04**
The **Credit No.** field should show the number 7
• Because credit memos are included in the numbering sequence for invoices, this number matches the number of the next blank invoice.
There is no PO No.
• Omit this field.
Tab to or click in **Item**
Click the drop-down list arrow in the Item column
Click **Training 2**
Tab to or click in **Quantity**
Type in **5**
Click the next blank line in the Description column
Type **Deduct 5 hours of additional training, which was not required. Reduce the amount due for Invoice #4.**
• This will print as a note or explanation to the customer.
Click the drop-down list arrow next to **Customer Message**
Click **It's been a pleasure working with you!**

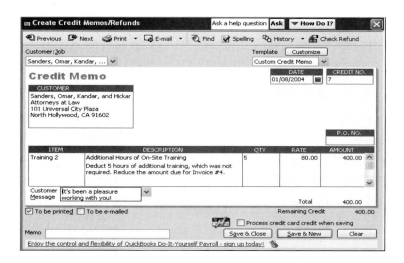

Click **Print** on **Create Credit Memos/Refunds**
Click **Print** on **Print One Credit Memo**
Click the **Save & Close** button on **Create Credit Memos/Refunds** to close
    Credit Memo

VIEW CUSTOMER BALANCE DETAIL REPORT

Periodically viewing reports allows you to verify the changes that have occurred to accounts. The Customer Balance Detail report shows all the transactions for each *credit* customer. Cash customers must be viewed through sales reports.

DO: Click **Reports Finder** on the QuickBooks Customers Navigator
- Customers & Receivables displays as the report type

    Double-click **Customer Balance Detail** on the list of reports displayed
    Scroll through the report
- Notice that the account for Sanders, Omar, Kandar, and Hickam shows Credit Memo No. 7 for $400.00. The total amount owed was reduced by $400 and is $2,815.00.

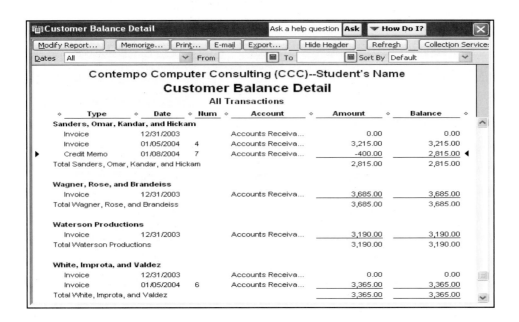

Click **Close** to close the report without printing
Close the **Report Finder**

ADD A NEW ACCOUNT TO THE CHART OF ACCOUNTS

Because account needs can change as a business is in operation, QuickBooks Pro allows you to make changes to the chart of accounts at any time. Some changes to the chart of accounts require additional changes to lists.

Brian Colbert has determined that CCC has received a lot of calls from customers for assistance with hardware installation. Even though Contempo Computer Consulting does not record revenue according to the employee performing the service, it does assign primary areas of responsibility to some of the personnel. Jason Jung will be responsible for installing hardware for customers. As a result of this decision, you will be adding a third income account. This account will be used when revenue from hardware installation is earned. In addition to adding the account, you will also have to add two new sales items to the Item list.

DO: Click the **Navigators** button at the top of the Customers Navigator
                Click **Company** on the drop-down list of QuickBooks Navigators
                Click the **Chart of Accounts** icon on the Navigator
- Remember that the Chart of Accounts is also the General Ledger.

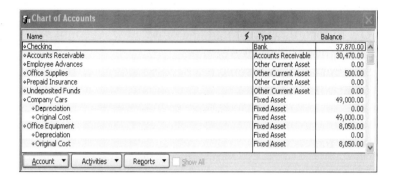

Click the **Account** button at the bottom of the Chart of Accounts screen

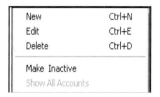

Click **New**
Click the drop-down list arrow next to **Type**
Click **Income**
Tab to or click in the text box for **Name**
Type **Installation Income**
Click the check box for **Subaccount of**
Click the drop-down list arrow for **Subaccount of**
Click **Income**
Tab to or click **Description**
Type **Hardware Installation Income**
Click the **Tax Line** drop-down list arrow
Click **Schedule C: Gross Receipts or Sales**

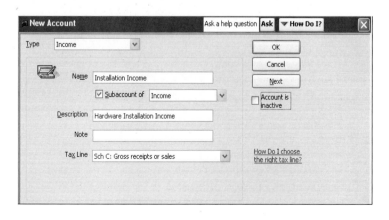

Click **OK** to record new account and close New Account screen
Scroll through the Chart of Accounts
Verify that Installation Income has been added under Income
Close **Chart of Accounts**

ADD NEW ITEMS TO LIST

In order to accommodate the changing needs of a business, all QuickBooks Pro lists allow you to make changes at any time. The Item List stores information about the services CCC provides. In order to use the new Hardware Installation Income account, two new items need to be added to the Item List.

DO: Click **Customers** on the Navigator bar
Click the **Items & Services** folder at the bottom of the QuickBooks Navigator
Click the **Item** button at the bottom of the **Item List** screen
Click **New**
Item Type is **Service**
Tab to or click **Item Name/Number**
Type **Install 1**
Tab to or click **Description**
Type **Initial Hour of Hardware Installation**
Tab to or click **Rate**
Type **95**
To indicate the general ledger account to be used to record the sale of this item, click the drop-down list arrow for **Account**
Click **Installation Income**

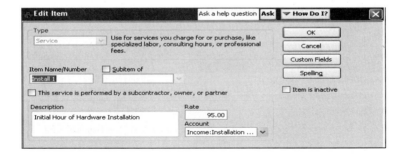

Click **Next** on the New Item dialog box
Repeat the steps above to add **Install 2**

The description is **Additional Hours of Hardware Installation**
The rate is **$80.00** per hour
When finished adding Install 2, click **OK** to add new items and to close **New Item** screen
- Whenever hardware installation is provided for customers, the first hour will be billed as Install 1, and additional hours will be billed as Install 2.
Verify the addition of Install 1 and Install 2 on the Item List
- If you find an error, click on the item with the error, click the **Item** button, click **Edit**, and make corrections as needed.

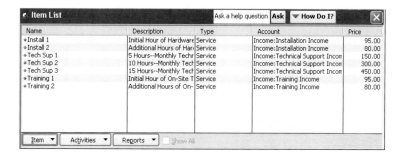

Close the **Item List**

ADD A NEW CUSTOMER

Because customers are the lifeblood of a business, QuickBooks Pro allows customers to be added "on the fly" as you create an invoice or sales receipt. You may choose between Quick Add (used to add only a customer's name) and Set Up (used to add complete information for a customer).

MEMO:

DATE: January 8, 2004

Prepare the following: <u>Invoice No. 8</u>—A new customer, Andrew Anderson, has purchased several upgrade items for his personal computer but needed assistance with the installation. Jason Jung spent two hours installing this hardware. Bill Mr. Anderson for 2 hours of hardware installation. His address is: 20985 Ventura Blvd., Woodland Hills, CA 91371. His telephone number is: 818-555-2058. He does not have a fax. His credit limit is $1,000; and the terms are Net 30.

DO: Record the above sale on account to a new customer:

Click **Invoices** on the Customers Navigator

In the Customer:Job dialog box, type **Anderson, Andrew**

Press **Tab**

- You will see a message box for **Customer:Job Not Found** with buttons for three choices:

  Quick Add (used to add only a customer's name)

  Set Up (used to add complete information for a customer)

  Cancel (used to cancel the **Customer:Job Not Found** message box)

Click **Set Up**

Complete the **New Customer** dialog box

- The name **Anderson, Andrew** is displayed in the Customer Name field and as the first line of Bill To in the Address section on the Address Info tab.

There is no Opening Balance, so leave this field blank

- An opening balance may be given only when the customer's account is created. It is the amount the customer owes you at the time the account is created. It is not the amount of any transaction not yet recorded.

Complete the information for the **Address Info** tab

Tab to or click the first line for **Bill To**

If necessary, highlight **Anderson, Andrew**

Type **Andrew Anderson**

- Entering the customer name in this manner allows for the Customer:Job List to be organized according to the last name, yet the bill will be printed with the first name, then the last name.

Press **Enter** or click the second line of the billing address

Type the address **20985 Ventura Blvd.**

Press **Enter** or click the third line of the billing address

Type **Woodland Hills, CA 91371**

There is no Contact person, so leave this blank

Tab to or click **Phone**

Type the phone number **818-555-2058**

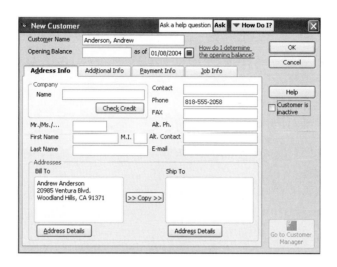

Click **Additional Info** tab
Tab to or click **Terms**
Click the drop-down list arrow
Click **Net 30**

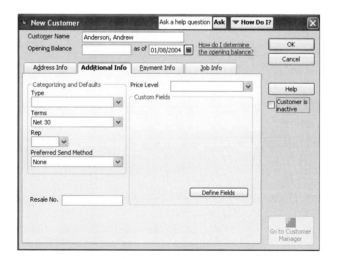

Click **Payment Info** tab
Tab to or click **Credit Limit**
Type the amount **1000**

- Do not use a dollar sign. QuickBooks Pro will insert the comma for you.

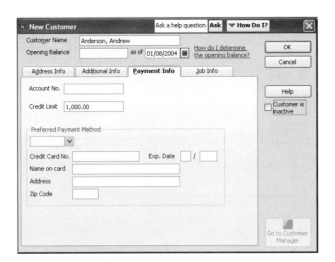

Click **OK** to return to Invoice

Enter Invoice information as previously instructed

Date of the invoice is **01/08/04**

Invoice No. is **8**

The bill is for 2 hours of hardware installation

- Remember to bill for the initial or first hour, then bill the other hour separately.

The message is **Thank you for your business.**

The invoice total should be $175.00

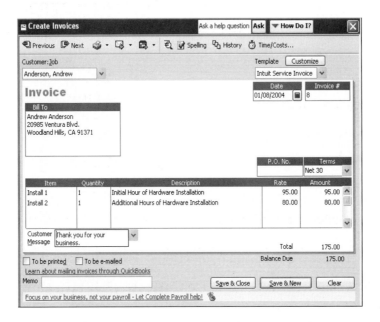

Print the invoice as previously instructed

Click **Save & Close** on the invoice to record and close the transaction

MODIFY CUSTOMER RECORDS

Occasionally, information regarding a customer will change. QuickBooks Pro allows you to modify customer accounts at any time by editing the Customer:Job List.

MEMO:

DATE: January 8, 2004

Update the following account: Design Creations has changed its fax number to 310-555-5959.

DO: Edit the above account:
Access the Customer:Job List:
There are four ways to access the Customer:Job List:
- Click **Lists** on the drop-down menu, click **Customer:Job**.
- Using QuickBooks Customer Navigator, click **Customers** folder.
- Click the **Cust** icon on the icon bar.
- Use the keyboard shortcut: **Ctrl+J**.

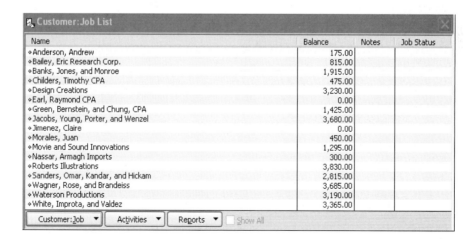

Select Design Creations and access the account in one of the following three ways:
- Click **Design Creations** on the **Customer:Job List:** click the **Customer:Job** button, click **Edit**.
- Click **Design Creations** on the **Customer:Job List**. Use the keyboard shortcut **Ctrl+E**.
- Double-click **Design Creations** on the **Customer:Job List**.

Change the fax number to 310-555-5959:
Click at the end of the fax number
Backspace to delete **11**
Type **59**
Click **OK**

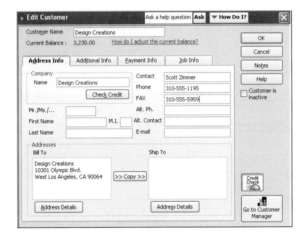

Close the **Customer:Job List**

RECORD CASH SALES

Not all sales in a business are on account. In many instances, payment is made at the time the
service is performed. This is entered as a cash sale. When entering a cash sale, you prepare a
sales receipt rather than an invoice. QuickBooks Pro records the transaction in the Journal and
places the amount of cash received in an account called Undeposited Funds. The funds received
remain in Undeposited Funds until you record a deposit to your bank account.

MEMO:

DATE: January 10, 2004

Prepare the following to record cash sales: Sales Receipt No. 1—Brian Colbert provided
5 hours of on-site training to Raymond Earl, CPA, and received Ray's Check No. 3287
for the full amount due. Prepare Sales Receipt No. 1 for this transaction. Use It's been a
pleasure working with you! as the message.

DO: Enter the following transaction as a cash sale:
           Use the QuickBooks Customer Navigator:

Click **Sales Receipts** icon
- If you get a message for a Merchant Account Service Manager, click **No**

Click the drop-down list arrow next to **Customer:Job**

Click **Earl, Raymond, CPA**

Tab to **Template**
- This should have **Custom Cash Sales** as the template. If not, click the drop-down list arrow and click **Custom Cash Sales**.

Tab to or click **Date**

Type **01/10/04**
- You may click on the calendar icon next to the date text box. Make sure the month is January and the year is 2004 then click 10

Sales No. should be **1**

Tab to or click **Check No.**

Type **3287**

Click the drop-down list arrow next to **Payment Method**

Click **Check**

Tab to or click beneath **Item**

Click the drop-down list arrow next to **Item**

Click **Training 1**

Tab to or click **Qty**

Type **1**
- The amount and total are automatically calculated when you move to the next field.

Tab to or click the second line for **Item**

Click the drop-down list arrow next to **Item**

Click **Training 2**

Tab to or click **Qty**

Type **4**
- The amount and total are automatically calculated when you go to the Customer Message or tab past Qty.

Click **Customer Message**

Click the drop-down list arrow for **Customer Message**

Click **It's been a pleasure working with you!**
- Message is inserted.

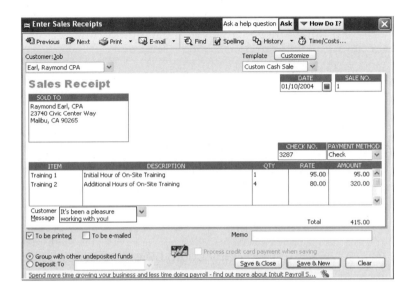

PRINT SALES RECEIPT

DO: Print the sales receipt immediately after entering information
Click **Print** button on the top of the **Enter Sales Receipts** screen
Check the information on the **Print One Sales Receipt Settings** tab:
Printer name (should identify the type of printer you are using):
Printer type: Page-oriented (Single sheets)
Print on: Blank paper
Do not print lines around each field check box should be selected
Number of copies should be **1**
Click **Print**
- This initiates the printing of the sales receipt through QuickBooks Pro. However, since not all classroom configurations are the same, check with your instructor for specific printing instructions.

Once the Sales Receipt has been printed, click **Save & Close** on the bottom of the **Enter Sales Receipts** screen

ENTER CASH SALES TRANSACTIONS WITHOUT STEP-BY-STEP INSTRUCTIONS

MEMO:

DATE: January 12, 2004

Sales Receipt No. 2—Raymond Earl needed additional on-site training to correct some error messages he received on his computer. Brian Colbert provided 1 hour of on-site training for Raymond Earl, CPA, and received Ray's Check No. 3306 for the full amount due. (Even though Mr. Earl has had on-site training previously, this is a new sales call and should have the first hour billed as Training 1.)

Sales Receipt No. 3—Brian Colbert provided 4 hours of on-site Internet training for Eric Bailey Research Corp. so the company could be online. Brian received Check No. 10358 for the full amount due.

DO: Record the two transactions listed above by repeating the procedures used to enter Sales Receipt No. 1:

- Remember, the <u>first hour for on-site training</u> is billed as <u>Training 1</u> and the <u>remaining hours</u> are billed as <u>Training 2</u>.
- Always use the Item List to determine the appropriate sales items for billing.
- Use <u>Thank you for your business.</u> as the message for these sales receipts.
- Print each sales receipt immediately after entering the information for it.
- If you make an error, correct it.
- To go from one sales receipt to the next, click the **Save & New** button on the bottom of the **Enter Sales Receipts** screen.
- Click **Save & Close** after you have entered and printed Sales Receipt No. 3.

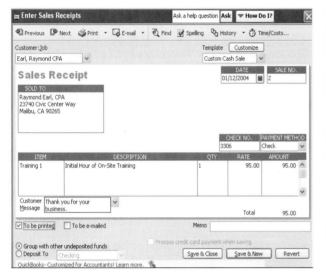 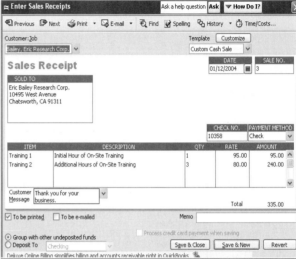

PRINT SALES BY CUSTOMER DETAIL REPORT

QuickBooks Pro has reports available that enable you to obtain sales information about sales items or customers. To get information about the total amount of sales to each customer during a specific period, print a Sales Report by Customer Detail. The total shown represents both cash and/or credit sales.

     DO: Click **Reports** on the menu bar

Point to **Sales**

Click **Sales by Customer Detail**

To remove the **Date Prepared**, **Time Prepared**, and **Report Basis** from the report, click the **Modify Report** button and follow the instructions given previously for deselecting the date prepared, time prepared, and report basis

Change the dates to reflect the sales period desired:

Click in or tab to **From**

Type **01/01/04**

Tab to **To**

Type **01/14/04**

Tab to generate the report

- Notice that the report information includes the type of sales to each customer, the date of the sale, the sales item(s), the quantity for each item, the sales price, the amount, and the balance.
- The report does not include information regarding opening or previous balances due.

- The scope of this report is to focus on sales.

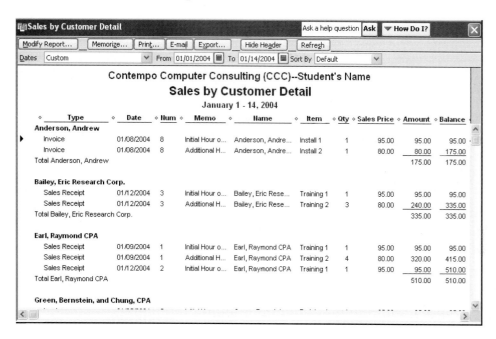

Click the **Print** button on the **Sales by Customer Detail** screen

On the **Print Report** screen, check the Settings tab to verify that **Print to**: Printer is selected and that the name of your printer is correct

Click **Landscape** to change the **Orientation** from Portrait

- Landscape changes the orientation of the paper so the report is printed 11-inches wide by 8½-inches long.

Verify that the **Range** is **All**

Make sure **Smart page breaks** have been selected

On the **Print Report** screen, click **Print**

- Do not select **Fit** report **to one page wide**. The printed report may require more than one page.

Close **Sales by Customer Detail Report**

CORRECT A SALES RECEIPT AND PRINT THE CORRECTED FORM

QuickBooks Pro makes correcting errors user friendly. When an error is discovered in a transaction such as a cash sale, you can simply return to the form where the transaction was recorded and correct the error. Thus, to correct a sales receipt, you would open a Sales Receipt, click the Previous button until you found the appropriate sales receipt, and then correct the error. However, because cash or checks received for cash sales are held in the Undeposited Funds account until the bank deposit is made, you can access the sales receipt through the Undeposited Funds account in the Chart of Accounts. Accessing the receipt in this manner allows you to see all the transactions entered in the account for Undeposited Funds.

When a correction for a sale is made, QuickBooks Pro not only changes the form, it also changes all journal and account entries for the transaction to reflect the correction. QuickBooks Pro then allows a corrected sales receipt to be printed.

MEMO:

DATE: January 14, 2004

After reviewing transaction information, you realize the date for the Sales Receipt No. 1 to Raymond Earl, CPA, was entered incorrectly. Change the date to 1/9/2004.

DO: Correct the error indicated in the memo above and print a corrected sales receipt:
Click **Chart of Accounts** on the QuickBooks Company Navigator
Click **Undeposited Funds**

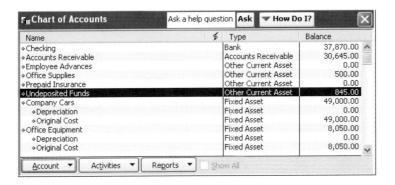

Click the **Activities** button
Click **Use Register**

- The register maintains a record of all the transactions recorded within the Undeposited Funds account.

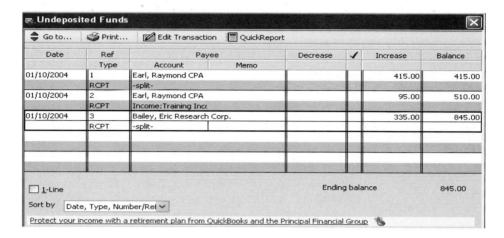

Click anywhere in the transaction for Sales Receipt No. 1 to Raymond Earl, CPA
- Look at the Ref/Type column to see the type of transaction.
- The number in the Ref line indicates the number of the sales receipt or the customer's check number.
- Type shows RCPT for a sales receipt.

Click the **Edit Transaction** button at the top of the register
- The sales receipt appears on the screen.

Tab to or click **Date** field
Change the Date to **01/09/04**
Tab to enter the date

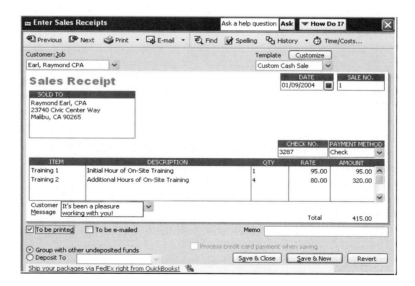

Click the **Print** button on the **Enter Sales Receipts** screen to print a corrected sales receipt

Click **Print** on the **Print One Sales Receipt** screen

Click **Save & Close** on the **Enter Sales Receipts** screen to record changes, close the sales receipt, and return to the Register for Undeposited Funds

Click **Yes** on the **Recording Transaction** dialog box

Do not close the register

VIEW A QUICKREPORT

After editing the sales receipt and returning to the register, you may get a detailed report regarding the customer's transactions by clicking the QuickReport button.

DO: After closing the sales receipt, you are returned to the register for the Undeposited Funds account

Click the **QuickReport** button to display the Register QuickReport for Raymond Earl, CPA

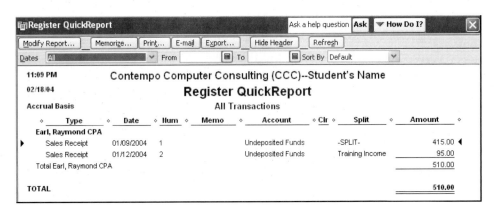

ANALYZE THE QUICKREPORT FOR RAYMOND EARL

DO: Notice that the date for Sales Receipt No. 1 has been changed to **01/09/2004**

- You may need to use the horizontal scroll bar to view all the columns in the report.

The account used is Undeposited Funds

The Split column contains the other accounts used in the transaction

- For Sales Receipt No. 2, the account used is **Training Income**.
- For Sales Receipt No. 1, you see the word **Split** rather than an account name.
- Split means that more than one account was used for this portion of the transaction.

View the accounts used for the Split by using QuickZoom to view the actual Sales
   Receipt
Use QuickZoom by double-clicking anywhere on the information for Sales
   Receipt No. 1
- The accounts used are Training 1 and Training 2.
Close the **Sales Receipt**
Close the **Register QuickReport** without printing
Close the **Register for Undeposited Funds**
Close the **Chart of Accounts**

ANALYZE SALES

To obtain information regarding the amount of sales by item, you can print or view sales reports.
Sales reports provide information regarding cash and credit sales. When information regarding
the sales according to the Sales Item is needed, a Sales by Item Summary Report is the
appropriate report to print or view. This report enables you to see how much revenue is being
generated by each sales item. This provides important information for decision making and
managing the business. For example, if a sales item is not generating much income, it might be
wise to discontinue that sales item.

DO: Print a summarized list of sales by item
Click **Report Finder** on the QuickBooks Company Navigator
Click the drop-down list arrow for **Select type of report**
Click **Sales**
Click **Sales by Item Summary** in **Select a report**
Click in **From** on the **Report Finder** screen
Enter **01/01/04**
Tab to or click **To**
Enter **01/15/04**
Click the **Display** button
Turn off the Date Prepared, Time Prepared, and Report Basis following
   instructions given previously
Tab to generate the report
Click **Print**
The Orientation should be **Portrait**
Click **Print** on **Print Reports** dialog box

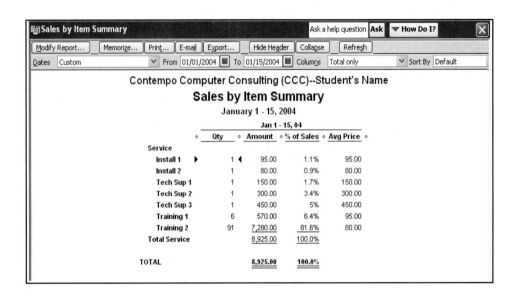

Close the report

DO: In order to obtain information regarding which transactions apply to each sales
             item, view a sales report by item detail
          Click **Sales By Item Detail** on the Report Finder
          Click in **From**
          Enter **01/01/04**
          Tab to **To**
          Enter **01/15/04**
          Click the **Display** button
          Change **Header/Footer** so **Date Prepared**, **Time Prepared**, and **Report Basis**
             do not print on the report
          Scroll through the report to view the types of sales and the transactions that
             occurred within each category
          • Notice how many transactions occurred in each sales item.

Close the report without printing
Close the **Report Finder**

RECORD CUSTOMER PAYMENTS ON ACCOUNT

When customers make a full or partial payment of the amount they owe, QuickBooks Pro places the money received in an account called Undeposited Funds. The money stays in the account until a bank deposit is made. When you start to record a payment made by a customer, you see the customer's balance, any credits made to the account, and a complete list of outstanding invoices. QuickBooks Pro automatically applies the payment received to the oldest invoice.

MEMO:

DATE: January 15, 2004

Record the following cash receipt: Received Check No. 0684 for $815 from Eric Bailey Research Corp. as payment on account.

DO: Record the above payment on account:
Click **Receive Payments** on the Customers Navigator

- Notice the flow chart line from Invoices to Receive Payments. This icon is illustrated in this manner because recording a payment receipt is for a payment made on account. This is <u>not</u> a cash sale.

Click the drop-down list arrow for **Received From**

Click **Bailey, Eric Research Corp.**

- Notice that the current date or the last transaction date shows in the **Date** column and the total amount owed appears as the balance.
- Also note that previous cash sales to Eric Bailey Research Corp. are not listed. This is because a payment receipt is used only for payments on account.
- In the middle of the screen the unpaid invoice for Eric Bailey Research Corp. shows in the Applied To: area.

Tab to or click **Date**

- If you click, you will need to delete the date. If you tab, the date will be deleted when you type 01/15/04.

Type date **01/15/04**

Tab to or click **Amount**

- If you click, you will need to delete the 0.00. If you tab, it will be deleted when you type in the amount.

Enter **815**

Tab to or click **Check No.**

- QuickBooks Pro will enter the **.00** when you tab to or click **Check No**.
- Notice that the cursor moves into the **Check No.** text box and that the payment amount is entered in the Payment column for Applied To:.

Enter **0684**

Click the drop-down list arrow for **Pmt. Method**

Click **Check**

- QuickBooks Pro automatically applies the payment to the oldest open invoice.

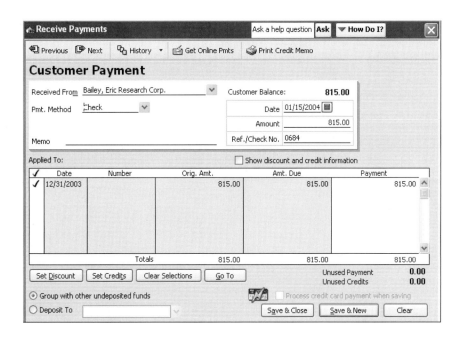

Click **Save & New**

RECORD ADDITIONAL PAYMENTS ON ACCOUNT WITHOUT STEP-BY-STEP INSTRUCTIONS

MEMO:

DATE: January 15, 2004

Received Check No. 1952 from Jacobs, Young, Porter, and Wenzel for $3,680.

Received Check No. 8925 for $2,000 from Roberts Illustrations in partial payment of account. This receipt requires a Memo notation of Partial Payment.

Received Check No. 39251 from Timothy Childers for $475.

Received Check No. 2051 for $2,190 from Waterson Productions in partial payment of account. Record a Memo of Partial Payment for this receipt.

Received Check No. 5632 from Juan Morales for $150

Received Check No. 80195 from Wagner, Rose, and Brandeiss for $3,685.

 DO: Refer to the previous steps listed to enter the above payments:

Click **Save & New** to go from one Receive Payments Screen to the next
Click the **Save & Close** button after all payments received have been recorded

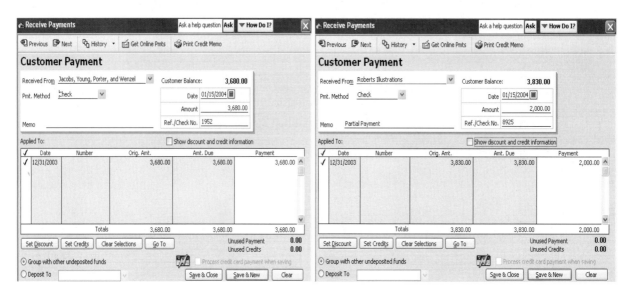

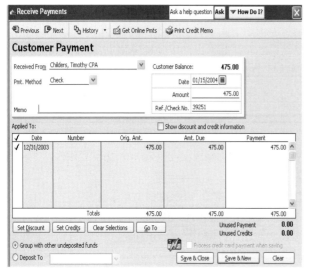

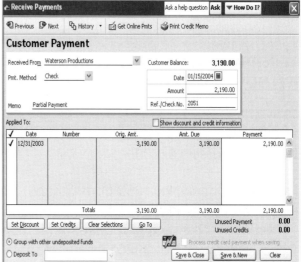

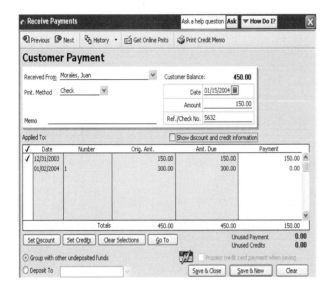
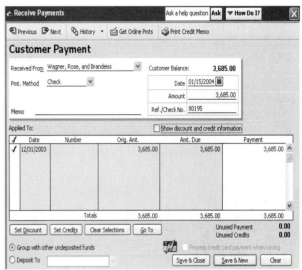

VIEW TRANSACTIONS BY CUSTOMER

In order to see the transactions for credit customers, you need to prepare a transaction report by customer. This report shows all sales, credits, and payments for each customer on account.

DO: Click **Reports** on the menu bar

Click **Customers & Receivables**

Click **Transaction List by Customer**

Follow steps presented earlier to remove the Date Prepared and the Time Prepared from the header

Tab to or click **From**

Enter **01/01/04**

Tab to or click **To**

Enter **01/15/04**

Tab to generate the report

Scroll through the report

- Notice that information is shown for the invoices, cash sales, credit memo, and payments made on the accounts.

- Notice that the **Num** column shows the invoice numbers, sales receipt numbers, credit memo numbers, and check numbers.

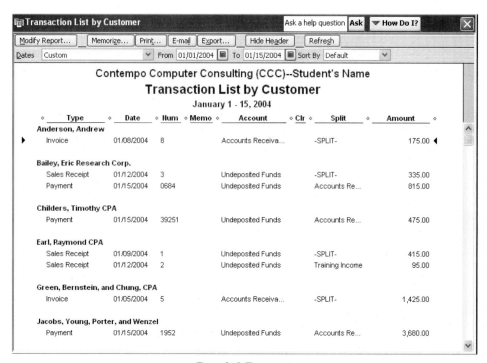

Partial Report

Click the **Close** button to exit the report

DEPOSIT CHECKS RECEIVED FOR CASH SALES AND PAYMENTS ON ACCOUNT

When you record cash sales and the receipt of payments on accounts, QuickBooks Pro places the money received in the Undeposited Funds account. Once the deposit is recorded, the funds are transferred from Undeposited Funds to the account selected when preparing the deposit.

MEMO:

DATE: January 15, 2004

Deposit all checks received for cash sales and payments on account.

DO: Deposit checks received:

Click **Deposits** on the Customers Navigator

- **Payments to Deposit** window shows all amounts received for cash sales and payments on account that have not been deposited in the bank.

- The column for **Type** contains RCPT, which means the amount is for a Sales Receipt (Cash Sale), and PMT, which means the amount received is for a payment on account.
- Notice that the √ column to the left of the Date column is empty.

Click the **Select All** button

- Notice the check marks in the √ column.

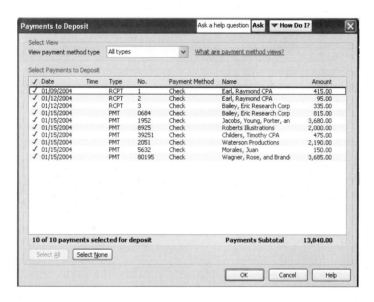

Click **OK** to close **Payments to Deposit** screen and open **Make Deposits** screen
On the **Make Deposits** screen, **Deposit To** should be **Checking**
Date should be **01/15/2004**

- Tab to date and change if not correct.

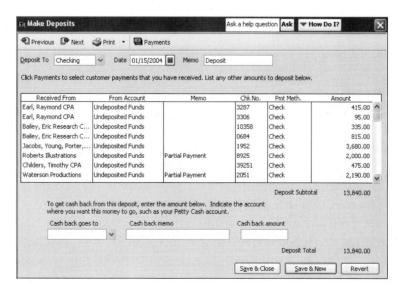

Click the **Print** button to print **Deposit Summary**
Select **Deposit summary only** on the **Print Deposit** dialog box, click **OK**

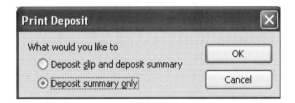

Check the **Settings** for **Print List**, click **Print**
* *Note:* QuickBooks Pro automatically prints the date that the Deposit Summary
  was printed on the report. It is the current date of your computer; and,
  therefore, it may not match the date shown in the answer key.
When printing is finished, click **Save & Close** on **Make Deposits** screen to
  record and close

PRINT JOURNAL

Even though QuickBooks Pro displays registers and reports in a manner that focuses on the
transaction—for example, entering a sale on account via an invoice—it still keeps a General
Journal. The Journal records each transaction and lists the accounts and the amounts for debit
and credit entries.

DO: Click **Report Finder** on the Customer Navigator
Click **Accountant & Taxes** as the Report type
Click **Journal**
Click in **From**
Enter **01/01/04**
Tab to **To** field
Enter **01/15/04**
Click **Display**
Modify the Report to change the **Header/Footer** so the **Date Prepared** and **Time
Prepared** are not selected, click **OK**
Scroll through the report to view the transactions
* You may find that your Trans # is not the same as shown. QuickBooks
  automatically numbers all transactions recorded. If you have deleted and re-
  entered transactions more than directed in the text, you may have different
  transaction numbers. Do not be concerned with this.

- Also notice that not all names, memos, and accounts are displayed in full. You will learn how to change this later in training.

Click **Print**

On the Print Reports screen, the settings will be the same used previously except:

Click **Landscape** to select Landscape orientation

Click on **Fit report to one page wide** to select this item

- The printer will print the Journal using a smaller font so the report will fit across the 11-inch width.

Click Print

- The Journal will be several pages in length.

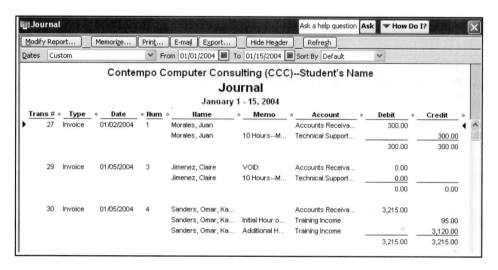

Close the report

PRINT THE TRIAL BALANCE

When all sales transactions have been entered, it is important to print the Trial Balance and verify that the total debits equal the total credits.

DO: Click **Trial Balance** on the Report Finder list of Accountant & Taxes reports

Enter the dates from **010104** to **011504**

Click the **Modify Report** button and change **Header/Footer** so **Date Prepared**, **Time Prepared**, and **Report Basis** do not print

Click the **Display** button

Click **Print**

On the **Print Reports** screen, click **Portrait** to select Portrait orientation

If necessary, click on **Fit report to one page wide** to deselect this item
Click **Print**

Contempo Computer Consulting (CCC)--Student's Name		
Trial Balance		
As of January 15, 2004		
	Jan 15, 04	
	Debit	**Credit**
Checking	51,710.00	
Accounts Receivable	17,650.00	
Office Supplies	500.00	
Undeposited Funds	0.00	
Company Cars:Original Cost	49,000.00	
Office Equipment:Original Cost	8,050.00	
Accounts Payable		850.00
Loan Payable	0.00	
Loan Payable:Company Cars Loan		35,000.00
Loan Payable:Office Equipment Loan		4,000.00
Brian Colbert, Capital		53,135.00
Brian Colbert, Capital:Investments		25,000.00
Retained Earnings	0.00	
Income:Installation Income		175.00
Income:Technical Support Income		900.00
Income:Training Income		7,850.00
TOTAL	**126,910.00**	**126,910.00**

Close the report

GRAPHS IN QUICKBOOKS® PRO

Once transactions have been entered, transaction results can be visually represented in a graphic form. QuickBooks Pro illustrates Accounts Receivable by Aging Period as a bar chart, and it illustrates Accounts Receivable by Customer as a pie chart. For further details, double-click on an individual section of the pie chart or chart legend to create a bar chart analyzing an individual customer. QuickBooks Pro also prepares graphs based on sales and will show the results of sales by item and by customer.

PREPARE ACCOUNTS RECEIVABLE GRAPHS

Accounts Receivable graphs illustrate account information based on the age of the account and the percentage of accounts receivable owed by each customer.

DO: Create graphs for accounts receivable:
Click **Customers & Receivables** on the Report Finder to select the type of report
Click **Accounts Receivable Graph** to select the report
Click the **Display** button
Click **Dates** on the QuickInsight: Accounts Receivable Graph screen

On the **Change Graph Dates** change **Show Aging As of** to **01/15/04**
Click **OK**

- QuickBooks Pro generates a bar chart illustrating Accounts Receivable by Aging Period and a pie chart illustrating Accounts Receivable by Customer

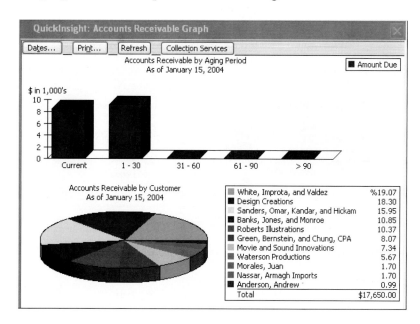

Printing is not required for this graph

- If you want a printed copy, click **Print** and print in Portrait mode

Click **Dates**

Enter **02/01/04** for the **Show Aging As of** date

Click **OK**

- Notice the difference in the aging of accounts.

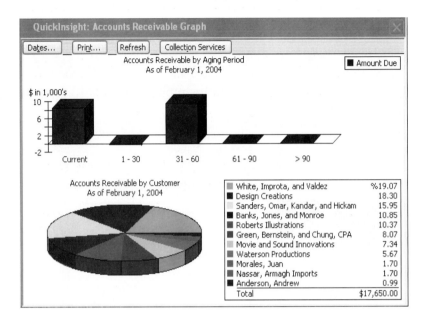

Click **Dates**

Enter **03/01/04**

Click **OK**

- Again, notice the difference in aging of accounts.

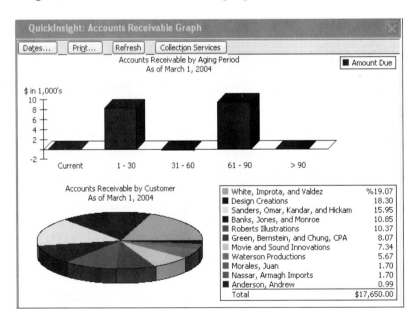

Click **Dates**

Enter **01/15/04**

Do not close the report

USE QUICKZOOM FEATURE TO OBTAIN INDIVIDUAL CUSTOMER DETAILS

It is possible to get detailed information regarding the aging of transactions for an individual customer by using the QuickZoom feature of QuickBooks Pro.

DO: Double-click on the section of the pie chart for **White, Improta, and Valdez**
- You get a bar chart aging the transactions of the customer.

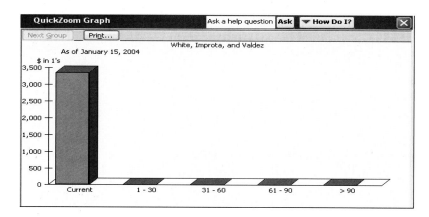

Printing is not required for this graph
- If a hard (printed) copy is desired, click **Print**.

Close the chart for White, Improta, and Valdez

Double-click the section of the pie chart for **Movie & Sound Innovations**
- Notice the age of the transactions for this customer.

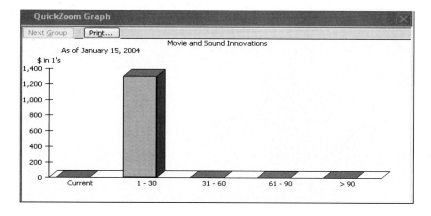

Printing is not required for this graph
- If you want a hard copy, click **Print**.

Close all charts

PREPARE SALES GRAPHS

Sales graphs illustrate the amount of cash and credit sales for a given period as well as the percentage of sales for each sales item.

DO: Click the drop-down list arrow to show the types of reports on **Report Finder**
Click **Sales**
Click **Sales Graph** and **Display**
Click **Dates**
Click the drop-down list arrow for **Graph Dates**
Click in **From**
Enter **01/01/04**
Tab to **To**
Enter **01/15/04**
Click **OK**
The **By Item** button should be indented
- You will see a bar chart representing Sales by Month and a pie chart displaying a Sales Summary by item.
- If the **By Customer** button is indented, you will see the same bar chart but the pie chart will display a Sales Summary by customer.
- If the **By Rep** button is indented, you will see the same bar chart but the pie chart will display a Sales Summary by sales rep.

Printing is not required for this graph
- If you want a printed copy, click **Print**.

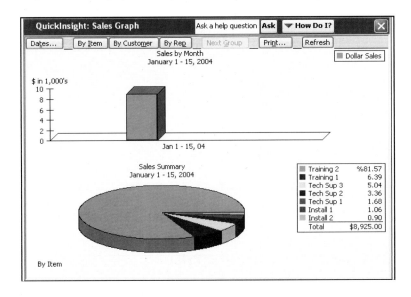

Click **By Customer**
- Again, you will see a bar chart representing Sales by Month; however, the pie chart will display a Sales Summary by customer.

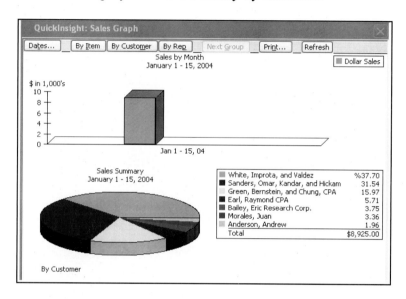

Printing is not required for this graph
- If you want a printed copy, click **Print**.

USE QUICKZOOM TO VIEW AN INDIVIDUAL ITEM OR CUSTOMER

It is possible to use QuickZoom to view details regarding an individual item's sales by month or an individual customer's sales by month.

DO: Sales Summary by Customer must be on the screen
In the chart legend, double-click **Andrew Anderson**
- You will see the Sales by Month for Andrew Anderson

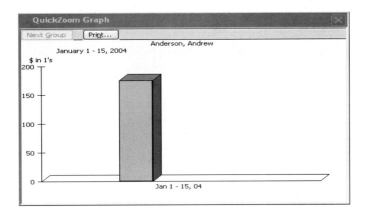

Close the QuickZoom graph for Andrew Anderson
Click **By Item**
You will see the Sales Summary by Item
In the chart legend, double-click **Install 1**

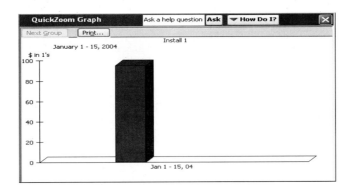

You will see the Sales by Month for Install 1
Do not **Print** the graph unless you want a hard (paper) copy
Close Graphs

BACK UP AND CLOSE COMPANY

When you use QuickBooks Pro to make a back up file, the program creates a condensed file that contains all the data for the entries made up to the time of the backup file. This file has an extension **.qbb** and cannot be used to record transactions. When new transactions are recorded, a new backup file must be made. In training, it is wise to make a daily backup as well as an end-of-chapter backup. If errors are made in training, the appropriate backup file can be restored. For example, if you back up Chapter 2 and make errors in Chapter 3, the Chapter 2 backup may be restored to a company file with the extension **.qbw**. The data entered for Chapter 3 will be erased and only the data from Chapter 2 will appear.

A duplicate copy of the file may be made using Windows. Instructions for this procedure are given in Appendix A. You may hear the duplicate copy referred to as a backup file. This is different from the QuickBooks backup file.

 DO: Back up the company
Click **File**
Click **Back Up...**
The **Back Up Company File** dialog box appears
File name for the backup copy of the company files is **Contempo Chapter 2.qbb**
Verify that the drive is A:
- Check with your instructor to see if this is the appropriate procedure for your course.
- QuickBooks Pro will back up the information for Contempo Computer Consulting on the **Contempo** data disk in the A: drive.

Click **OK** on the **QuickBooks Backup** screen
- When the back up is completed, QuickBooks Pro displays a dialog box stating that the backup was successful.

Click **OK**
- Your Contempo Chapter 2.qbb, contains all your work from Chapter 2. This will not contain transactions from the work you do in Chapter 3. This is helpful for those times when you have made errors and cannot figure out how to correct them. Restoring your Chapter 2 back up file will restore your work from Chapter 2 and eliminate any work completed in Chapter 3. This will allow you to start over at the beginning of Chapter 3. If you do not have a back up file for Chapter 2, you would need to re-enter all the transactions for Chapter 2 before beginning Chapter 3.
- You may wish to make a daily back up file. If so, you should make a second backup to save your work each day. Use Contempo.qbb as your daily backup file. This is helpful for those times when you have made errors and cannot figure out how to correct them but do not want to start over at the beginning of the chapter. Restoring your daily backup file will restore your work from the previous training session and eliminate the work completed in the current session.

Click **File**
Click **Close Company**
- Refer to Appendix A for the steps to follow to make a duplicate disk.

SUMMARY

In this chapter, cash and credit sales were prepared for Contempo Computer Consulting, a service business, using sales receipts and invoices. Credit memos were issued. Customer accounts were added and revised. Invoices and sales receipts were edited, deleted, and voided. Cash payments were received and bank deposits were made. All the transactions entered reinforced the QuickBooks Pro concept of using the business form to record transactions rather than enter information in journals. However, QuickBooks Pro does not disregard traditional accounting methods. Instead, it performs this function in the background. The Journal was accessed and changes to transactions were made via the Journal. The fact that the Customer:Job List functions as the Accounts Receivable Ledger and that the Chart of Accounts is the General Ledger in QuickBooks Pro was pointed out. The importance of reports for information and decision-making was illustrated. Exploration of the various sales and accounts receivable reports and graphs allowed information to be viewed from a sales standpoint and from an accounts receivable perspective. Sales reports emphasized both cash and credit sales according to the customer or according to the sales item generating the revenue. Accounts Receivable reports focused on amounts owed by credit customers. The traditional trial balance emphasizing the equality of debits and credits was prepared.

END-OF-CHAPTER QUESTIONS

TRUE/FALSE

ANSWER THE FOLLOWING QUESTIONS IN THE SPACE PROVIDED BEFORE THE QUESTION NUMBER.

_____ 1. A new customer can be added to a company's records on the fly.

_____ 2. In QuickBooks Pro, error correction for a sale on account can be accomplished by editing the invoice.

_____ 3. A Sales Item List stores information about products you purchase.

_____ 4. Once transactions have been entered, modifications to a customer's account may be made only at the end of the fiscal year.

_____ 5. In QuickBooks Pro all transactions must be entered with the traditional debit/credit method.

_____ 6. Checks received for cash sales are held in the Undeposited Funds account until the bank deposit is made.

_____ 7. When a correction for a transaction is made, QuickBooks Pro not only changes the form used to record the transaction, it also changes all journal and account entries for the transaction to reflect the correction.

_____ 8. QuickGraphs allow information to be viewed from both a sales standpoint and from an accounts receivable perspective.

_____ 9. QuickZoom allows you to print a report instantly.

_____ 10. A customer's payment on account is immediately recorded in the cash account.

MULTIPLE CHOICE

WRITE THE LETTER OF THE CORRECT ANSWER IN THE SPACE PROVIDED BEFORE
THE QUESTION NUMBER.

_____ 1.   To remove an invoice without a trace, it is ___.
A. voided
B. deleted
C. erased
D. reversed

_____ 2.   To enter a cash sale, ___ is completed.
A. a debit
B. an invoice
C. a sales receipt
D. receive payments

_____ 3.   Two primary types of lists used in this chapter are ___.
A. receivables and payables
B. invoices and checks
C. registers and navigator
D. customers and item

_____ 4.   When you enter an invoice, an error may be corrected by ___.
A. backspacing or deleting
B. tabbing and typing
C. dragging and typing
D. all of the above

_____ 5.   While in the Customer Balance Summary Report, it is possible to get an individual
customer's information by using ___.
A. QuickReport
B. QuickZoom
C. QuickGraph
D. QuickSummary

_____ 6.   Undeposited Funds represents ___.
A. cash or checks received from customers but not yet deposited in the bank
B. all cash sales
C. the balance of the accounts receivable account
D. none of the above

_____ 7.   QuickBooks Pro uses graphs to illustrate information about ___.
A. the chart of accounts
B. sales
C. the cash account
D. supplies

_____ 8.   Changes to the chart of accounts may be made ___.
A. at the beginning of a fiscal period
B. before the end of the fiscal year
C. at any time
D. once established, the chart of accounts may not be modified

_____ 9.   To obtain information about sales by item, you can view ___.
A. the income statement
B. the trial balance
C. receivables reports
D. sales reports

_____10.   When you add a customer using the Set Up method, you ___.
A. add complete information for a customer
B. add only a customer's name
C. add the customer's name, address, and telephone number
D. add the customer's name and telephone number

FILL-IN

IN THE SPACE PROVIDED, WRITE THE ANSWER THAT MOST APPROPRIATELY COMPLETES THE SENTENCE.

1. The report used to view all the balances on account of each customer is the _____.

2. The form prepared to show a reduction to a transaction is a(n) _____.

3. The report that proves that debits equal credits is the _____.

4. QuickBooks Pro generates a _____ illustrating Accounts Receivable by Aging Period.

5. To verify the company being used in QuickBooks Pro, you check the _____.

SHORT ESSAY

Explain how the method used to enter an Accounts Receivable transaction in QuickBooks Pro is different from the method used to enter a transaction according to an accounting textbook.

NAME_____

TRANSMITTAL

<u>CHAPTER 2: CONTEMPO COMPUTER CONSULTING</u>

Attach the following documents and reports:

Invoice No. 1: Juan Morales
Invoice No. 2: Timothy Childers
Invoice No. 3: Claire Jimenez
Invoice No. 4: Sanders, Omar, Kandar, and Hickam
Invoice No. 5: Green, Bernstein, and Chung
Invoice No. 6: White, Improta, and Valdez
Customer Balance Summary, January 5, 2004
Customer Balance Detail, Sanders, Omar, Kandar, and Hickam
Invoice No. 5: Green, Bernstein, and Chung
Transactions by Customer, January 1-7, 2004
Customer Balance Detail Report
Credit Memo No. 7: Sanders, Omar, Kandar, and Hickam
Invoice No. 8: Andrew Anderson
Sales Receipt No. 1: Raymond Earl
Sales Receipt No. 2: Raymond Earl
Sales Receipt No. 3: Eric Bailey Research Corp.
Sales by Customer Detail Report, January 1-14, 2004
Sales Receipt No. 1 (corrected): Raymond Earl
Sales by Item Summary, January 1-15, 2004
Deposit Summary
Journal
Trial Balance, January 15, 2004

END-OF-CHAPTER PROBLEM

SUPREME LAWN AND POOL MAINTENANCE

Supreme Lawn and Pool Maintenance is owned and operated by George Gordon. Melissa and Zack Gordon also work for the company. Melissa manages the office and keeps the books for the business. George provides lawn maintenance and supervises the lawn maintenance employees. Zack provides the pool maintenance. Supreme is located in Santa Barbara, California.

INSTRUCTIONS

Copy the company file for Supreme Lawn and Pool Maintenance, **Supreme.qbw**, to a new floppy disk and open the company. Add your name to the company name. The company name will be **Supreme Lawn and Pool Maintenance—Student's Name**. (Type your actual name, *not* the words *Student's Name*.) Record the following transactions using invoices, sales receipts, and receive payments. Make bank deposits as indicated. Print the reports as indicated.

The invoices and sales receipts are numbered consecutively. Invoice No. 25 is the first invoice number used in this problem. Sales Receipt No. 15 is the first sales receipt number used in this problem. Each invoice recorded should contain a message. Choose the one that you feel is most appropriate for the transaction. Print each invoice and sales receipt as it is completed. Remember that payments received on account should be recorded as Receive Payments and not as a Sales Receipt.

When recording transactions, use the following Sales Item chart to determine the item(s) billed. If the transaction does not indicate the size of the pool or property, use the first category for the item; for example, LandCom 1 or LandRes 1 would be used for standard-size landscape service. Remember that PoolCom 1 and PoolRes 1 are services for spas—not pools. The appropriate billing for a standard-size pool would be PoolCom 2 or PoolRes 2. .

When printing reports, always remove the Date Prepared, Time Prepared, and Report Basis from the Header/Footer.

SUPREME POOL AND LAWN MAINTENANCE
SALES ITEM LIST

ITEM	DESCRIPTION	AMOUNT
LandCom 1	Commercial Landscape Maintenance (Standard Size)	$150 mo.
LandCom 2	Commercial Landscape Maintenance (Medium)	250 mo.
LandCom 3	Commercial Landscape Maintenance (Large)	500 mo.
LandRes 1	Residential Landscape Maintenance (Standard Size)	$100 mo.
LandRes 2	Residential Landscape Maintenance (Medium)	200 mo.
LandRes 3	Residential Landscape Maintenance (Large)	350 mo.
PoolCom 1	Commercial Spa Service	$100 mo.
PoolCom 2	Commercial Pool Service (All pools unless specified as Large)	300 mo.
PoolCom 3	Commercial Pool Service (Large)	500 mo.
PoolRes 1	Residential Spa Service	$ 50 mo.
PoolRes 2	Residential Pool Service (All pools unless specified as Large)	100 mo.
PoolRes 3	Residential Pool Service (Large)	150 mo.
LandTrim	Trimming and Pruning	$75 hr.
LandPlant	Planting and Cultivating	50 hr.
LandWater	Sprinklers, Timers, etc.	75 hr.
LandGrow	Fertilize, Spray for Pests	75 hr.
PoolRepair	Mechanical Maintenance and Repairs	$75 hr.
PoolWash	Acid Wash, Condition	Price by the job
PoolStart	Startup for New Pools	500.00

RECORD TRANSACTIONS

May 1

Billed Ocean View Motel for monthly landscape services and monthly pool maintenance services, Invoice No. 25. (Use LandCom 1 to record the monthly landscape service fee and PoolCom 2 to record the monthly pool service fee. The quantity for each item is 1.) Terms are Net 15.

Billed Dr. Shapiro for monthly landscape and pool services at his home. Both the pool and landscaping are standard size. The terms are Net 30.

Billed Elegant Creations for 2 hours shrub trimming. Terms are Net 30.

Received Check No. 381 for $500 from Donna Lindsey for pool startup services at her home, Sales Receipt No. 15.

Received Check No. 8642 from Morris Mendoza for $150 as payment in full on his account.

May 15

Billed a new customer: Terry Ericsson (remember to enter the last name first for the customer name and change the billing name to first name first)—10824 Hope Ranch St., Santa Barbara, CA 93110, 805-555-9825, terms Net 30—for monthly service on his large pool and large residential landscape maintenance.

Received Check No. 6758 from Ocean View Motel in full payment of Invoice No. 25.

Received Check No. 987 from a new customer: William Chase (a neighbor of Terry Ericsson) for $75 for 1 hour of pool repairs. Even though this is a cash sale, do a complete customer setup: 10877 Hope Ranch St., Santa Barbara, CA 93110, 805-555-7175, fax 805-555-5717, E-mail wchase@abc.com, terms Net 30.

Billed Resorts by the Bay for maintenance on their large pool and large landscaping maintenance. Also bill for 5 hours planting, 3 hours trimming, and 2 hours spraying on the landscaping and for 3 hours pool repair services. Terms are Net 15.

May 30

Received Check No. 1247 for $525 as payment in full from Elegant Creations.

Received Check No. 8865 from June Singer for amount due.

Billed Blue Pacific Resorts for large pool and large landscaping maintenance. Terms are Net 15.

Billed Garden Street Apartments for standard-size commercial pool service and standard-size commercial landscape maintenance (LandCom 1). Terms are Net 30.

Deposit all cash receipts. Print Deposit Summary.

PRINT REPORTS

Customer Balance Detail Report for all transactions. Portrait orientation.
Sales by Item Summary Report for 5/1/2004 through 5/30/2004. Portrait orientation.
Journal for 5/1/2004 through 5/30/2004. Print in Landscape orientation, fit to one page wide.
Trial Balance. Portrait orientation.

NAME _____

TRANSMITTAL

CHAPTER 2: SUPREME LAWN AND POOL MAINTENANCE

Attach the following documents and reports:

Invoice No. 25: Ocean View Motel
Invoice No. 26: Dr. Michael Shapiro
Invoice No. 27: Elegant Creations
Sales Receipt No. 15: Donna Lindsey
Invoice No. 28: Terry Ericsson
Sales Receipt No. 16: William Chase
Invoice No. 29: Resort by the Bay
Invoice No. 30: Blue Pacific Resorts
Invoice No. 31: Garden Street Apartments
Deposit Summary
Customer Balance Detail
Sales by Item Summary
Journal
Trial Balance

PAYABLES AND PURCHASES: SERVICE BUSINESS

LEARNING OBJECTIVES

At the completion of this chapter you will be able to:

1. Understand the concepts for computerized accounting for payables.
2. Enter, edit, correct, delete, and pay bills.
3. Add new vendors and modify vendor records.
4. View Accounts Payable transaction history from the Enter Bills window.
5. View and/or print QuickReports for vendors, Accounts Payable Register, etc.
6. Use the QuickZoom feature.
7. Record and edit transactions in the Accounts Payable Register.
8. Enter vendor credits.
9. Print, edit, void, and delete checks.
10. Pay for expenses using petty cash.
11. Add new accounts.
12. Display and print the Accounts Payable Aging Summary Report, an Unpaid Bills Detail Report, a Vendor Balance Summary Report.
13. Display an Accounts Payable Graph by Aging Period.

ACCOUNTING FOR PAYABLES AND PURCHASES

In a service business, most of the accounting for purchases and payables is simply paying bills for expenses incurred in the operation of the business. Purchases are for things used in the operation of the business. Some transactions will be in the form of cash purchases, and others will be purchases on account. Bills can be paid when they are received or when they are due. Rather than use cumbersome journals, QuickBooks Pro continues to focus on recording transactions based on the business document; therefore, you use the Enter Bills and Pay Bills features of the program to record the receipt and payment of bills. QuickBooks Pro can remind you when payments are due and can calculate and apply discounts earned for paying bills early. Payments can be made by recording payments in the Pay Bills window or, if using the cash basis for accounting, by writing a check. A cash purchase can be recorded by writing a check or by using petty cash. Even though QuickBooks Pro focuses on recording transactions on the business forms used, all transactions are recorded behind the scenes in the General Journal. QuickBooks

Pro uses a Vendor List for all vendors with which the company has an account. QuickBooks Pro does not refer to the Vendor List as the Accounts Payable Ledger, yet that is exactly what it is. The total of the Vendor List/Accounts Payable Ledger will match the total of the Accounts Payable account in the Chart of Accounts/General Ledger.

As in Chapter 2, corrections can be made directly on the business form or within the Transaction Journal. New accounts and vendors may be added on the fly as transactions are entered. Reports illustrating vendor balances, unpaid bills, accounts payable aging, transaction history, and accounts payable registers may be viewed and printed. Graphs analyzing the amount of accounts payable by aging period provide a visual illustration of the accounts payable.

TRAINING TUTORIAL AND PROCEDURES

The following tutorial will once again work with Contempo Computer Consulting (CCC). As in Chapter 2, transactions will be recorded for this fictitious company. To maximize training benefits, you should:

1. Read the entire chapter *before* beginning the tutorial within the chapter.
2. Answer the end-of-chapter questions.
3. Be aware that transactions to be entered are given within a **MEMO**.
4. Complete all the steps listed for the Contempo Computer Consulting tutorial in the chapter.
   (Indicated by: **DO:**)
5. When you have completed a section, put an **X** on the button next to **DO:**.
6. If you do not complete a section, put the date in the margin next to the last step completed. This will make it easier to know where to begin when training is resumed.
7. As you complete your work, proofread carefully and check for accuracy. Double-check amounts of money.
8. If you find an error while preparing a transaction, correct it. If you find the error after the transaction has been entered, follow the steps indicated in this chapter to correct, void, or delete the transaction.
9. Print as directed within the chapter.
10. You may not finish the entire chapter in one computer session. Always use QuickBooks Pro to back up your work at the end of your work session as described in Chapter 1.
11. When you complete your computer session, always close your company. If you try to use a computer for CCC and a previous student did not close the company, QuickBooks Pro may freeze when you put in your disk. In addition, if you do not close the company as you leave, you may have problems with your company file, your disk may be damaged, and you may have unwanted .qbi (QuickBooks In Use) files that cause your data disk to become full.

OPEN QUICKBOOKS® PRO AND CONTEMPO COMPUTER CONSULTING—CCC

DO: Open QuickBooks Pro as instructed in Chapters 1 and 2
Open Contempo Computer Consulting (CCC):
> Click **File**
> Click **Open Company**
> Click **Contempo.qbw**
> Check to make sure you are using the disk in the A: drive
> - Verify the company file location with your instructor. Each classroom setting and environment may be set up in a manner that does not always match the steps indicated in the text.
Click **Open**
Check the title bar to verify that Contempo Computer Consulting (CCC)—
> Student's Name is the open company

BEGINNING THE TUTORIAL

In this chapter, you will be entering bills incurred by the company in the operation of the business. You will also be recording the payment of bills, purchases using checks, and purchases/payments using petty cash.

The Vendor List keeps information regarding the vendors with whom you do business and is the Accounts Payable Ledger. Vendor information includes the vendor names, addresses, telephone numbers, payment terms, credit limits, and account numbers. You will be using the following list for vendors with which CCC has an account:

Name	Balance	Notes
California Electric	0.00	
California Gas Co.	0.00	
California Water	0.00	
Communication Telephone Co.	0.00	
Computer Professionals Magazine	0.00	
Juan's Garage and Auto Services	0.00	
Lindsey Realtors	0.00	
Office & Sales Supplies Co.	350.00	
Southern California Insurance Company	0.00	
Speedy Delivery Service	0.00	
Universal Advertising	500.00	

Vendor ▼   Activities ▼   Reports ▼   ☐ Show All

All transactions are listed on memos. The transaction date will be the same date as the memo date unless specified otherwise within the transaction. Vendor names, when necessary, will be given in the transaction. Unless other terms are provided, the terms are Net 30. Once a specific type of transaction has been entered in a step-by-step manner, additional transactions of the same or a similar type will be made without having instructions provided. Of course, you may always refer to instructions given for previous transactions for ideas or for steps used to enter those transactions. To determine the account used in the transaction, refer to the Chart of Accounts. When you are entering account information on a bill, clicking on the drop-down list arrow will show a copy of the Chart of Accounts.

ENTER A BILL

QuickBooks Pro provides accounts payable tracking. Entering bills as soon as they are received is an efficient way to record your liabilities. Once bills have been entered, QuickBooks Pro will be able to provide up-to-date cash flow reports, and QuickBooks Pro will remind you when it is time to pay your bills. A bill is divided into two sections: a vendor-related section (the upper part of the bill that looks similar to a check and has a memo text box under it) and a detail section (the area that is divided into columns for Account, Amount, and Memo). The vendor-related section of the bill is where information for the actual bill is entered, including a memo with information about the transaction. The detail section is where the expense accounts, expense account amounts, and transaction explanations are indicated.

MEMO

DATE: January 16, 2004

Record the following bill: Universal Advertising prepared and placed advertisements in local business publications announcing our new hardware installation service. Received Universal's Invoice No. 9875 for $260 as a bill with terms of Net 30.

    DO: Record the above transaction
Click **Vendors** on the Navigator list
Click **Enter Bills**
Complete the vendor-related section of the bill:
    Verify that Bill is marked at the top of the form
    Click the drop-down list arrow next to **Vendor**
    Click **Universal Advertising**
    • Name is entered as the vendor.
    Tab to **Date**
    • When you tab to the date, it will be highlighted.
    • When you type in the new date, the highlighted date will be deleted.
    Type **01/16/04** as the date

Tab to **Amount Due**

Type **260**

- QuickBooks Pro will automatically insert the .00 after the amount.

Tab to **Terms**

Click the drop-down list arrow next to **Terms**

Click **Net 30**

- QuickBooks Pro automatically changes the Bill Due date to show 30 days from the transaction date.

Tab to **Ref. No.**

Type the vendor's invoice number: **9875**

- At this time nothing will be inserted as a memo in the text box between the vendor-related section of the bill and the detail section of the bill.

Complete the detail section of the bill using the **Expenses** tab:

Tab to or click in the column for **Account**

Click the drop-down list arrow next to **Account**

Click **Advertising Expense**

- Based on the accrual method of accounting, Advertising Expense is selected as the account used in this transaction because this expense should be matched against the revenue of the period.

The **Amount** column already shows **260.00**—no entry required

Tab to or click the first line in the column for **Memo**

Enter the transaction explanation of **Ads for Hardware Installation Services**

Do not click Save & Close

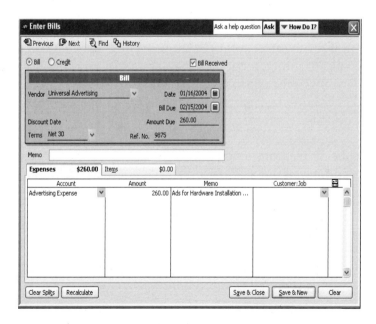

EDIT AND CORRECT ERRORS

If an error is discovered while you are entering information, it may be corrected by positioning the cursor in the field containing the error. You may do this by tabbing to move forward through each field or pressing Shift+Tab to move back to the field containing the error. If the error is highlighted, type the correction. If the error is not highlighted, you can correct the error by pressing the backspace or the delete key as many times as necessary to remove the error, then type the correction. (*Alternate method:* Point to the error, highlight it by dragging the mouse through the error, then type the correction.)

 DO: Practice editing and making corrections to the bill for Universal Advertising:
Click the drop-down list arrow for **Vendor**
Click **Communication Telephone Co.**
Tab to **Date**
To increase the date by one day, press +
- You may press shift and the = key next to the backspace key, or you may press the + key on the numerical keypad.

Press + two more times
- The date should be **01/19/04**.

To decrease the date by one day, press -
- You may type a hyphen (-) next to the number **0**, or you may press the hyphen (-) key on the numerical keypad.

Press - two more times
- The date should be **01/16/04**.

Change the date by clicking on the calendar next to the date

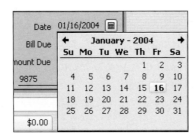

Click **19** on the calendar for January 2004
Click the calendar again
Click **16** to change the date back to 01/16/2004
To change the amount, click between the **2** and the **6** in **Amount Due**
Press the **Delete** key two times to delete the **60**
Key in **99** and press the **Tab** key
- The Amount Due should be **299.00**. The amount of 299.00 should also be shown in the Amount column in the detail section of the bill.

The transaction explanation has been entered in the Memo column in the detail area of the bill and shows the transaction explanation of Ads for Hardware Installation Services.

- This memo prints on all reports that include the transaction.
- The same information should be in the Memo text box in the vendor-related area of the bill so it will appear as part of the transaction in the Accounts Payable account as well as all reports that include the transaction.

Copy **Ads for Hardware Installation Services** from the Memo column to the Memo text box:

Click to the left of the letter **A** in Ads

Highlight the memo text—**Ads for Hardware Installation Services**:

    Hold down the primary mouse button

    While holding down the primary mouse button, drag through the memo text **Ads for Hardware Installation Services**

Click **Edit** on the menu bar

Click **Copy**

- Notice that the keyboard shortcut **Ctrl+C** is listed. This shortcut could be used rather than using the Edit menu and Copy.
- This actually copies the text and places it in a temporary storage area of Windows called the Clipboard.

Click in the **Memo** text box beneath the **Terms**

Click **Edit** on the menu bar

Click **Paste**

- Notice the keyboard shortcut **Ctrl+V**.
- This inserts a copy of the material in the Windows Clipboard into the Memo text box—**Ads for Hardware Installation Services**
- This explanation will appear in the Memo area for the transaction in the Accounts Payable account as well as in any report that used the individual transaction information.

Click the drop-down list arrow for **Vendor**

Click **Universal Advertising**

Click to the right of the last **9** in **Amount Due**

Backspace two times to delete the **99**

Key in **60**

- The Amount **Due** should once again show **260.00**

Click the **Terms** drop-down list arrow

Click **Net 30**

Click **Save & Close** button to record the bill and return to the main screen

Click **No** On the **Name Information Changed** dialog box.

- The dialog box states: You have changed the Terms for Universal Advertising. Would you like to have this new information appear next time?

PREPARE A BILL USING MORE THAN ONE EXPENSE ACCOUNT

MEMO
DATE: January 18, 2004

On the recommendation of the office manager, Maria Garcia, CCC is trying out several different models of fax machines on a monthly basis. Received a bill from Office & Sales Supplies Co. for one month's rental of a fax machine, $25, and for fax supplies, which were consumed during January, $20, Invoice No. 1035A, Terms Net 10.

 DO: Record the transaction listed in the above memo. This transaction involves two expense accounts:

Click **Enter Bills** on the Vendors Navigator
Complete the vendor-related section of the bill:
  Click the drop-down list arrow next to **Vendor**
  Click **Office & Sales Supplies Co.**
  Tab to or click **Date**
  • If you click in Date, you will have to delete the current date.
  Enter **01/18/04**
  Tab to or click **Amount Due**
  Enter **45**
  Tab to or click on the line for **Terms**
  Type **Net 10** on the line for Terms, press the Tab key
  • You will get a **Terms Not Found** message box.

Click **Set Up**
Complete the information required in the **New Terms** dialog box:
  Net 10 should appear as the Terms
  Standard should be selected
  Change the **Net due** from 0 to **10** days
  Discount percentage should be **0**
  Discount if paid within **0** days
  Click **OK**

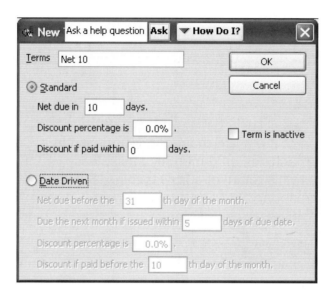

Tab to or click **Ref. No.**

Key in the vendor's invoice number: **1035A**

Tab to or click the **Memo** text box

Enter **Fax Rental and Fax Supplies for the Month** as the transaction description

Complete the **Detail Section** of the bill:

Tab to or click the first line for **Account**

Click the drop-down list arrow next to **Account**

Click **Equipment Rental**

- Because a portion of this transaction is for equipment that is being rented, Equipment Rental is the appropriate account to use.

Amount column shows **45.00**

Change this to reflect the actual amount of the Equipment Rental Expense

Tab to **Amount** to highlight

Type **25**

Tab to **Memo**

Enter **Fax Rental for the Month** as the transaction explanation

Tab to **Account**

Click the drop-down list arrow next to **Account**

Click **Office Supplies Expense**

- The transaction information indicates that the fax supplies will be used within the month of January. Using Office Supplies Expense account correctly charges the supplies expense against the period.
- If the transaction indicated that the fax supplies were purchased to have on hand, the appropriate account to use would be the asset Office Supplies.

The **Amount** column correctly shows **20.00** as the amount

Tab to or click **Memo**
Enter **Fax Supplies for the Month** as the transaction explanation

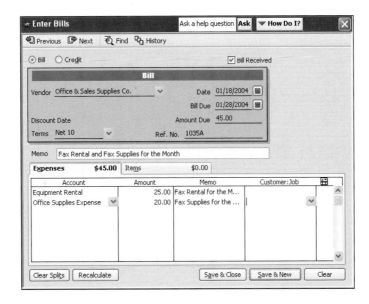

Click **Save & Close** to close the bill
- If you get a message regarding the change of Terms for Office & Sales Supplies Co., click **No**.

PRINT TRANSACTION BY VENDOR REPORT

To obtain information regarding individual transactions grouped by vendor, you prepare a transaction report by vendor. This allows you to view the vendors for which you have recorded transactions. The type of transaction is identified; for example, the word *Bill* appears when you have entered the transaction as a bill. The transaction date, any invoice numbers or memos entered when recording the transaction, the accounts used, and the transaction amount appear in the report.

DO: Prepare a **Transaction by Vendor Report**
Click **Report Finder** on the Vendors Navigator
- The type of report should be **Vendors & Payables**.
In the **Select a report** section of the Report Finder, click **Transaction List by Vendor**
Tab to or click **From**
Enter **01/01/04**
Tab to or click **To**
Enter **01/18/04**

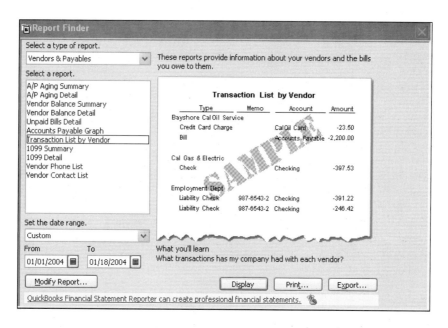

Click **Display**

Once the report is displayed, click the **Modify Report** button

Click the **Header/Footer** tab

Click **Date Prepared** and **Time Prepared** to deselect these features

Click **OK**

Analyze the report:

- Look at each vendor account.
- Note the type of transaction, any invoice numbers, and memos.
- The **Account** column shows **Accounts Payable** as the account.
- As in any traditional accounting transaction recording a purchase on account, the Accounts Payable account is credited.
- The **Split** column shows the other accounts used in the transaction.
- If the word **-SPLIT-** appears in this column, it indicates that more than one account was used.
- The transaction for Office & Sales Supplies Co. has -SPLIT- in the Split Column. This is because the transaction used two accounts: Equipment Rental and Office Supplies Expense for the debit portion of the transaction.

Click **Print**

Complete the information on the **Print Reports Screen**:

    Print to: The selected item should be **Printer**

- The printer name should appear in the printer text box. This may be different from the printer identified in this text.
- If the correct printer does not appear, click the drop-down list arrow, click the correct printer.

    Orientation: Click **Landscape** for this report

Page Range: **All** should be selected; if it is not, click **All**
Page Breaks: **Smart page breaks** should be selected
Click **Print** on the **Print Reports** screen

Contempo Computer Consulting (CCC)--Student's Name
Transaction List by Vendor
January 1 - 18, 2004

◇	Type	◇	Date	◇	Num	◇	Memo	◇	Account	◇	Clr	◇	Split	◇	Amount
Office & Sales Supplies Co.															
	Bill		01/18/2004		1035A		Fax Rental a...		Accounts Payable				-SPLIT-		-45.00
Universal Advertising															
	Bill		01/16/2004		9875		Ads for Har...		Accounts Payable				Advertising E...		-260.00

USE THE QUICKZOOM FEATURE

Maria Garcia wants more detailed information regarding the accounts used in the Split column of the report. Specifically, she wants to know what accounts were used for the transaction of January 18, 2004 for Office & Sales Supplies Co. In order to see these account names, Maria will use the QuickZoom feature of QuickBooks Pro.

DO: Point to the word **-SPLIT-** in the Split column
- The mouse pointer turns into a magnifying glass with a **Z** in it.
Double-click to **Zoom** in to see the accounts used in the transaction
- This returns you to the *original bill* entered for Office & Sales Supplies Co. for the transaction of 01/18/2004.
- The accounts used are Equipment Rental Expense and Office Supplies Expense.

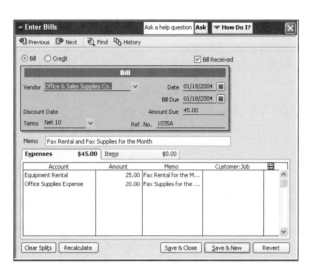

Click **Close** button to return to the Transaction by Vendor Report
Click **Close** button to close the report
- If you get a Memorize Report dialog box, click **No**
Close Report Finder

PREPARE BILLS WITHOUT STEP-BY-STEP INSTRUCTIONS

The accrual method of accounting matches the expenses of a period against the revenue of the period. Frequently when in training, there may be difficulty in determining whether something is recorded as an expense or as a prepaid expense. When you pay something in advance, it is recorded as an increase (debit) to an asset rather than an increase (debit) to an expense. When you have an expense that is paid for in advance, such as insurance, it is called a prepaid expense. At the time the prepaid asset is used (such as one month's worth of insurance), an adjusting entry is made to account for the amount used during the period. Unless otherwise instructed, use the accrual basis of accounting when recording the above entries. (Notice the exception in the first transaction.)

MEMO

DATE: January 19, 2004

Received a bill from Computer Professionals Magazine for a 6-month subscription for Brian Colbert, $74, Net 30 days, Invoice No. 1579-53. (Enter as an expense.)

Maria Garcia received office supplies from Office & Sales Supplies Co.,$450, terms Net 10 days, Invoice No. 8950S. These supplies will be used over a period of several months so enter as a prepaid expense. (Note: After you enter the vendor's name, the information from the previous bill appears on the screen. As you enter the transaction, simply delete any unnecessary information. This may be done by tabbing to the information and pressing the delete key until the information is deleted or by dragging through the information to highlight, then in either method entering the new information.)

While Monique McBride was on her way to a training session at Sanders, Omar, Kandar, and Hickam, the company car broke down. It was towed to Juan's Garage and Auto Services, where it was repaired. The total bill for the towing and repair is $575, Net 30 days, Invoice No. 630.

Received a bill from Southern California Insurance Company for the annual auto insurance premium, $2,850, terms Net 30, Invoice No. 3659 (Enter a memo for this bill.)

DO: Enter the four transactions in the memo above.
- Refer to the instructions given for the two previous transactions entered.
- Remember, when recording bills, you will need to determine the accounts used in the transaction. To determine the appropriate accounts to use, refer to the Chart of Accounts/General Ledger as you record the above transactions.
- Enter information for Memos where an explanation is needed for clarification.
- To go from one bill to the next, click the **Save & New** button.
- After entering the fourth bill, click **Save & Close** to record and exit the **Enter Bills** screen.

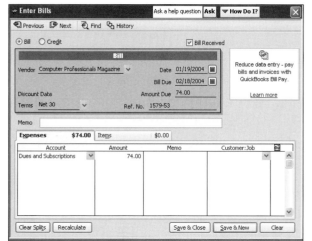

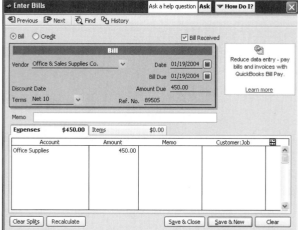

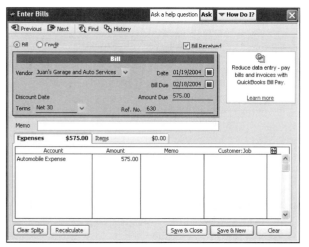

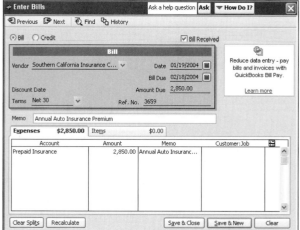

ENTER A BILL USING THE ACCOUNTS PAYABLE REGISTER

The Accounts Payable Register maintains a record of all the transactions recorded within the Accounts Payable account. Entering a bill directly into the Accounts Payable Register can be faster than filling out all of the information through Enter Bills.

MEMO
DATE: January 19, 2004

Speedy Delivery Service provides all of our delivery service for training manuals delivered to customers. Received monthly bill for January deliveries from Speedy Delivery Service, $175, terms Net 10, Invoice No. 88764.

DO: Use the **Accounts Payable Register** to record the above transaction:
Click the **Lists** menu, click **Chart of Accounts**
> OR

Use the keyboard shortcut **Ctrl+A**
Click **Accounts Payable**

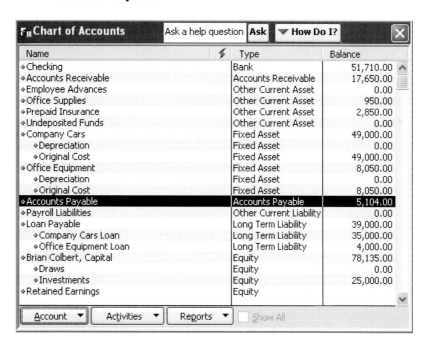

Click the **Activities** button at the bottom of the Chart of Accounts
Click **Use Register**
> OR

Use the keyboard shortcut **Ctrl+R**

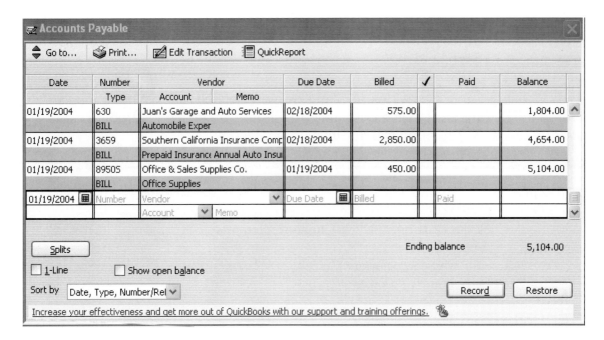

The date of **01/19/2004** is highlighted in the blank entry at the end of the
  Accounts Payable Register
- If it is not, click in the date column in the blank entry and key in **01/19/04** for
  the transaction date.
The word *Number* is in the next column
Tab to or click **Number**
- The word *Number* disappears.
Enter the Invoice Number **88764**
Tab to or click **Vendor**
Click the drop-down list arrow for **Vendor**
Click **Speedy Delivery Service**
Tab to or click **Due Date**
Verify the due date of **01/29/2004**
- If this is not the date showing, drag through the due date to highlight, then
  type **01/29/2004**.
Tab to or click **Billed**
Enter the amount **175**
Tab to or click **Account**
Click the drop-down list arrow for **Account**
Determine the appropriate account to use for the delivery expense
- If all of the accounts do not appear in the drop-down list, scroll through the
  accounts until you find the one appropriate for this entry.
Click **Postage and Delivery**
Tab to or click **Memo**
For the transaction memo, key **January Delivery Expense**

Click the **Record** button to record the transaction
Do not close the register

01/19/2004	88764	Speedy Delivery Service	01/29/2004	175.00			5,279.00
	BILL	Postage and Deli\ January Delivery					

EDIT A TRANSACTION IN THE ACCOUNTS PAYABLE REGISTER

Because QuickBooks Pro makes corrections extremely user friendly, a transaction can be edited or changed directly in the Accounts Payable Register as well as on the original bill. By eliminating the columns for Type and Memo, it is possible to change the register to show each transaction on one line. This can make the register easier to read.

MEMO

DATE: January 20, 2004

Upon examination of the invoices and the bills entered, Maria Garcia discovers two errors: The actual amount of the invoice for Speedy Delivery Services was $195. The amount recorded was $175. The amount of the Invoice for *Computer Professionals Magazine* was $79, not $74. Change the transaction amounts for these transactions.

DO: Correct the above transactions in the Accounts Payable Register
Click the check box for **1-line** to select
- Each Accounts Payable transaction will appear on one line.
Click the transaction for Speedy Delivery Service
Click between the **1** and **7** in the Amount column for the transaction
Press **Delete** to delete the 7
Type **9**
- The amount should be **195.00**.
Scroll through the register until the transaction for *Computer Professionals Magazine* is visible
Click the transaction for *Computer Professionals Magazine*
The **Recording Transaction** dialog box appears on the screen

Click **Yes** to record the changes to the Speedy Delivery Service transaction
- The transaction for *Computer Professionals Magazine* will be the active transaction.

Click between the **4** and the **decimal point**

Press the **Backspace** key one time to delete the 4

Type **9**
- The amount for the transaction should be **79.00**.

Click the **Record** button at the bottom of the register to record the change in the transaction

Do not close the register

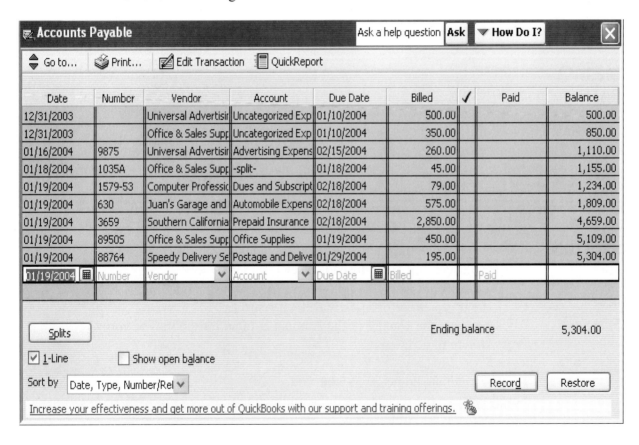

PREVIEW AND PRINT A QUICKREPORT
FROM THE ACCOUNTS PAYABLE REGISTER

After editing the transaction, you may want to view information about a specific vendor. This can be done quickly and efficiently by clicking the vendor's name within a transaction and clicking the QuickReport button at the top of the Register.

MEMO

DATE: January 20, 2004

Several transactions have been entered for Office & Sales Supplies Co. The owner, Brian Colbert, likes to view transaction information for all vendors that have several transactions within a short period of time.

DO: Prepare a QuickReport for Office & Sales Supplies Co.
Click any field in any transaction for Office & Sales Supplies Co.
Click the **QuickReport** button at the top of the Register
- The Register QuickReport for All Transactions for Office & Sales Supplies Co. appears on the screen.

To remove the **Date Printed**, **Time Prepared**, and **Report Basis**, click the **Modify Report** button
Click the **Header/Footer** tab
Click **Date Prepared**, **Time Prepared**, and **Report Basis** to deselect these options
Click **OK**
Click **Print**
Complete the information on the **Print Reports** screen:
  Print to: The selected item should be **Printer**
  - The printer name should appear in the **Printer** text box.
  Orientation: click **Landscape** for this report
  Page Range: All should be selected; if it is not, click **All**
  Page Breaks: Smart Page Breaks should be selected
Click **Preview** to view the report before printing
- The report appears on the screen as a full page.
- A full-page report on the screen usually cannot be read.

To read the text in the report, click the **Zoom In** button at the top of the screen
Use the scroll buttons and bars to view the report columns
Click **Zoom Out** to return to a full-page view of the report
When finished viewing the report, click **Close**
- You will return to the **Print Reports** screen.

If the report does not fit on one page, click **Fit report to one page wide** to select

Click **Print** button on the **Print Reports** screen

Contempo Computer Consulting (CCC)--Student's Name
Register QuickReport
All Transactions

Type	Date	Num	Memo	Account	Paid	Open Balance	Amount
Office & Sales Supplies Co.							
Bill	12/31/2003		Opening bal...	Accounts Payable	Unpaid	350.00	350.00
Bill	01/18/2004	1035A	Fax Rental a...	Accounts Payable	Unpaid	45.00	45.00
Bill	01/19/2004	8950S		Accounts Payable	Unpaid	450.00	450.00
Total Office & Sales Supplies Co.						845.00	845.00
TOTAL						**845.00**	**845.00**

Click the **Close** button to close each of the following: the **Register QuickReport**, the **Accounts Payable Register**, and the **Chart of Accounts**

PREPARE UNPAID BILLS DETAIL REPORT

It is possible to get information regarding unpaid bills by simply preparing a report—no more digging through tickler files, recorded invoices, ledgers, or journals. QuickBooks Pro prepares an Unpaid Bills Report listing each unpaid bill grouped and subtotaled by vendor.

MEMO

DATE: January 25, 2004

Maria Garcia prepares an Unpaid Bill Report for Brian Colbert each week. Even though CCC is a small business, Brian likes to have a firm control over cash flow so he determines which bills will be paid during the week.

DO: Prepare and print an Unpaid Bills Report
Click **Unpaid Bills Detail** in the Memorized Reports section of the **Vendors** Navigator
OR
Click **Report Finder** on the **Vendors** Navigator
The **Type of report** should be **Vendors & Payables**
In the **Select a report** section of the Report Finder, click **Unpaid Bills Detail**
Click **Display**

Remove the date and time prepared from the report by clicking the **Modify Report** button, clicking the **Header/Footer** tab**,** and clicking **Date Prepared** and **Time Prepared** to deselect these options

Click **OK**

Provide the report date by clicking in the text box for **Date**, dragging through the date to highlight, and typing **01/25/04**

Tab to generate the report

Click **Print**

Complete the information on the **Print Reports Screen**:

Print To: The selected item should be **Printer**

Orientation: click **Portrait** for this report

Page Range: All should be selected; if it is not, click **All**

Page Breaks: Smart page breaks should be selected

If necessary, click **Fit report to one page wide** to deselect

Click **Print**

Contempo Computer Consulting (CCC)-...
Unpaid Bills Detail
As of January 25, 2004

Type	Date	Num	Due Date	Aging	Open Balance
Computer Professionals Magazine					
Bill	01/19/2004	1579...	02/18/2004		79.00
Total Computer Professionals Magazine					79.00
Juan's Garage and Auto Services					
Bill	01/19/2004	630	02/18/2004		575.00
Total Juan's Garage and Auto Services					575.00
Office & Sales Supplies Co.					
Bill	12/31/2003		01/10/2004	15	350.00
Bill	01/18/2004	1035A	01/18/2004	7	45.00
Bill	01/19/2004	8950S	01/19/2004	6	450.00
Total Office & Sales Supplies Co.					845.00

Partial Report

Click **Close** to close the report

Click **No** if you get a Memorize Report dialog box

If necessary, click **Close** to close the **Report Finder**

DELETE A BILL

QuickBooks Pro makes it possible to delete any bill that has been recorded. No adjusting entries are required in order to do this. Simply access the bill or the Accounts Payable Register and delete the bill.

MEMO

DATE: January 26, 2004

After reviewing the Unpaid Bills Report, Maria Garcia realizes that the bill recorded for *Computer Professionals Magazine* should have been recorded for *Computer Technologies Magazine*.

 DO: Delete the bill recorded for *Computer Professionals Magazine*

Access the Chart of Accounts:
   Use the keyboard shortcut **Ctrl+A**
      OR
   Click the **Accnt** icon on the icon bar
      OR
   Use the menu bar, click **List**, click **Chart of Accounts**
With the Chart of Accounts showing on the screen, click **Accounts Payable**
Open the Accounts Payable Register:
   Use keyboard shortcut **Ctrl+R**
      OR
   Click **Activities Button**, click **Use Register**
Click on the bill for *Computer Professionals Magazine*
To delete the bill:
   Click **Edit** on the menu bar, click **Delete Bill**

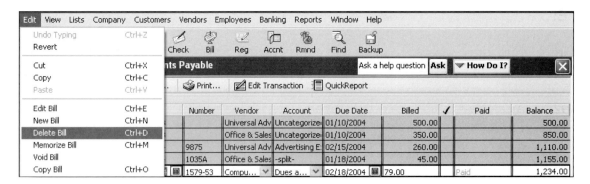

      OR
   Use the keyboard shortcut **Ctrl+D**
   • The **Delete Transaction** dialog box appears on the screen.

Click **OK** to delete the bill
- Notice that the transaction no longer appears in the Accounts Payable Register.

Close the **Accounts Payable Register**

Close the **Chart of Accounts**

ADD A NEW VENDOR WHILE RECORDING A BILL

When entering bills, typing the first letter(s) of a vendor name enters the name on the Vendor line. If the vendor is not in the Vendor List, QuickBooks Pro allows you to add a new vendor on the fly while entering a bill. If you key in the vendor name, a QuickBooks Pro dialog box for Vendor Not Found appears with choices for a Quick Add—adding just the vendor name—or Set Up—adding the vendor name and all vendor account information. When the new vendor information is complete, QuickBooks Pro fills in the blanks on the bill for the vendor, and you finish entering the rest of the transaction.

MEMO

DATE: January 26, 2004

Record the bill for a 6-month subscription to *Computer Technologies Magazine*. The transaction date is 01/19/04, amount $79, Terms Net 30, Invoice No. 1579-53. This is recorded as an expense. The address and telephone for *Computer Technologies Magazine* is 12405 Menlo Park Drive, Menlo Park, CA 94025, 510-555-3829.

DO: Record the above transaction
- Step-by-step instructions will be provided only for entering a new vendor.
- Refer to transactions previously recorded for all other steps used in entering a bill.

Access the **Enter Bills** screen
- When you key the first few letters of a vendor name, QuickBooks Pro will automatically enter a vendor name.

On the line for Vendor, type the **C** for *Computer Technologies Magazine*

- The vendor name **California Electric** appears on the vendor line and is highlighted.

Type **omp**

- The vendor name changes to **Computer Professionals Magazine**.

Finish typing **uter Technologies Magazine**

Press **Tab**

The **Vendor Not Found** dialog box appears on the screen with buttons for:

- **Quick Add**—adds only the name to the vendor list.
- **Set Up**—adds the name to the vendor list and allows all account information to be entered.
- **Cancel**—cancels the addition of a new vendor.

Click **Cancel**

- The name *Computer Technologies Magazine* is still on the Vendor line and is highlighted.

Click the drop-down list arrow for **Vendor**

Click **<Add New>**

Enter **Computer Technologies Magazine** in the Vendor Name text box

Enter the information needed for the **Address Info** tab:

    Tab to or click **Company Name**

    Key **Computer Technologies Magazine**

    Tab to or click the first line for **Address**

- Computer Technologies Magazine appears as the first line of the address.

    Press **Enter** or click the line beneath the company name (Do not tab)

    Type the address listed in the transaction

    Press **Enter** at the end of each line

    When finished with the address, tab to or click **Phone**

    Enter the telephone number

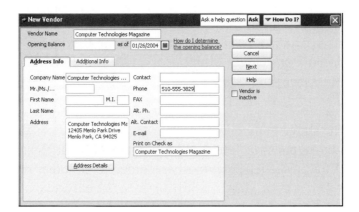

Enter the information for **Additional Info** tab

    Click **Additional Info** tab

    Click drop-down list arrow next to **Terms**

Click **Net 30**

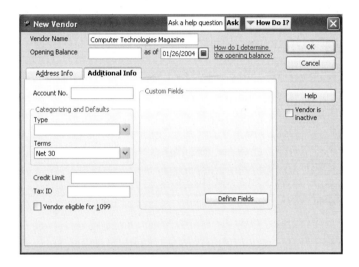

Click the **OK** button for **New Vendor** screen
- The information for Vendor, Terms, and the Dates is filled in on the Enter Bills screen.

If necessary, change the transaction date to **01/19/04**

Complete the bill using instructions previously provided for entering bills

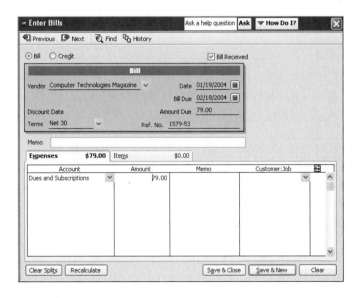

When finished, click **Save & Close** to close the bill and exit

MODIFY VENDOR RECORDS

Occasionally, information regarding a vendor will change. QuickBooks Pro allows vendor accounts to be modified at anytime by editing the Vendor List.

MEMO

DATE: January 26, 2004

Because Linda Scott received a promotion, the contact person for Speedy Delivery Service has been changed to Brenda Hermosa.

DO: Modify the vendor records for Speedy Delivery Service
Access the **Vendor List**:
> Click the **Vendor** menu, click **Vendor List**
>> OR
> Click the **Vendors** icon on the Vendors Navigator

If necessary, scroll through the Vendor List until **Speedy Delivery Service** appears

Click **Speedy Delivery Service**

Click the **Vendor** button at the bottom of the list, click **Edit**
> OR

Use the keyboard shortcut **Ctrl+E**
- The Edit Vendor screen appears.

Click the **Contact** text box

Drag through **Linda Scott** to highlight

Type **Brenda Hermosa**

Click **OK** to record the change

Click **Close** on **Vendor List** to close

ENTER A CREDIT FROM A VENDOR

Credit memos are prepared to record a reduction to a transaction. With QuickBooks Pro, you use the Enter Bills window to record credit memos received from vendors acknowledging a return of or an allowance for a previously recorded bill and/or payment. The amount of a credit memo is deducted from the amount owed.

MEMO

DATE: January 26, 2004

Received Credit Memo No. 789 for $5 from Office & Sales Supplies Co. for a return of fax paper that was damaged.

 DO: Access the **Enter Bills** window and record the credit memo shown above

On the **Enter Bills** screen, click **Credit** to select

- Notice that the word *Bill* changes to *Credit*.

Click the drop-down list arrow next to **Vendor**

Click **Office & Sales Supplies Co.**

Tab to or click the **Date**

Type **01/26/04**

Tab to or click **Credit Amount**

Type **5**

Tab to or click **Ref. No.**

Type **789**

Tab to or click in **Memo**

Enter **Returned Fax Paper**

Tab to or click the first line of **Account**

Click the drop-down list arrow

Because this was originally entered as an expense, click the account **Office Supplies Expense**

- The amount should show **5.00**; if not, enter **5**.
- The **Memo** column may be left blank.

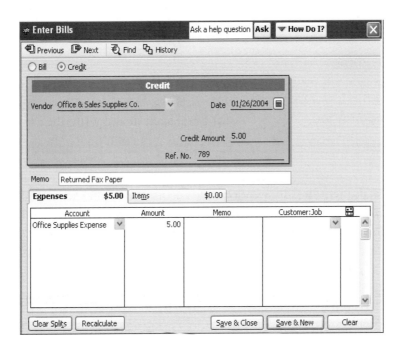

Click **Save & Close** to record the credit and exit **Enter Bills**

- QuickBooks Pro records the credit in the Accounts Payable account and shows the transaction type as BILLCRED in the Accounts Payable Register.

VIEW CREDIT IN ACCOUNTS PAYABLE REGISTER

When recording the credit in the last transaction, QuickBooks Pro listed the transaction type as BILLCRED in the Accounts Payable Register.

DO: Verify the credit from Office & Sales Supplies Co.

Follow steps previously provided to access the Accounts Payable Register

If a check mark shows in the **1-Line** check box, remove it by clicking the check box

- This changes the display in the Accounts Payable Register from 1-Line to multiple lines.

Look at the **Number/Type** column and verify the type **BILLCRED**

01/26/2004	789	Office & Sales Supplies Co.				5.00	5,299.00
	BILLCRED	Office Supplies Returned Fax P.					

Close the **Accounts Payable Register**
Close the **Chart of Accounts**

PAYING BILLS

When using QuickBooks Pro, you should pay any bills entered through "Enter Bills" directly from the pay bills command and let QuickBooks Pro write your checks for you and mark the bills "Paid." If you have not entered a bill for an amount you owe, you will need to write the checks yourself. If you have recorded a bill for a transaction and write the check for payment yourself, the bill will not be marked as being paid and will continue to show up as an amount due.

Using the Pay Bills window enables you to determine which bills to pay, the method of payment—check or credit card—and the appropriate account. When determining which bills to pay, QuickBooks Pro allows you to display the bills by due date, discount date, vendor, or amount. All bills may be displayed, or only those bills that are due by a certain date may be displayed.

MEMO
DATE: January 26, 2004

Whenever possible, Maria Garcia pays the bills on a weekly basis. With the Pay Bills window showing the bills due for payment before 01/31/2004, Maria compares the bills shown with the Unpaid Bills Report previously prepared. The report has been marked by Brian Colbert to indicate which bills should be paid. Maria will select the appropriate bills for payment and record the bill payment for the week.

DO: Pay the bills for the week
Access the **Pay Bills** window:
If necessary, click **Vendors** on the Navigator list; click **Pay Bills** on the Vendors Navigator
Determine the bills to be paid:
Click **Show All Bills** to select
Sort Bills by **Due Date**
- If this is not showing, click the drop-down list arrow next to the **Sort Bills By** text box, click **Due Date**.
Scroll through the list of bills
Click the drop-down list arrow next to the **Sort Bills By** text box
Click **Vendor**
- This shows you how much you owe each vendor.
Again, click the drop-down list arrow next to the **Sort Bills** text box
Click **Amount Due**
- This shows you your bills from the highest amount owed to the lowest.

Click drop-down list arrow next to the **Sort Bills** text box, click **Due Date**
- The bills will be shown according to the date due.

Click **Show bills due on or before** to select this option

Click in the text box for the date

Drag through the date to highlight, enter **01/31/04** as the date

Scroll through the list of bills due

Select the bills to be paid
- The bills shown on the screen are an exact match to the bills Brian Colbert marked to be paid.

Click **Select All Bills**
- To pay some of the bills but not all of them, mark each bill to be paid by clicking on the individual bill or using the cursor keys to select a bill and pressing the space bar.

The **Select All Bills** button changes to **Clear Selections** so bills can be unmarked and the bills to be paid may be selected again

Apply the $5 credit for Office Supply Wholesale by clicking in the √ column for the $45 transaction for Office & Sales Supplies Co. with a due date of 01/28/2004
- This will deselect the bill

Click the √ column again to select the bill

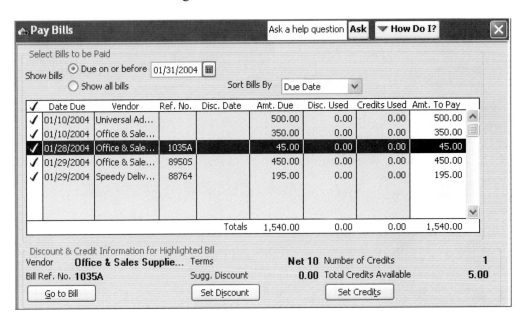

- Notice that the Set Credits button appears in bold and that a Total Credit of $5.00 is available.

Click the **Set Credits** button

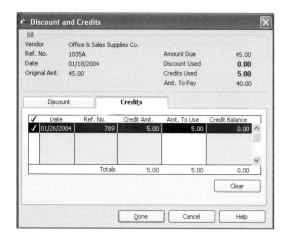

Click **Done** on the Discounts and Credits screen

- Notice that the Credits Used column for the transaction displays 5.00 and the Amt. To Pay for the bill is 40.00.

The **Payment Account** should be **Checking**

In the **Payment Method** section of the screen, make sure **Check** has been selected as the payment method

Make sure **To be printed** box has been selected

If it is not selected, click in the circle to select

Tab to or click **Payment Date**

Enter the Payment Date of **01/26/04**

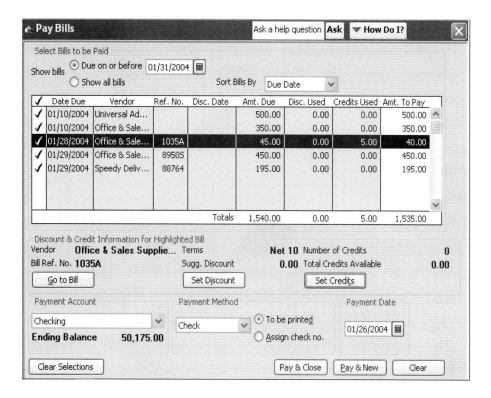

Click **Pay & Close** to record your payments and close the **Pay Bills** window

PRINTING CHECKS FOR BILLS

Once bills have been marked and recorded as paid, you may handwrite checks to vendors, or you may have QuickBooks Pro print the checks to vendors. If there is more than one amount due for a vendor, QuickBooks Pro totals the amounts due to the vendor and prints one check to the vendor.

DO: Print the checks for the bills paid

Click the **File** menu

Point to **Print Forms**

Click **Checks**

Bank Account should be **Checking**
- If this is not showing, click the drop-down list arrow, click **Checking**.

The **First Check Number** should be **1**
- If not, delete the number showing, and key **1**.

In the √ column, the checks selected to be printed are marked with a check mark

Click **OK** to print the checks
- The **Print Checks** screen appears.

Verify and if necessary change information on the **Settings** tab

    Printer name: The name of your printer should show in the text box
- If the correct printer name is not showing, click the drop-down list arrow, click the correct printer name.

    Printer type: Page-oriented (Single sheets) should be in the text box
- If this does not show or if you use Continuous (Perforated Edge) checks, click the drop-down list arrow, click the appropriate sheet style to select.

    Check style: Three different types of check styles may be used: Standard, Voucher, or Wallet

    If it is not in the check style text box, click **Standard Checks** to insert

    Print Company Name and Address: If the box does not have a check mark, click to select

    Use Logo should not be selected; if a check mark appears in the check box, click to deselect

Click **Print** to print the checks
- All three checks will print on one page. Verify the amounts of the checks: Universal Advertising, $500; Office & Sales Supplies Co., $840; and Speedy Delivery Service, $195.

Did check(s) print OK? dialog box appears

If checks printed correctly, click **OK**
- The checks have the address for Contempo Computer Consulting, the name and address of the company being paid, and the amount being paid.
- The actual checks will not have a check number printed because QuickBooks Pro is set up to work with preprinted check forms containing check numbers.
- In the memo section of the check, any memo entered on the bill shows.
- If there was no memo entered for the bill, the vendor account number appears as the memo.
- If you cannot get the checks to print on one page, it is perfectly acceptable to access the checks by clicking **Banking** on the Navigator list, clicking **Checks** on the Banking Navigator, and printing them one at a time. This method is also useful if you need to correct a check and reprint it.

If you get a message box regarding purchasing checks, click **No**

REVIEW BILLS THAT HAVE BEEN PAID

In order to avoid any confusion about payment of a bill, QuickBooks Pro marks the bill PAID. Scrolling through the recorded bills in the Enter Bills window, you will see the paid bills marked PAID.

 DO: Scroll the **Enter Bills** window to view PAID bills
Click **Enter Bills** on the Vendors Navigator
Click the **Previous** button to go back through all the bills recorded
- Notice that the bills paid for Office & Sales Supplies Co., Speedy Delivery Service, and Universal Advertising are marked **PAID**.

Click the **Close** button

PETTY CASH

Frequently, a business will need to pay for small expenses with cash. These might include expenses such as postage, office supplies, and miscellaneous expenses. For example, rather than write a check for postage due of 75 cents, you would use money from petty cash. QuickBooks Pro allows you to establish and use a petty cash account to track these small expenditures. Normally, a Petty Cash Voucher is prepared; and, if available, the receipt for the transaction is stapled to it. It is important in a business to keep accurate records of the petty cash expenditures, and procedures for control of the Petty Cash fund need to be established to prohibit access to and unauthorized use of the cash. Periodically, the petty cash expenditures are recorded so that the records of the company accurately reflect all expenses incurred in the operation of the business.

ADD PETTY CASH ACCOUNT TO THE CHART OF ACCOUNTS

QuickBooks Pro allows accounts to be added to the Chart of Accounts list at any time. Petty Cash is identified as a "Bank" account type so it will be placed at the top of the Chart of Accounts along with other checking and savings accounts.

MEMO
DATE: January 26, 2004

Occasionally, there are small items that should be paid for using cash. Maria Garcia needs to establish a petty cash account for $100

DO: Add Petty Cash to the **Chart of Accounts**
Access **Chart of Accounts**:
   Click **Lists** menu, click **Chart of Accounts**
      OR
   Click **Chart of Accounts** on the **Company** Navigator
Access **New Account** screen:
   Click the **Account** button at the bottom of the Chart of Accounts, click **New**
      OR
   Use the keyboard shortcut **Ctrl+N**
Create a new account:
   Type should be **Bank**
   • If it is not, click the drop-down list arrow next to the text box for **Type**, then click **Bank**.
   Enter **Petty Cash** in the **Name** text box
   Leave the following items blank:

Subaccount
Bank Acct. No.
Tax Line (Unassigned)
Opening Balance
- The Opening Balance is used only when setting up QuickBooks Pro, not when adding an account.

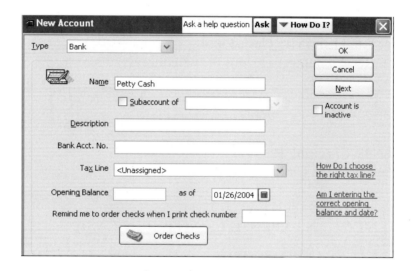

If the date of **01/26/04** is not shown for the **as of** date, enter it
Click **OK** to record the new account
Do not close the **Chart of Accounts**

ESTABLISH PETTY CASH FUND

Once the account has been established, the petty cash fund must have money in order to pay for small expenses. A cash withdrawal from checking must be made or a check must be written and cashed to obtain petty cash funds. This may be recorded in the Checking Register.

DO: Record the cash withdrawal of $100 from checking to establish petty cash:
To access the **Check Register**, click **Checking** account in the **Chart of Accounts**, click the **Activities** button, click **Use Register**
- The Check Register should be on the screen.
- If the cursor is not already in the Date column, click in the **Date** column for a new transaction at the end of the Check Register.
- The date should be highlighted; if it is not, drag through the date to highlight.
If the date is not 01/26/2004, enter **01/26/04**
Tab to or click **Number**
Enter **CASH**

Because this is a cash withdrawal, a Payee name will not be entered
Tab to or click **Payment**
Enter **100**
Tab to or click **Account**
Click the drop-down list arrow next to **Account**
Click **Petty Cash**
• The account shows Petty Cash and Type changed from CHK to TRANSFR.
Tab to or click **Memo**
Enter **Establish Petty Cash Fund**
Click **Record** button to record the withdrawal

01/26/2004	CASH			100.00			50,075.00
	TRANSFR	Petty Cash	Establish Petty Cash Fund				

Close the **Checking Register**
Do not close the **Chart of Accounts**

RECORD PAYMENT OF AN EXPENSE USING PETTY CASH

As petty cash is used to pay for small expenses in the business, these payments must be recorded. QuickBooks Pro makes it a simple matter to record petty cash expenditures directly into the Petty Cash Register.

MEMO
DATE: January 30, 2004

Maria Garcia needs to record the petty cash expenditures made during the week: postage due, 34 cents; purchased staples and paper clips, $3.57 (this is an expense); reimbursed Monique McBride for gasoline purchased for company car, $13.88.

DO: In the Petty Cash account, record a compound entry for the above expenditures:
Click **Petty Cash** on the **Chart of Accounts**
Access the **Register**:
    Ctrl+R
     OR
Click **Activities** button, click **Use Register**
Click in the **Date** column, highlight the date if necessary
Type **01/30/04**
• No entry is required for Number; QuickBooks Pro inserts **1** for the number.

- No entry is required for Payee.

Tab to or click **Payment**

Enter **17.79** (you must type the decimal point)

Tab to or click in **Account** text box

Click **Splits** at the bottom of the screen

- Splits is used because the total amount of the transaction will be split among three expense accounts.

In the **Account** column showing on the screen, click the drop-down list arrow

Scroll until you see **Postage and Delivery**

Click **Postage and Delivery**

Tab to **Amount** column

- Using the Tab key will highlight **17.79**.

Type **.34**

- Memo notations are not necessary because the transactions are self-explanatory.

Tab to or click the next blank line in **Account**

Repeat the steps listed above to record **3.57** for **Office Supplies Expense** and **13.88** for **Automobile Expense**

Click **Close** when all expenses have been recorded

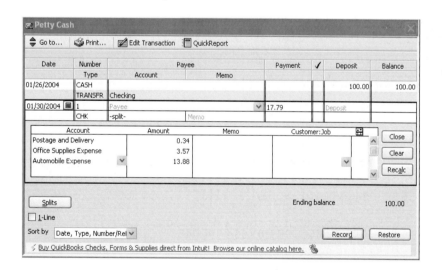

Click **Record** to record the transaction

- Notice that the word "payee," the account name, and memo are removed from the transaction. The only item indicated is **-split-**.
- Verify the account Ending Balance of 82.21.

Close **Petty Cash** and the **Chart of Accounts**

PAY BILLS BY WRITING CHECKS

Although it is more efficient to record all bills in the Enter Bills window and pay all bills through the Pay Bills window, QuickBooks Pro also allows bills to be paid by writing a check. The check window is divided into two main areas: the check face and the detail area. The check face includes information such as the date of the check, the payee's name, the check amount, the payee's address, and a line for a memo—just like a paper check. The detail area is used to indicate transaction accounts and amounts.

MEMO
DATE: January 30, 2004

Since these items were not previously recorded as bills, write checks to pay the following:

Lindsey Realtors—rent for the month, $1,500
Communication Telephone Co.—telephone bill for the month, $350
California Electric—electric bill for the month, $250
California Water—water bill for the month, $35
California Gas Co.—heating bill for the month, $175

DO: Write checks to pay the bills listed above:
     Access **Checking**:
         Click **Banking** menu, click **Write Checks**
            OR
         Click **Banking** on the Navigator list, click **Checks** on the Banking Navigator
            OR
         Use the keyboard shortcut **Ctrl+W**
            OR
         Click the **Check** icon on the icon bar
     Verify the bank account used for the check
         If the screen shows **Write Checks-Petty Cash**, click the drop-down list arrow
            for **Bank Account**, click **Checking**.
     •   If you get a message to set a default account, click **Ok**
     Tab to or click **Date**
     Enter **01/30/04**
     •   If the check has been written by hand, this will be left blank.
     Complete the check face:
         Click the drop-down list arrow next to **Pay to the Order of**
         Click **Lindsey Realtors**
         Tab to or click **Amount**

Enter the amount of the rent
Tab to or click **Memo**
Enter **Monthly Rent**
- This memo prints on the check, not on reports.

Click **To Be Printed** to indicate that the check needs to be printed
- When To Be Printed is selected, an icon for Order Checks appears on the check.

Complete the detail area:
On the **Expenses** tab, tab to or click the first line of **Account**
Click the drop-down list arrow for **Account**
Click **Rent**
- The total amount of the check is shown in Amount column.
- If you want a transaction description to appear in reports, enter the description in the Memo column—no entry is required because these are standard transactions.

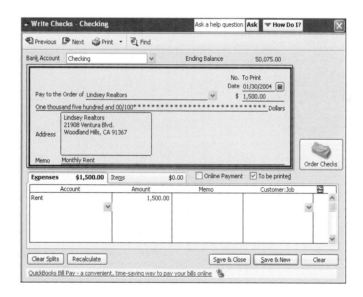

Do not print any of the checks being entered
Click **Save & New** to record the check and advance to the next check
Repeat the steps indicated above to record payment of the telephone, electric, water, and gas bills
- While entering the bills, you may see a dialog box on the screen, indicating that QuickBooks Pro allows you to do online banking. Online banking will not be used at this time. Click **OK** to close the dialog box.

ENTER THE CHECK FOR THE ELECTRIC BILL A SECOND TIME
Click the drop-down list arrow and click **California Electric**
- The first payment entered for the payment of the bill for electricity appears on the screen.

Click **Save & Close** to record the second payment for the electric bill and exit the **Write Checks** window

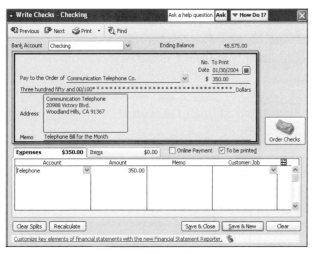

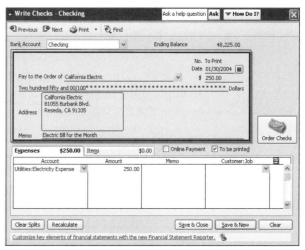

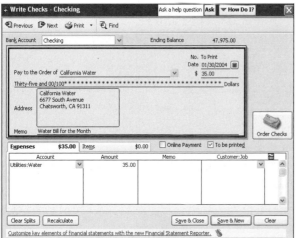

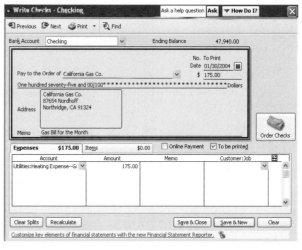

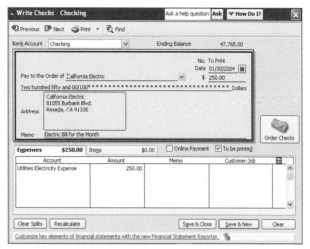

Duplicate Check

EDIT CHECKS

Mistakes can occur in business—even on a check. QuickBooks Pro allows for checks to be edited at anytime. You may use either the Check Register or the Write Checks window to edit checks.

MEMO

DATE: January 30, 2004

Once the check for the rent had been entered, Maria realized that it should have been for $1,600. Edit the check written to Lindsey Realtors.

DO: Revise the check written to pay the rent
  Open **Write Checks** as previously instructed
  Click **Previous** until you reach the check for Lindsey Realtors
  Click between the **1** and the **5** in the **Amount** column
  Press **Delete** to delete the **5**
  Type **6**, press the Tab key

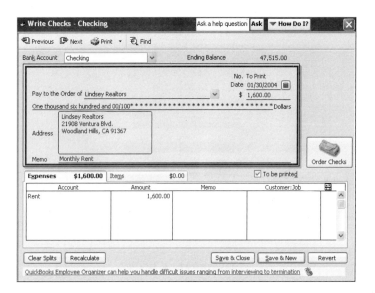

Do not print the check

Click **Save & Close**

Click **Yes** on the screen asking if you want to save the transaction that has been changed

VOID CHECKS

QuickBooks Pro allows checks to be voided. Rather than deleting the transaction, voiding a check changes the amount of the check to zero but keeps a record of the transaction.

MEMO

DATE: January 30, 2004

The telephone bill should not have been paid until the first week of February. Void the check written for the telephone expense.

DO: Use the steps given previously to access the Register for the **Checking** account

Void the check written for the telephone expense

Click anywhere in the check to Communication Telephone Co.

Click **Edit** on the menu bar at the top of the screen—not the Edit button

Click **Void Check**

- The amount of the check is now 0.00 and the memo shows VOID: Telephone Bill for the Month.

Click the **Record** button

Do not close the register for checking

01/30/2004		Communication Telephone Co.		0.00	✓		50,075.00
	CHK	Telephone VOID: Telephone Bill fo					

DELETE CHECKS

Deleting a check completely removes it and any transaction information for the check from QuickBooks Pro. Make sure you definitely want to remove the check before deleting it. Once it is deleted, a check cannot be recovered. It is often preferable to void a check than to delete it because a voided check is maintained in the company records; whereas, no record is kept of a deleted check.

MEMO

DATE: January 30, 2004

In reviewing the register for the checking account, Maria Garcia discovered that two checks were written to pay the electric bill. Delete the second check.

DO: Delete the second entry for the electric bill
- Notice that there are two transactions showing for California Electric.
Click anywhere in the second entry to California Electric
Click **Edit** on the menu bar at the top of the screen, click **Delete Check**
     OR
Use the keyboard shortcut **Ctrl+D**

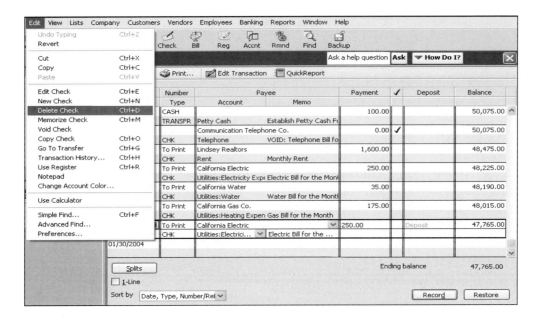

Click **OK** on the **Delete Transaction** dialog box

- After you have clicked the **OK** button, there is only one transaction in Checking for California Electric.

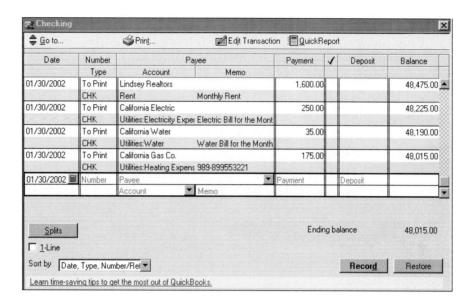

Close the **Checking Register** and the **Chart of Accounts**

PRINT CHECKS

Checks may be printed as they are entered, or they may be printed at a later time. When checks are to be printed, QuickBooks Pro inserts the words *To Print* rather than a check number in the Check Register. The appropriate check number is indicated during printing. Because QuickBooks Pro is so flexible, a company must institute a system for cash control. For example, if the check for rent of $1,500 had been printed, QuickBooks Pro would allow a second check for $1,600 to be printed. In order to avoid any impropriety, more than one person can be designated to review checks. As a matter of practice in a small business, the owner or a person other than the one writing checks should sign the checks. Pre-numbered checks should be used, and any checks printed but not mailed should be submitted along with those for signature. Lastly, QuickBooks optional audit trail feature detailing all transactions, including corrections, should be in use. This is turned on in the Preferences section on the Edit menu. The audit trail has not been turned on for use in training; however, it is strongly recommended that this feature by used in an actual business environment.

MEMO

DATE: January 30, 2004

Maria needs to print checks and obtain Brian Colbert's signature so the checks can be mailed.

DO: Print the checks for rent and utility bills paid by writing checks

Click the **File** menu, point to **Print Forms**, click **Checks**

Bank Account should be **Checking**

- If this is not showing, click the drop-down list arrow, click **Checking**

Because Check Nos. 1, 2, and 3 were printed previously, **4** should be the number in the **First Check Number** text box

- If not, delete the number showing, key **4**

In the √ column, the checks selected for printing are marked with a check mark

- If not, click the **Select All** button.

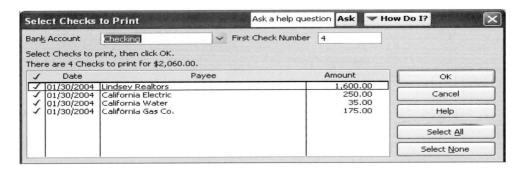

Click **OK** to print the checks

- The **Print Checks** screen appears.

Verify and if necessary change information on the **Settings** tab

Printer name: The name of your printer should show in the text box

Printer type: Page-oriented (Single sheets) should be in the text box

- If this does not show or if you use Continuous (Perforated Edge) checks, click the drop-down list arrow, click the appropriate sheet style to select.

Check style: Three different types of check styles may be used: Standard, Voucher, or Wallet

- If it is not in the check style text box, click **Standard Checks** to insert.

Print Company Name and Address: if the box does not have a check mark, click to select

Use Logo should not be selected

Click **Print** to print the checks

- The following shows the check portion of the Check window, not the entire printed check.

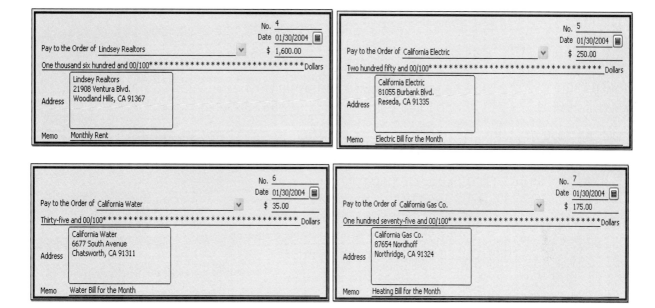

Did check(s) print OK? dialog box appears

If the checks printed correctly, click **OK**

- The checks have the address for Contempo Computer Consulting, the name and address of the company being paid, and the amount being paid. There is no check number printed on the checks because QuickBooks Pro is set up to use pre-numbered checks.
- In the memo section of the check, any memo entered when preparing the check shows. If there was no memo entered for the bill, the vendor account number appears as the memo.
- If you run into difficulties or find you made an error and want to correct and/or print an individual check, you may do so by printing directly from the check.

PREPARE CHECK DETAIL REPORT

Once checks have been printed, it is important to review information about checks. The Check Detail Report provides detailed information regarding each check, including the checks for 0.00 amounts. Information indicates the type of transaction, the date, the check number, the payee, the account used, the original amount, and the paid amount of the check.

MEMO

DATE: January 30, 2004

Now that the checks have been printed, Maria prints a Check Detail Report. She will give this to Brian Colbert to examine when he signs the printed checks.

DO: Print a Check Detail Report:

Click **Check Detail** in the Memorized Reports area of the Banking Navigator
 OR
Click **Report Finder** on the Banking Navigator
 Click **Check Detail** from the reports listed
  • The type of report should be Banking and Check Detail should appear in the area of Select a Report.
 Click **Display**
Remove the **Date Prepared** and **Time Prepared** from the report header
Provide report period:
 Click in the text box for **From**
 Drag through the date to highlight, type **01/01/04**
 Tab to **To**
 Enter **01/30/04**
Tab to generate report
 • *Note:* You may find that the transaction for Petty Cash appears in a different order than the screen shot. The position of the transaction does not matter as long as the transaction is included in the report.
Click **Print**
Complete the information on the **Print Reports Screen**:
 Print to: The selected item should be **Printer**
 Orientation: click **Landscape** for this report
 Page Range: All should be selected; if it is not, click **All**
 If necessary, click **Fit report to one page wide** to deselect
Click **Print**

Type	**Num**	**Date**	**Name**	**Item**	**Account**	**Paid Amount**	**Original Amount**
Check	1	01/30/2004			Petty Cash		-17.79
					Postage and Delive...	-0.34	0.34
					Office Supplies Ex...	-3.57	3.57
					Automobile Expense	-13.88	13.88
TOTAL						-17.79	17.79
Bill Pmt -Check	2	01/26/2004	Speedy Delivery...		Checking		-195.00
Bill	88764	01/19/2004			Postage and Delive...	-195.00	195.00
TOTAL						-195.00	195.00
Bill Pmt -Check	3	01/26/2004	Universal Adver...		Checking		-500.00
Bill		12/31/2003			Uncategorized Exp...	-500.00	500.00
TOTAL						-500.00	500.00

Contempo Computer Consulting (CCC)--Student's Name
Check Detail
January 1 - 30, 2004

Click **Close** to close the report

VIEW MISSING CHECKS REPORT

A Missing Checks Report lists the checks written for a bank account in order by check number. If there are any gaps between numbers or duplicate check numbers, this information is provided. The report indicates the type of transaction, Check or Bill Payment-Check, check date, check number, payee name, account used for the check, the split or additional accounts used, and the amount of the check.

MEMO

DATE: January 30, 2004

To see a listing of all checks printed, view a Missing Checks Report for all dates.

DO: View a Missing Checks Report
If necessary, open Report Finder
Click **Missing Checks** on the **Report Finder**
Click **Display**
- If **Checking** appears as the account on the **Missing Checks Report** dialog box, click **OK**.

- If it does not appear, click the drop-down list arrow, click **Checking**, click **OK**.

Examine the report:

Type	Date	Num	Name	Memo	Account	Split	Amount
Bill Pmt -Check	01/26/2004	1	Office & Sales Sup...	456-45623	Checking	Accounts Pa...	-840.00
Bill Pmt -Check	01/26/2004	2	Speedy Delivery S...	January Del...	Checking	Accounts Pa...	-195.00
Bill Pmt -Check	01/26/2004	3	Universal Advertis...	1-2567135-54	Checking	Accounts Pa...	-500.00
Check	01/30/2004	4	Lindsey Realtors	Monthly Rent	Checking	Rent	-1,600.00
Check	01/30/2004	5	California Electric	Electric Bill f...	Checking	Electricity Exp...	-250.00
Check	01/30/2004	6	California Water	Water Bill fo...	Checking	Water	-35.00
Check	01/30/2004	7	California Gas Co.	Heating Bill f...	Checking	Heating Expe...	-175.00

Contempo Computer Consulting (CCC)--Student's Name
Missing Checks
All Transactions

- The **Account** in all cases is **Checking**.
- The **Split** column indicates which accounts in addition to checking have been used in the transaction.
- Look at the **Type** column.
    - The checks written through Pay Bills indicate the transaction type as **Bill Pmt-Check**.
    - The bills paid by actually writing the checks show **Check** as the transaction type.

Close the report without printing
Close Report Finder

PURCHASE AN ASSET WITH A COMPANY CHECK

Not all purchases will be transactions on account. If something is purchased and paid for with a check, a check is written and the purchase is recorded.

MEMO
DATE: January 30, 2004

Having tried out several fax machines from Office & Sales Supplies Co. on a rental basis, Maria Garcia and Brian Colbert decide to purchase a fax machine from them. Because the fax machine is on sale if it is purchased for cash, Brian decides to buy it by writing a company check for the asset for $486.

DO: Record the check written for the purchase of a fax machine
Access **Write Checks - Checking** window as previously instructed
- This check was hand written by Brian Colbert and does not need printing.
- If a check mark appears in the box **To be printed**, click the box to deselect.
- The **No.** shows as **1**; do not change.
Click the drop-down list arrow for **Pay to the Order of**
Click **Office & Sales Supplies Co.**
The **Date** should be **01/30/2004**
Tab to or click **$0.00**
- If necessary, highlight 0.00.
Enter **486**
Tab to or click **Memo**
Enter **Purchase Fax Machine**
Tab to or click **Account** on the **Expenses** tab
Click the drop-down list arrow, scroll to the top of the **Chart of Accounts**, and
    click **Original Cost** under **Office Equipment**
- If you get a message to Track Fixed Assets, click **NO**
- **Amount** column shows the transaction total of **486.00**. This does not need to
    be changed.
Click **Memo**
Enter **Purchase Fax Machine**
Click **Save & Close** to record the check and exit the **Write Checks** window
QuickBooks Message dialog box appears on the screen indicating that another
    check already has number 1
- QuickBooks lets you know that you may reuse the check number and have
    more than one check with the same number.
Click **Cancel**

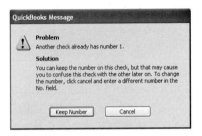

Click to the right of **1** in No.
Backspace to delete the 1
Because Check Nos. 1 through 7 have been printed, enter **8** for the check number

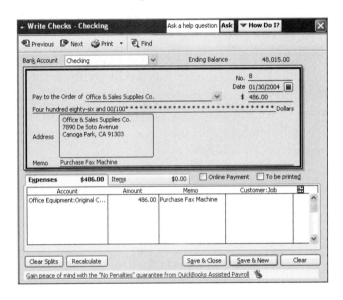

Click **Save & Close** to record the check and exit the **Write Checks - Checking** window

CUSTOMIZE REPORT FORMAT

The report format used in one company may not be appropriate for all companies that use QuickBooks Pro. In order to allow program users the maximum flexibility, QuickBooks Pro makes it very easy to customize many of the user preferences of the program. For example, you may customize menus, reminder screens, and reports and graphs.

DO: Customize the report preferences so the reports are automatically refreshed, and the date prepared, the time prepared, and the report basis do not print on reports: Click the **Edit** menu, click **Preferences**

Scroll through the items listed on the left side of the screen until you get to
   Reports and Graphs
Click **Reports and Graphs**
Click **Refresh Automatically** on the **My Preferences**
   tab

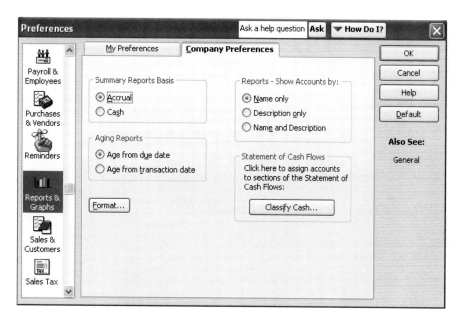

* Whenever data is changed and a report appears on
  the screen, QuickBooks will automatically update the report to reflect the
  changes.
Click the **Company Preferences** tab

Click the **Format** button
* If necessary, click the **Header/Footer** tab
Click **Date Prepared**, **Time Prepared**, and **Report Basis** to deselect

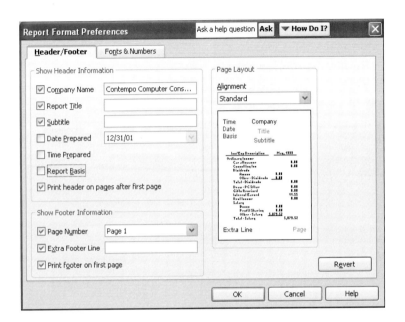

Click **OK** to save the change
Click **OK** to close **Preferences**

PRINT ACCOUNTS PAYABLE AGING SUMMARY

It is important in a business to maintain a good credit rating and to make sure that payments are made on time. In order to avoid overlooking a payment, the Accounts Payable Aging Summary lists the vendors to which the company owes money and shows how long the money has been owed.

MEMO

DATE: January 30, 2004

Prepare the Accounts Payable Aging Summary for Brian Colbert.

DO: Prepare an **Accounts Payable Aging Summary**
Click **Reports** on the menu bar, point to **Vendors & Payables**, click **A/P Aging Summary**
        OR
Click **Report Finder**
Click the drop-down list arrow for **Select a type of report**
Click **Vendors & Payables**, click **A/P Aging Summary**, click **Display**

- Notice that the date and time prepared do not appear as part of the heading information.

Tab to or click in the box for the **Date**

- If it is not highlighted, highlight the current date.

Enter **01/30/04**

- Tab through but leave Interval (days) as 30 and Through (days past due) as 90.
- The report will show the current bills as well as any past due bills.

Contempo Computer Consulting (CCC)--Student's Name						
A/P Aging Summary						
As of January 30, 2004						
	◇ Current ◇	1 - 30 ◇	31 - 60 ◇	61 - 90 ◇	> 90 ◇	TOTAL
Computer Technologies Magazine	▶ 79.00 ◀	0.00	0.00	0.00	0.00	79.00
Juan's Garage and Auto Services	575.00	0.00	0.00	0.00	0.00	575.00
Southern California Insurance Company	2,850.00	0.00	0.00	0.00	0.00	2,850.00
Universal Advertising	260.00	0.00	0.00	0.00	0.00	260.00
TOTAL	**3,764.00**	**0.00**	**0.00**	**0.00**	**0.00**	**3,764.00**

Follow instructions provided earlier to print the report in Portrait orientation

Close the **A/P Aging Summary** screen

PRINT UNPAID BILLS DETAIL REPORT

Another important report is the Unpaid Bills Detail Report. Even though it was already printed once during the month, it is always a good idea to print the report at the end of the month.

MEMO

DATE: January 30, 2004

At the end of every month, Maria Garcia prepares an Unpaid Bills Detail Report for Brian Colbert. Prepare the report.

DO: Follow instructions provided earlier in the chapter to prepare and print an **Unpaid Bills Detail Report** for **01/30/2004** in Portrait orientation

```
Contempo Computer Consulting (CCC)--Student's Name
                    Unpaid Bills Detail
                    As of January 30, 2004
     ◇    Type    ◇   Date   ◇  Num  ◇ Due Date  ◇ Aging  ◇  Open Balance
Computer Technologies Magazine
     Bill           01/26/2004  1579...  02/25/2004              79.00
Total Computer Technologies Magazine                             79.00

Juan's Garage and Auto Services
     Bill           01/19/2004  630     02/18/2004              575.00
Total Juan's Garage and Auto Services                          575.00

Southern California Insurance Company
     Bill           01/19/2004  3659    02/18/2004            2,850.00
Total Southern California Insurance Company                   2,850.00

Universal Advertising
     Bill           01/16/2004  9875    02/15/2004              260.00
Total Universal Advertising                                     260.00

TOTAL                                                         3,764.00
```

PRINT VENDOR BALANCE SUMMARY

There are two Vendor Balance Reports available in QuickBooks Pro. There is a Summary Report that shows unpaid balances for vendors and a Detail Report that lists each transaction for a vendor. In order to see how much is owed to each vendor, prepare a Vendor Balance Summary report.

MEMO
DATE: January 30, 2004

Prepare a Vendor Balance Summary Report to give to Brian Colbert.

   DO: Prepare and print a **Vendor Balance Summary Report**
            On the **Reports Finder**, click **Vendor Balance Summary**, click **Display**
            • The report should show only the totals owed to each vendor on January 30, 2004.
            • If it does not, tab to or click **From**, enter **01/30/04**. Then tab to or click **To**, enter **01/30/04**.
            Tab to generate the report

```
Contempo Computer Consulting (CCC)--Student's Name
                Vendor Balance Summary
                   All Transactions
                                          ◇ Jan 30, 04 ◇
        Computer Technologies Magazine    ▶    79.00 ◀
        Juan's Garage and Auto Services        575.00
        Southern California Insurance Company 2,850.00
        Universal Advertising                  260.00
              TOTAL                           3,764.00
```

Follow steps listed previously to print the report in Portrait orientation
Close the report; and, if necessary, close **Report Finder**

VIEW A QUICKREPORT FOR A VENDOR

A QuickReport for an individual vendor can be prepared by accessing the vendor's account via the Vendor List, clicking on the Vendor Name, and clicking the Report button. This QuickReport provides information regarding the type of transaction, the transaction date, vendor's invoice number, the account and the split account(s) used, and the amount owed.

DO: View a QuickReport for Juan's Garage and Auto Services
Click **Lists**, click **Vendor List** on the menu bar
Click **Juan's Garage and Auto Services**
Click the **Reports** button at the bottom of the Vendor List
Click **QuickReport: Juan's Garage and Auto Services**
   OR
Use the keyboard shortcut **Ctrl+Q**
Tab to or click **From**, enter **01/01/04**
Tab to or click **To**, enter **01/30/04**
Tab to generate the report
Analyze the report

```
            Contempo Computer Consulting (CCC)--Student's Name
                        Vendor QuickReport
                        January 1 - 30, 2004
 ◇   Type   ◇  Date  ◇ Num ◇ Memo ◇   Account   ◇ Clr ◇   Split    ◇  Amount
Juan's Garage and Auto Services
   Bill      01/19/2004  630          Accounts Payable  Automobile Expense  -575.00
```

Close the report without printing
Close the **Vendor List**

CREATE AN ACCOUNTS PAYABLE GRAPH BY AGING PERIOD

Graphs provide a visual representation of certain aspects of the business. It is sometimes easier to interpret data in a graphical format. For example, to determine if any payments are overdue for accounts payable accounts, use an Accounts Payable Graph to provide that information instantly on a bar chart. In addition, the Accounts Payable Graph feature of QuickBooks Pro also displays a pie chart showing what percentage of the total amount payable is owed to each vendor.

DO:　　Prepare an Accounts Payable Graph
　　　　　Click **Reports** on the menu bar
　　　　　Point to **Vendors & Payables**
　　　　　Click **Accounts Payable Graph**
　　　　　Click the **Dates** button at the top of the report
　　　　　Enter **01/30/04** for **Show Aging as of** in the **Change Graph Dates** text box

Click **OK**

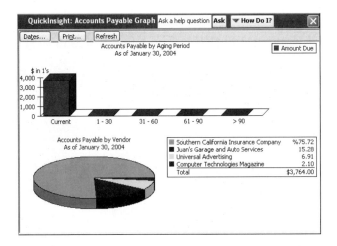

Click the **Dates** button again, enter **02/28/04** for the date
Click **OK**
- Notice that the bar moved from Current to 1-30. This means at the end of February the bills will be between 1 and 30 days overdue.

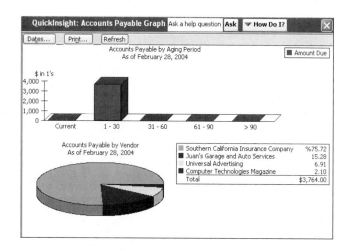

USE QUICKZOOM TO VIEW GRAPH DETAILS

To obtain detailed information from a graph, use the QuickZoom feature. For example, to see the overdue category of an individual account, double-click on a vendor in the pie chart, and this information will appear in a separate bar chart.

DO: Use QuickZoom to see how many days overdue the Southern California Insurance Company's bill will be at the end of February

Point to the section of the pie chart for **Southern California Insurance Company**

Double-click

- The bar chart shows the bill will be in the 1-30 day category at the end of February.

Close the QuickZoom Graph for Southern California Insurance Company

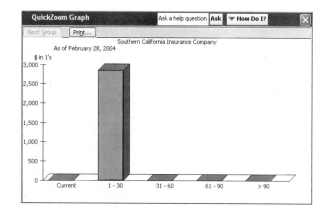

Click the **Dates** button on the **QuickInsight: Accounts Payable Graphs** screen

Change the date to **01/30/04**
In the legend of the pie chart, double-click on **Computer Technologies Magazine**
This payable is current as of January 30, 2004

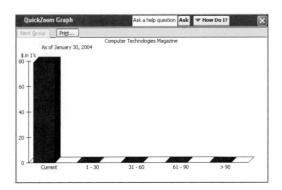

Close the **QuickZoom Graph**
Close the **QuickInsight: Accounts Payable Graph**

BACK UP CCC DATA AND CLOSE COMPANY

Whenever an important work session is complete, you should always back up your data. If your data disk is damaged or an error is discovered at a later time, the backup disk may be restored and the information used for recording transactions. As in previous chapters, you should close the company at the end of each work session.

 DO: Follow the instructions given in Chapters 1 and 2 to back up data for Contempo Computer Consultants and to close the company and refer to Appendix A for instructions on making a duplicate disk

SUMMARY

In this chapter, bills were recorded and paid, checks were written, and reports were prepared. The petty cash fund was established and used for payments of small expense items. Checks were voided, deleted, and corrected. Accounts were added and modified. QuickReports were accessed in various ways, and QuickZoom was used to obtain transaction detail while in various reports. Unpaid Vendor Reports provided information regarding bills that had not been paid. The graphing feature of QuickBooks Pro allowed you to determine Accounts Payable by aging period and to see the percentage of Accounts Payable for each vendor.

END-OF-CHAPTER QUESTIONS

TRUE/FALSE

ANSWER THE FOLLOWING QUESTIONS IN THE SPACE PROVIDED BEFORE THE QUESTION NUMBER.

_____ 1. Credit Memos are prepared to record a reduction to a transaction.

_____ 2. When you use QuickBooks Pro, checks may not be written in a checkbook.

_____ 3. QuickZoom is a QuickBooks Pro feature that allows detailed information to be displayed.

_____ 4. A cash purchase can be recorded by writing a check or by using petty cash.

_____ 5. Once a report format has been customized as a QuickBooks Pro preference for a company, QuickBooks Pro will automatically use the custom format for the company.

_____ 6. A graph is a visual representation of certain aspects of a business.

_____ 7. The accrual method of accounting matches the income of the period with the cash received for sales.

_____ 8. A Missing Check Report lists any duplicate check numbers or gaps between check numbers.

_____ 9. The Accounts Payable Register keeps track of all checks written in the business.

_____ 10. If a check has been edited, it cannot be printed.

MULTIPLE CHOICE

WRITE THE LETTER OF THE CORRECT ANSWER IN THE SPACE PROVIDED BEFORE THE QUESTION NUMBER.

_____ 1. When using QuickBooks Pro graphs, information regarding the percentage of accounts payable owed to each vendor is displayed as a ___.
   A. pie chart
   B. bar chart
   C. line chart
   D. both A and B

_____ 2. A check may be entered in ___.
   A. the Write Checks window
   B. the Check Register
   C. both A and B
   D. neither A nor B

_____ 3. When you enter a bill, typing the first letter(s) of a vendor's name on the Vendor line
   A. enters the vendor's name on the line if the name is in the Vendor List
   B. displays a list of vendor names
   C. displays the Address Info tab for the vendor
   D. indicates that you want to type the vendor name completely

_____ 4. To erase an incorrect amount in a bill, you may ___, then key the correction.
   A. drag through the amount to highlight
   B. position the cursor in front of the amount and press the delete key until the amount has been erased
   C. position the cursor after the amount and press the backspace key until the amount has been erased
   D. all of the above

_____ 5. When a document prints sideways, it is called ___ orientation.
   A. portrait
   B. landscape
   C. standard
   D. horizontal

_____ 6. A correction to a bill that has been recorded can be made on the bill or ___.
   A. not at all
   B. on the Accounts Payable Graph
   C. in the Accounts Payable Register
   D. none of the above

_____ 7. When a bill is deleted, ___.
    A. the amount is changed to 0.00
    B. the word *deleted* appears as the Memo
    C. it is removed without a trace
    D. a bill cannot be deleted

_____ 8. To increase the date on a bill by one day, ___.
    A. press the + key
    B. press the - key
    C. tab
    D. press the # key

_____ 9. If a bill is recorded in the Enter Bills window, it is important to pay the bill by ___.
    A. writing a check
    B. using the Pay Bills window
    C. using petty cash
    D. allowing QuickBooks Pro to generate the check automatically five days before the due date

_____ 10. When entering several bills at once on the Enter Bills screen, it is most efficient to ___ to go to the next blank screen.
    A. click Previous
    B. click Save & New
    C. click OK
    D. click Preview

FILL-IN

IN THE SPACE PROVIDED, WRITE THE ANSWER THAT MOST APPROPRIATELY COMPLETES THE SENTENCE.

1. The _____ section of a bill is used to record the information for the actual bill. The _____ section of a bill is used to record accounts used for the bill, amounts for each account, and transaction explanations.

2. An Accounts Payable Graph by Aging Period shows a _____ chart detailing the amounts due by aging period and a _____ chart showing the percentage of the total amount payable owed to each vendor.

3. Three different check styles may be used in QuickBooks Pro: _____, _____, or _____.

4. The keyboard shortcut to edit or modify a vendor's record is _____.

5. Petty Cash is identified as a _____ account type so it will be placed at the top of the Chart of Accounts along with checking and savings accounts.

SHORT ESSAY

When viewing a Transaction by Vendor Report that shows the entry of a bill for the purchase of office supplies and office equipment, you will see the term **-split-** displayed. Explain what the term **Split** means when used as a column heading and when used within the Split column for the bill indicated.

_____

_____

_____

_____

_____

_____

_____

NAME_____

TRANSMITTAL

CHAPTER 3: CONTEMPO COMPUTER CONSULTING

Attach the following documents and reports:

Transaction List by Vendor, January 1-18, 2004
Register QuickReport, Office & Sales Supplies Co.
Unpaid Bills by Vendor, January 25, 2004
Check No. 1: Office & Sales Supplies Co.
Check No. 2: Speedy Delivery Service
Check No. 3: Universal Advertising
Check No. 4: Lindsey Realtors
Check No. 5: California Electric
Check No. 6: California Water
Check No. 7: California Gas Co.
Check Detail Report
A/P Aging Summary, Current and Total
Unpaid Bills by Vendor
Vendor Balance Summary

END-OF-CHAPTER PROBLEM

SUPREME LAWN AND POOL MAINTENANCE

Chapter 3 continues with the transactions for bills, bill payments, and purchases for Supreme Lawn and Pool Maintenance. Even though it is a family-owned business, cash control measures have been implemented. Melissa prints the checks and any related reports; Zack initials his approval of the checks; and George, the owner, signs the checks.

INSTRUCTIONS

Continue to use the data disk for Supreme. Open the company—the file used is **Supreme.qbw**. Record the bills, bill payments, and purchases as instructed within the chapter. Always read the transactions carefully and review the Chart of Accounts when selecting transaction accounts. Print reports and graphs as indicated. If a bill is recorded on the Enter Bills screen, it should be paid on the Pay Bills screen—not by writing the check yourself.

RECORD TRANSACTIONS

May 1—Use Enter Bills to record the following bills:

Received a bill from Total Communications for cellular phone service, $485, Net 10, Invoice No. 1109, Memo: Cellular Telephone Services for May.

Received a bill from the Office 'N More for supplies purchased, $275, Net 30, Invoice No. 58-9826. (This is a prepaid expense so an asset account is used.) No memo is necessary.

Received a bill from Jerry's Motors for truck service and repairs, $519, Net 10, Invoice No. 1-62, Memo: Truck Service and Repairs. (Use Automobile Expense as the account for this transaction. We will change the name to something more appropriate in Chapter 4.)

Received a bill from State Street Gasoline for gasoline for the month, $375, Net 10, Invoice No. 853, Memo: Gasoline for Month.

Received a bill from Ryan's Cooler/Heating for a repair of the office air conditioner, $150, Net 30, Invoice No. 87626, Memo: Air Conditioner Repair. (The air conditioner is part of the building.)

May 15—Use Enter Bills to record the following bills:

Add a new expense account: Disposal Expense, Description: County Dump Charges, Tax Line is Schedule C: Other business expenses.

Received a bill from County Dump for disposing of lawn, tree, and shrub trimmings, $180, Net 30, Invoice No. 667, no memo necessary.

Received a bill from Continental Water Co., $25, Net 10, Invoice No. 098-1, no memo.

Change the QuickBooks Pro Company Preferences to customize the report format so that reports refresh automatically, and that the Date Prepared, the Time Prepared, and the Report Basis do not print as part of the header.

Print an Unpaid Bills Detail Report for May 1-15 in Portrait orientation.

Pay all bills *due on or before May 15*, print checks. (Use Pay Bills to pay bills that have been entered in the Enter Bills window.)

Record the receipt of a bill from Reliable Equipment Maintenance. Add this new vendor as you record the transaction. Additional information needed to do a complete Set Up is: 1234 State Street, Santa Barbara, CA 93110, 805-555-0770. The bill was for the repair of the lawn mower, $75, Invoice No. 5-1256, Net 10, no memo necessary.

Change the telephone number for County Dump. The new number is 805-555-3798.

Prepare and print the Vendor Balance Detail Report for all transactions.

May 30—Enter the transactions:

Received a $10 credit from Reliable Equipment Maintenance. The repair of the lawn mower wasn't as extensive as originally estimated.

Add Petty Cash to the Chart of Accounts.

Use the Register for Checking to transfer $50 from Checking to Petty Cash, Memo: Establish Petty Cash Fund.

Record the use of Petty Cash to pay for postage due 64 cents, and office supplies, $1.59 (this is a current expense). Memo notations are not necessary.

Write Check No. 5 to Reliable Equipment Maintenance to buy a lawn fertilizer spreader as a cash purchase of equipment, $349, Check Memo: Purchase of Lawn Fertilizer Spreader. Print the check. (If you get a dialog box indicating that you currently owe money to Reliable Equipment Maintenance, click **OK** and continue writing the check.)

Print an Unpaid Bills Detail Report for May 30.

Pay all bills *due on or before May 30*; print the checks. (Note: There may be some bills that were due after May 15 but before May 30. Be sure to pay these bills now. If any vendor shows a credit and has a bill that is due, apply it to the bill prior to payment. You may need to click on each bill individually in order to determine whether or not there is a credit to be applied.)

Prepare an Accounts Payable Graph as of 5/30/2004.

Prepare a QuickZoom Graph for County Dump as of 5/30/2004.

Back up your data and close the company.

NAME_____

TRANSMITTAL

CHAPTER 3: SUPREME LAWN AND POOL MAINTENANCE

Attach the following documents and reports:

Unpaid Bills Detail Report, May 15, 2004
Check No. 1: County Dump
Check No. 2: Jerry's Motors
Check No. 3: State Street Gasoline
Check No. 4: Total Communications
Vendor Balance Detail
Check No. 5: Reliable Equipment Maintenance
Unpaid Bills Report, May 30, 2004
Check No. 6: Continental Water Co.
Check No. 7: Reliable Equipment Maintenance

GENERAL ACCOUNTING AND END-OF-PERIOD PROCEDURES: SERVICE BUSINESS

LEARNING OBJECTIVES

At the completion of this chapter, you will be able to:

1. Complete the end-of-period procedures.
2. Change account names, delete accounts, and make accounts inactive.
3. View an account name change and its effect on subaccounts.
4. Record depreciation and enter the adjusting entries required for accrual-basis accounting.
5. Record owner's equity transactions for a sole proprietor including capital investment and owner withdrawals.
6. Reconcile the bank statement, record bank service charges, and mark cleared transactions.
7. Print Trial Balance, Profit and Loss Statement, and Balance Sheet.
8. Export a report to Microsoft® Excel
9. Perform end-of-period backup and close the end of a period.

GENERAL ACCOUNTING AND END-OF-PERIOD PROCEDURES

As previously stated, QuickBooks Pro operates from the standpoint of the business document rather than an accounting form, journal, or ledger. While QuickBooks Pro does incorporate all of these items into the program, in many instances they operate behind the scenes. QuickBooks Pro does not require special closing procedures at the end of a period. At the end of the fiscal year, QuickBooks Pro transfers the net income into the Retained Earnings account and allows you to protect the data for the year by assigning a closing date to the period. All of the transaction detail is maintained and viewable, but it will not be changed unless OK is clicked on a warning screen.

Even though a formal closing does not have to be performed within QuickBooks Pro, when you use accrual-basis accounting, several transactions must be recorded to reflect all expenses and income for the period. For example, bank statements must be reconciled and any charges or bank collections need to be recorded. During the business period, the CPA for the company will review things such as account names, adjusting entries, depreciation schedules, owner's equity adjustments, and so on. Sometimes the changes and adjustments will be made by the accountant on a separate disk called the Accountant's Copy of the business files. This disk is then merged with the company files that are used to record day-to-day business transactions, and all adjustments made by the CPA are added to the current company files. There are certain restrictions to the types of transactions that may be made on an Accountant's Copy of the business files.

Once necessary adjustments have been made, reports reflecting the end-of-period results of operations should be prepared. For archive purposes at the end of the fiscal year an additional backup disk is prepared and stored.

TRAINING TUTORIAL AND PROCEDURES

The following tutorial will once again work with Contempo Computer Consulting (CCC). As in Chapters 2 and 3, transactions will be recorded for this fictitious company. To maximize training benefits, you should:

1. Read the entire chapter *before* beginning the tutorial within the chapter.
2. Answer the end-of-chapter questions.
3. Be aware that transactions to be entered are given within a **MEMO**.
4. Complete all the steps listed for the Contempo Computer Consulting tutorial in the chapter. (Indicated by: **DO:**)
5. When you have completed a section, put an **X** on the button next to **DO:**.
6. If you do not complete a section, put the date in the margin next to the last step completed. This will make it easier to know where to begin when training is resumed.
7. As you complete your work, proofread carefully and check for accuracy. Double-check dates and amounts of money.
8. If you find an error while preparing a transaction, correct it. If you find the error after the transaction has been entered, follow the steps indicated in this chapter and/or the previous chapters to correct, void, or delete the transaction.
9. Print as directed within the chapter.
10. You may not finish the entire chapter in one computer session. Always use QuickBooks Pro to back up your work at the end of your work session as described in Chapter 1.
11. When you complete your computer session, always close your company. If you try to use a computer for CCC and a previous student did not close the company, QuickBooks Pro may freeze when you put in your disk. In addition, if you do not close the company as you leave, you may have problems with your company file, your disk may be damaged, and you may have unwanted .qbi (QuickBooks In Use) files that cause your data disk to become full.

OPEN QUICKBOOKS® PRO AND CONTEMPO COMPUTER CONSULTING

  DO: Open QuickBooks Pro as instructed in Chapters 1 and 2

Open Contempo Computer Consulting (CCC)
- To close an open company and open your copy of CCC, click **File**, click **Open Company**, click **Contempo.qbw**, check to make sure you are using the disk in **A:** (or the location you have been instructed to use), click **Open**.

Check the title bar to verify that CCC is the open company

BEGINNING THE TUTORIAL

In this chapter, you will be recording end-of-period adjustments, reconciling bank statements, changing account names, and preparing traditional end-of-period reports. Because QuickBooks Pro does not perform a traditional "closing" of the books, you will learn how to assign a closing date and to protect transactions and data recorded during previous accounting periods.

All transactions are listed on memos. The transaction date will be the same as the memo date unless otherwise specified within the transaction. Once a specific type of transaction has been entered in a step-by-step manner, additional transactions of the same or a similar type will be made without instructions being provided. Of course, you may always refer to instructions given for previous transactions for ideas or for steps used to enter those transactions. To determine the account used in the transaction, refer to the Chart of Accounts, which is also the General Ledger.

CHANGE THE NAME OF EXISTING ACCOUNTS IN THE CHART OF ACCOUNTS

Even though transactions have been recorded during the month of January, QuickBooks Pro makes it a simple matter to change the name of an existing account. Once the name of an account has been changed, all transactions using the "old" name are updated and show the "new" account name.

MEMO

DATE: January 31, 2004

Upon the recommendation from the company's CPA, Brian Colbert decided to change the account named Company Cars to Business Vehicles.

DO: Change the account name of Company Cars

Access the **Chart of Accounts**:

Click **Lists**, click **Chart of Accounts** on the menu bar

OR

Click **Chart of Accounts** on the Company Navigator

        OR

Use the keyboard shortcut **Ctrl+A**

        OR

Click the **Acct** icon on the icon bar

Scroll through accounts until you see Company Cars, click **Company Cars**

Click the **Account** button at the bottom of the Chart of Accounts, click **Edit**

        OR

Use the keyboard shortcut **Ctrl+E**

On the **Edit Account** screen, highlight **Company Cars**

Enter the new name **Business Vehicles**

- The balances of any subaccounts of Business Vehicles will be reflected in the account total on the Chart of Accounts and in reports.

Click **OK** to record the name change and to close the **Edit Account** screen

- Notice that the name of the account appears as Business Vehicles in the Chart of Accounts and that the balance of $49,000 shows.

Follow the steps above to change the names of:

    Company Cars Loan to **Business Vehicles Loan**

    Automobile Expense to **Business Vehicles Expense**

- Delete the Description Automobile Expense.

    Auto Insurance Expense to **Business Vehicles Insurance**

    Office Equipment to **Office Furniture and Equipment**

    Office Equipment Loan to **Office Furniture/Equipment Loan**

- Due to exceeding the allotted number of characters in an account name, the word "and" was omitted and the "/" was used.

    Loan Interest to **Interest on Loans**

- Leave the description as Loan Interest Expense

Do not close the **Chart of Accounts**

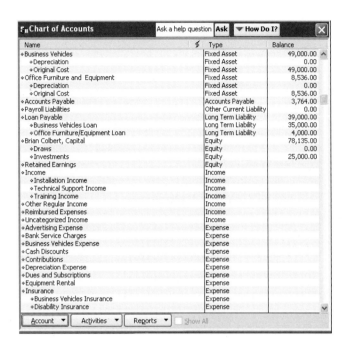

EFFECT OF AN ACCOUNT NAME CHANGE ON SUBACCOUNTS

Any account that uses Company Car as part of the account name needs to be changed. However, when the account name of Company Car was changed to Business Vehicles, the subaccounts of Company Car automatically became subaccounts of Business Vehicles.

DO: Examine the Depreciation and Original Cost accounts for Business Vehicles
Click **Depreciation** under Business Vehicles
Click the **Account** button at the bottom of the chart, click **Edit**
   OR
Use the keyboard shortcut **Ctrl+E**
Notice that the text box for **Subaccount of** shows as **Business Vehicles**

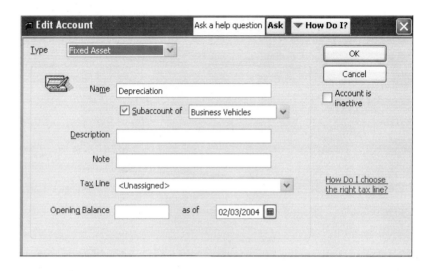

Click **Cancel**
- Repeat the above steps to examine the **Original Cost** account.
- Examine **Office Furniture and Equipment** and its subaccounts of **Depreciation** and **Original Cost**.

Do not close the **Chart of Accounts**

MAKE AN ACCOUNT INACTIVE

If you are not using an account and do not have plans to use it in the near future, the account may be made inactive. The account remains available for use, yet it does not appear on your chart of accounts unless you check the Show All check box.

MEMO

DATE: January 31, 2004

At present, CCC does not plan to purchase its own building. The accounts Interest Expense: Mortgage and Taxes: Property should be made inactive.

DO: Make the accounts listed above inactive
Click **Mortgage** under Interest Expense
Click the **Account** button at the bottom of the **Chart of Accounts**
Click **Make Inactive**
- The account no longer appears in the Chart of Accounts.

- If you wish to view all accounts including the inactive ones, click the **Show All** check box at the bottom of the **Chart of Accounts** and all accounts will be displayed.
- Notice the icon next to Mortgage. It marks the account as inactive.

◆Interest Expense	Expense
◆Finance Charge	Expense
◆Interest on Loans	Expense
✖ ◆Mortgage	Expense

Repeat the above to make **Taxes: Property** inactive

◆Taxes	Expense
◆Federal	Expense
◆Local	Expense
✖ ◆Property	Expense
◆State	Expense

DELETE AN EXISTING ACCOUNT FROM THE CHART OF ACCOUNTS

If you do not want to make an account inactive because you have not used it and do not plan to use it at all, QuickBooks Pro allows the account to be deleted at anytime. However, as a safeguard, QuickBooks Pro prevents the deletion of an account once it has been used even if it simply contains an opening or an existing balance.

MEMO

DATE: January 31, 2004

In addition to previous changes to account names, Brian Colbert finds that he does not use nor will he use the expense account: Contributions. Delete this account from the Chart of Accounts. In addition, Brian wants you to delete the Dues and Subscriptions account.

 DO: Delete the **Contributions** expense account
Scroll through accounts until you see Contributions, click **Contributions**
Click the **Account** button at the bottom of the Chart of Accounts, click **Delete**
    OR
Use the keyboard shortcut **Ctrl+D**

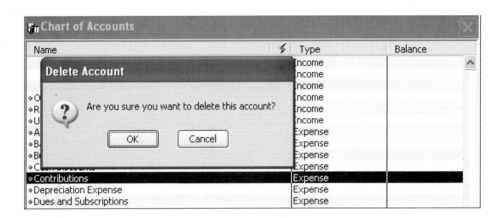

Click **OK** on the **Delete Account** dialog box
- The account has now been deleted.

Repeat the above steps for the deletion of **Dues and Subscriptions**
- As soon as you try to delete Dues and Subscriptions, a **QuickBooks Message** appears indicating that the account has a balance or is used in a transaction, an invoice item, or your payroll setup. QuickBooks offers a solution of making the account inactive.

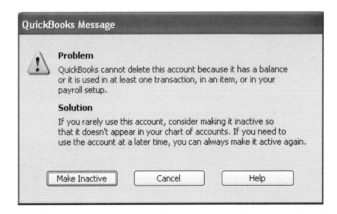

Click **Cancel**
- The account remains in the Chart of Accounts.

Close the **Chart of Accounts**

ADJUSTMENTS FOR ACCRUAL-BASIS ACCOUNTING

As previously stated, the accrual basis of accounting matches the income and the expenses of a period in order to arrive at an accurate figure for net income. Thus, the revenue is earned at the time the service is performed or the sale is made no matter when the actual cash is received. The cash basis of accounting records income or revenue at the time cash is received no matter when the sale was made or the service performed. The same holds true when a business buys things or pays bills. In accrual-basis accounting, the expense is recorded at the time the bill is received or the purchase is made regardless of the actual payment date. In cash-basis accounting, the expense is not recorded until it is paid.

There are several internal transactions that must be recorded when you are using the accrual basis of accounting. These entries arc called adjusting entries. For example, equipment does wear out and will eventually need to be replaced. Rather than wait until replacement to record the use of the equipment, one makes an adjusting entry to allocate the use of equipment as an expense for a period. This is called depreciation. Certain items used in a business are paid for in advance. As these are used, they become expenses of the business. For example, insurance for the entire year would be used up month by month and should, therefore, be a monthly expense. Commonly, the insurance is billed and paid for the entire year. Until the insurance is used, it is an asset. Each month, the portion of the insurance used becomes an expense for the month.

ADJUSTING ENTRIES—PREPAID EXPENSES

During the operation of a business, companies purchase supplies to have on hand for use in the operation of the business. In accrual-basis accounting, unless the supplies are purchased for immediate use and will be used up within the month, the supplies are considered to be prepaid expenses (an asset because it is something the business owns) until they are used in the operation of the business. As the supplies are used, the amount used becomes an expense for the period. The same system applies to other things paid for in advance, such as insurance. At the end of the period, an adjusting entry must be made to allocate the amount of prepaid expenses (assets) used to expenses.

The transactions for these adjustments may be recorded in the register for the account by clicking on the prepaid expense (asset) in the Chart of Accounts, or they may be made in the General Journal.

MEMO
DATE: January 31, 2004

NOTE from Brian—
Maria, remember to record the monthly adjustment for Prepaid Insurance. The $2,850 is the amount we paid for the year. Also, we used $350 worth of supplies this month. Please adjust accordingly.

DO: Record the adjusting entries for office supplies expense and business vehicle insurance expense in the General Journal.

Access the General Journal:

    Click **Company** or **Banking** on the menu bar, click **Make General Journal Entries**

        OR

    Open **Chart of Accounts** as previously instructed, click the **Activities** button, click **Make General Journal Entries**

        OR

    Access the **Banking** Navigator, click **Make General Journal Entries**

- If you get a screen regarding Assigning Numbers to Journal Entries, click **OK**

Record the adjusting entry for Prepaid Insurance

Enter **01/31/04** as the **Date**

- **Entry No.** is left blank unless you wish to record a specific number.

- Because all transactions entered for the month have been entered in the Journal as well as on an invoice or a bill, all transactions automatically have a Journal entry number.

Tab to or click the **Account** column

Click the drop-down list arrow for **Account**, click **Business Vehicles Insurance**

Tab to or click **Debit**

- The $2,850 given in the memo is the amount for the year; calculate the amount of the adjustment for the month by using QuickBooks QuickMath or the Calculator.

    Use QuickBooks QuickMath

        Press the + key on the 10-key numerical keypad or at the top of the keyboard

        Enter **2850** by:

            Using the mouse to click the numbers

                OR

            Typing the numbers at the top of the keyboard

                OR

            Keying the numbers on the **10-key pad** (preferred)

            - Be sure Num Lock is on. There should be a light by Num Lock on/or above the 10-key pad. If not, press Num Lock to activate.

        Press / for division

        Key **12**

        Press **Enter** to close QuickMath and enter the amount in the Debit column

    Use the Calculator

        Click **Edit** on the menu bar, click **Use Calculator**

        Enter **2850**

    Press / for division

    Key **12**

    Press = or **Enter**

    Click the **Close** button to close the **Calculator**

- For additional calculator instructions refer to Chapter 1.

Enter the amount of the adjustment **237.5** in the **Debit** column

- Notice that the amount must be entered by you when using Calculator; QuickBooks Math automatically enters the amount.

Tab to or click the **Memo** column

Type **Adjusting Entry, Insurance**

Tab to or click **Account**

Click the drop-down list arrow for **Account**

Click **Prepaid Insurance**

- The amount for the Credit column should be entered automatically. However, there are several reasons why an amount may not appear in the Credit column; if 237.50 does not appear, type it in the Credit column.

Tab to or click the **Memo** column

Type **Adjusting Entry, Insurance**

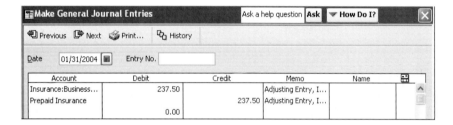

Click **Save & New** to record the adjustment and advance to the next **Make General Journal Entries** screen

Repeat the above procedures to record the adjustment for the office supplies used

- The amount given in the memo is the actual amount of the supplies used in January.
- Remember, when supplies are purchased to have on hand, the original entry recorded an increase to the asset Office Supplies. Once the supplies are used, the adjustment correctly records the amount of supplies used as an expense.

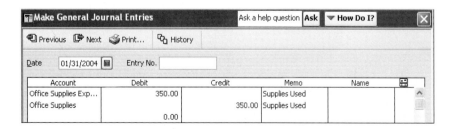

Click **Save & New**

ADJUSTING ENTRIES—DEPRECIATION

Using the accrual basis of accounting requires companies to record an expense for the amount of equipment used in the operation of the business. Unlike supplies—where you can actually see, for example, the paper supply diminishing—it is very difficult to see how much of a computer has been "used up" during the month. To account for the fact that machines do wear out and need to be replaced, an adjustment is made for depreciation. This adjustment correctly matches the expenses of the period against the revenue of the period.

The adjusting entry for depreciation can be made in the account register for Depreciation, or it can be made in the General Journal.

MEMO
DATE: January 31, 2004

Having received the necessary depreciation schedules, Maria records the adjusting entry for depreciation: Business Vehicles, $583 per month; Equipment, $142 per month.

   DO: Record a compound adjusting entry for depreciation of the equipment and the business vehicles in the **General Journal**:
If it is not automatically displayed, enter **01/31/04** as the **Date**
Entry No. is left blank
- Normally, the Debit portion of a Journal entry is entered first. However, in order to use the automatic calculation feature of QuickBooks Pro, you will enter the Credit entries first.
Tab to or click the **Account** column
Click the drop-down list arrow for **Account**, click **Depreciation** under **Business Vehicles**
- Make sure that you do not click the controlling account, Business Vehicles
Tab to or click **Credit**, enter **583**
Tab to or click **Memo**
Enter **Adjusting Entry January**
Tab to or click the **Account** column
- The amount of the 583 credit shows in the debit column temporarily.
Click the drop-down list arrow for **Account**, click **Depreciation** under **Office Furniture and Equipment**
- Again, make sure that you do not use the controlling account, Office Furniture and Equipment.
Tab to or click **Credit**
Enter **142**

- The 583 in the debit column is removed when you tab to or click **Memo**.

Tab to or click **Memo**

Enter **Adjusting Entry January**

Tab to or click the **Account** column

Click the drop-down list arrow for **Account**

Click **Depreciation Expense**

Debit column should automatically show **725**

- If 725 does not appear, enter it in the debit column.

Tab to or click **Memo**, enter **Adjusting Entry January**

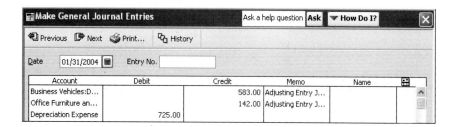

Click **Save & Close** to record the adjustment and close the **General Journal**

- If you get a message regarding Tracking Fixed Assets, click **OK.**

Close the **Chart of Accounts**, if necessary

VIEW GENERAL JOURNAL

Once transactions have been entered in the General Journal, it is important to view them. QuickBooks Pro also refers to the General Journal as the Journal and allows it to be viewed or printed at any time. Even with the special ways in which transactions are entered in QuickBooks Pro through invoices, bills, checks, and account registers, the Journal is still the book of original entry. All transactions recorded for the company may be viewed in the Journal even if they were entered elsewhere.

 DO: View the Journal for January

Click **Reports** on the menu bar, point to **Accountant & Taxes,** click **Journal**
   OR

Click **Report Finder** on a QuickBooks Navigator, click **Accountant & Taxes** as
   the type of report, click **Journal**, click **Display**

Tab to or click **From**

- If necessary, delete existing date.

Enter **01/01/04**

Tab to or click **To**

Enter **01/31/04**

Tab to generate the report

- Notice that the transactions do not begin with the adjustments entered directly into the Journal.
- The first transaction displayed is the entry for Invoice No. 1 to Juan Morales.
- If corrections or changes are made to entries, the transaction numbers may differ from the key. Since QuickBooks assigns transaction numbers automatically, disregard any discrepancies in transaction numbers.

Contempo Computer Consulting (CCC)--Student's Name
Journal
January 2004

Trans #	Type	Date	Num	Name	Memo	Account	Debit	Credit
27	Invoice	01/02/2004	1	Morales, Juan		Accounts Receiva...	300.00	
				Morales, Juan	10 Hours--M...	Technical Support...		300.00
							300.00	300.00
29	Invoice	01/05/2004	3	Jimenez, Claire	VOID:	Accounts Receiva...	0.00	
				Jimenez, Claire	10 Hours--M...	Technical Support...	0.00	
							0.00	0.00
30	Invoice	01/05/2004	4	Sanders, Omar...		Accounts Receiva...	3,215.00	
				Sanders, Omar...	Initial Hour o...	Training Income		95.00
				Sanders, Omar...	Additional H...	Training Income		3,120.00
							3,215.00	3,215.00
31	Invoice	01/05/2004	5	Green, Bernste...		Accounts Receiva...	1,425.00	
				Green, Bernste...	Initial Hour o...	Training Income		95.00
				Green, Bernste...	Additional H...	Training Income		880.00
				Green, Bernste...	15 Hours--M...	Technical Support...		450.00
							1,425.00	1,425.00

Partial Report

Scroll through the report to view all transactions recorded in the Journal
Verify the total Debit and Credit Columns of $46,530.29
- If your totals do not match, check for errors and make appropriate corrections.
Close the report without printing

OWNER WITHDRAWALS

In a sole proprietorship an owner cannot receive a paycheck because he or she owns the business. An owner withdrawing money from a business—even to pay personal expenses—is similar to withdrawing money from a savings account. A withdrawal simply decreases the owner's capital. QuickBooks Pro allows you to establish a separate account for owner withdrawals. If a separate account is not established, owner withdrawals may be subtracted directly from the owner's capital or investment account.

MEMO
DATE: January 31, 2004

Because Brian Colbert works in his business full time, he does not earn a paycheck. Prepare his check for his monthly withdrawal, $2,500.

DO: Write Check No. 9 to Brian Colbert for $2,500 withdrawal

Open the **Write Checks - Checking** window:

Click **Banking** on the menu bar, click **Write Checks**

OR

Access the **Banking** Navigator, click **Checks** on the Banking Navigator

OR

Use the keyboard shortcut **Ctrl+W**

OR

Click **Check** on the icon bar

The Check No. should be **To Print**

- If not, click the check box **To be printed**

Date should be **01/31/04**

Enter **Brian Colbert** on the **Pay to the Order of** line

Press the **Tab** key

- Because Brian's name was not added to any list when the company was created, the **Name Not Found** dialog box appears on the screen.

Click **Quick Add** to add Brian's name to a list

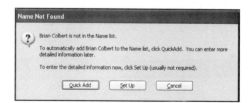

The **Select Name Type** dialog box appears
Click **Other**
Click **OK**

- Brian's name is added to a list of "Other" names, which are used for owners, partners, and other miscellaneous names.

Tab to or click in the area for the amount of the check

- If necessary, delete any numbers showing for the amount (0.00).

Enter **2500**

Tab to or click **Memo** on the check

Enter **Owner Withdrawal for January**

Tab to or click in the **Account** column at the bottom of the check

Click the drop-down list arrow, click the Equity account **Draws**

- The amount 2,500.00 should appear in the **Amount** column.
- If it does not, tab to or click in the **Amount** column and enter 2500.

Click **Print** to print the check

The **Print Check** dialog box appears

Printed Check Number should be **9**

- If necessary, change the number to 9.

Click **OK**

Print the check as previously instructed

Once the check has printed successfully, click **OK** to close the **Did check(s) print OK?** dialog box

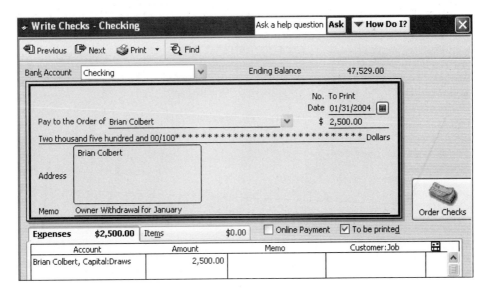

Click **Save & Close** to record the check

ADDITIONAL CASH INVESTMENT BY OWNER

An owner may decide to invest more of his or her personal cash in the business at any time. The new investment is entered into the owner's investment account and into cash. The investment may be recorded in the account register for checking or in the register for the owner's investment account. It may also be recorded in the Journal.

MEMO
DATE: January 31, 2004

Brian Colbert received money from a certificate of deposit. Rather than reinvest in another certificate of deposit, he decided to invest an additional $5,000 in CCC.

DO: Record the additional cash investment by Brian Colbert in the Journal
Access the General Journal as previously instructed
The **Date** should be **01/31/04**
- Nothing is needed for Entry No.
Debit **Checking, $5,000**
Credit **Investments, $5,000**
- This account is listed as a subaccount of Brian Colbert, Capital
The memo for both entries should be **Cash Investment**

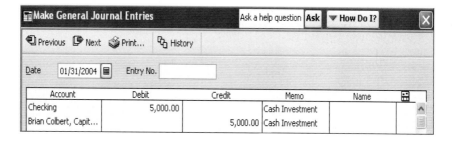

Click **Save & New** to record and go to the next blank **Make General Journal Entries** screen

NONCASH INVESTMENT BY OWNER

An owner may make investments in a business at any time. The investment may be cash; but it may also be something such as reference books, equipment, tools, buildings, and so on. Additional investments by an owner(s) are added to owner's equity. In the case of a sole proprietor, the investment is added to the Capital account for Investments.

MEMO

DATE: January 31, 2004

Originally, Brian Colbert planned to have an office in his home as well as in the company and purchased new office furniture for his home. He decided the business environment would appear more professional if the new furniture were in the office rather than his home. Brian gave the new office furniture to CCC as an additional owner investment. The value of the investment is $3,000.

DO: Record the additional investment by Brian Colbert in the Journal
The **Date** should be **01/31/04**
Nothing is needed for Entry No.
Debit **Office Furniture and Equipment: Original Cost, $3,000**
- Make sure you Debit the subaccount Original Cost not the controlling account Office Furniture and Equipment.

Credit **Investments, $3,000**
- This account is listed as a subaccount of Brian Colbert, Capital

The memo for both entries should be **Investment of Furniture**
- If you wish to copy the memo for the second entry rather than retype it, drag through the memo text to highlight; press Ctrl+C; position the cursor in the memo area for the second entry; press Ctrl+V.

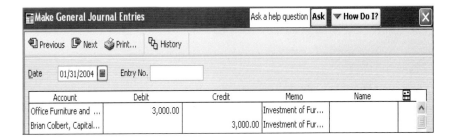

Click **Save & Close** to record and exit
- If you get a message regarding Tracking Fixed Assets, click **OK.**

VIEW BALANCE SHEET

Prior to the owner's making an additional investment in the business, there had been no withdrawals, and the drawing account balance was zero. Once the owner makes a withdrawal, that amount is carried forward in the owner's drawing account. Subsequent withdrawals are added to this account. When you view the Balance Sheet, notice the balance of the Drawing account after the check for the withdrawal was written. Also notice the Net Income account that appears in the equity section of the Balance Sheet. This account is automatically added by QuickBooks Pro to track the net income for the year.

   DO: View a Standard Balance Sheet:
Click **Reports** on the menu bar, point to **Company & Financial**, click **Balance Sheet Standard**
    OR
Click **Report Finder** on a QuickBooks Navigator, click **Company & Financial**, click **Balance Sheet Standard**, click **Display**
Tab to or click **As of**
- If necessary, delete existing date.
Enter **01/31/04**
Tab to generate the report
Scroll through the report
- Notice the Equity section, especially Net Income.

```
Contempo Computer Consulting (CCC)--Student's Name
                    Balance Sheet
                 As of January 31, 2004
                                            Jan 31, 04
        Business Vehicles Loan              35,000.00
        Office Furniture/Equipment Loan      4,000.00
        Total Loan Payable                             39,000.00

        Total Long Term Liabilities                    39,000.00

    Total Liabilities                                  42,764.00

    Equity
        Brian Colbert, Capital
            Draws                           -2,500.00
            Investments                     33,000.00
            Brian Colbert, Capital - Other  53,135.00
        Total Brian Colbert, Capital                   83,635.00

        Net Income                                      4,385.71
    Total Equity                                       88,020.71

    TOTAL LIABILITIES & EQUITY                        130,784.71
```

Partial Report

Close the report and, if necessary, Report Finder

BANK RECONCILIATION

Each month, the checking account should be reconciled with the bank statement to make sure that the balances agree. The bank statement will rarely have an ending balance that matches the balance of the checking account. This is due to several factors: outstanding checks (written by the business but not paid by the bank), deposits in transit (deposits that were made too late to be included on the bank statement), bank service charges, interest earned on checking accounts, collections made by the bank, and errors made in recording checks and/or deposits by the company or by the bank.

In order to have an accurate amount listed as the balance in the checking account, it is important that the differences between the bank statement and the checking account be reconciled. If something such as a service charge or a collection made by the bank appears on the bank statement, it needs to be recorded in the checking account.

Reconciling a bank statement is an appropriate time to find any errors that may have been recorded in the checking account. The reconciliation may be out of balance because a transposition was made (recording $94 rather than $49), a transaction was recorded backwards, a transaction was recorded twice, or a transaction was not recorded at all. If a transposition was made, the error may be found by dividing the difference by 9. For example, if $94 was recorded and the actual transaction amount was $49, you would subtract 49 from 94 to get 45. The number 45 can be divided by 9, so your error was a transposition. If the error can be evenly divided by 2, the transaction may have been entered backwards. For example, if you were out of balance $200, look to see if you had any $100 transactions. Perhaps you recorded a $100 debit, and it should have been a credit (or vice versa).

BEGIN RECONCILIATION

To begin the reconciliation, you need to open the Reconcile - Checking window. Verify the information shown for the checking account. The Opening Balance should match the amount of the final balance on the last reconciliation, or it should match the starting account balance.

MEMO

DATE: January 31, 2004

Received the bank statement from Southern California Bank. The bank statement is dated January 30, 2004. Maria Garcia needs to reconcile the bank statement and print a Detail Reconciliation Report for Brian Colbert.

DO: Reconcile the bank statement for January
Open the **Begin Reconciliation** window and enter preliminary information
Open **Chart of Accounts** as previously instructed, click **Checking**, click
    Activities, click **Reconcile**
    OR
Access the **Banking** Navigator, click **Reconcile** on the Banking Navigator
The **Account To Reconcile** should be **Checking**
    If not, click the drop-down list arrow, click **Checking**
Opening Balance should be **12,870**
- This is the same amount as the checking account starting balance.
The Account should be **Checking**
- You may see several previous dates listed. Disregard them at this time.

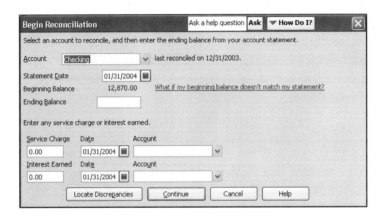

ENTER BANK STATEMENT INFORMATION FOR BEGIN RECONCILIATION

Some information appearing on the bank statement is entered into the Begin Reconciliation window as the next step. This information includes bank service charges and interest earned.

 DO: Continue to reconcile the following bank statement with the checking account

SOUTHERN CALIFORNIA BANK
12345 West Colorado Avenue
Woodland Hills, CA 91377
(818) 555-3880

BANK STATEMENT FOR:

Contempo Computer Consulting
2895 West Avenue
Woodland Hills, CA 91367

Acct. # 123-456-7890   **January 2004**

Beginning Balance 1/1/04			$12,870.00
01/02/04 Deposit	25,000.00		37,870.00
1/15/04 Deposit	13,840.00		51,710.00
1/26/04 Cash Transfer		110.00	51,600.00
1/26/04 Check 1		840.00	50,760.00
1/26/04 Check 2		195.00	50,565.00
1/26/04 Check 3		500.00	50,065.00
1/30/04 Vehicle Loan Pmt.: $467.19 Principal, $255.22 Interest		722.41	49,342.59
1/30/04 Office Equip. Loan Pmt.: $29.17 Principal, $53.39 Interest		82.56	49,260.03
1/30/04 Service Chg.		8.00	49,252.03
1/30/04 Interest	66.43		49,318.46
Ending Balance 1/30/04			49,318.46

Enter the **Statement Date** of **01/30/04**

Enter the **Ending Balance** from the Bank Statement, **49,318.46**

Tab to or click **Service Charge**

Enter **8.00**

Tab to or click Service Charge **Date**; if necessary, change to **01/30/2004**

- Don't forget to check the date. If you leave an incorrect date, you will have errors in your accounts and in your reports.

Tab to or click **Account**

Click the drop-down list arrow for **Account**

Click **Bank Service Charges**

Tab to or click **Interest Earned**, enter **66.43**

Tab to or click Interest Earned **Date**; if necessary, change to **01/30/2004**

Tab to or click **Account**

Click the drop-down list arrow for **Account**
Click **Interest Income**

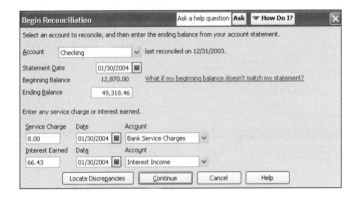

Click **Continue**

MARK CLEARED TRANSACTIONS FOR BANK RECONCILIATION

Once bank statement information for service charges and interest has been entered, compare the checks and deposits listed on the statement with the transactions for the checking account. Remember, the dates shown for the checks on the bank statement are the dates the checks were processed by the bank, not the dates the checks were written. If a deposit or a check is listed correctly on the bank statement and in the Reconcile - Checking window, it has cleared and should be marked. An item may be marked individually by positioning the cursor on the deposit or the check and clicking the primary mouse button. If all deposits and checks match, click the Mark All button. To remove all the checks, click the Unmark All button. To unmark an individual item, click the item to remove the check mark.

DO: Mark cleared checks and deposits
Compare the bank statement with the **Reconcile - Checking** window
Click the items that appear on both statements
- *Note*: The date next to the check or the deposit on the bank statement is the date the check or deposit cleared the bank, not the date the check was written or the deposit was made.
- If you are unable to complete the reconciliation in one session, click the **Leave** button to leave the reconciliation and return to it later. Under no circumstances should you click **Reconcile Now** until the reconciliation is complete.
- Include Petty Cash transaction on 1/26/04 even though the bank statement shows 110 and the check register shows 100.

Look at the bottom of the **Reconcile - Checking** window

You have marked cleared:

    4 Deposits, Interest and Other Credits for 38,906.43

- This includes interest earned and the voided check to Communication Telephone Co.

    5 Checks, Payments, and Service Charges for 1,643.00

- This includes the $100 for petty cash and the $8 service charge.

    The Ending Balance is 49,318.46

    The Cleared Balance is 50,133.43

    There is a Difference of -814.97

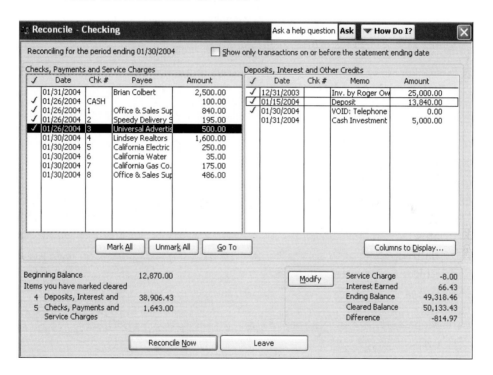

ADJUSTING AND CORRECTING ENTRIES—BANK RECONCILIATION

As you complete the reconciliation, you may find errors that need to be corrected or transactions that need to be recorded. Anything entered as a service charge or interest earned will be entered automatically when the reconciliation is complete and the Reconcile Now button is clicked. To correct an error such as a transposition, click on the entry, then click the Go To button. The original entry will appear on the screen. The correction can be made and will show in the Reconcile - Checking window. If there is a transaction, such as an automatic loan payment to the bank, you need to access the register for the account used in the transaction and enter the payment.

DO: Correct the error on the transfer into Petty Cash and enter the automatic loan
          payments shown on the bank statement.
          Correct the entry for the transfer of cash into Petty Cash:
               In the section of the reconciliation for **Checks and Payments**, click the entry
                    for **Cash** made on **01/26/04**

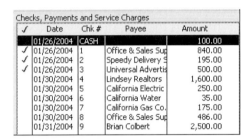

               Click **Go To**
               Change the amount on **Transfer Funds Between Accounts** from 100 to **110**

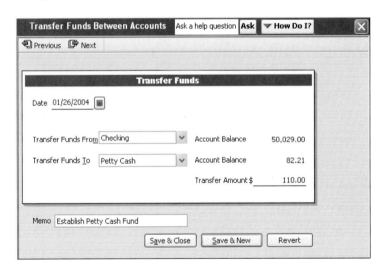

               Click **Save & Close**
               Click **Yes** on the **Change Transaction** dialog box
               • Notice that the amount for the Petty Cash transaction now shows 110.
               If necessary, click the Petty Cash transaction to mark it.
          With the **Reconcile - Checking** window still showing, enter the automatic loan
               payments:
               Click **Edit** on the menu bar, click **Use Register**
                    OR
               Use the keyboard shortcut **Ctrl+R**
               In the blank transaction at the bottom of the Checking register enter the **Date**,
                    01/30/04

Tab to or click **Number**
Enter **Transfer**
Tab to or click **Payee**
Enter **Southern California Bank**
Tab to or click the **Payment** column
- Because Southern California Bank does not appear on any list, you will get a **Name Not Found** dialog box when you move to another field.

Click the **Quick Add** button to add the name of the bank to the Name list
Click **Other**

Click **OK**
- Once the name of the bank has been added to the Other list, the cursor will be positioned in the **Payment** column.
Enter **722.41** in the **Payment** column
Click the **Account** column
Click the **Splits** button at the bottom of the register
Click the drop-down list arrow for **Account**
Click **Interest on Loans** under Interest Expense
Tab to or click **Amount**, delete the amount 722.41 shown
Enter **255.22** as the amount of interest
Tab to or click **Memo**
Enter **Interest Business Vehicles Loan**
Tab to or click **Account**
Click the drop-down list arrow for **Account**
Click **Business Vehicles Loan** under Loan Payable
- The correct amount of principal, 467.19, should be showing for the amount.

Tab to or click **Memo**

Enter **Payment Business Vehicles Loan**

Account	Amount	Memo	Customer:Job		
Interest Expense:Interest on...	255.22	Interest Business Vehic...			Close
Loan Payable:Business Ve...	467.19	Payment Business Vehi...			Clear
					Recalc

Click **Close**

- This closes the window for the information regarding the way the transaction is to be "split" between accounts.

For the **Memo** in the Checking Register, record **Loan Pmt., Business Vehicles**

Click the **Record** button to record the transaction

- Because the Register organizes transactions according to date, you will notice that the loan payment will not appear as the last transaction in the Register. You may need to scroll through the Register to see the transaction.

01/30/2004	Transfer	Southern California Bank		722.41			49,342.59
	CHK	-split- Loan Pmt., Business Vehi					

Repeat the procedures to record the loan payment for office equipment

- When you enter the Payee as Southern California Bank, the amount for the previous transaction (722.41) appears in Amount.

Enter the new amount, **82.56**

Click **Splits** button

Click the appropriate accounts and enter the correct amount for each item

- Refer to the bank statement for details regarding the amount of the payment for interest and the amount of the payment applied to principal.
- *Note*: The amounts for the previous loan payment automatically appear. You will need to enter the amounts for both accounts in this transaction.

Account	Amount	Memo	Customer:Job		
Interest Expense:Interest on...	53.39	Interest Office Equipm...			Close
Loan Payable:Office Furni...	29.17	Loan Pmt., Office Equi...			Clear
					Recalc

Click **Close** to close the window for the information regarding the "split" between accounts

Enter the transaction Memo **Loan Pmt., Office Equipment**

Click **Record** to record the loan payment

| 01/30/2004 | Transfer | Southern California Bank | | 82.56 | | | 49,260.03 |
| | CHK | -split- | Loan Pmt., Office Equipm | | | | |

Close the **Checking** Register
- You should return to **Reconcile - Checking**.

Scroll to the top of **Checks and Payments**
- Notice the two entries for the payments in **Checks and Payments**.

Mark the two entries
- At this point, the **Ending Balance** and **Cleared Balance** should be equal—$49,318.46 with a difference of 0.00.

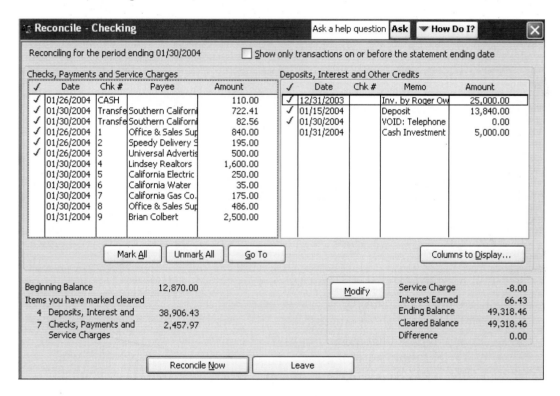

If your entries agree with the above, click **Reconcile Now** to finish the reconciliation
- If your reconciliation is not in agreement, do not click **Reconcile Now** until the errors are corrected.
- Once you click **Reconcile Now**, you may not return to this **Reconciliation - Checking** window.
- If you get an Information screen referring to online banking, click **OK**

PRINT A RECONCILIATION REPORT

As soon as the Ending Balance and the Cleared Balance are equal or when you finish marking and click Reconcile Now, a screen appears allowing you to select the level of Reconciliation report you would like to print. You may select Summary and get a report that lists totals only or Detail and get all the transactions that were reconciled on the report. You may print the report at the time you have finished reconciling the account or you may print the report later by returning to the Reconciliation window. QuickBooks Pro keeps your last two reconciliation reports in memory. If you think you may want to print the report again in the future, print the report to a file to save it permanently.

 DO: Print a **Detail Reconciliation Report**

On the **Select Reconciliation Report** screen, click **Detail**
Click the **Print** button
Print as previously instructed:
    Printer should be default printer
    Orientation is **Landscape**
    Page Range is **All**
If your report printed correctly, close the report

VIEW THE CHECKING ACCOUNT REGISTER

Once the bank reconciliation has been completed, it is wise to scroll through the Check register to view the effect of the reconciliation on the account. You will notice that the check column shows a check mark for all items that were marked as cleared during the reconciliation. If at a later date an error is discovered, the transaction may be changed, and the correction will be reflected in the Beginning Balance on the reconciliation.

 DO: View the register for the Checking account

Access the register as previously instructed

To display more of the register, click the check box for **1-Line**

Scroll through the register

- Notice that the transactions are listed in chronological order.
- Even though the bank reconciliation transactions were recorded after the checks written on January 31, the bank reconciliation transactions appear before the checks because they were recorded with the date of January 30.

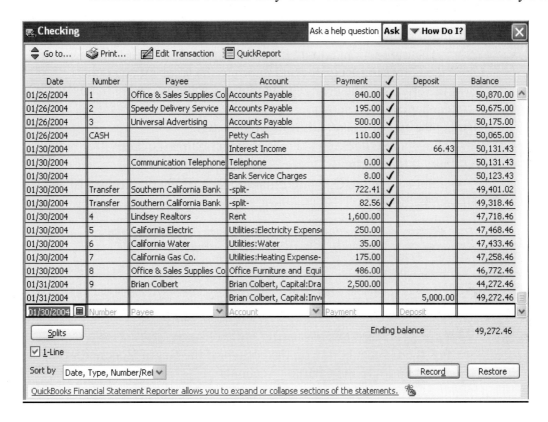

EDIT CLEARED TRANSACTIONS

DO: Edit transactions that were marked and cleared during the bank reconciliation:

Edit the **Petty Cash** transaction:

Click in the entry for the transfer of funds to **Petty Cash** on January 26

Change the **Payment** amount to **100**

Click **Record**

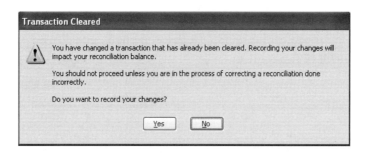

Click **Yes** on the **Transaction Cleared** dialog box
- The transaction amount has been changed.

Close the **Checking Register** and return to the Chart of Accounts
View the effects of the change to the Petty Cash transaction in the Begin Reconciliation window:
Display the **Begin Reconciliation** window by:
Making sure **Checking** is highlighted, clicking the **Activities** button, and clicking **Reconcile**
- Notice that the Opening Balance has been increased by $10 and shows $49,328.46.

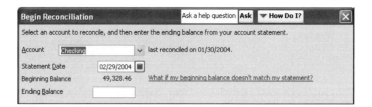

Click the **Cancel** button on the bottom of the **Begin Reconciliation** screen and return to the Chart of Accounts
Open the **Checking** account register
Change the amount for the **Petty Cash** transaction back to **110**
Click **Record** to record the change
Click **Yes** on the **Transaction Cleared** dialog box

01/26/2004	3		Universal Advertising	Accounts Payable	500.00	✓			50,175.00
01/26/2004	CASH	Payee		Petty Cash	110.00	✓	Deposit		50,065.00
01/30/2004				Interest Income		✓		66.43	50,131.43

Close the **Checking Register** and the **Chart of Accounts**

VIEW THE JOURNAL

After entering several transactions, it is helpful to view the Journal. In the Journal, all transactions, regardless of the method of entry are shown in traditional debit/credit format.

DO: View the **Journal** for January
Click **Reports** on the menu bar, click **Accountant & Taxes**, click **Journal**
    OR
Click **Report Finder** tab on a QuickBooks Navigator, click **Accountant & Taxes**
    as the type of report on the **Reports Finder**, click **Journal**, click **Display**
Tab to or click **From**
- If necessary, delete existing date.

Enter **01/01/04**
Tab to or click **To**
Enter **01/31/04**
Tab to generate the report
Scroll through the report
Verify the total of $57,919.69
Close the **Journal** without printing

PREPARE TRIAL BALANCE

After all adjustments have been recorded and the bank reconciliation has been completed, it is wise to prepare the Trial Balance. As in traditional accounting, the QuickBooks Pro Trial Balance proves that debits equal credits.

MEMO

DATE: January 31, 2004

Because adjustments have been entered, prepare a Trial Balance.

 DO: Prepare a Trial Balance
Access Report Finder as previously instructed
When Report Finder is displayed on the screen, click **Accountant & Taxes** as the
    type of report, click **Trial Balance,** click **Display**
Enter the **As of Date** as **01/31/04**
Tab to generate the report
Scroll through the report and study the amounts shown
- Notice that the final totals of debits and credits are equal: $138,119.07.

USE QUICKZOOM IN TRIAL BALANCE

QuickZoom is a QuickBooks Pro feature that allows you to make a closer observation of transactions, amounts, and other entries. With QuickZoom you may zoom in on an item when the mouse pointer turns into a magnifying glass with a Z inside. If you point to an item and you do not get a magnifying glass with a Z inside, you cannot zoom in on the item. For example, if you point to Interest Expense, you will see the magnifying glass with the Z inside. If your Trial Balance had Retained Earnings and you pointed to the account, the mouse pointer would not change from the arrow. This means that you can see transaction details for Interest Expense but not for Retained Earnings.

DO: Use QuickZoom to view the details of Interest Expense:
Scroll through the Trial Balance until you see Interest Expense
Position the mouse pointer over the amount of Interest Expense: Interest on Loans, **308.61**
- Notice that the mouse pointer changes to a magnifying glass with a Z.
Double-click the primary mouse button
- A Transactions by Account Report appears on the screen showing the payment of loan interest as of 01/31/2004.
Enter the From date **010104** and the To date **013104**
Tab to generate the report
Scroll through the report
Close the report without printing

PRINT THE TRIAL BALANCE

Once the Trial Balance has been prepared, it may be printed.

DO: Print the Trial Balance
Click the **Print** button at the top of the **Trial Balance**
Verify the **Settings**
    Printer should be selected
    Orientation is **Portrait**
    Page Range is **All**
    Smart Page Breaks should be selected
    Do not use **Fit report to one page wide**
Click the **Preview** button to view a miniature copy of the report
- This helps determine the orientation and whether you need to select the feature to print one page wide.
Click **Close**

Click **Print**
Close the **Trial Balance**; and, if necessary, the **Report Finder**

SELECT ACCRUAL-BASIS REPORTING PREFERENCE

QuickBooks Pro allows a business to customize the program and select certain preferences for reports, displays, graphs, accounts, and so on. There are two report preferences available in QuickBooks Pro: Cash and Accrual. You need to choose the one you prefer. If you select Cash as the report preference, income on reports will be shown as of the date payment is received and expenses will be shown as of the date you pay the bill. If Accrual is selected, QuickBooks Pro shows the income on the report as of the date of the invoice and expenses as of the bill date. Prior to printing end-of-period reports, it is advisable to verify which reporting basis is selected. If cash has been selected and you are using the accrual method, it is imperative that you change your report basis.

MEMO
DATE: January 31, 2004

Prior to printing reports, check the report preference selected for CCC. If necessary, choose Accrual. After the selection has been made, print a Standard Profit and Loss and a Standard Balance Sheet for Brian Colbert.

   DO: Select **Accrual** as the **Summary Reports Basis**
Click **Edit** on the menu bar, click **Preferences**
Scroll through the Preferences list until you see **Reports & Graphs**
Click **Reports & Graphs**
Click the **Company Preferences** tab
If necessary, click **Accrual** to select the **Summary Reports Basis**

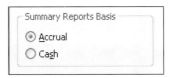

Click **OK** to close the **Preferences** window

PREPARE AND PRINT CASH FLOW FORECAST

In planning for the cash needs of a business, QuickBooks Pro can prepare a Cash Flow Forecast. This report is useful when determining the expected income and disbursement of cash. It is important to know if your company will have enough cash on hand to meet its obligations. A company with too little cash on hand may have to borrow money to pay its bills, while another company with excess cash may miss out on investment, expansion, or dividend opportunities. QuickBooks Pro Cash Flow Forecast does not analyze investments. It simply projects the amount you will be receiving if all those who owe you money pay on time and the amounts you will be spending to pay your accounts payable on time.

MEMO
DATE: January 31, 2004

Prepare Cash Flow Forecast for January 1-31, 2004, and February 1-28, 2004.

DO: Prepare Cash Flow Forecast for January and February
Click the **Report Finder** tab on a QuickBooks Navigator, click **Company & Financial** in the type of reports section, scroll through the list of reports, click **Cash Flow Forecast**, click **Display**
Enter the **From** date of **01/01/04** and the **To** date of **01/31/04**
Tab to generate the report

- Notice that **Periods** show **Week**. Use Week, but click the drop-down list arrow to see the periods available for the report.
- Analyze the report for January: The Beginning Balance for Accounts Receivable shows the amounts due from customers as of 12/31/01.
- The amounts for A/R and A/P for the future weeks are for the customer payments you expect to receive and the bills you expect to pay. This information is based on the due dates for invoices and bills.
- The bank account amount for future weeks is based on deposits made or deposits that need to be made.
- Net Inflows summarizes the amounts that should be received and the amounts that should be paid to get a net inflow of cash.
- The projected balance is the total in all bank accounts if all customer and bill payments are made on time.

Contempo Computer Consulting (CCC)--Student's Name
Cash Flow Forecast
January 2004

	Accnts Receivable	Accnts Payable	Bank Accnts	Net Inflows	Proj Balance
Beginning Balance	9,570.00	0.00	37,870.00		47,440.00
Jan 1 - 3, 04	0.00	0.00	0.00	0.00	47,440.00
Week of Jan 4, 04	-400.00	0.00	845.00	445.00	47,885.00
Week of Jan 11, 04	0.00	0.00	12,995.00	12,995.00	60,880.00
Week of Jan 18, 04	0.00	0.00	0.00	0.00	60,880.00
Week of Jan 25, 04	0.00	0.00	-2,345.33	-2,345.33	58,534.67
Jan 04	-400.00	0.00	11,494.67	11,094.67	
Ending Balance	**9,170.00**	**0.00**	**49,364.67**		**58,534.67**

Change the dates: **From** is **02/01/04** and **To** is **02/28/04**
Tab to generate the report

Contempo Computer Consulting (CCC)--Student's Name
Cash Flow Forecast
February 1 - 28, 2004

	Accnts Receivable	Accnts Payable	Bank Accnts	Net Inflows	Proj Balance
Beginning Balance	9,170.00	0.00	49,364.67		58,534.67
Week of Feb 1, 04	8,480.00	0.00	0.00	8,480.00	67,014.67
Week of Feb 8, 04	0.00	0.00	0.00	0.00	67,014.67
Week of Feb 15, 04	0.00	3,685.00	0.00	-3,685.00	63,329.67
Week of Feb 22, 04	0.00	79.00	0.00	-79.00	63,250.67
Feb 1 - 28, 04	8,480.00	3,764.00	0.00	4,716.00	
Ending Balance	**17,650.00**	**3,764.00**	**49,364.67**		**63,250.67**

- Compare the differences between the two reports.

Print the report for February in **Landscape**
Use **Preview** to determine if it is necessary to use **Fit report to one page wide**
Close the report
Do not close Report Finder

STATEMENT OF CASH FLOWS

Another report that details the amount of cash flow in a business is the Statement of Cash Flows. This report organizes information regarding cash in three areas of activities: Operating Activities, Investing Activities, and Financing Activities. The report also projects the amount of cash at the end of a period.

```
┌─────────────────────────────────────────────────────────────────────┐
│ MEMO                                                                  │
│ DATE: January 31, 2004                                                │
│                                                                       │
│ Prepare Statement of Cash Flows for January 1-31, 2004.               │
└─────────────────────────────────────────────────────────────────────┘
```

    DO: Prepare Statement of Cash Flows for January
               If necessary, click **Company & Financial** in the **Type of reports** section on the Report Finder, scroll through the list of reports, click **Statement of Cash Flows**, click **Display**
               Enter the **From** date of **01/01/04** and the **To** date of **01/31/04**
               Tab to generate the report

Contempo Computer Consulting (CCC)--Student's Name
Statement of Cash Flows
January 2004

	Jan 04
Net cash provided by Operating Activities	9,252.03
INVESTING ACTIVITIES	
Business Vehicles:Depreciation	583.00
Office Furniture and Equipment:Depreciation	142.00
Office Furniture and Equipment:Original Cost	-3,486.00
Net cash provided by Investing Activities	-2,761.00
FINANCING ACTIVITIES	
Loan Payable:Business Vehicles Loan	-467.19
Loan Payable:Office Furniture/Equipment Loan	-29.17
Brian Colbert, Capital:Draws	-2,500.00
Brian Colbert, Capital:Investments	8,000.00
Net cash provided by Financing Activities	5,003.64
Net cash increase for period	11,494.67
Cash at beginning of period	37,870.00
Cash at end of period	**49,364.67**

               Print the report in Portrait mode following previous instructions
               Close the report

PRINT STANDARD PROFIT AND LOSS STATEMENT

Because all income, expenses, and adjustments have been made for the period, a Profit and Loss Statement can be prepared. This statement is also known as the Income Statement. QuickBooks Pro has several different types of Profit and Loss statements available: <u>Standard</u>—summarizes income and expenses; <u>Detail</u>—shows the year-to-date transactions for each income and expense account; <u>YTD Comparison</u>—is like the Standard Profit and Loss but summarizes your income and expenses for this month and compares them to your income and expenses for the current fiscal year; <u>Prev Year Comparison</u>—is like the standard statement but summarizes your income and expenses for both this month and this month last year; <u>By Job</u>—is like the Standard Profit and Loss statement, but has columns for each customer and job and amounts for this year to date; <u>By Class</u>—is like the Standard Profit and Loss statement, but has columns for each class and sub-class with the amounts for this year to date, and <u>Unclassified</u>—is like the Standard Profit and Loss statement, but shows how much you are making or losing within segments of your business that are not assigned to a QuickBooks class so you can identify transactions to which you have not assigned a class..

DO: Print a **Standard Profit and Loss Report**
If necessary, click **Company & Financial** as the type of report on Report Finder, click **Profit & Loss Standard**, click **Display**
Tab to or click **From**, enter **01/01/04**
Tab to or click **To**, enter **01/31/04**
Tab to generate the report
Scroll through the report to view the income and expenses listed

```
Contempo Computer Consulting (CCC)--Student's Name
                    Profit & Loss
                      January 2004
                                          ◇    Jan 04    ◇
            Telephone                              0.00
            Utilities
                Electricity Expense         250.00
                Heating Expense--Gas        175.00
                Water                         35.00
                Total Utilities                  460.00

            Total Expense                        4,855.90

         Net Ordinary Income                      4,069.10


         Other Income/Expense
            Other Income
                Interest Income                     66.43
            Total Other Income                      66.43

         Net Other Income                           66.43

         Net Income                              4,135.53
```

Partial Report

Print the report in **Portrait** orientation
Close the **Profit and Loss Report**
Do not close Report Finder

PRINT STANDARD BALANCE SHEET

The Balance Sheet proves the fundamental accounting equation: Assets = Liabilities + Owner's
Equity. When all transactions and adjustments for the period have been recorded, a balance sheet
should be prepared. QuickBooks Pro has several different types of Balance Sheet statements
available: Standard—shows as of today the balance in each balance sheet account with subtotals
provided for assets, liabilities, and equity; Detail—which is a more detailed version of the
standard balance sheet report; Summary—shows amounts for each account type but not for
individual accounts; and Prev. Year Comparison—has columns for a year ago today, $ change,
and % change. For each account, the report shows the starting balance at the beginning of last
month, transactions entered in the account for this month to date, and the ending balance as of
today.

    DO: Print a **Standard Balance Sheet Report**
                   If necessary, click **Company & Financial** as the **Type of report**
                   Click **Balance Sheet Standard**, click **Display**
                   Tab to or click **As of**, enter **01/31/04**, tab to generate the report

Scroll through the report to view the assets, liabilities, and equities listed
- Notice the Net Income account listed in the Equity section of the report. This is the same amount of Net Income shown on the Profit and Loss Statement.

Contempo Computer Consulting (CCC)--Student's Name		
Balance Sheet		
As of January 31, 2004		
		Jan 31, 04
Loan Payable		
Business Vehicles Loan	34,532.81	
Office Furniture/Equipment Loan	3,970.83	
Total Loan Payable		38,503.64
Total Long Term Liabilities		38,503.64
Total Liabilities		42,267.64
Equity		
Brian Colbert, Capital		
Draws	-2,500.00	
Investments	33,000.00	
Brian Colbert, Capital - Other	53,135.00	
Total Brian Colbert, Capital		83,635.00
Net Income		4,135.53
Total Equity		87,770.53
TOTAL LIABILITIES & EQUITY		130,038.17

Print the report in **Portrait** orientation
Do not close the **Standard Balance Sheet**

ADJUSTMENT TO TRANSFER NET INCOME/RETAINED EARNINGS INTO BRIAN COLBERT, CAPITAL

Because Contempo Computer Consulting is a sole proprietorship, the amount of net income should appear as part of Brian Colbert's capital account rather than set aside in Retained Earnings as QuickBooks Pro does automatically. In many instances, this is the type of adjustment the CPA makes on the Accountant's Copy of the QuickBooks Pro company files. The adjustment may be made before the closing date for the fiscal year, or it may be made after the closing has been performed. Because QuickBooks Pro automatically transfers Net Income into Retained Earnings, the closing entry will transfer the net income into the Owner's Capital account. This adjustment is made in a Journal entry that debits Retained Earnings and credits the Owner's Capital account. When you view a report before the end of the year, you will see an amount in Net Income and the same amount as a negative in Retained Earnings. If you view a report after the end of the year, you will not see any information regarding Retained Earnings or Net Income because the adjustment correctly transferred the amount to the Owner's Capital account.

If you prefer to use the power of the program and not make the adjustment, QuickBooks Pro simply carries the amount of Retained Earnings forward. Each year net income is added to Retained Earnings. On the Balance Sheet, Retained Earnings and/or Net Income appears as part of the equity section. The owner's drawing and investment accounts are kept separate from Retained Earnings at all times. If Contempo Computer Consulting had used a traditional QuickBooks Pro set up for the Equity section of the Balance Sheet, it would appear as:

> **Equity**
> > **Owner's Capital**
> > > **Owner's Draw**
> > > **Owner's Investment**
> > > **Total Owner's Capital**
>
> > **Retained Earnings**
> > **Net Income**
>
> > **Total Equity**

DO: Transfer the net income into Brian Colbert, Capital account after year end:
Open the General Journal by clicking on **Company** or **Banking** on the menu bar, and clicking **Make General Journal Entries**
Enter the date of **01/31/04**
The first account used is **Retained Earnings**
Debit **Retained Earnings**, **4,135.53**
- Note: if the entire General Journal disappears during the transaction entry, simply open the Journal again and continue recording the transaction.
For the Memo record, **Transfer Net Income into Capital**
The other account used is **Brian Colbert, Capital**
4,135.53 should appear as the credit amount for **Brian Colbert, Capital**
Enter the same Memo

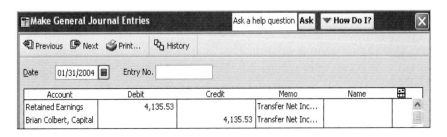

Click **Save & Close** to record and close the **General Journal**

PRINT STANDARD BALANCE SHEET

Once the adjustment for Net Income/Retained Earnings has been performed, viewing or printing the Balance Sheet will show you the status of the Owner's Equity.

> **DO:** Print a **Standard Balance Sheet** for January 2004
> The Standard Balance Sheet should still be showing on the screen
> Scroll through the report
> - Notice the Equity section, especially Retained Earnings and Net Income.
>
> Prior to printing, change the title of the report by clicking **Modify Report**, clicking the **Header/Footer** tab, clicking at the end of **Balance Sheet** in the Report Title dialog box and keying **(After Transfer of Net Income)**, click **OK**
>
> Print the **Balance Sheet** for January 2004 in **Portrait** orientation
> - The Balance Sheet shows on the screen after printing is complete.

Contempo Computer Consulting (CCC)--Student's Name
Balance Sheet (After Transfer of Net Income)
As of January 31, 2004

	Jan 31, 04
Office Furniture/Equipment Loan	3,970.83
Total Loan Payable	38,503.64
Total Long Term Liabilities	38,503.64
Total Liabilities	42,267.64
Equity	
Brian Colbert, Capital	
Draws	-2,500.00
Investments	33,000.00
Brian Colbert, Capital - Other	57,270.53
Total Brian Colbert, Capital	87,770.53
Retained Earnings	-4,135.53
Net Income	4,135.53
Total Equity	87,770.53
TOTAL LIABILITIES & EQUITY	**130,038.17**

Partial Report After Adjusting Entry

Change the **As of** date to **01/31/05**
- Because you did not close the report, the title does not change
- Notice the Equity section.
- Nothing is shown for Retained Earnings or Net Income.
- The Net Income has been added to the account Brian Colbert, Capital - Other.
- Verify this by adding the net income of 4,135.53 to 53,135.00, the balance of the Brian Colbert, Capital - Other account on the Balance Sheet printed before the adjusting entry was made. The total should equal 57,270.53, which is the amount of Brian Colbert, Capital - Other on the 2005 Balance Sheet.

Contempo Computer Consulting (CCC)--Student's Name
Balance Sheet (After Transfer of Net Income)
As of January 31, 2005

	Jan 31, 05
Long Term Liabilities	
Loan Payable	
Business Vehicles Loan	34,532.81
Office Furniture/Equipment Loan	3,970.83
Total Loan Payable	38,503.64
Total Long Term Liabilities	38,503.64
Total Liabilities	42,267.64
Equity	
Brian Colbert, Capital	
Draws	-2,500.00
Investments	33,000.00
Brian Colbert, Capital - Other	57,270.53
Total Brian Colbert, Capital	87,770.53
Total Equity	87,770.53
TOTAL LIABILITIES & EQUITY	**130,038.17**

Partial Report

Print the **Balance Sheet** for January 2005
Close the **Balance Sheet**; do not close Report Finder

PRINT JOURNAL

It is always wise to have a printed or "hard copy" of the data on disk. After all entries and adjustments for the month have been made, print the Journal for January. This copy should be kept on file as an additional backup to the data stored on your disk. If something happens to your disk to damage it, you will still have the paper copy of your transactions available for re-entry into the system.

DO: Print the Journal for January
With the Report Finder displayed on the screen, click **Accountant & Taxes** as the type of reports, click **Journal**
Tab to or click **From**, enter **01/01/04**
Tab to or click **To**, enter **01/31/04**
Click **Display**
- Notice that the report contains all the transactions from Chapters 2, 3, and 4
Verify that the final total for debits and credits is $62,055.22
- If it is not, make the necessary corrections to incorrect transactions. Frequent errors include incorrect dates, incorrect accounts used, and incorrect amounts.
Print in **Landscape** orientation, select **Fit report to one page wide**
Close the **Journal**

EXPORTING REPORTS TO EXCEL

Many of the reports prepared in QuickBooks Pro can be exported to Microsoft® Excel. This allows you to take advantage of extensive filtering options available in Excel, hide detail for some but not all groups of data, combine information from two different reports, change titles of columns, add comments, change the order of columns, and to experiment with "what if" scenarios. In order to use this feature of QuickBooks Pro you must also have Microsoft® Excel 97 or higher.

DO: Optional Exercise: Export a report from QuickBooks Pro to Excel
With Report Finder on the screen, click **Trial Balance**
Enter the **From** date as **01/01/04** and the **To** date as **01/31/04**
Click the **Export...** button

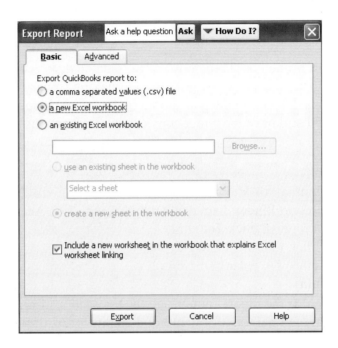

Make sure the Export QuickBooks Report to: is **a new Excel workbook**
Click **Export**
- The Trial Balance will be displayed in Excel.

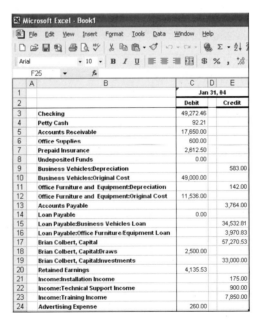

Partial Trial Balance in Excel

Click in Cell C1, change the heading by typing **JANUARY 31, 2004**
Click in Cell C2, type **DEBIT** to change Debit to all capitals

Click in Cell E2, type **CREDIT** to change Credit to all capitals

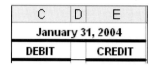

Click the **Close** button in the top right corner of the Excel title bar to close Excel

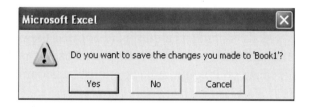

Click **No** to close Book1 without saving
Close **Report Finder**

END-OF-PERIOD BACKUP

Once all end-of-period procedures have been completed, a regular backup and a second backup of the company data should be made. The second backup should be filed as an archive copy. Preferably this copy will be located someplace other than on the business premises. The archive or file copy is set aside in case of emergency or in case damage occurs to the original and current backup copies of the company data.

DO: Back up company data and prepare an archive copy of the company data
Your **Contempo** disk should be in **A:**
Click **File** on the menu bar, click **Back Up**
In the **Name** text box enter **Contempo Archive 1-31-04.qbb** as the name for the backup
- In actual practice, the company (.qbw) file would be on your hard drive and the backup (.qbb) file would be stored on a floppy disk. For class purposes, if you are saving your work using the A: drive, you will also save your backup file on A:.
- Check with your instructor for specific classroom procedures for creating an archive copy based on your individual classroom configuration. Also, if your disk becomes full, check with your instructor for alternate procedures.
Click **OK**
Once the backup has been made, click **OK** on the QuickBooks Pro Information dialog box to acknowledge the successful backup

Optional: Use Windows Explorer and create a duplicate disk as previously instructed.

Label this disk **Archive, 1-31-2004**

- An archive disk is made as a duplicate copy of the company data files. It is advised that this disk be kept off the premises in case of fire or other situations that could cause your original backup disk to become unusable.

PASSWORDS

Not every employee of a business should have access to all the financial records for the company. In some companies, only the owner will have complete access. In others, one or two key employees will have full access while other employees are provided limited access based on the jobs they perform. Passwords are secret words used to control access to data. QuickBooks Pro has several options available when assigning passwords.

In order to assign any passwords at all, you must have an administrator. The administrator has unrestricted access to all QuickBooks Pro functions, sets up users and user passwords for QuickBooks and for Windows, and assigns areas of transaction access for each user. Areas of access can be limited to transaction entry for certain types of transactions or a user may have unrestricted access into all areas of QuickBooks Pro and company data. To obtain more information regarding QuickBooks' passwords, refer to the Help Index.

A password should be kept secret at all times. It should be something that is easy for the individual to remember, yet difficult for someone else to guess. Birthdays, names, initials, and similar devices are not good passwords because the information is too readily available. Never write down your password where it can be easily found or seen by someone else. Make sure your password is something you won't forget. Otherwise, you will not be able to access your Company file.

Since the focus of the text is in training in all aspects of QuickBooks Pro, no passwords will be assigned.

SET THE CLOSING DATE FOR THE PERIOD

A closing date assigned to transactions for a period prevents change to data from the period without acknowledging that a transaction has been changed for a closed period. This is helpful to discourage casual changes or transaction deletions to a period that has been closed. Setting the closing date is done by accessing Preferences in QuickBooks Pro.

MEMO

DATE: January 31, 2004

Maria, now that the closing transactions have been performed, protect the data by setting the closing date to 1/31/04.

DO: Assign the closing date of **01/31/04** to the transactions for the period ending 1/31/04
Click **Edit** on the menu bar, click **Preferences**
Scroll through the list of Preferences until you see **Accounting**
Click **Accounting**
Click **Company Preferences**
Enter **013104** as the date through which the books are closed
Do not assign a closing password at this time
Click **OK** to close the period and to close Preferences

ACCESS TRANSACTION FOR PREVIOUS PERIOD

Even though the month of January has been "closed," transactions still appear in the account registers, the Journal, and so on. The transactions shown may not be changed unless you click Yes on the screen warning you that you have changed a transaction to a closed period.

DO: Change Prepaid Insurance to 2,500
Access the **Chart of Accounts** as previously instructed
Click **Prepaid Insurance**
Click **Activities** at the bottom of the Chart of Accounts, click **Use Register**
OR
Use the keyboard shortcut, **Ctrl+R**
Click the **Increase** column showing **2,850** paid to Southern California Insurance Co.
Highlight 2,850, enter **2,500**

Click **Record**
The **QuickBooks** dialog box allowing the transaction to be changed appears

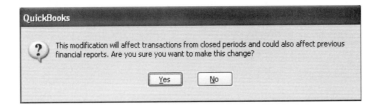

Click **No**
Click **Restore** to restore the transaction to the original 2,850
Close the **Prepaid Insurance** account
Do not close the **Chart of Accounts**

EDIT TRANSACTION FROM PREVIOUS PERIOD

If it is determined that an error was made in a previous period, QuickBooks Pro does allow the correction. Before it will record any changes for previous periods, QuickBooks Pro requires that Yes be clicked on the dialog box warning of the change to a transaction date that is prior to the closing date for the company. The adjusting entry used to transfer retained earnings/net income into the owner's capital account also needs to be adjusted as a result of any changes to transactions. Increasing the amount of supplies on hand by $25 will decrease the amount of expense incurred and will result in a $25 increase in net income/retained earnings.

MEMO
DATE: February 1, 2004

After reviewing the journal and reports printed at the end of January, Brian Colbert finds that the amount of supplies used was $325, not $350. Make the correction to the adjusting entry of January 31.

    DO: Change Office Supplies adjusting entry to $325 from $350
                Click **Office Supplies** account
                Use the keyboard shortcut **Ctrl+R** to use the register
                   OR
                Click **Activities** at the bottom of the **Chart of Accounts**
                Click **Use Register**
                Click the **Decrease** column for the Adjusting Entry recorded to the account on
                   01/31/04
                Change 350 to **325**

Click **Record**

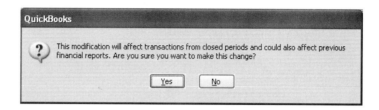

Click **Yes** on the QuickBooks screen
- The change to the transaction has been made.
- Notice that the Balance for the Office Supplies account now shows 625 instead of 600.

01/31/2004				325.00			625.00
	GENJRNL	Office Supplies Expense	Supplies Used				

Close the **Register for Office Supplies**
- Since the correction to Office Supplies decreased the amount of the expense by $25, there is an additional $25 that will need to be included in the net income.

Click **Brian Colbert, Capital**

Click **Activities** at the bottom of the **Chart of Accounts**

Click **Make General Journal Entries**

Click **Previous** until you find the entry adjusting Retained Earnings

Change the Debit to Retained Earnings from 4135.53 to **4160.53**

Change the Credit to Brian Colbert, Capital from 4135.53 to **4160.53**

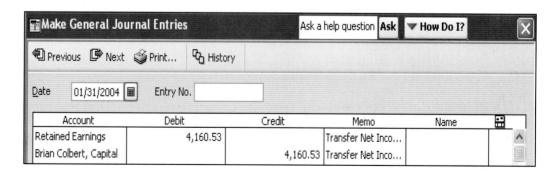

Click **Save & Close**

Click **Yes** on the **QuickBooks** dialog boxes

Close the **Chart of Accounts**

PRINT POST-CLOSING TRIAL BALANCE

After "closing" has been completed, it is helpful to print a Post-Closing Trial Balance. This proves that debits still equal credits.

MEMO

DATE: February 1, 2004

Print a Post-Closing Trial Balance, a Post-Closing Profit and Loss Statement, and a Post-Closing Balance Sheet for Brian Colbert. The dates should be as of or for 02/01/04.

DO: Print a Post-Closing Trial Balance to prove debits still equal credits
Click **Report Finder** on a QuickBooks Navigator, click **Accountant & Taxes** in the type of reports section, click **Trial Balance**, click **Display**
Enter the As of date **02/01/04**
Tab to generate the report
Change the Header so the report title is **Post-Closing Trial Balance**
Scroll through the report and study the amounts shown
- Notice that the final totals of debits and credits are equal.
Click the **Print** button at the top of the Trial Balance
Click **Preview** to view a miniature copy of the report
- Notice that the report appears in Landscape orientation. Using Preview helps determine if you should still use Landscape orientation or change to Portrait.
- Preview also helps you determine whether you need to select the feature to print one page wide.
Click **Close**
Print the report in **Portrait** orientation

Contempo Computer Consulting (CCC)--Student's Name
Post-Closing Trial Balance
As of February 1, 2004

	Feb 1, 04	
	Debit	Credit
Income:Training Income		7,850.00
Advertising Expense	260.00	
Bank Service Charges	8.00	
Business Vehicles Expense	588.88	
Depreciation Expense	725.00	
Dues and Subscriptions	79.00	
Equipment Rental	25.00	
Insurance:Business Vehicles Insurance	237.50	
Interest Expense:Interest on Loans	308.61	
Office Supplies Expense	343.57	
Postage and Delivery	195.34	
Rent	1,600.00	
Telephone	0.00	
Utilities:Electricity Expense	250.00	
Utilities:Heating Expense--Gas	175.00	
Utilities:Water	35.00	
Interest Income		66.43
TOTAL	142,279.60	142,279.60

Close the **Trial Balance**

PRINT POST-CLOSING PROFIT AND LOSS STATEMENT

Because February 1 is after the closing date of January 31, 2004, the Profit and Loss Statement for February 1 is the Post-Closing Profit and Loss Statement. To verify the closing, print a Profit and Loss statement for February 1.

DO: Print a **Standard Profit and Loss Report** as the Post-Closing Profit and Loss report for February
Using **Report Finder**, click **Company & Financial** as the type of report, click **Profit & Loss Standard**, click **Display**
Tab to or click **From**, enter **02/01/04**
Tab to or click **To**, enter **02/01/04**
Tab to generate the report
Change the Header so the report title is **Post-Closing Profit & Loss**
Print the report in **Portrait** orientation
Close the **Profit and Loss Report**
• The Net Income is **0.00**.

Contempo Computer Consulting (CCC)--Student's Name
Post-Closing Profit & Loss
February 1 - 4, 2004

◇ Feb 1 - 4, 04 ◇
Net Income ▶   <u>0.00</u> ◀

PRINT POST-CLOSING BALANCE SHEET

Proof that assets are equal to liabilities and owner's equity needs to be displayed in a Post-Closing Balance Sheet. The Balance Sheet for February 1 is considered to be a Post-Closing Balance Sheet because it is prepared after the closing of the period. Most of the adjustments were for the month of January 2004. Because this report is for a month, the adjustment to Retained Earnings and Net Income will result in both accounts being included on the Balance Sheet. If, however, this report were prepared for the year, neither account would appear.

DO: Print a **Standard Balance Sheet Report** for February 1, 2004, and February 1, 2005

Prepare a **Standard Balance Sheet** as previously instructed

Tab to or click **As of**, enter **02/01/04**

Tab to generate the report

Change the Header so the report title is **Post-Closing Balance Sheet**

Scroll through the report to view the assets, liabilities, and equities listed

- Because this report is for a one-month period, both Retained Earnings and Net Income are included on this report.

Print the report in **Portrait** orientation

Contempo Computer Consulting (CCC)--Student's Name
Post-Closing Balance Sheet
As of February 1, 2004

	Feb 1, 04	
Business Vehicles Loan	34,532.81	
Office Furniture/Equipment Loan	3,970.83	
Total Loan Payable		38,503.64
Total Long Term Liabilities		38,503.64
Total Liabilities		42,267.64
Equity		
Brian Colbert, Capital		
Draws	-2,500.00	
Investments	33,000.00	
Brian Colbert, Capital - Other	57,295.53	
Total Brian Colbert, Capital		87,795.53
Retained Earnings		-4,160.53
Net Income		4,160.53
Total Equity		87,795.53
TOTAL LIABILITIES & EQUITY		130,063.17

Change the date to **02/01/05**, tab to generate the report

Change the Header so the report title is **Balance Sheet**

Scroll through the report to view the assets, liabilities, and equities listed

- Because this report is prepared after the end of the fiscal year, neither Retained Earnings nor Net Income is included on this report.

Print the report in **Portrait** orientation then close the **Balance Sheet** and **Report Finder**

```
┌─────────────────────────────────────────────────────────────┐
│        Contempo Computer Consulting (CCC)--Student's Name     │
│                       Balance Sheet                           │
│                    As of February 1, 2005                     │
│                                             ◇   Feb 1, 05   ◇  │
│         Long Term Liabilities                                 │
│           Loan Payable                                        │
│             Business Vehicles Loan           34,532.81        │
│             Office Furniture/Equipment Loan   3,970.83        │
│             Total Loan Payable                      38,503.64 │
│                                                               │
│           Total Long Term Liabilities               38,503.64 │
│                                                               │
│         Total Liabilities                           42,267.64 │
│                                                               │
│         Equity                                                │
│           Brian Colbert, Capital                              │
│             Draws                            -2,500.00         │
│             Investments                      33,000.00         │
│             Brian Colbert, Capital - Other   57,295.53         │
│             Total Brian Colbert, Capital            87,795.53 │
│                                                               │
│         Total Equity                                87,795.53 │
│                                                               │
│         TOTAL LIABILITIES & EQUITY                 130,063.17 │
└─────────────────────────────────────────────────────────────┘
```

END-OF-CHAPTER BACKUP AND CLOSE COMPANY

As in previous chapters, you should back up your company and close the company.

 DO: Follow instructions previously provided to back up company files, close CCC, and make a duplicate disk

SUMMARY

In this chapter, end-of-period adjustments were made, a bank reconciliation was performed, backup and archive disks were prepared, and a period was closed. The use of Net Income and Retained Earnings accounts was explored and interpreted for a sole proprietorship. Account name changes were made, and the effect on subaccounts was examined. Even though QuickBooks Pro focuses on entering transactions on business forms, a Journal recording each transaction is kept by QuickBooks Pro. This chapter presented transaction entry directly into the Journal. The differences between accrual-basis and cash-basis accounting were discussed. Company preferences were established for reporting preferences. Owner withdrawals and additional owner investments were made. Many of the different report options available in QuickBooks Pro were examined, and the exporting of reports to Excel was explored. A variety of reports were printed. Correction of errors was explored, and changes to transactions in "closed" periods were made. The fact that QuickBooks Pro does not require an actual closing entry at the end of the period was examined.

END-OF-CHAPTER QUESTIONS

TRUE/FALSE

ANSWER THE FOLLOWING QUESTIONS IN THE SPACE PROVIDED BEFORE THE QUESTION NUMBER.

_____   1. Accrual-basis accounting matches the income from the period and the expenses for the period in order to determine the net income or net loss for the period.

_____   2. In QuickBooks Pro, the Journal is called the book of final entry.

_____   3. An account may be deleted at any time.

_____   4. In a sole proprietorship, an owner's name is added to the Vendor List for recording withdrawals.

_____   5. Additional investments made by an owner may be cash or noncash items.

_____   6. QuickBooks Pro keeps a Journal record of every transaction.

_____   7. QuickBooks Pro keeps the last two Bank Reconciliation reports in memory.

_____   8. Once an account has been used in a transaction, no changes may be made to the account name.

_____   9. Anything entered as a service charge or as interest earned during a bank reconciliation will be entered automatically when the reconciliation is complete.

_____   10. A Balance Sheet is prepared to prove the equality of debits and credits.

MULTIPLE CHOICE

WRITE THE LETTER OF THE CORRECT ANSWER IN THE SPACE PROVIDED BEFORE THE QUESTION NUMBER.

_____ 1. To close a period, you must ___.
   A. have a closing password
   B. change company preferences for Accounting
   C. change company preferences for Reports
   D. enter the traditional closing entries in debit/credit format in the General Journal

_____ 2. When an account name such as "cars" is changed to "automobile," the subaccount "car depreciation" ___.
   A. needs to be changed to "automobile depreciation"
   B. is automatically changed to "automobile depreciation"
   C. cannot be changed
   D. must be deleted and re-entered

_____ 3. The report that proves Assets = Liabilities + Owner's Equity is the ___.
   A. Trial Balance
   B. Income Statement
   C. Profit and Loss Statement
   D. Balance Sheet

_____ 4. If the adjusting entry to transfer net income/retained earnings into the owner's capital account is made prior to the end of the year, the Balance Sheet shows ___.
   A. Retained Earnings
   B. Net Income
   C. both Net Income and Retained Earnings
   D. none of the above because the income/earnings has been transferred into capital

_____ 5. The type of Profit and Loss Report showing year-to-date transactions instead of totals for each income and expense account is a(n) ___ Profit and Loss Report.
   A. Standardized
   B. YTD Comparison
   C. Prev Year Comparison
   D. Detailed

_____ 6. A bank statement may ___.
   A. show service charges or interest not yet recorded
   B. be missing deposits in transit or outstanding checks
   C. both of the above
   D. none of the above

_____ 7. The Journal shows ___.
    A. all transactions no matter where they were recorded
    B. only those transactions recorded in the General Journal
    C. only transactions recorded in account registers
    D. only those transactions that have been edited

_____ 8. A QuickBooks backup file ___.
    A. is a condensed file containing company data
    B. is prepared in case of emergencies or errors on current disks
    C. must be restored before information can be used
    D. all of the above

_____ 9. An error known as a transposition can be found by ___ during reconciliation.
    A. dividing the amount out of balance by 9
    B. dividing the amount out of balance by 2
    C. multiplying the difference by 9, then dividing by 2
    D. dividing the amount out of balance by 5

_____ 10. The type of Balance Sheet Report showing information for today and a year ago is a(n) ___ Balance Sheet.
    A. Standard
    B. Summary
    C. Comparison
    D. Detailed

FILL-IN

IN THE SPACE PROVIDED, WRITE THE ANSWER THAT MOST APPROPRIATELY COMPLETES THE SENTENCE.

1. Bank reconciliations should be performed on a(n) _____ basis.

2. Exporting report data from QuickBooks Pro to _____ can be made in order to perform "what if" scenarios.

3.   An owner's paycheck is considered a(n) _____.

4. The two types of reporting are _____ basis and _____ basis.

5. The Cash Flow Forecast _____ column shows the total in all bank accounts if all customer and bill payments are made on time.

SHORT ESSAY

Describe the four types of Balance Sheet Reports available in QuickBooks Pro.

_____

_____

_____

_____

_____

_____

_____

NAME_____

TRANSMITTAL

CHAPTER 4: CONTEMPO COMPUTER CONSULTING

Attach the following documents and reports:

Check No. 9: Brian Colbert
Reconciliation Detail Report
Trial Balance, January 1-31, 2004
Cash Flow Forecast, February 1-28, 2004
Statement of Cash Flows, January 2004
Profit and Loss Statement, January 31, 2004
Balance Sheet, January 31, 2004
Balance Sheet (After Transfer of Net Income), January 31, 2004
Balance Sheet (After Transfer of Net Income), January 31, 2005
Journal, January 1-31, 2004
Post-Closing Trial Balance, February 1, 2004
Post-Closing Profit and Loss, February 1, 2004
Post-Closing Balance Sheet, February 1, 2004
Balance Sheet, February 1, 2005

END-OF-CHAPTER PROBLEM

SUPREME LAWN AND POOL MAINTENANCE

Chapter 4 continues with the end-of-period adjustments, bank reconciliation, archive disks, and closing the period for Supreme Lawn and Pool Maintenance. The company does use a certified professional accountant for guidance and assistance with appropriate accounting procedures. The CPA has provided information for Melissa to use for adjusting entries and so on.

INSTRUCTIONS

Continue to use the student data disk for Supreme. Open the company—the file used is **Supreme.qbw**. Record the adjustments and other transactions as you were instructed in the chapter. Always read the transaction carefully and review the Chart of Accounts when selecting transaction accounts. Print the reports and journals as indicated.

RECORD TRANSACTIONS

<u>May 31</u>—Enter the following:
Change the names of the following accounts:

> **Business Trucks** to **Business Vehicles** (also change the subaccounts so they reflect the name Business Vehicles)
> **Automobile Expense** to **Business Vehicles Expense**
> **Business Trucks Loan** to **Business Vehicles Loan**
> **Auto Insurance Expense** to **Business Vehicles Insurance**

Make the following accounts inactive:

> **Recruiting**
> **Travel & Ent**
> > **Travel & Ent: Entertainment**
> > **Travel & Ent: Meals**
> > **Travel & Ent: Travel**

Delete the following accounts:

> **Sales**
> **Services**
> **Amortization Expenses**
> **Contributions**
> **Interest Expense: Mortgage**
> **Taxes: Property**

Print the Chart of Accounts by clicking **Reports** on the menu bar, pointing to **List**, clicking **Account Listing.** Use Landscape orientation.

May 31—Enter the following:

Enter adjusting entries in the Journal for:

Office Supplies Used, $185. Memo: Office Supplies Used for May

Depreciation for the month (Use a compound entry):

Business Vehicles, $950

Equipment, $206.25

Memo for all accounts used: Depreciation Expense May

The amount of insurance remaining in the Prepaid Insurance account is for three months of insurance on the business vehicles. Record the business vehicles insurance expense for the month, $250. Memo: Insurance Expense May

Enter transactions for Owner's Equity:

Owner withdrawal $1,000. Memo: Withdrawal for May (Print the check.)

Additional cash investment by George Gordon, $2,000. Memo: Investment: Cash

Additional noncash investment by owner, $1,500 of lawn equipment. Memo: Investment: Equipment (Note: The value of the lawn equipment is the original cost of the asset.)

Prepare Bank Reconciliation and Enter Adjustments for the Reconciliation for May 31, 2004

- Be sure to enter automatic payments, service charges, and interest. Pay close attention to the dates.

SANTA BARBARA BANK

1234 Coast Highway
Santa Barbara, CA 93100 (805) 555-9310

BANK STATEMENT FOR

Supreme Lawn and Pool Maintenance
18527 State Street
Santa Barbara, CA 93103
Acct. #987-352-9152   May 31, 2004

Beginning Balance, May 2, 2004			$23,850.00
5/18/04, Check 1		180.00	23,670.00
5/18/04, Check 2		669.00	23,001.00
5/18/04, Check 3		375.00	22,626.00
5/18/04, Check 4		485.00	22,141.00
5/31/04, Service Charge		10.00	22,131.00
5/31/04, Business Vehicles Loan Pmt.: Interest, 795.54; Principal, 160.64		956.18	21,174.82
5/31/04, Interest	59.63		21,234.45
Ending Balance, 5/31/04			$21,234.45

Print a Detailed Reconciliation Report in Landscape orientation
Change Preferences: Verify or change reporting preferences to accrual basis

Print:
        Trial Balance
        Standard Profit & Loss Statement
        Standard Balance Sheet

Transfer Net Income/Retained Earnings into Capital Account
Prepare a Balance Sheet Standard, add **(After Transfer of Net Income)** to the header, and print
Close the period: The end-of-period closing date is **05/31/04**

Edit a Transaction from a closed period:
        Discovered an error in the amount of office supplies used. The amount used should be
            $175, not $185. (Don't forget to adjust Retained Earnings and Capital.)

June 1, 2004—Print the following in Portrait orientation unless specified as Landscape:
>   Journal for May, 2004 (Landscape orientation, Fit report to one page wide)
>   Post-Closing Trial Balance, June 1, 2004 (Add the words **Post-Closing** to the report title)
>   Cash Flow Forecast for June 1-30 (Landscape orientation), 2004
>   Statement of Cash Flows, May 1-31, 2004
>   Post-Closing Profit & Loss Statement, June 1, 2004 (Add the words **Post-Closing** to the
>   report title)
>   Post-Closing Balance Sheet, June 1, 2004 (Add the words **Post-Closing** to the report
>   title)

June 1, 2005—Print the following:
>   Standard Balance Sheet

NAME_____

TRANSMITTAL

CHAPTER 4: SUPREME LAWN AND POOL MAINTENANCE

Attach the following documents and reports:

Account Listing, May 31, 2004
Check No. 8: George Gordon
Reconciliation Report
Trial Balance, May 31, 2004
Profit and Loss, May 2004
Balance Sheet, May 31, 2004
Balance Sheet, May 31, 2004 (After Transfer of Net Income)
Journal, May 2004
Post-Closing Trial Balance, June 1, 2004
Cash Flow Forecast, June 2004
Statement of Cash Flows, May 2004
Post-Closing Profit and Loss, June 1, 2004
Post-Closing Balance Sheet, June 1, 2004
Balance Sheet, June 1, 2005

HELP 4 YOU PRACTICE SET: SERVICE BUSINESS AND PAYROLL

The following is a comprehensive practice set combining all the elements of QuickBooks Pro studied in the text. In this practice set, you will keep the books for a company for one month. Entries will be made to record invoices, receipt of payments on invoices, cash sales, receipt and payment of bills, credit memos for invoices and bills, and payment of the payroll. Account names will be added, changed, deleted, and made inactive. Customer, vendor, and owner names will be added to the appropriate lists. Reports will be prepared to analyze sales, bills, and receipts. Formal reports including the Trial Balance, Profit and Loss Statement, and Balance Sheet will be prepared. Adjusting entries for depreciation, supplies used, and insurance expense will be recorded. A bank reconciliation will be prepared.

HELP 4 YOU

Located in Beverly Hills, California, Help 4 You is a service business providing assistance with errands, shopping, home repairs, simple household chores, and transportation for children and others who do not drive. Rates are on a per-hour basis and differ according to the service performed.

Help 4 You is a sole proprietorship owned and operated by Pamela Deschamps. Pamela has one assistant, Gail Hsing, helping her with errands, scheduling of duties, and doing the bookkeeping for Help 4 You. In addition, a part-time employee, Greta Gunderssen, works weekends for Help 4 You.

INSTRUCTIONS

To work with transactions for Help 4 You, copy the file **Help 4 You.qbw** from the CD-ROM onto a new disk. Label the disk **Help 4 You**.

The following lists are used for all sales items, customers, vendors, and employees. You will be adding additional customers and vendors as the company is in operation. When entering transactions, you are responsible for any memos or customer messages you wish to include in transactions. Unless otherwise specified, the terms for each sale or bill will be the terms specified on the Customer or Vendor List. (Choose Edit for the individual customers or vendors, and select the Additional Info tab to see the terms for each customer or vendor.)

Customers:

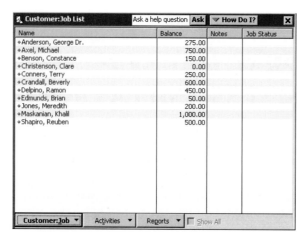

Vendors:

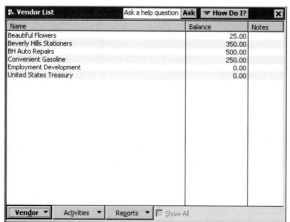

Sales Items:

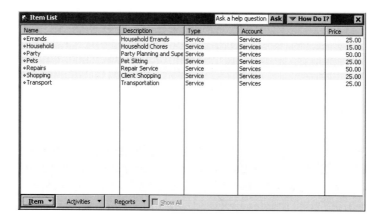

Each Item is priced per hour. Unless otherwise specified within the transactions, a minimum of one hour is charged for any service provided. As you can see, there is no difference in amount between the first hour of a service and subsequent hours of service.

RECORD TRANSACTIONS

Enter the transactions for Help 4 You and print as indicated. Always print invoices, sales receipts, checks, and so on as they are entered.

Week 1: September 1-6, 2004:

Add your name to the company name. The company name will be **Help 4 You—Student's Name**. (Type your actual name, *not* the words *Student's Name*.)

Change Report Preferences: Reports should refresh automatically, Report Header/Footer should *not* include the Date Prepared, Time Prepared, or the Report Basis

Find all accounts with the name **Automobile** as part of the account name. Change every occurrence of Automobile to **Business Vehicle**.

Find all accounts with the name **Office Equipment** as part of the account name. Change every occurrence of Office Equipment to **Office Furniture/Equipment**.

Make the following inactive: **Interest Expense: Mortgage**, **Taxes: Property**, **Travel & Ent**

Delete the following accounts: **Sales, Recruiting, Contributions, Amortization Expense,** and **Professional Development**

Add **Petty Cash** to the Chart of Accounts. Transfer $100 from checking to Petty Cash to fund the account.

Print an Account Listing in Portrait orientation. (From the Report menu select List and Account Listing)

Prior to recording any transactions, print a Trial Balance as of September 1, 2004.

9/1/04

Clare Christenson is having a party in two weeks. Bill Clare Christenson for 3 hours of party planning. Refer to the Item Detail List for the appropriate sales item. Invoice No. 35, terms, Net 30. Print the invoice.

Dr. Shapiro has arranged for you to feed and walk his dogs every day. Bill Dr. Shapiro for pet sitting, 1 hour per day for 7 days (put this all on one bill).

We were out of paper, toner cartridges for the laser printer, computer disks, and various other office supplies that we need to have on hand. Received a bill—Invoice No. 1806-1—from Beverly Hills Stationers for $350 for the office supplies we received today.

Every week we put fresh flowers in the office in order to provide a welcoming environment for any customers who happen to come to the office. Received a bill—Invoice No. 887—from Beautiful Flowers for $25 for office flowers for the week. (Miscellaneous Expense)

9/2/04

Dr. Anderson almost forgot his anniversary. He called Help 4 You with an emergency request for assistance. The store will bill the doctor for the actual gift purchased. Bill Dr. George Anderson, 3 hours of shopping for his wife's birthday gift.

Constance Benson needed to have her shelves relined. You did part of the house this week and will return next week to continue the work. Bill her for 5 hours of household chores for this week.

9/3/04

Ramon's mother has several doctor appointments. Mr. Delpino has asked Help 4 You to take her to these appointments. Bill Ramon Delpino for 3 hours of transportation.

9/4/04

Received a bill—Invoice No. 81056—from Convenient Gasoline, $125 for the weekly gasoline charge.

Received checks from the following customers on account: Dr. George Anderson, Check No. 713 for $275; Terry Conners, Check No. 3381 for $250; Ramon Delpino, Check No. 6179 for $450; Khalil Maskanian, Check No. 38142 for $1000.

9/5/04

Fionna Jones has a birthday party to attend. Her mother, Meredith, has hired Help 4 You to take her to the party and stay with her while she is there. Bill Meredith Jones 3 hours of transportation for the birthday party. (This transportation charge also includes the time at the party.)

9/6/04

Prepare Sales Receipt No. 22 to record a cash sale. Received Check No. 2894 for 1 hour of errands for a new customer: Carolyn Roberts, 18062A Camden Drive, Beverly Hills, CA 90210, 310-555-7206, Fax 310-555-6027, E-mail C Roberts@abc.com, terms Net 10 days. (*Note:* Remember to key the last name first for the customer name.) Print the sales receipt.

Prepare Unpaid Bills Detail Report. Print the report.

Pay bills for the amount owed to Beautiful Flowers and Convenient Gasoline on August 31. (Refer to the Vendor List on Page 284 or to the Unpaid Bills Detail Report to determine the amounts for the checks. Remember that the due dates will not be 8/31/04.) Print the checks using a Standard check style—they may be printed on one page or individually.

Make the bank deposit for the week. The date of the deposit is 9/6/04. Print a Deposit Summary.

Print Trial Balance.

Back up your work for the week. Use **Help 4 You Week 1.qbb** as the file name.

Week 2: September 7-13, 2004
9/7/04

Clare Christenson is having a party September 19. Bill Clare Christenson for 4 hours of party planning.

Ramon's mother has several additional doctor appointments. Mr. Delpino has asked Help 4 You to take her to these appointments. Bill Ramon Delpino for 4 hours of transportation.

Dr. Shapiro was pleased with Help 4 You' service and has arranged to have Help 4 You feed and walk his dogs every day on a permanent basis. Bill Dr. Shapiro for pet sitting, 1 hour per day for 7 days.

9/8/04

Beverly Crandall really likes the floral arrangements in the office of Help 4 You. She has asked that flowers be brought to her home and arranged throughout the house. When Pamela completes the placement of the flowers in the house, Beverly gives her Check No. 387 for $40. This is payment in full for 1 hour of errands and 1 hour of household chores.

9/9/04

Received checks from the following customers: Dr. Shapiro, No. 7891, $500; Ms. Jones, No. 97452, $200; Ms. Crandall, No. 395, $600; Mr. Edmunds, No. 178, $50; Mr. Axel, No. 3916, $750.

Received a bill—Invoice No. 943—from Beautiful Flowers for $25 for office flowers for the week.

Received a bill—Invoice No. 81085—from Convenient Gasoline, $100 for the weekly gasoline charge.

9/10/04

Khalil Maskanian has arranged for Help 4 You to supervise and coordinate the installation of new tile in his master bathroom. Bill Mr. Maskanian for 4 hours of repair service for hiring the subcontractor, scheduling the installation for 9/15 and 9/16, and contract preparation.

9/11/04

Constance Benson needed to have her shelves relined. Pamela did part of the house last week and completed the work today. Bill Ms. Benson for 5 hours of household chores for this week.

Returned faulty printer cartridge. Received Credit Memo No. 5 from Beverly Hills Stationers, $75.

9/13/04

Pay all bills for the amounts due on or before September 13. (*Hint:* Are there any credits to apply?) There should be three checks. Print the checks–all on one page or individually.

Correct the invoice issued to Constance Benson on 9/11/04. The number of hours billed should be 7 instead of 5. Print the corrected invoice.

Make the bank deposit for the week. The date of the deposit is 9/13/04. Print a Deposit Summary.

After depositing checks, print A/R Aging Detail Report as of 9/13/04. Use Landscape orientation.

Back up your work for the week. Use **Help 4 You Week 2.qbb** as the file name.

Week 3: September 14-20, 2004
9/14/04
Clare Christenson is having a party the 19th. Bill Clare Christenson for 2 more hours of party planning.

9/15/04
Pay postage due 64 cents. Use Petty Cash.

Print Petty Cash Account QuickReport. Fit report to one page wide.

Beverly Crandall was really pleased with the floral arrangements Pamela did last week. She has asked that flowers be brought to her home and arranged throughout the house on a weekly basis. This week when Pamela completes the placement of the flowers in the house, Beverly gives her Check No. 421 for 1 hour of errands and 1 hour of household chores.

9/17/04
Received a bill—Invoice No. 81109—from Convenient Gasoline, $150 for the weekly gasoline charge.

Received a bill—Invoice No. 979—from Beautiful Flowers for $25 for office flowers for the week.

The bathroom tile was installed on 9/15 and 9/16. The installation was completed to Mr. Maskanian's satisfaction. Bill him for 16 hours of repair service.

9/18/04
Beverly Crandall's neighbor, Dr. Jackson Greene, really liked the flowers in Beverly's house and asked Pamela to bring flowers to his home and office. This week he gave her Check No. 90-163 for 1 hour of errands and 1 hour of household chores. Add him to the customer list: Dr. Jackson Greene, 236 West Canon Drive, Beverly Hills, CA 90210, 310-555-0918, Net 10.

9/19/04
Tonight is Clare's big party. She has arranged for both Pamela and Greta to supervise the party from 3 p.m. until 1 a.m. Bill Clare Christenson for 20 hours of party planning and supervision.

Print a Customer Balance Summary Report.

9/20/04
Record the checks received from customers for the week: Mr. Delpino, No. 9165, $175; Ms. Benson, No. 7-303, $150; Dr. Shapiro, No. 89162, $175; Ms. Jones, No. 5291, $75.

Make the bank deposit for the week. The date of the deposit is 9/20/04. Print a Deposit Summary.

Back up your work for the week. Use **Help 4 You Week 3.qbb** as the file name.

Week 4: September 21-27, 2004
9/22/04

Beverly Crandall gave Pamela Check No. 439 for 1 hour of errands and 1 hour of household chores in payment for the flowers that were brought to her home and arranged throughout the house this week.

9/23/04

Use Petty Cash to pay for a box of file folders to be used immediately in reorganizing some of the files in the office, $4.23. (This is an expense.)

Print a Petty Cash Account QuickReport. Fit the report to one page wide.

Clare's party went so smoothly on the 19th that Pamela went home at 11 p.m. rather than 1 a.m. Issue a Credit Memo to Clare Christenson for 2 hours of party planning and supervision.

Brian Edmunds arranged to have his pets cared for by Help 4 You during the past 7 days. Bill him for 1 hour of pet sitting each day. Brian wants to add a doggie door and a fenced area for his dog. Bill him 20 hours of repair service for the planning and overseeing of the project.

9/24/04

Pamela arranged for theater tickets and dinner reservations for Dr. Anderson to celebrate his wife's birthday. Bill him for 1 hour of errands, 3 hours shopping for the gift, and 5 hours of party planning for the after-theater surprise party.

Received a bill—Invoice No. 81116—from Convenient Gasoline, $110 for the weekly gasoline charge.

Received a bill—Invoice No. 1002—from Beautiful Flowers for $25 for office flowers for the week.

Write a check to Beverly Hills Stationers for the purchase of a new printer for the office, $500. (*Note:* If you get a warning to use Pay Bills because we owe the company money, disregard the warning.) Print the check using standard-style checks.

9/27/04

Dr. Shapiro has arranged for Help 4 You to feed and walk his dogs every day. Bill him for pet sitting, 1 hour per day for the past two weeks. In addition, Dr. Shapiro is going to have a party and wants Help 4 You to plan it for him. Bill him for 20 hours party planning. When the dogs were puppies they did some damage to the interior of the house. In order to prepare for the party several areas in the house need to be reorganized and repaired. Bill him for 15 hours of household chores and 15 hours of repairs.

Write checks to pay bills for rent and utilities. The utility companies and the rental agent will need to be added to the Vendor List. Vendor information is provided in each transaction. Print the checks using standard-style checks. They may be printed as a batch or individually.

> Monthly telephone bill: $192, Beverly Hills Telephone, 2015 Wilshire Boulevard, Beverly Hills, CA 90210, 310-555-8888, Net 30 days.
>
> Monthly rent for office space: $1,500, Rentals for You, 3016 Robertson Boulevard, Beverly Hills, CA 90210, 310-555-1636, Net 30 days.
>
> Monthly water bill: $153, California Water, 9916 Sunset Boulevard, Beverly Hills, CA 90210, 310-555-1961, Net 30 days.
>
> Monthly gas and electric bill: $296, Beverly Hills Power, 10196 Olympic Boulevard, West Los Angeles, CA 90016, 310-555-9012, Net 30 days.

Prepare and print in Portrait orientation an Unpaid Bills Detail Report for September 27.

Pay bills for all amounts due on or before September 27.

Prepare a Check Detail Report from 9/1/04 to 9/27/04. Use Landscape orientation and fit report to one page wide.

Record payments received from customers: Ms. Christenson, No. 4692, $150; Dr. Shapiro, No. 7942, $175; Mr. Edmunds, No. 235, $175; Dr. Anderson, No. 601, $75; Ms. Benson, No. 923-10, $75.

Make the bank deposit for the week. The date of the deposit is 9/27/04. Print a Deposit Summary.

Print Customer Balance Detail Report in Portrait orientation. Fit report to one page wide.

Record adjusting entries for:

> Business Vehicle Insurance, $200
> Office Supplies Used, $150
> Depreciation:
>> Business Vehicles, $500
>> Office Furniture and Equipment, $92

Write a check for a withdrawal by Pamela Deschamps, $1,000.

Because a fax machine is a business necessity, Pamela decided to give her new fax machine to Help 4 You. Record this additional $350 investment of equipment by Pamela Deschamps.

Because they are remodeling the offices, Rentals for You decreased the amount of rent to $1,000 per month. Correct and reprint the check for rent.

Back up your work for the week. Use **Help 4 You Week 4.qbb** as the file name.

End of the Month: September 30, 2004

Prepare the bank reconciliation using the following bank statement. Record any adjustments necessary as a result of the bank statement. Print a Detailed Reconciliation Report.

Beverly Hills Bank, 1234 Rodeo Drive, Beverly Hills, CA 90210

Help 4 You, 27800 Beverly Boulevard, Beverly Hills, CA 90210

Beginning Balance, 9/1/04			$15,350.00
9/1/04, Transfer		100.00	15,250.00
9/6/04, Deposit	2,000.00		17,250.00
9/7/04, Check 1		25.00	17,225.00
9/7/04, Check 2		250.00	16,975.00
9/13/04, Check 3		25.00	16,950.00
9/13/04, Deposit	2,140.00		19,090.00
9/15/04, Check 5		500.00	18,590.00
9/16/04, Check 4		275.00	18,315.00
9/20/04, Deposit	655.00		18,970.00
9/28/04, Check 6		500.00	18,470.00
9/29/04, Check 8		1,000.00	17,470.00
9/30/04, Payment: Business Vehicle Loan: interest $445.15; principal $86.06		531.21	16,938.79
9/30/04, Payment: Office Equipment Loan: interest $53.42; principal $10.33		63.75	16,875.04
9/30/04, Service Charge		15.00	16,860.04
9/30/04, Interest	42.50		16,902.54
9/30/04, Ending Balance			16,902.54

Print the following reports as of 9/30/04:
> Journal from 9/1/04 through 9/30/04 in Landscape orientation and Fit to one page wide.
> Trial Balance from 9/1/04 through 9/30/04 in Portrait orientation.
> Cash Flow Forecast from 9/1/04 through 9/30/04 in Landscape orientation.
> Statement of Cash Flows from 9/1/04 through 9/30/04 in Portrait orientation.
> Standard Profit and Loss Statement from 9/1/04 through 9/30/04 in Portrait orientation.
> Standard Balance Sheet for 9/30/04 in Portrait orientation.

Transfer the net income/retained earnings to owner's capital account.

Prepare a Standard Balance Sheet as of 9/30/04. Change the title to **Balance Sheet After Transfer of Net Income** and print

Back up your work for the week. Use **Help 4 You Complete.qbb** as the file name.

NAME _____

TRANSMITTAL

HELP 4 YOU PRACTICE SET: SERVICE BUSINESS

Attach the following documents and reports:

Week 1
Account Listing
Trial Balance, September 1, 2004
Invoice No. 35: Clare Christenson
Invoice No. 36: Reuben Shapiro
Invoice No. 37: George Anderson
Invoice No. 38: Constance Benson
Invoice No. 39: Ramon Delpino
Invoice No. 40: Meredith Jones
Sales Receipt No. 22: Carolyn Roberts
Unpaid Bills Detail, September 6, 2004
Check No. 1: Beautiful Flowers
Check No. 2: Convenient Gasoline
Deposit Summary, September 6, 2004
Trial Balance, September 6, 2004

Week 2
Invoice No. 41: Clare Christenson
Invoice No. 42: Ramon Delpino
Invoice No. 43: Reuben Shapiro
Sales Receipt No. 23: Beverly Crandall
Invoice No. 44: Khalil Maskanian
Invoice No. 45: Constance Benson
Check No. 3: BH Auto Repairs
Check No. 4: Beverly Hills Stationers
Check No. 5: Beautiful Flowers
Invoice No. 45 (Corrected): Constance Benson
Deposit Summary, September 13, 2004
A/R Aging Detail, September 13, 2004

Week 3
Invoice No. 46: Clare Christenson
Petty Cash QuickReport, September 15, 2004 (May be in Portrait or Landscape)
Sales Receipt No. 24: Beverly Crandall
Check 6: Paycheck for Gail Hsing
Check 7: Paycheck for Greta Billesdon
Invoice No. 47: Khalil Maskanian
Sales Receipt No. 25: Jackson Greene
Invoice No. 48: Clare Christenson
Customer Balance Summary
Deposit Summary, September 20, 2004

Week 4
Sales Receipt No. 26: Beverly Crandall
Petty Cash QuickReport, September 23, 2004 (May be in Portrait or Landscape)
Credit Memo No. 49: Clare Christenson
Invoice No. 50: Brian Edmunds
Invoice No. 51: George Anderson
Check No. 8: Beverly Hills Stationers
Invoice No. 52: Reuben Shapiro
Check No. 9: Beverly Hills Telephone
Check No. 10: Rentals for You
Check No. 11: California Water
Check No. 12: Beverly Hills Power
Unpaid Bills Detail, September 27, 2004
Check No. 13: Beautiful Flowers
Check Detail, September 1-27, 2004
Deposit Summary, September 27, 2004
Customer Balance Detail
Check No. 14: Pamela Deschamps
Check No. 10 (Corrected): Rentals for You
Check 15: Paycheck for Gail Hsing
Check 16: Paycheck for Greta Billesdon
Payroll Transactions by Payee
Bank Reconciliation Report
Journal, September 2004
Trial Balance, September 30, 2004
Cash Flow Forecast, September 2004
Statement of Cash Flows, September 2004
Profit and Loss, September 2004
Balance Sheet, September 30, 2004
Balance Sheet (After adjustment for net income), September 30, 2004

SALES AND RECEIVABLES: MERCHANDISING BUSINESS

LEARNING OBJECTIVES

At the completion of this chapter, you will be able to:

1. Enter sales transactions for a retail business.
2. Prepare invoices that use sales tax, have sales discounts, and exceed a customer's credit limit.
3. Prepare transactions for cash sales with sales tax.
4. Add new accounts to the Chart of Accounts and new sales items to the Item List.
5. Add new customers and modify existing customer records.
6. Delete and void invoices.
7. Prepare credit memos with and without refunds.
8. Record customer payments on account with and without discounts.
9. Deposit checks and credit card receipts for sales and customer payments.
10. Customize report preferences and prepare and print Customer Balance Detail Reports, Open Invoice Reports, and Sales Reports.
11. View a QuickReport and use the QuickZoom feature.
12. Use the Customer Center to obtain information regarding credit customers.
13. Use the Customer Detail Center to obtain information for an individual customer.
14. Prepare accounts receivable and sales graphs.

ACCOUNTING FOR SALES AND RECEIVABLES IN A MERCHANDISING BUSINESS

Rather than using a traditional Sales Journal to record transactions using debits and credits and special columns, QuickBooks Pro uses an invoice to record sales transactions for accounts receivable in the Accounts Receivable Register. Because cash sales do not involve accounts receivable, a Sales Receipt is prepared, and QuickBooks Pro puts the money from a cash sale into the Undeposited Funds account until a deposit to a bank account is made. Instead of being recorded within special journals, cash receipt transactions are entered as activities. However, all transactions, regardless of the activity, are placed in the Journal behind the scenes. A new account, sales item, or customer can be added *on the fly* as transactions are entered. Customer information may be changed by editing the Customer List.

For a retail business, QuickBooks Pro tracks inventory, maintains information on reorder limits, tracks the quantity of merchandise on hand, maintains information on the value of the inventory, and can inform you of the percentage of sales for each inventory item. Discounts to certain types of customers can be given as well as early-payment discounts. Different price levels may be created for sales items and/or customers.

Unlike many computerized accounting programs, QuickBooks Pro makes error correction easy. A sales form may be edited, voided, or deleted in the same window where it was created or via an account register. If a sales form has been printed prior to correction, it may be reprinted after the correction has been made.

A multitude of reports are available when using QuickBooks Pro. Accounts receivable reports include Customer Balance Summary and Customer Balance Detail reports. Sales reports provide information regarding the amount of sales by item. Transaction Reports by Customer are available as well as the traditional accounting reports such as Trial Balance, Profit and Loss, and Balance Sheet. QuickBooks Pro also has graphing capabilities so that you can see and evaluate your accounts receivable and sales at the click of a button. Reports created in QuickBooks Pro may be exported to Microsoft® Excel.

TRAINING TUTORIAL

The following tutorial is a step-by-step guide to recording receivables (both cash and credit) for a fictitious company with fictitious employees. This company is called Year Round Sports. In addition to recording transactions using QuickBooks Pro, you will prepare several reports and graphs for Year Round Sports. The tutorial for Year Round Sports will continue in Chapters 6 and 7, when accounting for payables, bank reconciliations, financial statement preparation, and closing an accounting period for a merchandising business will be completed.

COMPANY PROFILE: YEAR ROUND SPORTS

Year Round Sports is a sporting goods store located in Mammoth Lakes, California. Previously, the company was open only during the winter. As a result Year Round Sports specializes in equipment, clothing, and accessories for skiing and snowboarding. They have plans to expand into year-round operation and will eventually provide merchandise for summer sports and activities. The company is a partnership between Andy McBride and Tim Bailey. Each partner has a 50 percent share of the business, and both devote all of their efforts to Year Round Sports. They have several part-time employees who work in the evenings and on the weekends during ski season. There is a full-time bookkeeper and manager, Rhonda Spears, who oversees purchases, maintains the inventory, and keeps the books for the company.

OPEN A COMPANY—YEAR ROUND SPORTS

As in previous chapters, make a duplicate of **Year Round.qbw** to a new disk labeled **Year Round**, access QuickBooks Pro, and open the company.

DO: Start the computer
Insert your **Year Round** data disk in **A:**
Access QuickBooks Pro
Open the company Year Round Sports

VERIFYING AN OPEN COMPANY

DO: Verify the title bar heading:

Year Round Sports--Your Name - QuickBooks Pro 2004

ADD YOUR NAME TO THE COMPANY NAME

As with previous companies, each student in the course will be working for the same company and printing the same documents. Personalizing the company name to include your name will help identify many of the documents you print during your training.

DO: Add your name to the company name
Click **Company** on the menu bar
Click **Company Info**
Click to the right of **Year Round Sports**
Drag through the word **Your Name** to highlight
Type **–your real name**
- Type your real name, *not* the words *Your Real Name*. For example, Pamela Iverson would type—**Pamela Iverson**.

Click **OK**
- The title bar now shows Year Round Sports—Student's Name.

BEGINNING THE TUTORIAL

In this chapter you will be entering both accounts receivable transactions and cash sales transactions for a retail company that charges its customers sales tax. Much of the organization of QuickBooks Pro is dependent on lists. The two primary types of lists you will use in the tutorial for receivables are a Customer List and a Sales Item List.

The names, addresses, telephone numbers, credit terms, credit limits, balances, and tax terms for all established credit customers are contained in the Customer List. The Customer List is also the Accounts Receivable Ledger. You will be using the following Customer List for established credit customers:

Sales are often made up of various types of income. In Year Round Sports there are several income accounts. In addition, there are sales categories within an income account. For example, each sales item represents an inventory item and is a subaccount of an income account—Ski Boots is a sales item and is a subaccount of Equipment Income. QuickBooks Pro uses lists to organize sales items. Using lists for sales items allows for flexibility in billing and a more accurate representation of the way in which income is earned. If the company charges a standard price for an item, the price of the item will be included on the list. In Year Round Sports, all items sell at different prices, so the price given for each item is listed at 0.00. In a retail business with an inventory, the number of units on hand can be tracked; and, when the amount on hand gets to a predetermined limit, an order can be placed. The following Item List for the various types of merchandise and sales categories will be used for Year Round Sports:

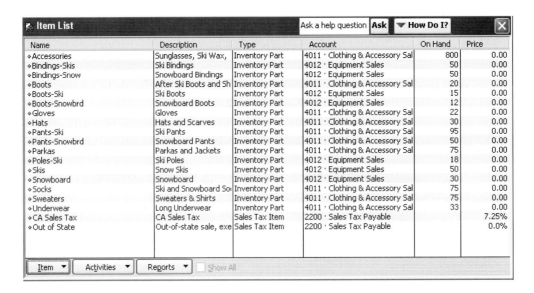

As in previous chapters, all transactions are listed on memos. The transaction date will be the same date as the memo date unless otherwise specified within the transaction. Customer names, when necessary, will be given in the transaction. Unless otherwise specified, all terms for customers on account are Net 30 days. If a memo contains more than one transaction, there will be a horizontal line separating the transactions.

Even when you are instructed to enter a transaction step by step, you should always refer to the memo for transaction details. Once a specific type of transaction has been entered in a step-by-step manner, additional transactions will be made without having instructions provided. Of course, you may always refer to instructions given for previous transactions for ideas or for steps used to enter those transactions.

CUSTOMIZE REPORT FORMAT

The report format used in one company may not be appropriate for all companies that use QuickBooks Pro. The preferences selected in QuickBooks Pro are only for the current company. In Section 1 of the text, report preferences were changed for Contempo Computer Consulting, but those changes have no effect on Year Round Sports. The header/footer for reports in Year Round Sports must be customized to eliminate the printing of the current date as part of a report heading.

MEMO
DATE: January 1, 2004

Before recording any transactions or preparing any reports, customize the report format by removing the date prepared, time prepared, and report basis from report headings. In addition, have reports refresh automatically.

DO: Customize the report preferences as indicated in the memo
Click **Edit**, click **Preferences**
Scroll through the items listed on the left side of the screen until you get to
    Reports and Graphs
Click **Reports and Graphs**
On the **My Preferences** tab, click **Refresh automatically**
Click the **Company Preferences** tab
Click the **Format** button
Click the **Header/Footer** tab
Click **Date Prepared**, **Time Prepared**, and **Report Basis** to deselect

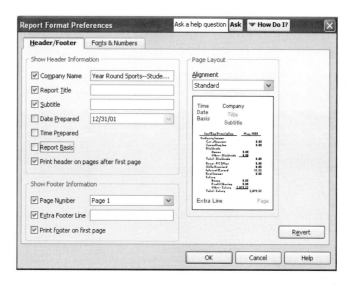

Click **OK** to save the change
Click **OK** to close **Preferences**

CUSTOMIZE BUSINESS FORMS

In QuickBooks it is possible to customize the business forms used in recording transactions. In earlier chapters some student names did not print on the same line as the company name. In order to provide more room for the company title, QuickBooks' Layout Designer must be used. When you access an invoice, for example, QuickBooks uses a ready-made form. This is called a *template*. In order to make changes to a template, you must first duplicate the template and then make changes to it. Other business forms may be changed without duplicating the form.

MEMO

DATE: January 2, 2004

Customize the Sales Receipt form, the Credit Memo form, and the template used for Product Invoices.

 DO: Customize the Sales Receipt and the Product Invoice
Open a **Sales Receipt** as previously instructed
Click the **Customize** button next to Template
Click the **Edit** button on the Customize Template dialog box

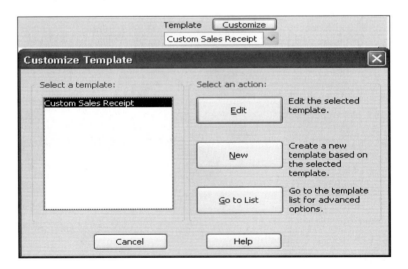

Click the **Layout Designer** button on the Customize Sales Receipt screen
Point to the black squares (sizing handles) on the frame around Sales Receipt
When the cursor turns into a double arrow, hold the primary (left) mouse button
and drag until the size of the frame begins at **6** on the ruler bar

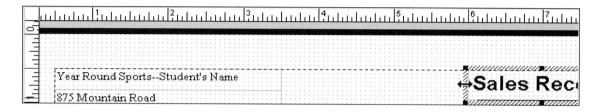

Click **Year Round Sports—Student's Name**
Drag the border of the frame until it is a **5 ¾** on the ruler bar

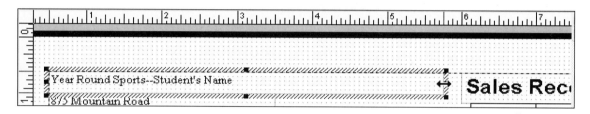

Click **OK** on Layout Designer
Click **OK** on Customize Sales Receipt
Close the **Enter Sales Receipts** screen
Click **Lists** on the menu bar
Click **Templates**

- *Note:* The Custom Sales Receipt has been added to the Template list

From the Templates List repeat the steps previously listed to customize the Credit Memo

When finished with the customization of the Credit Memo, click **Intuit Product Invoice**

Click the **Templates** button

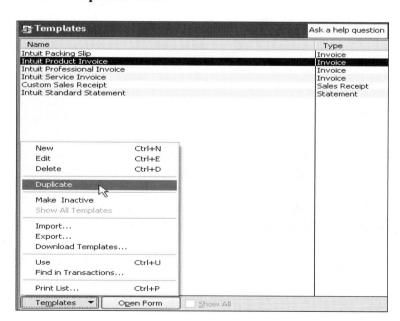

Click **Duplicate**

On the Select Template Type make sure Invoice is selected and click **OK**

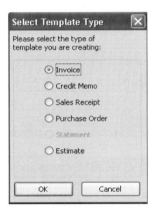

Make sure **DUP: Intuit Product Invoice** is selected

Click the **Templates** button, click **Edit**
    OR
Ctrl+E

Click the **Layout Designer** button and change the layout as instructed for Sales
    Receipts

Click **OK** until you return to the Template List
Close the Template List

ENTER SALES ON ACCOUNT

Because QuickBooks Pro operates on a business form premise, a sale on account is entered via
an invoice. When you sell merchandise on account, you prepare an invoice including sales tax
and payment terms and QuickBooks Pro records the transaction in the Journal and updates the

customer's account automatically. QuickBooks allows you to set up different price levels for customers. Since our small company has not established sales prices for each item it sells, we will not be using Price Levels in this tutorial. For information on Price Levels, refer to Appendix C.

MEMO

DATE: January 2, 2004

Bill the following: Invoice No. 1—An established customer, Rick Woods, purchased a pair of after-ski boots for $75.00 on account. Terms are Net 15.

 DO: Record the sale on account shown in the invoice above. This invoice is used to bill a customer for a sale using one sales item:

Access a blank invoice as previously instructed in Chapter 2

Click the drop-down list arrow next to **Customer:Job**

Click **Woods, Rick**

Click the drop-down list arrow next to Intuit Product Invoice

Click **DUP: Intuit Product Invoice** to use your customized invoice

Tab to **Date**

- When you tab to the date, it will be highlighted. When you type in the new date, the highlighted date will be deleted.

Type **01/02/2004** as the date

Invoice No. 1 should be showing in the **Invoice No.** box

There is no PO No. to record

Terms should be indicated as **Net 15**

- If not, click the drop-down list arrow next to **Terms** and click **Net 15**

Tab to or click **Quantity**

Type **1**

- The quantity is one because you are billing for one pair of after-ski boots.

Tab to or click the first line beneath **Item Code**

Click the drop-down list arrow next to **Item Code**

- Refer to the memo above and the Item list for appropriate billing information.

Click **Boots** to bill for one pair of after-ski boots

- The Description *After Ski Boots and Shoes* is automatically inserted.

Tab to or click **Price Each**

- If necessary, highlight the 0.00 amount shown by holding down the primary mouse button and dragging through the amount. Press the **Delete** key.

Type in the amount of the after-ski boots **75**

- Because the price on ski boots differs with each style, QuickBooks Pro has not been given the price in advance. It must be inserted during the invoice preparation. If you chose to set up separate sales items for each type of ski boot, sales prices could and should be assigned. In addition, different price levels could be given for the item.

Click in the box for **Customer Message**

- QuickBooks Pro will automatically calculate the total in the **Amount** column.
- Because this is a taxable item, QuickBooks Pro inserts **Tax** in the **Tax** column.

Click the drop-down list arrow next to **Customer Message**

Click **Thank you for your business.**

- Message is inserted in the **Customer Message** box.
- Notice that QuickBooks Pro automatically calculates the tax for the invoice and adds it to the invoice total.

EDIT AND CORRECT ERRORS

If an error is discovered while entering invoice information, position the cursor in the field containing the error. As in previous chapters, you may do this by positioning the mouse pointer in the field and clicking the primary key, by tabbing to move forward through each field, or pressing Shift+Tab to move back to the field containing the error. If the error is highlighted, type the correction. If the error is not highlighted, you can correct the error by pressing the Backspace or the Delete key as many times as necessary to remove the error, then typing the correction. (*Alternate method*: point to error, highlight by dragging the mouse through the error, then type the correction.)

DO: If you are not comfortable correcting errors, do the following on Invoice No. 1:
Click the drop-down list arrow next to **Customer:Job**
Click **Chau, Mei-Hwa**

- If the message, "Switching between customers may alter tax codes" appears, click **OK**.
- Name is changed in Customer:Job, and Bill To information is also changed.

Click to the left of the first number in the **Date**—this is **0**

Hold down primary mouse button and drag through the date to highlight.

Type **11/19/2004** as the date

- This removes the 01/02/2004 date originally entered.

Click to the right of the **1** in **Quantity**

Backspace and type a **2**

To eliminate the changes made to Invoice No. 1, click the drop-down list arrow next to **Customer:Job**

Click **Woods, Rick**

Click the cursor so it is in front of the **1** in the **Date**

Press the **Delete** until the date is removed

Type **01/02/2004**

Click to the right of the **2** in **Quantity**

Backspace and type a **1**

Press the **Tab** key

- This will cause QuickBooks Pro to calculate the amount and the total for the invoice and will move the cursor to the **Description** field.
- Invoice No. 1 has been returned to the correct customer, date, and quantity.

Compare the information you entered with the information provided in the memo and on the following:

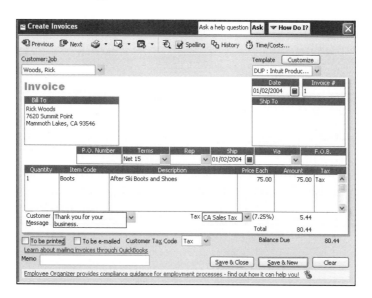

PRINT AN INVOICE

DO: With Invoice No. 1 on the screen, print the invoice immediately after entering the corrected information

Click **Print** at the top of the **Create Invoices** screen

If you get a message regarding printing Shipping Labels, click **OK**

Check the information on the **Print One Invoice Settings** tab:

Printer name (should identify the type of printer you are using):

Printer Type: Page-oriented (Single sheets)

Print On: Blank paper

Do not print lines around each field check box: should not have a check mark

- If there is a check mark in the box, lines will not print around each field.
- If a check is not in the box, lines will print around each field.

Number of Copies should be 1

Click the **Print** button

- This initiates the printing of the invoice through QuickBooks Pro. However, because not all classroom configurations are the same, check with your instructor for specific printing instructions.
- When the form has been printed, you will return to the invoice.

Click the **Save & New** button on the bottom of the **Create Invoices** screen to record the invoice and go to a blank invoice

ENTER TRANSACTIONS USING MORE THAN ONE SALES ITEM AND SALES TAX

Frequently, sales to customers will be for more than one item. For example, new bindings are usually purchased along with a new pair of skis. Invoices can be prepared to bill a customer for several items at once.

MEMO

DATE: January 3, 2004

Bill the following: Invoice No. 2—Every year Dr. Jose Morales gets new ski equipment. Bill him for his equipment purchase for this year: skis, $425; bindings, $175; ski boots, $250; and ski poles, $75.

DO: Record a transaction on account for a sale involving several taxable sales items:

Click the drop-down list arrow next to **Customer:Job**

Click **Morales, Jose Dr.**

- Name is entered as Customer:Job and Bill To information is completed automatically.

Verify the Template as **DUP: Intuit Product Invoice**

Tab to or click **Date**

Delete the current date, if showing

- Refer to instructions for Invoice No. 1 or to editing practice if necessary.

Type **01/03/04** as the date

Make sure the number **2** is showing in the **Invoice No.** box

There is no PO No. to record

Terms should be indicated as **2% 10 Net 30**

Tab to or click **Quantity**

Type **1**

Tab to or click the first line beneath **Item Code**

- Refer to memo and Item List for appropriate billing information.

Click the drop-down list arrow next to **Item Code**

Click **Skis**

- **Skis** is inserted as the item code.
- **Snow Skis** is inserted as the **Description**.

Tab to or click **Price Each**

Delete **0.00**

Enter **425**

- Total is automatically calculated when you go to the next line. Notice that the amount is $425.00.
- Notice that the **Customer is taxable** because the Customer Tax Code indicates **Tax**.
- Because Dr. Morales is a taxable customer, sales tax is indicated by **Tax** in the **Tax** column.

Tab to or click the second line for **Quantity**

Type **1**

Tab to or click the second line for **Item Code**

Click the drop-down list arrow next to **Item Code**

Click **Bindings-Skis**

- **Ski Bindings** is inserted as the **Description**.

Tab to or click **Price Each**

Delete **0.00**

Enter **175**

- Total is automatically calculated when you go to the next line. Notice that the amount is $175.00.
- Notice that sales tax is indicated by **Tax** in the **Tax** column.

Repeat the above steps to enter the information for the ski boots and the ski poles

Click the drop-down list arrow next to **Customer Message**

Click **Thank you for your business.**

- Message is inserted in the Customer Message box.
- Notice that QuickBooks Pro automatically calculates the tax for the invoice and adds it to the invoice total.

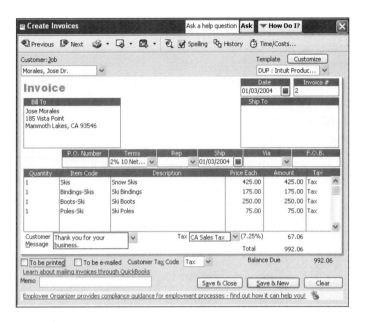

Print the invoice by following the instructions provided for Invoice No. 1

E-MAIL INVOICES

In addition to printing and mailing invoices, QuickBooks® Pro 2004 allows invoices to be sent to customers e-mail. While this text will not actually require sending invoice by e-mail, it is important to be aware of this time-saving feature of QuickBooks.

DO: Explore e-mailing an invoice:
Click the drop-down list arrow next to **Send**
Click **E-mail Invoice**
- Notice that the e-mail text has automatically been completed.
- Look at the message that will accompany the electronic copy of the invoice.

Click **Cancel**

PREPARE INVOICES WITHOUT STEP-BY-STEP INSTRUCTIONS

MEMO **DATE:** January 3, 2004
Bill the following: <u>Invoice No. 3</u>—We give Mountain Schools a special rate on equipment and clothing for the ski team. This year the school purchases 5 pairs of skis, $299 each; 5 pairs of bindings, $100 each; and 5 sets of ski poles, $29 each. Terms 2/10 Net 30.
<u>Invoice No. 4</u>—Sally Princeton purchased a new ski outfit: 1 parka, $249; a hat, $25; a sweater, $125; 1 pair of ski pants, $129; long underwear, $68; ski gloves, $79; ski socks, $15.95; sunglasses, $89.95; and a matching ski boot carrier, $2.95. Terms Net 15.
<u>Invoice No. 5</u>—Trent Trudeau broke his snowboard when he was going down his favorite run, Dragon's Back. He purchased a new one without bindings for $499.95, Terms 1/10 Net 30.
<u>Invoice No. 6</u>—Rick Woods decided to buy some new powder skis and bindings. Bill him for snow skis, $599, and ski bindings, $179. Terms Net 15.

DO: If Invoice 2 is still on the screen, click **Next**

Enter the four transactions in the memo above. Refer to instructions given for the two previous transactions entered.

- Always use the Item List to determine the appropriate sales items for billing.
- Use *Thank you for your business.* as the message for these invoices.
- If you make an error, correct it.
- If you get a suggestion from Spell check; i.e., **Snowboard**, and the word is spelled correctly, click **Ignore All**.
- Print each invoice immediately after you enter the information for it, and print lines around each field.
- To go from one invoice to the next, click **Save & New** at the bottom of the **Create Invoices** screen or click **Next** at the top of the invoice.

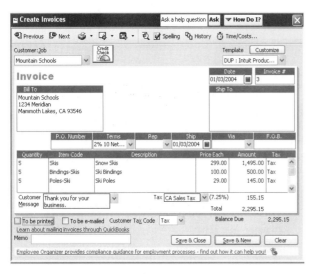

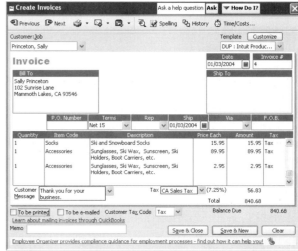

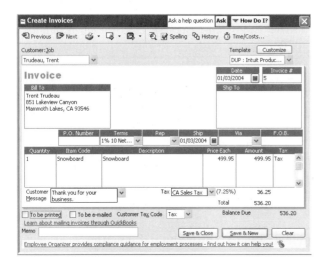

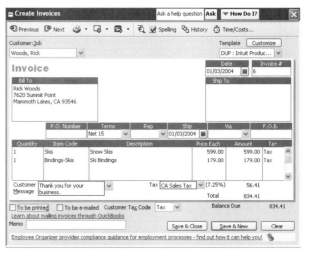

ENTER A TRANSACTION EXCEEDING A CUSTOMER'S CREDIT LIMIT AND ADD A WORD TO THE SPELLING DICTIONARY

When a customer is added to the Customer List and a complete setup is performed, the file tab for Additional Info will appear. Additional Info contains a dialog box in which a credit limit can be established for a customer. QuickBooks Pro does allow transactions for a customer to exceed the established credit limit, but a dialog box appears with information regarding the transaction amount and the credit limit for a customer.

As was experienced in the last set of transactions, QuickBooks Pro has a spelling check. When the previous invoices were printed, QuickBooks Spell Check identified snowboard as being misspelled. In fact, the word is spelled correctly. It just needs to be added to the QuickBooks dictionary. This is done by clicking the Add button when the word is highlighted in spell check.

MEMO

DATE: January 5, 2004

Bill the following: Invoice No. 7—Mei-Hwa Chau decided to get a new snowboard, $489.95; bindings, $159.99; snowboard boots, $249; and a special case to carry her boots, $49.95. Terms are Net 30.

DO: Prepare and print Invoice No. 7 as instructed previously
- Always use the Item List to determine the appropriate sales items for billing.
- Use Thank *you for your business.* as the message for the invoice.
- If you make an error, correct it.
- Print the invoice immediately after you enter the information for it.
- Print lines around each field.

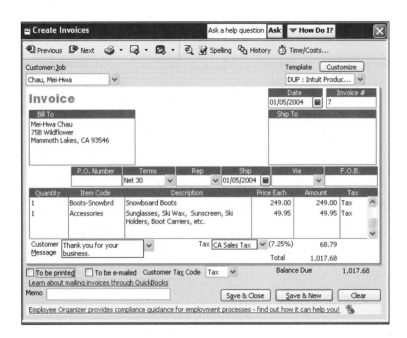

Click **Save & Close** after Invoice No. 7 has been entered and printed.

- If you click **No**, you are returned to the invoice in order to make changes.
- If you click Yes, the transaction is recorded.

Click **Yes** to record the transaction

When the **Check Spelling on Form** appears and the word **Snowboard** is highlighted, click the **Add** button

ACCOUNTS RECEIVABLE REPORTS

A variety of reports are available regarding accounts receivable. Data regarding customers may be displayed on the basis of account aging, open invoices, collections reports, customer balances, or they may be itemized according to the sales by customer. Many reports may be printed in a summarized form while other reports provide detailed information.

PREPARE CUSTOMER BALANCE DETAIL REPORT

The Customer Balance Detail Report lists information regarding each customer. The information provided for each customer includes all invoices on which there is a balance, the date of the invoice, the invoice number, the account used to record the invoice, the amount of each invoice, the balance after each invoice, and the total balance due from each customer.

MEMO

DATE: January 5, 2004

Prepare and print a Customer Balance Detail Report so that the owners can see exactly how much each customer owes to Year Round Sports.

 DO: Prepare a Customer Balance Detail Report for all customers for all transactions:

Click **Reports** on the menu bar, point to **Customers & Receivables**, click
  Customer Balance Detail
  OR
Click **Customer Balance Detail** in the Memorized Reports section of the
  Customers Navigator
- *Note:* When opening a report in this manner, the date prepared, time prepared, and report basis are shown. These will need to be removed by modifying the report header/footer.
  OR
Use Report Finder on a QuickBooks Navigator:
  Click **Report Finder** on a QuickBooks Navigator
  Select **Customers & Receivables** as the type of report, click **Customer
    Balance Detail**, click **Display**
  Dates should be **All**
- If not, click the drop-down list arrow next to the **Dates** text box, click **All**.
- Scroll through the report. See how much each customer owes for each invoice.
- Notice that the amount owed by Mei-Hwa Chau for Invoice No. 7 is $1,017.68 and that her total balance is $1,071.25.
Do not close the **Customer Balance Detail Report**

USE THE QUICKZOOM FEATURE

QuickZoom is a feature of QuickBooks Pro that allows you to view additional information within a report. For example, an invoice may be viewed when the Customer Balance Detail Report is on the screen simply by using the QuickZoom feature.

MEMO
DATE: January 5, 2004

The bookkeeper, Rhonda Spears, could not remember if Invoice No. 7 was for ski equipment or snowboard equipment. With the Customer Balance Detail Report on the screen, use QuickZoom to view Invoice No. 7.

DO: Use QuickZoom to view Invoice No. 7
Position the cursor over any part of the report showing information about Invoice
No. 7
- The cursor will turn into a magnifying glass with a letter **Z** inside.
  Double-click
- Invoice No. 7 appears on the screen.
- Check to make sure the four items on the invoice are: Snowboard, Bindings-Snow, Boots-Snowbrd, and Accessories.
  With Invoice No. 7 on the screen, proceed to the next section.

CORRECT AN INVOICE AND PRINT THE CORRECTED FORM

QuickBooks Pro allows corrections and revisions to an invoice even if the invoice has been printed. The invoice may be corrected by going directly to the original invoice or by accessing the original invoice via the Accounts Receivable Register. An invoice can be on view in QuickZoom and still be corrected.

MEMO
DATE: January 5, 2004

While viewing Invoice No. 7 for Mei-Hwa Chau in QuickZoom, the bookkeeper, Rhonda Spears, realizes that the snowboard should be $499.95, not the $489.95 that is on the original invoice. Make the correction and reprint the invoice.

DO: Correct Invoice No. 7 while showing on the screen in QuickZoom

Click in the **Price Each** column

Change the amount to **499.95**

Press Tab to change the **Amount** calculated for the Snowboard

Print the corrected Invoice No. 7

Click **Save & Close** at the bottom of the **Create Invoice** screen to record and close the invoice

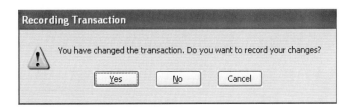

When the **Recording Transaction** message box appears, click **Yes**

A **Recording Transaction** message box appears on the screen regarding the credit limit of $500 for Mei-Hwa Chau

Click **Yes** to accept the current balance of $1,081.98

- This closes the invoice and returns you to the Customer Balance Detail Report.
- Notice that the total amount for Invoice No. 7 is $1,028.41 and that Mei-Hwa Chau's total balance is $1,081.98

Click **Print** at the top of the **Customer Balance Detail Report**

Complete the information on the **Print Report Settings** tab:

Print to: The selected item should be **Printer**

Orientation: Click **Portrait** to select Portrait orientation for this report

Page Range: **All** should be selected; if it is not, click **All**

Smart page breaks should be selected

Do not select **Fit report to one page wide**

Click **Print** on the **Print Reports** screen

After the report is printed, click **Close** to close the **Customer Balance Detail Report**

Year Round Sports--Student's Name
Customer Balance Detail
All Transactions

Type	Date	Num	Account	Amount	Balance
Chau, Mei-Hwa					
Invoice	12/31/2003		1200 · Accounts R...	53.57	53.57
Invoice	01/05/2004	7	1200 · Accounts R...	1,028.41	1,081.98
Total Chau, Mei-Hwa				1,081.98	1,081.98
Childers, Irene Dr.					
Invoice	12/31/2003		1200 · Accounts R...	417.00	417.00
Total Childers, Irene Dr.				417.00	417.00
Clary, Anne					
Invoice	12/31/2003		1200 · Accounts R...	455.00	455.00
Total Clary, Anne				455.00	455.00

ADDING NEW ACCOUNTS TO THE CHART OF ACCOUNTS

Because account needs can change as a business is in operation, QuickBooks Pro allows you to make changes to the Chart of Accounts at any time. Some changes to the Chart of Accounts require additional changes to other lists, such as the Item List. An account may be added by accessing the Chart of Accounts. It is also possible to add an account to the Chart of Accounts while adding an item to another list.

ADD NEW ITEMS TO LIST

In order to accommodate the changing needs of a business, all QuickBooks Pro lists allow you to make changes at any time. New items may be added to the list via the Item List or *on the fly* while entering invoice information. The Item List stores information about the items Year Round Sports sells. Since Year Round Sports does not use price levels, it would be appropriate to have an item allowing for sales discounts. Having a discount item allows discounts to be recorded on the sales form. A discount can be a fixed amount or a percentage. A discount is calculated only on the line above it on the sales form. To allow the entire amount of the invoice to receive the discount, an item for a subtotal will also need to be added. When you complete the sales form, the subtotal item will appear before the discount item.

MEMO
DATE: January 5, 2004

Add an item for Sales Discounts and a Subtotal Item. Add a new expense account, 6130 Sales Discount, to the Chart of Accounts. The description for the account should be Discount on Sales.

DO: Use QuickBooks Navigator for Customer:
> Click **Customers** on the Navigator list
> Click **Items & Services** folder on the QuickBooks' Customers Navigator

Click **Item** button at the bottom of the **Item List** screen
Click **New**
Item Type is **Discount**
Tab to or click **Item Name/Number**
Type **Nonprofit Discount**
Tab to or click **Description**
Type **10% Discount to Nonprofit Agencies**
Tab to or click **Amount or %**
Type in **10%**
- The % sign must be included in order to differentiate between a $10 discount and a 10% discount.

Click the drop-down list arrow for **Account**
Type **Sales Discount**
- **Account Not Found** dialog box appears on the screen.

Click **Set Up** on the **Account Not Found** dialog box
Complete the information for a New Account:
> **Type** should be **Expense**
> - If **not**, click the drop-down list arrow next to the text box for Type.
> - **Click Expense**.
> Tab to or click in the **Number** text box
> Enter the Account Number **6130**
> Tab to or click **Name**

Type **Sales Discounts**
Tab to or click **Description**
Enter **Discount on Sales**
Click **OK** to add the **Sales Discounts** account and close the **New Account** dialog box

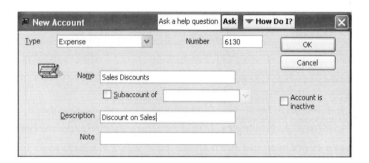

- At the bottom of the screen you should see the Tax Code as **Tax** and the statement **Discount is applied before sales tax** should be displayed.

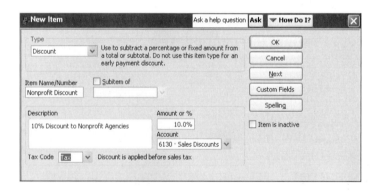

Click **Next** on the **New Item** dialog box

- A **discount** is calculated only on the line above it on the sales form. To allow the entire amount of the invoice to receive the discount, an item for a subtotal will also need to be added.

Repeat the steps for adding a New Item to add **Subtotal**
Type should be **Subtotal**
Item Name/Number is **Subtotal**
The description is **Subtotal**

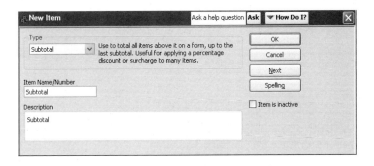

Click **OK** to add the new items and to close the **New Item** screen

- Verify the addition of Nonprofit Discount and Subtotal on the Item List. If everything is correct, close the **Item List**.
- If you find an error, click on the item with the error, click the **Item** button, click **Edit**, make corrections as needed.

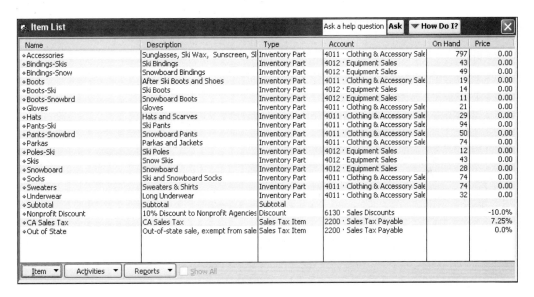

Close the **Item List**

CORRECT AN INVOICE TO INCLUDE SALES DISCOUNT

> **MEMO**
> **DATE:** January 6, 2004
>
> Now that the appropriate accounts for sales discounts have been created, use the Accounts Receivable Register to correct Invoice 3 for Mountain Schools to give the schools a 10% discount as a nonprofit organization.

DO: Correct invoice to Mountain Schools by opening the Chart of Accounts

Use the keyboard shortcut, **Ctrl+A**

OR

Click **Lists** on the menu bar, click **Chart of Accounts**

OR

Use QuickBooks Navigator:

Click **Company** on the Navigator list

Click **Chart of Accounts**

In the Chart of Accounts, click **Accounts Receivable**

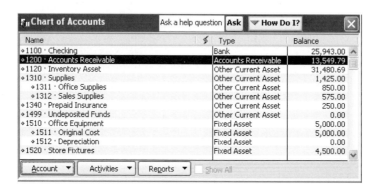

Double-click **Accounts Receivable**

OR

Click **Activities**

Click **Use Register**

- The **Accounts Receivable Register** appears on the screen with information regarding each transaction entered into the account.

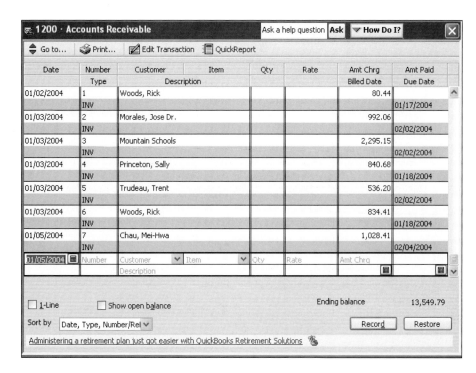

If necessary, scroll through the register until the transaction for **Invoice No. 3** is on the screen

- **Look** at the **Number/Type** column to identify the number of the invoice and the type of transaction.
  - On the **Number** line you will see a <u>check number</u> or an <u>invoice number</u>.
  - On **the Type** line **PMT** indicates a payment was received on account, and **INV** indicates a sale on account.

Click anywhere in the transaction for Invoice No. 3 to Mountain Schools

Click **Edit Transaction** at the top of the register

- Invoice No. 3 appears on the screen.

Click in **Item Code** beneath the last item, Poles-Ski

Click the drop-down list arrow for **Item Code**

Click **Subtotal**

- You may need to scroll through the Item List until you find Subtotal.
- Remember that QuickBooks Pro must subtotal the items on the invoice in order to calculate a discount on all items on the invoice.

Tab to or click the next blank line in **Item Code**

Click **Nonprofit Discount**

- You may need to scroll through the Item List until you find Nonprofit Discount.

Click **Print** on the **Create Invoices** screen to print a corrected invoice

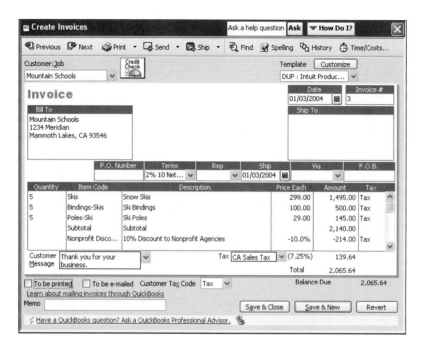

- Notice the subtotal of $2,140.00, the discount of $214, and the new invoice total of $2,065.64.

Click **Save & Close** on the **Create Invoices** screen to save the corrected invoice and return to the Accounts Receivable Register

Click **Yes** on the **Recording Transaction** screen

- Notice the new Amt Chg of $2,065.64 for Invoice No. 3 in the register.

Do not close the **Accounts Receivable Register**

VIEW A QUICKREPORT

After editing the invoice and returning to the register, you may get a detailed report regarding the customer's transactions by clicking the QuickReport button.

DO: With the cursor in Invoice No. 3, click **QuickReport** button to view the **Mountain Schools** account

ANALYZE THE QUICKREPORT FOR MOUNTAIN SCHOOLS

DO: Notice that the total of Invoice No. 3 is $2,065.64

Year Round Sports--Student's Name
Register QuickReport
All Transactions

Type	Date	Num	Memo	Account	Paid	Open Balance	Amount
Mountain Schools							
Invoice	01/03/2004	3		1200 · Accounts Receivable	Unpaid	2,065.64	2,065.64
Total Mountain Schools						2,065.64	2,065.64
TOTAL						2,065.64	2,065.64

Close the **QuickReport** without printing
Close the **Accounts Receivable Register**
Close the **Chart of Accounts**

ADD A NEW CUSTOMER

QuickBooks Pro allows customers to be added at any time. They may be added to the company records through the Customer List, or they may be added *on the fly* as you create an invoice or sales receipt. When adding *on the fly*, you may choose between Quick Add (used to add only a customer's name) and Set Up (used to add complete information for a customer).

Memo

DATE: January 8, 2004

Rhonda was instructed to add a new customer. The information provided for the new customer is: Mountain Recreation Center, 985 Old Mammoth Road, Mammoth Lakes, CA 93546, Contact: Kathleene Clark, Phone: 909-555-2951, Fax: 909-555-1592, E-mail: mountainrec@abc.com Terms: 1%10 Net 30, Tax Code is Tax, Tax Item: CA Sales Tax, Credit Limit: 5,000, as of 1/8/2004 there is a 0.00 opening balance for the customer.

DO: Add a new customer using the Customer:Job List
Click **List** menu, click **Customer:Jobs**
   OR
Use QuickBooks Navigator:
   Click **Customers** on the Navigator list, click the **Customers** icon
With the Customer List showing on the screen
   Use the keyboard shortcut **Ctrl+N** to create a new customer
      OR
   Click **Customer:Job** button at the bottom of the list, click **New**
In the **Customer** text box, enter **Mountain Recreation Center**

Tab to or click **Company Name**
Enter **Mountain Recreation Center**
Tab to or click the second line in **Bill To**
Enter the address listed above
Tab to or click **Contact**
Enter the name of the person to contact
Tab to or click **Phone**, enter the telephone number
Tab to or click **FAX**, enter the fax number
Tab to or click **E-mail**, enter the e-mail address

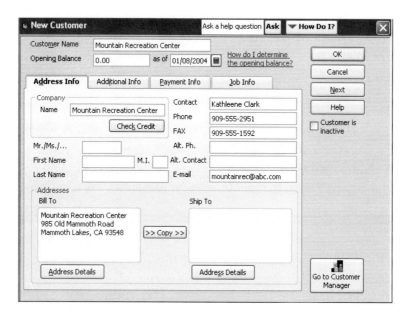

Click the **Additional Info** tab
Enter the terms and sales tax information for **Additional Info**

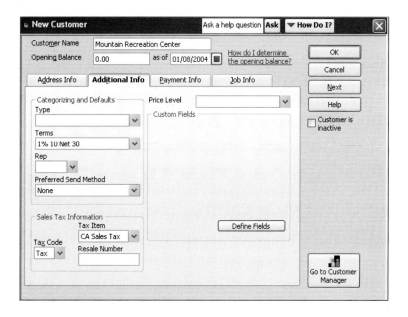

Click the **Payment Info** tab and enter the credit limit

Click **OK** to complete the addition of Mountain Recreation Center as a customer

- Verify the addition of Mountain Recreation Center to the Customer:Job List.

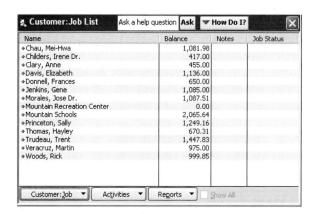

Close the **Customer:Job List**

RECORD A SALE TO A NEW CUSTOMER

Once a customer has been added, sales may be recorded for a customer.

> **MEMO**
> **DATE:** January 8, 2004
>
> Record a sale of 5 sleds at $119.99 each and 5 toboggans at $229.95 each to Mountain Recreation Center. Because the sale is to a nonprofit organization, include a nonprofit discount.

DO: Record the above sale on account to a new customer:
Click **Invoices** on the Navigator bar
> OR

Use QuickBooks Navigator:
> Click **Customers** on the Navigator bar, click **Invoices** on the Customer Navigator

Enter invoice information for **Mountain Recreation Center** as previously instructed
Date of the invoice is **01/08/2004**
Invoice No. is **8**
Tab to or click **Quantity**
Enter **5**
Tab to or click **Item Code**
Because sleds is not on the Item List, type **Sleds** for the **Item Code**, press **Enter**
Click **Set Up** on the **Item Not Found** dialog box

On the **New Item** screen, click **Inventory Part** for **Type**
- If necessary, click the drop-down list menu to get a list of choices for **Type**.

Item Name/Number should be **Sleds**
- If not, tab to or click in the text box for Item Name/Number, type **Sleds**.

Complete **Purchase Information**:
- This section provides information to be used for orders of sleds for Year Round Sports.

  Description on Purchase Transactions: enter **Sleds**
  Cost: 0.00

- • Year Round Sports has elected to keep the item list simple and not use different items for different styles and models of sleds. Thus, sleds are purchased at different prices so the Cost is left at 0.00.

    COGS Account: **5000 Cost of Goods Sold**
    - • If this account is not in the **COGS Account** text box, click the drop-down list arrow, click **5000 Cost of Goods Sold**.

    Preferred Vendor: Leave blank

Complete **Sales Information**:
- • This section provides the information used when Year Round Sports sells sleds to customers.

    Description on Sales Transactions: Should be **Sleds**
    - • If Sleds was not inserted at the same time as the Purchase Information Description, enter **Sleds** for the description.

    Sales Price: Leave 0.00
    - • Year Round Sports has elected to keep the item list simple and not use different items for different styles and models of sleds. Thus, sleds are sold at different prices; and the Sales Price remains as 0.00.

    Tax Code: Should be **Tax**
    - • If not, click the drop-down list arrow and click **Tax**.

    Click the drop-down list arrow for **Income Account**

    Click **4012 Equipment Sales**

Complete the **Inventory Information**:
- • QuickBooks Pro uses this information to track the amount of inventory on hand and to provide reorder information.

    Asset Account: Should be **1120 Inventory Asset**
    - • If this account is not in the Asset Account text box, click the drop-down list arrow, click **1120 Inventory Asset**.

    Tab to or click **Reorder Point**

    Enter **5**

    Tab to or click **Qty on Hand**

    Enter **10**

    Tab to or click **Total Value**
    - • Five of the ten sleds were purchased by Year Round Sports for $75 each. The other five sleds were purchased for $60 each.

    Enter **675** for the **Total Value**

    Tab to or click **As of**

    Enter the As of date of **01/08/04**

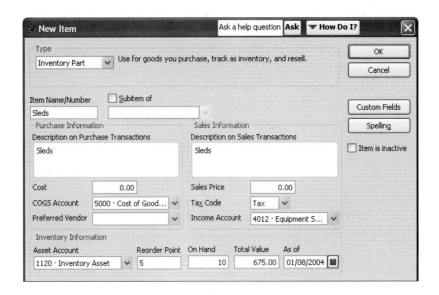

Click **OK** to add Sleds as a sales item

On the invoice, tab to or click **Price Each**

Enter **119.99**

Tab to or click the second line in **Quantity**

Enter **5**

Tab to or click **Item Code**

Click the drop-down list arrow for **Item Code**

- There is no item listed for Toboggans.

Click <**Add New**> at the top of the **Item List**

Complete the information for **New Item**

On the **New Item** screen, click **Inventory Part** for **Type**

- If necessary, click the drop-down list menu to get a list of choices for **Type**.

Tab to or click **Item Name/Number**

Enter **Toboggans**

Complete **Purchase Information**:

    Description on Purchase Transactions: Enter **Toboggans**

    Cost: **0.00**

    COGS Account: **5000 Cost of Goods Sold**

    Preferred Vendor: Leave blank

Complete **Sales Information**:

    Description on Sales Transactions: Should be **Toboggans**

    - If Toboggans was not inserted at the same time as the Purchase Information Description, enter **Toboggans** for the description.

    Sales Price: Leave **0.00**

    Tax Code: Should be **Tax**

Click the drop-down list arrow for **Income Account**

Click **4012 Equipment Sales**

Complete the **Inventory Information**:

Asset Account: Should be **1120 Inventory Asset**

- If this account is not in the **Asset Account** text box, click the drop-down list arrow, click **1120 Inventory Asset**.

Tab to or click **Reorder Point**

Enter **5**

Tab to or click **Qty on Hand**

Enter **10**

Tab to or click **Total Value**

- Five of the ten toboggans were purchased by Year Round Sports for $125 each. The other five toboggans were purchased for $150 each.

Enter **1375** for the **Total Value**

Tab to or click **As of**

Enter the As of date of **01/08/04**

Click **OK** to add Toboggans as a sales item

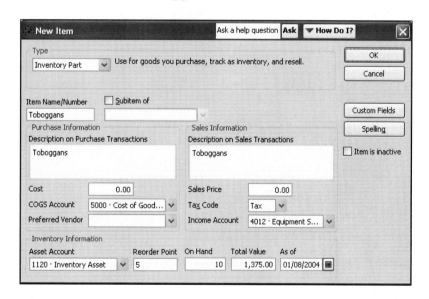

Complete the invoice

- Remember that Mountain Recreation Center is a nonprofit organization and is entitled to a Nonprofit Discount.

The message is **Thank you for your business.**

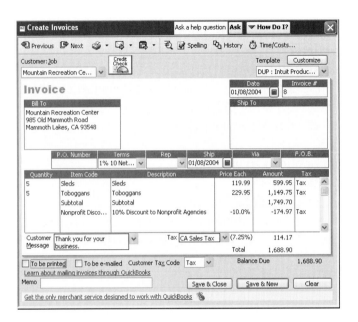

Print the invoice as previously instructed

Click **Save & Close** to record the invoice and close the transaction

MODIFY CUSTOMER RECORDS

Occasionally information regarding a customer will change. QuickBooks Pro allows customer accounts to be modified at any time by editing the Customer List.

MEMO

DATE: January 8, 2004

In order to update Mei-Hwa Chau's account, change her credit limit to $2,500.00.

DO: To edit the above account, access the **Customer List**

Access the **Customer List** by using one of the four methods listed:

Click **Lists** on the menu bar, click **Customer:Job**.

Use QuickBooks Navigator: Click **Customers** on the Navigator list, click the **Customers** folder.

Click Cust on the Icon bar.

Use the keyboard shortcut: **Ctrl+J**.

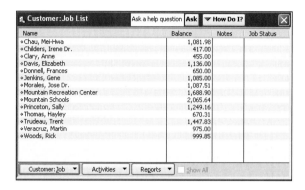

Access Mei-Hwa Chau's account in one of the following three ways:
> Click **Chau, Mei-Hwa** on the Customer:Job List, click **Customer:Job** button, click **Edit**.
>
> Click **Chau, Mei-Hwa** on the Customer:Job List, use the keyboard shortcut **Ctrl+E**.
>
> Double-click **Chau, Mei-Hwa** on the Customer:Job List.

Click the **Payment Info** tab

Tab to or click **Credit Limit**

Enter **2500** for the amount

- You may have to delete the existing credit limit of 500.00.
- You do not have to enter a comma between the 2 and the 5. You do not need to enter a decimal point and the two zeros. QuickBooks Pro will format the number for you automatically.

Click **OK** to record the change and exit the information for Mei-Hwa Chau

Close the **Customer:Job List**

VOID AND DELETE SALES FORMS

Deleting an invoice or sales receipt permanently removes it from QuickBooks Pro without leaving a trace. If you want to correct financial records for the invoice that you no longer want, it is more appropriate to void the invoice. When an invoice is voided, it remains in the QuickBooks Pro system, but QuickBooks Pro does not count it. Voiding an invoice should be used only if there have been no payments made on the invoice. If any payment has been received, a Credit Memo would be appropriate for recording a return.

Void an Invoice

MEMO
DATE: January 8, 2004

Rick Woods returned the after-ski boots he purchased for $80.44 including tax on January 2. He had not made any payments on this purchase. Void the invoice.

     DO: Void the above transaction using **Advanced Find** to locate the invoice:
- **Advanced Find** is useful when you have a large number of invoices and want to locate an invoice for a particular customer.
- Using Advanced **Find** will locate the invoice without requiring you to scroll through all the invoices for the company. For example, if customer Sanderson's transaction was on Invoice No. 7 and the invoice on the screen was 784, you would not have to scroll through 777 invoices because Find would locate Invoice No. 7 instantly.

To use **Advanced Find**:
   Click **Edit** menu, click **Advanced Find**
   In the list displayed under **Filter**, click **Name**
   In the **Name** dialog box, click the drop-down list arrow, click **Woods, Rick**
   Click the **Find** button on the **Find** dialog box
- QuickBooks Pro will find all transactions recorded for Rick Woods.

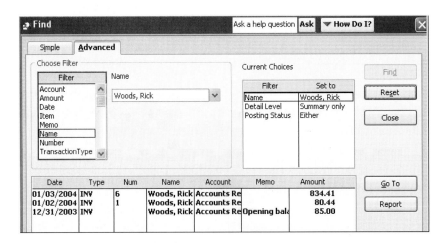

- Because there are several invoices, another filter would need to be defined in order to find the invoice with the exact amount of 80.44.

This would be done by selecting a second filter:
   Click **Amount** under **Filter**
   Click the **Select** box in front of the = sign

Key in **80.44** in the text box
Press the **Tab** key
- The first two lines of the Current Choices Box shows *Filter: Amount* and *Set to: 80.44:* followed by *Filter: Name* and *Set to: Woods, Rick.*

Click the **Find** button on the **Find** dialog box

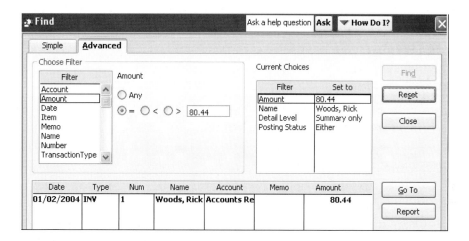

Click the line for **Invoice No. 1**
Click **Go To** button
- Invoice No. 1 appears on the screen.

With the invoice on the screen, click **Edit** menu, click **Void Invoice**

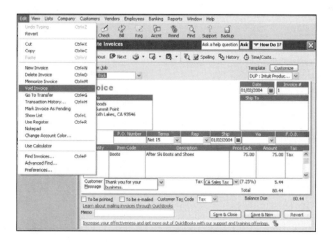

- Notice that the amount and the total for Invoice No. 1 are no longer 80.44. Both are **0.00**. Also note that the Memo box contains the word Void.

Click **Save & Close** button on the **Create Invoices** screen to close the invoice
Click **Yes** on the **Recording Transaction** screen
- Invoice No. 1 is no longer displayed on the **Advanced Find** screen.

Click **Close** button to close **Find**

Delete an Invoice

MEMO
DATE: January 8, 2004

Trent Trudeau lost his part-time job. He decided to repair his old snowboard and return the new one he purchased from Year Round Sports. Delete Invoice No. 5.

DO: Delete Invoice No. 5 by going directly to the original invoice
Use **QuickBooks Navigator**:
> Click **Customers** on the Navigator list, click **Invoice** on QuickBooks Customers Navigator
- You may also access the invoice via the register for Accounts Receivable.
Click the **Previous** button until you get to Invoice No. 5
With Invoice No. 5 on the screen, click the **Edit** menu
Click **Delete Invoice**

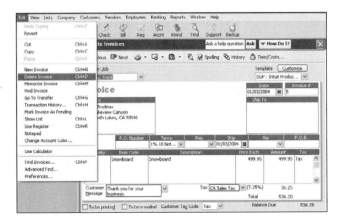

Click **OK** in the **Delete Transaction** dialog box

- The cursor is now positioned on Invoice No. 6.

Click **Previous**

- Now the cursor is positioned on Invoice No. 4.

Click **Close** on the **Create Invoices** screen to close the invoice

View the **Customer Balance Detail Report**

Click **Reports** on the menu bar, point to **Customer & Accounts Receivable,** click **Customer Balance Detail**

Scroll through the report

- Look at Trent Trudeau's account. Notice that Invoice No. 5 does not show up in the account listing. When an invoice is deleted, there is no record of it anywhere in the report.
- Notice that the Customer Balance Detail Report does not include the information telling you which amounts are opening balances.
- The report does give information regarding the amount owed on each transaction plus the total amount owed by each customer.
- Look at Rick Woods's account. The amount for Invoice No. 1 shows as **0.00**.

Year Round Sports--Student's Name
Customer Balance Detail
All Transactions

Type	Date	Num	Account	Amount	Balance
Total Thomas, Hayley				670.31	670.31
Trudeau, Trent					
Invoice	12/31/2003		1200 · Accounts Receivable	911.63	911.63
Total Trudeau, Trent				911.63	911.63
Veracruz, Martin					
Invoice	12/31/2003		1200 · Accounts Receivable	975.00	975.00
Total Veracruz, Martin				975.00	975.00
Woods, Rick					
Invoice	12/31/2003		1200 · Accounts Receivable	85.00	85.00
Invoice	01/02/2004	1	1200 · Accounts Receivable	0.00	85.00
Invoice	01/03/2004	6	1200 · Accounts Receivable	834.41	919.41
Total Woods, Rick				919.41	919.41
TOTAL				**14,392.54**	**14,392.54**

Close the report without printing

PREPARE CREDIT MEMOS

Credit memos are prepared to show a reduction to a transaction. If the invoice has already been sent to the customer, it is more appropriate and less confusing to make a change to a transaction by issuing a credit memo rather than voiding the invoice and issuing a new invoice. A credit memo notifies a customer that a change has been made to a transaction.

MEMOS

DATE: January 10, 2004

Prepare Credit Memo No. 9 for Mei-Hwa Chau to show a reduction to her account for the return of the boot carrying case purchased for $49.95 on Invoice No. 7.

DO: Prepare the Credit Memo shown above
Use QuickBooks Navigator

> Click **Customers** on the Navigator list, click **Refunds and Credit** on the
> Customers Navigator

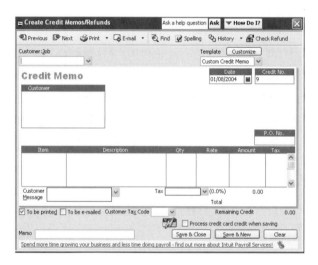

Click the down arrow for the drop-down list box next to **Customer:Job**
Click **Chau, Mei-Hwa**
Tab to **Template**

- It should say **Custom Credit Memo**.
- If not, click the drop-down list arrow and click **Custom Credit Memo**.

Tab to or click **Date**
Type in the date of the Credit Memo—**01/10/04**
The **Credit No.** field should show the number **9**

- Because Credit Memos are included in the numbering sequence for invoices, this number matches the number of the next blank invoice.

There is no PO No.
Tab to or click in **Item**
Click the drop-down list arrow next to **Item**, click **Accessories**
Tab to or click in **Quantity**, type in **1**
Tab to or click **Rate**, enter **49.95**
Press tab to enter 49.95 in the **Amount** column

Click the drop-down list arrow next to **Customer Message**
Click **Thank you for your business.**

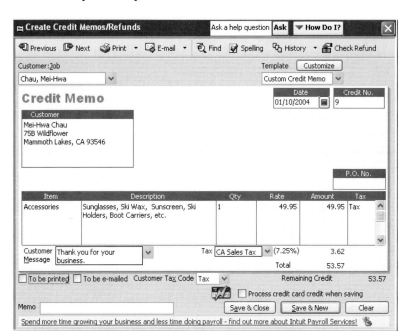

Click **Print** on **Create Credit Memo/Refunds**

Check the print settings

To print with lines around each field, the check box for *Do not print lines around each field* should not have a check mark

- If it is checked, click the box to remove the check mark.

Click **Print** on **Print One Credit Memo**

Click **Save & Close** on **Create Credit Memo/Refunds** to close the **Credit Memo**

PRINT OPEN INVOICES REPORT

To determine which invoices are still open—they have not been paid—QuickBooks Pro allows you to print a report titled Open Invoices. This report shows information regarding the type of transaction (Invoice or Credit Memo), the transaction date, the Invoice or Credit Memo number, a Purchase Order number (if there is one), terms of the sale, due date, aging, and the amount of the open balance. The total amount due from each customer for all open invoices less credit memos is also listed.

When you view and a print report, each column of information is separated by a diamond between the column headings. These diamonds may be used to change the size/width of a column. This is useful if the report is too wide to view on screen, if a column is taking up too much room, or a column does not contain any information.

MEMO

DATE: January 10, 2004

Rhonda needs to prepare and print an Open Invoices Report to give to the owners, Andy and Tim, so they can see which invoices are open. When preparing the report, eliminate the column for P.O. # and adjust the width of the columns. The report should be one page wide without selecting the print option *Fit report to one page wide*.

DO: Prepare and print an Open Invoices Report
Click **Reports** menu, point to **Customers & Receivables**, click **Open Invoices**
   OR
On the QuickBooks Customers Navigator, click **Report Finder**
On Report Finder the type should be Customers & Receivables, click **Open Invoices** to select the report, click **Display**
Tab to or click the text box for the **Date**, enter **011004** or **01/10/04**
Press the **Tab** key to generate the report
Click **Print**
- Be sure the orientation is Portrait and that *Fit report to one page wide* is not selected.
Click **Preview**
Click **Next Page** to see all of the pages in the report
Click **Zoom In** to see what information is contained in the report
Click **Close** to close the **Preview**
Click **Cancel** to close **Print Reports**
Hide columns or resize the width of the columns so the report will fit on one page wide
- The column for P.O. # does not contain any information.
To hide the column from view, position the cursor on the diamond between **P.O. #** and **Terms**
   - The cursor turns into a plus with arrows pointing left and right.
   Hold down the primary mouse button
   Drag the cursor from the diamond between **P.O. #** and **Terms** to the diamond between **P.O. #** and **Num**
      - You will see a dotted vertical line while you are dragging the mouse and holding down the primary mouse button.
      - When you release the primary mouse button, the column for **P.O. #** will not show on the screen.

Click **Print**
- Verify that **Fit report to one page wide** is not selected.
- If it is selected, click the check box to remove the check mark.

Click **Preview**
- The report will now fit on one page wide.

Click **Close** to close the **Preview**

Click **Print**

Year Round Sports--Student's Name						
Open Invoices						
As of January 10, 2004						
Type	Date	Num	Terms	Due Date	Aging	Open Balance
Chau, Mei-Hwa						
Invoice	12/31/2003			12/31/2003	10	53.57
Credit Memo	01/10/2004	9		01/10/2004		-53.57
Invoice	01/05/2004	7	Net 30	02/04/2004		1,028.41
Total Chau, Mei-Hwa						1,028.41
Childers, Irene Dr.						
Invoice	12/31/2003			12/31/2003	10	417.00
Total Childers, Irene Dr.						417.00
Clary, Anne						
Invoice	12/31/2003			12/31/2003	10	455.00
Total Clary, Anne						455.00

Close the **Open Invoices Report** and **Report Finder** if it was used

RECORD CASH SALES WITH SALES TAX

Not all sales in a business are on account. In many instances, payment is made at the time the merchandise is purchased. This is entered as a cash sale. Sales with cash, credit cards, or checks as the payment method are entered as cash sales. When entering a cash sale, you prepare a Sales Receipt rather than an Invoice. QuickBooks Pro records the transaction in the Journal and places the amount of cash received in an account called *Undeposited Funds*. The funds received remain in Undeposited Funds until you record a deposit to your bank account.

Memo

DATE: January 11, 2004

Record the following cash sale: Sales Receipt No. 1—Received <u>cash</u> from a customer who purchased a pair of sunglasses, $29.95; a boot carrier, $2.99; and some lip balm, $1.19. Use *Thank you for your business.* as the message.

DO: Enter the above transaction as a cash sale to a cash customer

    Click **Customers** on the Navigator bar, click **Sales Receipts** on the QuickBooks Customers Navigator

    Enter **Cash Customer** in the **Customer:Job** text box

    Tab to **Template**

    Because Year Round Sports does not have a customer named Cash Customer, a **Customer:Job Not Found** dialog box appears on the screen.

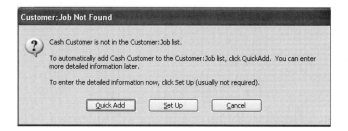

    Click **Quick Add** to add the customer name Cash Customer to the Customer List

- Details regarding Cash Customer are not required, so Quick Add is the appropriate method to use to add the name to the list.
- Now that the customer name has been added to the Customer:Job List, the cursor moves to the **Template** field.

    Template should be **Custom Sales Receipt**

- If not, click the drop-down list arrow and click Custom Cash Sales.

    Tab to or click **Date**, type **01/11/04**

    Sales No. should be **1**

    Click the drop-down list arrow next to **Payment Method**, click **Cash**

    Tab to or click beneath **Item**

    Click the drop-down list arrow next to **Item**, click **Accessories**

    Tab to or click **Qty**, type **1**

    Tab to or click **Rate**, enter **29.95**

- When you move to the next field, the total for **Amount** is calculated automatically.

    Tab to or click the next line in **Item**

Click the drop-down list arrow next to **Item**, click **Accessories**
Tab to or click **Qty**, type **1**
Tab to or click **Rate**, enter **2.99**
- The Total for **Amount** is calculated when you move to the next field.
Repeat the steps above to enter $1.19 for the lip balm
- Total for **Amount** is calculated when you go to the **Customer Message**.
Click **Customer Message**
Click the drop-down list arrow for Customer Message, click **Thank you for your business.**
- The message is inserted.

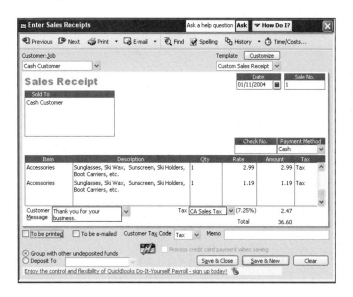

PRINT SALES RECEIPT

DO: Print the Sales Receipt immediately after entering information
Click **Print** button at the top of the **Enter Sales Receipts** screen
To print with lines around each field, the check box for *Do not print lines around each field* should not have a check mark
- If it is checked, click the box to remove the check mark.
Print the Sales Receipt following printing methods in earlier chapters
Click **Save & New** on the bottom of the **Enter Sales Receipts** screen to save the Sales Receipt and go to the next one

ENTERING A CREDIT CARD SALE

A credit card sale is treated exactly like a cash sale. When you prepare the Sales Receipt, the payment method selected is credit card. The credit cards available on the Payment Method List are American Express, Discover, MasterCard, and Visa. Except for American Express, the credit card deposits are made into the checking or bank account, and bank fees for the charge cards are deducted directly from the bank account. Because American Express is not a *bank* charge card, charge receipts are sent to American Express, and American Express sends a check to the company for the amount of the charge, less American Express fees.

MEMO

DATE: January 11, 2004

Enter a sale to a customer using a Visa card. Identify the customer as Cash Customer. The sale was for a sled, $199.95. Use *Thank you for your business.* as the message.

    DO: Record the credit card sale
Click the drop-down list arrow next to **Customer:Job**, click **Cash Customer**
Tab to **Template**, template should be **Custom Sales Receipt**
- If not, click the drop-down list arrow and click **Custom Sales Receipt**.
Tab to or click **Date**, type **01/11/04**
Sales No. should be **2**
Click the drop-down list arrow next to **Payment Method**, click **VISA**
Tab to or click beneath **Item**
Click the drop-down list arrow next to **Item**, click **Sleds**
Tab to or click **Qty**, type **1**
Tab to or click **Rate**, enter **199.95**
Click the drop-down list arrow for **Customer Message**, click **Thank you for your business.**

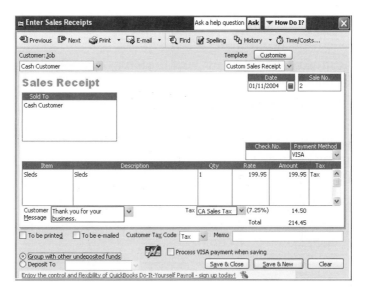

Print the sales receipt immediately after entering information
Click **Next** to go to Sales Receipt No. 3

RECORD SALES PAID BY CHECK

A sale paid for with a check is considered a cash sale. A sales receipt is prepared to record the sale.

MEMO

DATE: January 11, 2004

We do take checks for sales even if a customer is from out of town. Record the sale of 2 pairs of socks at $15.99 each to a cash customer using Check No. 5589. The message for the Sales Receipt is *Thank you for your business.*

DO: With Sales Receipt No. 3 on the screen, enter the information for the above
transaction
Click the drop-down list arrow next to **Customer:Job**, click **Cash Customer**
Tab to **Template**
- This should have **Custom Sales Receipt** as the template. If not, click the
drop-down list arrow and click **Custom Sales Receipt**.
Tab to or click **Date**, type **01/11/04**
Sales No. should be **3**
Tab to or click **Check No.**, type **5589**

Click the drop-down list arrow next to **Payment Method**, click **Check**
Tab to or click beneath **Item**
Click the drop-down list arrow next to **Item**, click **Socks**
Tab to or click **Qty**, type **2**
Tab to or click **Rate**, enter **15.99**

- Total is automatically calculated when you go to the Customer Message.

Click the drop-down list arrow for **Customer Message**, click **Thank you for your business.**
Print Sales Receipt No. 3

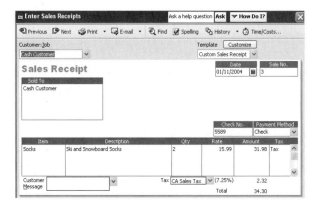

Click **Next** to go to Sales Receipt No. 4

ENTER CASH SALES TRANSACTIONS WITHOUT STEP-BY-STEP INSTRUCTIONS

MEMO

DATE: January 12, 2004

After a record snowfall, the store is really busy. Use Cash Customer as the customer name for the transactions. Record the following cash, check, and credit card sales:

Sales Receipt No. 4—A cash customer used Check No. 196 to purchase a ski parka, $249.95; ski pants, $129.95; and a ski sweater, $89.95.

Sales Receipt No. 5—A cash customer used a MasterCard to purchase a snow-board, $389.95; snowboard boots, $229.95; and snowboard bindings, $189.95.

Sales Receipt No. 6—A cash customer purchased gloves for $89.95.

      DO: Repeat the procedures used to enter Sales Receipt Nos. 1, 2, and 3 to record the additional transactions listed above:

- Always use the Item List to determine the appropriate sales items for billing.
- Use **Thank you for your business.** as the message for these sales receipts.
- Print each Sales Receipt immediately after entering the information for it.
- If you make an error, correct it.
- To go from one Sales Receipt to the next, click the **NEXT** button on the top of the Enter Cash Sales screen.
- If you get a message about Merchant Account Services, click Not Now.
- Click **Save & Close** after you have entered and printed Sales Receipt No. 6.

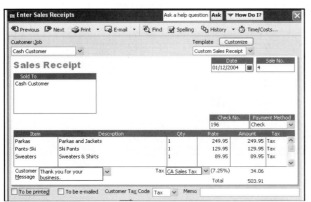

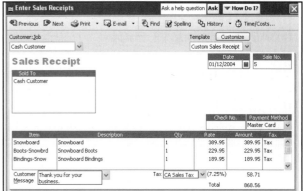

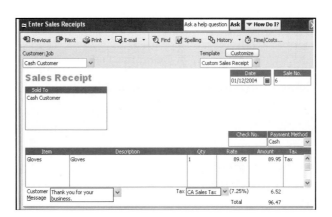

PRINT SALES BY ITEM SUMMARY REPORT

The Sales by Item Summary Report analyzes the quantity of merchandise on hand by item, gives the amount or value of the merchandise, gives the percentage of the total sales of each item, and calculates the average price per item, the cost of goods sold for each item, the average cost of goods sold for each item, the gross margin for each item, and the percentage of gross margin for each item. Information regarding the total inventory is also provided. This includes the value of the total inventory, the cost of goods sold for the inventory, and the gross margin for the inventory of merchandise.

MEMO
DATE: January 13, 2004

Near the middle of the month, Rhonda prepares a Summary Sales by Item Report to obtain information about sales, inventory, and merchandise costs. Prepare this report in landscape form for 1/1/2004-1/13/2004. Adjust the widths of the columns so the report prints on one page without selecting the print option *Fit report to one page wide*

DO: Prepare the above report
Click **Reports** on the menu bar, point to **Sales Reports**, click **Sales By Item Summary**
OR
Click **Report Finder** on QuickBooks Navigator, click **Sales** as the type of report, click **Sales By Item Summary**, click **Display**
Tab to or click **From**, enter **010104**
- The diagonal (/) between the elements of the date is optional.
Tab to or click **To**, enter **011304**
Tab to generate the report
Scroll through the report
Click **Print**
Click **Landscape** to select **Orientation: Landscape**
Click **Preview**
Click **Next Page**
- Notice that the report does not fit on one page wide.
Click **Close** to close the Preview
Click **Cancel** to return to the report
Position the cursor on the diamond between columns
Drag to resize the columns
- The names of the column headings should appear in full and should not have **...** as part of the heading.

If you get a **Resize Columns** dialog box wanting to know if all columns should be the same size, click **No**

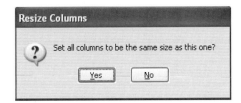

When the columns have been resized, click **Print** and **Preview**

Year Round Sports--Student's Name
Sales by Item Summary
January 1 - 13, 2004

	Qty	Amount	% of Sales	Avg Price	COGS	Avg COGS	Gross Margin	Gross Margin %
Inventory								
Accessories	5	127.03	1.5%	25.41	18.30	3.66	108.73	85.6%
Bindings-Skis	7	854.00	10%	122.00	525.00	75.00	329.00	38.5%
Bindings-Snow	2	349.94	4.1%	174.97	150.00	75.00	199.94	57.1%
Boots	0.00	0.00	0.0%	0.00	0.00	0.00	0.00	0.0%
Boots-Ski	1	250.00	2.9%	250.00	75.00	75.00	175.00	70.0%
Boots-Snowbrd	2	478.95	5.6%	239.48	150.00	75.00	328.95	68.7%
Gloves	2	168.95	2%	84.48	30.00	15.00	138.95	82.2%
Hats	1	25.00	0.3%	25.00	8.00	8.00	17.00	68.0%
Pants-Ski	2	258.95	3%	129.48	60.00	30.00	198.95	76.8%
Parkas	2	498.95	5.8%	249.48	116.66	58.33	382.29	76.6%
Poles-Ski	6	220.00	2.6%	36.67	180.00	30.00	40.00	18.2%
Skis	7	2,519.00	29.5%	359.86	700.00	100.00	1,819.00	72.2%
Sleds	6	799.90	9.4%	133.32	405.00	67.50	394.90	49.4%
Snowboard	2	889.90	10.4%	444.95	200.00	100.00	689.90	77.5%
Socks	3	47.93	0.6%	15.98	9.00	3.00	38.93	81.2%
Sweaters	2	214.95	2.5%	107.48	50.00	25.00	164.95	76.7%
Toboggans	5	1,149.75	13.5%	229.95	687.50	137.50	462.25	40.2%
Underwear	1	68.00	0.8%	68.00	8.00	8.00	60.00	88.2%
Total Inventory		8,921.20	104.6%		3,372.46		5,548.74	62.2%

When the report fits on one page wide, print the report

CORRECT A SALES RECEIPT AND PRINT THE CORRECTED FORM

QuickBooks Pro makes correcting errors user friendly. When an error is discovered in a transaction such as a cash sale, you can simply return to the form where the transaction was recorded and correct the error. Thus, to correct a sales receipt, you could click Customers on the menu bar, click Enter Sales Receipts, click the Previous button until you found the appropriate sales receipt, and then correct the error. Since cash or checks received for cash sales are held in the Undeposited Funds account until the bank deposit is made, a sales receipt can be accessed through the Undeposited Funds account in the Chart of Accounts. Accessing the receipt in this manner allows you to see all the transactions entered in the account for Undeposited Funds.

When a correction for a sale is made, QuickBooks Pro not only changes the form, it also changes all Journal and account entries for the transaction to reflect the correction. QuickBooks Pro then allows a corrected sales receipt to be printed.

MEMO

DATE: January 13, 2004

After reviewing transaction information, you realize that the date for Sales Receipt No. 1 was entered incorrectly. Change the date to 1/8/2004.

DO: Correct the error indicated in the memo above, and print a corrected Sales Receipt
Open the **Chart of Accounts**:
Click **Lists** menu, click **Chart of Accounts**
    OR
Use the keyboard shortcut **Ctrl+A**
Click **Undeposited Funds**

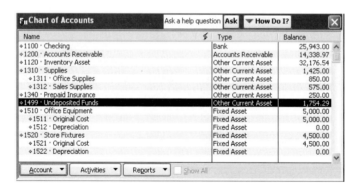

Click **Activities**
Click **Use Register**
- The register maintains a record of all the transactions recorded within the Undeposited Funds account.
Click anywhere in the transaction for Sale No. 1
- Look at the **Ref/Type** column to see the type of transaction.
- The number in the Ref column indicates the number of the sales receipt or the customer's check number.
- Type shows **RCPT** for a sales receipt.

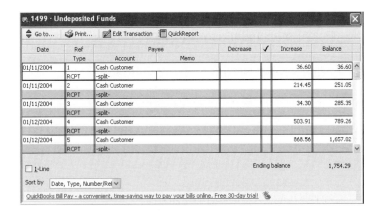

Click **Edit Transaction**
- The sales receipt appears on the screen.

Tab to or click **Date** field

Change the Date to **01/08/04**

Click **Print** on the **Enter Sales Receipts** screen to print a corrected sales receipt

Click **Print** on the **Print One Sales Receipt** screen

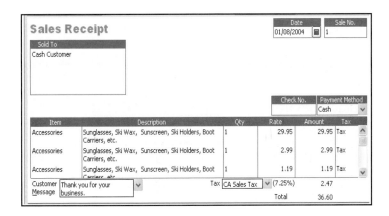

Click **Save & Close** on the **Enter Sales Receipts** screen to record changes, close the **Sales Receipt**, and return to the **Register for Undeposited Funds**

Click **Yes** on the **Recording Transactions** dialog box

Do not close the register

VIEW A QUICKREPORT

After editing the sales receipt and returning to the register, you may get a detailed report regarding the customer's transactions by clicking the QuickReport button. If you use Cash Customer for all cash sales, a QuickReport will be for all the transactions of Cash Customer.

DO: After closing the sales receipt, you returned to the register for the Undeposited Funds account

Click the **QuickReport** button to display the Register QuickReport for **Cash Customer**

Because there are no entries in the Memo and Clr columns, drag the diamond between columns to eliminate the columns for **Memo** and **Clr**

Widen the **Account** column until the account name **Undeposited Funds** appears in full

Year Round Sports--Student's Name
Register QuickReport
All Transactions

Type	Date	Num	Account	Split	Amount
Cash Customer					
Sales Receipt	01/08/2004	1	1499 · Undeposited Funds	-SPLIT-	36.60
Sales Receipt	01/11/2004	2	1499 · Undeposited Funds	-SPLIT-	214.45
Sales Receipt	01/11/2004	3	1499 · Undeposited Funds	-SPLIT-	34.30
Sales Receipt	01/12/2004	4	1499 · Undeposited Funds	-SPLIT-	503.91
Sales Receipt	01/12/2004	5	1499 · Undeposited Funds	-SPLIT-	868.56
Sales Receipt	01/12/2004	6	1499 · Undeposited Funds	-SPLIT-	96.47
Total Cash Customer					1,754.29
TOTAL					**1,754.29**

ANALYZE THE QUICKREPORT FOR CASH CUSTOMER

DO: All transactions for Cash Customer appear in the report

- Notice that the date for Sales Receipt No. 1 has been changed to **01/08/2004**.

The account used is Undeposited Funds

The Split column contains the other accounts used in the transactions

- For all the transactions you see the word **-SPLIT-** rather than an account name.
    - Split means that more than one account was used for this portion of the transaction.
    - In addition to a variety of sales items, sales tax was charged on all sales, so each transaction will show **-SPLIT-** even if only one item was sold as in Sales Receipt No. 2.

View the accounts used for the Split by using QuickZoom to view the actual sales receipt

Use QuickZoom by double-clicking anywhere on the information for Sales Receipt No. 2

- The accounts used are Sleds and CA Sales Tax.

Close **Sales Receipt No. 2**

Close the report without printing
Close the register for **Undeposited Funds**
Do not close the **Chart of Accounts**

VIEW SALES TAX PAYABLE REGISTER

The Sales Tax Payable Register shows a detailed listing of all transactions with sales tax. The option of 1-Line may be selected in order to view each transaction on one line rather than the standard two lines. The account register provides information regarding the vendor and the account used for the transaction.

DO: View the register for the Sales Tax Payable account
Click **Sales Tax Payable** in the Chart of Accounts
Click the **Activities** button at the bottom of the Chart of Accounts, click **Use Register**
OR
Use the keyboard shortcut, **Ctrl+R**
Once the register is displayed on the screen, click **1-Line** to view the transactions on single lines

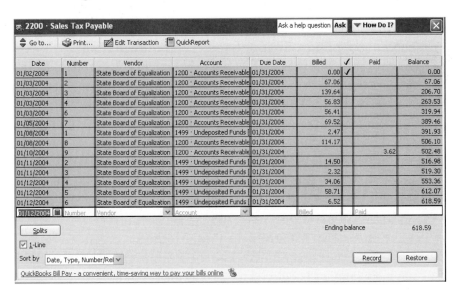

Close the register for **Sales Tax Payable**, and close the **Chart of Accounts**

RECORD CUSTOMER PAYMENTS ON ACCOUNT

Whenever money is received, whether it is for a cash sale or when customers pay the amount they owe on account, QuickBooks Pro uses the account called *Undeposited Funds* rather than a cash/checking account. The money stays in the account until a bank deposit is made. When you start to record a payment on account, you see the customer's balance, any credits made to the account, and a complete list of outstanding invoices. QuickBooks Pro automatically applies the payment received to the oldest invoice.

MEMO
DATE: January 13, 2004

Record the following receipt of Check No. 765 for $975 from Martin Veracruz as payment in full on his account.

DO: Record the above payment on account:

Click **Customers** on the Navigator list, click **Receive Payments** on the QuickBooks Customers Navigator

Since Year Round Sports offers customers early payment discounts and may have issued credit memos to customers, click the checkbox for **Show discount and credit information**

Click the drop-down list for **Received From**, click **Veracruz, Martin**

- Notice that the current date shows in the **Date** column and that the total amount owed appears as the Customer Balance.
- At the bottom of the **Receive Payments** screen, notice that the unpaid invoice for Martin Veracruz shows in the Applied To section of the screen.

Tab to or click **Date**, type **01/13/04**

Tab to or click **Amount**, enter **975**

- QuickBooks Pro will enter the **.00** when you tab to or click **Ref./Check No.**

Tab to or click **Check No.**, enter **765**

Click the drop-down list arrow for **Pmt. Method**

- Notice that the cursor moves into the **Pmt. Method** text box and that the payment amount is entered in the **Payment** column for Outstanding Invoices/Statement Charges.

Click **Check**

- QuickBooks places a check mark in the check mark column to indicate the invoice for which the payment is received. When there is more than one open invoice, QuickBooks Pro automatically applies the payment to the oldest open invoice.

Click **Next** to record this payment and advance to the next **Receive Payments** screen

RECORD CUSTOMER PAYMENT ON ACCOUNT AND APPLY CREDIT

If there are any existing credits (such as a Credit Memo) on an account that have not been applied to the account, they may be applied to a customer's account when a payment is made.

MEMO

DATE: January 13, 2004

Mei-Hwa Chau sent Check No. 1026 for $1,028.41 to pay her account in full. Apply unused credits when recording her payment on account.

DO: Record the payment by Mei-Hwa Chau and apply her unused credits
Click the drop-down list for **Received From**, click **Chau, Mei-Hwa**
- Notice the Customer Balance shows the total amount owed by the customer and does not reflect any credits.
- In the lower portion of the **Receive Payments** screen, notice the list of unpaid invoices for Mei-Hwa Chau.
- At the bottom of the Receive Payments window is information regarding Unused Credits. Mei-Hwa has $53.57 in unused credits that may be applied to her account.

Tab to or click **Date**, type the date **01/13/04**

Tab to or click **Amount**, enter **1028.41**

- Notice that this amount is different from the balance of $1,081.98.

Tab to or click **Check No.**, enter **1026**

Click the drop-down list arrow for **Pmt. Method**

Click **Check**

- Because the amount of the payment matched the amount due for the invoice, Invoice 7 has a check in the Applied to: column.

Complete the information to apply the Credits:

- Notice the Unused Credits of $53.57

Click the button to **Set Credits**

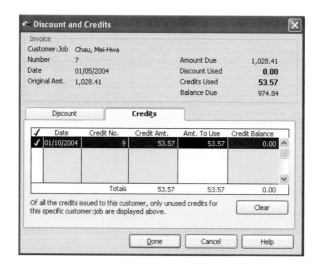

Click **Done**

- The Unused Credits now show 0.00 and $53.57 shows in the Credits column.

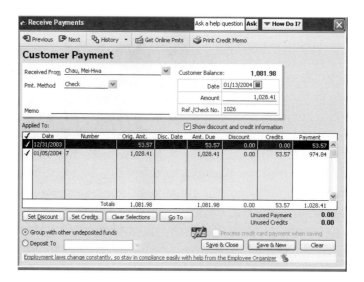

Check Unused Payment:
- If the Unused Payment shows $0.00, click **Next** to record this payment and to advance to the next **Receive Payments** screen.
- If the Unused Payment shows $53.57, click the check column for the 12/31/2003 Beginning Balance of $53.57. This should mark the invoice and change the Unused Payment to $0.00. Click **Next** to record this payment and to advance to the next **Receive Payments** screen.

RECORD PAYMENT ON ACCOUNT FROM A CUSTOMER QUALIFYING FOR AN EARLY-PAYMENT DISCOUNT

Each customer may be assigned terms as part of the customer information. When terms such as 1% 10 Net 30 or 2% 10 Net 30 are given, customers whose payments are received within ten days of the invoice date are eligible to deduct 1% or 2% from the amount owed when making their payments.

MEMO

DATE: January 13, 2004

Received payment from Mountain Recreation Center for Invoice No. 8. Check No. 981-13 for $1672.01 was received as full payment. Record the payment and the 1% discount for early payment under the invoice terms of 1% 10 Net 30.

DO: Record the receipt of the check and apply the discount to the above transaction
Click the drop-down list for **Received From**
Click **Mountain Recreation Center**
- The total amount owed, $1,688.90, appears as the Customer Balance.
- In the lower portion of the **Receive Payments** screen, notice that the unpaid Invoice 8 for Mountain Recreation Center is shown
Tab to or click **Date**, type date **01/13/04**
Tab to or click **Amount**, enter **1672.01**
- Notice that this amount is different from the balance of $1,688.90.
Tab to or click **Check No.**, enter **981-13**
Click the drop-down list arrow for **Pmt. Method**
- Notice that the payment amount is entered in the **Payment** column for Invoice 8.

Click **Check**

Tab to or click **Memo**, type **Includes Early Payment Discount**

- Since the columns for Disc. Date, Discount, and Credits are displayed, you will see that the Invoice is being paid within the discount date and is eligible to receive a discount

Click the button for **Set Discount**

- QuickBooks displays the 1% discount amount, which was calculated on the total amount due

Click the drop-down list arrow for **Discount Account**, click **6130 Sales Discounts**

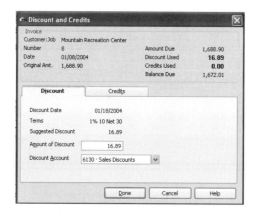

Click **Done** to apply the discount of $16.89

- Notice that the Original Amount stays the same, the Amount Due on Invoice No. 8 changes to $1,672.01, the discount amount of $16.89 shows in the Discount column, and the Payment shows $1,672.01.

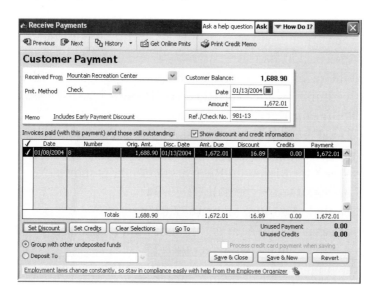

- If you make an error in applying the discount, click the Clear or Clear Selection button and re-enter the transaction.

Click **Next** to record this payment and to advance to the next **Receive Payments** screen

RECORD ADDITIONAL PAYMENTS ON ACCOUNT
WITHOUT STEP-BY-STEP INSTRUCTIONS

MEMO

DATE: January 14, 2004

Received Check No. 152 from Rick Woods for $919.41

Received Check No. 8252 dated January 11 and postmarked 1/12 for $2,024.33 from Mountain Schools. This receipt requires an item as a Memo. The memo is: *Includes Early Payment Discount.* Even though the date we are recording the payment is after the discount date, the check was postmarked within the discount period. Apply the discount for early payment to this transaction. Since the payment is being recorded after the discount date, you may need to enter the amount of the 2% discount when you click the Set Discount button.

Received Check No. 3951 from Dr. Jose Morales for $1,087.51 (no discount).

Received Check No. 1051 for $500 from Elizabeth Davis in partial payment of account. Record the memo: Partial Payment.

Received Check No. 563 from Sally Princeton for $408.48 in payment of the 12/31/2003 balance.

Received Check No. 819 from Trent Trudeau for $100 in partial payment of his account.

DO: Refer to the previous steps listed to enter the above payments:

Click **NEXT** to go from one Receive Payments screen to the next

- Any discounts or partial payments should be noted as a Memo on the Customer Payment slip.
- Be sure to display the discount and credit information.

Click the **Save & Close** button after all payments received have been recorded

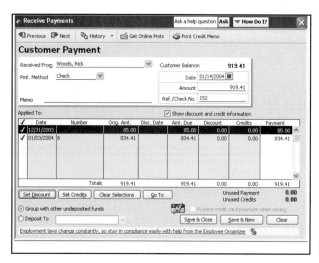

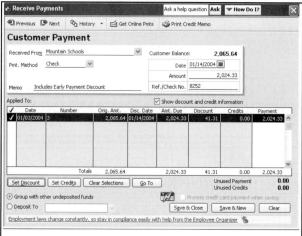

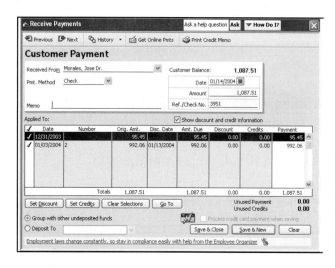

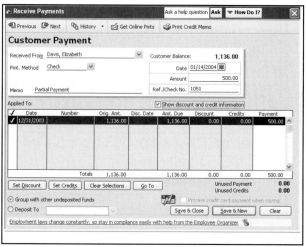

VIEW TRANSACTION LIST BY CUSTOMER

In order to see the transactions for customers, you need to prepare a report called Transaction List by Customer. This report shows all sales, credits, and payments for each customer on account and for the customer named Cash Customer. The report does not show the balance remaining on account for the individual customers.

DO: Click **Report Finder** on QuickBooks Navigator
Click **Customers & Receivables** as the type of report
Click **Transaction List by Customer**, click **Display**
Tab to or click **From**, enter **01/01/04**
Tab to or click **To**, enter **01/14/04**
Tab to generate the report
Scroll through the report
- Information is shown for the Invoices, Sales Receipts, Credit Memos, and payments made on the accounts and the **Num** column shows the Invoice numbers, Sales Receipt numbers, Credit Memo numbers, and Check numbers.

Year Round Sports--Student's Name
Transaction List by Customer
January 1 - 14, 2004

◇ Type ◇	Date	◇ Num ◇	Memo	◇	Account	◇ Clr ◇	Split	◇	Amount ◇
Cash Customer									
Sales Receipt	01/08/2004	1			1499 · Undeposited Funds		-SPLIT-		36.60
Sales Receipt	01/11/2004	2			1499 · Undeposited Funds		-SPLIT-		214.45
Sales Receipt	01/11/2004	3			1499 · Undeposited Funds		-SPLIT-		34.30
Sales Receipt	01/12/2004	4			1499 · Undeposited Funds		-SPLIT-		503.91
Sales Receipt	01/12/2004	5			1499 · Undeposited Funds		-SPLIT-		868.56
Sales Receipt	01/12/2004	6			1499 · Undeposited Funds		-SPLIT-		96.47
Chau, Mei-Hwa									
Invoice	01/05/2004	7			1200 · Accounts Receiva...		-SPLIT-		1,028.41
Credit Memo	01/10/2004	9			1200 · Accounts Receiva...		-SPLIT-		-53.57
Payment	01/13/2004	1026			1499 · Undeposited Funds		1200 · Account...		1,028.41
Davis, Elizabeth									
Payment	01/14/2004	1051	Partial Payment		1499 · Undeposited Funds		1200 · Account...		500.00
Morales, Jose Dr.									
Invoice	01/03/2004	2			1200 · Accounts Receiva...		-SPLIT-		992.06
Payment	01/14/2004	3951			1499 · Undeposited Funds		1200 · Account...		1,087.51

Click **Close** to exit the report

PRINT CUSTOMER BALANCE SUMMARY

A report that will show you the balance owed by each customer is the Customer Balance Summary. The report presents the total balance owed by each customer as of a certain date.

MEMO
DATE: January 14, 2004

The owners, Andy and Tim, want to see how much each customer owes to Year Round Sports. Print a Customer Balance Summary Report.

     DO: With Report Finder still on the screen, click **Customer Balance Summary** from the list of reports available for Customers & Receivables
Print the report using **Portrait Orientation**

	Year Round Sports--Student's Name
	Customer Balance Summary
	All Transactions

	◇ Jan 14, 04 ◇
Childers, Irene Dr. ▶	417.00 ◀
Clary, Anne	455.00
Davis, Elizabeth	636.00
Donnell, Frances	650.00
Jenkins, Gene	1,085.00
Princeton, Sally	840.68
Thomas, Hayley	670.31
Trudeau, Trent	811.63
TOTAL	5,565.62

Close the report and **Report Finder**

DEPOSIT CHECKS AND CREDIT CARD RECEIPTS
FOR CASH SALES AND PAYMENTS ON ACCOUNT

When cash sales are made and payments on accounts are received, QuickBooks Pro places the money received in the *Undeposited Funds* account. Once the deposit is recorded, the funds are transferred from *Undeposited Funds* to the account selected when preparing the deposit.

MEMO
DATE: January 14, 2004

Deposit all cash, checks and credit card receipts for cash sales and payments on account into the Checking account.

DO: Deposit cash, checks and credit card receipts
Click **Banking** on the menu bar, click **Make Deposits**
  OR
Use QuickBooks Navigator:
  Click **Customers** on the Navigator bar
  Click **Deposits** on the QuickBooks Customers Navigator
The View payment method type should be **All types**

- The **Payments to Deposit** window shows all amounts received for cash sales (including bank credit cards) and payments on account that have not been deposited in the bank.
- Notice that the **check** column to the left of the Date column is empty.

Click the **Select All** button

- Notice the check marks in the check column.

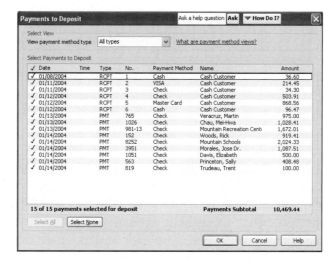

Click **OK** to close the **Payments to Deposit** screen and open the **Make Deposits** screen
On the **Make Deposits** screen, **Deposit To** should be **1100 Checking**
Date should be **01/14/2004**

- Tab to date and change if not correct.

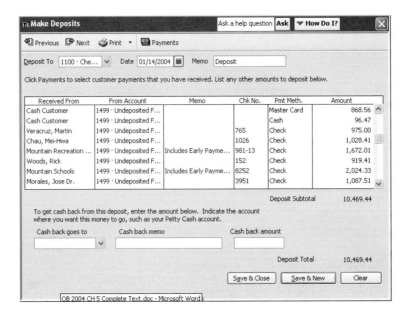

Click **Print** to print **Deposit Summary**
Select **Deposit summary only** and click **OK** on the **Print Deposit** dialog box

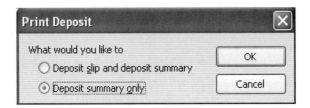

Click **Print** on the **Print Lists** dialog box
When printing is finished, click **Save & Close** on **Make Deposits**

RECORD THE RETURN OF A CHECK BECAUSE OF NONSUFFICIENT FUNDS

If a customer pays you with a check and the check cannot be processed by the bank because there are insufficient funds in the customer's bank account, the amount of the check and the associated bank charges need to be subtracted from the account where the check was deposited; and the Accounts Receivable account needs to be updated to show the amount the customer owes you for the check that "bounced." This type of check is also called *nonsufficient funds* or *NSF*. In order to track the amount of a bad check and to charge a customer for the bank charges and any penalties you impose, Other Charge items may need to be created.

MEMO
DATE: January 15, 2004

The bank returned Trent Trudeau's Check No. 819 for $100 marked NSF. The bank imposed a $10 service charge for the NSF check. Year Round Sports charges a $15 fee for NSF checks. Record the NSF and related charges on an invoice to Trent Trudeau. Add any necessary items for Other Charges to the Items List.

DO: Prepare an invoice to record the NSF check and related charges indicated above
- The invoice is prepared to increase the amount that Trent Trudeau owes. That amount will include the bad check and the fees for the bad check.

Access Invoice No. 10 as previously instructed
Click the drop-down list arrow for **Customer:Job**, click **Trudeau, Trent**
Tab to or click **Date**, enter **011504**
Click drop-down list arrow for **Terms**, click **Due on receipt**
Click the drop-down list arrow for **Item Code**
- You need to add an item that will identify the transaction as a bad check. Because you are preparing an invoice to record the NSF check, using this item will keep the bad check from being incorrectly identified as a sale.

Click **<Add New>**
Click **Other Charge**
Enter **Bad Check** as the **Item Name/Number**
Tab to or click **Description**
Enter **Check returned by bank**
Amount or % should be **0.00**
Click the drop-down-list arrow for **Tax Code**
Click **Non-Taxable**
Click the drop-down list arrow for **Account**
Click **1100 Checking**

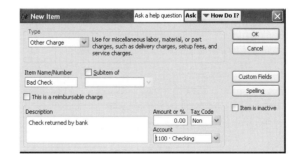

Click **OK**
Click or tab to **Price Each** on the Invoice

Enter **100**

- This is the amount of Trent's bad check.
- QuickBooks Pro will insert the decimal point and two zeros.

Tab to or click the next line for **Item Code**, click the drop-down list arrow for **Item Code**

- Another item needs be added in order to identify the amount that Trent owes for the NSF charges from the bank and from Year Round Sports.

Click **<Add New>**

- The list for **Type** automatically appears.

Click **Other Charge** for **Type**

Tab to or click **Item Name/Number**

Enter **Bad Check Charges**

Tab to or click **Description**

Enter **Bank and other charges for returned check.**

Amount or % should be **0.00**

The **Tax Code** should be **Non-Taxable**

Click the drop-down list arrow for **Account**

Scroll through the list of accounts

- There are no appropriate accounts for this item.

Add a new account to the Chart of Accounts by clicking **<Add New>** at the top of the list for the Accounts

Type of account is **Income**

Enter **4040** for the **Number**

Tab to or click **Name**

Enter **Returned Check Service Charges**

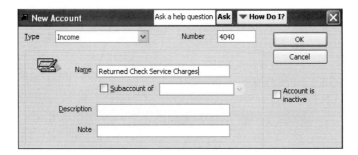

Click **OK** to record the new account in the **Chart of Accounts**

Account 4040 is inserted as the **Account** for the **New Item**

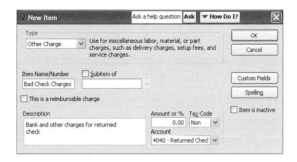

Click **OK** to add Bad Check Charge to the Item List

Tab to or click **Price Each** on the Invoice

Enter **25**

- This is the total amount of the charges Trent has incurred for the NSF check.

Click the drop-down list arrow for **Customer Message**, click **Please remit to above address.**

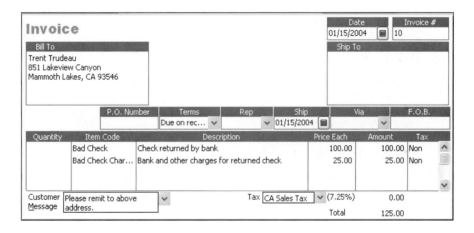

Print the Invoice

Click **Save & Close** to save and exit **Create Invoices**

- You may get a message box regarding the change in terms for Trent Trudeau.

Click **No**

ISSUE A CREDIT MEMO AND A REFUND CHECK

If merchandise is returned and the invoice has been paid in full or the sale was for cash, a refund check may be issued at the same time as the credit memo is prepared. Simply clicking a Check Refund button instructs QuickBooks Pro to prepare the refund check for you.

Memo

DATE: January 15, 2004

Dr. Jose Morales returned the ski poles he purchased for $75 January 3 on Invoice No. 2. He has already paid his bill in full. Record the return and issue a check refunding the $75 plus tax.

DO: Prepare a Credit Memo to record the return of the ski poles and issue a refund check

Issue a Credit Memo as previously instructed

Use the Customer Message **Thank you for your business.**

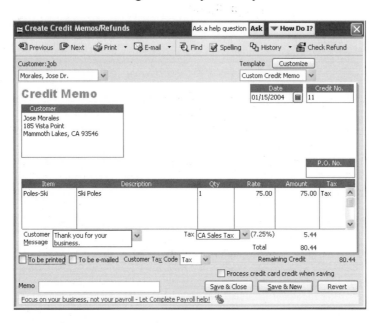

Once the Credit Memo is complete, click **Check Refund** at the top of the screen

The completed check appears on the screen

Make sure the date of the check is **01/15/2004**; if not, change it

- You do not have to change any account information.

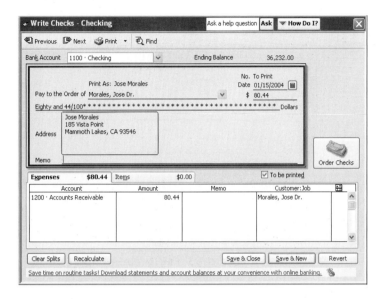

Click **Print** to print the check
Click **OK** on the **Print Check** dialog box to print Check No. 1

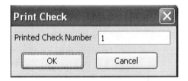

Click **Print** on the **Print Checks** dialog box
- Make sure **Standard** is selected as the check style.

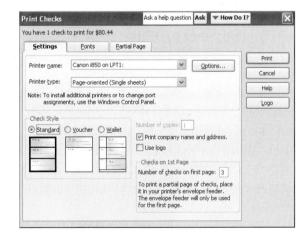

When finished printing the check, click **OK** for **Did check(s) print OK?**

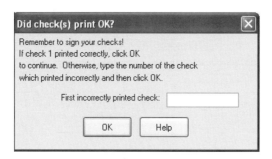

- If you get a message to Set Check Reminder, click No

Click **Save & Close** on the **Write Checks** screen

Click **Print** on the **Credit Memo** to print Credit Memo No. 11

- Print on blank paper with lines around each field.

Click **Save & Close** to record the **Credit Memo** and exit

PRINT JOURNAL

Even though QuickBooks Pro displays registers and reports in a manner that focuses on the transaction—that is, entering a sale on account via an invoice rather than a Sales Journal or a General Journal—it still keeps a General Journal. The Journal records each transaction and lists the accounts and the amounts for debit and credit entries.

DO: Print the Journal

Click **Report Finder**, click **Accountant & Taxes** as the type of report, click **Journal** to select the report

Click **From** date, enter **01/01/04**

Tab to or click **To** field, enter **01/15/04**

Click **Display**

Scroll through the report to view the transactions

- For each item sold, you will notice that the Inventory Asset account is credited and the Cost of Goods Sold account is debited. This moves the value of the item out of your assets and into the cost of goods sold. The amount is not the same amount as the one in the transaction. This is because QuickBooks uses the average cost method of inventory valuation and records the transaction based on the average cost of an item rather than the specific cost of an item.

Resize the columns by positioning the cursor on the diamond and dragging

- Make sure that the account names are displayed in full

Click **Print**

On the **Print Reports** screen, the settings will be the same as those used previously except:

Click **Landscape** to select Landscape orientation
Use Print Preview to make sure that the report fits on one-page wide and that
the account names are displayed in full

Year Round Sports--Student's Name
Journal
January 1 - 15, 2004

Trans #	Type	Date	Num	Name	Memo	Account	Debit	Credit
48	Invoice	01/02/2004	1	Woods, Rick	VOID:	1200 · Accounts Receivable	0.00	
				Woods, Rick	After Ski Boot...	4011 · Clothing & Accessory Sales	0.00	
				State Board of Equalization	CA Sales Tax	2200 · Sales Tax Payable	0.00	
							0.00	0.00
49	Invoice	01/03/2004	2	Morales, Jose Dr.		1200 · Accounts Receivable	992.06	
				Morales, Jose Dr.	Snow Skis	4012 · Equipment Sales		425.00
				Morales, Jose Dr.	Snow Skis	1120 · Inventory Asset		100.00
				Morales, Jose Dr.	Snow Skis	5000 · Cost of Goods Sold	100.00	
				Morales, Jose Dr.	Ski Bindings	4012 · Equipment Sales		175.00
				Morales, Jose Dr.	Ski Bindings	1120 · Inventory Asset		75.00
				Morales, Jose Dr.	Ski Bindings	5000 · Cost of Goods Sold	75.00	
				Morales, Jose Dr.	Ski Boots	4012 · Equipment Sales		250.00
				Morales, Jose Dr.	Ski Boots	1120 · Inventory Asset		75.00
				Morales, Jose Dr.	Ski Boots	5000 · Cost of Goods Sold	75.00	
				Morales, Jose Dr.	Ski Poles	4012 · Equipment Sales		75.00
				Morales, Jose Dr.	Ski Poles	1120 · Inventory Asset		30.00
				Morales, Jose Dr.	Ski Poles	5000 · Cost of Goods Sold	30.00	
				State Board of Equalization	CA Sales Tax	2200 · Sales Tax Payable		67.06
							1,272.06	1,272.06

Click **Print**
Close the report

PRINT THE TRIAL BALANCE

When all sales transactions have been entered, it is important to print the trial balance and verify
that the total debits equal the total credits.

DO: Click **Trial Balance** to select the type of report on the Accountant & Taxes
section of Report Finder
The report dates are **From 01/01/2004 To 01/15/2004**
Click **Display**
Print the Trial Balance in **Portrait** orientation

Year Round Sports--Student's Name
Trial Balance
As of January 15, 2004

	Jan 15, 04	
	Debit	Credit
1200 · Accounts Receivable	5,690.62	
1120 · Inventory Asset	32,206.54	
1311 · Office Supplies	850.00	
1312 · Sales Supplies	575.00	
1340 · Prepaid Insurance	250.00	
1499 · Undeposited Funds	0.00	
1511 · Original Cost	5,000.00	
1521 · Original Cost	4,500.00	
2000 · Accounts Payable		8,500.00
2100 · Visa		150.00
2200 · Sales Tax Payable		613.15
2510 · Office Equipment Loan		3,000.00
2520 · Store Fixtures Loan		2,500.00
3000 · Retained Earnings	0.00	
3010 · Bailey & McBride Capital		25,459.44
3011 · Andy McBride, Investment		20,000.00
3012 · Tim Bailey, Investment		20,000.00
4011 · Clothing & Accessory Sales		1,409.76
4012 · Equipment Sales		7,436.44
4040 · Returned Check Service Charges		25.00
5000 · Cost of Goods Sold	3,342.46	
6130 · Sales Discounts	447.17	
TOTAL	89,093.79	89,093.79

Click **Print**

Close the report and Report Finder

CUSTOMER CENTER

In the Customer Center, you will see a list of all customers who have open balances, including the amount each customer owes you. You will see QuickBooks alerts. By default the Unbilled Job-related Expenses and Customers with Overdue Balances are shown as tables at the bottom of the Customer Center.

DO: Click **Customer Center** on the QuickBooks Customers Navigator (Note: Depending on the date of your computer, your amounts may be different than those shown on this page. Disregard the differences and simply view the Customer Center as it appears.)

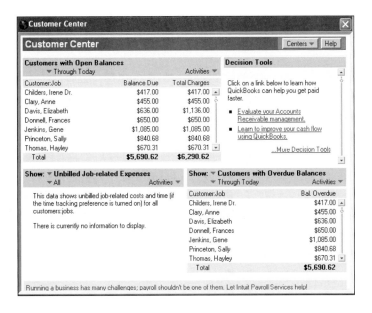

CUSTOMER DETAIL CENTER

Use the Customer Detail Center to manage your business with individual customers. Once the Customer Detail Center has been accessed, use the drop-down list at the top of the window to choose the customer whose information you want to see. At the top of the Center, you will see the Customer Contact Information for the selected customer. Click Edit/More Info to see further information about the customer or to edit the information. You will also see QuickBooks alerts. By default, the tables shown at the bottom of the Customer Detail Center show Open Invoices/Charges and Payments Received and Credits Issued. In addition, if inventory tracking is on, you can change either of the tables to show Outstanding Items on Order.

DO: Click **Centers** at the top of the Customer Center
Click **Customer Detail Center**
Click the drop-down list arrow on the **Customer Detail**
Click **Davis, Elizabeth** (Note: Open Invoices and Payments may not match the
following because your computer date may not match the date in the chapter.)

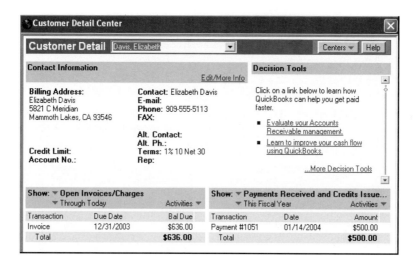

Click **Edit/More Info** for Elizabeth Davis

Click in the **E-mail** textbox on the **Edit Customer** screen

Enter **edavis@hotmail.com** as the e-mail address

Click **OK**

Her e-mail address is now shown in the customer information displayed on the screen

Close the **Customer Detail Center** and the **Customer Center**

GRAPHS IN QUICKBOOKS® PRO

Once transactions have been entered, transaction results can be visually represented in a graphic form. QuickBooks Pro illustrates Accounts Receivable by Aging Period as a bar chart, and it illustrates Accounts Receivable by Customer as a pie chart. For further details, double-click on an individual section of the pie chart or chart legend to create a bar chart analyzing an individual customer. QuickBooks Pro also prepares graphs based on sales and will show the results of sales by item and by customer.

PREPARE ACCOUNTS RECEIVABLE GRAPHS

Accounts Receivable graphs illustrate account information based on the age of the account and the percentage of accounts receivable owed by each customer.

DO: Prepare an Accounts Receivable Graph

Click **Customers & Receivables** on the Report Finder

Click **Accounts Receivable Graph**, click **Display**

Click **Dates** button on the **QuickInsight: Accounts Receivable Graphs**

On the **Change Graph Dates**, change **Show Aging As of** to **01/15/2004**
Click **OK**
- QuickBooks Pro generates a bar chart illustrating Accounts Receivable by Aging Period and a pie chart illustrating Accounts Receivable by Customer.

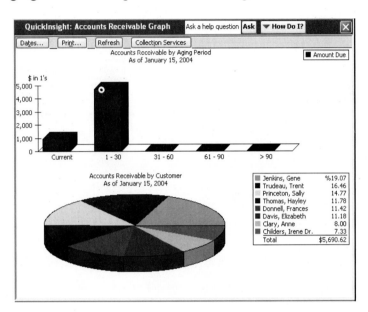

Click **Dates**
Enter **02/01/2004** for the **Show Aging As of** date
Click **OK**
- Notice the difference in the aging of accounts.
Click **Dates**, enter **03/01/2004**
Click **OK**
- Again, notice the difference in aging of accounts.
Close the graph

PREPARE SALES GRAPHS

Sales graphs illustrate the amount of cash and credit sales for a given period as well as the percentage of sales for each sales item.

DO: Click **Sales** as the type of report
Click **Sales Graph**
Click **Display**
Click **Dates**
Click the drop-down list arrow next to **Graph Dates**
Click in **From**, enter **01/01/04**

Tab to **To**, enter **01/15/04**

Click **OK**

By Item button should be indented

- You will see a bar chart representing Sales by Month and a pie chart displaying a Sales Summary by Item.

Printing is not required for this chart

- If you want a printed copy, click **Print**.

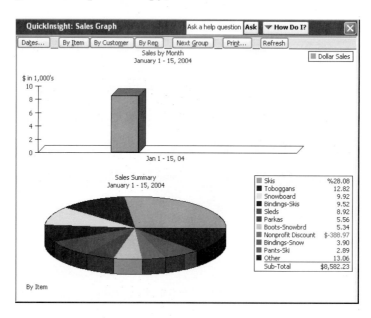

Close the graph and **Report Finder**

BACK UP YEAR ROUND SPORTS DATA

Whenever an important work session is complete, you should always back up your data. If your data disk is damaged or an error is discovered at a later time, the backup disk may be restored and the information used for recording transactions. No matter what type of business, the backup procedure remains the same. In addition, it is always wise to make a duplicate of your data disk just in case the disk is damaged in some way.

DO: Follow the instructions given in Chapters 1 and 2 to back up data for Year Round Sports. Follow the instructions in Appendix A to make a duplicate disk.

SUMMARY

In this chapter, cash, bank charge card, and credit sales were prepared for Year Round Sports, a retail business, using sales receipts and invoices. Credit memos and refund checks were issued, and customer accounts were added and revised. Invoices and sales receipts were edited, deleted, and voided. Cash payments were received, and bank deposits were made. New accounts were added to the Chart of Accounts, and new items were added to the Item List while entering transactions. Inventory items were added and sold. All the transactions entered reinforced the QuickBooks Pro concept of using the business form to record transactions rather than entering information in journals. However, QuickBooks Pro does not disregard traditional accounting methods. Instead, it performs this function in the background. The Journal was accessed, analyzed, and printed. The importance of reports for information and decision-making was illustrated. Exploration of the various sales and accounts receivable reports and graphs allowed information to be viewed from a sales standpoint and from an accounts receivable perspective. Sales reports emphasized both cash and credit sales according to the customer or according to the sales item generating the revenue. Accounts receivable reports focused on amounts owed by credit customers. The traditional trial balance emphasizing the equality of debits and credits was prepared.

END-OF-CHAPTER QUESTIONS

TRUE/FALSE

ANSWER THE FOLLOWING QUESTIONS IN THE SPACE PROVIDED BEFORE THE QUESTION NUMBER.

_____ 1.   If an invoice has been paid in full, a refund check is issued along with a credit memo.

_____ 2.   QuickBooks Pro automatically applies a payment received to the most current invoice.

_____ 3.   Sales tax will be calculated automatically on an invoice if a customer is marked taxable.

_____ 4.   A new sales item may be added only at the beginning of a period.

_____ 5.   A new customer may be added _on the fly_.

_____ 6.   Report formats may be customized.

_____ 7.   The Set Discount button on the Receive Payments window allows discounts to be applied to invoices being paid by clicking Cancel.

_____ 8.   Cash sales are recorded on invoices and marked paid.

_____ 9.   If a customer issues a check that is returned marked NSF, you may charge the customer the amount of the bank charges and any penalty charges you impose.

_____ 10. Sales tax must be calculated manually and added to sales receipts.

MULTIPLE CHOICE

WRITE THE LETTER OF THE CORRECT ANSWER IN THE SPACE PROVIDED BEFORE THE QUESTION NUMBER.

_____ 1. Information regarding details of a customer's balance may be obtained by viewing
.
A. the Trial Balance
B. the Customer's Balance Summary Report
C. the Customer's Balance Detail Report
D. an invoice for the customer

_____ 2. Even though transactions are entered via business documents such as invoices and sales receipts, QuickBooks Pro keeps track of all transactions ___.
A. in a chart
B. in the register
C. on a graph
D. in the Journal

_____ 3. If a transaction is ___, it will not show up in the Customer Balance Detail Report.
A. voided
B. deleted
C. corrected
D. canceled

_____ 4. A credit card sale is treated exactly like a ___.
A. cash sale
B. sale on account until reimbursement is received from a bank
C. sale on account
D. bank deposit

_____ 5. If the word -Split- appears in the Split column of a report rather than an account name, it means that the transaction is split between two or more ___.
A. accounts or items
B. customers
C. journals
D. reports

_____   6. When adding a customer *on the fly*, you may choose to add just the customer's name by selecting ___.
A. Quick Add
B. Set Up
C. Condensed
D. none of the above—a customer cannot be added *on the fly*

_____   7. The Item List stores information about ___.
A. each item that is out of stock
B. each item in stock
C. each customer with an account
D. each item a company sells

_____   8. A report prepared to obtain information about sales, inventory, and merchandise costs is a ___.
A. Stock Report
B. Income Statement
C. Sales by Vendor Summary Report
D. Sales by Item Summary Report

_____   9. If a customer has a balance for an amount owed and a return is made, a credit memo is prepared and ___.
A. a refund check is issued
B. the amount of the return may be applied to the balance owed at the time the invoice is paid
C. the customer determines whether to apply the amount to the balance owed or to get a refund check
D. all of the above

_____   10. Purchase information regarding an item sold by the company is entered ___.
A. in the Invoice Register
B. when adding a sales item
C. only when creating the company
D. when the last item in stock is sold

FILL-IN

IN THE SPACE PROVIDED, WRITE THE ANSWER THAT MOST APPROPRIATELY COMPLETES THE SENTENCE.

1. A report showing all sales, credits, and payments for each customer on account but not the remaining balance on the account is the _____ report.

2. When you make a bank deposit, the _____ window shows all amounts received for cash sales and payments on account that have not been deposited in the bank.

3. If the Quantity and Price Each are entered on an invoice, pressing the _____ key will cause QuickBooks Pro to calculate and enter the correct information in the Amount column of the invoice.

4. QuickBooks Pro allows you to view additional information within a report by using the _____ feature.

5. When you receive payments from customers, QuickBooks Pro places the amount received in an account called _____.

SHORT ESSAY

Describe the use of Find. Based on chapter information, what is used to instruct Find to limit its search?

_____

_____

_____

_____

_____

NAME _____

TRANSMITTAL

CHAPTER 5: YEAR ROUND SPORTS

Attach the following documents and reports:

Invoice No. 1: Rick Woods
Invoice No. 2: Jose Morales
Invoice No. 3: Mountain Schools
Invoice No. 4: Sally Princeton
Invoice No. 5: Trent Trudeau
Invoice No. 6: Rick Woods
Invoice No. 7: Mei-Hwa Chau
Invoice No. 7 (Corrected): Mei-Hwa Chau
Customer Balance Detail
Invoice No. 3 (Corrected): Mountain Schools
Invoice No. 8: Mountain Recreation Center
Credit Memo No. 9: Mei-Hwa Chau
Open Invoices by Customer, January 10, 2004
Sales Receipt No. 1: Cash Customer
Sales Receipt No. 2: Cash Customer
Sales Receipt No. 3: Cash Customer
Sales Receipt No. 4: Cash Customer
Sales Receipt No. 5: Cash Customer
Sales Receipt No. 6: Cash Customer
Sales by Item Summary, January 1-13, 2004
Sales Receipt No. 1 (Revised): Cash Customer, January 8, 2004
Customer Balance Summary
Deposit Summary
Invoice No. 10: Trent Trudeau
Check No. 1: Jose Morales
Credit Memo No. 11: Jose Morales
Journal, January 1-15, 2004
Trial Balance, January 1-15, 2004

END-OF-CHAPTER PROBLEM

GREAT ESCAPES CLOTHING

Great Escapes Clothing is a men's and women's clothing store located in San Luis Obispo, California, specializing in resort wear. The store is owned and operated by Kahala Mahalo and Leilani Ohana. Leilani keeps the books and runs the office for the store, and Kahala is responsible for buying merchandise and managing the store. Both partners sell merchandise in the store, and they have some college students working part time during the evenings and on the weekends.

INSTRUCTIONS

As in previous chapters, copy **Great Escapes.qbw** to a new disk. Open the company, and record the following transactions using invoices and sales receipts. Great Escapes accepts cash, checks, and credit cards for *cash* sales. Make bank deposits as instructed. Print the reports and graphs as indicated. Add new accounts, items, and customers where appropriate.

When recording transactions, use the Item List to determine the item(s) sold. All transactions are taxable unless otherwise indicated. Terms for sales on account are the standard terms assigned to each customer individually. If a customer exceeds his or her credit limit, accept the transaction. When receiving payment for sales on account, always check to see if a discount should be given. A customer's beginning balance is not eligible for a discount. The date of the sale begins the discount period. A check should be received or postmarked within ten days of the invoice in order to qualify for a discount. If the customer has any credits to the account because of a return, apply the credits when payments are received. If the customer makes a return and does not have a balance on account, prepare a refund check for the customer. Invoices begin with number 15, are numbered consecutively, and have lines printed around each field. Sales Receipts begin with number 25, are also numbered consecutively, and have lines printed around each field. Each invoice and sales receipt should contain a message. Use the one you feel is most appropriate.

If you write any checks, keep track of the check numbers used. QuickBooks Pro does not always display the check number you are expecting to see. Remember that QuickBooks Pro does not print check numbers on checks because most businesses use checks with the check numbers preprinted.

If a transaction can be printed, print the transaction when it is entered.

LISTS

The Item List and Customer List are displayed for your use in determining which sales item and customer to use in a transaction.

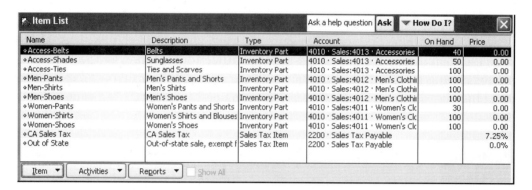

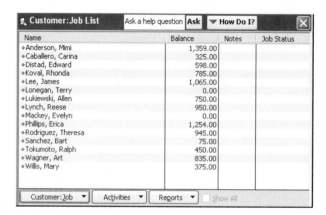

RECORD TRANSACTIONS

January 3, 2005:

Add your name to the company name. The company name will be **Great Escapes Clothing—Student's Name**. (Type your actual name, *not* the words *Student's Name*.)

Customize the Invoice, the Sales Receipt, and the Credit Memo so that there is enough room to display your name in full on the same line as the company name. Change the company preferences so that the date prepared, time prepared, and report basis do not print as part of the heading on reports. Have the reports refresh automatically.

Prepare Invoice No. 15 to record the sale on account for 1 belt for $29.95, 1 pair of shorts for $39.95, and a shirt for $39.95 to Terry Lonegan. Print the invoice.

Received Check No. 3305 from Carina Caballero for $325 in payment of her bill in full.

Record the sale on account of 1 pair of sunglasses for $89.95 to Ralph Tokumoto. (Remember to approve any transaction that exceeds a customer's credit limit.)

CHAPTER 5–SALES AND RECEIVABLES: MERCHANDISING BUSINESS 355

Record the sale of a dress on account to Erica Phillips for $79.95. (Add a new sales item: Women-Dress, Women's Dresses, preferred vendor is Sun Clothes, Income Account is 4011 Women's Clothing, Reorder Point is 20, Qty on Hand 25, Total Value $750, as of 01/01/2004.)

Add a new customer: San Luis Obispo Rec Center, 451 Marsh Street, San Luis Obispo, CA 93407, Contact person is Katie Gregg, 805-555-2241, Credit Terms are 2% 10 Net 30, Credit Limit $1,000, they are taxable for CA Sales Tax.

Sold 5 men's Hawaiian shirts on account to San Luis Recreation Center for $29.95 each, 5 pair of men's shorts for $29.95 each. Because San Luis Recreation Center is a nonprofit organization, include a subtotal for the sale and apply a 10% sales discount for a nonprofit organization. (Create any new sales items necessary by following the instructions given in the chapter. If you need to add a Sales Discounts account to the Chart of Accounts, assign account number 6130.)

Sold 1 woman's blouse for $59.95 to Julee Gardener. Received Check No. 378 for the full amount including tax. Record the sale as a cash customer. (If necessary, refer to steps provided within the chapter for instructions on creating a cash customer.) Issue and print Sales Receipt No. 25 for this transaction.

Received a belt returned by Art Wagner. The original price of the belt was $49.95. Prepare a Credit Memo.

Sold a dress to a customer for $99.95. The customer paid with her Visa. Record the sale.

Sold a scarf for $19.95 plus tax for cash. Record the sale.

Received payments from the following customers:
Edward Distad, $598.00, Check No. 145
Mary Willis, $375, Check No. 4015
Allen Lukiewski, $750, Check No. 8915-02
Art Wagner, $781.43, Check No. 6726

January 5:
Deposit all cash, checks, and credit card receipts. Print a Deposit Summary.

January 15:
Received an NSF notice from the bank for the check for $325 from Carina Caballero. Enter the necessary transaction for this nonsufficient funds check. The bank's charges are $15, and Great Escapes Clothing charges $15 for all NSF checks. (If necessary, refer to steps provided within the chapter for instructions on adding accounts or items necessary to record this transaction.)

Allen Lukiewski returned a shirt he had purchased for $54.99 plus tax. Record the return. Check the balance of his account. If there is no balance, issue a refund check.

Sold 3 men's shirts to Richard Ralph, a cash customer, for $39.95 each plus tax. Richard used his Master Card for payment.

Sold on account 1 dress for $99.99, 1 pair of sandals for $79.95, and a belt for $39.95 to Rhonda Koval.

Sold 1 pair of women's shorts for $34.95 to a cash customer. Accepted Check No. 8160 for payment.

Received a partial payment on account from James Lee, $250, Check No. 2395.

Received payment in full from Bart Sanchez, Check No. 9802.

Received $1,338.03 from Erica Phillips as payment in full on account, Check No. 2311. The payment was postmarked 1/11/2005. (Because both the 12/31/2004 Invoice for $1,254 and Invoice No. 17 are being paid with this check, the payment will be applied to both invoices. In order to apply the discount to Invoice No. 17, click both the beginning balance and Invoice No. 17 to deselect; then click in the check mark column for Invoice No. 17; click Set Discount; calculate the 2 percent discount and enter the amount on the Discounts and Credits screen, select the appropriate account for the sales discount, click Done to apply the discount; and, finally, click in the check mark column for the 12/31/2004 invoice.)

Sold 3 pairs of men's pants for $75.00 each, 3 men's shirts for $50.00 each, 3 belts for $39.99 each, 2 pairs of men's shoes for $90.00 each, 2 ties for $55.00 each, and 1 pair of sunglasses for $75.00 to Theresa Rodriguez on account. (If the amount of the sale exceeds Theresa's credit limit, accept the sale anyway.)

Sold on account 1 pair of sunglasses for $95.00, 2 dresses for $99.95 each, and 2 pairs of women's shoes for $65.00 each to Mary Willis.

Print Customer Balance Detail Report. Adjust column widths so the account names are shown in full and the report is one page wide without selecting Fit report to one page wide. The report length may be longer than one page.

Print a Sales by Item Detail Report for 01/01/2005 to 01/15/2005 in Landscape orientation. Adjust column widths so the report fits on one page wide. Do not select Fit report to one page wide.

Deposit all payments, checks, and charges received from customers. Print the Deposit Summary.

Print a Trial Balance for 01/01/2005 to 01/15/2005.

NAME _____

TRANSMITTAL

CHAPTER 5: GREAT ESCAPES CLOTHING

Attach the following documents and reports:

Invoice No. 15: Terry Lonegan
Invoice No. 16: Ralph Tokumoto
Invoice No. 17: Erica Phillips
Invoice No. 18: San Luis Obispo Rec Center
Sales Receipt No. 25: Cash Customer
Credit Memo No. 19: Art Wagner
Sales Receipt No. 26: Cash Customer
Sales Receipt No. 27: Cash Customer
Deposit Summary, January 5, 2005
Invoice No. 20: Carina Caballero
Check No. 1: Allen Lukiewski
Credit Memo No. 21: Allen Lukiewski
Sales Receipt No. 28: Cash Customer
Invoice No. 22: Rhonda Koval
Sales Receipt No. 29: Cash Customer
Invoice No. 23: Theresa Rodriguez
Invoice No. 24: Mary Willis
Customer Balance Detail
Itemized Sales by Item Report, January 1-15, 2005
Deposit Summary, January 15, 2005
Trial Balance, January 1-15, 2005

PAYABLES AND PURCHASES: MERCHANDISING BUSINESS

LEARNING OBJECTIVES

At the completion of this chapter you will be able to:

1. Understand the concepts for computerized accounting for payables in a merchandising business.
2. Customize a Purchase Order template.
3. Prepare, view, and print purchase orders and checks.
4. Enter items received against purchase orders.
5. Enter bills, enter vendor credits, and pay bills.
6. Edit and correct errors in bills and purchase orders.
7. Add new vendors, modify vendor records, and add new accounts.
8. View accounts payable transaction history from the Enter Bills window.
9. View, use the QuickZoom feature, and/or print QuickReports for vendors, accounts payable register, and so on.
10. Record and edit transactions in the Accounts Payable Register.
11. Edit, void, and delete bills, purchase orders, and checks.
12. Use various payment options including writing checks, using Pay Bills to write checks, and company credit cards.
13. Display and print a Sales Tax Liability Report, an Accounts Payable Aging Summary Report, an Unpaid Bills Detail Report, and a Vendor Balance Summary Report.
14. Use the Vendor Detail Center to obtain information for an individual vendor.
15. Display Accounts Payable Graph by Aging Period.

ACCOUNTING FOR PAYABLES AND PURCHASES

In a merchandising business, much of the accounting for purchases and payables consists of ordering merchandise for resale and paying bills for expenses incurred in the operation of the business. Purchases are for things used in the operation of the business. Some transactions will be in the form of cash purchases; others will be purchases on account. Bills can be paid when they are received or when they are due. Merchandise received must be checked against purchase orders, and completed purchase orders must be closed. Rather than use cumbersome journals, QuickBooks Pro continues to focus on recording transactions based on the business document; therefore, you use the Enter Bills and Pay Bills features of the program to record the receipt and payment of bills. While QuickBooks Pro does not refer to it as such, the Vendor List is the same as the Accounts Payable Subsidiary Ledger.

QuickBooks Pro can remind you when inventory needs to be ordered and when payments are due. Purchase orders are prepared when ordering merchandise. The program automatically tracks inventory and uses the average cost method to value the inventory. QuickBooks Pro can calculate and apply discounts earned for paying bills early. Payments can be made by recording payments in the Pay Bills window or, if using the cash basis for accounting, by writing a check. Merchandise purchased may be paid for at the same time the items and the bill are received, or it may be paid for at a later date. A cash purchase can be recorded by writing a check, by using a credit card, or by using petty cash. Even though QuickBooks Pro focuses on recording transactions on the business forms used, all transactions are recorded behind the scenes in the General Journal.

As in previous chapters, corrections can be made directly on the bill or within the transaction journal. New accounts and vendors may be added *on the fly* as transactions are entered. Purchase orders, bills, or checks may be voided or deleted. Reports illustrating vendor balances, unpaid bills, accounts payable aging, sales tax liability, transaction history, and accounts payable registers may be viewed and printed. Graphs analyzing the amount of accounts payable by aging period provide a visual illustration of the accounts payable.

TRAINING TUTORIAL AND PROCEDURES

The following tutorial will once again work with Year Round Sports. As in Chapter 5, transactions will be recorded for this fictitious company. Refer to procedures given in Chapter 5 to maximize training benefits.

OPEN QUICKBOOKS® PRO AND YEAR ROUND SPORTS

DO: Open QuickBooks Pro as instructed in previous chapters
Open Year Round Sports
Check the title bar to verify that Year Round Sports is the open company and that your name appears.

Year Round Sports--Student's Name - QuickBooks Pro 2004

BEGINNING THE TUTORIAL

In this chapter you will be entering purchases of merchandise for resale in the business and entering bills incurred by the company in the operation of the business. You will also be recording the payment of bills and purchases using checks and credit cards.

The Vendor List keeps information regarding the vendors with which you do business. This information includes the vendor names, addresses, telephone number, fax number, e-mail address, payment terms, credit limits, and account numbers. You will be using the following list for vendors with which Year Round Sports has an account:

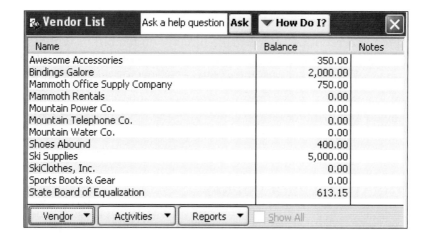

All transactions are listed on memos. The transaction date will be the same date as the memo date unless otherwise specified within the transaction. Vendor names, when necessary, will be given in the transaction. Unless otherwise specified, terms are 2% 10 Net 30. Once a specific type of transaction has been entered in a step-by-step manner, additional transactions of the same or a similar type will be made without having instructions provided. Of course, you may always refer to instructions given for previous transactions for ideas or for steps used to enter those transactions. To determine the account used in the transaction, refer to the Chart of Accounts. When entering account information on a bill, clicking the drop-down list arrow will show a copy of the Chart of Accounts.

VIEW THE REMINDERS LIST TO DETERMINE MERCHANDISE TO ORDER

QuickBooks Pro has a Reminders List that is used to remind you of things that need to be completed. The center section of the Company Navigator displays the Reminders List. If the list is not visible on the screen when you wish to view it, you may also display it by simply clicking the Company menu and clicking Reminders. Information on the Reminders List may be displayed in summary (collapsed) form or in detailed (expanded) form.

MEMO
DATE: January 16, 2004

Display the Reminders List to determine which items need to be ordered.

 DO: Display the **Reminders List**
Use QuickBooks Company Navigator
- The Reminders List appears on the screen in Summary form.
To view the list, click the drop-down list arrow for **View** on the Reminders
Overview, click **Expand All**
- Note: Your Reminders List Summary (Collapsed) form and Reminders List
Detail (Expanded) form may not match the ones displayed in the text. This is
due to the fact that your computer date may be different from the date used in
the chapter. Disregard any differences.

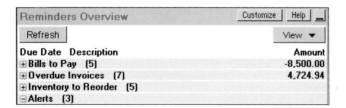

- The expanded view shows the bills that need to be paid as well as overdue
invoices, inventory to reorder, any items that need to be printed, and alerts.

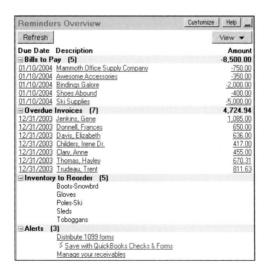

Collapse the Reminders Overview

PRINT THE REMINDERS LIST

The Reminders Overview is displayed on the Company Navigator but is not a list that may be printed. In order to print the Reminders List must be displayed as a list. To use the Reminders List as an aid in reordering merchandise, it is helpful to have it available in printed form. As with all other lists, QuickBooks Pro allows the Reminders List to be printed.

DO: Display the expanded Reminders List on the screen, print the list
Click **Reminders** on the Company Navigator
Click **Expand All**
Use the keyboard shortcut **Ctrl+P**
     OR
Click **File** on the Menu bar, click **Print List**
- Verify that the printer, **Portrait** orientation, and print **All** pages are selected on the Print List dialog box.

Click the **Print** button
When printing is complete, close the **Reminders List**

CUSTOMIZE PURCHASE ORDERS

As instructed in Chapter 5, business forms may be customized. Prior to recording your first purchase order, it should be customized.

DO: Customize a Purchase Order
Click **Purchase Orders** on the **Vendor** navigator
Click the **Customize** button next to **Template**
Click **Edit**
Click the **Layout Designer** button
Change the size for **Purchase Order** to begin at **5**
Expand the area for the **Company Name** to 4 ¾
Click **OK** to close the Layout Designer
Click **OK** to close the Custom Purchase Order template
Do not close the Purchase Order

PURCHASE ORDERS

Using the QuickBooks Pro Purchase Order feature helps you track your inventory. Information regarding the items on order or the items received may be obtained at any time. Once merchandise has been received, QuickBooks Pro marks the purchase order *Received in full*. The Purchase Order feature must be selected as a Preference when setting up the company, or it may be selected prior to processing your first purchase order. QuickBooks Pro will automatically set up an account called Purchase Orders in the Chart of Accounts. The account does not affect the balance sheet or the profit and loss statement of the company. As with other business forms, QuickBooks Pro allows you to customize your purchase orders to fit the needs of your individual company or to use the purchase order format that comes with the program.

VERIFY PURCHASE ORDERS ACTIVE AS A COMPANY PREFERENCE

Verify that the Purchase Order feature of QuickBooks Pro is active by checking the Company Preferences.

MEMO
DATE: January 16, 2004

Prior to completing the first purchase order, verify that Purchase Orders are active.

DO: Verify that Purchase Orders are active by accessing the Company Preferences
Click **Edit** menu, click **Preferences**
Scroll through Preference List until you see **Purchases & Vendors**
Click **Purchases & Vendors**
Click the **Company Preferences** tab
- Make sure there is a check mark in the check box for **Inventory and purchase orders are active**.
- If not, click the check box to select.

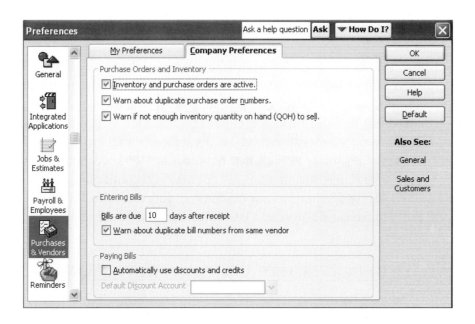

Click **OK** to accept and close

PREPARE PURCHASE ORDERS TO ORDER MERCHANDISE

Once the Purchase Order feature is selected, purchase orders may be prepared. Primarily, purchase orders are prepared to order merchandise; but they may also be used to order non-inventory items like supplies or services.

MEMO

DATE: January 16, 2004

With only 10 pairs of snowboard boots in stock in the middle of January, Andy and Tim decide to order an additional 25 pairs of boots in assorted sizes from Sports Boots & Gear for $75 per pair. Prepare Purchase Order No. 1.

DO: Prepare Purchase Order No. 1 for 25 pairs of snowboard boots
Click **Vendors** menu, click **Create Purchase Orders**
   OR
Click **Vendors** on the Navigator list, click **Purchase Orders** on the QuickBooks Vendor Navigator
Click the drop-down list arrow for **Vendor**, click **Sports Boots & Gear**
Tab to or click **Date**, enter **01/16/2004**

- P.O. No. should be 1.
- If not, enter 1 as the P.O. No.

Tab to or click **Item**, click **Boots-Snowbrd**

Tab to or click **Qty**, enter **25**

- The cost of the item was entered when Boots-Snowbrd was created. The Rate should appear automatically as **75.00**

Tab to generate Amount

Click **Print** to print the **Purchase Order**

Check printer settings:

- Make sure the appropriate printer is selected.
- **Printer type** is Page-oriented (Single sheets).
- **Print on** Blank paper.
- Print lines around each field.

Click **Print**

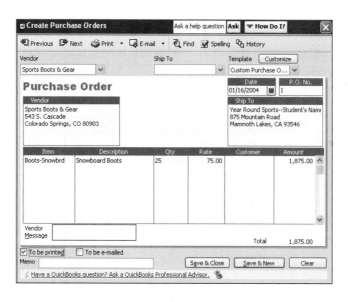

Click **Next** or **Save & New** to go to the next purchase order

PREPARE A PURCHASE ORDER FOR MORE THAN ONE ITEM

If more than one item is purchased from a vendor, all items purchased can be included on the same purchase order.

MEMO

DATE: January 16, 2004

Prepare a purchase order for 3 sleds @ $50 each, and 2 toboggans @ $110 each from a new vendor: Snowfall Gear, 7105 Camino del Rio, Durango, CO 81302, Contact: Leo Jenkins, Phone: 303-555-7765, Fax: 303-555-5677, E-mail: snowfallgear@ski.com, Terms: 2% 10 Net 30, Credit Limit: $2000.

DO: Prepare a purchase order and add a new vendor
Click the drop-down list arrow for **Vendor**, click < **Add New** >
Enter **Snowfall Gear** for the **Vendor** name and the **Company** name
Click the second line of the address, enter **7105 Camino del Rio**
Click the third line of the address, enter **Durango, CO 81302**
Click Address Details

- Verify that **Show this window again when address is incomplete or unclear** has a check mark. This means that the **Edit Address Information** window will appear if the address is incomplete or unclear.

Click **OK**
Tab to or click **Contact**, enter **Leo Jenkins**
Tab to or click **Phone**, enter **303-555-7765**
Tab to or click **FAX**, enter **303-555-5677**
Tab to or click **E-mail**, enter **snowfallgear@ski.com**
Click **Additional Info** tab, click the drop-down list arrow for **Terms**, click **2% 10 Net 30**
Tab to or click **Credit Limit**, enter **2000**
Click **OK** to add Vendor

- The **Date** should be **01/16/2004**. If it is not, delete the date shown and enter **01/16/04**.
- P.O. No. should be **2**. If it is not, enter **2**.

Tab to or click the first line in the column for **Item**

Click the drop-down list arrow for **Item**, click **Sleds**

Tab to or click **Qty**, enter **3**

Tab to or click **Rate**, enter **50**

- The purchase cost was not entered when the item was created, so it must be entered on the purchase order as the Rate.

Tab to generate the total for **Amount**

Repeat steps necessary to enter the information to order 2 toboggans at $110 each

Print **Purchase Order No. 2**

Click **Next** to save **Purchase Order No. 2** and go to the next purchase order

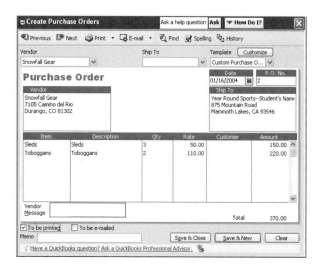

ENTER PURCHASE ORDERS WITHOUT STEP-BY-STEP INSTRUCTIONS

MEMO

DATE: January 16, 2004

Prepare purchase orders for the following:
25 pairs of gloves @ 15.00 each from SkiClothes, Inc.
12 sets of ski poles @ 30.00 each from Ski Supplies.

DO: Prepare and print the purchase orders indicated above.

Compare your completed purchase orders with the ones below:

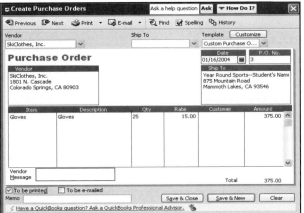

VIEW PURCHASE ORDERS LIST

To see a list of purchase orders, select Purchase Orders from the Vendor menu or on the QuickBooks Vendor Navigator. Another method used to see a list of purchase orders is to select Chart of Accounts from the Lists menu, select Purchase Orders, click the Reports button, and choose QuickReport from the menu shown.

MEMO

DATE: January 16, 2004

Andy and Tim need to see which purchase orders are open. View the Purchase Orders List.

DO: View the open purchase orders for Year Round Sports
Click **Vendors** menu, click **Purchase Orders List**
   OR
Click **Vendors** on the Navigator list, click **PO List** on the
   QuickBooks Vendor Navigator

- The list shows all open purchase orders, the date of the purchase order, and the number of the purchase order.

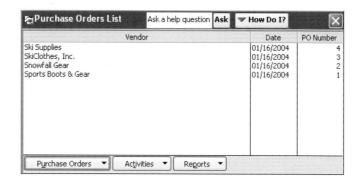

Close the **Purchase Order List**

CHANGE MINIMUM REORDER LIMITS FOR AN ITEM

Any time that you determine your reorder limits are too low or too high, you can change the Reorder Point by editing the Item in the Item List.

MEMO

DATE: January 16, 2004

View the Item List to see the amount on hand for each item. In viewing the list, Andy and Tim determine that they should have a minimum of 35 sets of long underwear on hand at all times. Currently, there are 32 sets of long underwear in stock. Change the reorder point for long underwear to 35.

DO: View the **Item List**
Click **Lists** menu, click **Items**
   OR
Click **Items & Services** icon on the QuickBooks Vendor Navigator
Scroll through Item List, click **Underwear**
Click **Item** button at the bottom of the **Item List**, click **Edit**
Click in **Reorder Point**
Change 30 to **35**

Items & Services

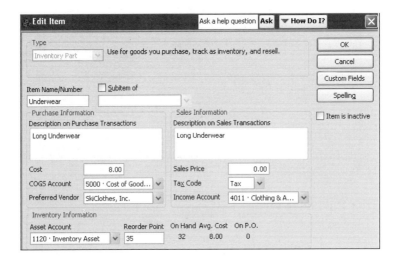

Click **OK** to save and exit
Close the **Item List**

VIEW EFFECT OF REORDER POINT ON REMINDERS LIST

Once the reorder point has been changed and the quantity on hand is equal to or falls below the new minimum, the item will be added to the Reminders List so you will be reminded to order it.

MEMO
DATE: January 16, 2004

Look at the Reminders Overview to see what items need to be ordered.

DO: Look at the **Reminders Overview**
Click **Company** Navigator
- Notice the small box with a plus sign next to Inventory to Reorder. This means that this section of the reminder may be expanded.

In the Reminders Overview, click on **Inventory to Reorder (1)**
- Reminders will be expanded and show **Inventory to Reorder**.
- The small box next to Inventory to Reorder shows a minus sign. This means that this section of the reminder may be collapsed by clicking Inventory to Reorder.

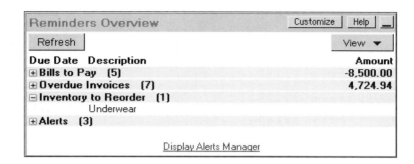

Collapse Inventory to Reorder

VIEW INVENTORY STOCK STATUS BY ITEM REPORT

Several Inventory Reports are available for viewing and/or printing. One report is the Inventory Stock Status by Item report. This report provides information regarding the stock on hand, the stock on order, and the stock that needs to be reordered.

MEMO

DATE: January 16, 2004

More detailed information regarding the stock on hand, stock ordered, and stock needed to be ordered needs to be provided. View the report for Inventory Stock Status by Item.

DO: View the **Inventory Stock Status by Item Report**
       Click the **PO List** icon on the QuickBooks Vendor Navigator
       Click the **Reports** button at the bottom of the **Purchase Order List**, point to
           Inventory, click **Inventory Stock Status by Item**
       Tab to or click **From**, delete the date shown, and enter **01/01/04**
       Tab to or click **To**, delete the date shown, and enter **01/16/04**
       Tab to generate the report
       Scroll through the report
       •   Notice the items in stock.
       •   Notice the reorder point for items.
       •   Find the items marked as needing to be ordered.
       •   Notice the dates of the items that have been ordered.

Year Round Sports--Student's Name
Inventory Stock Status by Item
January 1 - 16, 2004

	Pref Vendor	Reorder Pt	On Hand	Order	On Purchase Order	Next Deliv	Sales/Week
Inventory							
Accessories	Awesome Ac...	100	795		0		2.2
Bindings-Skis	Bindings Galore	10	43		0		3.1
Bindings-Snow	Bindings Galore	5	48		0		0.9
Boots	Shoes Abound	10	20		0		0
Boots-Ski	Sports Boots...	10	14		0		0.4
Boots-Snowbrd	Sports Boots...	10	10		25	01/16/2004	0.9
Gloves	SkiClothes, Inc.	20	20		25	01/16/2004	0.9
Hats	Awesome Ac...	20	29		0		0.4
Pants-Ski	SkiClothes, Inc.	10	93		0		0.9
Pants-Snowbrd	SkiClothes, Inc.	10	50		0		0
Parkas	SkiClothes, Inc.	25	73		0		0.9
Poles-Ski	Ski Supplies	15	13		12	01/16/2004	2.2
Skis	Ski Supplies	15	43		0		3.1
Sleds		5	4		3	01/16/2004	2.6
Snowboard	Ski Supplies	15	28		0		0.9
Socks	Sports Boots...	25	72		0		1.3
Sweaters	SkiClothes, Inc.	25	73		0		0.9
Toboggans		5	5		2	01/16/2004	2.2
Underwear	SkiClothes, Inc.	35	32	✓	0		0.4

Close the report without printing
Close the **Purchase Order List**

PRINT A PURCHASE ORDER QUICKREPORT

It is possible to prepare a QuickReport providing information about purchase orders. The QuickReport can be prepared by accessing Purchase Orders through the Chart of Accounts.

MEMO
DATE: January 16, 2004

Prepare and print a QuickReport of purchase orders as of January 16.

DO: Prepare a QuickReport of Purchase Orders
Access Chart of Accounts as instructed in other chapters
Scroll through the Chart of Accounts until you find **Purchase Orders**
- Purchase Orders is the last item in the Chart of Accounts.

Click **Purchase Orders**
Click the **Reports** button at the bottom of the Chart of Accounts
Click **QuickReport: 2-Purchase Orders**
    OR
Use the keyboard shortcut **Ctrl+Q**
Insert the appropriate dates:

From **01/01/04** To **01/16/04**

Tab to generate the report

Resize the columns as previously instructed to:

> Eliminate the **Memo** column
>
> Be able to view the account name in full in the **Split** column
>
> Be able to print in Portrait orientation on one page without using Fit to one page wide

Click **Print** to print the report

Year Round Sports--Student's Name

Account QuickReport

As of January 16, 2004

Type	Date	Num	Name	Split	Amount
2 · Purchase Orders					
Purchase Order	01/16/2004	1	Sports Boots & Gear	1120 · Inventory Asset	-1,875.00
Purchase Order	01/16/2004	2	Snowfall Gear	-SPLIT-	-370.00
Purchase Order	01/16/2004	3	SkiClothes, Inc.	1120 · Inventory Asset	-375.00
Purchase Order	01/16/2004	4	Ski Supplies	1120 · Inventory Asset	-360.00
Total 2 · Purchase Orders					-2,980.00
TOTAL					**-2,980.00**

Close the report

Close the **Chart of Accounts**

RECEIVING ITEMS ORDERED

The form used to record the receipt of items in QuickBooks Pro depends on the way in which the ordered items are received. Items received may be recorded in three ways. If the items are received without a bill and you pay later, record the receipt on an item receipt. If the items are received at the same time as the bill, record the item receipt on a bill. If the items are received and paid for at the same time, record the receipt of items on a check or a credit card.

RECORD RECEIPT OF ITEMS NOT ACCOMPANIED BY A BILL

The ability to record inventory items prior to the arrival of the bill keeps quantities on hand, quantities on order, and the inventory up to date. Items ordered on a purchase order that arrive before the bill is received are recorded on an item receipt. When the bill arrives, it is recorded.

MEMO

DATE: January 18, 2004

The sleds and toboggans ordered from Snowfall Gear, arrive without a bill. Record the receipt of the 3 sleds and 2 toboggans.

 DO: Record the receipt of the items above
Click **Vendors** menu, click **Receive Items**
      OR
Use QuickBooks Vendor Navigator:
   Click the **Receive Items** icon
         OR
   Click the **PO List** icon, click **Activities**, click **Receive Items**
Click the drop-down list arrow for **Vendor**, click **Snowfall Gear**

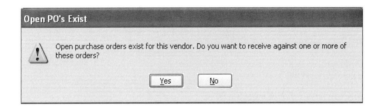

Click **Yes** on the **Open PO's Exist** message box
- An **Open Purchase Orders** dialog box appears showing all open purchase orders for the vendor, Snowfall Gear
Point to any part of the line for P.O. No. 2
Click to select **Purchase Order No. 2**
- This will place a check mark in the check mark column.
Click **OK**

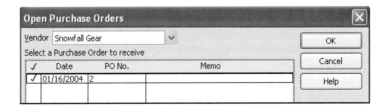

- Notice the completed information for the **Items** tab indicating how many sleds and toboggans were received.
- Notice the **Memo** box beneath the **Item Receipt**. It states *Received items (bill to follow).*
- If necessary, change the date to **01/18/2004**.

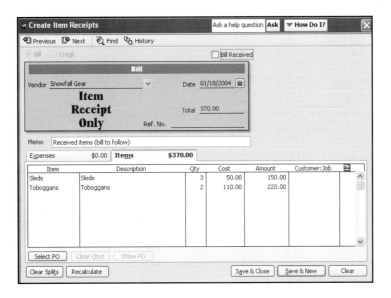

Click **Save & Close**
If necessary, close **Purchase Order List**

VERIFY THAT PURCHASE ORDER IS MARKED RECEIVED IN FULL

Once items have been marked as received, QuickBooks Pro stamps the Purchase Order *Received in Full* and marks each item received in full as *Clsd*.

MEMO

DATE: January 18, 2004

View the original Purchase Order No. 2 to verify that it has been stamped Received in Full and each item received is marked Clsd.

DO: Verify that Purchase Order No. 2 is marked Received in Full and all items received are Closed
Access Purchase Orders as previously instructed
Click **Previous** until you get to **Purchase Order No. 2**
- The Purchase Order should be stamped **RECEIVED IN FULL**.
- Next to the **Amount** column, you will see two new columns: **Rcv'd** and **Clsd**.
  - **Rcv'd** indicates the number of the items received.

- **Clsd** indicates that the number of items were received in full so the Purchase Order has been closed for that Item.

Purchase Order					Date	01/16/2004	P.O. No.	2

Vendor
Snowfall Gear
7105 Camino del Rio
Durango, CO 81302

RECEIVED IN FULL

Ship To
Year Round Sports--Student's Name
875 Mountain Road
Mammoth Lakes, CA 93546

Item	Description	Qty	Rate	Customer	Amount	Rcv'd	Clsd
Sleds	Sleds	3	50.00		150.00	3	✓
Toboggans	Toboggans	2	110.00		220.00	2	✓

Vendor Message

Total 370.00

Close **Create Purchase Orders** window

ENTER RECEIPT OF A BILL FOR ITEMS ALREADY RECEIVED

For items that have been received prior to the bill, the receipt of items is recorded as soon as the items arrive. When the bill is received, it must be recorded. To do this, indicate that the bill is for items received and mark the Receive Items List as bill received. When completing a bill for items already received, QuickBooks Pro fills in all essential information on the bill. A bill is divided into two sections: a vendor-related section (the upper part of the bill that looks similar to a check and has a memo text box under it) and a detail section (the area that has two tabs marked Items and Expenses). The vendor-related section of the bill is where information for the actual bill is entered, including a memo with information about the transaction. The detail section is where the information regarding the items ordered, the quantity ordered and received, and the amounts due for the items received is indicated.

MEMO

DATE: January 19, 2004

Record the bill for the sleds and toboggans already received from Snowfall Gear Vendor's Invoice No. 97 dated 01/18/2004, Terms 2% 10 Net 30.

DO: Record the above bill for items already received
Click **Vendors**, click **Enter Bill for Received Items**
OR

Use QuickBooks Vendor Navigator:

Click **Receive Bill**

  OR

Click **PO List**, click **Activities**, click **Enter Bill for Received Items**

On the **Select Item Receipt**, click the drop-down list arrow for **Vendor**, click **Snowfall Gear**

- Snowfall Gear is entered as the vendor.

Click anywhere on the line **01/18/2004 Received items (bill to follow)** to select the Item Receipt

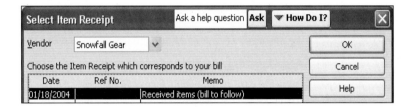

Click **OK**

- QuickBooks Pro displays the **Enter Bills** screen and the completed bill for Snowfall Gear
- The date shown is the date the items were received **01/18/2004**.

Tab to or click **Ref No.**, type the vendor's invoice number **97**

- Notice that the **Amount Due** of **370** has been inserted.
- Terms of **2% 10 Net 30** and the due date are shown.
- The discount date does not always appear on the bill. If you change the date on the bill and press tab, the discount date may appear. With terms of 2% 10 Net 30, the discount date, if it appears, will be ten days from the date of the invoice or 01/28/2004.

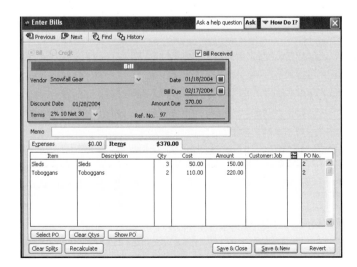

Click **Save & Close**

- If you get a Recording Transaction message box regarding the fact that the transaction has been changed, click **Yes**.

RECORD RECEIPT OF ITEMS AND A BILL

When ordered items are received and accompanied by a bill, the receipt of the items is recorded while entering the bill.

MEMO

DATE: January 19, 2004

Received 25 pairs of snowboard boots and a bill from Sports Boots & Gear. Record the bill dated 01/18/2004 and the receipt of the items.

DO: Record the receipt of the items and the bill

Click **Receive Items with Bill** on QuickBooks Vendor Navigator
   OR
Click **PO List** on QuickBooks Vendor Navigator, click **Activities**, click **Receive Items & Enter Bill**
   OR
Click **Vendors** on the menu bar, click **Receive Items and Enter Bill**
Click the drop-down list for **Vendor**, click **Sports Boots & Gear**
Click **Yes** on the **Open PO's Exist** message box

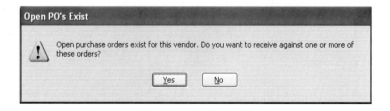

Click anywhere in P.O. No. 1 line to select

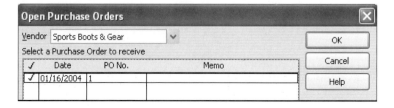

Click **OK**
- The bill appears on the screen and is complete.
- Because no invoice number was given in the transaction, leave the **Ref. No.** blank.

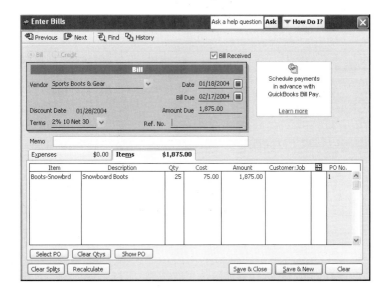

Click **Save & Close**
- If necessary, close any open **Item List** or **Purchase Orders List**.

EDIT A PURCHASE ORDER

As with any other form, purchase orders may be edited once they have been prepared. Purchase orders may be accessed by clicking on the Purchase Order icon in QuickBooks Vendor Navigator or by displaying the Purchase Order List and clicking the Activities button and Edit.

MEMO
DATE: January 19, 2004

Rhonda realized that Purchase Order No. 4 should be for 15 pairs of ski poles. Change the purchase order and reprint.

DO: Change Purchase Order No. 4
          Access Purchase Order No. 4:

> Click the **Purchase Order** icon in QuickBooks Vendor Navigator, click **Previous** until you see P.O. 4
> OR
> Click the **PO List** icon on QuickBooks Vendor Navigator, click **Ski Supplies**, click the **Purchase Order** button, click **Edit**
> Click in **Qty**, change the number from 12 to **15**
> Tab to recalculate the amount due for the purchase order

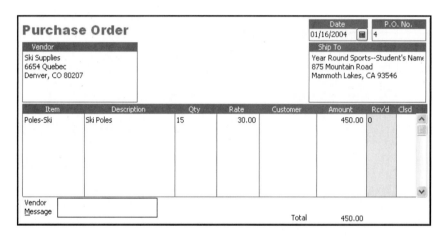

> Print the **Purchase Order** as previously instructed
> Click **Save & Close** to record the changes and exit
> Click **Yes** on the **Recording Transaction** dialog box to save the changes
> - If it is open, close the **Purchase Order List**.

RECORD A PARTIAL RECEIPT OF MERCHANDISE ORDERED

Sometimes when items on order are received, they are not received in full. The remaining items may be delivered as back-ordered items. This will usually occur if an item is out of stock, and you must wait for delivery until more items are manufactured and/or received by the vendor. With QuickBooks Pro you record the number of items you actually receive, and the bill is recorded for that amount.

> ## MEMO
> **DATE:** January 19, 2004
>
> Record the bill and the receipt of 20 pairs of gloves ordered on Purchase Order No. 3. On the purchase order, 25 pairs of gloves were ordered. SkiClothes, Inc., will no longer be carrying these gloves, so the remaining 5 pairs of gloves on order will not be shipped. Manually close the purchase order. The date of the bill is 01/18/2004.

DO: Record the receipt of and the bill for 20 pairs of gloves from SkiClothes, Inc.

Access **Receive Items with Bill** or **Receive Items & Enter Bill** as previously instructed

If necessary, change the **Date** of the bill to **01/18/2004**

Click the drop-down list arrow for **Vendor**, click **SkiClothes, Inc.**

Click **Yes** on **Open PO's Exist** dialog box

Click anywhere in the line for **P.O. 3** on **Open Purchase Orders** dialog box

Click **OK**

Click the **Qty** column on the Items tab at the bottom of the Enter Bills window

Change the quantity to **20**

Tab to change **Amount** to **300**

- Notice the **Amount Due** on the bill also changes.

Click **Save & Close** to record the items received and the bill

CLOSE PURCHASE ORDER MANUALLY

If you have issued a purchase order and it is determined that you will not be receiving the items on order, a purchase order can be closed manually.

DO: Close Purchase Order No. 3

Use **Find** to locate Purchase Order No. 3

Click **Edit** on the menu bar, click **Advanced Find**

Scroll through **Choose Filter**

- Filter helps to narrow the search for locating something.

Click **Transaction Type**, click the drop-down list arrow for **Transaction Type**, click **Purchase Order**

Click **Find**

- A list of all purchase orders shows on the screen.

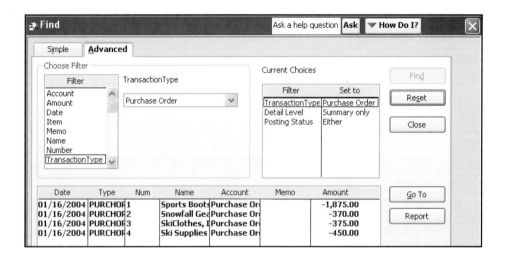

Click **Purchase Order No. 3** for **SkiClothes, Inc**.
Click **Go To**
Click the **Clsd** column to mark and close the purchase order
- Notice that the ordered **Qty** is 25 and **Rcv'd** is 20.

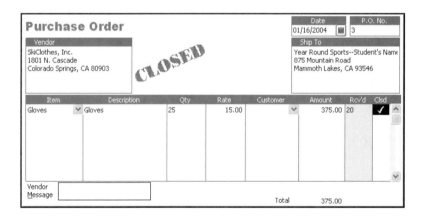

Click **Save & Close** to close the purchase order
Close **Find**

ENTER A CREDIT FROM A VENDOR

Credit memos are prepared to record a reduction to a transaction. With QuickBooks Pro you use the Enter Bills window to record credit memos received from vendors acknowledging a return of or an allowance for a previously recorded bill and/or payment. The amount of a credit memo can be applied to the amount owed to a vendor when paying bills.

MEMO

DATE: January 21, 2004

Upon further inspection of merchandise received, Rhonda Spears found that one of the sleds received from Snowfall Gear, was cracked. The sled was returned. Received Credit Memo No. 9912 from Snowfall Gear, for $50, the full amount on the return of 1 sled.

DO: Prior to recording the above return, check the **Item List** to verify how many sleds are currently on hand

Access **Item List** as previously instructed

- Look at Sleds to verify that there are 7 sleds in stock.

Close the **Item List**

Access the **Enter Bills** window and record the credit memo shown above

On the **Enter Bills** screen, click **Credit** to select

- The word *Bill* changes to *Credit*.

Click the drop-down list arrow next to **Vendor**, click **Snowfall Gear**

Tab to or click the **Date**, type **01/21/04**

Tab to or click **Credit Amount**, type **50**

Tab to or click **Ref. No.**, type **9912**

Tab to **Memo**, enter **Returned 1 Sled**

Tab to or click the **Items** tab

Tab to or click the first line in the **Item** column, click the drop-down list arrow, click **Sleds**

Tab to or click **Qty**, enter **1**

Tab to or click **Cost**, enter **50**

Tab to enter the **50** for **Amount**

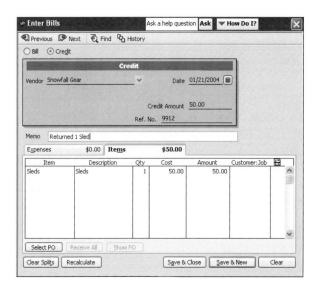

Click **Save & Close** to record the credit and exit the **Enter Bills** window

- QuickBooks Pro decreases the quantity of sleds on hand and creates a credit with the vendor that can be applied when paying the bill. The Credit Memo also appears in the Accounts Payable account in the **Paid** column, which decreases the amount owed and shows the transaction type as BILLCRED in the Accounts Payable register.

Access the **Item List**

- Verify that there are 6 sleds in stock after the return.

Close the list

Access the **Chart of Accounts** as previously instructed, click **Accounts Payable**

Click the **Activities** button, click **Use Register**

Scroll through the register until you see the BILLCRED for Snowfall Gear

01/21/2004	9912	Snowfall Gear					50.00	10,995.00
	BILLCRED	1120 · Inventory Asset Returned 1 Sled						

Close the **Accounts Payable Register**

Close the **Chart of Accounts**

MAKE A PURCHASE USING A CREDIT CARD

Some businesses use credit cards as an integral part of their finances. Many companies have a credit card used primarily for gasoline purchases for company vehicles. Other companies use credit cards as a means of paying for expenses or purchasing merchandise or other necessary items for use in the business.

MEMO

DATE: January 21, 2004

Rhonda discovered that she was out of paper. She purchased a box of paper to have on hand to be used for copies, for the laser printer, and for the fax machine from Mammoth Office Supply Company for $21.98. Rather than add to the existing balance owed to the company, Andy and Tim decided to have Rhonda pay for the office supplies using the company's Visa card.

DO: Purchase the above office supplies using the company's Visa card

Click the **Banking** menu, click **Record Credit Card** Charges, then click **Enter Credit Card Charges**

OR

Click **Banking** on the Navigator list

On the QuickBooks Banking Navigator, click **Credit Card Charges**

Credit Card should indicate **2100 Visa**

Click the drop-down list arrow for **Purchased From**, click **Mammoth Office Supply Company**

Click **OK** on the **Warning** screen

Date should be **01/21/2004**

Ref No. is blank

Tab to or click **AMOUNT**, enter **21.98**

Tab to or click **Memo**, enter **Purchase Paper**

Tab to or click the **Account** column on the **Expenses** tab, click the drop-down list arrow for **Account**, click **1311 Office Supplies**

Click **Next** to record the charge and go to the next credit card entry

PAY FOR INVENTORY ITEMS ON ORDER USING A CREDIT CARD

It is possible to pay for inventory items using a credit card. The payment may be made using the Pay Bills window, or it may be made by recording an entry for Credit Card Charges. If you are purchasing something that is on order, you may record the receipt of merchandise on order first, or you may record the receipt of merchandise and the credit card payment at the same time.

MEMO

DATE: January 21, 2004

Note from Andy: Rhonda, record the receipt of 10 ski poles from Ski Supplies. Pay for the ski poles using the company's Visa.

DO: Pay for the ski poles received using the Visa
Click the drop-down list for **Purchased From** click **Ski Supplies**
Click the **Yes** button on the **Open PO's Exist** message box

To select P.O. No. 4, click the line containing information regarding P.O. No. 4 on the **Open Purchase Orders** dialog box

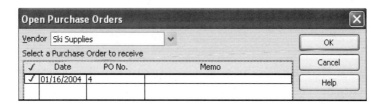

Click **OK**
- If you get a warning screen regarding outstanding bills, click **OK.**

Click the **Clear Qtys** button on the bottom of the screen to clear 15 from the Qty column

Tab to or click **Qty**, enter **10**

Tab to change the Amount to 300

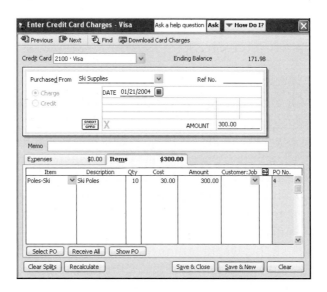

Click **Save & Close** to record and close the transaction

CONFIRM THE RECORDING OF THE SKI POLES RECEIVED ON PURCHASE ORDER NO. 4

> **MEMO**
>
> **DATE:** January 21, 2004
>
> View Purchase Order No. 4 to determine whether or not the amount of ski poles received was recorded.

DO: Access Purchase Order No. 4 as previously instructed
- The **Rcv'd** column should show **10**.
- Notice that the **Qty** column shows **15** and **Clsd** is not marked. This indicates that 5 sets of ski poles are still on order.

Click the **Save & Close** button to close Purchase Order No. 4

ENTER BILLS

Whether the bill is to pay for expenses incurred in the operation of a business or to pay for merchandise to sell in the business, QuickBooks Pro provides accounts payable tracking for all vendors to which the company owes money. Entering bills as soon as they are received is an efficient way to record your liabilities. Once bills have been entered, QuickBooks Pro will be able to provide up-to-date cash flow reports, and QuickBooks Pro will remind you when it's time to pay your bills. As previously stated, a bill is divided into two sections: a vendor-related section (the upper part of the bill that looks similar to a check and has a memo text box under it) and a detail section (the area that is divided into columns for Account, Amount, and Memo). The vendor- related section of the bill is where information for the actual bill is entered, including a memo with information about the transaction. If the bill is for paying an expense, the Expenses tab is used for the detail section. Using this tab allows you to indicate the expense accounts for the transaction, to enter the amounts for the various expense accounts, and to provide transaction explanations. If the bill is for merchandise, the Items tab will be used to record the receipt of the items ordered.

MEMO
DATE: January 23, 2004

Took out an ad in the *Mammoth Lakes News* announcing our February sale. Received a bill for $95.00 from *Mammoth Lakes News*, Terms Net 30, Invoice No. 381-22. The newspaper is a new vendor. The address is 1450 Main Street, Mammoth Lakes, CA 93546, Contact: Fran Falco, Phone: 909-555-2525, Fax: 909-555-5252, E-mail: mammothlakesnews@ski.com.

DO: Record the receipt of the bill from *Mammoth Lakes News* and add the newspaper as a new vendor

Use QuickBooks Navigator:

Click **Vendors** on the Navigator list, click **Enter Bills** on the QuickBooks Vendor Navigator

Complete the **Vendor-Related Section** of the bill:

    Click the drop-down list arrow next to **Vendor**, click **<Add New>**

    Enter the **Vendor** name as **Mammoth Lakes News**

    Tab to or click **Company Name**, enter **Mammoth Lakes News**

    Tab to or click the second line in the **Address**, enter **1450 Main Street**, press **Enter**

    Key in **Mammoth Lakes, CA 93546**

    Tab to or click **Contact**, key in **Fran Falco**

    Tab to or click **Phone**, enter **909-555-2525**

    Tab to or click **FAX**, enter **909-555-5252**

    Tab to or click **E-mail**, enter **mammothlakesnews@ski.com**

    Click **OK** to exit and add the name to the Vendor List

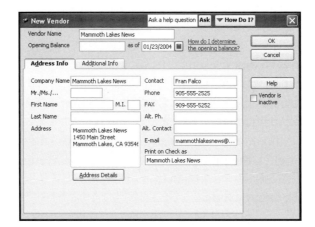

- Mammoth Lakes News is entered as the vendor on the bill.
  Tab to **Date**, type **01/23/04** as the date
  Tab to **Amount Due**, type **95**
  Tab to **Terms**, click the drop-down list arrow next to **Terms**, click **Net 30**
  - QuickBooks Pro automatically changes the Bill Due date to show 30 days from the transaction date.
  - At this time no change will be made to the Bill Due date, and nothing will be inserted as a memo.
  Tab to **Ref No.**, type the vendor's invoice number **381-22**

Complete the **Detail Section** of the bill:
  - If necessary, click the **Expenses** tab so it is the area of the detail section in use.
  Tab to or click in the column for **Account**, click the drop-down list arrow next to **Account**, scroll through the list to find **Advertising Expense**
  Because the account does not appear, click **<Add New>**
  - **Type** of account should show **Expense**. If not, click drop-down list arrow and click **Expense**.
  Enter **6140** as the account number in **Number**
  Tab to or click **Name**, enter **Advertising Expense**

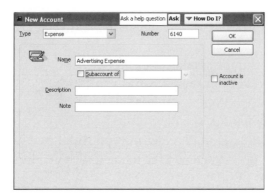

Click **OK**
6140 Advertising Expense shows as the Account
- Based on the accrual method of accounting, **Advertising Expense** is selected as the account for this transaction because this expense should be matched against the revenue of the period.
- The Amount column already shows **95.00**—no entry required
Tab to or click the first line in the column for **Memo**
Enter the transaction explanation of:
Ad for February Sale

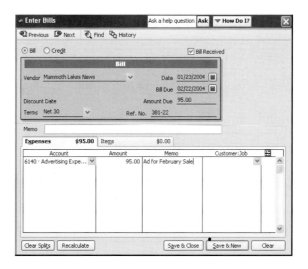

Click **Save & Close**
- If you get a dialog box for **Name Information Changed**, click **No**.

CHANGE EXISTING VENDORS' TERMS

Once a vendor has been established, changes can be made to the vendor's account information. The changes will take effect immediately and will be reflected in any transactions recorded for the vendor.

MEMO

DATE: January 23, 2004

Rhonda Spears realizes that no terms were recorded for Mountain Power Company, Mountain Telephone Company, and Mountain Water Company when vendor accounts were established. Change the terms for the three companies to Net 30.

DO: Change the terms for all of the vendors listed above
Access the **Vendor List** as previously instructed
Click **Mountain Power Co.**, click **Vendor**, click **Edit**
    OR
Double-click on **Mountain Power Co.**
Click **Additional Info** tab
Click the drop-down list arrow for terms, click **Net 30**
Click **OK**
Repeat for the other vendors indicated in the memo above

Close the **Vendor List** when all changes have been made

PREPARE BILLS WITHOUT STEP-BY-STEP INSTRUCTIONS

It is more efficient to record bills in a group or batch than it is to record them one at a time. If an error is made while preparing the bill, correct it. Year Round Sports uses the accrual basis of accounting. In the accrual method of accounting the expenses of a period are matched against the revenue of the period. Unless otherwise instructed, use the accrual basis of accounting when recording entries.

MEMO
DATE: January 25, 2004

Record the receipt of the following bills:

Mountain Power Company electrical power for January, $359.00, Invoice No. 3510-1023, Net 30.
Mountain Telephone Company telephone service for January, $156.40, Invoice No. 7815-21, Net 30.
Mountain Water Company water for January, $35.00, Invoice No. 3105, Net 30.

 DO: Enter the three transactions in the memo above.
- Refer to the instructions given for previous transactions.
- Remember, when recording bills, you will need to determine the accounts used in the transaction. To determine the appropriate accounts to use, refer to the Chart of Accounts as you record the transactions.
- Enter information for Memos where transaction explanation is needed for clarification.
- To go from one bill to the next, click **NEXT** button at the top of the bill or the **Save & New** button at the bottom of the bill.
- After entering the last bill, click **Save & Close** to record and exit the **Enter Bills** screen.

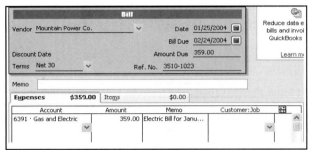

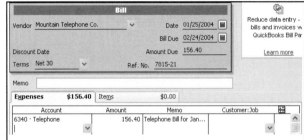

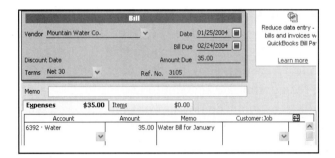

ENTER A BILL USING THE ACCOUNTS PAYABLE REGISTER

The Accounts Payable Register maintains a record of all the transactions recorded within the Accounts Payable account. Not only is it possible to view all of the account activities through the account's register, it is also possible to enter a bill directly into the Accounts Payable register. This can be faster than filling out all of the information through Enter Bills.

MEMO

DATE: January 25, 2004

Received a bill for the rent from Mammoth Rentals. Use the Accounts Payable Register and record the bill for rent of $950, Invoice No. 7164, due February 4, 2004.

DO: Use the Accounts Payable Register to record the above transaction:
Click the **Lists** menu, click **Chart of Accounts**

OR
Use the keyboard shortcut, **Ctrl+A**
Double-click **Accounts Payable**
- This will open the Accounts Payable register

Click in the blank entry at the end of the register
The date is highlighted, key in **01/25/04** for the transaction date
The word *Number* is in the next column
Tab to or click **Number**
- The word *Number* disappears.

Enter the Invoice Number **7164**
Tab to or click **Vendor**, click the drop-down list arrow for the Vendor, click
    Mammoth Rentals
If necessary, Tab to or click **Due Date**, and enter the due date **02/04/04**
Tab to or click **Billed**, enter the amount **950**
Tab to or click **Account**, click the drop-down list arrow for **Account**
Determine the appropriate account to use for rent
- If all of the accounts do not appear in the drop-down list, scroll through the accounts until you find the one appropriate for this entry.

Click **6300 Rent**
Tab to or click Memo, key **Rent**
Click **Record** to record the transaction

01/25/2004	7164	Mammoth Rentals	02/04/2004	950.00		12,590.40
	BILL	6300 · Rent Rent				

Do not close the register

EDIT A TRANSACTION IN THE ACCOUNTS PAYABLE REGISTER

Because QuickBooks Pro makes corrections extremely user friendly, a transaction can be edited or changed directly in the Accounts Payable Register as well as on the original bill. By eliminating the columns for Type and Memo, it is possible to change the register to show each transaction on one line. This can make the register easier to read.

> **MEMO**
>
> **DATE:** January 25, 2004
>
> Upon examination of the invoices and the bills entered, Rhonda discovers an error: The actual amount of the bill from the water company was **$85**, not $35. Change the transaction amount for this bill.

DO: Correct the above transaction in the Accounts Payable Register
Click the check box for **1-line** to select
- Each Accounts Payable transaction will appear on one line.

Click the transaction for Mountain Water Co.
Change the amount of the transaction from $35.00 to **$85.00**
Click the **Record** button at the bottom of the register to record the change in the transaction

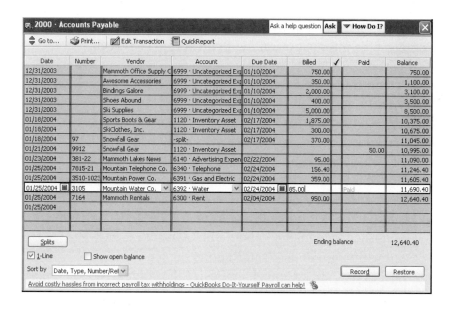

Do not close the register

PREVIEW AND PRINT A QUICKREPORT
FROM THE ACCOUNTS PAYABLE REGISTER

After editing the transaction, you may want to view information about a specific vendor. Clicking the vendor's name within a transaction and clicking the QuickReport button at the top of the register can do this quickly and efficiently.

MEMO
DATE: January 25, 2004

More than one transaction has been entered for Snowfall Gear. The owners, Andy and Tim, like to view transaction information for all vendors that have several transactions within a short period of time.

DO: Prepare a QuickReport for Snowfall Gear
Click any field in any transaction for Snowfall Gear
Click the **QuickReport** button at the top of the Register
- The Register QuickReport for All Transactions for Snowfall Gear appears on the screen.
Resize the columns so the Account is shown in full and the report will print on one page in Landscape orientation
Click **Print**
Click **OK** on the screen for smart page breaks
Complete the information on the **Print Reports Screen**:
   Print to: Printer
   Orientation: Landscape
   Page Range: All
Click **Preview** to view the report before printing
- The report appears on the screen as a full page.
- A full-page report usually cannot be read on the screen.
To read the text in the report, click the **Zoom In** button at the top of the screen
Use the scroll buttons and bars to view the report columns
Click the **Zoom Out** button to return to a full-page view of the report
When finished viewing the report, click **Close**
- You will return to the Print Reports Screen.
- If necessary, click **Cancel** and resize the columns so the reports will print on one-page wide.
When the columns are shown appropriately, click **Print** button on the Print Reports Screen

Year Round Sports--Student's Name
Register QuickReport
All Transactions

Type	Date	Num	Memo	Account	Paid	Open Balance	Amount
Snowfall Gear							
Bill	01/18/2004	97		2000 · Accounts Payable	Unpaid	370.00	370.00
Credit	01/21/2004	9912	Returned 1 Sled	2000 · Accounts Payable	Unpaid	-50.00	-50.00
Total Snowfall Gear						320.00	320.00
TOTAL						320.00	320.00

Click the **Close** button to close the report

Close the Accounts Payable register by double-clicking on the **Control Menu Button** or **Icon** in the top left corner of the Accounts Payable title bar

Click the **Close** button to close the **Chart of Accounts**

PREPARE AND PRINT UNPAID BILLS DETAIL REPORT

It is possible to get information regarding unpaid bills by simply preparing a report. No more digging through tickler files, recorded invoices, ledgers, or journals. QuickBooks Pro prepares an Unpaid Bills Detail Report listing each unpaid bill grouped and subtotaled by vendor.

MEMO

DATE: January 25, 2004

Rhonda Spears prepares an Unpaid Bill Report for Andy and Tim each week. Because Year Round Sports is a small business, the owners like to have a firm control over cash flow so they can determine which bills will be paid during the week.

DO: Prepare and print an **Unpaid Bills Detail Report**

Click **Reports** on the menu bar, point to **Vendors & Payables**, click **Unpaid Bills Detail**

OR

Use QuickBooks Navigator Report Finder: Click **Report Finder** on any QuickBooks Navigator, click **Vendors & Payables** for the type of Report click **Unpaid Bills Detail**, click **Display**

- The **Unpaid Bills Detail Report** shows on the screen.

Enter the date of **01/25/04** as the report date

Tab to generate report

Click the **Print** button, use Portrait orientation

```
                    Year Round Sports--Student's Name
                         Unpaid Bills Detail
                         As of January 25, 2004
     ◇    Type      ◇   Date  ◇ Num ◇  Due Date ◇ Aging ◇  Open Balance  ◇
   Ski Supplies
     Bill              12/31/2003         01/10/2004    15        5,000.00
   Total Ski Supplies                                             5,000.00


   SkiClothes, Inc.
     Bill              01/18/2004         02/17/2004               300.00
   Total SkiClothes, Inc.                                          300.00


   Snowfall Gear
     Credit            01/21/2004  9912                            -50.00
     Bill              01/18/2004  97     02/17/2004               370.00
   Total Snowfall Gear                                             320.00


   Sports Boots & Gear
     Bill              01/18/2004         02/17/2004              1,875.00
   Total Sports Boots & Gear                                      1,875.00

   TOTAL                                                         12,640.40
```

Click **Close** to close the report; if necessary, close the Report Finder

PAYING BILLS

When using QuickBooks Pro, you may choose to pay your bills directly from the Pay Bills command and let QuickBooks Pro write your checks for you, or you may choose to write the checks yourself. If you recorded a bill, you should use the Pay Bills feature of QuickBooks Pro to pay the bill. If no bill was recorded, you should pay the bill by writing a check in QuickBooks Pro. Using the Pay Bills window enables you to determine which bills to pay, the method of payment—check, or credit card—and the appropriate account. When you are determining which bills to pay, QuickBooks Pro allows you to display the bills by due date, discount date, vendor, or amount. All bills may be displayed, or only those bills that are due by a certain date may be displayed. In addition, when a bill has been recorded and is paid using the Pay Bills feature of QuickBooks Pro, the bill will be marked *Paid in Full* and the amount paid will no longer be shown as a liability. If you record a bill and pay it by writing a check and *not* using the Pay Bills feature of QuickBooks, the bill won't be marked as paid and it will show up as a liability.

MEMO

DATE: January 25, 2004

Whenever possible, Rhonda Spears pays the bills on a weekly basis. Show all the bills in the Pay Bills window. Select the bills, except the bill for Snowfall Gear, with discounts dates of 1/28/2004 for payment.

DO: Pay the bills that are eligible for a discount

Access the **Pay Bills** window:

    Click the **Vendors** menu, click **Pay Bills**

        OR

    Use QuickBooks Navigator: Click **Vendors** on the Navigator list, click **Pay Bills** on the QuickBooks Vendor Navigator

Determine the bills to be paid:

    Click **Show All Bills** to select

    Sort Bills by **Due Date**

- If this is not showing, click the drop-down list arrow next to the **Sort Bills** text box, click **Due Date**.
- At the bottom of the **Pay Bills** window, verify the following items: **1100 Checking** is the account used, **Payment Method** shows **Check**, and **To be printed** is selected.

    Tab to or click **Payment Date, enter 01/25/04**

Scroll through the list of bills

- The bills will be shown according to the date due.

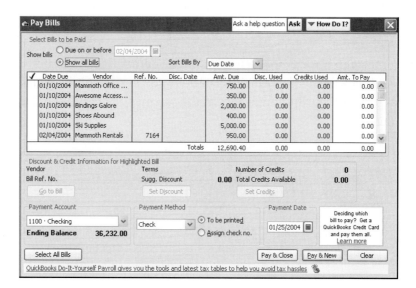

Select the bills to be paid and apply the discounts:
Click in the check mark column for the transaction for Sports Boots & Gear with
    a due date of 2/17/2004
Click the **Set Discount** button

- Verify the amount of the discount.
- If necessary, select account **4030 Purchases Discounts** as the discount
  account. Notice that the discount account is an income account. QuickBooks
  Pro considers discounts earned by early payment a type of income and lists
  purchases discounts as income and not as part of cost of goods sold.

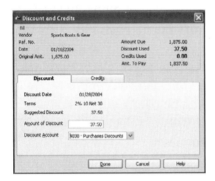

Click **Done** to record the discount
Repeat the steps for the other transaction eligible for a discount

- Remember to skip the transaction for Snowfall Gear

✓	Date Due	Vendor	Ref. No.	Disc. Date	Amt. Due	Disc. Used	Credits Used	Amt. To Pay
	01/10/2004	Ski Supplies			5,000.00	0.00	0.00	0.00
	02/04/2004	Mammoth Rentals	7164		950.00	0.00	0.00	0.00
	02/17/2004	Snowfall Gear	97	01/28/2004	370.00	0.00	0.00	0.00
✓	02/17/2004	Sports Boots & Gear		01/28/2004	1,875.00	37.50	0.00	1,837.50
✓	02/17/2004	SkiClothes, Inc.		01/28/2004	300.00	6.00	0.00	294.00

- Once you click **Done** to accept the discount, the amount due and amount paid
  amounts change to reflect the amount of the discount taken.

Click **Pay & New** button to record the payments and go to the next **Pay Bills**
    screen

PAY A BILL QUALIFYING FOR A PURCHASE DISCOUNT AND APPLY CREDIT AS PART OF PAYMENT

When paying bills, it is a good idea to apply credits received for returned or damaged
merchandise to the accounts as payment is made.

┌───┐
│ **MEMO**   │
│ **DATE:** January 25, 2004   │
│   │
│ As she is getting ready to pay bills, Rhonda looks for any credits   │
│ that may be applied to the bill as part of the payment. In addition, │
│ Rhonda looks for bills that qualify for an early-payment discount.   │
│ Apply the credit received from Snowfall Gear, as part of the   │
│ payment for the bill, then apply the discount, and pay the bill   │
│ within the discount period.   │
└───┘

DO: Apply the credit received from Snowfall Gear, as part of the payment for the bill and pay bill within the discount period

Verify **Payment Date of 01/25/2004**

Verify the **Payment Method** as **Check** and **To be printed** is marked

Verify **1100 Checking** is the **Payment Account**

Select **Show all bills**

Click the drop-down list for **Sort Bills By**, click **Vendor**

Scroll through transactions until you see the transaction for Snowfall Gear

Click the transaction to select it

- *Note:* This must be completed before applying the discount or credit to the bill.
- Notice that both the Set Credits and Set Discount buttons are now active and that information regarding credits and discounts is displayed.

Click **Set Discount** button

Verify the amount of the discount **7.40** and the discount account **4030 Purchases Discounts**

Click the **Credits** tab

Click the Check column for the credit amount of **50.00**

- On the Discounts and Credits screen, verify the amount due of **370**, the discount used of **7.40**, and the credit used of **50.00**, leaving an amount to pay of **312.60**
- QuickBooks calculates the discount on the original amount of the invoice rather than the amount due after subtracting the credit. If you need to recalculate the discount on the amount due after the credit, you may change the amount of the discount on the Discount screen. At this point in training, we will accept the discount calculated by QuickBooks.

Click the **Done** button

✓	Date Due	Vendor	Ref. No.	Disc. Date	Amt. Due	Disc. Used	Credits Used	Amt. To Pay
	02/04/2004	Mammoth Rentals	7164		950.00	0.00	0.00	0.00
	02/24/2004	Mountain Power Co.	3510-1...		359.00	0.00	0.00	0.00
	02/24/2004	Mountain Telepho...	7815-21		156.40	0.00	0.00	0.00
	02/24/2004	Mountain Water Co.	3105		85.00	0.00	0.00	0.00
	01/10/2004	Shoes Abound			400.00	0.00	0.00	0.00
	01/10/2004	Ski Supplies			5,000.00	0.00	0.00	0.00
✓	02/17/2004	Snowfall Gear	97	01/28/2004	370.00	7.40	50.00	312.60

Click **Pay & Close** to record the payment

VERIFY THAT BILLS ARE MARKED PAID

 DO: Access **Enter Bills** as previously instructed
Click **Previous** and view all the bills that were paid in Pay Bills to verify that
they are marked as paid
Close the Enter Bills screen

PRINT CHECKS TO PAY BILLS

Once bills have been selected for payment and any discounts taken or credit applied, the checks should be printed, signed, and mailed. QuickBooks Pro has two methods that may be used to print checks. Checks may be accessed and printed one at a time. This allows you to view the Bill Payment Information for each check. A more efficient way to print checks is to click the File menu and select checks from the Print Forms menu. This method will print all checks that are marked *To be printed* but will not allow you to view the bill payment information for any of the checks as you would if you printed each check separately. QuickBooks does not separate checks it writes in Pay Bills from the checks that are written when using the Write Checks feature of the program.

MEMO

DATE: January 25, 2004

Rhonda needs to print the checks for bills that have been paid. She decides to print checks individually so she can view bill payment information for each check while printing. When she finishes with the checks, she will give them to Andy for his approval and signature.

 DO: Print the checks for bills that have been paid
To access checks, click the **Banking** menu, click **Write Checks**

OR

Click **Banking** on the Navigator bar, click **Checks** on the QuickBooks Banking Navigator

OR

Use the keyboard shortcut **Ctrl+W**

- A blank check will show on the screen.

Click **Previous** until you get to the check for **SkiClothes, Inc.**

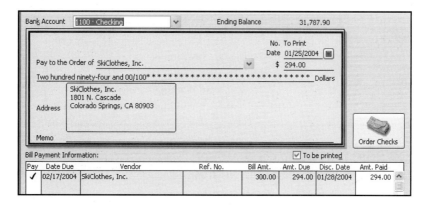

Click **Print** at the top of the window to print the check

Click **OK** on the Print Check screen to select Check No. 2

- Check No. 1 was issued in Chapter 5 to Dr. Jose Morales for a return. If Check No. 2 is not on the Print Check screen, change the screen so that the check number is 2.

- On the **Print Checks** screen, verify the printer name, printer type, and the selection of Standard check style.

Print Company Name and Address should be selected

- If is not marked with a check, click the check box to insert a check mark and select.

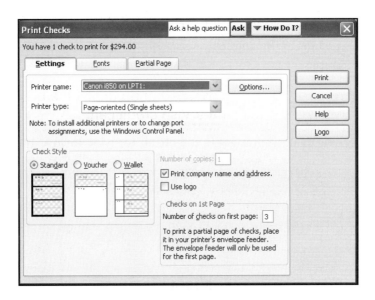

Click **Print** to print the check

Click **OK** on **Did check(s) print OK?**

- If you get a **Set Check Reminder** screen, click **No**

Click **Previous** or **Next** and repeat the steps to print Check No. 3 for Sports Boots & Gear, and Check No. 4 for Snowfall Gear

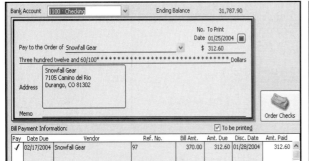
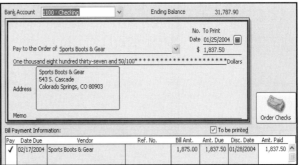

- Notice that the amount of the check to Snowfall Gear, is $312.60. This allows for the original bill of $370 less the return of $50 and the discount of $7.40.

Click **Save & Close** to close the **Write Checks** window.

PAY BILLS USING A CREDIT CARD

A credit card may be used to pay a bill rather than a check. Use the Pay Bills feature, but select Pay By Credit Card rather than Pay By Check.

> # MEMO
> **DATE:** January 25, 2004
>
> In viewing the bills due, Andy and Tim direct Rhonda to pay the bills to Awesome Accessories and Shoes Abound using the Visa credit card.

DO: Pay the above bills with a credit card

Access **Pay Bills** as previously instructed

Select **Show all bills**

In **Payment Method** click the drop-down list arrow, click **Credit Card** to select

- Payment Account should show 2100 Visa. If it does not, click the drop-down list arrow and click **2100 Visa**.

Payment Date should be **01/25/2004**

Scroll through the list of bills and select **Awesome Accessories** and **Shoes Abound** by clicking in the check mark column

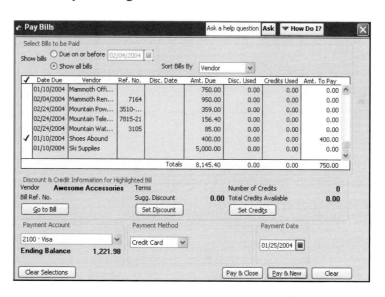

Click **Pay & Close** to record the payment

VERIFY THE CREDIT CARD PAYMENT OF BILLS

Paying bills with a credit card in Pay Bills automatically creates a Credit Card transaction in QuickBooks Pro. This can be verified through the Visa account register in the Chart of Accounts and through Enter Credit Card Charges. The entry into QuickBooks does not actually charge the credit card. It only records the transaction.

MEMO

DATE: January 25, 2004

Verify the credit card charges for Awesome Accessories and Shoes Abound.

 DO: Verify the credit card charges

Access the Visa account register in the **Chart of Accounts**

Scroll through the register to see the charges for Awesome Accessories and Shoes Abound

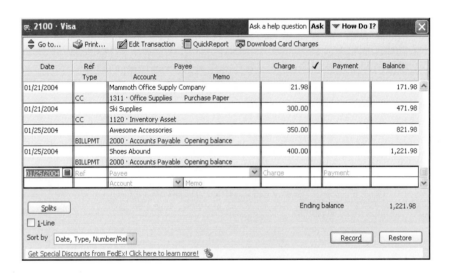

Close the register and the **Chart of Accounts**

SALES TAX

When a company is set up in QuickBooks Pro, a Sales Tax Payable liability account is automatically created if the company indicates that it charges sales tax on sales. The Sales Tax Payable account keeps track of as many tax agencies as the company needs. As invoices are written, QuickBooks Pro records the tax liability in the Sales Tax Payable account. To determine the sales tax owed, a Sales Tax Liability Report is prepared.

PRINT SALES TAX LIABILITY REPORT

The Sales Tax Liability Report shows your total taxable sales, the total nontaxable sales, and the amount of sales tax owed to each tax agency.

MEMO
DATE: January 25, 2004

Prior to paying the sales tax, Rhonda prepares the Sales Tax Liability Report.

DO: Prepare the Sales Tax Liability Report
Click **Report Finder** on any QuickBooks Navigator, select **Vendors & Payables** as the type of report, click **Sales Tax Liability Report**
The Report Dates are **From 01/01/2004 To 01/25/2004**
Click **Display**
Print in Landscape orientation
- If necessary, adjust the column widths so the report will fit on one page.
- If you get a message box asking if all columns should be the same size as the one being adjusted, click **No**.

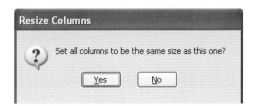

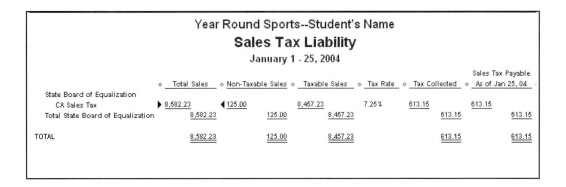

Close the report and the **Report Finder**

PAYING SALES TAX

Use the Pay Sales Tax window to determine how much sales tax you owe and to write a check to the tax agency. QuickBooks Pro will update the sales tax account with payment information.

> **MEMO**
>
> **DATE:** January 25, 2004
>
> **Note from Tim:** Rhonda, pay the sales taxes owed.

DO: Pay the sales taxes owed
Click the **Vendors** menu, click **Pay Sales Tax**
  OR
Click **Vendors** on the Navigator list, click the **Pay Sales Tax**
  icon on the QuickBooks Vendor Navigator
Pay From Account is **1100 Checking**
Check Date is **01/25/2004**
Show sales tax due through is **01/25/2004**
To be printed should be selected with a check mark in the check box.
Click the **Pay All Tax** button

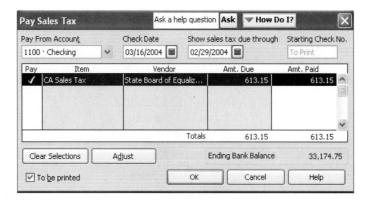

- Once **Pay All Tax** has been clicked and the item selected, the **Ending Bank Balance** changes to reflect the amount in checking after the tax has been paid.
Click **OK**
Print Check No. 5:
  Click **File**, point to **Print Forms**, click **Checks**

- Verify the Bank Account 1100 Checking, the First Check No. 5, and the check mark in front of State Board of Equalization.

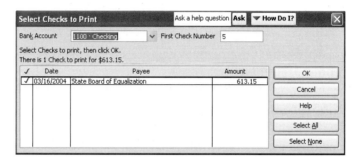

Click **OK**, click **Print**, click **OK** to answer *Did check(s) print Ok?*

VOIDING AND DELETING PURCHASE ORDERS, BILLS, CHECKS, AND CREDIT CARD PAYMENTS

QuickBooks Pro is so user friendly it allows any business form to be deleted. Some accounting programs do not allow error corrections, except as adjusting entries, once an entry has been made. QuickBooks Pro, however, allows a purchase order, a bill, a credit card payment, or a check to be voided or deleted. If a business form is voided, the form remains as a transaction. The transaction shows as a zero amount. This is useful when you want a record to show that an entry was made. If the form is deleted, all trace of the form is deleted. QuickBooks Pro allows a company to keep an audit trail if it wants a complete record of all transactions entered. The audit trail includes information regarding deleted transactions as well as transactions that appear on business forms, in the Journal, and in reports. An audit trail helps to eliminate misconduct such as printing a check and then deleting the check from the company records.

The procedures for voiding and deleting business forms are the same whether the business is a retail business or a service business. For actual assignments and practice in voiding and deleting business forms, refer to Chapters 2, 3, and 5.

VENDOR DETAIL CENTER

The Vendor Detail Center is used to obtain information regarding individual vendors. Use the drop-down list at the top of the window to choose the vendor whose information you want to see. At the top of the Center, you'll see the Vendor Contact Information for the selected vendor. Click Edit/More Info to see further information about the vendor or to edit the information.

At the bottom of the Vendor Detail Center, you can display two of the three tables available. The three tables are: Bills I Haven't Paid, Outstanding Purchase Orders (if inventory tracking is on), and Payments Issued.

DO: Click the **Vendor** menu
            Click **Vendor Detail Center**
            Click the drop-down list arrow for **Vendor Detail**, click **Ski Supplies**
            Click **Edit/More Info** to change the vendor information for the company
            Complete the Vendor information:
                  Company Name: **Ski Supplies**
                  Address: **1274 Boulder Avenue, Lafayette, CO 80026**
                  Contact: **Robert Carrillo**
                  Telephone: **303-555-1263**
                  FAX: **303-555-6321**
                  E-mail: **supplies@co.com**
            Click **OK**
            Select **Bills I Haven't Paid** and **Payments Issued** as the two tables to be
                  displayed at the bottom of the Vendor Detail Center
            • You may need to click the inverted triangle next to **Show:**

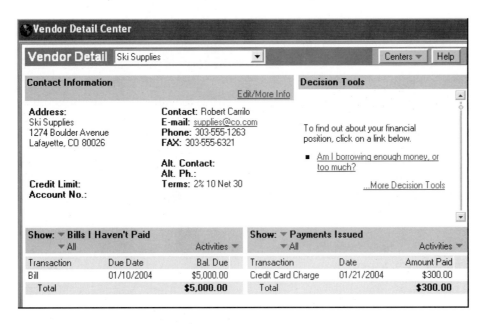

            • Note: The amounts shown above may be different on your screen. This is due
                  to the date of the computer being different from the date used in the chapter.
            Display some of the other vendors and select from among the available tables
            Close the **Vendor Detail Center**

CREATE AN ACCOUNTS PAYABLE GRAPH BY AGING PERIOD

Graphs provide a visual representation of certain aspects of the business. It is sometimes easier to interpret data in a graphical format. For example, to determine if any payments are overdue for Accounts Payable accounts, an Accounts Payable graph will provide that information instantly on a bar chart. In addition, the Accounts Payable graph feature of QuickBooks Pro also displays a pie chart showing what percentage of the total amount payable is owed to each vendor.

DO: Prepare an Accounts Payable Graph

Click **Reports** on the menu bar, point to **Vendors & Payables**, click **Accounts Payable Graph**

If necessary, click the **Dates** button at the top of the report, enter **01/25/2004** for **Show Aging as of** text box, and click **OK**

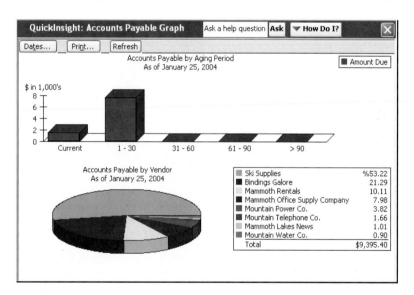

Close without printing

BACK UP YEAR ROUND SPORTS DATA

Whenever an important work session is complete, you should always back up your data. If your data disk is damaged or an error is discovered at a later time, the backup disk may be restored and the information used for recording transactions.

DO: Follow the instructions given in previous chapters to back up data for Year Round Sports, and follow the instructions in Appendix A to prepare a duplicate disk.

SUMMARY

In this chapter, purchase orders were completed, inventory items were received, and bills were recorded. Payments for purchases and bills were made by cash and by credit card. Sales taxes were paid. Vendors, inventory items, and accounts were added while transactions were being recorded. Various reports and graphs were prepared to determine the unpaid bills, the sales tax liability, and the aging of Accounts Payable accounts.

END-OF-CHAPTER QUESTIONS

TRUE/FALSE

ANSWER THE FOLLOWING QUESTIONS IN THE SPACE PROVIDED BEFORE THE QUESTION NUMBER.

_____ 1.   Receipt of purchase order items is never recorded before the bill arrives.

_____ 2.   A bill can be paid by check or credit card.

_____ 3.   A purchase order can be entered via the Reminders List.

_____ 4.   Voiding a purchase order removes all trace of the purchase order from the company records.

_____ 5.   QuickBooks Pro can prepare a bar chart illustrating the overdue Accounts Payable accounts.

_____ 6.   A single purchase order can be prepared and sent to several vendors.

_____ 7.   A Sales Tax account is automatically created if a company indicates that it charges sales tax on sales.

_____ 8.   A credit received from a vendor for the return of merchandise can be applied to a payment to the vendor.

_____ 9.   A new vendor cannot be added while recording a transaction.

_____ 10. A purchase order is closed automatically when a partial receipt of merchandise is recorded.

MULTIPLE CHOICE

WRITE THE LETTER OF THE CORRECT ANSWER IN THE SPACE PROVIDED BEFORE THE QUESTION NUMBER.

_____ 1. If you change the minimum quantity for an item, it becomes effective ___.
- A. immediately
- B. the beginning of next month
- C. as soon as outstanding purchase orders are received
- D. the beginning of the next fiscal year

_____ 2. If an order is received with a bill but is incomplete, QuickBooks Pro will ___.
- B. record the bill for the full amount ordered
- C. record the bill only for the amount received
- D. not allow the bill to be prepared until all the merchandise is received
- E. close the purchase order

_____ 3. The Purchase Order feature must be selected as a preference ___.
- F. when setting up the company
- G. prior to recording the first purchase order
- H. is automatically set when the first purchase order is prepared
- I. either A or B

_____ 4. A faster method of entering bills can be entering the bills ___.
- J. while writing the checks for payment
- K. in the Pay Bills window
- L. in the Accounts Payable Register
- M. none of the above

_____ 5. When items ordered are received with a bill, you record the receipt ___.
- N. on an item receipt form
- O. on the bill
- P. on the original purchase order
- Q. in the Journal

_____ 6. Sales tax is paid by using the ___ window.
- R. Pay Bills
- S. Pay Sales Tax
- T. Write Check
- U. Credit Card

_____ 7. An individual vendor's percentage of the total amount for Accounts Payable is displayed in a ___.
A. pie chart
B. bar chart
C. line graph
D. 3-dimensional line graph

_____ 8. Checks to pay bills may be printed ___.
A. individually
B. all at once
C. as the checks are written
D. all of the above

_____ 9. When recording a bill for merchandise received, you click the ___ tab on the vendor section of the bill.
A. Memo
B. Expenses
C. Items
D. Purchase Order

_____ 10. The ___ matches income for the period against expenses for the period.
A. cash basis of accounting
B. credit basis of accounting
C. accrual basis of accounting
D. debit/credit basis of accounting

FILL-IN

IN THE SPACE PROVIDED, WRITE THE ANSWER THAT MOST APPROPRIATELY COMPLETES THE SENTENCE.

1. Orders for merchandise are prepared using the QuickBooks Pro _____ form.

2. Information on the Reminders List may be displayed in _____ or _____ form.

3. The _____ Report shows the total taxable sales and the amount of sales tax owed.

4. A purchase order can be closed _____ or _____.

5. To see the bill payment information, checks must be printed _____.

SHORT ESSAY

Describe the cycle of obtaining merchandise. Include the process from ordering the merchandise through paying for it. Include information regarding the QuickBooks Pro forms prepared for each phase of the cycle, the possible ways in which an item may be received, and the ways in which payment may be made.

_____

_____

_____

_____

_____

NAME_____

TRANSMITTAL

CHAPTER 6: YEAR ROUND SPORTS

Attach the following documents and reports:

Reminders List
Purchase Order No. 1: Sports Boots & Gear
Purchase Order No. 2: Snowfall Gear
Purchase Order No. 3: SkiClothes, Inc.
Purchase Order No. 4: Ski Supplies
Account QuickReport, Purchase Orders, January 16, 2004
Purchase Order No. 4 (Revised): Ski Supplies
Register Quick Report, Snowfall Gear
Unpaid Bills by Vendor, January 25, 2004
Check No. 2: SkiClothes, Inc.
Check No. 3: Sports Boots & Gear
Check No. 4: Snowfall Gear
Sales Tax Liability Report, January 1-25, 2004
Check No. 5: State Board of Equalization

END-OF-CHAPTER PROBLEM

GREAT ESCAPES CLOTHING

Chapter 6 continues with the transactions for purchase orders, merchandise receipts, bills, bill payments, and sales tax payments. Leilani prints the checks, purchase orders, and any related reports; and Kahala signs the checks. This procedure establishes cash control procedures and lets both owners know about the checks being processed.

INSTRUCTIONS

Continue to use the copy of Great Escapes you used in Chapter 5. Open the company—the file used is **Great Escapes.qbw**. Record the purchase orders, bills, payments, and other purchases as instructed within the chapter. Always read the transactions carefully and review the Chart of Accounts when selecting transaction accounts. Print reports and graphs as indicated. Add new vendors and minimum quantities where indicated. Print all purchase orders and checks issued. The first purchase order used is Purchase Order No. 1. When paying bills, always check for credits that may be applied to the bill, and always check for discounts.

In addition to the Item List and the Chart of Accounts, you will need to use the Vendor List when ordering merchandise and paying bills.

RECORD TRANSACTIONS

January 5, 2005:
Customize a Purchase Order template so the Company Name is expanded to 4 ¾ and Purchase Order begins at 6.

Change the reorder point for dresses from 20 to 25.

Change the reorder point for women's pants to 30.

Display and print an expanded Reminders List.

Prepare and print an Inventory Stock Status by Item Report for January 1-5 in Landscape orientation. Manually adjust column widths so the item descriptions and the vendors' names are shown in full and the report prints on one page.

Prepare Purchase Orders for all items marked Order on the Stock Status by Item Inventory Report. Refer to the Stock Status by Item Report for vendor information. The quantity for each item ordered is 10. The rate is $35 for dresses and $20 for pants. Print purchase orders with lines around each field.

Order an additional 10 dresses from a new vendor: The Clothes Rack, 9382 Grand Avenue, San Luis Obispo, CA 93407, Contact person is Mitchell Rogers, 805-555-5512, Fax is 805-555-2155, E-mail is clothesrack@slo.com, Credit terms are 2% 10 Net 30, Credit limit is $2000. The rate for the dresses is $25.

Print a Purchase Order QuickReport in Landscape orientation for January 1-5. Adjust column widths so all columns are displayed in full and the report prints on one page.

January 8, 2005:
Received pants ordered from Contempo Clothing Supply, Inc. without the bill. Enter the receipt of merchandise. The transaction date is 01/08/2005.

Received dresses from Sun Clothes with Bill C309. Enter the receipt of the merchandise and the bill.

Received 8 dresses from The Clothes Rack. Enter the receipt of the merchandise and Bill 406.

After recording the receipt of merchandise, view the three purchase orders. Notice which ones are marked Received in Full and Clsd.

January 9, 2005:
Received Bill 239 for pants. The bill was dated 01/08/2005.

Pay for the dresses from The Clothes Rack with a credit card. (Take a purchase discount if the transaction qualifies for one. Use 4030 Purchases Discounts Income account for any discounts.)

January 10, 2005:
Discovered unstitched seams in two pairs of women's pants ordered on PO 2. Return the pants for credit. Use 2340 as the Reference number.

January 15, 2005:
Record bill for rent of $1150. (Vendor is SLO Rental Company, 301 Marsh Street, San Luis Obispo, CA 93407, Contact person is Matt Ericson, 805-555-4100, Fax 805-555-0014, Terms Net 30.)

Record bill for telephone service of $79.85. (Vendor is Telephone Service Company, 8851 Hwy. 58, San Luis Obispo, CA 93407, 805-555-1029. No terms or credit limits have been given.)

January 18, 2005:

Pay all bills that are eligible for a discount. Take any discounts for which you are eligible. If there are any credits to an account, apply the credit prior to paying the bill. Pay the bill(s) by check.

Print Check Nos. 2 and 3 for the bills that were paid.

January 25, 2005:

Purchase office supplies to have on hand for $250 with a credit card from Office Masters, 8330 Grand Avenue, Arroyo Grande, CA 93420, Contact person is Larry Thomas, 805-555-9915, Fax 805-555-5199, E-mail OfficeMasters@slo.com,Terms Net 30, Credit limit $500.

Print Unpaid Bills Detail Report in Portrait orientation.

Pay bills for rent and telephone. Print the checks prepared for these bills.

January 30, 2005:

Prepare Sales Tax Liability Report from 01/01/2005 to 01/30/2005. Print the report in Landscape orientation. Change columns widths, if necessary, so the report will fit on one page.

Pay Sales Tax and print the check.

Prepare a Vendor Balance Detail Report as of 01/30/2005. Print in Portrait orientation. Adjust column widths so the report will display the account names in full and will print on one page without selecting Fit report on one page wide.

Print a Trial Balance for 01/01/2005 to 01/30/2005.

Back up data.

NAME_____

TRANSMITTAL

CHAPTER 6: GREAT ESCAPES CLOTHING

Attach the following documents and reports:

Reminders List
Inventory Stock Status by Item, January 1-5, 2005
Purchase Order No. 1: Sun Clothes
Purchase Order No. 2: Contempo Clothing Supply, Inc.
Purchase Order No. 3: The Clothes Rack
Account QuickReport, Purchase Orders
Check No. 2: Sun Clothes
Check No. 3: Contempo Clothing Supply, Inc.
Unpaid Bills Detail, January 25, 2005
Check No. 4: SLO Rental Company
Check No. 5: Telephone Service Company
Sales Tax Liability Report
Check No. 6: State Board of Equalization
Vendor Balance Detail, January 30, 2005
Trial Balance, January 1-30, 2005

GENERAL ACCOUNTING AND END-OF-PERIOD PROCEDURES: MERCHANDISING BUSINESS

LEARNING OBJECTIVES

At the completion of this chapter, you will be able to:

1. Complete the end-of-period procedures.
2. Change the name of existing accounts in the Chart of Accounts, view the account name change, and view the effect of an account name change on subaccounts.
3. Delete an existing account from the Chart of Accounts.
4. Enter the adjusting entries required for accrual-basis accounting.
5. Record depreciation and an adjustment for Purchases Discounts.
6. Understand how to record owners' equity transactions for a partnership.
7. Enter a transaction for owner withdrawals, and transfer owner withdrawals and net income to the owners' capital accounts.
8. Reconcile the bank statement, record bank service charges, and mark cleared transactions.
9. Reconcile a credit card statement.
10. Undo a reconciliation and customize the layout of the reconciliation screen.
11. Print the Journal.
12. Print reports such as Trial Balance, Profit and Loss Statement, and Balance Sheet.
13. Export a report to Microsoft® Excel and import data from Excel
14. Perform end-of-period backup, close a period, record transactions in a closed period, and adjust inventory quantities.

GENERAL ACCOUNTING AND END-OF-PERIOD PROCEDURES

As stated in previous chapters, QuickBooks Pro operates from the standpoint of the business document rather than an accounting form, journal, or ledger. While QuickBooks Pro does incorporate all of these items into the program, in many instances they operate behind the scenes. Many accounting programs require special closing procedures at the end of a period. QuickBooks Pro does not require special closing procedures at the end of a period. At the end of the fiscal year, QuickBooks Pro transfers the net income into the Retained Earnings account and allows you to protect the data for the year by assigning a closing date to the period. All of the transaction detail is maintained and viewable, but it will not be changed unless OK is clicked on a warning screen.

Even though a formal closing does not have to be performed within QuickBooks Pro, when using accrual-basis accounting, several transactions must be recorded in order to reflect all expenses and income for the period accurately. For example, bank statements and credit cards must be reconciled; and any charges or bank collections need to be recorded. An adjustment to transfer purchase discounts from income to cost of goods sold needs to be made. Other adjusting entries such as depreciation, office supplies used, and so on will also need to be made. These adjustments may be recorded by the CPA or by the company's accounting personnel. At the end of the year, net income for the year and the owner withdrawals for the year should be transferred to the owners' capital accounts.

As in a service business, the CPA for the company will review things such as account names, adjusting entries, depreciation schedules, owner's equity adjustments, and so on. There are several ways for accountant entries to be made.

If the CPA makes the changes and adjustments, they may be made on the Accountant's Copy of the business files. This disk is then merged with the company files that are used to record day-to-day business transactions. All adjustments made by the CPA are added to the current company files. There are certain restrictions to the types of transactions that may be made on an accountant's copy of the business files.

In some instances, the accountant will make adjustments on a backup copy of the company data. This method may be used because there are no restrictions on the types of entries that may be made. If the backup is used, the transactions entered by the accountant on backup company files will also need to be entered in the company files used to record day-to-day transactions. The two sets of company files cannot be merged.

Another method to use for an accountant is to allow your accountant to access your QuickBooks company file remotely. This may be done if your accountant is using QuickBooks® Premier: Accountant Edition. When a file is accessed remotely, the accountant may enter the appropriate transactions directly into your company file. During the session, the accountant controls QuickBooks on your computer. All the transactions are shown on your screen in real-time. When the session is complete, your company file contains all the transactions made by the accountant.

Once necessary adjustments have been made, reports reflecting the end-of-period results of operations should be prepared. For archive purposes, at the end of the fiscal year, an additional backup disk is prepared and stored.

TRAINING TUTORIAL AND PROCEDURES

The following tutorial will once again work with Year Round Sports. As in Chapters 5 and 6, transactions will be recorded for this fictitious company. Refer to procedures given in Chapter 5 to maximize training benefits.

OPEN QUICKBOOKS® PRO AND YEAR ROUND SPORTS

    DO: Open **QuickBooks Pro** as instructed in previous chapters
              Open **Year Round Sports**
              • Check the title bar to verify that Year Round Sports is the open company.

BEGINNING THE TUTORIAL

In this chapter you will be recording end-of-period adjustments, reconciling bank and credit card statements, changing account names, and preparing traditional end-of-period reports. Because QuickBooks Pro does not perform a traditional closing of the books, you will learn how to close the period to protect transactions and data recorded during previous accounting periods.

As in previous chapters, all transactions are listed on memos. The transaction date will be the same as the memo date unless otherwise specified within the transaction. Once a specific type of transaction has been entered in a step-by-step manner, additional transactions of the same or a similar type will be made without having instructions provided. Of course, you may always refer to instructions given for previous transactions for ideas or for steps used to enter those transactions. To determine the account used in the transaction, refer to the Chart of Accounts.

CHANGE THE NAME OF EXISTING ACCOUNTS IN THE CHART OF ACCOUNTS

Even though transactions have been recorded during the month of January, QuickBooks Pro makes it a simple matter to change the name of an existing account. Once the name of an account has been changed, all transactions using the old name are updated and show the new account name.

MEMO

DATE: January 31, 2004

On the recommendation of the company's CPA, Andy and Tim decided to change the account named Freight Income to Delivery Income.

  DO: Change the account name of Freight Income

Access the Chart of Accounts using the keyboard shortcut **Ctrl+A**

Scroll through accounts until you see Freight Income, click **Freight Income**

Use the keyboard shortcut **Ctrl+E**

On the **Edit Account** screen, highlight **Freight Income**

Enter the new name **Delivery Income**

Change the description from **Freight Income** to **Delivery Income**

Click **OK** to record the name change and to close the **Edit Account** screen

- Notice that the name of the account appears as Delivery Income in the Chart of Accounts.

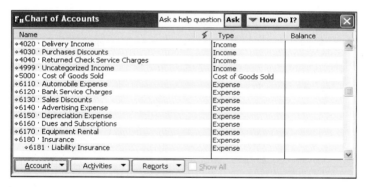

Partial List

Do not close the **Chart of Accounts**

MAKE AN ACCOUNT INACTIVE

If you are not using an account and do not have plans to do so in the near future, the account may be made inactive. The account remains available for use, yet it does not appear on your Chart of Accounts unless you check the Show All check box.

MEMO

DATE: January 31, 2004

At this time, Year Round Sports does not plan to rent any equipment. The account Equipment Rental should be made inactive. In addition, Andy and Tim do not plan to use Franchise Fees. Make these accounts inactive.

     DO: Make the accounts listed above inactive
Click **Equipment Rental**
Click **Account** at the bottom of the Chart of Accounts, click **Make Inactive**
- The account no longer appears in the Chart of Accounts.
Make **Franchise Fees** inactive
Click **Franchise Fees**
Use the keyboard shortcut **Ctrl+E**
On the Edit Account screen, click the **Account is inactive** check box
Click **OK**
- If you wish to view all accounts, including the inactive ones, click the **Show All** check box at the bottom of the Chart of Accounts, and all accounts will be displayed.
- Notice the icons that mark Equipment Rental and Franchise Fees as inactive accounts.

✖ ◦6170 · Equipment Rental	Expense	
◦6180 · Insurance	Expense	
◦6181 · Liability Insurance	Expense	
◦6182 · Disability Insurance	Expense	
◦6210 · Interest Expense	Expense	
◦6211 · Finance Charge	Expense	
◦6212 · Loan Interest	Expense	
◦6213 · Mortgage	Expense	
◦6230 · Licenses and Permits	Expense	
◦6240 · Miscellaneous	Expense	
◦6250 · Postage and Delivery	Expense	
◦6260 · Printing and Reproduction	Expense	
◦6270 · Filing Fees	Expense	
◦6280 · Professional Fees	Expense	
◦6281 · Legal Fees	Expense	
◦6282 · Accounting	Expense	
✖ ◦6290 · Franchise Fees	Expense	

Do not close the **Chart of Accounts**

DELETE AN EXISTING ACCOUNT FROM THE CHART OF ACCOUNTS

If you do not want to make an account inactive because you have not used it and do not plan to use it at all, QuickBooks Pro allows the account to be deleted at anytime. However, as a safeguard, QuickBooks Pro does prevent the deletion of an account once it has been used even if it simply contains an opening or an existing balance.

MEMO
DATE: January 31, 2004

In addition to previous changes to account names, Andy and Tim find that they do not use nor will they use the expense accounts: Interest Expense: Mortgage, Taxes: Property, and Travel & Ent. Delete these accounts from the Chart of Accounts.

DO: Delete the account Interest Expense: Mortgage
Scroll through Chart of Accounts until you see Interest Expense: Mortgage, click
   Interest Expense: Mortgage
Click the **Account** button at the bottom of the Chart of Accounts, click **Delete**
Click **OK** on the **Delete Accounts** dialog box
- The account has now been deleted.
Use the keyboard shortcut **Ctrl+D** to delete **Taxes: Property**
Also follow the same procedures to delete the subaccounts of **Travel & Ent.**
- *Note:* Whenever an account has subaccounts, the subaccounts must be deleted before QuickBooks Pro will let you delete the main account. This is what you must do before you can delete Travel & Ent. A subaccount is deleted the same as any other account. In fact, Taxes: Property was a subaccount of Taxes.
When the subaccounts of Travel & Ent. have been deleted, delete **Travel & Ent.**
Close the **Chart of Accounts**

FIXED ASSET MANAGEMENT

QuickBooks contains a Fixed Asset Manager in the program. When you purchase <u>fixed assets</u> that you need for your business, it's important to keep good records so you can track their cost, the cost of repairs and upgrades, and how much they <u>depreciate</u> from year to year. These amounts affect the worth of your business and the size of your tax bill.

Fixed asset items provide a way to keep important information about your assets in one convenient place.

You can create an item to track a fixed asset at several points during the asset's life cycle; however, it is recommended that you create the item when you buy the asset or setup the company.

You can create a fixed asset item from the Fixed Asset List or from a Transaction.

MEMO
DATE: January 31, 2004

When Year Round Sports was setup in QuickBooks, Office Equipment and Store Fixtures were designated as Fixed Assets and added to the Fixed Asset List. To work with the Fixed Asset List, the Fixed Asset Store Fixtures will be deleted and readded.

DO: Delete the Fixed Asset Item Store Fixtures
            Click **Lists** on the menu bar
            Click **Fixed Asset Item List**
            Click the item **Store Fixtures**
            Use the keyboard shortcut **Ctrl+D** to delete the item
            Click **OK** to delete the item
            Use the keyboard shortcut **Ctrl+N** to create a new item

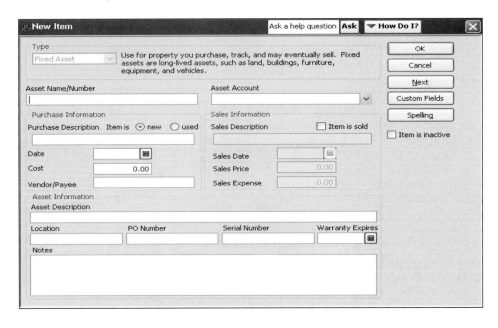

Complete the information for the new item:
        The **Asset Name** is **Store Fixtures**
        The Item is **new**
        The **Purchase Description** should be **Store Fixtures**
        The **Date** is **12/31/03**
        The **Cost** is **4500**
        The **Asset Account** is **1520**

The **Asset Description** is **Store Fixtures**

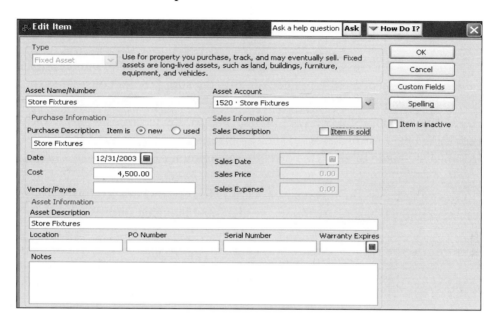

When the information is entered for Store Fixtures, click **OK**
Close the Fixed Asset List

ADJUSTMENTS FOR ACCRUAL-BASIS ACCOUNTING

In accrual-basis accounting, the income from a period is matched against the expenses of a period in order to arrive at an accurate figure for net income. Thus, the revenue is earned at the time the service is performed or the sale is made regardless of when the cash is actually received. The same holds true when a business buys things or pays bills. In the accrual basis of accounting, the expense is recorded at the time the bill is received or the product or service is delivered regardless of the actual payment date. The cash basis of accounting records income or revenue at the time cash is received regardless of when the sale was made or the service performed. In cash-basis accounting, the expense is not recorded until it is paid.

There are several internal transactions that must be recorded when using the accrual basis of accounting. These entries are called adjusting entries. For example, equipment does wear out and will eventually need to be replaced. Rather than waiting until replacement to record the use of the equipment, an adjusting entry is made to allocate the use of equipment as an expense for a period. This is called *depreciation*. Certain items used in a business are paid for in advance. As these are used, they become expenses of the business. For example, insurance for the entire year would be used up month by month and should, therefore, be a monthly expense. Commonly, the insurance is billed and paid for the entire year. Until the insurance is used, it is an asset. Each month the portion of the insurance used becomes an expense for the month.

ADJUSTING ENTRIES—PREPAID EXPENSES

During the operation of a business, companies purchase supplies to have on hand for use in the operation of the business. In accrual-basis accounting, the supplies are considered to be prepaid assets (something the business owns) until they are used in the operation of the business. As the supplies are used, the amount used becomes an expense for the period. The same rationale applies to other things paid for in advance, such as insurance. At the end of the period, an adjusting entry must be made to allocate correctly the amount of prepaid assets to expenses.

The transactions for these adjustments may be recorded in the register for the account by clicking on the prepaid asset in the Chart of Accounts, or they may be made in the General Journal.

MEMO

DATE: January 31, 2004

NOTE from Tim: Rhonda, remember to record the monthly adjustment for Prepaid Insurance. The $250 is the amount we paid for two months of liability insurance coverage. Also, we have a balance of $521.98 in office supplies and a balance of $400 in sales supplies. Please adjust accordingly.

DO: Record the adjusting entries for insurance expense, office supplies expense, and sales supplies expense in the General Journal.
Access the **General Journal**:
   Click **Company** or **Banking** on the menu bar, click **Make General Journal Entries**
   OR
   Open **Chart of Accounts** as previously instructed, click **Prepaid Insurance**, click **Activities**, click **Make General Journal Entries**
   OR
   Click **Banking** on the Navigator list, click **Make Journal Entry** on the QuickBooks Banking Navigator
Record the adjusting entry for Prepaid Insurance
   Click **OK** on the Assigning Numbers to Journal Entries screen
   Enter **01/31/04** as the **Date**
   • Entry No. is left blank unless you wish to record a specific number.
   • Because all transactions entered for the month have been entered in the Journal as well as on an invoice or a bill, all transactions automatically have a Journal entry number. When the Journal is printed, your transaction number may be different from the answer key. Disregard the transaction

number because it can change based on how many times you delete
transactions, etc.

Tab to or click the **Account** column, click the drop-down list arrow for
Account, click **6181 Liability Insurance Expense**

Tab to or click **Debit**

- The $250 given in the memo is the amount for two months.

Calculate the amount of the adjustment for the month:

Press the = sign

QuickBooks calculator shows and adding machine tape

Delete the 0.00 and enter **250**

Press / for division

Key **2**

Press **Enter**

- The calculation is performed and the amount is entered in the Debit
column.

Tab to or click the **Memo** column, type **Adjusting Entry, Insurance**

Tab to or click **Account**, click the drop-down list arrow for Account, click
1340 Prepaid Insurance

- The amount for the **Credit** column should have been entered
automatically. If not, enter **125**.

Enter the Memo information by using the copy command:

Click the **Memo** column for the Debit entry

Drag through the memo **Adjusting Entry, Insurance**

When the memo is highlighted, use the keyboard command **Ctrl+C** to
copy the memo

Click in the **Memo** column for the Credit entry

Use the keyboard command **Ctrl+V** to paste the memo into the column

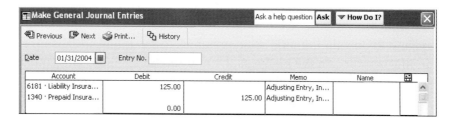

Click **NEXT** to record the adjustment and to advance to the next General Journal
Entry screen

Repeat the above procedures to record the adjustment for the office supplies used

- The amount given in the memo is the balance of the account after the supplies
have been used.

- The actual amount of the supplies used in January must be calculated.

Determine the balance of the Office Supplies account by using the keyboard
shortcut **Ctrl+A** to access the Chart of Accounts

Use the QuickBooks Calculator or the Windows Calculator to determine the amount of the adjustment

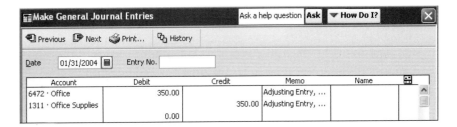

When the entry is complete, click **Next**

Repeat the above procedures to record the adjustment for the sales supplies used

- The amount given in the memo is the balance of the account after the supplies have been used. The actual amount of the supplies used in January must be calculated.

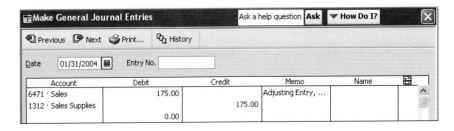

When the entry is complete, click **Save & Close**

If necessary, close **Chart of Accounts** and **General Journal**

ADJUSTING ENTRIES—DEPRECIATION

Using the accrual basis of accounting requires companies to record an expense for the amount of equipment used in the operation of the business. Unlike supplies, where you can actually see the paper supply diminishing, it is very difficult to see how much of a cash register has been used up during the month. To account for the fact that machines do wear out and need to be replaced, an adjustment is made for depreciation. This adjustment correctly matches the expenses of the period against the revenue of the period.

The adjusting entry for depreciation can be made in the depreciation account register, or it can be made in the General Journal.

MEMO
DATE: January 31, 2004

Having received the necessary depreciation schedules, Rhonda records the adjusting entry for depreciation:

Office Equipment, $85 per month
Store Fixtures, $75 per month

DO: Record a compound adjusting entry for depreciation of the office equipment and the store supplies in the General Journal:
Access the **General Journal** as previously instructed
Enter **01/31/04** as the **Date**
Entry No. is left blank
- In order to use the automatic calculation feature of QuickBooks Pro, the credit entries will be entered first.
Tab to or click the **Account** column, click the drop-down list arrow for **Account**, click **1512 Depreciation** under **Office Equipment**
Tab to or click **Credit**, enter **85**
Tab to or click **Memo**, enter **Adjusting Entry, Depreciation**
Tab to or click the **Account** column, click the drop-down list arrow for **Account**, click **1522 Depreciation** under **Store Fixtures**
- Disregard the 85 that shows as a debit. Entering an amount in the credit column and pressing the tab key will eliminate the debit.
Tab to or click **Credit**, enter **75**
Tab to or click **Memo**, enter **Adjusting Entry, Depreciation**
Tab to or click the **Account** column, click the drop-down list arrow for **Account**, click **6150 Depreciation Expense**
Debit column should automatically show **160**
Tab to or click **Memo**, enter **Adjusting Entry, Depreciation**

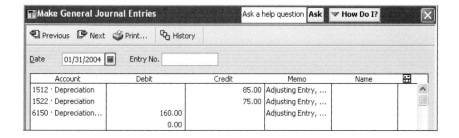

Click **Save & Close** to record the adjustment and close the General Journal

- If you get a message regarding tracking fixed assets on journal entries, click **OK**.

Close the **Chart of Accounts**, if necessary

VIEW PROFIT AND LOSS STATEMENT TO DETERMINE NEED FOR AN ADJUSTMENT TO PURCHASE DISCOUNTS

QuickBooks Pro records purchase discounts as a form of income and does not allow this to be changed to a cost of goods sold account. Because paying for merchandise within the discount period reduces the amount you pay for an item, the amount of income is increased. However, income is taxed in many areas and to leave the purchase discounts as an income item would make it subject to tax.

DO: View Profit and Loss Statement to see how Purchase Discounts are shown as income

Click **Reports** menu, point to **Company & Financial**, click **Profit & Loss Standard**

Enter the Dates: **From 01/01/04** and **To 01/31/04**

Tab to generate the report

Year Round Sports--Student's Name
Profit & Loss
January 2004

	Jan 04
Ordinary Income/Expense	
Income	
4010 · Sales	
4011 · Clothing & Accessory Sales	▶ 1,409.76
4012 · Equipment Sales	7,436.44
Total 4010 · Sales	8,846.20
4030 · Purchases Discounts	50.90
4040 · Returned Check Service Charges	25.00
Total Income	8,922.10
Cost of Goods Sold	
5000 · Cost of Goods Sold	3,352.46
Total COGS	3,352.46
Gross Profit	5,569.64

Partial Report

- Notice that 4030 Purchases Discounts is shown as a form of income and not as a reduction to the Cost of Goods Sold.

Close the report

ADJUSTING ENTRY TO TRANSFER PURCHASES DISCOUNTS INCOME TO COST OF GOODS SOLD

To conform to generally accepted accounting procedures, purchase discounts should be shown as a reduction to the cost of goods sold. It is necessary to prepare an adjusting entry to transfer the Income account 4030 Purchases Discounts to a Cost of Goods Sold Purchases Discounts account. This adjustment places the discount where it belongs—as a reduction to the cost of merchandise rather than income.

MEMO

DATE: January 31, 2004

Note from Andy: Rhonda, create a Cost of Goods Sold account 5100 Purchases Discounts. Transfer the amount of Purchases Discounts from Income account 4030 to Cost of Goods Sold account 5100.

DO: Create new account 5100 Purchases Discounts as a subaccount of Cost of Goods Sold

Open the **Chart of Accounts** as previously instructed
Click **Account**, click **New**
   OR
Use the keyboard shortcut **Ctrl+N**
Click the drop-down list arrow for **Type**, click **Cost of Goods Sold**
Tab to or click **Number**, enter **5100**
Tab to or click **Name**, enter **Purchases Discounts**
Click **Subaccount of** to select, click the drop-down list arrow for **Subaccount**, click **5000 Cost of Goods Sold**

Click **OK**
With the Chart of Accounts still showing on the screen, click the **Activities** button
Click **Make General Journal Entries**
• Verify that the date is **01/31/04**. If not, change the date to 01/31/04.
Click the drop-down list arrow for **Account**, click **4030 Purchases Discounts**
Tab to or click the **Debit** column, enter the amount of Purchases Discounts **50.90**

Tab to or click **Memo**, enter **Transfer to CoGS** as the Memo
Click the drop-down list arrow for **Account**, click **5100 Purchases Discounts**
- The credit amount of 50.90 is already entered.

Tab to or click **Memo**, enter **Transfer to CoGS** as the Memo

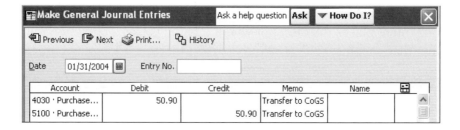

Click **Save & Close**
Close the **Chart of Accounts**

PREPARE PROFIT AND LOSS STATEMENT

MEMO

DATE: January 31, 2004

Print a Profit and Loss Statement for January 1-31, 2004.

DO: To view the effect of the adjustment, print a Profit and Loss Statement for January 1-31, 2004
Prepare the report as previously instructed
- Notice that the amount of 4030 Purchases Discounts is **0.00**.
- The amount of 5100 Purchases Discounts is **-50.90**.
- The amount of Cost of Goods Sold is now **$3,301.56** rather than $3,352.46.
- The Total Income is **$8,871.20** rather than $8,922.10.

```
                    Year Round Sports--Student's Name
                              Profit & Loss
                              January 2004
                                                  ◇        Jan 04

    Ordinary Income/Expense
        Income
            4010 · Sales
                4011 · Clothing & Accessory Sales    ▶ 1,409.76
                4012 · Equipment Sales                 7,436.44
            Total 4010 · Sales                                    8,846.20

            4030 · Purchases Discounts                               0.00
            4040 · Returned Check Service Charges                   25.00
        Total Income                                              8,871.20

        Cost of Goods Sold
            5000 · Cost of Goods Sold
                5100 · Purchases Discount              -50.90
                5000 · Cost of Goods Sold - Other     3,352.46
            Total 5000 · Cost of Goods Sold                       3,301.56

        Total COGS                                                3,301.56
```

Partial Report

Print the report in **Portrait** orientation
Close the report

VIEW GENERAL JOURNAL

Once transactions have been entered in the General Journal, it is important to view them.
QuickBooks Pro also refers to the General Journal as the Journal and allows it to be viewed or
printed at any time. Even with the special ways in which transactions are entered in QuickBooks
Pro through invoices, bills, checks, and account registers, the Journal is still the book of original
entry. All transactions recorded for the company may be viewed in the Journal even if they were
entered elsewhere.

DO: View the Journal for January
Click **Reports** on the menu bar, point to **Accountant & Taxes**, click **Journal**
  OR
Click **Report Finder** on any QuickBooks Navigator, click **Accountant & Taxes**
  to select the type of report, click **Journal**, click **Display**
Tab to or click **From**
• If necessary, delete existing date.
Enter **01/01/04**
Tab to or click **To**, enter **01/31/04**
Tab to generate the report

Year Round Sports--Student's Name

Journal

January 2004

Trans #	Type	Date	Num	Name	Memo	Account	Debit	Credit
48	Invoice	01/02/2004	1	Woods, Rick	VOID:	1200 · Accounts Receivable	0.00	
				Woods, Rick	After Ski Boots and Shoes	4011 · Clothing & Accessory Sales	0.00	
				State Board of Equ...	CA Sales Tax	2200 · Sales Tax Payable	0.00	
							0.00	0.00
49	Invoice	01/03/2004	2	Morales, Jose Dr.		1200 · Accounts Receivable	992.06	
				Morales, Jose Dr.	Snow Skis	4012 · Equipment Sales		425.00
				Morales, Jose Dr.	Snow Skis	1120 · Inventory Asset		100.00
				Morales, Jose Dr.	Snow Skis	5000 · Cost of Goods Sold	100.00	
				Morales, Jose Dr.	Ski Bindings	4012 · Equipment Sales		175.00
				Morales, Jose Dr.	Ski Bindings	1120 · Inventory Asset		75.00
				Morales, Jose Dr.	Ski Bindings	5000 · Cost of Goods Sold	75.00	
				Morales, Jose Dr.	Ski Boots	4012 · Equipment Sales		250.00
				Morales, Jose Dr.	Ski Boots	1120 · Inventory Asset		75.00
				Morales, Jose Dr.	Ski Boots	5000 · Cost of Goods Sold	75.00	
				Morales, Jose Dr.	Ski Poles	4012 · Equipment Sales		75.00
				Morales, Jose Dr.	Ski Poles	1120 · Inventory Asset		30.00
				Morales, Jose Dr.	Ski Poles	5000 · Cost of Goods Sold	30.00	
				State Board of Equ...	CA Sales Tax	2200 · Sales Tax Payable		67.06
							1,272.06	1,272.06

Partial Report

Scroll through the report to view all transactions recorded in the Journal

- Only the transactions made from January 1 through January 31, 2004 are displayed. Since opening balances have also been entered during the creation of the company, note that the first transaction shown is 48—Invoice No. 1.
- Viewing the Journal and checking the accounts used in transactions, the dates entered for transactions, and the amounts recorded for the transactions is an excellent way to discover errors and determine corrections that need to be made.

Close the report without printing

DEFINITION OF A PARTNERSHIP

A partnership is a business owned by two or more individuals. Because it is unincorporated, each partner owns a share of all the assets and liabilities. Each partner receives a portion of the profits based on the percentage of his or her investment in the business or according to any partnership agreement drawn up at the time the business was created. Because the business is owned by the partners, they do not receive a salary. Any funds obtained by the partners are in the form of withdrawals against their share of the profits. QuickBooks Pro makes it easy to set up a partnership and create separate accounts, if desired, for each partner's equity, investment, and withdrawals.

OWNER WITHDRAWALS

In a partnership, owners cannot receive a paycheck because they own the business. An owner withdrawing money from a business—even to pay personal expenses—is similar to an individual withdrawing money from a savings account. A withdrawal simply decreases the owners' capital. QuickBooks Pro allows you to establish a separate account for owner withdrawals for each owner. If a separate account is not established, owner withdrawals may be subtracted directly from each owner's capital or investment account.

MEMO

DATE: January 31, 2004

Because Andy McBride and Tim Bailey work in the business full time, they do not earn a paycheck. Prepare checks for Andy's monthly withdrawal of $1,000 and Tim's monthly withdrawal of $1,000.

DO: Write Check No. 6 to Andy McBride for $1,000 withdrawal

Open the **Write Checks - Checking** window:

Click **Banking** on the menu bar, click **Write Checks**

OR

Click the **Checks** icon on the **Banking** Navigator

OR

Use the keyboard shortcut **Ctrl+W**

Click the check box **To be printed**, the Check No. should be **To Print**

Date should be **01/31/04**

Enter **Andy McBride** on the **Pay to the Order of** line, press the **Tab** key

- Because Andy's name was not added to any list when the company was created, the **Name Not Found** dialog box appears on the screen.

Click **Quick Add** to add Andy's name to a list

The **Select Name Type** dialog box appears

Click **Other**

Click **OK**

- Andy's name is added to a list of *Other* names, which is used for owners, partners, and other miscellaneous names.

Tab to or click in the area for the amount of the check

- If necessary, delete any numbers showing for the amount (0.00).

Enter **1000**

Tab to or click **Memo**, enter **Owner Withdrawal for January**

Tab to or click in the Account column at the bottom of the check, click the drop-down list arrow, click the Equity account **3013 Andy McBride, Drawing**

- The amount 1,000.00 should appear in the Amount column.
- If it does not, tab to or click in the Amount column and enter 1000.
- Make sure there To be printed is selected.

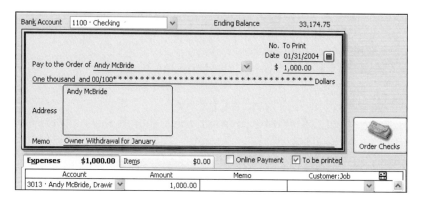

Click **Next** to record the check and advance to the next check

Repeat the above procedures to prepare Check No. 7 for Tim Bailey for $1,000 withdrawal

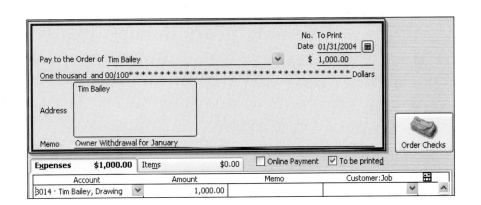

Click **Next**

Click the drop-down list arrow for **Print**

Click **Print Batch**

The **Select Checks to Print** dialog box appears

The **First Check Number** should be **6**

- If necessary, change the number to **6**.

If both checks have a check mark, click **OK**, if not, click **Select All** and then click **OK**

Once the check has printed successfully, click **OK** to close **Did check(s) print OK?** dialog box

Close **Write Checks - Checking**

PREPARE BALANCE SHEET

A balance sheet proves that assets equal liabilities plus owners' equity; however, the owners' equity in a partnership may be organized in a manner that is more meaningful than is currently shown.

DO: View the Balance Sheet for January 31, 2004

Click **Reports** on the menu bar, point to **Company & Financial**, click **Balance Sheet Standard**

OR

Click **Report Finder** on any QuickBooks Navigator, click **Company & Financial** as the type of report, click **Balance Sheet Standard**, click **Display**

Tab to or click **As of**

- If necessary, delete existing date.

Enter **01/31/04**

Tab to generate the report

Scroll through the report

- Notice the Equity section, especially the Investment and Drawing accounts for each owner.
- Also notice the Bailey & McBride Capital account balance. When the capital for both owners is combined into one account, the report does not indicate how much of the capital is for each owner.

Year Round Sports--Student's Name

Balance Sheet

As of January 31, 2004

	Jan 31, 04
Long Term Liabilities	
2510 · Office Equipment Loan	3,000.00
2520 · Store Fixtures Loan	2,500.00
Total Long Term Liabilities	5,500.00
Total Liabilities	16,730.53
Equity	
3010 · Bailey & McBride Capital	
3011 · Andy McBride, Investment	20,000.00
3012 · Tim Bailey, Investment	20,000.00
3013 · Andy McBride, Drawing	-1,000.00
3014 · Tim Bailey, Drawing	-1,000.00
3010 · Bailey & McBride Capital - Other	25,459.44
Total 3010 · Bailey & McBride Capital	63,459.44
Net Income	2,667.07
Total Equity	66,126.51
TOTAL LIABILITIES & EQUITY	82,857.04

Do not close the report

TRANSFER COMBINED CAPITAL INTO AN INDIVIDUAL CAPITAL ACCOUNT FOR EACH OWNER

A better display of owners' equity would be to show all equity accounts for each owner grouped together by owner. In addition, each owner should have an individual capital account.

MEMO

DATE: January 31, 2004

Change the account number of Bailey & McBride, Capital, to 3100. Create separate Capital accounts for Andy McBride and Tim Bailey. Name the accounts 3110 Andy McBride, Capital, and 3120 Tim Bailey, Capital. In addition, renumber Andy's Investment account to 3111 and his Drawing account to 3112. Make these subaccounts of his Capital account. Do the same for Tim's accounts: 3121 Investment and 3122 Drawing.

DO: Create separate Capital accounts and change subaccounts for existing owners' equity accounts

Access the **Chart of Accounts** as previously instructed

Click **3010 Bailey & McBride, Capital**

Click **Account** at the bottom of the **Chart of Accounts**, click **Edit**
   OR
Use the keyboard shortcut **Ctrl+E**

Change the account number to **3100**

Click **OK**

Click **Account** at the bottom of the **Chart of Accounts**, click **New**
   OR
Use the keyboard shortcut **Ctrl+N**

Click the drop-down list arrow for **Type**, click **Equity**

Tab to or click **Number**, enter **3110**

Tab to or click **Name**, enter **Andy McBride, Capital**

Click **Subaccount**, click the drop-down list arrow next to **Subaccount**, click **3100 Bailey & McBride, Capital**

Click **OK**

Click **Andy McBride, Investment**

Edit the account following steps previously listed

Change the account number to **3111**

Make this a subaccount of **3110 Andy McBride, Capital**

Click **OK** when the changes have been made

Make the following changes to **Andy McBride, Drawing**: Account number is **3112**, Subaccount of **3110**

Create the Equity account **3120 Tim Bailey, Capital**: Account 3120 is a subaccount of **3100**

Change **3012 Tim Bailey, Investment** to **3121**: Account 3121 is a subaccount of **3120**

Change **3014 Tim Bailey, Drawing** to **3122**: Account 3122 is a subaccount of
3120

◇3000 · Retained Earnings	Equity	
◇3100 · Bailey & McBride Capital	Equity	63,459.44
◇3110 · Andy McBride, Capital	Equity	19,000.00
◇3111 · Andy McBride, Investment	Equity	20,000.00
◇3112 · Andy McBride, Drawing	Equity	-1,000.00
◇3120 · Tim Bailey, Capital	Equity	19,000.00
◇3121 · Tim Bailey, Investment	Equity	20,000.00
◇3122 · Tim Bailey, Drawing	Equity	-1,000.00

Close the **Chart of Accounts**

- Since the Balance Sheet is still on the screen, the changes made to the Capital accounts will be shown in the report. If you get a screen asking if you would like to refresh the report, click **Yes**.
- Notice the change in the Equity section of the Balance Sheet.

Year Round Sports--Student's Name
Balance Sheet
As of January 31, 2004

	◇	Jan 31, 04
Equity		
3100 · Bailey & McBride Capital		
3110 · Andy McBride, Capital		
3111 · Andy McBride, Investment	20,000.00	
3112 · Andy McBride, Drawing	-1,000.00	
Total 3110 · Andy McBride, Capital		19,000.00
3120 · Tim Bailey, Capital		
3121 · Tim Bailey, Investment	20,000.00	
3122 · Tim Bailey, Drawing	-1,000.00	
Total 3120 · Tim Bailey, Capital		19,000.00
3100 · Bailey & McBride Capital - Other		25,459.44
Total 3100 · Bailey & McBride Capital		63,459.44
Net Income		2,667.07
Total Equity		66,126.51
TOTAL LIABILITIES & EQUITY		**82,243.89**

Partial Report

Do not close the report

DISTRIBUTE CAPITAL TO EACH OWNER

As you view the Balance Sheet, you will notice that the balance for Bailey & McBride, Capital, is $25,459.44. Because Bailey & McBride, Capital, is a combined Capital account, the report does not indicate how much of the capital should be distributed to each partner. In order to clarify this section of the report, the capital should be distributed between the two owners. Each owner has contributed an equal amount as an investment in the business, so the capital should be divided equally between Andy and Tim.

DO: Make an adjusting entry to distribute capital between the two owners
Access the **General Journal Entry** screen as previously instructed
Transfer the amount in the account **3100 Bailey & McBride, Capital –Other** to the owners' individual capital accounts by debiting Account 3100 for **25459.44**
Memo for all entries in the transaction is **Transfer Capital to Individual Accounts**
Transfer one-half of the amount debited to **3110 Andy McBride, Capital**, by crediting this account
- To determine one-half of the amount, you may use the Calculator or QuickMath as previously instructed.
Credit **3120 Tim Bailey, Capital**, for the other half of the amount

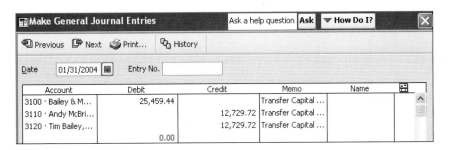

Click **Save & Close** to record
- Notice the change in the Equity section of the Balance Sheet.
- Total of 3100 Bailey & McBride, Capital, is still 63,459.44; however, accounts 3110 Andy McBride, Capital-Other and 3120 Tim Bailey, Capital-Other each show 12,729.72, which is the amount of capital for each owner.

```
                 Year Round Sports--Student's Name
                          Balance Sheet
                       As of January 31, 2004
                                        ◇          Jan 31, 04
       3100 · Bailey & McBride Capital
         3110 · Andy McBride, Capital
           3111 · Andy McBride, Investment    20,000.00
           3112 · Andy McBride, Drawing       -1,000.00
           3110 · Andy McBride, Capital - Other  12,729.72
           Total 3110 · Andy McBride, Capital           31,729.72

         3120 · Tim Bailey, Capital
           3121 · Tim Bailey, Investment      20,000.00
           3122 · Tim Bailey, Drawing         -1,000.00
           3120 · Tim Bailey, Capital - Other   12,729.72
           Total 3120 · Tim Bailey, Capital             31,729.72

         Total 3100 · Bailey & McBride Capital          63,459.44

         Net Income                                      2,667.07
       Total Equity                                     66,126.51

     TOTAL LIABILITIES & EQUITY                         82,243.89
```

Partial Report

Close the report

BANK RECONCILIATION

Each month the Checking account should be reconciled with the bank statement to make sure both balances agree. The bank statement will rarely have an ending balance that matches the balance of the Checking account. This is due to several factors: outstanding checks (written by the business but not paid by the bank), deposits in transit (deposits that were made too late to be included on the bank statement), bank service charges, interest earned on checking accounts, collections made by the bank, errors made in recording checks and/or deposits by the company or by the bank, etc.

In order to have an accurate amount listed as the balance in the Checking account, it is important that the differences between the bank statement and the Checking account be reconciled. If something such as a service charge or a collection made by the bank appears on the bank statement, it needs to be recorded in the Checking account.

Reconciling a bank statement is an appropriate time to find any errors that may have been recorded in the Checking account. The reconciliation may be out of balance because a transposition was made (recording $45 rather than $54), a transaction was recorded backwards, a transaction was recorded twice, or a transaction was not recorded at all.

OPEN RECONCILE – CHECKING

To begin the reconciliation, the Reconcile - Checking window needs to be opened. Verify the information shown for the Checking account. The Beginning Balance should match the amount of the final balance on the last reconciliation, or it should match the starting account balance.

The Begin Reconciliation screen initiates the account reconciliation. On this screen, information regarding the ending balance, service charges, and interest earned is entered.

MEMO
DATE: January 31, 2004

Received the bank statement from Mammoth Bank. The bank statement is dated January 30, 2004. Rhonda needs to reconcile the bank statement and print a Reconciliation Report for Andy and Tim.

DO: Reconcile the bank statement for January

ENTER BANK STATEMENT INFORMATION AND COMPLETE BEGIN RECONCILIATION

Information appearing on the bank statement is entered into the Begin Reconciliation window as the first step in the reconciliation process. The information entered includes the ending balance, bank service charges, and interest earned.

MAMMOTH BANK
12345 Old Mammoth Road
Mammoth Lakes, CA 93546
(909) 555-3880

Year Round Sports
875 Mountain Road
Mammoth Lakes, CA 93546

Acct. # 123-456-7890   **January 2004**

Beginning Balance 1/1/04	25,943.00		$25,943.00
1/18/04 Deposit	10,469.44		36,412.44
1/20/04 NSF Returned Check		100.00	36,312.44
1/20/04 Check 1		80.44	36,232.00
1/25/04 Check 2		294.00	35,938.00
1/25/04 Check 3		1,837.50	34,100.50
1/25/04 Check 4		312.60	33,787.90
1/25/04 Check 5		613.15	33,174.75
1/31/04 Office Equip. Loan Pmt.: $10.33 Principal, $53.42 Interest		63.75	33,111.00
1/31/04 Store Fixtures Loan Pmt.: $8.61 Principal, $44.51 Interest		53.12	33,057.88
1/31/04 Service Chg.		8.00	33,049.88
1/31/04 NSF Charge		10.00	33,039.88
1/31/04 Interest	54.05		33,093.93
Ending Balance 1/31/04			33,093.93

DO: Open the **Reconcile - Checking** window and enter preliminary information on the Begin Reconciliation screen

Open the **Chart of Accounts** as previously instructed, click **Checking**, click **Activities**, click **Reconcile**
OR
Click **Banking** on the Navigator list, click **Reconcile** on the QuickBooks Banking Navigator

- *Note:* If you need to exit the Begin Reconciliation screen before it is complete, click **Cancel**.

The **Account To Reconcile** should be **1100 Checking**

- If not, click the drop-down list arrow, click **Checking**.

The **Statement Date** should be **01/31/04**
Beginning Balance should be **25,943.00**
- This is the same amount as the Checking account starting balance.

Enter the **Ending Balance** from the bank statement, **33,093.93**
Tab to or click **Service Charge**, enter the **Service Charge**, **18.00**
- Note that this includes both the service charge of $8.00 and the $10.00 charge for Trent Trudeau's NSF check in Chapter 5.

Tab to or click Service Charge **Date**, the date should be **01/31/04**; if not, change it
Tab to or click **Account**, click the drop-down list arrow for **Account**, click **6120 Bank Service Charges**
Tab to or click **Interest Earned**, enter **54.05**
Tab to or click Interest Earned **Date**, the date should be **01/31/04**; if not, change it
Tab to or click **Account**, enter the account number **7010** for Interest Income

Click **Continue**

MARK CLEARED TRANSACTIONS FOR BANK RECONCILIATION

Once bank statement information for the ending balance, service charges, and interest has been entered, compare the checks and deposits listed on the statement with the transactions for the Checking account. If a deposit or a check is listed correctly on the bank statement and in the Reconcile - Checking window, it has cleared and should be marked. An item may be marked individually by positioning the cursor on the deposit or the check and clicking the primary mouse button. If all deposits and checks match, click the Mark All button to mark all the deposits and checks at once. To remove all the checks, click the Unmark All button. To unmark an individual item, click the item to remove the check mark.

DO: Mark cleared checks and deposits

- *Note:* If you need to exit the Reconcile - Checking screen before it is complete, click **Leave**. If you click **Reconcile Now**, you must Undo the reconciliation and start over.
- If you need to return to the Begin Reconciliation window, click the **Modify** button.

Compare the bank statement with the **Reconcile - Checking** window

Click the items that appear on both statements

Look at the bottom of the **Reconcile - Checking** window

You have marked cleared:

2 Deposits and Other Credits for 10,523.49

- This includes interest earned.

7 Checks and Payments for 3,255.69

- This includes the $100 NSF check returned, the $10 charge for the return of the NSF check, and the $8 service charge.

The Ending Balance is 33,093.96

The Cleared Balance is 33,210.80

There is a Difference of -116.87

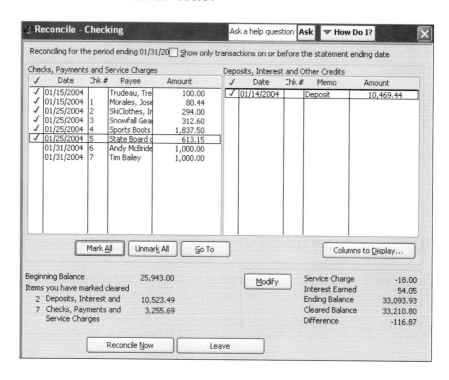

The bank statement should remain on the screen while you complete the next section

ADJUSTING AND CORRECTING ENTRIES—BANK RECONCILIATION

As you complete the reconciliation, you may find errors that need to be corrected or transactions that need to be recorded. Anything entered as a service charge or interest earned will be entered automatically when the reconciliation is complete and the Reconcile Now button is clicked. To correct an error such as a transposition, click on the entry then click the Go To button. The original entry will appear on the screen. The correction can be made and will show in the Reconcile - Checking window. If there is a transaction, such as an automatic loan payment to the bank, access the register for the account used in the transaction and enter the payment.

DO: Enter the automatic loan payments shown on the bank statement
Open the register for the **1100 Checking** account:
Use the keyboard shortcut **Ctrl+R**
In the blank transaction at the bottom of the register, enter the **Date, 01/31/04**
Tab to or click **Number**, enter **Transfer**
Tab to or click **Payee**, enter **Mammoth Bank**
Tab to or click the **Payment** column
- Because Mammoth Bank does not appear on any list, you will get a **Name Not Found** dialog box when you move to another field.

Click the **Quick Add** button to add the name of the bank to the Name List
Click **Other**

Click **OK**
- Once the name of the bank has been added to the Other List, the cursor will be positioned in the **Payment** column.
Enter **63.75** in the **Payment** column

Click the **Account** column

Click **Splits** at the bottom of the register

Click the drop-down list arrow for **Account**, click **6212 Loan Interest**

Tab to or click **Amount**, delete the amount 63.75 shown

Enter **53.42** as the amount of interest

Tab to or click **Memo**, enter **Interest Office Equipment Loan**

Tab to or click **Account**, click the drop-down list arrow for **Account**, click **2510 Office Equipment Loan**

- The correct amount of principal, **10.33**, should be shown as the amount. Tab to or click **Memo**, enter **Payment Office Equipment Loan**

Account	Amount	Memo	Customer:Job	
6212 · Loan Interest	53.42	Interest Office Equip...		
2510 · Office Equipment L...	10.33	Payment Office Equi...		

Click **Close**

- This closes the window for the information regarding the way the transaction is to be "split" between accounts.

For the **Memo** in the Checking Register, record **Loan Payment, Office Equipment**

Click the **Record** button to record the transaction

- Because the register organizes transactions according to date, you will notice that the loan payment will not appear as the last transaction in the register.

01/31/2004	Transfer	Mammoth Bank		63.75			33,111.00
	CHK	-split- Loan Payment, Offic					

Repeat the procedures to record the loan payment for store fixtures

- When you enter the Payee as Mammoth Bank, the amount for the previous transaction (63.75) appears in amount.

Enter the new amount **53.12**

Click **Splits**

Click the appropriate accounts and enter the correct amount for each item

- The accounts used for the office equipment loan payment may appear. Click the drop-down list arrow and select the appropriate accounts for the store fixture loan payment.

- Refer to the bank statement for details regarding the amount of the payment for interest and the amount of the payment applied to principal.

Account	Amount	Memo	Customer:Job	
6212 · Loan Interest	44.51	Interest Store Fixtur...		
2520 · Store Fixtures L...	8.61	Loan Payment Store ...		

Click **Close** to close the window for the information regarding the "split" between accounts

Enter the transaction **Memo**

Click **Record** to record the loan payment

01/31/2004	Transfer	Mammoth Bank		53.12		33,057.88
	CHK	-split-　　　　　Loan Payment, Store				

Close the **Checking Register**
- You should return to **Reconcile - Checking**.

Scroll to the top of **Checks and Payments**
- Notice the two entries for the payments in Checks and Payments.

Mark the two entries
- At this point the Ending Balance and Cleared Balance should be equal— $33,093.93 with a difference of 0.00.

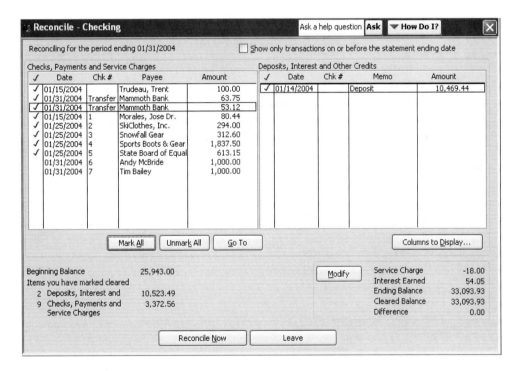

If your entries agree with the above, click **Reconcile Now** to finish the reconciliation
- If your reconciliation is not in agreement, do not click **Reconcile Now** until the errors are corrected.
- Once you click **Reconcile Now**, you may not return to this **Reconciliation - Checking** window. You would have to Undo the reconciliation and start over.

PRINT A RECONCILIATION REPORT

As soon as the Ending Balance and the Cleared Balance are equal or when you finish marking and click Reconcile Now, a screen appears allowing you to select the level of Reconciliation Report you would like to print. You may select Detail, which shows all the transactions that were reconciled, or Summary, which shows the beginning balance, the totals of the deposits and checks, and the ending balance. You may print the report at the time you have finished reconciling the account, or you may print the report later by returning to the Reconciliation window. QuickBooks Pro keeps your last two Reconciliation Reports in memory. If you think you may want to print the report after it is no longer one of the two reconciliation reports in memory, you can print the report to a file to save it permanently.

    DO: Print a Detail Reconciliation report
On the **Reconciliation Complete** screen, click **Detail**, click **Display**

    Adjust the column widths so the report will print on one page and all information
        is displayed in full
    Print as previously instructed:
    Printer should be **default printer**
    Orientation is **Portrait**
    Page Range is **All**
    When the report finishes printing, close the report

VIEW THE CHECKING ACCOUNT REGISTER

Once the bank reconciliation has been completed, it is wise to scroll through the Check Register to view the effect of the reconciliation on the account. You will notice that the check column shows a check mark for all items that were marked as cleared during the reconciliation. If at a later date an error is discovered, the transaction may be changed, and the correction will be reflected in the Beginning Balance on the reconciliation.

DO: View the register for the Checking account
Access the register as previously instructed
To display more of the register, click the check box for **1-Line**
Scroll through the register

- Notice that the transactions are listed in chronological order. Even though the bank reconciliation transactions were recorded after the checks written on January 31, the bank reconciliation transactions appear before the checks because they were recorded as a Transfer.

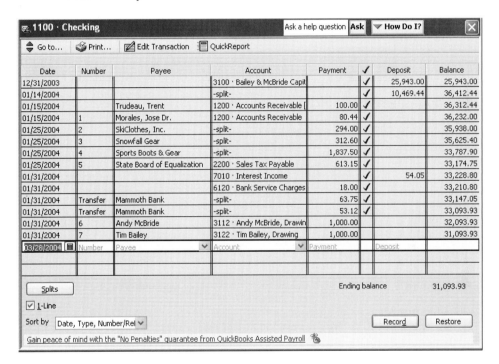

Date	Number	Payee	Account	Payment	✓	Deposit	Balance
12/31/2003			3100 · Bailey & McBride Capit		✓	25,943.00	25,943.00
01/14/2004			-split-		✓	10,469.44	36,412.44
01/15/2004		Trudeau, Trent	1200 · Accounts Receivable [	100.00	✓		36,312.44
01/15/2004	1	Morales, Jose Dr.	1200 · Accounts Receivable	80.44	✓		36,232.00
01/25/2004	2	SkiClothes, Inc.	-split-	294.00	✓		35,938.00
01/25/2004	3	Snowfall Gear	-split-	312.60	✓		35,625.40
01/25/2004	4	Sports Boots & Gear	-split-	1,837.50	✓		33,787.90
01/25/2004	5	State Board of Equalization	2200 · Sales Tax Payable	613.15	✓		33,174.75
01/31/2004			7010 · Interest Income		✓	54.05	33,228.80
01/31/2004			6120 · Bank Service Charges	18.00	✓		33,210.80
01/31/2004	Transfer	Mammoth Bank	-split-	63.75	✓		33,147.05
01/31/2004	Transfer	Mammoth Bank	-split-	53.12	✓		33,093.93
01/31/2004	6	Andy McBride	3112 · Andy McBride, Drawin	1,000.00			32,093.93
01/31/2004	7	Tim Bailey	3122 · Tim Bailey, Drawing	1,000.00			31,093.93
03/28/2004	Number	Payee	Account	Payment		Deposit	

Ending balance 31,093.93

Splits

☑ 1-Line

Sort by Date, Type, Number/Rel ∨

Record   Restore

Gain peace of mind with the "No Penalties" guarantee from QuickBooks Assisted Payroll

- Notice that the final balance of the account is $31,093.93.
Close the register
Leave the Chart of Accounts open

CREDIT CARD RECONCILIATION

Any account used in QuickBooks Pro may be reconciled. As with a checking account, it is a good practice to reconcile the Credit Card account each month. When the credit card statement is received, the transactions entered in QuickBooks Pro should agree with the transactions shown on the credit card statement. A reconciliation of the credit card should be completed on a monthly basis.

MEMO

DATE: January 31, 2004

The monthly bill for the Visa has arrived and is to be paid. Prior to paying the monthly credit card bill, reconcile the Credit Card account.

DO: Reconcile and pay the credit card bill
Click **2100 Visa** in the Chart of Accounts, click the **Activities** button, click
Reconcile Credit Card
The Beginning Balance should be **150.00**

MAMMOTH BANK
VISA
12345 Old Mammoth Road
Mammoth Lakes, CA 93546
(619) 555-3880

Year Round Sports
875 Mountain Road
Mammoth Lakes, CA 93546   Acct. # 098-776-4321

Beginning Balance 1/1/04		150.00	$150.00
1/23/04 Mammoth Office Supply Company		21.98	171.98
1/23/04 Ski Supplies		300.00	471.98
1/25/04 Awesome Accessories		350.00	821.98
1/25/04 Shoes Abound		400.00	1,221.98
Ending Balance 1/31/04			1,221.98

Minimum Payment Due: $50.00   Payment Due Date: February 15, 2004

Compare the credit card statement with the **Reconcile Credit Card - Visa**
Enter the **Statement Date** of **01/31/04**
Enter the **Ending Balance** of **1,221.98** in the **Begin Reconciliation** window

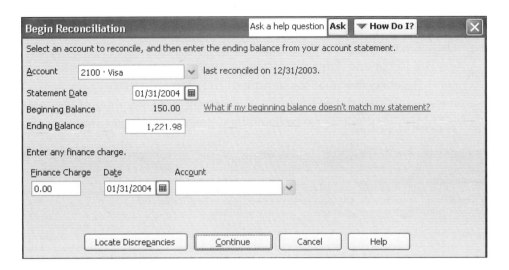

> Click **Continue**
> Mark each item that appears on both the statement and in the reconciliation <u>EXCEPT</u> for the $**400** transaction for Shoes Abound

RECORD AN ADJUSTMENT TO A RECONCILIATION

In QuickBooks Pro 2004, adjustments to reconciliations may be made during the reconciliation process. In addition, account reconciliations may be eliminated by clicking an Undo button.

DO: Verify that all items are marked <u>EXCEPT</u> the last charge for $**400**

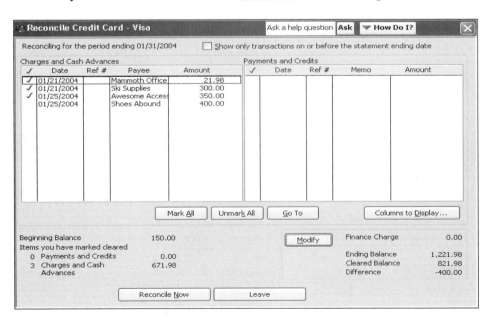

Click **Reconcile Now**

- The Reconcile Adjustment screen appears because there was a $400 Difference shown at the bottom of the reconciliation.
- Even though the error on the demonstration reconciliation is known, an adjustment will be entered and then deleted at a later time.

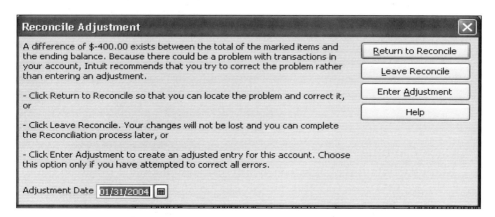

Click **Enter Adjustment**

Click **Cancel** on the Make Payment screen

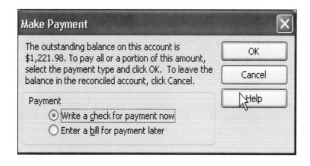

- The Reconciliation report is generated

Display the Detail report

Year Round Sports--Student's Name
Reconciliation Detail
2100 · Visa, Period Ending 01/31/2004

Type	Date	Num	Name	Clr	Amount	Balance
Beginning Balance						150.00
Cleared Transactions						
Checks and Payments - 4 items						
Credit Card Charge	01/21/2004		Mammoth Office Supply Company	✓	-21.98	-21.98
Credit Card Charge	01/21/2004		Ski Supplies	✓	-300.00	-321.98
Bill Pmt -CCard	01/25/2004		Awesome Accessories	✓	-350.00	-671.98
General Journal	01/31/2004			✓	-400.00	-1,071.98
Total Checks and Payments					-1,071.98	-1,071.98
Total Cleared Transactions					-1,071.98	-1,071.98
Cleared Balance					1,071.98	1,221.98
Uncleared Transactions						
Checks and Payments - 1 item						
Bill Pmt -CCard	01/25/2004		Shoes Abound		-400.00	-400.00
Total Checks and Payments					-400.00	-400.00
Total Uncleared Transactions					-400.00	-400.00
Register Balance as of 01/31/2004					1,471.98	1,621.98

- Notice that there is a General Journal entry for $400 in the Clear Transactions section of the report. This is the Adjustment made by QuickBooks.
- Also note that Uncleared Transactions shows the $400 for Shoes Abound.

Close the Reconciliation Detail report without printing

UNDO A PREVIOUS RECONCILIATION, DELETE AN ADJUSTMENT, AND REDO A RECONCILIATION

If an error is discovered after an account reconciliation has been completed, the reconciliation may be removed by using the Undo Reconciliation feature located on the Locate Discrepancies screen. If an adjusting entry for a reconciliation has been made, it may be deleted. This is useful if you had a discrepancy when making the reconciliation and found the error at a later date.

DO: Undo the credit card reconciliation and delete the adjusting entry made by QuickBooks

Access the **Reconcile Credit Card** window as previously instructed

Click **Locate Discrepancies** on the Begin Reconciliation screen

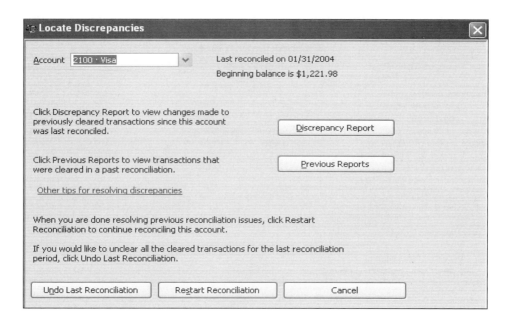

Click the **Undo Last Reconciliation** button

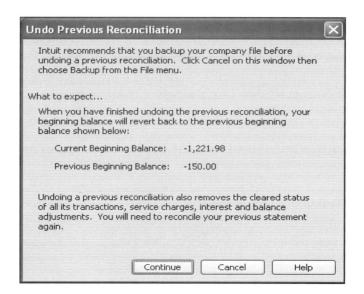

Click **Continue** on the Undo Previous Reconciliation screen

Click **OK** on the Undo Previous Reconcile Complete screen

Click the **Restart Reconciliation** button on the Locate Discrepancies screen
- You will return to the Begin Reconciliation screen.

Make sure the **Statement Date** is **01/31/04**

Enter the **Ending Balance** of **1221.98**

Click **Continue**

Mark all the items listed on the Credit Card Statement <u>INCLUDING</u> the $400 for Shoes Abound

Click the Adjusting entry for 01/31/04

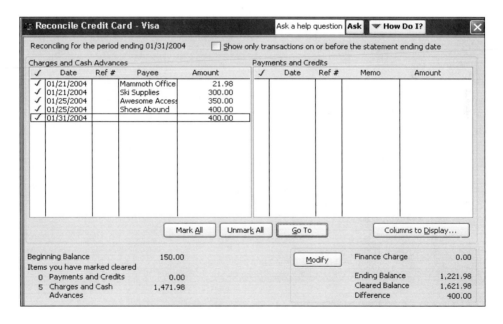

Click **Go To**
- You will go to the Make General Journal Entries screen

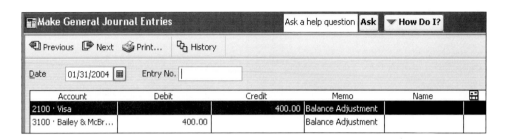

Use the keyboard shortcut **Ctrl+D** to delete the entry

After the adjustment has been deleted, close the Journal

Verify that the adjusting entry has been deleted and that the Ending and Cleared Balances are 1,221.98 and the Difference is 0.00

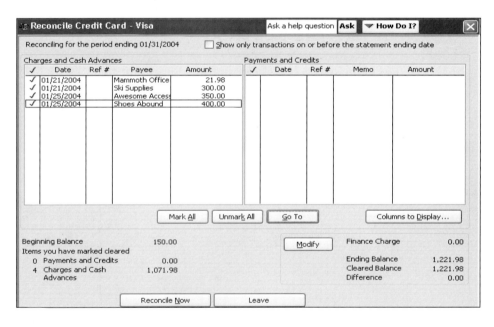

Click **Reconcile Now**

Print a **Detail Report** following the procedures given for the Bank Reconciliation Report

When the **Make Payment** dialog box appears on the screen

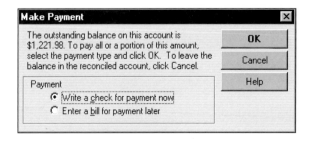

Make sure **Write a check for payment now** is selected, click **OK**

- If it is not selected, click **Write a check for payment now** to select, then click **OK**.

Display and print a Reconciliation Detail report

Close the Reconciliation Detail report

The payment check should appear on the screen

Enter **8** as the check number

The **Date** of the check should be **01/31/04**

Click the drop-down list next to **Pay to the Order of**, click **Mammoth Bank**

- If you get a dialog box for **Auto Recall**, click **No**.

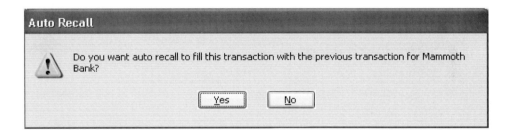

Tab to or click **Memo** on the bottom of the check

Enter **January Visa Payment** as the memo

Print the check as previously instructed

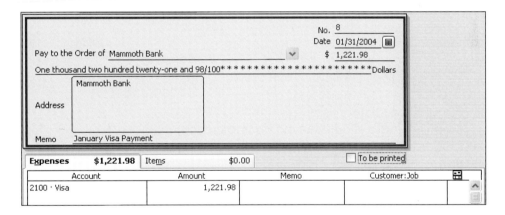

When the check has printed successfully, click **Save & Close** to record and exit **Write Checks**

Close the Chart of Accounts

VIEW THE JOURNAL

After entering several transactions, it is helpful to view the Journal. In the Journal all transactions regardless of the method of entry are shown in traditional debit/credit format.

DO: View the **Journal** for January
Click **Report Finder** on any QuickBooks Navigator, click **Accountant & Taxes**
        as the type of report, click **Journal**
Tab to or click **From**, enter **01/01/04**
Tab to or click **To**, enter **01/31/04**
Click **Display**
Scroll through the Journal and view all the transactions that have been made

Year Round Sports--Student's Name

Journal

January 2004

Trans #	Type	Date	Num	Name	Memo	Account	Debit	Credit
111	Check	01/31/2004	Transfer	Mammoth Bank	Loan Payment, Store Fixtures	1100 · Checking		53.12
				Mammoth Bank	Interest Store Fixtures Loan	6212 · Loan Interest	44.51	
				Mammoth Bank	Loan Payment Store Fixtures	2520 · Store Fixtures Loan	8.61	
							53.12	53.12
112	Check	01/31/2004			Service Charge	1100 · Checking		18.00
					Service Charge	6120 · Bank Service Charges	18.00	
							18.00	18.00
113	Dep...	01/31/2004			Interest	1100 · Checking	54.05	
					Interest	7010 · Interest Income		54.05
							54.05	54.05
115	Check	01/31/2004	8	Mammoth Bank	January Visa Payment	1100 · Checking		1,221.98
				Mammoth Bank	January Visa Payment	2100 · Visa	1,221.98	
							1,221.98	1,221.98
TOTAL							72,797.15	72,797.15

Partial Report

Close the **Journal** without printing
Report Finder should remain on the screen

PREPARE TRIAL BALANCE

After all adjustments have been recorded and the bank reconciliation has been completed, it is wise to prepare the Trial Balance. As in traditional accounting, the QuickBooks Pro Trial Balance proves that debits equal credits.

MEMO
DATE: January 31, 2004

Because adjustments have been entered, prepare a Trial Balance.

DO: Prepare a trial balance using Report Finder
Verify that the type of report is **Accountant & Taxes**
Click **Trial Balance**
- If necessary, enter the dates **From 01/01/04** and **To 01/31/04**
Click **Display**
Scroll through the report and study the amounts shown
- Notice that the final totals of debits and credits are equal: $89,472.05.
Do not close the report

USE QUICKZOOM IN TRIAL BALANCE

QuickZoom is a QuickBooks Pro feature that allows you to make a closer observation of transactions, amounts, etc. With QuickZoom you may zoom in on an item when the mouse pointer turns into a magnifying glass with a Z inside. If you point to an item and you do not get a magnifying glass with a Z inside, you cannot zoom in on the item. For example, if you point to Store Fixtures Loan, you will see the magnifying glass with the Z inside.

DO: Use QuickZoom to view the details of Office Supplies:
Scroll through the Trial Balance until you see **1311 Office Supplies**
Position the mouse pointer over the amount of Office Supplies, **521.98**
- Notice that the mouse pointer changes to a magnifying glass with a Z.
Double-click the primary mouse button
- A **Transactions by Account Report** appears on the screen showing the two transactions entered for office supplies.
Scroll through the report

			Year Round Sports--Student's Name					
			Transactions by Account					
			As of January 31, 2004					
Type	Date	Num	Name	Memo	Clr	Split	Amount	Balance
1310 · Supplies								**850.00**
1311 · Office Supplies								**850.00**
Credit Card Charge	01/21/2004		Mammoth Office S...	Purchase Pa...		2100 · Visa	21.98	871.98
General Journal	01/31/2004			Adjusting En...		6472 · Office	-350.00	521.98
Total 1311 · Office Supplies							-328.02	521.98
Total 1310 · Supplies							-328.02	521.98
TOTAL							**-328.02**	**521.98**

Close the report

PRINT THE TRIAL BALANCE

Once the trial balance has been prepared, it may be printed.

DO: Print the **Trial Balance**
Click the **Print** button at the top of the Trial Balance
Click **Preview** to view a miniature copy of the report
- This helps determine the orientation, whether you need to select the feature to print one page wide, or whether you need to adjust the column widths.

Click **Close**
Use **Portrait** orientation
Click **Print**
Close the **Trial Balance** and close **Report Finder**

SELECT ACCRUAL-BASIS REPORTING PREFERENCE

QuickBooks Pro allows a business to customize the program and select certain preferences for reports, displays, graphs, accounts, and so on. There are two report preferences available in QuickBooks Pro: Cash and Accrual. You need to select the preference you prefer. If you select Cash as the report preference, income on reports will be shown as of the date payment is received, and expenses will be shown as of the date you pay the bill. If Accrual is selected, QuickBooks Pro shows the income on the report as of the date of the invoice and expenses as of the bill date. Prior to printing end-of-period reports, it is advisable to verify which reporting basis is selected. If Cash has been selected and you are using the Accrual method, it is imperative that you change your report basis.

MEMO
DATE: January 31, 2004

Prior to printing the Balance Sheet, Profit and Loss or Income Statement, or any other reports, check the report preference. If necessary, choose Accrual. After the selection has been made, print a Standard Profit and Loss and a Standard Balance Sheet for Year Round Sports.

DO: Select **Accrual** as the Summary Report Basis
Click **Edit** on the menu bar, click **Preferences**
Scroll through the Preferences List until you see **Reports & Graphs**
Click **Reports & Graphs** and the **Company Preferences** tab
If necessary, click **Accrual** to select the Summary Reports Basis

Reports & Graphs

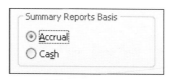

Click **OK** to close the **Preferences** window

PRINT STANDARD PROFIT AND LOSS STATEMENT

Because all income, expenses, and adjustments have been made for the period, a Profit and Loss Statement can be prepared. This statement is also known as the Income Statement. QuickBooks Pro has several different types of Profit and Loss Statements available: Standard—summarizes income and expenses; Detail—shows year-to-date transactions for each income and expense account; YTD Comparison—like the Standard Profit and Loss but summarizes your income and expenses for this month and compares them to your income and expenses for the current fiscal year; Prev Year Comparison—summarizes your income and expenses for both this month and this month last year and shows $ change and % change; By Job—like the Standard Profit and Loss statement, but with columns for each customer and job and amounts for this year to date; and By Class—like the Standard Profit and Loss statement, but with columns for each class and subclass with the amounts for this year to date. Unclassified shows how much you are making or losing within segments of your business that are not assigned to a QuickBooks class.

DO: Print a **Standard Profit and Loss Report**

Click **Reports** on the menu bar, point to **Company & Financial**, click **Profit &**
  Loss Standard
  OR
Click **Report Finder** on any QuickBooks Navigator, click **Company &**
  Financial as the type of report, click **Profit & Loss Standard**, click **Display**
Tab to or click **From**, enter **01/01/04**
Tab to or click **To**, enter **01/31/04**
Tab to generate the report
Scroll through the report to view the income and expenses listed
Print the report
Use **Portrait** orientation

Year Round Sports--Student's Name
Profit & Loss
January 2004

	Jan 04	
6392 · Water	85.00	
Total 6390 · Utilities		444.00
6470 · Supplies Expense		
6471 · Sales	175.00	
6472 · Office	350.00	
Total 6470 · Supplies Expense		525.00
Total Expense		3,018.50
Net Ordinary Income		2,551.14
Other Income/Expense		
Other Income		
7010 · Interest Income		54.05
Total Other Income		54.05
Net Other Income		54.05
Net Income		2,605.19

Partial Report

Close the **Profit and Loss Report**

VIEW A STANDARD BALANCE SHEET

The Balance Sheet proves the fundamental accounting equation: Assets = Liabilities + Owners'
Equity. When all transactions and adjustments for the period have been recorded, a Balance
Sheet should be prepared. QuickBooks Pro has several different types of Balance Sheet
statements available: Standard—shows as of today the balance in each Balance Sheet account
with subtotals provided for assets, liabilities, and equity; Detail—This report is a more detailed
version of the Standard Balance Sheet Report, Summary—shows amounts for each account type

but not for individual accounts; and <u>Comparison</u>—has columns for today, a year ago today, $ change, and % change;. For each account, the report shows the starting balance at the beginning of last month, transactions entered in the account for this month to date, and the ending balance as of today.

DO: View a **Standard Balance Sheet Report**
Click **Reports** on the menu bar, point to **Company & Financial**, click **Balance Sheet Standard**
OR
Use Report Finder and select **Company & Financial** as the type of report, click **Balance Sheet Standard**, click **Display**
Tab to or click **As of,** enter **01/31/04**
Tab to generate the report
Scroll through the report to view the assets, liabilities, and equities listed
- Notice the Net Income account listed in the **Equity** section of the report. This is the same amount of Net Income shown on the Profit and Loss Statement.

Year Round Sports--Student's Name
Balance Sheet
As of January 31, 2004

	Jan 31, 04
Equity	
3100 · Bailey & McBride Capital	
3110 · Andy McBride, Capital	
3111 · Andy McBride, Investment	20,000.00
3112 · Andy McBride, Drawing	-1,000.00
3110 · Andy McBride, Capital - Other	12,729.72
Total 3110 · Andy McBride, Capital	31,729.72
3120 · Tim Bailey, Capital	
3121 · Tim Bailey, Investment	20,000.00
3122 · Tim Bailey, Drawing	-1,000.00
3120 · Tim Bailey, Capital - Other	12,729.72
Total 3120 · Tim Bailey, Capital	31,729.72
Total 3100 · Bailey & McBride Capital	63,459.44
Net Income	2,605.19
Total Equity	66,064.63
TOTAL LIABILITIES & EQUITY	**80,941.09**

Partial Report

Do not close the report

ADJUSTMENT TO TRANSFER NET INCOME/RETAINED EARNINGS INTO ANDY MCBRIDE, CAPITAL, AND TIM BAILEY, CAPITAL:

Because Year Round Sports is a partnership, the amount of net income should appear as part of each owner's Capital account rather than appear as Retained Earnings. In many instances, this is the type of adjustment the CPA makes on the Accountant's Copy of the QuickBooks Pro company files. The adjustment may be made before the closing date for the fiscal year, or it may be made after the closing has been performed. Because QuickBooks Pro automatically transfers the amount in the Net Income account into Retained Earnings, the closing entry for a partnership will transfer the net income into each owner's Capital account. This adjustment is made by debiting Retained Earnings and crediting the owners' individual capital accounts. When you view a report before the end of the year, you will see an amount in Net Income and the same amount as a negative in Retained Earnings. If you view a report after the end of the year, you will not see any information regarding Retained Earnings or Net Income because the adjustment correctly transferred the amount to the owners' capital accounts.

If you prefer to use the power of the program and not make the adjustment, QuickBooks Pro simply carries the amount of Retained Earnings forward. Each year the amount of net income is added to Retained Earnings.

On the Balance Sheet, Retained Earnings and/or Net Income appear as part of the equity section. The owners' Drawing and Investment accounts are kept separate from Retained Earnings at all times. If Year Round Sports had used a traditional QuickBooks Pro setup for the Equity section of the Balance Sheet, it would appear as:

Equity
  Retained Earnings
  Owners' Equity
    Owners' Investment
    Owners' Draw
  Total Owners' Equity

  Net Income

Total Equity

 DO: Evenly divide and transfer the net income into the Andy McBride, Capital, and Tim Bailey, Capital, accounts after year end:
  Open the **General Journal** as previously instructed
  The **Date** is **01/31/04**
  The first account used is **3000 Retained Earnings**

Debit **3000 Retained Earnings**, **2,605.19**

For the Memo record **Transfer Net Income into Capital**

The other accounts used are **3110 Andy McBride, Capital**, and **3120 Tim Bailey, Capital**

1,302.60 should be entered as the credit amount for **3110 Andy McBride, Capital**

- QuickBooks Pro enters **1,302.59** as the credit amount for **3120 Tim Bailey, Capital**.
- Bcause QuickBooks Pro accepts only two numbers after a decimal point, the cents must be rounded. Thus, there is a 1¢ difference in the distribution between the two owners. If there is an uneven amount in the future, Tim will receive the extra amount.

Enter the same Memo as entered for Retained Earnings

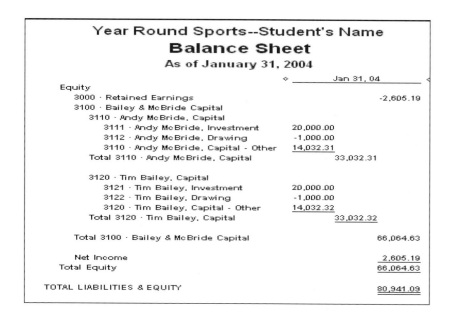

Click **Save & Close** to record and close the **General Journal**

- Since you did not close the report, the Balance Sheet should still be on the screen.

- Notice the change in the **Equity** section of the Balance Sheet.
- Not all companies have a profit each month. If your business has a negative amount for net income, the appropriate adjustment would be to debit each owner's individual capital account and to credit Retained Earnings. For example, if Net Income was -500.00, you would record the following: 3110 Andy McBride, Capital—debit 250; 3120 Tim Bailey, Capital—debit 250; and 3000 Retained Earnings—credit 500.

Do not close the report

PRINT STANDARD BALANCE SHEET

Once the adjustment for Net Income/Retained Earnings has been performed, viewing or printing the Balance Sheet will show you the status of the Owners' Equity.

DO: Print a **Standard Balance Sheet** for January 2005
Click **Print**
- The Balance Sheet still appears on the screen after printing is complete.

Change the **As of** date to **01/31/2005**
- Notice the Equity section.
- Nothing is shown for Retained Earnings or Net Income.
- The net income has been added to the owners' Capital accounts.

	Year Round Sports--Student's Name		
	Balance Sheet		
	As of January 31, 2005		
			Jan 31, 05
Equity			
3100 · Bailey & McBride Capital			
3110 · Andy McBride, Capital			
3111 · Andy McBride, Investment		20,000.00	
3112 · Andy McBride, Drawing		-1,000.00	
3110 · Andy McBride, Capital - Other		14,032.31	
Total 3110 · Andy McBride, Capital			33,032.31
3120 · Tim Bailey, Capital			
3121 · Tim Bailey, Investment		20,000.00	
3122 · Tim Bailey, Drawing		-1,000.00	
3120 · Tim Bailey, Capital - Other		14,032.32	
Total 3120 · Tim Bailey, Capital			33,032.32
Total 3100 · Bailey & McBride Capital			66,064.63
Total Equity			66,064.63
TOTAL LIABILITIES & EQUITY			80,941.09

Partial Report

Print the **Balance Sheet** for January 2005
Do not close the report
Change the **As of** date for the Balance Sheet to **01/31/04**

CLOSE DRAWING AND TRANSFER INTO OWNERS' CAPITAL ACCOUNTS

In traditional accrual-basis accounting, there are four entries that need to be made at the end of a fiscal year. These entries close income, expenses, and the drawing accounts and transfer the net income into owners' equity. When preparing reports during the next fiscal year, QuickBooks Pro will not show any amounts in the income and expense accounts for the previous year. However, QuickBooks Pro does not close the owners' drawing accounts, nor does it transfer the net income into the owners' Capital accounts. If you prefer to use the power of the program and omit the last two closing entries, QuickBooks Pro will keep a running account of the owner withdrawals, and it will put net income into a Retained Earnings account. However, transferring the net income and drawing into the owners' Capital accounts provides a clearer picture of the value of the owners' equity.

The entry transferring the net income into the owners' Capital accounts has already been made. While this is not the actual end of the fiscal year for Year Round Sports, the closing entry for the Drawing accounts will be entered at this time so that you will have experience in recording this closing entry.

MEMO

DATE: January 31, 2004

Record the closing entry to close 3112 Andy McBride, Drawing, and 3122 Tim Bailey, Drawing, into each owner's Capital account.

DO: Record the closing entry for each owner's Drawing account
Access the **General Journal** as previously instructed
Debit **3110 Andy McBride, Capital**, for the amount of the drawing account
1,000
The Memo for the transaction is **Close Drawing**
Credit **3112 Andy McBride, Drawing**, for **1,000**
Use the same Memo for this portion of the transaction

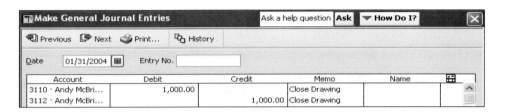

Click **Next**
Repeat the above steps to close **3122 Tim Bailey, Drawing**

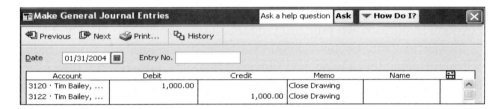

Click **Save & Close**

- Notice the change in the **Equity** section of the Balance Sheet.

Year Round Sports--Student's Name
Balance Sheet
As of January 31, 2004

	Jan 31, 04
Equity	
3000 · Retained Earnings	-2,605.19
3100 · Bailey & McBride Capital	
3110 · Andy McBride, Capital	
3111 · Andy McBride, Investment	20,000.00
3110 · Andy McBride, Capital - Other	13,032.31
Total 3110 · Andy McBride, Capital	33,032.31
3120 · Tim Bailey, Capital	
3121 · Tim Bailey, Investment	20,000.00
3120 · Tim Bailey, Capital - Other	13,032.32
Total 3120 · Tim Bailey, Capital	33,032.32
Total 3100 · Bailey & McBride Capital	66,064.63
Net Income	2,605.19
Total Equity	66,064.63
TOTAL LIABILITIES & EQUITY	**80,941.09**

Partial Report

Print the **Balance Sheet**
Close the report
Do not close Report Finder

EXPORTING REPORTS TO EXCEL

Many of the reports prepared in QuickBooks Pro can be exported to Microsoft® Excel. This allows you to take advantage of extensive filtering options available in Excel, hide detail for some but not all groups of data, combine information from two different reports, change titles of columns, add comments, change the order of columns, and experiment with "what if" scenarios. In order to use this feature of QuickBooks Pro you must also have Microsoft Excel 97 or higher.

DO: Optional Exercise: Export a report from QuickBooks Pro to Excel
With Report Finder on the screen, click **Balance Sheet Standard**
Enter the **From** date as **01/01/04** and the **To** date as **01/31/04**
Click the **Export** button

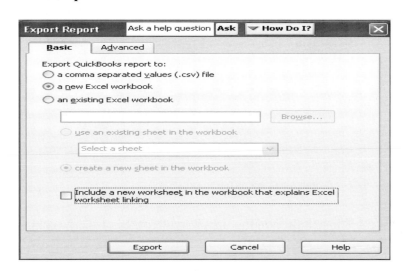

Make sure the Export Report screen has **a new Excel workbook** selected as the
File option and that **Include a new worksheet in the workbook that
explains Excel worksheet linking** is not selected
Click **Export**
• The Balance Sheet will be displayed in Excel.

	A	B	C	D	E	F
1						Jan 31, 04
2	ASSETS					
3		Current Assets				
4			Checking/Savings			
5				1100 · Checking		29,871.95
6			Total Checking/Savings			29,871.95
7			Accounts Receivable			
8				1200 · Accounts Receivable		5,690.62
9			Total Accounts Receivable			5,690.62
10			Other Current Assets			
11				1120 · Inventory Asset		34,991.54
12				1310 · Supplies		
13					1311 · Office Supplies	521.98
14					1312 · Sales Supplies	400.00
15				Total 1310 · Supplies		921.98
16				1340 · Prepaid Insurance		125.00
17			Total Other Current Assets			36,038.52
18		Total Current Assets				71,601.09

Partial Report

Scroll through the report and click in Cell A60
Type **BALANCE SHEET IMPORTED TO EXCEL**

	A	B	C	D	E	F
1						Jan 31, 04
60	BALANCE SHEET IMPORTED TO EXCEL					

Click the **Close** button in the upper right corner of the Excel title bar to close
Excel

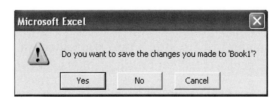

Click **No** to close **Book1** without saving

IMPORTING DATA FROM EXCEL

You may have Excel or .csv (comma separated value) files that contain important business
information about customers, vendors, and sales that are not contained in your QuickBooks
Company File. That information can now be imported directly into QuickBooks and customized
as desired. An import file must conform to a specific structure for QuickBooks to interpret the
data in the file correctly.

It is recommended that you set up your import file correctly in order to transfer the data properly and avoid errors. This includes preparing the file for import into QuickBooks, mapping the data from your file to QuickBooks, and previewing the imported data. QuickBooks has a built in Reference Guide for Importing Files that may be accessed and printed through Help.

PRINT JOURNAL

It is always wise to have a printed or hard copy of the data on disk. After all entries and adjustments for the month have been made, print the Journal for January. This copy should be kept on file as an additional backup to the data stored on your disk. If something happens to your disk to damage it, you will still have the paper copy of your transactions available for re-entry into the system.

DO: Print the **Journal** for January
Click **Reports** on the menu bar, point to **Accountant & Taxes**, click **Journal**
  OR
Click **Report Finder** on any QuickBooks Navigator, click **Taxes and Accountant** as the type of report, click **Journal**, click **Display**
Tab to or click **From**, enter **01/01/04**
Tab to or click **To**, enter **01/31/04**
Tab to generate the report
Resize the columns so all names and accounts are shown in full and the report prints on one-page wide
Print the report in **Landscape** orientation
Close the **Journal** and, if necessary, **Report Finder**

END-OF-PERIOD BACKUP

Once all end-of-period procedures have been completed, in addition to a regular backup copy of company data and a duplicate disk, a second duplicate disk of the company data should be made and filed as an archive disk. Preferably, this copy will be located someplace other than on the business premises. The archive disk or file copy is set aside in case of emergency or in case damage occurs to the original and current backup copies of the company data.

DO: Back up company data and prepare an archive copy of the company data
Prepare a Back Up as previously instructed
- In the **File** Name text box enter **Year Round Archive 1-31-04.qbb** as the name for the backup
Also prepare a duplicate disk as instructed in Appendix A

- Label this disk **Archive, 1-31-04**

PASSWORDS

Not every employee of a business should have access to all the financial records. In some companies, only the owner(s) will have complete access. In others, one or two key employees will have full access while other employees are provided limited access based on the jobs they perform. Passwords are secret words used to control access to data. QuickBooks Pro has several options available to assign passwords.

In order to assign any passwords at all, you must have an administrator. The administrator has unrestricted access to all QuickBooks Pro functions and sets up users, user passwords, and assigns areas of transaction access for each user. Areas of access can be limited to transaction entry for certain types of transactions or a user may have unrestricted access into all areas of QuickBooks Pro and company data.

A password should be kept secret at all times. It should be something that is easy for the individual to remember, yet difficult for someone else to guess. Birthdays, names, initials, and other similar devices are not good passwords because the information is too readily available. Never write down your password where it can be easily found or seen by someone else.

Even though the password feature is available, we will not be assigning passwords during training. If a password is forgotten, QuickBooks cannot be accessed until the appropriate password is entered.

SET THE CLOSING DATE FOR THE PERIOD

A closing date assigned to transactions for a period prevents change to data from the period without acknowledging that a transaction has been changed for a closed period. This is helpful to discourage casual changes or transaction deletions to a period that has been closed. Setting the closing date is done by accessing Set Up Users in QuickBooks Pro.

MEMO
DATE: January 31, 2004

Now that the closing transactions have been performed, Andy and Tim want to protect the data by setting the closing date to 1/31/04.

DO: Assign the closing date of **01/31/04** to the transactions for the period ending
1/31/04
Click **Edit** on the menu bar, click **Preferences**
Scroll through the preference list until you see the icon for Accounting
Click **Accounting**
Click **Company Preferences**
Enter **01/31/04** as the closing date in the Closing Date section of the Company
Preferences for Accounting

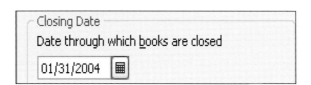

Click **OK**

ACCESS TRANSACTION FOR PREVIOUS PERIOD

Even though the month of January has been closed, transactions still appear in the account
registers, the Journal, etc. The transactions shown may not be changed unless you click Yes on
the screen warning you that you have changed a transaction to a closed period.

DO: Try to change Prepaid Insurance to 2,500
Access the **Chart of Accounts** as previously instructed, click **Prepaid Insurance**
Click **Activities** at the bottom of the **Chart of Accounts**, click **Use Register**
OR
Use the keyboard shortcut **Ctrl+R**
Click the **Increase** column showing **250**
Highlight 250, enter **2,500**
Click **Record**
A **QuickBooks** dialog box allowing the transaction to be changed appears

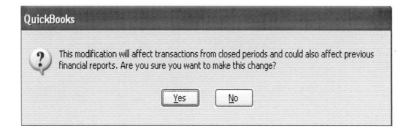

Click **No**

Click **Restore** to restore the transaction to the original 250
Close the **Prepaid Insurance** account
Do not close the **Chart of Accounts**

EDIT TRANSACTION FROM PREVIOUS PERIOD

If it is determined that an error was made in a previous period, QuickBooks Pro does allow the correction. Before it will record any changes for previous periods, QuickBooks Pro requires that Yes is clicked on the dialog box warning of the change to a transaction date that is prior to the closing date for the company.

MEMO

DATE: January 31, 2004

After entering the closing date, Rhonda reviews the Journal and reports printed at the end of January. She finds that $25 of the amount of Office Supplies should have been recorded as Sales Supplies. Record an entry in the Journal to transfer $25 from Office Supplies to Sales Supplies.

DO: Transfer $25 from Office Supplies to Sales Supplies
Access the **General Journal** as previously instructed
Enter the date of **01/31/04**
Tab to or click **Account**, click the drop-down list arrow for **Account**, click **1312 Sales Supplies**
Enter the debit of **25.00**
Enter the Memo **Correcting Entry**
Tab to or click **Account**, click the drop-down list arrow for Account, click **1311 Office Supplies**
- A credit amount of 25.00 should already be in the credit column. If not, enter the amount.

Enter the Memo **Correcting Entry**

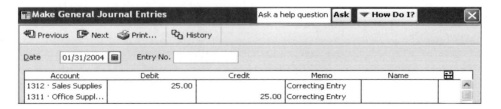

Click **Save & Close**

Click **Yes** on the **QuickBooks** dialog box

VERIFY THE CORRECTION TO OFFICE AND SALES SUPPLIES

Once the correction has been made, it is important to view the change in the accounts. The transfer of an amount of one asset into another will have no direct effect on the total assets in your reports. The account balances for Office Supplies and Sales Supplies will be changed. To view the change in the account, open the Chart of Accounts and look at the balance of each account. You may also use the account register to view the correcting entry as it was recorded in each account.

MEMO

DATE: January 31, 2004

Access the Chart of Accounts and view the change in the account balances and the correcting entry in each account's register.

DO: View the correcting entry in each account
If necessary, open the **Chart of Accounts** as previously instructed
- Notice that the balance for Office Supplies has been changed from 521.98 to 496.98.
- Notice that the balance for Sales Supplies has been changed from 400.00 to 425.00.

◆1310 · Supplies	Other Current Asset	921.98
◆1311 · Office Supplies	Other Current Asset	496.98
◆1312 · Sales Supplies	Other Current Asset	425.00

Double-click **Office Supplies** to open the account register
- Verify that the correcting entry was recorded for Office Supplies.

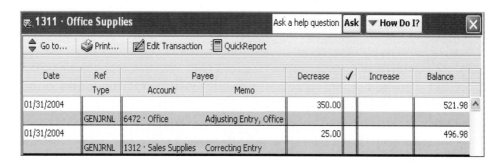

Close the **Office Supplies Register**
Repeat the steps to view the correcting entry in Sales Supplies

Date	Ref	Payee		Decrease	✓	Increase	Balance
	Type	Account	Memo				
12/31/2003					✓	575.00	575.00
	DEP	3100 · Bailey & McBride (Account Opening Balance					
01/31/2004				175.00			400.00
	GENJRNL	6471 · Sales					
01/31/2004						25.00	425.00
	GENJRNL	1311 · Office Supplies	Correcting Entry				

1312 · Sales Supplies Ask a help question [Ask] ▼ How Do I? [×]
♦ Go to...   Print...   Edit Transaction   QuickReport

Close the **Sales Supplies Register**
Close the **Chart of Accounts**

INVENTORY ADJUSTMENTS

In a business that has inventory, it is possible that the number of items on hand is different from the quantity shown in QuickBooks Pro when a physical inventory is taken. This can be caused by a variety of items: loss due to theft, fire, or flood; damage to an item in the stockroom; an error in a previous physical inventory. Even though QuickBooks Pro uses the average cost method of inventory valuation, the value of an item can be changed as well. For example, assume that several pairs of after-ski boots are discounted and sold for a lesser value during the summer months. QuickBooks Pro allows the quantity and value of inventory to be adjusted.

MEMO
DATE: January 31, 2004

After taking a physical inventory, Andy and Tim discover two hats were placed next to the cleaning supplies and are discolored because bleach was spilled on them. These hats must be discarded. Record this as an adjustment to the quantity of inventory. Use the Expense account 6190 Merchandise Adjustments to record this adjustment.

DO: Click **Vendors** on the Navigator list, click **Adjust Qty on Hand** at the bottom of the QuickBooks Vendors Navigator
Enter the adjustment date of **013104**
Click the drop-down list arrow next to **Adjustment Account**
Click **<Add New>**

> Enter the new account information:
> > Type **Expense**
> > Number **6190**
> > Name **Merchandise Adjustments**
> Click **OK** to add the account
> Click in the **New Qty** column for Hats
> Enter **27**
> Tab to enter the change

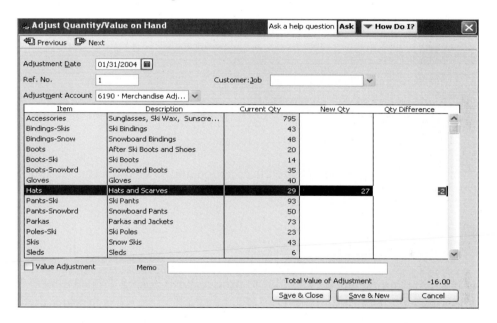

> Click **Save & Close**
> Click **Yes** on the **QuickBooks** dialog box

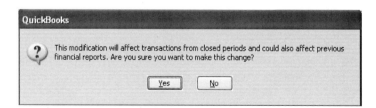

ADJUST THE JOURNAL ENTRY FOR NET INCOME/RETAINED EARNINGS

The adjustment to inventory reduced the value of the inventory asset by $16.00 and increased the expenses of the business by $16.00. The change decreased the net income by $16.00; thus, the adjusting entry for net income/retained earnings made previously needs to be changed.

DO: Click **Banking** on the menu bar
Click **Make Journal Entry**
Click **Previous** until you get to the entry debiting Retained Earnings for 2,605.19
Change that amount to **2,589.19**
Change the credit amount for Andy McBride to **1,294.60**
Change the credit amount for Tim Bailey to **1,294.59**

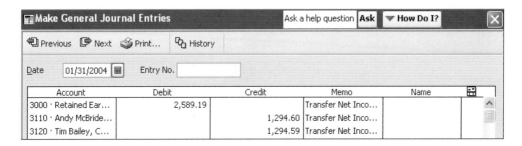

Click **Save & Close**
Click **Yes** to save the changed transaction and to record a transaction for a closed period

PRINT POST-CLOSING TRIAL BALANCE

After closing has been completed, it is helpful to print a Post-Closing Trial Balance. This proves that debits still equal credits. Printing the Trial Balance on February 1 is printing the Post-Closing Trial Balance for January 31.

MEMO

DATE: February 1, 2004

Print a Post-Closing Trial Balance, a Post-Closing Profit and Loss Statement, and a Post-Closing Balance Sheet for Year Round Sports. The dates should be as of or for 02/01/04.

DO: Print a **Post-Closing Trial Balance** to prove debits still equal credits
Click **Report Finder** on any QuickBooks Navigator, click **Accountant & Taxes** as the type of report, click **Trial Balance**,
Tab to or click **From**, enter the date **02/01/04**
Tab to or click **To**, enter the date **02/01/04**
Click **Display**

Scroll through the report and study the amounts shown
- Notice that the final totals of debits and credits are equal.

Click the **Print** button at the top of the Trial Balance

Click the **Preview** button to view a miniature copy of the report
- This helps determine the orientation, whether you need to select the feature to print one page wide, or whether you need to adjust column widths.

Click **Close**

Print in **Portrait** orientation

Year Round Sports--Student's Name		
Trial Balance		
As of February 1, 2004		
	Feb 1, 04	
	Debit	Credit
5000 · Cost of Goods Sold	3,352.46	
5100 · Purchases Discount		50.90
6120 · Bank Service Charges	18.00	
6130 · Sales Discounts	447.17	
6140 · Advertising Expense	95.00	
6150 · Depreciation Expense	160.00	
6181 · Liability Insurance	125.00	
6190 · Merchandise Adjustments	16.00	
6212 · Loan Interest	97.93	
6300 · Rent	950.00	
6340 · Telephone	156.40	
6391 · Gas and Electric	359.00	
6392 · Water	85.00	
6471 · Sales	175.00	
6472 · Office	350.00	
7010 · Interest Income		54.05
TOTAL	90,061.24	90,061.24

Partial Report

Close the **Trial Balance**

PRINT POST-CLOSING PROFIT AND LOSS STATEMENT

Because February 1 is after the closing date of January 31, 2004, the Profit and Loss Statement for February 1 is the Post-Closing Profit and Loss Statement. To verify the closing, print a Profit and Loss Statement for February 1.

DO: Print a **Standard Profit and Loss Report** for February
Using Report Finder, click **Company & Financial** as the type of report, click **Profit & Loss Standard**
Tab to or click **From**, enter **02/01/04**

Tab to or click **To**, enter **02/01/04**
Click **Display**
- The Net Income is **0.00**.
Print the report in **Portrait** orientation

Year Round Sports--Student's Name
Profit & Loss
February 1, 2004

	◇ Feb 1, 04 ◇
Net Income ▸	**0.00** ◂

Close the **Profit and Loss Report**

PRINT POST-CLOSING BALANCE SHEET

The proof that assets equal liabilities and owners' equity after the closing entries have been made needs to be displayed in a Post-Closing Balance Sheet. The Balance Sheet for February 1 is considered to be a Post-Closing Balance Sheet because it is prepared after the closing of the period. Most of the adjustments were for the month of January 2004. Because this report is for a month, the adjustment to Retained Earnings and Net Income will result in both of the accounts being included on the Balance Sheet. If, however, this report were prepared for the year, neither account would appear.

 DO: Print a Standard Balance Sheet report for February 1, 2004, and February 1, 2005
On Report Finder, click **Balance Sheet Standard**
If necessary, enter the To and From dates as **02/01/04**
Click **Display**
Scroll through the report to view the assets, liabilities, and equities listed
- Because this report is for a one-month period, both Retained Earnings and Net Income are included on this report.
Print the report, orientation is **Portrait**

Year Round Sports--Student's Name
Balance Sheet
As of February 1, 2004

	Feb 1, 04
Equity	
3000 · Retained Earnings	-2,589.19
3100 · Bailey & McBride Capital	
3110 · Andy McBride, Capital	
3111 · Andy McBride, Investment	20,000.00
3110 · Andy McBride, Capital - Other	13,024.32
Total 3110 · Andy McBride, Capital	33,024.32
3120 · Tim Bailey, Capital	
3121 · Tim Bailey, Investment	20,000.00
3120 · Tim Bailey, Capital - Other	13,024.31
Total 3120 · Tim Bailey, Capital	33,024.31
Total 3100 · Bailey & McBride Capital	66,048.63
Net Income	2,589.19
Total Equity	66,048.63
TOTAL LIABILITIES & EQUITY	80,925.09

Partial Report

Change the date to **02/01/2005**
Tab to generate the report
Scroll through the report to view the assets, liabilities, and equities listed
- Because this report is prepared after the end of the fiscal year, neither Retained Earnings nor Net Income is included on this report.

Print the report

```
                Year Round Sports--Student's Name
                         Balance Sheet
                     As of February 1, 2005
                                              ◇          Feb 1, 05        ◁
        Equity
            3100 · Bailey & McBride Capital
                3110 · Andy McBride, Capital
                    3111 · Andy McBride, Investment        20,000.00
                    3110 · Andy McBride, Capital - Other   13,024.32
                Total 3110 · Andy McBride, Capital                    33,024.32

                3120 · Tim Bailey, Capital
                    3121 · Tim Bailey, Investment          20,000.00
                    3120 · Tim Bailey, Capital - Other     13,024.31
                Total 3120 · Tim Bailey, Capital                      33,024.31

            Total 3100 · Bailey & McBride Capital                              66,048.63

        Total Equity                                                          66,048.63

        TOTAL LIABILITIES & EQUITY                                            80,925.09
```

Partial Report

Close the **Balance Sheet**

SUMMARY

In this chapter, end-of-period adjustments were made, a bank reconciliation and a credit card reconciliation were performed, backup (duplicate) and archive disks were prepared, and adjusting entries were made. The use of Drawing, Net Income, and Retained Earnings accounts were explored and interpreted for a partnership. The closing date for a period was assigned. Account names were changed, and new accounts were created. Even though QuickBooks Pro focuses on entering transactions on business forms, a Journal recording each transaction is kept by QuickBooks Pro. This chapter presented transaction entry directly into the Journal. The difference between accrual-basis and cash-basis accounting was discussed. Company preferences were established for accrual-basis reporting preferences. Owner withdrawals and distribution of capital to partners were examined. Many of the different report options available in QuickBooks Pro were explored, and a report was exported to Microsoft® Excel. A variety of reports were printed. Correction of errors was analyzed, and corrections were made after the period was closed and adjustments were made to inventory. The fact that QuickBooks Pro does not require an actual closing entry at the end of the period was addressed.

END-OF-CHAPTER QUESTIONS

TRUE/FALSE

ANSWER THE FOLLOWING QUESTIONS IN THE SPACE PROVIDED BEFORE THE QUESTION NUMBER.

_____ 1. The owner's Drawing account should be transferred to capital each week.

_____ 2. Even if entered elsewhere, all transactions are recorded in the Journal.

_____ 3. You must access Set Up Users in order to close a period.

_____ 4. If Show All is selected, inactive accounts will not appear in the Chart of Accounts.

_____ 5. When you reconcile a bank statement, anything entered as a service charge will automatically be entered as a transaction when the reconciliation is complete.

_____ 6. Once an account has been used, the name cannot be changed.

_____ 7. The adjusting entry for depreciation may be made in the Depreciation account register.

_____ 8. At the end of the year, QuickBooks Pro transfers the net income into retained earnings.

_____ 9. A withdrawal by an owner in a partnership reduces the owner's capital.

_____ 10. As with other accounting programs, QuickBooks Pro requires that a formal closing be performed at the end of each year.

MULTIPLE CHOICE

WRITE THE LETTER OF THE CORRECT ANSWER IN THE SPACE PROVIDED BEFORE THE QUESTION NUMBER.

_____ 1. To print a Reconciliation Report that lists only totals, select ___.
A. none
B. summary
C. detail
D. complete

_____ 2. The report that proves debits equal credits is the ___.
A. Sales Graph
B. Balance Sheet
C. Profit and Loss Statement
D. Trial Balance

_____ 3. If reports are prepared as of January 31, net income will appear in the ___.
A. Profit and Loss Statement
B. Balance Sheet
C. both A and B
D. neither A nor B

_____ 4. In QuickBooks Pro, you export reports to Microsoft® Excel in order to ___.
A. print the report
B. explore "what if" scenarios with data from QuickBooks Pro
C. prepare checks
D. all of the above

_____ 5. QuickBooks Pro automatically records Purchases Discount as ___.
A. income
B. a decrease to cost of goods sold
C. an expense
D. an asset

_____ 6. If a transaction is recorded in the Journal, it may be viewed ___.
A. in the Journal
B. in the register for each account used in the transaction
C. by preparing an analysis graph
D. both A and B

_____ 7. Entries for bank collections ___.
A. are automatically recorded at the completion of the bank reconciliation
B. must be recorded after the bank reconciliation is complete
C. should be recorded while one is reconciling the bank statement
D. should be recorded on the first of the month

_____ 8. The accounts that may be reconciled are ___.
A. Checking
B. Credit Card
C. all accounts
D. both A and B

_____ 9. The closing entry for drawing transfers the balance of an owner's drawing account into the ___ account.
A. Retained Earnings
B. Net Income
C. Capital
D. Investment

_____ 10. A Balance Sheet that shows amounts for each account type but not for individual accounts is the ___ Balance Sheet.
A. Standard
B. Summary
C. Detail
D. Comparison

FILL-IN

IN THE SPACE PROVIDED, WRITE THE ANSWER THAT MOST APPROPRIATELY COMPLETES THE SENTENCE.

1. _____-basis accounting matches income and expenses against a period, and _____-basis accounting records income when the money is received and expenses when the purchase is made or the bill is paid.

2. The _____ proves that Assets = Liabilities + Owners' Equity.

3. In a partnership, each owner has a share of all the _____ and _____ based on the percentage of his or her investment in the business or according to any partnership agreements.

4. In order to close a period, a closing _____ must be provided.

5. No matter where transactions are recorded, they all appear in the _____.

SHORT ESSAY

Describe the adjustment required for Purchase Discounts, and explain why this adjustment should be made.

_____

_____

_____

_____

_____

NAME_____

TRANSMITTAL

<u>CHAPTER 7: YEAR ROUND SPORTS</u>

Attach the following documents and reports:

Profit and Loss, January 2004
Check No. 6: Andy McBride
Check No. 7: Tim Bailey
Bank Reconciliation Detail Report, January 30, 2004
Credit Card Reconciliation Detail Report, January 31, 2004
Check No. 8: Mammoth Bank
Trial Balance, January 31, 2004
Standard Profit and Loss Statement, January 2004
Standard Balance Sheet, January 31, 2004 (After adjustment to close Net Income)
Standard Balance Sheet, January 31, 2005
Standard Balance Sheet, January 31, 2004 (After adjustment to close Drawing accounts)
Journal, January 2004
Post-Closing Trial Balance, February 1, 2004
Post-Closing Profit and Loss, February 1, 2004
Post-Closing Balance Sheet, February 1, 2004
Post-Closing Balance Sheet, February 1, 2005

END-OF-CHAPTER PROBLEM

GREAT ESCAPES CLOTHING

Chapter 7 continues with the end-of-period adjustments, bank and credit card reconciliations, archive disks, and closing the period for Great Escapes Clothing. The company does use a certified public accountant for guidance and assistance with appropriate accounting procedures. The CPA has provided information for Leilani to use for adjusting entries, etc.

INSTRUCTIONS

Continue to use the copy of Great Escapes you used in the previous chapters. Open the company—the file used is **Great Escapes.qbw**. Record the adjustments and other transactions as you were instructed in the chapter. Always read the transaction carefully and review the Chart of Accounts when selecting transaction accounts. Print the reports and journals as indicated.

RECORD TRANSACTIONS

January 31, 2005—Enter the following:
Change the names and/or the account numbers of the following accounts:

> 6260 **Printing and Reproduction** to 6260 **Printing and Duplication**
> 6350 **Travel & Ent** to 6350 **Travel**
> 3010 **Mahalo & Ohana Capital** to 3100 **Mahalo & Ohana, Capital**

(Note: Check the description for each account to see if it needs to be changed as well.)

Add the following accounts:

> Cost of Goods Sold account **5010 Purchases Discounts** (subaccount of **5000**)
> Equity account **3110 Kahala Mahalo, Capital** (subaccount of **3100**)
> Equity account **3120 Leilani Ohana, Capital** (subaccount of **3100**)

Change the following accounts:

> 3011 **Kahala Mahalo, Investment** to 3111 **Kahala Mahalo, Investment** (subaccount of **3110**)

(Note: Since 3110 is a subaccount of 3100, you may not see the entire name of the subaccount listing. Cursor through the subaccount name to read it completely.)

> 3013 **Kahala Mahalo, Drawing** to 3112 **Kahala Mahalo, Drawing** (subaccount of **3110**)
> 3012 **Leilani Ohana, Investment** to 3121 **Leilani Ohana, Investment** (subaccount of **3120**)
> 3014 **Leilani Ohana, Drawing** to 3122 **Leilani Ohana, Drawing** (subaccount of **3120**)

Make the following accounts inactive:

> 6291 **Building Repairs**
> 6351 **Entertainment**

Delete the following accounts:
   6182 Disability Insurance
   6213 Mortgage
   6823 Property
Print the Chart of Accounts (Do *not* show inactive accounts. Use the File menu to print the list.)

Create a Fixed Asset Item List for:
   Office Equipment, Date is 12/31/05, Cost is $8,000, Account is 1510
   Store Fixtures, Date is 12/31/05, Cost is $9,500, Account is 1520

Enter the following adjustment:
   Transfer the amount of purchases discounts from Income: 4030 Purchases Discounts to Cost
   of Goods Sold: 5010 Purchases Discounts (Memo: Transfer to CoGS)
(Remember, you may not see 5010 in full because it is a subaccount of 5000.)

Enter adjusting entries in the Journal and use the memo Adjusting Entry for the following:
   Office Supplies Used, the amount used is $35
   Sales Supplies Used, account balance (on hand) at the end of the month is $1,400
   Record a compound entry for depreciation for the month: Office Equipment, $66.67 and
      Store Fixtures, $79.17
   The amount of insurance remaining in the Prepaid Insurance account is for six months of
      liability insurance. Record the liability insurance expense for the month

Each owner withdrew $500. (Memo: Withdrawal for January) Print Check Nos. 7 and 8 for the
owners' withdrawals.

Prepare Bank Reconciliation and Enter Adjustments for the Reconciliation:
(Refer to the chapter for appropriate Memo notations)

CENTRAL COAST BANK
1234 Coast Highway
San Luis Obispo, CA 93407
(805) 555-9300

Great Escapes Clothing
784 Marsh Street
San Luis Obispo, CA 93407

Acct. # 987-352-9152   January 31, 2005

Beginning Balance, January 1, 2005			$32,589.00
1/15/05, Deposit	3,022.33		35,611.33
1/15/05, Deposit	1,829.05		37,440.38
1/15/05, NSF Returned Check		325.00	37,115.38
1/15/05, Check 1		58.98	37,056.40
1/18/05, Check 2		156.00	36,900.40
1/18/05, Check 3		343.00	36,557.40
1/25/05, Check 4		1,150.00	35,407.40
1/25/05, Check 5		79.85	35,327.55
1/31/05, Service Charge		10.00	35,317.55
1/31/05, NSF Charge		15.00	35,302.55
1/31/05, Office Equipment Loan Pmt.: $44.51 Interest, $8.61 Principal		53.12	35,249.43
1/31/05, Store Fixtures Loan Pmt.: $53.42 Interest, $10.33 Principal		63.75	35,185.68
1/31/05, Interest	73.30		35,258.98
Ending Balance, 1/31/05			35,258.98

Print a Detailed Reconciliation Report. Adjust column widths so the report fits on one page

Reconcile the Visa account

CENTRAL COAST BANK
VISA DEPARTMENT
1234 Coast Highway
San Luis Obispo, CA 93407
(805) 555-9300

Great Escapes Clothing
784 Marsh Street
San Luis Obispo, CA 93407

VISA Acct. # 9187-52-9152   January 31, 2005

Beginning Balance, January 1, 2005			0.00
1/9/05, The Clothes Rack		196.00	196.00
1/18/05, Office Masters		250.00	446.00
Ending Balance, 1/20/05			446.00

Minimum Payment Due: $50.00
Payment Due Date: February 5, 2005

Print a Detailed Reconciliation Report. Pay Central Coast Bank for the Visa bill using Check No. 9. Print Check No. 9

Distribute capital to each owner: divide the balance of 3100 Mahalo & Ohana, Capital equally between the two partners. Record an entry to transfer each owner's portion of capital to her individual capital account. (Memo: Transfer Capital to Individual Accounts)

Verify or change reporting preferences to accrual basis

Print the following for January 1-31, 2005, or as of January 31, 2005:
  Trial Balance
  Standard Profit and Loss Statement
  Standard Balance Sheet

Divide in half and transfer Net Income/Retained Earnings into owners' individual Capital accounts.

Close Drawing accounts into owner's individual Capital accounts

Print a Standard Balance Sheet

Close the period as of January 31, 2005

Edit a transaction from a closed period:
  Discovered an error in the amount of Office Supplies and Sales Supplies: Transfer $40 from Office Supplies to Sales Supplies on 01/31/05

Found one damaged tie. Adjust the quantity of ties on 01/31/05 using the Expense account
    6190 Merchandise Adjustments

Change the net income/retained earnings adjustment to reflect the merchandise adjustment for
    the ties

February 1, 2005—Print the following:
    Journal for 01/01/05-02/01/05 (Landscape orientation, Fit to one page wide)
    Post-Closing Trial Balance, February 1, 2005
    Post-Closing Standard Profit and Loss Statement, February 1, 2005
    Post-Closing Standard Balance Sheet, February 1, 2005

February 1, 2006—Print the following:
    Standard Balance Sheet, February 1, 2006

NAME_____

TRANSMITTAL

<u>CHAPTER 7: GREAT ESCAPES CLOTHING</u>

Attach the following documents and reports:

Chart of Accounts (Revised)
Check No. 7: Kahala Mahalo
Check No. 8: Leilani Ohana
Bank Reconciliation, January 31, 2005
Visa Reconciliation, January 31, 2005
Check No. 9: Central Coast Bank
Trial Balance, January 31, 2005
Standard Profit and Loss, January 2005
Standard Balance Sheet, January 31, 2005
Standard Balance Sheet, January 31, 2005
Journal, January 1-February 1, 2005
Post-Closing Trial Balance, February 1, 2005
Post-Closing Profit and Loss, February 1, 2005
Post-Closing Balance Sheet, February 1, 2005
Balance Sheet, February 1, 2006

DESERT GOLF SHOP PRACTICE SET: MERCHANDISING BUSINESS

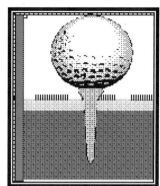

The following is a comprehensive practice set combining all the elements of QuickBooks Pro studied in the merchandising section of the text. In this practice set you will keep the books for a company for the month of January 2005. Entries will be made to record invoices, receipt of payments on invoices, cash sales, credit card sales, receipt and payment of bills, orders and receipts of merchandise, credit memos for invoices and bills, sales tax payments, and credit card payments. Account names will be added, changed, deleted, and made inactive. Customer, vendor, owner names, and fixed assets will be added to the appropriate lists. Reports will be prepared to analyze sales, bills, receipts, and items ordered. Formal reports including the Trial Balance, Profit and Loss Statement, and Balance Sheet will be prepared. Adjusting entries for depreciation, supplies used, insurance expense, and automatic payments will be recorded. Both bank and credit card reconciliations will be prepared. Entries to transfer purchase discounts from income to cost of goods sold will be made. Entries to display partnership equity for each partner will be made. The owners' Drawing accounts will be closed and the period will be closed.

DESERT GOLF SHOP

Located in Palm Springs, California, Desert Golf Shop is a full-service golf shop that sells golf equipment and golf clothing. Desert Golf Shop is a partnership owned and operated by Wayne Anderson and Ann Bailey. Each partner contributed an equal amount to the partnership. Wayne buys the equipment and manages the store. Ann buys the clothing and accessory items and keeps the books for Desert Golf Shop. There are several part-time employees working for Desert Golf Shop selling merchandise.

INSTRUCTIONS

Copy the file **Desert.qbw** to a new disk and open the company. The following lists are used for all sales items, customers, and vendors. You will be adding additional customers and vendors as the company is in operation. When entering transactions, you are responsible for any memos you wish to include in transactions. Unless otherwise specified, the terms for each sale or bill will be the term specified on the Customer or Vendor List. (Choose edit for the individual customers or vendors and select the Additional Info tab to see the terms for each customer or vendor.) Customer Message is usually *Thank you for your business*. However, any other message that is appropriate may be used. If a customer's order exceeds the established credit limit, accept the order and process it. If the terms allow a discount for a customer, make sure to apply the discount if payment is made within the discount period. Use 6130 Sales Discounts as the discount account. On occasion, a payment may be made within the discount period but not received or recorded within the discount period. Information within the transaction will indicate whether or not the payment is equivalent to a full payment. For example, if you received $98 for an invoice for $100 shortly after the discount period and the transaction indicated payment in full, apply the discount. If a customer has a credit and has a balance on the account, apply the credit to payments received for the customer. If there is no balance for a customer and a return is made, issue a credit memo and a refund check. Always pay bills in time to take advantage of purchase discounts. Remember that the discount due date will be ten days from the date of the bill.

Invoices, purchase orders, and other business forms should be printed as they are entered. Print with lines around each field. Most reports will be printed in Portrait orientation; however, if the report (such as the Journal) will fit across the page using Landscape, use Landscape orientation. Whenever possible, adjust the column widths so that reports fit on one page wide *without* selecting Fit report to one page wide.

Back up your work at the end of each week.

Sales Items:

Name	Description	Type	Account	On Hand	Price
◆Bags	Golf Bags	Inventory Part	4000 · Sales:4010 · Accessory S	15	0.00
◆Clubs-Irons	Golf Clubs: Irons	Inventory Part	4000 · Sales:4030 · Equipment S	150	0.00
◆Clubs-Sets	Golf Clubs: Sets	Inventory Part	4000 · Sales:4030 · Equipment S	50	0.00
◆Clubs-Woods	Golf Clubs: Woods	Inventory Part	4000 · Sales:4030 · Equipment S	150	0.00
◆Gift Sets	Golf Gift Sets	Inventory Part	4000 · Sales:4010 · Accessory S	10	0.00
◆Gloves	Golf Gloves	Inventory Part	4000 · Sales:4010 · Accessory S	35	0.00
◆Golf Balls	Golf Balls	Inventory Part	4000 · Sales:4010 · Accessory S	60	0.00
◆Hats	Golf Hats	Inventory Part	4000 · Sales:4010 · Accessory S	20	0.00
◆Men's Jackets	Men's Jackets	Inventory Part	4000 · Sales:4020 · Clothing Sale	12	0.00
◆Men's Pants	Men's Pants	Inventory Part	4000 · Sales:4020 · Clothing Sale	15	0.00
◆Men's Shirts	Men's Shirts	Inventory Part	4000 · Sales:4020 · Clothing Sale	15	0.00
◆Men's Shoes	Men's Shoes	Inventory Part	4000 · Sales:4020 · Clothing Sale	18	0.00
◆Men's Shorts	Men's Shorts	Inventory Part	4000 · Sales:4020 · Clothing Sale	12	0.00
◆Tees	Golf Tees	Inventory Part	4000 · Sales:4010 · Accessory S	30	0.00
◆Towels	Golf Towels	Inventory Part	4000 · Sales:4010 · Accessory S	10	0.00
◆Women's Jacket	Women's Jackets	Inventory Part	4000 · Sales:4020 · Clothing Sale	12	0.00
◆Women's Pants	Women's Pants	Inventory Part	4000 · Sales:4020 · Clothing Sale	12	0.00
◆Women's Shirt	Women's Shirts	Inventory Part	4000 · Sales:4020 · Clothing Sale	12	0.00
◆Women's Shoes	Women's Shoes	Inventory Part	4000 · Sales:4020 · Clothing Sale	20	0.00
◆Women's Short	Women's Shorts	Inventory Part	4000 · Sales:4020 · Clothing Sale	15	0.00
◆CA Sales Tax	CA Sales Tax	Sales Tax Item	2200 · Sales Tax Payable		7.25%
◆Out of State	Out-of-state sale, exempt	Sales Tax Item	2200 · Sales Tax Payable		0.0%

Note: Individual golf clubs are categorized as irons or woods. A complete set of clubs would be categorized as a set. The type of material used in a golf club makes no difference in a sales item. For example, graphite is a material used in the shaft of a golf club. A set of graphite clubs would refer to a set of golf clubs. Titanium is a type of metal used in the head of a golf club. A titanium wood would be sold as a wood. Golf balls are sold in packages called sleeves; thus, a quantity of one would represent one package of golf balls.

Vendors:

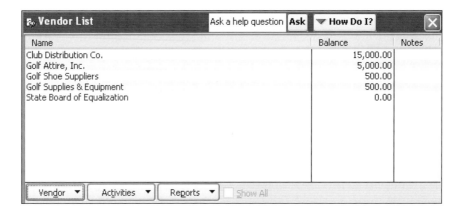

Customers:

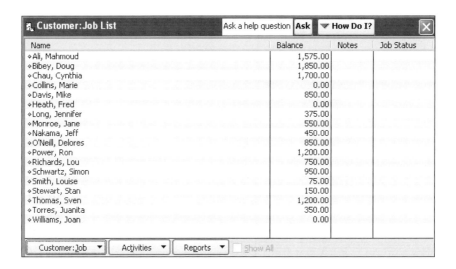

RECORD TRANSACTIONS:

Enter the transactions for Desert Golf Shop and print as indicated.

Week 1—January 2-8, 2005:

Add your name to the company name. The company name will be **Desert Golf Shop—Student's Name**. (Type your actual name *not* the words Student's Name.)

Change Preferences: Reports should refresh automatically, the Report Header/Footer should *not* include the Date Prepared, Time Prepared, or Report Basis. Inventory and purchase orders should be active

Change the names and, if necessary, the descriptions of the following accounts:

    4200 Sales Discounts to **4200 Purchases Discounts**

    6130 Cash Discounts to **6130 Sales Discounts**

6350 Travel & Ent to **6350 Travel**

6381 Marketing to **6381 Sales** (this is a subaccount of **6380 Supplies Expense**)

Delete the following accounts:

4050 Reimbursed Expenses

4070 Resale Discounts

4090 Resale Income

4100 Freight Income

6140 Contributions

6182 Disability Insurance

6213 Mortgage

6265 Filing Fees

6285 Franchise Fees

6351 Entertainment

Make the following accounts inactive:

6311 Building Repairs

6413 Property

Add the following accounts:

Equity account: **3010 Wayne Anderson, Capital** (subaccount of **3000**)

Equity account: **3020 Ann Bailey, Capital** (subaccount of **3000**)

Cost of Goods Sold account: **5010 Purchases Discounts** (subaccount of **5000**)

Change the following accounts:

Wayne Anderson, Investment to **3011 Wayne Anderson, Investment** (subaccount of **3010**)

Wayne Anderson, Drawing to **3012 Wayne Anderson, Drawing** (subaccount of **3010**)

Ann Bailey, Investment to **3021 Ann Bailey, Investment** (subaccount of **3020**)

Ann Bailey, Drawing to **3022 Ann Bailey, Drawing** (subaccount of **3020**)

Print the Chart of Accounts using print lists on the File menu. Do *not* show inactive accounts.

Add Store Fixtures to the Fixed Asset Item List. Use the purchase date of 12/31/04. Use the appropriate account, item names, etc. Use the Office Equipment item on the list as a reference.

Prior to recording any transactions, print a Trial Balance as of January 1, 2005.

Customize Sales Receipts, Invoices, and Purchase Orders so your name will print on the same line as the company name.

Print invoices, checks, and other items as they are entered in the transactions.

1/2/2005

Sold 2 pairs of women's shorts @ $64.99 each, 2 women's shirts @ $59.99 each, 1 women's jacket @ $129.99, and 1 pair of women's shoes @ $179.99 to Joan Williams. (Remember: Print Invoice No. 1 when the transaction is entered.)

Having achieved her goal of a handicap under 30, Marie treated herself to the new clubs she had been wanting. Sold 1 set of graphite clubs for $750, 1 golf bag for $129.95, and 5 sleeves (packages) of golf balls @ $6.95 each to Marie Collins. (Remember to accept sales that are over the credit limit.)

Fred heard that titanium would give him extra yardage with each shot. Sold 4 titanium woods to Fred Heath @ $459.00 each.

Sold 5 golf bags @ $59.99 each and 5 sets of starter clubs @ $159.99 each to Palm Springs Schools for the high school golf team. Palm Springs Schools located at 99-4058 South Palm Canyon Drive, Palm Springs, CA 92262 is a nonprofit organization. The telephone number is 760-555-4455, and the contact person is Claudia Colby. The terms are Net 30. Even though this is a nonprofit organization, it does pay California Sales Tax on all purchases. The credit limit is $1,500. Include a subtotal for the sale and apply a 10% sales discount for a nonprofit organization. (Create any new sales items necessary.)

Correct the invoice to Marie Collins. The price of the golf bag should be $179.95. Reprint the invoice.

Received Check No. 2285 from Mahmoud Ali in full payment of his account.

Received Check No. 102-33 from Sven Thomas, $600, in partial payment of his account.

1/3/2005

Sold 3 gift sets @ $14.99 each and 3 sleeves (packages) of golf balls @ $8.95 each to Louise Smith to be given away as door prizes at an upcoming ladies' club tournament.

Sold 2 pairs of men's shorts @ $49.95 each, 2 men's shirts @ $59.99 each, and 1 pair of golf shoes @ $119.99 to Stan Stewart.

Received Check No. 815 from Mike Davis for $850 in full payment of his account.

Sold 2 golf towels @ $9.95 each to a cash customer. (Cash is the payment method. Remember to print Sales Receipt No. 1.)

Sold 1 pair of women's golf shoes @ $149.95 to a new customer: Lisa Hamilton, 45-2215 PGA Drive, Rancho Mirage, CA 92270, 760-555-3322, Terms 1% 10 Net 30, taxable customer for California Sales Tax, Credit Limit $1,000

Received Check No. 2233 for $950 from Ron Power in partial payment of his account.

Sold a golf bag for $99.95 to a cash customer using a Visa card.

1/5/2005

Check Reminders List to see if any merchandise needs to be ordered. Use Expand All to display the list in detail. Print the list

Prepare and print an Inventory Stock Status by Item Report for January 1-5 in Landscape orientation.

Prepare Purchase Orders for all items marked Order on the Inventory Stock Status by Item Report. Place all orders with the preferred vendors. Prepare only one purchase order per vendor. For all items ordered, the Qty on Hand should exceed the Reorder Point by 10 when the new merchandise is received. (For example, if the reorder point is 5 and you have 4 items on hand, you will need to order 11 items. This would make the quantity 15 when the order is received. This would exceed the reorder point by 10.) The cost of golf bags are $40 each, gift sets are $3 each, men's shorts are $20 each, towels are $2 each, and women's shirts are $20 each. (Remember to print the purchase orders.)

Order 5 women's hats @ $10.00 each from a new vendor: Hats and More, 45980 West Los Angeles Street, Los Angeles, CA 90025, Contact Chris Griswald, Phone 310-555-8787, Fax 310-555-7878, E-mail hats@la.com, Terms 2% 10 Net 30, Credit Limit $500. Add a new inventory sales item: Women's Hats with Hats and More as the preferred vendor. The purchase and sales description is Women's Golf Hats. The COGS account is 5000. Leave the sales price at 0.00. The hats are taxable. The Income account is 4000-Sales: 4010-Accessory Sales. The Asset account is 1120-Inventory Asset. The reorder point is 10. Quantity on Hand is 0 as of 01/05/2005.

Change the current sales item Hats from Item Name: Hats to Men's Hats. The purchase and sales descriptions should be Men's Golf Hats. Change the reorder point from 15 to 12.

Print a Purchase Order QuickReport in Landscape orientation for January 1-5.

1/8/2005

Received Check No. 1822 for a cash sale of 2 men's golf hats @ $49.95 each.

Deposit all receipts (checks, credit cards, and/or cash) for the week. Print the Deposit Summary.

Backup your work for Week 1. Name your backup file **Desert Week 1.qbb**

Week 2—January 9-15:
1/10/2005

Received the order from Hats and More without the bill.

Received the orders from Golf Supplies & Equipment and Golf Attire, Inc., along with the bills for the merchandise received. All items were received in full except the golf bags. Of the 12 bags ordered, only 8 were received. Use 01/10/2005 for the bill date for both transactions.

Louise Smith returned 1 of the gift sets purchased on January 3. Issue a credit memo.

Mike Davis returned 1 pair of men's golf shorts that had been purchased for $59.95. (The shorts had been purchased previously and were part of his $850 opening balance.) Issue the appropriate items.

Sold 1 complete set of golf clubs on account to Jeff Nakama for $1,600.00.

Sold a graphite sand wedge and a graphite gap wedge @ $119.95 each to a customer using a Visa card. (Both clubs are classified as irons.)

1/12/2005

Received the telephone bill for the month, $85.15 from Desert Telephone Co., 11-092 Highway 111, Palm Springs, CA 92262, 760-555-9285. The bill is due January 25.

Purchased $175 of office supplies to have on hand from Indio Office Supply, 3950 46th Avenue, Indio, CA 92201, Contact Cheryl Lockwood, Phone 760-555-1535, Fax 760-555-5351. Used the company Visa card for the purchase.

1/14/2005

Received the bill for the order from Hats and More. Use 01/14/2005 for the bill date.

Received a bill from the Sunshine Electric Co., 995 Date Palm Drive, Cathedral City, CA 92234, 760-555-4646 for the monthly electric bill. The bill is for $275.00 and is due January 30.

Received the monthly water bill for $65 from Indian Wells Water, 84-985 Jackson Street, Indian Wells, CA 92202, 760-555-5653. The bill is due January 30.

Sold a set of golf clubs on account to Lisa Hamilton for $895.00.

Received Check No. 3801 for $1,949.42 from Fred Heath in full payment of his bill. (The payment includes the discount since the check was dated 01/10/05.)

Received Check No. 783 for $594.53 from Joan Williams in full payment of her bill. (The payment includes the discount since the check was dated 01/11/05.)

Deposit all receipts (checks, credit cards, and/or cash) for the week. Print the Deposit Summary.

Back up your work for the week.

Week 3—January 16-22:
1/17/2005
Received Check No. 1822 back from the bank. This check was for $107.14 from a cash customer: William Jones, 8013 Desert Drive, Desert Hot Springs, CA 92270, 760-555-0100. Payment is due on receipt. Charge William the bank charge of $15 plus Desert Golf Shop's own NSF charge of $15. Add any necessary customers, items and/or accounts. (Returned check service charges should be Income account 4040.)

Received Check No. 67-086 for $135.95 from Louise Smith in full payment of her account.

Received the remaining 4 golf bags and the bill from Golf Supplies & Equipment on earlier purchase order. The date of the bill is 01/16/2005.

1/18/2005
Pay all bills that are eligible to receive a discount if paid between January 18 and 22. Use account 4200 Purchases Discounts as the Discount Account. (Print the checks. You may use Print Forms or you may print the checks individually.)

Sold 1 golf bag @ $199.95, 1 set of graphite golf clubs @ $1,200.00, 1 putter @ $129.95 (record the putter as Golf Clubs: Irons), and 3 sleeves of golf balls @ $9.95 each to Louise Smith.

Returned 2 men's shirts that had poorly stitched seams at a cost of $20 each to Golf Attire, Inc. Received a credit memo from the company.

1/20/2005
Sold 1 men's golf hat @ $49.95 and 1 men's golf jacket at $89.95 to a customer using a Master Card.

Sold 1 towel @ $9.95, 2 packages of golf tees @ $1.95 each, and 1 sleeve of golf balls at $5.95 to a customer for cash.

Received Check No. 1256 in full payment of account from Cynthia Chau.

Ron Power bought a starter set of golf clubs for his son @ $250.00 and a new titanium driver for himself @ $549.95 (a driver is categorized as Golf Club: Woods).

A businessman in town with his wife bought them each a set of golf clubs @ $1,495.00 per set and a new golf bag for each of them @ $249.95 per bag. He purchased a men's jacket for $179.95. His wife purchased a pair of golf shoes for $189.99 and a women's jacket for $149.99. He used his Visa to pay for the purchases.

Prepare and print an Inventory Stock Status by Item Report for January 1-20. Prepare Purchase Orders to order any inventory items indicated on the report. As with earlier orders, use the preferred vendor, issue only one purchase order per vendor, and order enough to have 10 more than the minimum quantity of the ordered items on hand. (Golf balls cost $3.50 per sleeve, men's and women's jackets cost $20 each, and women's hats cost $10 each.)

Deposit all receipts (checks, credit cards, and/or cash) for the week. Print the Deposit Summary.

Back up your work for the week.

Week 4 and End of Period—January 23-31:
1/23/2005

Pay all bills eligible to receive a discount if paid between January 23 and 30 and pay the telephone bill in full.

Louise Smith was declared Club Champion and won a prize of $500. She brought in the $500 cash as a payment to be applied to the amount she owes on her account.

Sold Louise Smith 5 Women's Golf Hats @ $25.99 each to give away as prizes at her next ladies' club tournament.

1/24/2005

Received the bill and all the items ordered from Golf Attire, Inc., and Golf Supplies & Equipment. The bills are dated 01/23/2005.

Received Check No. 5216 from Doug Bibey as payment in full on his account.

Received Check No. 1205 from Marie Collins as payment in full on her account.

Received a letter of apology for the NSF check and a new check for $137.14 from William Jones to pay his account in full. The new check is Check No. 9015.

1/25/2005

Received the bill and all the hats ordered from Hats and More. The date of the bill is 01/23/2005.

Received the bill for $3,000 rent from Palm Springs Rentals, 11-2951 Palm Canyon Drive, Palm Springs, CA 92262, Contact Tammi Moreno, Phone 619-555-8368, Fax 619-555-8638. The rent is due February 1.

Purchased sales supplies to have on hand for $150 from Indio Office Supply. Used the company Visa for the purchase.

Prepare an Unpaid Bills Detail Report for January 25, 2005. Print the report.

Pay $1,000 to Golf Attire, Inc., for the amount owed on 12/31/2004. (NOTE: Select the bill you want to pay. Apply the credit you have from Golf Attire, Inc., because of returned merchandise. You want to pay $1,000 plus use the $40 credit and reduce the amount owed by $1,040, *not*

$960. Once the credit is applied, you will see the amount owed as $4,960. Since you are not paying the full amount owed, click in Amt. Paid column and enter the amount you are paying. In this case, enter 1,000 as the amount you are paying. When the payment is processed, $1,000 will be deducted from cash to pay for this bill and the $40 credit will be applied.)

Pay $5,000 to Club Distribution Co. toward the amount owed on 12/31/2004; pay $500 to Golf Supplies & Equipment to pay the amount owed on 12/31/2004; pay $500 to Golf Shoe Suppliers to pay the amount owed on 12/31/2004. Also pay the rent, the electric bill, and the water bill.

1/26/2005

Prepare and print an Unpaid Bills Detail Report by Vendor for January 26, 2005. (*Note:* check Golf Attire, Inc., the amount owed should be $4,360. If your report does not show this, check to see how you applied the credit when you paid bills. If necessary, QuickBooks Pro does allow you to delete the previous bill payment and redo it. If this is the case, be sure to apply the credit, and record $1,000 as the payment amount.)

Received $1,000 from Jeff Nakama, Check No. 3716, in partial payment of his account.

Received payment in full from Sven Thomas, Check No. 102-157.

Sold 15 sleeves of golf balls @ $5.95 each to a cash customer to use as prizes in a retirement golf tournament for an employee of his company. Paid with Check No. 2237.

1/29/2005

Deposit all checks and credit card receipts for the week.

1/30/2005

Prepare Sales Tax Liability Report from January 1-30, 2005. Adjust the column widths and print the report in Landscape orientation. The report should fit on one page.

Pay sales tax and print the check.

Print a Sales by Item Summary Report for January 1-30. Use Landscape orientation and, if necessary, adjust column widths so the report fits on one page wide.

Prepare and review a Sales by Item graph for January 1-30.

Prepare and review a Sales by Customer graph for January 1-30.

Print a Trial Balance for January 1-30 in Portrait orientation.

Transfer the amount of purchases discounts from Income: 4200 Purchases Discounts to Cost of Goods Sold: 5010 Purchases Discounts.

Enter the following adjusting entries:

Office Supplies Used for the month is $125.

The balance of the Sales Supplies is $650 on January 30.

The amount of Prepaid Insurance represents the liability insurance for 12 months. Record the adjusting entry for the month of January.

Depreciation for the month is: Office Equipment, $83.33, and Store Fixtures, $100.

Record the transactions for owner's equity:

Each owner's withdrawal for the month of January is $2,000.

Divide the amount in account 3000-Anderson & Bailey, Capital, and transfer one-half the amount into each owner's individual Capital account. Prepare a Standard Balance Sheet for January 30 to determine the amount to divide.

01/31/2005

Use the following bank statement to prepare a bank reconciliation. Enter any adjustments. Print a Reconciliation Detail Report.

DESERT BANK
1234-110 Highway 111
Palm Springs, CA 92270

(760) 555-3300

Desert Golf Shop
55-100 PGA Boulevard
Palm Springs, CA 92270   Acct. # 9857-32-922

January 2005

Beginning Balance, January 1, 2005			$35, 275.14
1/8/2005, Deposit	4,210.68		39,485.82
1/10/2005, Check 1		64.30	39,421.52
1/14/2005, Deposit	2,801.24		42,222.76
1/16/2005, NSF Check		107.14	42,115.62
1/18/2005, Check 2		392.00	41,723.62
1/25/2005, Check 3		365.54	41,358.08
1/23/2005, Check 4		85.15	41,272.93
1/23/2005, Check 5		156.80	41,116.13
1/23/2005, Check 6		49.00	41,067.13
1/25/2005, Deposit	6,307.77		47,374.90
1/25/2005, Check 7		1,000.00	46.374.90
1/25/2005, Check 13		275.00	46,099.90
1/25/2005, Check 12		3,000.00	43,099.90
1/25/2005, Check 11		65.00	43,034.90
1/25/2005, Check 8		5,000.00	38,034.90
1/25/2005, Check 9		500.00	37,534.90
1/25/2005, Check 10		500.00	37,034.90
1/31/2005, Service Charge, $15, and NSF Charge, $14		30.00	37,004.90
1/31/2005, Store Fixtures Loan Pmt.: $89.03 Interest, $17.21 Principal		106.24	36,898.66
1/31/2005, Office Equipment Loan Pmt: $53.42 Interest, $10.33 Principal		63.75	36,834.91
1/31/2005, Interest	76.73		36,911.64
Ending Balance, 1/31/2005			36,911.64

Received the Visa bill. Prepare a Credit Card Reconciliation and pay the Visa bill. Print the check for payment to Desert Bank and a Reconciliation Summary Report

DESERT BANK			
VISA DEPARTMENT			
1234-110 Highway 111			
Palm Springs, CA 92270		(760) 555-3300	
Desert Golf Shop			
55-100 PGA Boulevard			
Palm Springs, CA 92270			
VISA Acct. # 9287-52-952		January 2005	
Beginning Balance, January 1, 2005			0.00
1/12/2005, Indio Office Supply		175.00	175.00
1/25/2005, Indio Office Supply		150.00	325.00
Ending Balance, 1/25/2005			325.00
Minimum Payment Due, $50.00	Payment Due Date: February 7, 2005		

Make sure the reporting preference is for accrual basis.

Print the following reports for January 1-31, 2005, or as of January 31, 2005: Trial Balance, Standard Profit & Loss Statement, Standard Balance Sheet

Divide the Net Income/Retained Earnings in half and transfer one-half into each owner's individual capital account.

Close the drawing account for each owner into the owner's individual capital account.

Print a Standard Balance Sheet for January 31, 2005.

Close the period using the closing date of 01/31/2005.

Edit a transaction from the closed period: Discovered an error in the Supplies accounts. Transfer $50 from 1320-Sales Supplies to 1310-Office Supplies.

Adjust the number of tees on hand to 24. Use the expense account 6190 for Merchandise Adjustments. Be sure to correct the adjustment for net income/ retained earnings.

2/1/2005
Print the following:
Journal (Landscape orientation, Fit on one page wide) for January 1, 2005-February 1, 2005
Trial Balance, February 1, 2005
Standard Profit and Loss Statement, February 1, 2005
Standard Balance Sheet, February 1, 2005

2/1/2006
Print a Standard Balance Sheet for February 1, 2006

NAME_____

TRANSMITTAL

DESERT GOLF SHOP: PRACTICE SET
MERCHANDISING BUSINESS

Attach the following documents and reports:

Week 1
Chart of Accounts
Trial Balance, January 1, 2005
Invoice No. 1: Joan Williams
Invoice No. 2: Marie Collins
Invoice No. 3: Fred Heath
Invoice No. 4: Palm Springs Schools
Invoice No. 2 (Corrected): Marie Collins
Invoice No. 5: Louise Smith
Invoice No. 6: Stan Stewart
Sales Receipt No. 1: Cash Customer
Invoice No. 7: Lisa Hamilton
Sales Receipt No. 2: Cash Customer
Reminders List
Inventory Stock Status by Item Report,
    January 1-5, 2005
Purchase Order No. 1: Golf Supplies &
    Equipment
Purchase Order No. 2: Golf Attire, Inc.
Purchase Order No. 3: Hats and More
Purchase Order QuickReport,
    January 5, 2005
Sales Receipt No. 3: Cash Customer
Deposit Summary, January 8, 2005

Week 2
Credit Memo No. 8: Louise Smith
Check No. 1: Mike Davis
Credit Memo No. 9: Mike Davis
Invoice No. 10: Jeff Nakama
Sales Receipt No. 4: Cash Customer
Invoice No. 11: Lisa Hamilton
Deposit Summary, January 14, 2005

Week 3
Invoice No. 12: William Jones
Check No. 2: Golf Attire, Inc.
Check No. 3: Golf Supplies & Equipment
Invoice No. 13: Louise Smith
Sales Receipt No. 5: Cash Customer
Sales Receipt No. 6: Cash Customer
Invoice No. 14: Ron Power
Sales Receipt No. 7: Cash Customer
Inventory Stock Status by Item,
    January 1-20, 2005
Purchase Order No. 4: Golf Supplies &
    Equipment
Purchase Order No. 5: Golf Attire, Inc.
Purchase Order No. 6: Hats and More
Deposit Summary, January 20, 2005

Week 4 and End of Period

Check No. 4: Desert Telephone
Check No. 5: Golf Supplies & Equipment
Check No. 6: Hats and More
Invoice No. 15: Louise Smith
Unpaid Bills Detail, January 25, 2005
Check No. 7: Golf Attire, Inc.
Check No. 8: Club Distribution Co.
Check No. 9: Golf Shoe Suppliers
Check No. 10: Golf Supplies & Equipment
Check No. 11: Indian Wells Water
Check No. 12: Palm Springs Rentals
Check No. 13: Sunshine Electric Co.
Unpaid Bills Detail, January 26, 2005
Sales Receipt No. 8: Cash Customer
Deposit Summary, January 30, 2005
Sales Tax Liability Report,
    January 1-30, 2005
Check No. 14: State Board of Equalization
Sales by Item Summary, January 1-30, 2005
Trial Balance, January 30, 2005
Check No. 15: Wayne Anderson
Check No. 16: Ann Bailey
Bank Reconciliation, January 31, 2005
Check No. 17: Desert Bank
Credit Card Reconciliation,
    January 31, 2005
Trial Balance, January 31, 2005
Standard Profit and Loss, January 2005
Standard Balance Sheet, January 31, 2005
Standard Balance Sheet After Owner Equity
    Adjustments, January 31, 2005
Journal, January 2005
Post-Closing Trial Balance,
    February 1, 2005
Post-Closing Standard Profit and Loss
    Statement, February 1, 2005
Post-Closing Standard Balance Sheet,
    February 1, 2005
Standard Balance Sheet, February 1, 2006

PAYROLL

8

LEARNING OBJECTIVES

At the completion of this chapter, you will be able to:

1. Create, preview, and print payroll checks.
2. Adjust pay stub information.
3. Correct, void, and delete paychecks.
4. Change employee information and add a new employee.
5. Print a Payroll Summary by Employee Report.
6. View an Employee Journal Report.
7. Pay Taxes and Other Liabilities.
8. Prepare and print Forms 941 and 940.
9. Prepare and preview W-2 forms.

PAYROLL

Many times, a company begins the process of computerizing simply to be able to do the payroll using the computer. It is much faster and easier to let QuickBooks Pro look at the tax tables and determine how much withholding should be deducted for each employee than to have an individual perform this task. Because tax tables change frequently, QuickBooks Pro requires its users to enroll in a payroll service plan. In order to enroll in a payroll service plan, you must have a company tax identification number and a registered copy of QuickBooks. QuickBooks Pro has three types of payroll service plans: Do-It-Yourself Payroll, Assisted Payroll, and Complete Payroll. These are available for an additional charge. If you do not subscribe to a payroll plan, you must calculate and enter the payroll taxes manually.

The Do-It-Yourself plan allows you to subscribe to the QuickBooks Pro Tax Table Service for a small annual fee, currently $169 per year. Tax table updates will be received throughout the year by using QuickBooks Pro and the Internet to update the tax tables. Once a registered user of QuickBooks Pro has subscribed to the Do-It-Yourself Payroll plan, you will be able to use QuickBooks Pro to automatically calculate taxes on paychecks. Without a subscription to Do-It-Yourself Payroll, QuickBooks Pro will continue to provide earnings, additions, and non-tax deductions but will not process tax withholdings automatically.

The Assisted Payroll service calculates your payroll, makes your federal and state payroll tax deposits from your payroll accounts, prepares and files federal and state payroll tax forms, prepares and delivers W-2 and W-3 forms, automatically updates your QuickBooks accounts, and provides technical support. The amount of the fees charged depend on the number of employees in the company, the frequency of the payroll, and the number of states in which payroll taxes are filed.

The third type of payroll service Intuit offers is QuickBooks Complete Payroll that lets the subscriber submit payroll information and then processes and print checks, takes care of payroll tax deposits, and delivers paychecks to the company. This plan offers a full range of payroll and payroll tax services, including tax payment, preparation and filing of payroll forms, customized reports, Direct Deposit, and more (additional fees apply). The fees vary depending on the number of employees, the payroll frequency, the number of states in which payroll taxes are filed, and the extent of services provided.

Since all of our businesses are fictitious in this text, we will not be subscribing to any of the QuickBooks Pro Payroll Services; therefore, we will be entering all tax information for paychecks manually based on data provided in the text. Calculations will be made for vacation pay, sick pay, medical and dental insurance deductions, and so on. Paychecks will be created, printed, corrected, and voided. Tax reports, tax payments, and tax forms will be prepared.

TRAINING TUTORIAL

Miller & Myer, Inc. is a medical clinic located in Long Beach, California, which is owned and operated by Dr. Greg Miller and Dr. Richard Myer. Dr. Miller and Dr. Myer operate the clinic as a corporation. They have a thriving practice and currently employ six people. Andrea Dubin is the office manager and is responsible for the smooth operation of the medical clinic and for all the employees. Currently, her salary is $33,500 per year. Winston Mohammed is also a salaried employee at $29,500 per year. Winston is responsible for the bookkeeping and the insurance billing. The company is advertising for a part-time billing clerk so that the insurance claims can be processed a little faster. The other employees are the nurse, Linda Mitchell; the medical assistant, Trang Nguyen; the receptionist, Jenny Chau; and the lab technician, Delores Liebman. These employees are paid on an hourly basis, and any hours in excess of 80 for the pay period will be paid as overtime. Paychecks for all employees are issued on a semimonthly basis.

 DO: Make a copy of **Miller.qbw** to a new disk as previously instructed
Back up your work periodically
Open the company.
Change the words "Your Name" in the company name to your actual name
Change the preferences for reports to refresh automatically and for headers to
    eliminate the date prepared, the time prepared, and the report basis

SELECT A PAYROLL OPTION

Before entering any payroll transactions, QuickBooks Pro must be informed of the type of payroll service you are selecting. Once QuickBooks Pro knows what type of payroll process has been selected for the company, clicking on the QuickBooks Employees Navigator, the Employees icon on the Navigator bar, or the Employees menu to create paychecks allows you to select which employees will be receiving paychecks.

    DO: Select **Manual** as the payroll option
                Click **Set Up Payroll** on the Employees Navigator
                Click **Choose a Payroll Option**
                Scroll through the list of options
                At the very end of the description of the options, click **Learn more** next to **If you don't want to use a QuickBooks Payroll Service, you can still use QuickBooks to prepare your payroll.**
                Click **To calculate payroll taxes manually**
                Click the button **I choose to manually calculate payroll taxes**

> I choose to manually calculate payroll taxes

                Click **Done**

CREATE PAYCHECKS

Once the manual payroll option has been selected, paychecks may be created. You may enter hours and preview the checks before creating them, or, if using a payroll service, you may create the checks without previewing. Once the payroll has been processed, checks may be printed.

MEMO
DATE: January 15, 2004

Since you chose to process the payroll manually, you will enter the payroll data for withholdings and deductions rather than have QuickBooks Pro automatically calculate the amounts for you. QuickBooks Pro will still enter other payroll items such as medical and dental insurance deductions, and it will calculate the total amount of the checks. Create and print paychecks for January 15, 2004. Use the above date as the pay period ending date and the check date. Pay all employees using the hours and deductions listed in the following table.

PAYROLL TABLE: JANUARY 15, 2004						
	ANDREA DUBIN	**DELORES LIEBMAN**	**JENNY CHAU**	**LINDA MITCHELL**	**TRANG NGUYEN**	**WINSTON MOHAMMED**
HOURS						
REGULAR	80	80	40	40	75	20
OVERTIME		5				
SICK					5	20
VACATION				40		40
DEDUCTIONS OTHER PAYROLL ITEMS: EMPLOYEE						
DENTAL INS.	25.00	25.00	25.00	25.00	25.00	25.00
MEDICAL INS.	67.00	67.00	45.00	50.00	35.00	75.00
CREDIT UNION	50.00					
DEDUCTIONS: COMPANY						
CA-EMPLOYMENT TRAINING TAX	55.83	36.75	15.20	40.00	33.60	49.17
SOCIAL SECURITY	86.54	56.96	23.56	62.00	52.08	76.21
MEDICARE	20.24	13.32	5.51	14.50	12.18	17.82
FEDERAL UNEMPLOYMENT	11.17	7.35	3.04	8.00	6.72	9.83
CA-UNEMPLOYMENT	55.83	36.75	15.20	40.00	33.60	49.17
DEDUCTIONS: EMPLOYEE						
FEDERAL WITHHOLDING	83.00	29.00	0.00	110.00	109.00	116.00
SOCIAL SECURITY	86.54	56.96	23.56	62.00	52.08	76.21
MEDICARE	20.24	13.32	5.51	14.50	12.18	17.82
CA-WITHHOLDING	37.81	0.00	0.00	13.52	16.92	7.15
CA-DISABILITY	6.98	4.59	1.90	5.00	4.20	6.15

DO: Create checks for the above employees
Click **Employees** on the Navigator List; click **Pay Employees** on the
QuickBooks Employee Navigator
OR
Click **Employees** menu, click **Pay Employees**
If you get a message to Manager Your Employees Better, click **No**

The **Select Employees to Pay** screen should use **Payroll Checking** as the bank account

- If not, click the drop-down list for Bank Account and select Payroll Checking

Click **To be printed**

Select **Enter hours and tax amounts before creating paychecks**

Check Date is **01/15/04** and the **Pay Period Ends 01/15/04**

Click **Mark All** to select all employees to be paid

- Notice the check mark in front of each employee name.

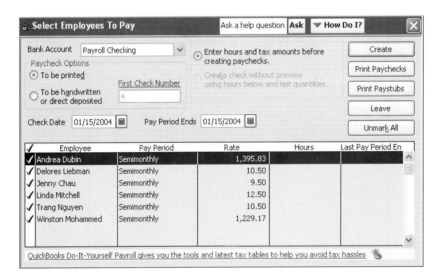

Click **Create**

- A **Payroll Subscription warning screen** may appear.

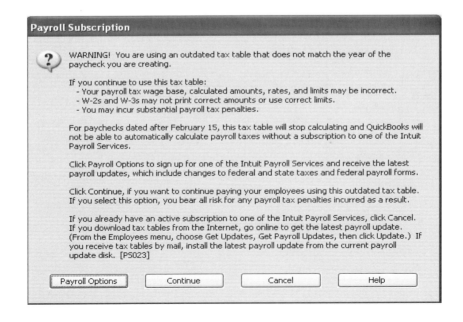

- If it does, click **Continue**

The **Preview Paycheck** screen for Andrea Dubin appears.

- As you record the information for each employee, refer to the payroll chart listed earlier in the chapter. Remember, if you subscribe to QuickBooks Pro payroll services you will not enter the taxes manually. QuickBooks Pro will calculate them and enter them for you. Since tax tables change frequently, the taxes calculated by QuickBooks Pro may not be the same as the amounts listed on the Payroll Table in the text.

Tab to or click **Hours**, enter **80**

The section for Other Payroll Items is completed by QuickBooks Pro

Complete the Company Summary information:

 Click in the **Amount** column for **CA-Employment Training Tax,** enter **55.83**

 Click in the **Amount** column for **Social Security Company**, enter **86.54**

 For **Medicare Company** enter **20.24**

 Federal Unemployment is **11.17**

 CA-Unemployment Company is **55.83**

Complete the Employee Summary information:

 Click in the **Amount** column for **Federal Withholding**, enter **83.00**

 For **Social Security Employee** enter **86.54**

 Medicare Employee is **20.24**

 CA-Withholding is **37.81**

 CA-Disability Employee is **6.98**

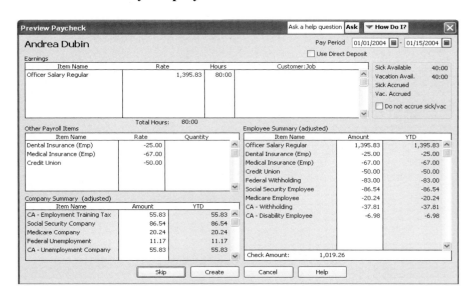

After verifying that everything was entered correctly, click **Create**

The next Preview Paycheck screen should be for Delores Liebman

Tab to or click the **Hours** column next to **Hourly Regular Rate** for **Delores Liebman**, enter **80**

Tab to or click the **Hours** column next to **Overtime Hourly Rate 1**, enter **5**

Refer to the Payroll Table for January 15, 2004, and enter the company and employee deductions for Delores

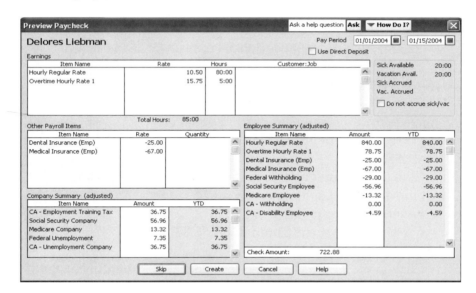

- Notice the amount of overtime pay in the Employee Summary.

Click **Create**

Pay **Jenny Chau** for **40** hours of **Hourly Regular Rate**

Following the steps previously indicated, enter the company and employee deductions from the Payroll Table for January 15, 2004

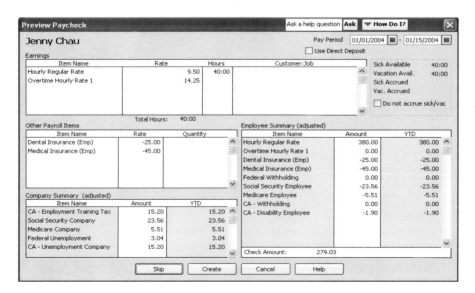

Pay **Linda Mitchell**

- Notice that the number of Vacation Hours listed in **Vacation Available** is **40.00**.

Tab to or click the **Hours** column for **Hourly Regular Rate**, enter **40**

In the **Item Name** column under **Earnings**, click on the blank line beneath Overtime Hourly Rate 1, click the drop-down list arrow that appears, click **Vacation Hourly Rate**, tab to or click the **Hours** column, enter **40**

Click in the **Amount** column for **CA-Employment Training Tax**

- Notice that the number of Vacation Hours in **Vacation Available** is 0.00.

Complete the paycheck information

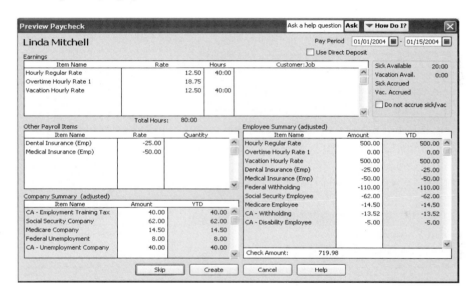

Process the paycheck for **Trang Nguyen**

- Follow the procedures indicated when paying Linda Mitchell except click **Sick Hourly Rate** rather than Vacation Hourly Rate and enter **5** hours of sick time. Remember her regular hours will be **75**.

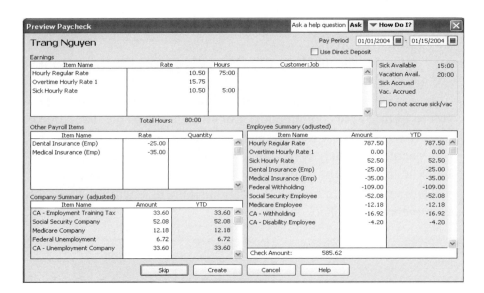

Process the paycheck for Winston Mohammed, select Payroll Items for Officer Salary Regular, Officer Sick Salary, and Officer Vac Salary

- Do not make any changes to the amounts listed in the Rate column. QuickBooks Pro will automatically allocate a portion of the salary to each of the accounts.

Enter the deductions listed on the Payroll Table

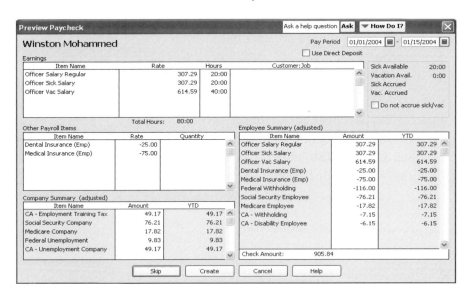

Click **Create** for Winston Mohammed

- **Select Employees To Pay** appears on the screen. Notice that the check marks have been removed, the Hours column has the hours for each employee, and the Last Pay Period End is 01/15/2004 for all employees.

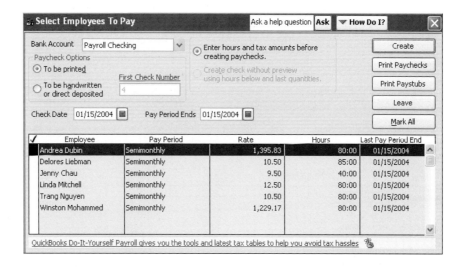

Do not close the Select Employees to Pay Screen

PRINT PAYCHECKS

Paychecks may be printed one at a time or all at once; however, they must be printed separately from other checks. You may use the same printer setup as your other checks in QuickBooks Pro or you may print using a different printer setup. If you use a voucher check, the pay stub is printed as part of the check. If you do not use a voucher check, you may print the pay stub separately. The pay stub information includes the employee's name, address, Social Security number, the pay period start and end dates, pay rate, the hours, the amount of pay, all deductions, sick and vacation time used and available, net pay, and year-to-date amounts.

MEMO

DATE: January 15, 2004

Print the paychecks for all employees using a voucher-style check with 2 parts. Print the company name on the checks.

DO: Print the January 15 paychecks

Click **Print Paychecks** on the **Select Employees To Pay** screen

Bank Account should be **Payroll Checking**; if it is not, click the drop-down list for Bank Account, click Payroll Checking.

Select All employees, **First Check Number** is **1**; if it is not, change it to 1

- Notice that there are 6 Paychecks to be printed for a total of $4,232.61.
- QuickBooks can process payroll for direct deposit or printed paychecks. Even though we are not processing direct deposit paychecks, leave **Show** as **Both**

Click the **Preferences** button and verify that all items for Payroll Printing Preferences for Paycheck Vouchers and Paystubs have been selected
Click **OK**

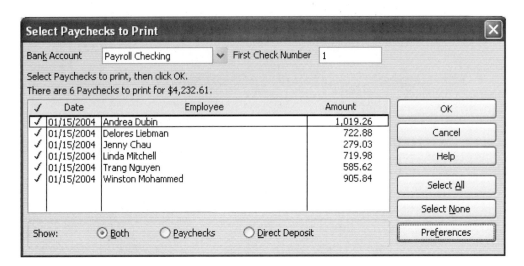

Click **OK** on the Select Paychecks to Print screen
- Printer Name and Printer Type will be the same as in the earlier chapters.
Click **Voucher Checks** to select as the check style
- If necessary, click **Print company name and address** to select. There should not be a check mark in Use logo. **Number of copies** should be **1**.
Click **Print**, click **OK** for **Did checks print OK?**
- *Note*: The pay stub information may be printed on the check two times. This is acceptable.
- If you get a message about ordering checks, click **No**
When the checks have been printed, click **Leave** on **Select Employees To Pay**

CHANGE EMPLOYEE INFORMATION

Whenever a change occurs for an employee, it may be entered at any time.

MEMO
DATE: January 16, 2004

Effective today, Andrea Dubin will receive a pay raise to $35,000 annually.

DO: Change the salary for Andrea
Click the **Employees** icon on the QuickBooks Employee Navigator
OR

Click the **Lists** menu or the **Employees** menu, click **Employee List**
Click **Andrea Dubin**
Ctrl+E
> OR
Click the **Employee** button, click **Edit**
> OR
Double-click on **Andrea Dubin**
Click the drop-down list arrow for **Change Tabs**
Click **Payroll and Compensation Info**
On the **Payroll Info** tab, change the **Hourly/Annual Rate** to **35,000**, click **OK**

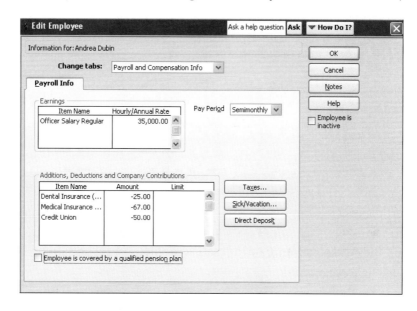

Do *not* close the **Employee List**

ADD A NEW EMPLOYEE

As new employees are hired, they should be added.

MEMO
DATE: January 24, 2004

Effective 01/24/04 hired a part-time employee to help process insurance claims.
Ms. Amy Riach, SS. No. 100-55-6936, Female, Birth date 02/14/80, 102 Bayshore
Drive, Long Beach, CA 90713, 562-555-9874, Paid an hourly rate of $7.00 semimonthly.
Federal and state withholding: Single, 0 Allowances. No local taxes, dental insurance,
medical insurance, sick time, or vacation time.

DO: Add Amy Riach
Ctrl+N
OR
Click **Employee**, click **New**
On the **Personal** tab, click in the text box for **Mr./Ms./...**, enter **Ms.**
Tab to or click in each field and enter the information provided in the Memo

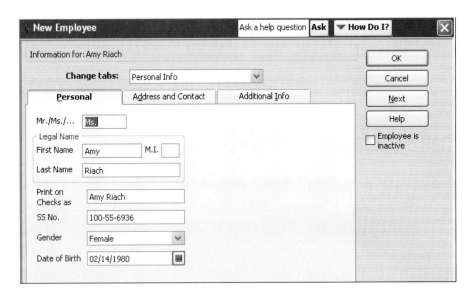

Click the **Address and Contact** tab and enter the information provided in the
Memo

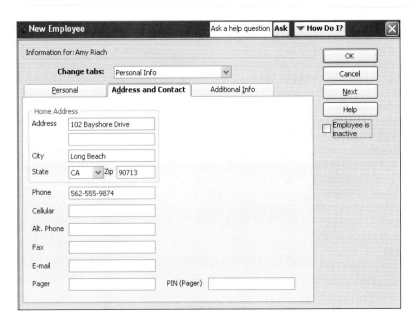

Click the drop-down list arrow for Changes Tabs and select **Payroll and Compensation Info**

Click **Item Name** column under **Earnings**, click the drop-down list arrow that appears, click **Hourly Regular Rate**

Tab to or click **Hourly/Annual Rate**, enter the hourly rate she will be paid

Verify a **Semimonthly** pay period

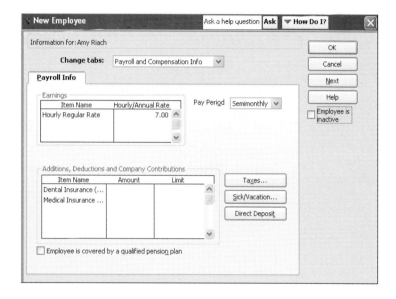

Click the **Taxes** button and complete the information as follows:

Federal taxes should show **Filing Status: Single, Allowances: 0, Extra Withholding: 0.00,**

Subject to: should have **Medicare**, **Social Security**, and **Federal Unemployment Tax (Company Paid)** selected

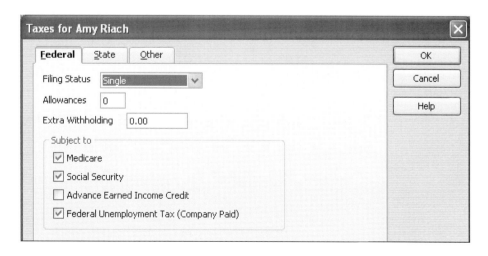

Click the **State** tab and complete the information as follows:

State Worked: CA; SUI and **SDI** should be selected

State Lived: CA; Filing Status: Single, Allowances: 0, Extra Withholding: 0.00; Estimated Deductions: 0

Click **Other** tab
Click the drop-down list arrow for **Item Name**
Click **CA-Employment Training Tax**

Click **OK**

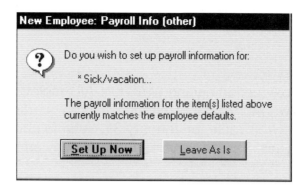

Since Amy does not have any sick/vacation hours, click **Leave As Is** on the New
     Employee: Payroll Info (other)
Click the drop-down list arrow for **Change Tabs**
Click **Employment Info**
The **Hire Date** should be **01/24/04** and **Employment Details Type** should be
     Regular

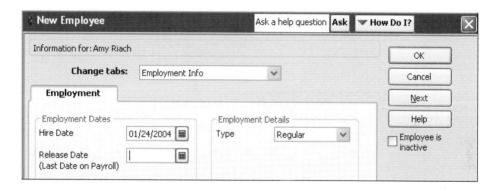

Click **OK** to add the employee
Close the Employee List

CREATE PAYCHECKS FOR THE NEXT PAY PERIOD

If using one of the QuickBooks Pro Payroll services, paychecks may be created automatically
without previewing. This is used if hours, and other details from the previous pay period have
not changed. In the case in which you are not subscribing to a QuickBooks Pro Payroll service,
you must enter the paycheck information for each pay period.

MEMO

DATE: January 31, 2004

Enter the payroll for the pay period ending 01/31/04. All employees worked 80 hours except Amy Riach, who worked 20 hours. No one worked overtime or used sick or vacation time. Use the Payroll Table for January 31, 2004 to obtain the amounts of the deductions for all employees. Print the checks for the hourly employees.

PAYROLL TABLE: JANUARY 31, 2004

	AMY RIACH	ANDREA DUBIN	DELORES LIEBMAN	JENNY CHAU	LINDA MITCHELL	TRANG NGUYEN	WINSTON MOHAMMED
HOURS							
REGULAR	20	80	80	80	80	80	80
DEDUCTIONS OTHER PAYROLL ITEMS: EMPLOYEE							
DENTAL INS.		25.00	25.00	25.00	25.00	25.00	25.00
MEDICAL INS.		67.00	67.00	45.00	50.00	35.00	75.00
CREDIT UNION		50.00					
DEDUCTIONS: COMPANY							
CA-EMPLOYMENT TRAINING TAX	5.60	55.83	33.60	30.40	40.00	33.60	49.17
SOCIAL SECURITY	8.68	90.42	52.08	47.12	62.00	52.08	76.21
MEDICARE	2.03	21.14	12.18	11.02	14.50	12.18	17.82
FEDERAL UNEMPLOYMENT	1.12	11.17	6.72	6.08	8.00	6.72	9.83
CA-UNEMPLOYMENT	5.60	55.83	33.60	30.40	40.00	33.60	49.17
DEDUCTIONS: EMPLOYEE							
FEDERAL WITHHOLDING	0.00	93.00	17.00	39.00	110.00	109.00	116.00
SOCIAL SECURITY	8.68	90.42	52.08	47.12	62.00	52.08	76.21
MEDICARE	2.03	21.14	12.18	11.02	14.50	12.18	17.82
CA-WITHHOLDING	0.00	42.81	0.00	7.89	13.52	16.92	7.15
CA-DISABILITY	0.70	7.29	4.20	3.80	5.00	4.20	6.15

DO: Process the payroll for January 31

Access **Pay Employees** as previously instructed

Click **Mark All** to place a check in the check mark column next to each
employee, click **Create**

If you get the Payroll Subscription screen, click **Continue**

Enter **20** hours for **Hourly Regular Rate** for Amy Riach

Enter the deductions for Amy from the Payroll Table for January 31, 2004

Click **Create**

Enter **80** hours for **Hourly Regular Rate** or **Officer Salary Regular** for the
remaining employees

If necessary, highlight and delete any overtime, sick, or vacation hours listed

Enter the deductions as shown on the Payroll Table for January 31, 2004

Click **Create** for each employee

When finished entering paycheck information, click **Leave**

VIEW CHECKS, MAKE CORRECTIONS, AND PRINT CHECKS INDIVIDUALLY

As in earlier chapters, checks may be viewed individually and printed one at a time. A paycheck
differs from a regular check. Rather than list accounts and amounts, it provides a Payroll
Summary and an option to view Paycheck Detail at the bottom of the screen. When you are
viewing the paycheck detail, corrections may be made and will be calculated for the check.

MEMO

DATE: January 31, 2004

Print each paycheck separately. Andrea Dubin used two hours of sick time during this
pay period. The sick time was not entered when the paycheck was calculated. When
viewing the check for Andrea Dubin, correct the paycheck. In addition, the deductions
given for Andrea were incorrect. Change the deductions to the following:
CA-Employment Training Tax, 58.33; Federal Unemployment, 11.67;
CA-Unemployment Company, 58.33

 DO: View, correct, and print the paychecks as indicated

To view the paychecks, use the keyboard shortcut **Ctrl+W**

Click **Previous** until you get to the check for **Amy Riach** for **01/31/04**

Click **Paycheck Detail** button to view the withholding details, click **OK**

Click **Print**, **Printed Check Number** should be **7**; if it is not, change the number
to **7**, click **OK** on **Print Paycheck**

Go to Andrea Dubin's paycheck and click **Paycheck Detail**

Change the Officer Salary Regular Hours to **78**

Tab to or click in the **Item Name** column for **Earnings**, click the drop-down list
arrow, click **Officer Sick Salary**

Tab to or click in the **Hours** column, enter **2**

Enter the changes to the various deductions and withholding amounts

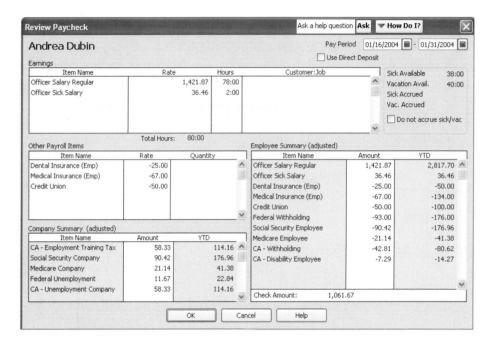

Click **OK** to save the changes to the paycheck
Click **OK** on the change transaction screen
Print check number 8 for Andrea Dubin
Print the checks for the remaining employees

VOIDING AND DELETING CHECKS

As with regular checks, paychecks may be voided or deleted. A voided check still remains as a check, but it has an amount of 0.00 and a Memo that says VOID. If a check is deleted, it is completely removed from the company records. The only way to have a record of the deleted check would be if an audit trail had been selected as a company preference. If you have prenumbered checks and the original check is misprinted, lost, or stolen, you should void the check. If an employee's check is lost or stolen and needs to be replaced and you are not using prenumbered checks, it may be deleted and reissued. For security reasons, it is better to void a check than to delete it.

MEMO
DATE: January 31, 2004

Jenny Chau lost her paycheck for the January 15 pay period. Void the check, issue and print a new one. Remember that she worked 40 hours.

DO: Void Jenny's January 15 paycheck and issue a new one
If necessary, open the Write Checks screen
Click **Previous** until Jenny's paycheck for *January 15, 2004*, appears on the screen, click **Edit** menu, click **Void Paycheck**

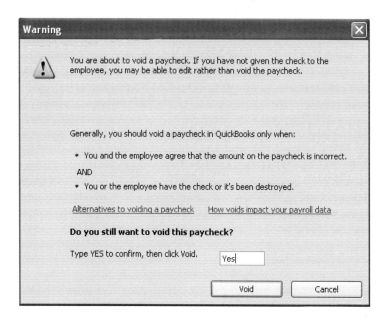

Enter **Yes** on the Warning Screen and click **Void**

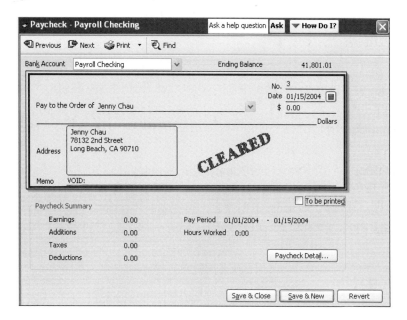

- Notice that the amount is 0.00 and that the Memo is VOID:.
Print the voided check as Check No. 3

Click **Save & Close** to close Paycheck-Payroll Checking

To issue Jenny's replacement check, click **Pay Employees** on the QuickBooks
    Employees Navigator

The Bank Account is **Payroll Checking**

Select: **To be printed** and **Enter hours and tax amounts before creating
    paychecks**

The Check Date is **01/31/04** and the Pay Period Ends **01/15/04**

Select **Jenny Chau**, click **Create**

Pay Period is **01/01/04 - 01/15/04**

Jenny worked **40** hours at the Hourly Regular Rate

Enter the deductions listed on the Payroll Table for January 15, 2004

Click **Create**

Click **Print Paychecks**

Print the replacement check as Check No. **14**

Click **OK** on the **Select Paychecks to Print** screen

Print the check

Click **Leave**

PAYROLL SUMMARY REPORT

The Payroll Summary Report shows gross pay, sick and vacation hours and pay, deductions from
gross pay, adjusted gross pay, taxes withheld, deductions from net pay, net pay, and employer-
paid taxes and contributions for each employee individually and for the company.

MEMO

DATE: January 31, 2004

Dr. Miller and Dr. Myer have Winston print a Payroll Summary Report at the end of
every month.

DO: Print the Payroll Summary Report for January

Click **Report Finder** on the QuickBooks Employees Navigator

Click the drop-down list arrow for the type of report

Click **Employees & Payroll**

Click **Payroll Summary**

If necessary, enter the dates from **01/01/04** to **01/31/04** as the report dates

Click **Display**

If necessary, remove the current date from the header as instructed in previous
    chapters

- View the information listed for each employee and for the company.

- If you adjust the width of the Hours, Rate, and Jan '04 columns for each employee by pointing to the diamond separating the columns and dragging it to resize the column, it may be possible to have the report fit on fewer pages

Print the report in Landscape orientation

Close the report

PREPARE THE EMPLOYEE EARNINGS SUMMARY REPORT

The Employee Earnings Summary Report lists the same information as the Payroll Summary Report above. The information for each employee is categorized by payroll items.

MEMO
DATE: January 31, 2004

Prepare the Employee Earnings Summary Report.

DO: Refer to the instructions in the preceding section to prepare the report, click **Employee Earnings Summary** as the report
Use the same dates as the Payroll Summary Report
Scroll through the report
- Notice the way in which payroll amounts are grouped by item rather than employee.
Do not print the report

PAYROLL LIABILITY BALANCES REPORT

The third payroll report is the Payroll Liability Balances Report. This report lists the company's payroll liabilities that are unpaid as of the report date.

MEMO
DATE: January 31, 2004

Prior to paying taxes, the doctors have Winston print the Payroll Liability Balances Report.

DO: Prepare and print the above report

Click **Payroll Liability Balances** as the report
The report dates should be **01/01/04** to **01/31/04**
Print in Portrait orientation

Miller & Myer, Inc.--Student's Name	
Payroll Liability Balances	
January 2004	
	◇ **BALANCE** ◇
Payroll Liabilities	
Federal Withholding	▶ 931.00 ◀
Medicare Employee	174.44
Social Security Employee	745.94
Federal Unemployment	96.25
Medicare Company	174.44
Social Security Company	745.94
CA - Withholding	163.69
CA - Disability Employee	60.16
CA - Unemployment Company	481.25
CA - Employment Training Tax	481.25
Credit Union	100.00
Dental Insurance (Emp)	300.00
Medical Insurance (Emp)	678.00
Total Payroll Liabilities	**5,132.36**

Close the report

PAY TAXES AND OTHER LIABILITIES

QuickBooks Pro keeps track of the payroll taxes and other payroll liabilities that you owe. When it is time to make your payments, QuickBooks Pro allows you to choose to pay all liabilities or to select individual liabilities for payment. When the liabilities to be paid have been selected, QuickBooks Pro will consolidate all the amounts for one vendor and prepare one check for that vendor.

MEMO

DATE: January 31, 2004

Based on the information in the Payroll Liabilities Report, Winston has been instructed to pay all the payroll liabilities.

DO: Pay all the payroll liabilities
Click the **Pay Liabilities** icon on QuickBooks Employees Navigator
Enter the dates of **01/01/04** to **01/31/04** on the **Select Date Range For Liabilities**
screen

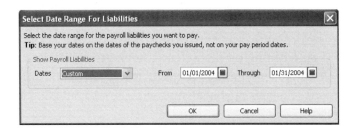

Click **OK**

If necessary, select **To be printed**

Checking Account should be **Payroll Checking**; if it is not, select it from the
drop-down list.

Check Date is **01/31/04**

Show payroll liabilities from **01/01/04** to **01/31/04**

Sort by **Payable To**

- Other sort options are alphabetically by payroll item or in descending order by
  amount.

Click in the check column to place a check mark next to each liability listed; be
sure to scroll through the list to view and mark each liability

- This selects the liabilities for payment.
- Notice the check marks next to each item.

Create liability check without reviewing should be selected

- If you wanted to preview the check in order to enter any other expenses or
  penalties, you would select **Review liability check to enter
  expenses/penalties**.

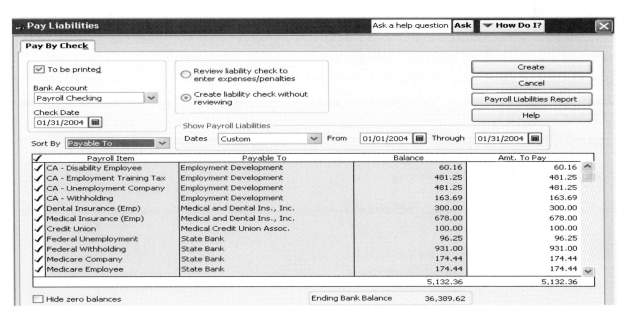

Click **Create**

To print the checks

Access the checks by **Ctrl+W**

Click the drop-down list arrow next to **Print** at the top of the window

Click **Print Batch**, on the **Select Checks to Print** screen

- The first check number should be 15. The names of the agencies receiving the checks and the check amounts should be listed and marked with a check.

Click **OK**

When the checks have printed successfully, click **OK** on the screen asking if checks printed correctly

Close the Checks window

FILE PAYROLL TAX FORMS

QuickBooks Pro creates and prints your Form 941—Employer's Quarterly Federal Tax Return, Schedule B—Employer's Record of Federal Tax Liability, and your Form 940—Employer's Annual Federal Unemployment Tax Return. These forms are accurate and updated with each release of QuickBooks Pro. You may also create a custom tax form that may be submitted in conjunction with any state taxes paid. Because each state has different reporting requirements, we will not create a customized state form in this chapter. Even though the forms are for the quarter and for the year, we will prepare them for the month of January to provide experience in the preparation of these items.

PREPARE AND PRINT FORM 941 AND SCHEDULE B

Form 941 for the Employer's Federal Tax Return is prepared to report federal income tax withheld, Social Security tax, and Medicare tax. The taxes are based on the total wages paid. QuickBooks Pro guides you through the completion of the form step by step.

MEMO

DATE: January 31, 2004

Prepare and print Form 941 for January.

    DO: Prepare and print Form 941 for January

Click **Process Payroll Forms** on the QuickBooks Employees Navigator

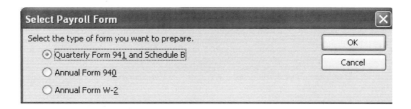

If necessary, click **Form 941 and Schedule B** to select

Click **OK**

- If you get a message about the Tax Form being from a different year, click **OK.**
- The tax form used in the answer key shows the year 2002. While there may be slight changes in the form for 2004, the basic content is the same. Disregard any discrepancies.

CA is the state in which the deposit is made

03/31/04 is the date the quarter ended

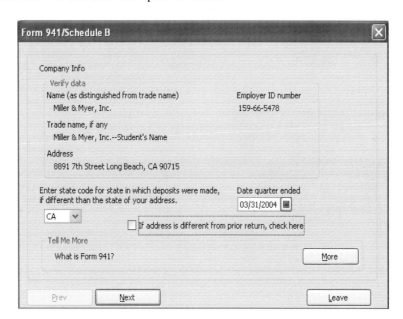

Click **Next** to continue

Because nothing needs to be selected on the following screen, click **Next**

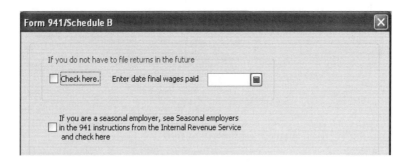

Enter **7** as the number of employees paid during the first quarter

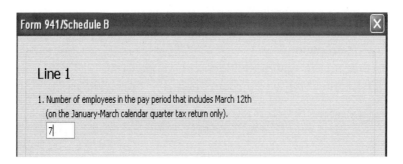

Click **Next**

No adjustments are required for Summary lines 2 to 5

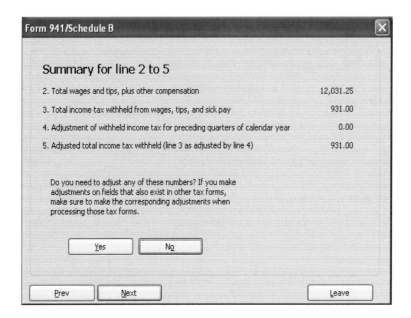

Click **No** or **Next**

- The summary for lines 6 to 10 is correct.

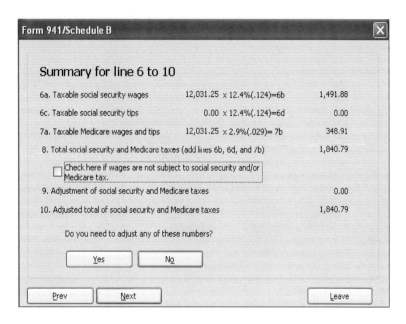

Click **No** or **Next**
As with the earlier summaries, lines 11 to 14 are correct

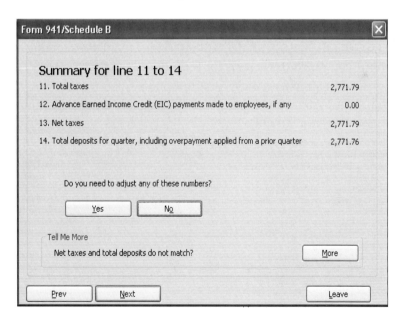

Click **No** or **Next**
There are no changes to make to lines 15 and 16
You must indicate whether the company is a semiweekly or monthly depositor
Click **Monthly or quarterly depositor**

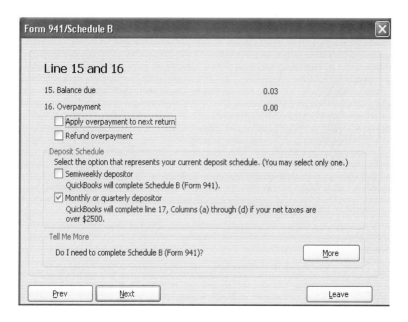

Click **Next** to continue

There are no adjustments to be made to liabilities and taxes in line 17

- There is a 3 cent difference between the liability calculated by QuickBooks Pro and the Net Taxes. This is due to rounding numbers when compiling the amounts for paycheck deductions. This can be corrected by clicking **Prev** until you reach the screen for Summary Lines 6 to 10 and clicking **Yes** to make adjustments. Click **Next** until an adjustment can be entered for Line 9. Click in **Fraction of Cents** and enter **-0.03**. However, at this time we will not make this adjustment.

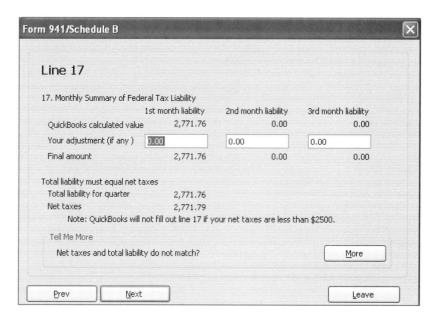

Click **Next**

The form is now complete, click **Print Form 941** to print the form

- The printed form is a government-approved form printed on blank paper and includes a payment voucher.

Check to be sure printer selected is correct, print range is all, click **OK**

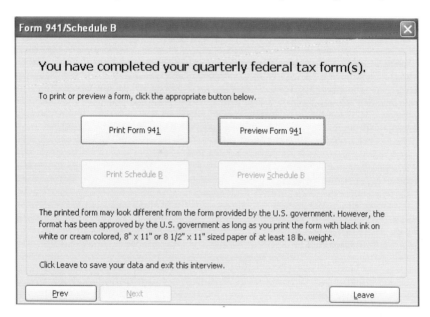

Click **Leave** to exit Form 941

PREPARE AND PRINT FORM 940

The preparation of Form 940 for the Employer's Annual Federal Unemployment Tax Return (FUTA) is similar to the preparation of Form 941.

MEMO

DATE: January 31, 2004

Even though Form 940 for FUTA is filed as an annual tax return, Winston has been asked to prepare this form for January.

 DO: Click **Process Payroll Forms**

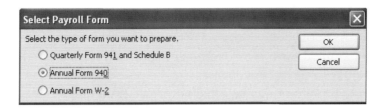

Click **Form 940** and **OK**

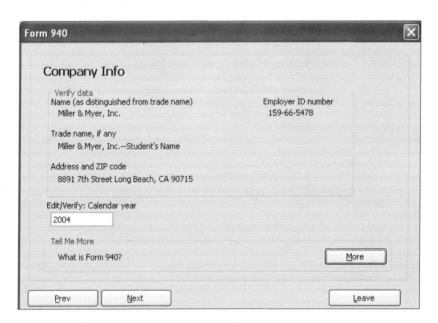

Calendar year is **2004**, click **Next**
Click **Yes** for Questions A, B, and C

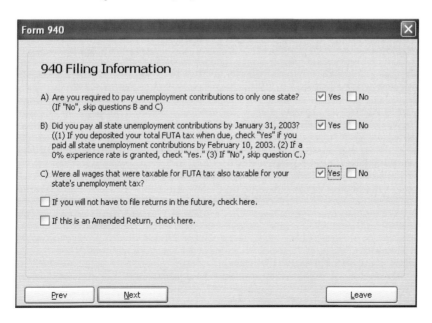

Click **Next**

No adjustments are required for Part I

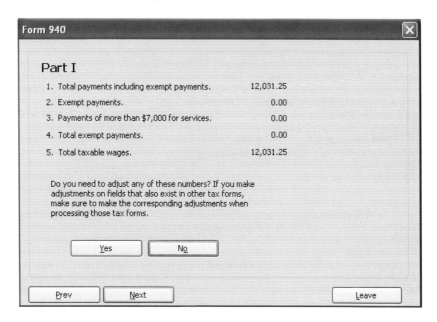

Click **No** or **Next**

The Part II Summary is correct

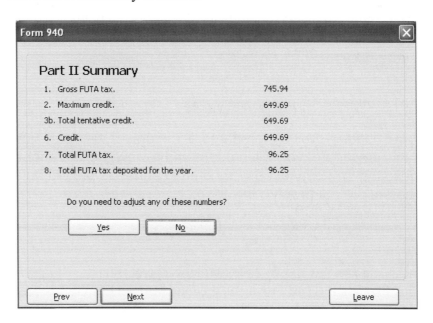

Click **No** or **Next**

Nothing is due

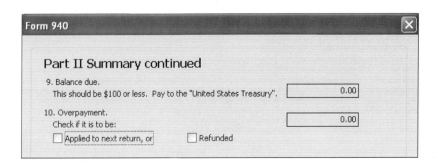

Click **Next**

Print all pages of the Form 940, click **Leave** to exit

- The printed tax form in the answer key shows the year 2002. Disregard any discrepancies.

PREPARE AND PREVIEW EMPLOYEES' W-2 FORMS

The W-2 form is prepared at the end of the year, mailed to each employee, and mailed to the Social Security Administration. The wages earned and taxes withheld for the individual employee for the year are shown on the form. A W-3 form is a summary of all the W-2 forms you are submitting to the federal government and cannot be printed unless the W-2s have been printed. QuickBooks Pro is set up to fill in this information on blank W-2 and W-3 forms. You may not print the W-2s on blank paper unless you subscribe to a QuickBooks payroll service. Electronic filing of W-2s for companies employing 250 or more is required. QuickBooks Pro does not support electronic filing of W-2s unless you subscribe to a QuickBooks payroll service.

MEMO
DATE: January 31, 2004

W-2s and the corresponding W-3 are prepared at the end of the year. However, for experience with this procedure, you will prepare and review the W-2s for each employee. Because the W-3 cannot be viewed and cannot be printed unless all W-2s have been printed, we will not prepare this form.

DO: Prepare and review the W-2s for Miller & Myer, Inc.
Click **Process Payroll Forms** on the QuickBooks Employees Navigator
Click **Form W-2** and click **OK**
If you get a warning screen regarding tax tables, click **OK**
The year should be **2004**

Click **Mark All**

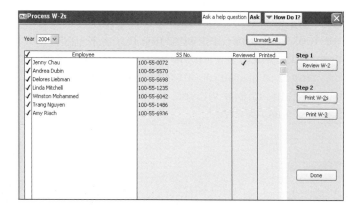

Click **Review W-2**

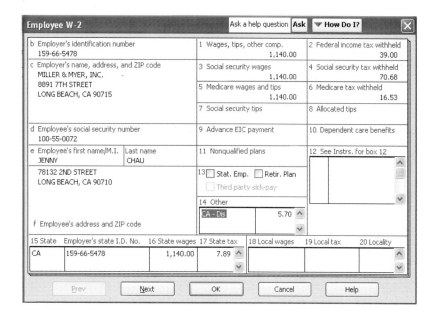

Review Jenny Chau's W-2
Click **OK**

• If you get a warning screen regarding a State Tax ID number, click **OK**
Click **Done**

BACK UP

Follow the instructions provided in previous chapters to make a backup copy of Miller & Myer, Inc. Refer to Appendix A to make a duplicate disk.

SUMMARY

In this chapter, paychecks were generated for employees who worked their standard number of hours, took vacation time, took sick time, and were just hired. Rather than have QuickBooks Pro calculate the amount of payroll deductions, a table was provided and deductions to paychecks were inserted manually. Changes to employee information were made, and a new employee was added. Payroll reports were printed and/or viewed, payroll liabilities were paid, Forms 941 and 940 were prepared, and a W-2 was reviewed.

END-OF-CHAPTER QUESTIONS

TRUE/FALSE

ANSWER THE FOLLOWING QUESTIONS IN THE SPACE PROVIDED BEFORE THE QUESTION NUMBER.

_____ 1.   You cannot enter payroll deductions manually on paychecks.

_____ 2.   Once a paycheck has been printed, you may not edit it.

_____ 3.   Paychecks and regular checks may be printed at the same time.

_____ 4.   A W-3 is printed and mailed to all employees at the end of the year.

_____ 5.   Checks may be created and previewed or created without previewing when entering the payroll manually.

_____ 6.   QuickBooks Pro includes an accurate and up-to-date Form 941 and Form 940.

_____ 7.   If several taxes are owed to a single agency, QuickBooks Pro generates a separate check to the agency for each tax liability item.

_____ 8.   If a salaried employee uses vacation pay, QuickBooks Pro will automatically distribute the correct amount of earnings to Officer Vac Salary once the number of vacation hours has been entered.

_____ 9.   Processing the Payroll Liabilities Report also generates the checks for payment of the liabilities.

_____ 10.   All W-2s must be printed before a W-3 can be printed.

MULTIPLE CHOICE

WRITE THE LETTER OF THE CORRECT ANSWER IN THE SPACE PROVIDED BEFORE THE QUESTION NUMBER.

_____ 1. When completing paychecks manually, ___.
   A. you must provide the information about hours worked
   B. QuickBooks Pro will use the same hours as the last paycheck unless you change them
   C. you must preview all checks
   D. all of the above

_____ 2. The form sent to the government as a summary of the forms sent to all the individual employees of the company is the ___ form.
   A. W-2
   B. 940
   C. W-3
   D. 941

_____ 3. When paying tax liabilities, you ___.
   A. may pay all liabilities at one time
   B. may select individual tax liabilities and pay them one at a time
   C. may pay all the tax liabilities owed to a vendor
   D. all of the above

_____ 4. A new employee may be added ___.
   A. at any time
   B. only at the end of the week
   C. only at the end of the pay period
   D. only when current paychecks have been printed

_____ 5. Pay stub information may be printed ___.
   A. as part of a voucher check
   B. separate from the paycheck
   C. only as an individual employee report
   D. both A and B

_____ 6. The QuickBooks ___ Navigator is used to access Pay Employees.
   A. Employees
   B. Banking
   C. Company
   D. none of the above

_____ 7. A voided check ___.
   A. shows an amount of 0.00
   B. has a Memo of VOID
   C. remains as part of the company records
   D. all of the above

_____ 8. When liabilities to be paid have been selected, QuickBooks Pro will ___.
   A. create a separate check for each liability
   B. consolidate liabilities paid and create one check for each vendor
   C. automatically process a Payroll Liability Balances Report
   D. prepare any tax return forms necessary

_____ 9. If you do not subscribe to a QuickBooks payroll service, you must purchase blank _____forms, and QuickBooks Pro will fill them in when printing.
   A. 940
   B. 941
   C. state tax
   D. W-2

_____ 10. Changes made to an employee's pay rate will become effective ___.
   A. immediately
   B. at the end of the next payroll period
   C. at the end of the quarter
   D. after a W-2 has been prepared for the employee

FILL-IN

IN THE SPACE PROVIDED, WRITE THE ANSWER THAT MOST APPROPRIATELY COMPLETES THE SENTENCE.

1. The form created for the Employer's Quarterly Federal Tax Return is Form _____.

2. The _____ must be printed for each employee before the _____ can be printed.

3. The reports that show an employee's gross pay, sick and vacation hours and pay, deductions, taxes, and other details are _____ and _____.

4. When the Employee List is on the screen, the keyboard shortcut used to add a new employee is _____.

5. The report listing the company's unpaid payroll liabilities as of the report date is the _____ Report.

SHORT ESSAY

What is the difference between voiding a paycheck and deleting a paycheck? Why should a business prefer to void paychecks rather than delete them?

_____

_____

_____

_____

_____

_____

NAME _____

TRANSMITTAL

CHAPTER 5: MILLER & MYER, INC.

Attach the following documents and reports:

Check No. 1: Andrea Dubin, 1/15/04
Check No. 2: Delores Liebman, 1/15/04
Check No. 3: Jenny Chau, 1/15/04
Check No. 4: Linda Mitchell, 1/15/04
Check No. 5: Trang Nguyen, 1/15/04
Check No. 6: Winston Mohammed, 1/15/04
Check No. 7: Amy Riach, 1/31/04
Check No. 8: Andrea Dubin, 1/31/04
Check No. 9: Delores Liebman, 1/31/04
Check No. 10: Jenny Chau, 1/31/04
Check No. 11: Linda Mitchell, 1/31/04
Check No. 12: Trang Nguyen, 1/31/04
Check No. 13: Winston Mohammed, 1/31/04
Check No. 3: Jenny Chau, 1/15/04, (Voided check)
Check No. 14: Jenny Chau, 1/15/04
Payroll Summary Report, January 2004
Payroll Liability Balances, January 2004
       Check Nos. 15-18 may not be in the same order as listed below:
Check No. 15: Employment Development
Check No. 16: Medical and Dental Ins., Inc.
Check No. 17: Medical Credit Union Assoc.
Check No. 18: State Bank
Employer's Quarterly Federal Tax Return, Form 941
Employer's Annual Federal Unemployment (FUTA) Tax Return, Form 940

END-OF-CHAPTER PROBLEM

SUN AND FUN MFG.

Sun and Fun Mfg. is a surfboard manufacturing company located in Newport Beach, California. The company is owned and operated by equal partners, Keith Bibey and Greg Iverson. Keith and Greg handle all the sales and marketing for the company. Business is booming, and Sun and Fun Mfg. currently has several advertisements for factory workers in the local newspapers.

Michelle Andrews is the office manager and is responsible for the smooth operation of the company and for all the employees. Michelle's salary is $37,500 per year. The assistant manager is responsible for the bookkeeping, ordering, delivery schedules, and so on. Le Tam is the assistant manager and earns $32,500 per year. Joe Morgan is the lead line person and supervisor in the factory and earns $15.00 per hour. The senior line assistant is Helen Powers. She earns $12.50 per hour. Regular line personnel earn $9.50 per hour. Currently, Jill Crane and Tom Douglas are regular line personnel. The employees typically work 80 hours within a semimonthly pay period. Any hourly employee working more than 80 hours will be paid overtime for extra hours.

INSTRUCTIONS

As in previous chapters, make a copy of **Sun.qbw** to a new disk and open the company.

RECORD TRANSACTIONS:

January 15, 2004

Open **Sun.qbw** and add your name to the company name. The title bar for the company name will be **Sun and Fun Mfg.--Student's Name**. If your entire name will not fit, use your last name or your first initial and your last name.

Have reports update automatically and remove the date prepared, time prepared, and report basis from the header on reports.

Choose a Payroll Option and Select Manual processing

Use the following Payroll Table to prepare and print checks for the semimonthly pay period from January 1-January 15, 2004: The beginning check number should be 1.

PAYROLL TABLE: JANUARY 15, 2004

	Helen Powers	Jill Crane	Joe Morgan	Le Tam	Michelle Andrews	Tom Douglas
HOURS						
Regular	75	80	80	40	80	80
Overtime			20			8
Sick	5					
Vacation				40		
DEDUCTIONS OTHER PAYROLL ITEMS: EMPLOYEE						
Dental Ins.	25.00	25.00	25.00	25.00	25.00	25.00
Medical Ins.	65.00	45.00	50.00	75.00	65.00	35.00
Credit Union					50.00	
DEDUCTIONS: COMPANY						
CA-Employment Training Tax	40.00	30.40	66.00	54.17	62.50	34.96
Social Security	62.00	47.12	102.30	83.96	96.88	54.19
Medicare	14.50	11.02	23.93	19.64	22.66	12.67
Federal Unemployment	8.00	6.08	13.20	10.83	12.50	6.99
CA-Unemployment	40.00	30.40	66.00	54.17	62.50	34.96
DEDUCTIONS: EMPLOYEE						
Federal Withholding	41.00	39.00	207.00	135.00	108.00	115.00
Social Security	62.00	47.12	102.30	83.96	96.88	54.19
Medicare	14.50	11.02	23.93	19.64	22.66	12.67
CA-Withholding	0.00	7.89	37.05	12.06	51.78	18.28
CA-Disability	5.00	3.80	8.25	6.77	7.81	4.37

Print the company name and address on the voucher checks. Checks begin with number 1.

Michelle hired two new employees effective 01/15/04 as line trainees at $6.50 per hour and time-and-a-half overtime at $9.75 per hour. The pay period is semi-monthly. Both employees are subject to Federal Taxes: Medicare, Social Security, and Federal Unemployment Tax, State Taxes: SUI, and SDI; Other Taxes: CA-Employment Training Tax. Neither employee receives medical or dental insurance, sick leave, or vacation time. Both are Regular employees.
Ron Raymond, Social Security No. 100-55-2145; male, Date of Birth 04/23/1977, 230 Coast Way, Newport Beach, CA 92660; 714-555-2323; Federal and State withholding: Single, 0;
Vince Strozer, Social Security No. 100-55-8487; male, Date of Birth 07/27/1970, 7821 Laguna Canyon Drive, Newport Beach, CA 92660; 714-555-3257; Federal and State withholding: Married (one income), 2

Change Joe Morgan's check to a total of 105 hours and reprint Check No. 3. Because of the additional 5 hours of overtime, his deductions change as follows: CA-Employment Training Tax: 70.50; Social Security Company and Employee: 109.28; Medicare Company and Employee: 25.56; Federal Unemployment: 14.10; CA-Unemployment: 70.50; Federal Withholding: 224.00; CA-Withholding: 42.61; and CA-Disability: 8.81.

January 24, 2004:
Effective today, hired an additional person to work in the office taking orders and answering telephones: Ms. Laine W. Rhodes; Social Security No. 100-55-1147; female, Date of Birth 12/07/1955; 890 Cove Lane, Newport Beach, CA 92660; 714-555-2233; $7.50 per hour and time-and-a-half overtime (calculate); The pay period is semi-monthly. She is subject to Federal Taxes: Medicare, Social Security, and Federal Unemployment Tax, State Taxes: SUI, and SDI; Other Taxes: CA-Employment Training Tax. Federal and State withholding: Head of Household, 1; dental $25; medical $25; no sick or vacation time. Laine is classified as a Regular employee.

Joe Morgan received a raise to $16.00 per hour for his regular hourly rate. Enter the new rate. Calculate the new rate for time-and-a-half overtime and enter as Overtime Hourly Rate 1.

Helen Powers changed her telephone number to 714-555-5111. Edit the employee on the employee list and record the change.

January 31, 2004:
Prepare and print checks beginning with Check No. 7 for the semimonthly pay period from January 16-January 31, 2004:

	Helen Powers	Jill Crane	Joe Morgan	Laine Rhodes	Le Tam	Michelle Andrews	Ron Raymond	Tom Douglas	Vince Strozer
PAYROLL TABLE: JANUARY 31, 2004									
HOURS									
Regular	65	80	80	40	80	60	80	78	80
Overtime			10						
Sick	15								

PAYROLL TABLE: JANUARY 31, 2004									
	Helen Powers	Jill Crane	Joe Morgan	Laine Rhodes	Le Tam	Michelle Andrews	Ron Raymond	Tom Douglas	Vince Strozer
Vacation						20		2	
DEDUCTIONS OTHER PAYROLL ITEMS: EMPLOYEE									
Dental Ins.	25.00	25.00	25.00	25.00	25.00	25.00		25.00	
Medical Ins.	65.00	45.00	50.00	25.00	75.00	65.00		35.00	
Credit Union						50.00			
DEDUCTIONS: COMPANY									
CA-Employment Training Tax	40.00	30.40	60.80	12.00	54.16	62.50	20.80	30.40	20.80
Social Security	62.00	47.12	94.24	18.60	83.96	96.87	32.24	47.12	32.24
Medicare	14.50	11.02	22.04	4.35	19.63	22.65	7.54	11.02	7.54
Federal Unemployment	8.00	6.08	12.16	2.40	10.84	12.50	4.16	6.08	4.16
CA-Unemployment	40.00	30.40	60.80	12.00	54.16	62.50	20.80	30.40	20.80
DEDUCTIONS: EMPLOYEE									
Federal Withholding	41.00	39.00	188.00	11.00	135.00	108.00	61.00	97.00	21.00
Social Security	62.00	47.12	94.24	18.60	83.96	96.87	32.24	47.12	32.24
Medicare	14.50	11.02	22.04	4.35	19.63	22.65	7.54	11.02	7.54
CA-withholding	0.00	7.89	31.85	0.00	12.06	51.78	6.06	13.72	1.18
CA-Disability	5.00	3.80	7.60	1.50	6.77	7.82	2.60	3.80	2.60

Vince spilled coffee on his check. Void his check for January 31, print the voided check, reissue the paycheck, and print it using Check No. 16.

Vince and Ron have completed their first two weeks of training. Because both are doing well, change their regular pay to $7.00 per hour. In addition, calculate and enter their time-and-a-half Overtime Hourly Rate 1.

Prepare and print the Payroll Summary Report for January 1-31, 2004 in Landscape orientation.

Prepare and print the Payroll Liabilities Report for January 1-31, 2004 in Portrait orientation.

Pay all the taxes and other liabilities for January 1-31, 2004; and print the checks.

Prepare and print Form 941 for the quarter ending 3/31/04. You are a monthly/quarterly depositor and want any overpayments applied to the next return. Do not make adjustments to the report. Prepare and print Form 940. Do not make adjustments to the report.

NAME _____

TRANSMITTAL

<u>CHAPTER 5: SUN AND FUN MFG.</u>

Attach the following documents and reports:

Check No. 1: Helen Powers
Check No. 2: Jill Crane
Check No. 3: Joe Morgan
Check No. 4: Le Tam
Check No. 5: Michelle Andrews
Check No. 6: Tom Douglas
Check No. 3 (Revised): Joe Morgan
Check No. 7: Helen Powers
Check No. 8: Jill Crane
Check No. 9: Joe Morgan
Check No. 10: Laine W. Rhodes
Check No. 11: Le Tam
Check No. 12: Michelle Andrews
Check No. 13: Ron Raymond
Check No. 14: Tom Douglas
Check No. 15: Vince Strozer
Check No. 15 (Voided): Vince Strozer
Check No. 16: Vince Strozer
Payroll Summary, January 31, 2004
Payroll Liability Balances, January 2004
      Check Nos. 17-20 may be in a different order
Check No. 17: Employment Development
Check No. 18: Medical and Dental Ins., Inc.
Check No. 19: Medical Credit Union Assoc.
Check No. 20: State Bank
Employer's Quarterly Federal Tax Return, Form 941
Employer's Annual Federal Unemployment (FUTA) Tax Return, Form 940

COMPUTERIZING A MANUAL ACCOUNTING SYSTEM

LEARNING OBJECTIVES

At the completion of this chapter, you will be able to:

1. Set up a company using the EasyStep Interview.
2. Establish a Chart of Accounts for a company.
3. Create lists for receivables, payables, items, customers, vendors, and others.
4. Add payroll items.
5. Transfer Uncategorized Income and Expenses to the owner's equity account.
6. Create an Employee Template and add employees to an Employee List.
7. Specify a company logo.
8. Customize reports and company preferences.

COMPUTERIZING A MANUAL SYSTEM

In previous chapters, QuickBooks Pro was used to record transactions for businesses that were already set up for use in QuickBooks Pro. In this chapter, you will actually set up a business, create a chart of accounts, create various lists, add names to lists, and delete unnecessary accounts. QuickBooks Pro makes setting up the records for a business user-friendly by going through the process using the EasyStep Interview. Once the basic accounts, items, lists, and other items are established via the EasyStep Interview, you will make some refinements to accounts, add detail information regarding customers and vendors, transfer Uncategorized Income and Expenses to the owner's equity account, customize report and company preferences, and create a company logo for use on business forms.

TRAINING TUTORIAL

The following tutorial is a step-by-step guide to setting up the fictitious company Movies & More. Company information, accounts, items, lists, and other items must be provided before transactions may be recorded in QuickBooks Pro. The EasyStep Interview will be used to set up company information. Once the basic company information has been entered via the EasyStep Interview, changes and modifications to the company data will be made. As in earlier chapters, information for the company setup will be provided in memos. Information may also be shown in lists or within the step-by-step instructions provided.

COMPANY PROFILE: MOVIES & MORE

Movies & More is a fictitious company that sells and rents videos and DVDs. In addition, Movies & More has a service department that cleans, conditions, and repairs VCRs and DVD players. Movies & More is located in San Diego, California, and is a sole proprietorship owned by David Watson. Mr. Watson is involved in all aspects of the business. Movies & More has two full-time employees who are paid a salary: Morris Carter, who manages the store and is responsible for all the employees, and Colleen Benson, whose duties include all the ordering, managing the office, and keeping the books. There are two full-time hourly employees: James Hansen, who works in the service/repairs department, and Sandra Roberts, who works in the store selling and renting videos. There will be other employees who work part time selling and renting videos and who are paid an hourly rate.

CREATE A NEW COMPANY

Since Movies & More is a new company, it does not appear as a company file if you select Open Company on the File menu. A new company may be created by clicking New Company on the File menu.

MEMO

DATE: July 1, 2005

Because this is the beginning of the fiscal year for Movies & More, it is an appropriate time to set up the company information in QuickBooks Pro. Use the EasyStep Interview in QuickBooks Pro.

DO: Open QuickBooks Pro as previously instructed
        If a company is open, click **File** menu, click **Close Company**
- If you do not close an open company, QuickBooks Pro will close it as soon as you begin to create a new company.

        Insert a formatted blank disk in the **A:** drive (or the storage location you have been instructed to use by your instructor)
        Click **File** menu, click **New Company**

The first screen of the EasyStep Interview will appear on the screen.

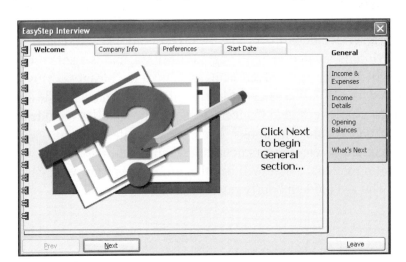

THE EASYSTEP INTERVIEW

The EasyStep Interview is a step-by-step guide to entering your company information as of a single date called a start date. It also provides tips regarding a chart of accounts, standard industry practices, and other items for the type of company indicated. The Interview is divided into five different sections. The sections appear as tabs along the right side of the EasyStep Interview screen. The General section is used to enter general company information, select a preset Chart of Accounts, indicate preferences such as payroll and inventory, and select a start date. The Income & Expenses section allows you to add additional income and expense accounts to the Chart of Accounts, which is also the General Ledger for the company. Income Details is used to indicate and set up items to track the services and products your company sells and/or provides. It is also used to set up inventory items. The Opening Balances section allows you to input opening balances of customers, vendors, and accounts. What's Next includes recommendations for other tasks that need to be completed as part of the company creation.

Each section is divided into topics, which are shown as tabs at the top of the screen. For example, the first screen in the General section is the Welcome screen. Once a screen has been read and any required items have been filled in or questions answered, the Next button is clicked to tell QuickBooks Pro to advance to the next screen. If you need to return to a previous screen, click the Previous button.

When a topic or section is complete, QuickBooks Pro places a large check mark on the section and/or topic tab. If you need to stop the Interview before completing everything, you may exit by clicking the Leave button in the bottom right corner of the screen or by clicking the close button at the top right corner of the EasyStep Interview screen. It is best to complete an entire topic before exiting.

GENERAL SECTION OF THE INTERVIEW

The General section of the EasyStep Interview has several tasks to be performed. The most important task is to provide a start date and to set up a chart of accounts. In order to complete the General section of the Interview, you need complete company data regarding the name and address of the company, the federal tax ID number, first month of the income tax year and the first month of the fiscal year, the type of business, a chart of accounts if you have one, and the start date you plan to use.

WELCOME TOPIC

The Welcome topic of the EasyStep Interview introduces you to the procedures followed during the Interview. It also allows you to tell QuickBooks Pro whether or not you are upgrading from another Intuit product.

MEMO
DATE: July 1, 2005

In preparation for setting up the company records for Movies & More, complete the Welcome and Company Information sections of the EasyStep Interview.

DO: Complete Welcome and Company Information section of the EasyStep Interview
Read the screens in the Welcome section for the EasyStep Interview, click **Next** to advance from one screen to the next
Read then click **Next** for obtaining assistance in setting up QuickBooks

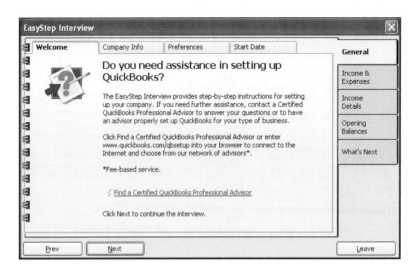

Since we are not converting Quicken data to QuickBooks, click **Next** to continue

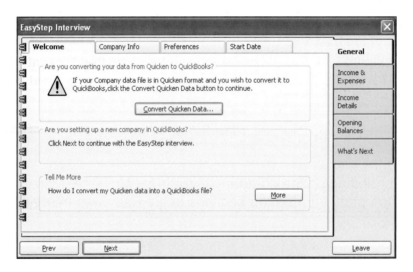

Read then click **Next for** Setting up a new QuickBooks Pro company

- Notice the Skip Interview button. This allows you to set up the company without going through the EasyStep Interview. This is a procedure that may be used if you are familiar with setting up a company in QuickBooks Pro, have an established Chart of Accounts, and know which preferences you want to select within the QuickBooks Pro program. Do *not* click this button.

Read then click **Next** for Navigating around the interview

Read then click **Next** for Sections and topics

Read then click **Next** for Feel free to change your answers!

Read then click **Next** for Welcome completed!

- When the Welcome section is complete, notice the check mark on the Welcome tab.

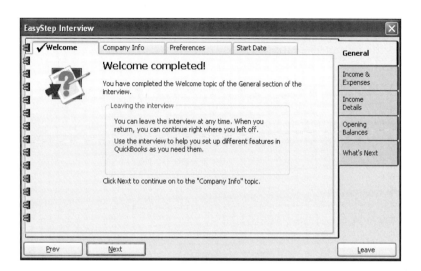

COMPANY INFO TOPIC

The Company Info topic sets up the company file, creates a Chart of Accounts designed for your specific type of business, and establishes the beginning of a company's fiscal year and income tax year.

MEMO

DATE: July 1, 2005

In preparation for setting up Movies & More company records, the following information is provided to Colleen by Mr. Watson:

Company: Movies & More--Your Name (*Key in your actual name*)
Address: 8795 Mission Bay Drive, San Diego, CA 92109
Telephone: 760-555-7979
Fax: 760-555-9797
E-mail: MoviesnMore@info.com
Web: www.MoviesnMore.com
Federal Tax ID: 159-88-8654
First Month in Tax and Fiscal Year: July
Income Tax form: None
Type of Business: Retail
Inventory: Yes
File Name: Movies & More—Student's Name.qbw

DO: Complete the Company Info topic

Read the General Company Information screen, click **Next**

Enter the Company Name **Movies & More–Your Name**, press the Tab key

- Movies & More–Your Name is entered as the Legal name when the Tab key is pressed. Do not actually enter the words "Your Name" as part of the company name. Instead, type your own name. For example, Mary Hernandez would show **Movies & More—Mary Hernandez**. This makes it easier for you to identify your work when you print.

Click **Next**

Enter the Company Address information in the spaces provided, tab to or click in the blanks to move from item to item

- *Note*: For the state, California, type C and QuickBooks Pro will fill in the rest or click the drop-down list arrow for State.
- The country is automatically filled in as US.

Enter the telephone number, fax number, e-mail address, and Web address as given in the Memo

Click **Next**

Complete the next screen:

Click **More** to see information regarding federal tax ID numbers, income tax year, and fiscal year

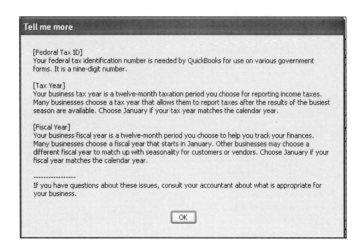

Click **OK**

Tab to or click **Tax ID number**, enter **159-88-8654**

Tab to or click **income tax year**, click the drop-down list arrow, click **July**

Tab to or click **fiscal year**, click the drop-down list arrow, click **July**

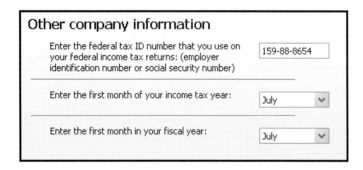

Click **Next**

Leave the **company income tax form** as **<Other/None>**

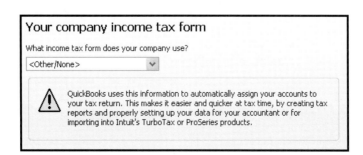

Click **Next**
A **Tax Form** message box appears on the screen, click **OK**

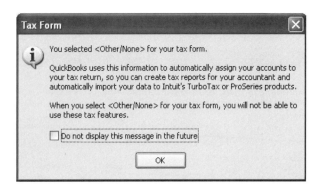

Scroll through the list of the types of businesses
Click **Retail: General**

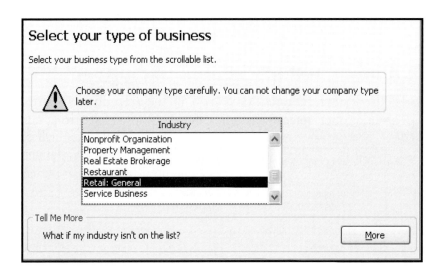

Click **Next**
Read the **Setup tips for your business** screen, click **Next**

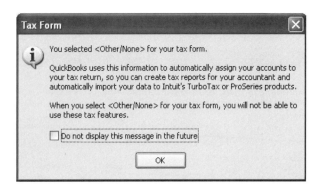

Read the screen about setting up your company file

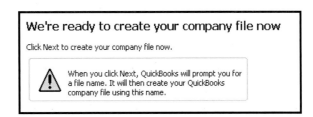

Insert a blank disk into the **A:** drive, click **Next**

- If necessary, click the drop-down list for **Save in:** and click **3 ½ Floppy (A:)**.
- The File name should show Movies & More—your actual name.qbw. If not, click in the textbox for File name and enter the appropriate name.
- Save as type: should show QuickBooks Files (*.QBW, *.QBA)

Click **Save**

Since we are using QuickBooks Pro to assist us with our company configuration, click **Yes** to use the income and expense accounts chosen by QuickBooks Pro

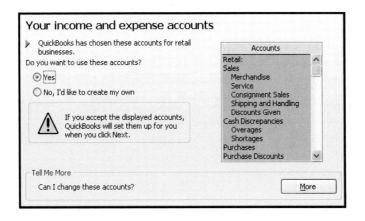

- Some accounts will not be appropriate for use by Movies & More. These will be deleted and/or changed after the EasyStep Interview is complete.

Click **Next**

You will be asked how many people should have access to your company files

Get more information about this by clicking the **More** button

Click **OK**

Leave the number of people at **0**, click **Next**

QuickBooks will provide a screen in which you are asked to create passwords for the Administrator; DO NOT enter any passwords

- If your company has a password for the Administrator and you forget what it is, you will not be able to access the company file for use. In a business environment, it would be essential to assign passwords to the administrator and anyone else given access to QuickBooks. However, in training passwords may be forgotten or misspelled so we will not be assigning passwords.

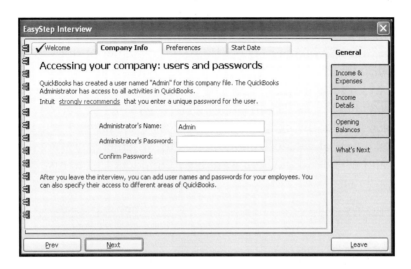

Click **Next**

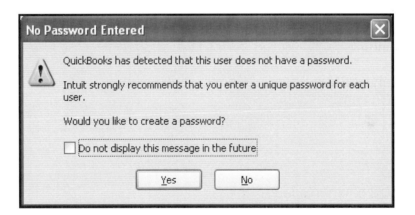

Click **No** on the No Password Entered screen

Company Information is complete, click **Next**

PREFERENCES TOPIC

The Preferences topic allows you to tell QuickBooks Pro whether or not you want to use certain features of the QuickBooks Pro program. If you answer a question one way and then decide to change, you can always reset your preferences after you exit the Interview. Preferences include whether or not to use QuickBooks Pro inventory feature, whether or not you collect sales tax, selection of an invoice format, the number of employees on the payroll, whether or not you use classes as an additional way of categorizing transactions, whether you want to enter bills first and pay them later, and whether or not you want the Reminders List to display automatically when you start the program.

MEMO
DATE: July 1, 2005

The information necessary to complete the Preferences topic is:

Collect sales tax: Yes, at a single rate for a single tax agency
Sales tax name and description: CA Sales Tax
Tax rate: 7.25%
Government agency: State Board of Equalization
Invoice format: Custom
Payroll feature: Yes
Estimates: No
Track time: No
Classes: No
Enter bills first and payments later
Reminders List: When I ask for it
Accrual-based reports

DO: Complete the Preferences topic
Click **Next** until you get to the **Sales tax** screen
Click **Yes** for collecting Sales tax

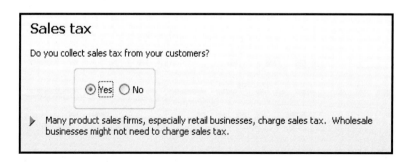

Click **Next**

- From this point forward, click **Next** whenever you want to move from one screen to the next. The step-by-step instructions will no longer remind you to click **Next** each time.

Single or multiple sales tax rates?

Select one of the following options:

- ⦿ I collect single tax rate paid to a single tax agency
- ◯ I collect multiple tax rates OR have multiple tax agencies

If you choose a single tax rate payable to a single tax agency, you can enter the sales tax information on the next screen.

If you choose multiple tax rates or agencies, you need to set up your sales tax outside the interview.

Select: **I collect single tax rate paid to a single tax agency**

Complete the screen for Sales Tax Information:

Tab to or click the text box for **Enter a short name for the sales tax.** Enter **CA Sales Tax**

Enter the same information for the description for Invoices

Tab to or click the box for the sales tax rate, enter **7.25%**

Tab to or click the box for the government agency, enter **State Board of Equalization**

Sales tax information

Enter a short name for the sales tax. This name will be used in QuickBooks reports and drop-down lists:	CA Sales Tax
Enter a sales tax description to be printed on invoices:	CA Sales Tax
Enter your sales tax rate here as a percentage (e.g., "5.2%"):	7.25%
Enter the name of the government agency to which you pay sales tax:	State Board of Equalization

---

Click **Custom** for the Invoice format

- *Note*: A custom invoice will be created later in the chapter.

Click **Yes** to use the QuickBooks payroll feature

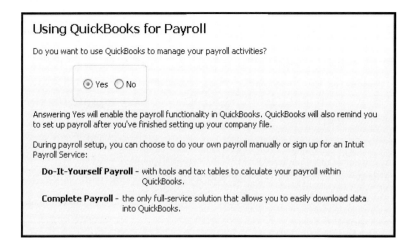

- In this text, we will not be subscribing to any of the QuickBooks Payroll services, so we will be entering our payroll manually and indicating the fact that we want to calculate payroll manually later in the chapter

Click **No** for written or verbal estimates

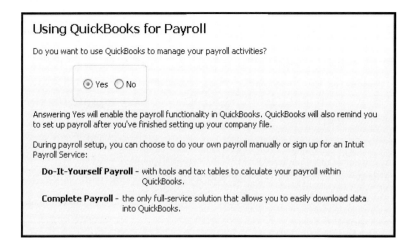

Click **No** for time tracking

Time tracking

Would you like to track the time that you or your employees spend on each job or project?

○ Yes ◉ No

▶ Most retailers do not track employee time by project or job. However, you may choose to
track employee time by project for services you sell.

- Time tracking would be useful in a business where a particular job or client is billed based on the time actually spent working the specific job or working for a specific client. Examples would include a construction job or the hours an attorney spends on an individual client's case.

Click **No** for tracking segments of your business with classes

To select the bill-paying method, click **Enter the bills first and then enter the payments later.**

Two ways to handle bills and payments

Choose one of the two following ways to track your bills and payments.

○ Enter the checks directly.
◉ Enter the bills first and then enter the payments later.

The first option is simple since it only involves one step.

The second option is a two-step process. QuickBooks reminds you when your bills are due, so that you can pay at the last possible moment or in time to get early payment discounts.

- By selecting to enter the bills first and then enter the payments later, you are actually choosing to use QuickBooks' Accounts Payable feature. In addition, this is the appropriate choice when using accrual-basis accounting. If you don't record an expense or a bill until the check is written, it may not be recorded within the period in which it occurred.

Click **When I ask for it** to display the Reminders List

Reminders list

The reminders window is a list of all things that are due or that you need to act on. It includes such things as bills to pay, overdue invoices, checks to print, and your To Do items.

How often would you like to see your Reminders List?

○ At start up ◉ When I ask for it ○ Rarely

Select **Accrual-based reporting** for your accounting reports

Accrual- or cash-based reporting

Do you prefer to view reports on an accrual or cash basis?

○ Cash-based reports

◉ Accrual-based reports

For cash-based reports, income is reported when you receive the payment on an invoice, and an expense is reported when you pay a bill.

For accrual-based reports, income is reported as soon as you write an invoice, and an expense is reported as soon as you receive a bill.

▶ If you haven't already done so, consider using accrual-based reporting, since it may give you a more accurate picture of your business than cash-based reporting.

Preferences have been completed, click **Next** to continue

START DATE

The start date is the date you select to give QuickBooks Pro the financial information for your company. Once a start date is entered, historical information will need to be entered in order to record transactions that occurred between your start date and the current date to make all records accurate. Otherwise, you will not receive correct data when preparing reports, paying taxes, and so on. For example, if the start date entered is May 1 and it is now July 1, two months of transactions (May and June) will need to be entered into QuickBooks Pro. This could be a tremendous task if you have a busy company with many transactions to record. If you did not enter the two months of transactions, then all reports and accounts would not show income, expenses, changes in assets, changes in liabilities, or changes in owner's equity for May and June. If you enter the start date and it is also the beginning of your fiscal year, you will not have to enter any previous transactions, and all reports and accounts will be accurate for the entire year. Some companies choose to begin using QuickBooks Pro at the beginning of their fiscal year to avoid having to enter all the transaction history; however, it is possible to begin using QuickBooks Pro at any time of the year. In this text, we are creating our company at the beginning of the fiscal year.

MEMO

DATE: July 1, 2005

Colleen: Use the memo date as the start date for the company. Because this is the first day of the fiscal year, historical data will not need to be entered.

DO: Read each screen carefully as you advance through the screens for Start Date
If **I want to start entering detailed transactions as of:** shows **07/01/2005,** click
to select
OR

Select **I want to start entering detailed transactions as of:** and enter **07/01/2005**

- Unless you change the date of your computer to match the date used in the text, you will probably have a different date shown. If this is the case, choose the second option.

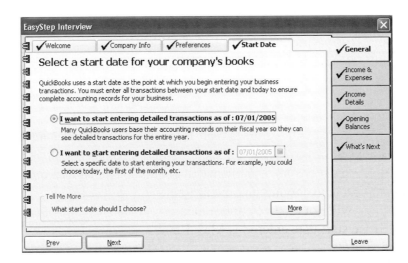

- The General section of the EasyStep Interview is complete. Notice the check marks on each of the topic tabs and on the General tab.

INCOME & EXPENSES SECTION

In the General section, QuickBooks Pro established a basic Chart of Accounts or General Ledger. Because this Chart of Accounts is based on a representation of the accounts most frequently used within an industry, it will not have all the accounts that are used by an individual company. Using the preset Chart of Accounts is helpful in providing a general setup. In the Income & Expenses section of the Interview, new income and expense accounts are added.

Any accounts created by QuickBooks Pro that are not appropriate for your individual company will be deleted after the setup procedure and EasyStep Interview are completed. QuickBooks Pro accounts can have both account names and account numbers. The EasyStep Interview displays only account names. If account numbers are used, the numbers are added outside the Interview. In addition, changing account names, changing subaccounts, and making accounts inactive will be completed after the Interview.

INCOME ACCOUNTS TOPIC

> **MEMO**
> **DATE:** July 1, 2005
>
> Because Movies & More sells videos and DVDs, rents videos and DVDs, and repairs VCRs and DVD players, income accounts need to be established for all three types of revenue. Because QuickBooks Pro has established a Sales account, accounts for Rental Income and Repair Income need to be added.

DO: Add income accounts for Rental Income and Repair Income
Click **Next** until you see the screen **Here are your income accounts**
- QuickBooks Pro has established a Sales account that will be used for the sale of videos. It has not established accounts for rental and repair income.
Click **Yes** to add another income account

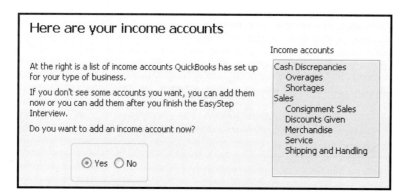

Click **Next**
Enter **Rental Income** as the account name

Click **Next**
Repeat the procedures to add Repair Income

- Tax lines will not be assigned at this time.
Click **Next**
Repeat the procedures to add Repair Income

Because you do not want to add any more income accounts, click **No** after Repair Income has been added

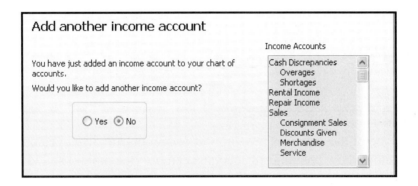

Complete the Income Accounts Topic

EXPENSE ACCOUNTS TOPIC

QuickBooks Pro has created some expense accounts in the Chart of Accounts already. This topic allows you to add additional expense accounts to the Chart of Accounts. Expense accounts may be categorized further by making an expense a subaccount of another account. For example, rather than lump all insurance together in one insurance expense account, the insurance expenses will be listed separately in individual accounts, such as Disability Insurance, Liability Insurance, and so on. These accounts will be grouped together as subaccounts under Insurance Expense.

MEMO
DATE: July 1, 2005

Add the following expense accounts: Fire Insurance (subaccount of Insurance), Supplies, and Sales Supplies (subaccount of Supplies).

   DO: Add the accounts as indicated above
Click **More Details** and read the screens to get additional information about accounts and subaccounts, click **Next**

- One of the screens shows how subaccounts are displayed on reports. This shows how creating subaccounts can provide more detailed information about expenses.

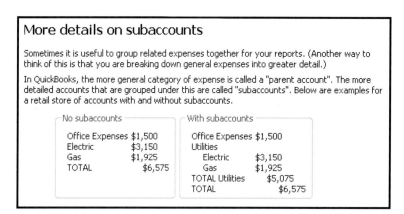

Click **Next** then scroll through the list of accounts created by QuickBooks Pro
- Notice that there is not an account for Fire Insurance, nor is there an account for Sales Supplies.

Click **Yes**, then click **Next** to enter more expense accounts
Enter **Fire Insurance** as the account name
Click **This is a subaccount**

Click the drop-down list arrow next to **Parent account**
Click **Insurance**

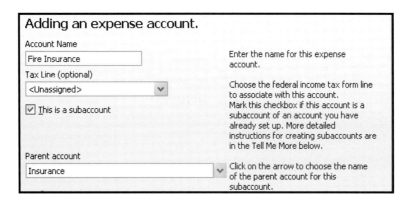

Repeat the procedures indicated to add a Supplies account
Add an additional account for Sales Supplies as a subaccount of Supplies
Scroll through the Chart of Accounts
Verify the addition of the three new accounts

Click **No** to add expense accounts
* Income & Expenses section is complete. Notice the check marks on the topic and section tabs.

INCOME DETAILS SECTION

The Income Details section of the EasyStep Interview allows you to track the sources of the company's income from the services and products it sells. This section also allows you to identify the service, product, and inventory items used in the various income accounts of the company. Accounts receivable features that will be used are identified in this section as well.

INTRODUCTION TOPIC

This topic tells QuickBooks Pro the information it needs to determine which parts of the Accounts Receivable features it will use for the business and whether or not you will be using invoices for each transaction or monthly statements.

    DO: Complete the Introduction of the Income Details Section
For Receipt of payment, click **Sometimes**

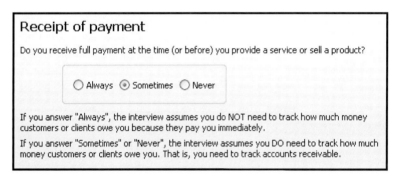

Click **No** for Statement Charges

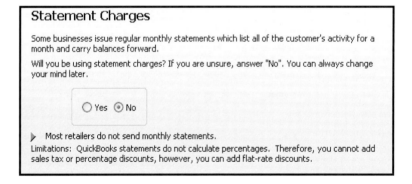

- *Note*: Statement Charges allow you to enter all transactions for an individual customer into the customer's account and send one statement at the end of the month rather than complete an invoice for each transaction.

ITEMS TOPIC

The Income Details: Items topic is the section of the Interview where Items to track services performed and products sold for income are created. The Items List is used in conjunction with the income accounts previously created.

MEMO
DATE: July 1, 2005

The following service and product items are used by Movies & More (Information is listed in the order of **Item Name, Sales Description, Sales Price, Taxable Item, Income Account**):

Video & DVD Rental, Video & DVD Rental, 3.00, Yes, Rental Income
VCR & DVD Repair, VCR & DVD Repair, 0.00, No, Repair Income
VCR & DVD Service, VCR & DVD Service, 19.95, No, Repair Income

---

DO: Add the three service items above to the Items List
Click **More** on the Income Details: Items screen to get additional information about items and income accounts

Click **OK** on the **Tell me more** screen

> **Service Items**
>
> Do you want to set up a service item for any work or service?
>
> ● Yes ○ No
>
> In QuickBooks Pro, Premier, or Enterprise Solutions, you use service items to charge customers for work or services performed by owners, partners, employees, and subcontractors.

Click **Yes** on the **Service Items** screen
Enter Item Name **Video & DVD Rental**
Tab to or click Sales Description, enter **Video & DVD Rental**
Tab to or click Sales Price, enter **3.00**
Click **Taxable Item** to select

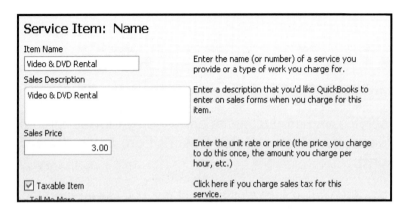

On the next screen, click the drop-down list arrow for **Income Account**
Click **Rental Income**

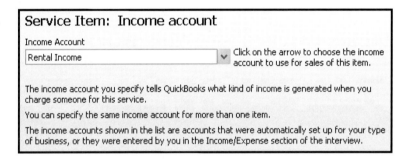

Click **No** for **Subcontracted expenses**

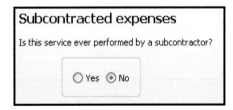

Repeat for the other two items listed in the Memo above

When all Items have been entered, click **No** on **Set up another service item**
Click **No** for Non-Inventory parts

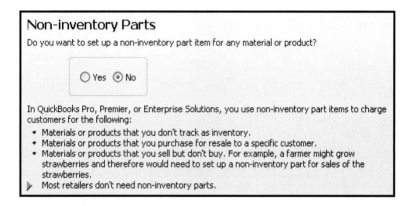

- Non-inventory parts are parts that are purchased and then immediately sold or installed. They are not kept as an in-stock item.
  Click **No** for Other Charges

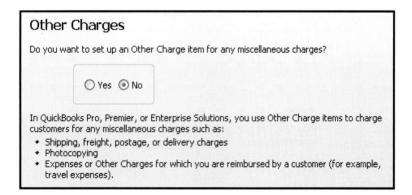

- As indicated, Other Charges are charges that you want to pass on to customers, not expenses you have paid for on behalf of customers. In Movies & More there doesn't appear to be a need for an account for other charges. If it is determined that the account is needed, it can be added at a later date.
- The Items topic is complete.

INVENTORY TOPIC

The Inventory topic is completed in order to set up your inventory part items. Inventory part items are the things you purchase, hold in inventory, and then sell.

MEMO

DATE: July 1, 2005

Enter the following Inventory items (information is listed in the order of Item Name, Sales Description, Sales Price, Taxable Item, Income Account, Purchase Description, Cost, Reorder Point, Quantity on Hand, Value):

Action DVD, Action DVD, 0.00, Yes, Sales, Action DVD, 0.00, 100, 550, 5,500
Action Video, Action Video, 0.00, Yes, Sales, Action Video, 0.00, 100, 550, 5,500
Children DVD, Children's DVD, 0.00, Yes, Sales, Children's DVD, 0.00, 100, 250, 2,500
Children Video, Children's Video, 0.00, Yes, Sales, Children's Video, 0.00, 100, 250,
    2,500
Comedy DVD, Comedy DVD, 0.00, Yes, Sales, Comedy DVD, 0.00, 100, 500, 5,000
Comedy Video, Comedy Video, 0.00, Yes, Sales, Comedy Video, 0.00, 100, 500, 5,000
Drama DVD, Drama DVD, 0.00, Yes, Sales, Drama DVD, 0.00, 100, 450, 4,500
Drama Video, Drama Video, 0.00, Yes, Sales, Drama Video, 0.00, 100, 450, 4,500

     DO: Use the information above to add the Inventory Items indicated

Income Details: Inventory

In the General section of this interview, you indicated that you did not need to track inventory.

Click Next to skip over the Inventory Items topic.

If you would like to set up inventory items, click "I want to set up inventory items" and then click Next.

○ Skip inventory items

◉ I want to set up inventory items

▷ Many retailers decide to track inventory outside QuickBooks.

Click **I want to set up inventory items**

Click **Yes** to begin adding inventory items

Enter **Action DVD** as the Item Name

Tab to or click Sales Description, enter **Action DVD**

- Because DVDs are sold for different amounts, Sales Price remains 0.00.

Click **Taxable Item**

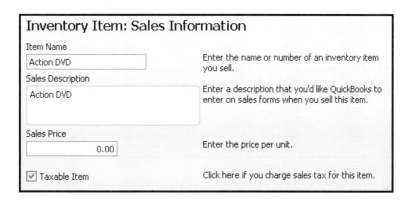

Click the drop-down list arrow next to **Income Account**, click **Sales**

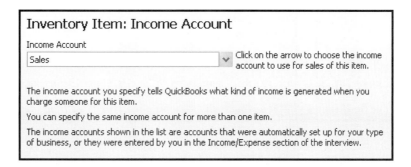

Enter **Action DVD** as the Purchases Description

- Because DVDs are purchased for different amounts, Cost remains 0.00.

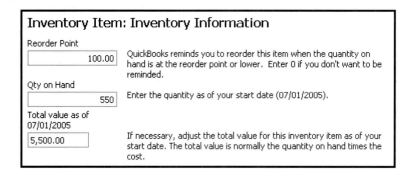

Enter **100** for the **Reorder Point**
Tab to or click **Qty on Hand**, enter **550**
Tab to or click Total value as of **07/01/05**, enter **5500**

Inventory Item: Inventory Information

Reorder Point

100.00 — QuickBooks reminds you to reorder this item when the quantity on hand is at the reorder point or lower. Enter 0 if you don't want to be reminded.

Qty on Hand

550 — Enter the quantity as of your start date (07/01/2005).

Total value as of 07/01/2005

5,500.00 — If necessary, adjust the total value for this inventory item as of your start date. The total value is normally the quantity on hand times the cost.

Repeat for the other seven items listed in the Memo above

- Only the first screen of next three inventory items is shown above.
  Click **No** when all inventory items have been entered
- The Inventory topic and the Income Details section are now complete.

OPENING BALANCES SECTION

As the name implies, the Opening Balances section is the section of the EasyStep Interview where opening balances for customers, vendors, and certain General Ledger accounts are entered as of the start date previously indicated. Detail information such as the address, the credit limit, and so on regarding individual customers and vendors will be entered as a separate procedure after the Interview is complete.

When setting up your company, you should have the current bank statement, value of your assets, liabilities, credit cards, and other balance sheet accounts as of the start date, the customer names and amounts owed as of the start date, and the vendor names and the amount you owe as of the start date.

  DO: Read the screens and complete the Introduction

CUSTOMERS TOPIC

The Customers topic is completed to add customers who have an opening balance with the company. Only customer names and balances are added at this point. The only time an opening balance can be entered is when a customer is added. If there are customers with whom you usually do business but that do not have an existing balance, they may be set up within the Interview or they may be added at a later date. Complete customer information is added after the EasyStep Interview is complete.

MEMO
DATE: July 1, 2005

Add the following customers and the balances they owe to Movies & More:
Goldin, Bernard: $50   Morales, Raul: $550
Reese, Yvonne: $350   Thompsen, Rick: $75

  DO: Add the customers and the amount they owe to Movies & More
            Click **Yes**, if necessary, to Enter customers
            Click **No**, if necessary, to Customer job tracking
            Enter **Goldin, Bernard** in Customer Name
            • Add the last name first so that the customer list is alphabetized according to the last name.

Tab to or click **Balance due on start date**, enter **50**

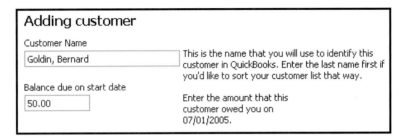

Repeat the steps above to add the remaining customers and their balances
- Verify the accuracy of the Balance due on start date. Remember, the only time you can enter an opening balance for a customer is when the customer is created. If you have an error in the opening balance, you will have to delete the customer and add the customer again.

When all the customers and their balances have been added, compare your Customer:Jobs List with the following QuickBooks list

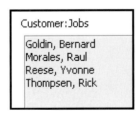

Notice that the balances are not shown on the list.
- The customer's names were added last name, first name so that QuickBooks Pro could alphabetize the customers by their last names. If customers are added first name then last name, the customers will be alphabetized by their first names.

Click **No** to end adding customers

VENDORS TOPIC

As with the Customer topic, the Vendor topic is used to set up a list of vendors and the balances owed to the vendors. If there are vendors with which you usually do business but that do not have an existing balance, they may be set up within the Interview or they may be added at a later date. This topic simply adds a vendor's name and the balance due. It does not allow you to enter information regarding credit terms, credit limits, vendor addresses, and so forth. That information must be entered after you leave the interview.

MEMO
DATE: July 1, 2005

Colleen:

Add the following vendors and the balances owed: DVD and Video Supplies, $3,000; Films and Disks Galore, $4,000; Rental Properties, Inc., $0.00.

   DO: Add the vendors and the balances listed above
Click **Yes** on the **Adding Vendors with open balances** screen

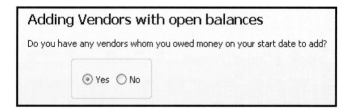

Enter **DVD and Video Supplies** as the Vendor Name
Tab to or click **Balance due on start date**, enter **3,000**

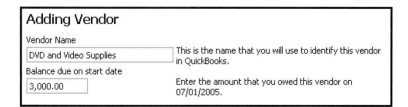

Repeat the steps above to add the other two vendors

Click **No** for **Adding another vendor**
- If a person's name was part of a vendor name, you would enter the name last name, first name.
- The Vendors topic is complete.

ACCOUNTS TOPIC

In this section of the Interview, balances will be entered for balance sheet accounts. Balance Sheet accounts are the assets (things owned), liabilities (things owed), and the owner's equity (owner's Capital, Investment, and Drawing accounts).

MEMO

DATE: July 1, 2005

Set up the following Balance Sheet accounts and balances:

MasterCard, Statement date: 6/30/05, $500
Store Equipment Loan, $3,000, Long-term liability
Store Fixtures Loan, $3,500, Long-term liability
Checking, Statement date: 6/30/05, $16,586, Bank Account No. 123-456-7890
Prepaid Insurance, Other Current Asset, $1,200
Office Supplies, Other Current Asset, $350
Sales Supplies, Other Current Asset, $500
Store Equipment, Fixed Asset, Depreciation: Yes, Original Cost: $8,000, Depreciation as of 07/01/05: $800
Store Fixtures, Fixed Asset, Depreciation: Yes, Original Cost: $15,000, Depreciation as of 07/01/05: $1,500

DO: Add the accounts and balances listed above
             Click **More**, read the information about Balance Sheet accounts, click **OK**

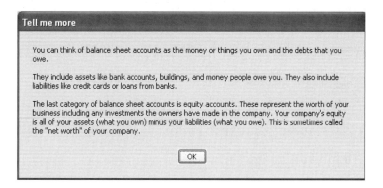

Click **Yes** to set up a credit card account

Enter **MasterCard** as the **name**

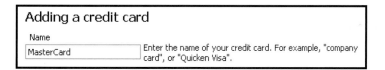

Enter **063005** as the Statement Ending Date
Tab to or click **Statement Ending Balance**, enter **500**

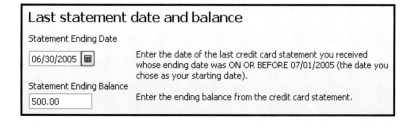

Because there are no additional credit cards to be added, click **No**

Adding another credit card

You have just added a credit card account. To the right is your current list of credit card accounts.

Do you want to add another credit card account?

○ Yes ⊙ No

Credit Card Accounts

MasterCard

Click **No** for **Adding lines of credit**

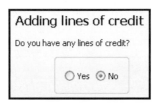

Adding lines of credit

Do you have any lines of credit?

○ Yes ⊙ No

Because there are loans for store fixtures and store equipment, click **Yes** to add Loans and Notes Payable

Loans and Notes Payable

Would you like to set up an account to track a loan or note payable? Loans and notes payable are tracked in "liability" accounts.

⊙ Yes ○ No

You must set up a separate QuickBooks liability account for each loan account you have.

Loans and notes are the two most common examples of liability accounts. QuickBooks sets up some kinds of liability accounts for you automatically if you charge sales tax, use payroll, or use accounts payable.

If you have other kinds of liabilities you would like to track with QuickBooks, enter them now as well.

Enter **Store Equipment Loan** as the Name
Tab to or click **Unpaid Balance on**, enter **3,000**
Since the store equipment loan is longer than one year, click **Long Term Liability**

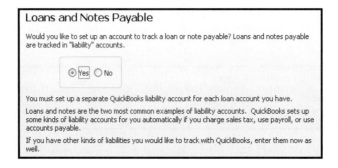

Adding a loan (liability) account

Name

Store Equipment Loan

Enter the name of your loan.

Unpaid Balance on 07/01/2005

3,000.00

Enter the balance of the loan (NOT the original amount of the loan) as of your start date. If you obtained this loan after your start date, enter 0 for the balance of the loan. After you finish the EasyStep interview, use QuickBooks to enter a loan deposit for the date on which you received the loan.

☑ Long Term Liability

Click here if this loan will not be paid off in a year. See Tell Me More below for further explanation.

Click **Yes** to add the remaining **Loan and Notes Payable** account

- Does your list of liabilities match the following?

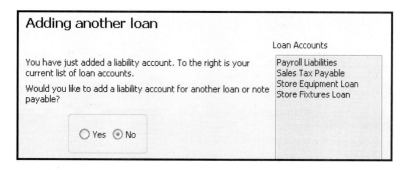

Click **No** for Adding another loan
Click **Yes** to Add a bank account

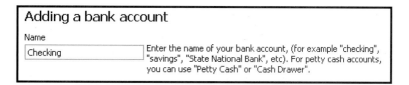

Enter **Checking** as the name of the account
- Traditionally, the main bank account is called *Cash*. However, Checking is a more appropriate name than Cash because it really defines the account.

Enter **063005** as the Statement Ending Date
Tab to or click **Statement Ending Balance**, enter **16586**
Enter the Bank Account number **123-456-7890**
Do not enter a check reorder number

Bank account setup

Statement Ending Date

| 06/30/2005 🔳 | Enter the date of the last bank statement you received whose ending date was ON OR BEFORE 07/01/2005 (the date you chose as the starting date for transaction entry).

Statement Ending Balance

| 16,586.00 | Enter the ending balance from the statement

Bank Account Number

| 123-456-7890 | Enter bank account number.

Check Reorder Number

| _____ | Remind me to order checks when I print this check number

Click **No** for Adding another bank account

Adding another bank account

Bank Accounts

You have just added a bank account. To the right is your current list of bank accounts.

| Checking

Would you like to add another bank account?

○ Yes ⊙ No

Remember, QuickBooks classifies all checking, savings, and money market accounts as bank accounts. We also recommend that you set up your petty cash accounts as bank accounts.

Click **Yes** for printing checks and deposit slips in QuickBooks
Read the screen for Introduction to assets
Click **Yes** to set up Asset accounts
Enter **Prepaid Insurance** as the Name
Click **More** to get additional information regarding fixed, current, and other assets

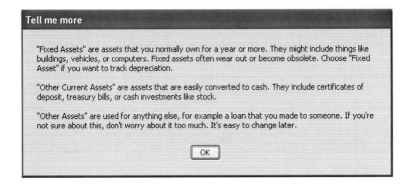

Tell me more

"Fixed Assets" are assets that you normally own for a year or more. They might include things like buildings, vehicles, or computers. Fixed assets often wear out or become obsolete. Choose "Fixed Asset" if you want to track depreciation.

"Other Current Assets" are assets that are easily converted to cash. They include certificates of deposit, treasury bills, or cash investments like stock.

"Other Assets" are used for anything else, for example a loan that you made to someone. If you're not sure about this, don't worry about it too much. It's easy to change later.

[OK]

Click the drop-down list arrow for **Type**, click **Other Current Asset**
Enter **1,200** as the Asset value

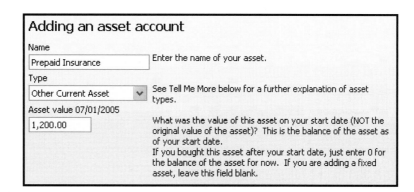

Add the additional Other Current Asset accounts listed in the Memo

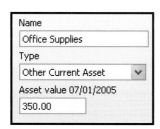 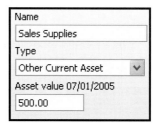

Add the Fixed Asset accounts listed in the Memo

Enter **Store Equipment** as the Name

Click the drop-down list arrow for **Type**, click **Fixed Asset**

- Notice that the Asset Value section becomes a gray color and cannot be accessed.

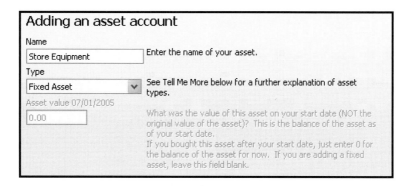

Click **Yes** to track **Depreciation**

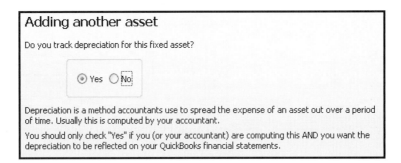

Enter **8,000** as the Original Cost

Tab to or click **Depreciation as of 07/01/05**, enter **800**

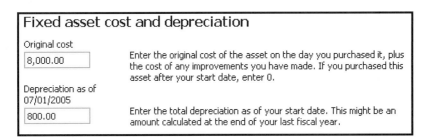

Add the other fixed asset

Click **No** when all assets have been added

Compare your list of assets to those shown below:

Read the **Introduction to Equity Accounts**

- Notice that QuickBooks Pro has automatically set up two equity accounts: Opening Balance Equity (this is actually the owner's capital account) and Retained Earnings (where QuickBooks Pro accumulates the Net Income for the business year after year unless an adjustment is made).

Your equity accounts

	Equity Accounts
To the right is the list of equity accounts which QuickBooks has added for you.	Opening Bal Equity Retained Earnings

- The Opening Balance section and Accounts topic are complete.

WHAT'S NEXT SECTION

This section contains recommendations for additional tasks that can be handled as part of the EasyStep Interview.

MEMO
DATE: July 1, 2005

None of the items listed applies to Movies & More at this time. Complete the EasyStep Interview.

 DO: Click **Next** and read each of the screens in this section

What's Next recommendations

We have recommendations for tasks that you may want to handle next.

- Create a backup copy of your new QuickBooks company.
- Enter your "historical" transactions.
- Set up your users and passwords.
- Customize your forms.
- Set up your 1099 tracking.
- Sign-up for Intuit Payroll Service.
- Visit our QuickBooks web site at: www.quickbooks.com.
- Order QuickBooks checks and forms.

Press Next to see more detail.

Click **Leave** to end the EasyStep Interview

PREFERENCES

Many preferences for the use of QuickBooks Pro are selected during the EasyStep Interview. However, there may be some preferences you would like to select in addition to those marked during the interview. The Preferences section has 18 areas that may be customized: Accounting, Checking, Desktop View, Finance Charge, General, Integrated Applications, Jobs & Estimates, Payroll & Employees, Purchases & Vendors, Reminders, Reports & Graphs, Sales & Customers, Sales Tax, Send Forms, Service Connection, Spelling, Tax: 1099, and Time Tracking. Not all the possible changes will be discussed in this chapter; however, some of the choices will be explored.

MEMO

DATE: July 1, 2005

Open the Preferences screen and explore the choices available for each of the 18 areas.

DO: In the following sections, click on the icons for the category and explore the choices available on both the My Preferences tabs and the Company tabs, but do not make any changes
Access Preferences from the Edit menu

ACCOUNTING PREFERENCES

This screen is accessed to select the use of account numbers. Selecting Use Account Numbers provides an area for each account to be given a number during editing. Use audit trail is an important choice if you want QuickBooks Pro to track all transactions (including any and all changes made to transactions). This allows an owner to see everything that has been entered, including deleted transactions, error corrections, etc. This is an important choice if there is a possibility of an employee making unauthorized changes. The closing date for a period is entered on the Company Preferences tab for Accounting Preferences.

CHECKING PREFERENCES

The preferences listed for checking allows QuickBooks Pro to print account names on check vouchers, warn of duplicate check numbers, change the check date when a check is printed, start with the payee field on a check, and set default accounts to use for payroll checks.

DESKTOP VIEW PREFERENCES

 The Desktop View preference allows you to set My Preferences to customize your QuickBooks screens, to display navigators, to save the desktop, select color schemes, and sounds.

FINANCE CHARGE PREFERENCES

 This preference allows you to provide information about finance charges if they are collected. You can even tell QuickBooks Pro if you want to collect finance charges. The information you may provide includes the annual interest rate, the minimum finance charge, the grace period, the finance charge account, and whether to calculate finance charges from the due date or from the invoice/billed date.

GENERAL PREFERENCES

 General preferences is used to set the time format, to display the year as four digits, to indicate decimal point placement, to set warning screens and beeps, to turn on messages, and to automatically recall the last transaction for a name.

INTEGRATED APPLICATIONS PREFERENCES

 Integrated preferences are used to manage all applications that interact with the current QuickBooks company file.

JOBS & ESTIMATES PREFERENCES

 This preference allows you to indicate the status of jobs and to choose whether or not to use estimates.

PAYROLL & EMPLOYEES PREFERENCES

 Payroll preferences include selecting the payroll features, if any, you wish to use. Items for printing on checks and vouchers are selected. You may choose the method by which employees are sorted. Employee Defaults may be accessed from this screen. Once accessed, the Employee Defaults may be changed and/or modified.

PURCHASES & VENDORS PREFERENCES

This section allows you to activate the inventory and purchase orders feature of the program. Warnings if there is not enough inventory to sell, warnings regarding duplicate purchases orders, and warnings for duplicate bill numbers are set on this screen. The number of days for bill due dates is also selected in the Purchases & Vendors preferences. QuickBooks can be instructed to automatically apply discounts and credits.

REMINDERS PREFERENCES

Items to include on the Reminders List are selected in the Reminders preferences. In this section you may also select whether or not to have the Reminders List appear when the QuickBooks Pro program is started.

REPORTS & GRAPHS PREFERENCES

Accrual or cash reporting is selected on this screen. Preferences for report aging and account display within reports are selected in this section. Drawing graphs in 2D or using patterns is an available option. QuickBooks Pro can be instructed to show a prompt to refresh reports and graphs or to refresh them automatically. We can tell QuickBooks assign accounts to the sections of the Statement of Cash Flows. In addition, report formats may be customized on this screen. In previous chapters, we have changed the preferences to have the reports refresh automatically and have modified the report format to remove the Date Prepared, Time Prepared, and Report Basis by accessing this preference.

SALES & CUSTOMERS PREFERENCES

Shipping methods, markup percentages, and usual FOB (free on board) preferences may be indicated on this screen. In addition, selections to automatically apply payments, to track reimbursed expenses as income, to warn about duplicate invoice numbers, and whether or not to use price levels are made in this section.

SALES TAX PREFERENCES

 The Sales Tax preferences indicate whether or not you charge sales tax. If you do collect sales tax, the default sales tax codes, when you need to pay the sales tax, when sales tax is owed, the most common sales tax, and whether or not to mark taxable amounts are selected on this screen.

SEND FORMS PREFERENCES

 Default text for invoices, estimates, and statements are prepared for invoices that are sent to customers by e-mail.

SERVICE CONNECTION PREFERENCES

 You can specify how you and other company file users log in to QuickBooks Business Services. You may select to automatically connect to QuickBooks Business Services network without passwords or require passwords before connecting. This preference is used to select whether or not Service updates are automatically downloaded from the Intuit server to your computer.

SPELLING PREFERENCES

 You can check the spelling in the Description, Memo, and Message fields of most sales forms invoices, estimates, sales receipts, credit memos, and purchase orders, and text fields on certain forms and lists. You can run Spell Checker automatically or change the preference and run the Spell Checker manually.

TAX: 1099 PREFERENCES

 This preference is used to indicate whether or not you file 1099-MISC forms. If you do file 1099s, you are given categories; you may select accounts and thresholds for the categories on this screen.

TIME TRACKING PREFERENCES

The Time Tracking preference is used to tell QuickBooks Pro to track time. Tracking time is useful if you bill by the hour.

CHART OF ACCOUNTS

Using the EasyStep Interview to set up a company is a user-friendly way to establish the basic structure of the company. However, the Chart of Accounts created by QuickBooks Pro may not be the exact Chart of Accounts you wish to use in your business. The Chart of Accounts is not only a listing of the account names and balances but also the General Ledger used by the business. As in textbook accounting, the General Ledger/Chart of Accounts is the book of final entry. In earlier chapters, instructions directed you to view the Register for an account. This is actually a procedure used to view all of the transaction details listed for one General Ledger account.

In many of the earlier chapters, account names were changed, accounts were deleted, and accounts were made inactive. This was done to give you experience in customizing a QuickBooks Pro Chart of Accounts/General Ledger. In QuickBooks Pro your General Ledger accounts may or may not have account numbers. If your company uses account numbers, they must be added after the EasyStep Interview is complete. To add account numbers, each account must be edited individually.

MEMO
DATE: July 1, 2005

Since Movies & More does not use account numbers, they do not need to be added.
However, the Chart of Accounts/General Ledger should be customized by:

Deleting: Automobile Expense, Franchise Fees, Travel & Ent. including subaccounts.
Also delete the subaccounts listed under Sales.

Changing the name: Equity Account: Opening Bal Equity to **David Watson, Capital**;
Income Account: Sales to **Sales Income**

Changing a subaccount: Expense Account: **Office Supplies** a subaccount of Supplies

Making inactive: Merchant Fees

Adding:
Equity Account: **David Watson, Investment**; Subaccount of David Watson, Capital;
Balance, $5,000
Equity Account: **David Watson, Drawing**; Subaccount of David Watson, Capital;
Balance, $0.00

DO: Make the changes indicated above

Open the Chart of Accounts as instructed in previous chapters

Position the cursor on **Automobile Expense**, **Ctrl+D**, click **OK** to delete

Repeat to delete the other accounts listed in the memo

Position the cursor on **Opening Bal Equity**, click the **Account** button, click **Edit**,
enter **David Watson, Capital** as the account name, click **OK**

Repeat basic procedures to rename the other accounts listed in the memo

Edit the **Office Supplies** account, click the drop-down list arrow for Subaccount,
click **Supplies**, click **OK**

Position the cursor on **Merchant Fees**, click the **Account** button, click **Make
Inactive**

Click **Account** button, click **New**, click drop-down list arrow next to **Type**, click
Equity, tab to or click **Name**, enter **David Watson, Investment**, click
Subaccount, click **David Watson, Capital**, tab to or click **Balance**, enter
5,000 (if necessary, enter **07/01/05** as the date), click **OK**

Repeat basic procedures to add the other accounts listed in the Memo

When all changes have been made, print the **Chart of Accounts** in Portrait
orientation

Click the **Account** button, click **Print List**, click **OK** on the List Reports
screen, click **Print**

CUSTOMER INFORMATION

When customers were added during the EasyStep Interview, only the customer names and balances were entered. QuickBooks Pro actually keeps much more detailed information regarding customers. This includes a customer's name, address, telephone and fax numbers, credit terms, credit limits, and sales tax information. This detailed information must be added after the EasyStep Interview is completed. The Customer List is also known as the Accounts Receivable Subsidiary Ledger. Whenever a transaction is entered for a customer, it is automatically posted to the General Ledger account and the Accounts Receivable Subsidiary Ledger account.

MEMO
DATE: July 1, 2005

Add information for the customers (all terms are Net 30, all customers are taxable, and pay CA Sales Tax):

Goldin, Bernard: 1980 A Street, San Diego, CA 92101; 760-555-3694; Credit Limit $500.

Morales, Raul: 719 4th Avenue, San Diego, CA 92101; 760-555-5478; Credit Limit $1,000.

Reese, Yvonne: 37601 State Street, San Diego, CA 92101; 760-555-2235; E-mail Yvonne@123.com; Credit Limit $750.

Thompsen, Rick: 2210 Columbia Street, San Diego, CA 92101; 760-555-7632; Credit Limit $300.

DO: Add the customer information to each customer's account

Open Customer List as described in previous chapters

Click **Goldin, Bernard**, **Ctrl+E** to edit, tab to or click in the fields where information is to be entered on the Address Info, Additional Info, and Payment Info tabs, enter the appropriate information for each tab, click **OK** when finished

- Make sure the Bill To section shows Bernard Goldin

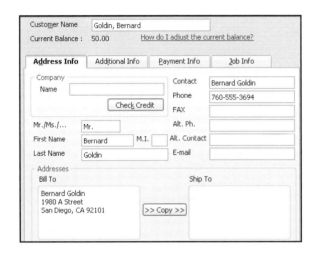

Repeat for each customer

Print the Customer:Job List in Portrait orientation, click **Customer:Job** button, click **Print List**, click **OK** on the Print List screen, click **Print**, close the list

VENDOR INFORMATION

When vendors were added during the EasyStep Interview, only the vendor names and balances were entered. QuickBooks Pro actually keeps much more detailed information regarding vendors. This includes the vendor's name, address, contact person, telephone and fax numbers, credit terms, and credit limits. This detailed information must be added after the EasyStep Interview is completed. The Vendor List is also known as the Accounts Payable Subsidiary Ledger. Whenever a transaction is entered for a vendor, it is automatically posted to the General Ledger account and the Accounts Payable Ledger account.

MEMO

DATE: July 1, 2005

Add the information for the individual vendors (all terms are 2% 10 Net 30):

DVD and Video Supplies: 10855 Western Avenue, Los Angeles, CA 90012; Contact Dennis Gonzalez; Phone 310-555-6971; Fax 310-555-1796; Credit Limit $15,000
Films and Disks Galore: 7758 Broadway Avenue, San Diego, CA 92101; Contact Dori Kwan; Phone 760-555-4489; Fax 760-555-9844; Credit Limit $10,000
Rental Properties, Inc.: 2687 University Avenue, San Diego, CA 92110; Contact Valerie Green; Phone 760-555-2589; Fax 760-555-9852; Credit Limit $5,000

The vendors who receive tax and withholding payments need to be edited and/or added. There are no terms and no credit limits:

State Board of Equalization: 7829 West 17th Street, Sacramento, CA 94267; Phone 916-555-1000
Employment Development Department; 10327 Wilshire Boulevard, Los Angeles, CA 90007; Phone 310-555-8877
CA State Bank; 302 Second Street, San Diego, CA 92114; Phone 760-555-9889
Medical and Dental Ins., Inc.; 20865 Wilshire Boulevard, Santa Monica, CA 90321; Phone 310-555-4646

DO: Add the information for the vendors listed above

Open the **Vendor List** as described in previous chapters

Click **DVD and Video Supplies**, **Ctrl+E** to edit, tab to or click in the fields where information is to be entered on the Address Info and the Additional Info tabs, enter the appropriate information for each field, click **OK** when finished

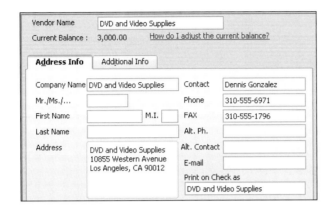

Repeat for each vendor
Print the **Vendor List** in Portrait orientation, click the **Vendor:Job** button, click
   Print List, click **Print**, close the list

EMPLOYEES

As with customers and vendors, employees may be added, deleted, or made inactive at any time.
Once an employee template is created and tax liabilities are associated with a vendor, employees
are added.

COMPLETE THE PAYROLL SETUP INTERVIEW

Before adding employees, you complete the payroll setup interview. It guides you through
setting up the payroll in QuickBooks. It helps you select your payroll option, set up payroll taxes
for your company, and set up common compensation and benefits correctly. Then it leads you
through setting up individual employees and year-to-date payroll amounts so you can start doing
payroll through QuickBooks. When establishing the Employee Defaults, you will specify which
payroll items apply to all or most of the employees of the company. Payroll items are used to
identify and/or track the various amounts that affect a paycheck. There are items for salaries and
wages, each kind of tax, each type of other deduction, commissions, and company-paid benefits.
QuickBooks Pro automatically sets up the payroll items for salaries, federal taxes, and state
taxes. Payroll tax liabilities and payroll withholding items need to be associated with a vendor in
order to have payments processed appropriately. Establishing a pay period, identifying payroll
items, providing tax information, and determining sick/vacation defaults creates an Employee
Template, which you can use to automatically fill in information when you set up individual
employees. Once the Employee Template has been created and payroll setup is complete, the
template will be used to add employees. When you use the Employee List to add a new
employee, the Employee Template appears on the screen, and you fill in the blanks.

MEMO

DATE: July 1, 2005

Complete the Payroll Setup Interview.

The Payroll Option is Manual Calculation
The Company Payroll State is CA
Accept the Federal Payroll Tax information shown
California EDD Account number is 999-9999-9
CA-State Unemployment Tax is 4% for each quarter
Payroll list items for wages, tips, and taxable fringe benefits are:
    Salary Regular, Salary Sick, Salary Vacation
    Hourly Wage Regular, Hourly Wage Overtime, Hourly Wage Sick, Hourly Wage
        Vacation
Insurance Benefits are:
    Health Insurance Emp (Taxable), Dental Insurance Emp (Taxable)
Retirement Benefits: None
Other Payments and Deductions: None

Vendors for Payroll Liabilities:
    Federal Withholding, Federal Unemployment, Social Security, Medicare: State Bank
    CA Withholding, CA Unemployment Company, CA Disability Employee, CA
        Employment Training Tax: Employment Development Department
    Dental Insurance and Health Insurance: Medical and Dental Ins., Inc.

Employee Defaults:
    Pay Period: Semimonthly
    Additions, Deductions and Company Contributions: Dental Insurance Emp Taxable,
        Health Insurance Emp Taxable
    Federal Taxes: Medicare, Social Security, Federal Unemployment Tax (Company
        Paid)
    State Taxes: State Worked and State Subject to Withholding CA, SUI (Company
        Paid), SDI
    Other: CA-Employment Training Tax
    Sick/Vacation: Beginning of year accrual period

DO: Click **Setup Payroll** on the Employees Navigator or on the Employees menu

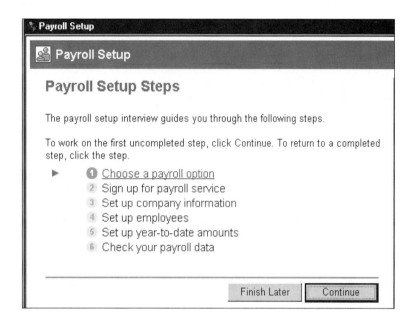

Click **Choose a Payroll Option**

Since we are processing the payroll manually and do not wish to use a
     QuickBooks Payroll service, scroll through the payroll options until you get to
     the bottom of the screen, and click **Learn more** at the end of the statement
     "If you don't want to use an Intuit Payroll Service, you can still use
     QuickBooks to prepare your payroll. Learn more"

Scroll down the screen until you see

I choose to manually calculate payroll taxes

Click **I choose to manually calculate payroll taxes**
Click **Setup company information**
Click **Setup Payroll Taxes**
Click **California** for the Company Payroll State
Click **Continue**
Accept everything on the payroll taxes screen by clicking **Continue**
Enter **999-9999-9** for the California EDD Account number
Enter **4** as the percentage for each quarter CA Unemployment for the Company
Accept everything else on the California Payroll Taxes screen by clicking
     Continue

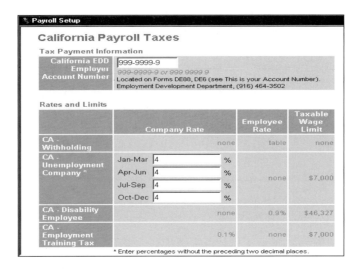

Click **Setup wages, tips, benefits, and misc. payroll items**

On the first of the four screens of commonly used Payroll Items, click Salary Regular, Salary Sick, Salary Vacation, Hourly Wage Regular, Hourly Wage Overtime, Hourly Wage Sick, and Hourly Wage Vacation

Click **Create** to add to My Payroll Items

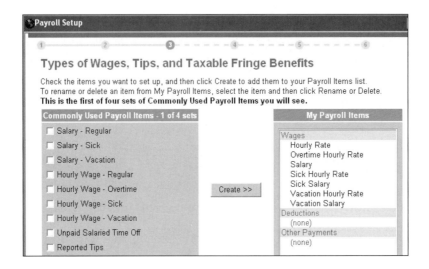

Click **Continue**

On the Insurance Benefits window, click **Health Insurance Emp (taxable)** and **Dental Insurance Emp (taxable)**

Click **Create**, click **Continue**

There are no Retirement Benefits, click **Continue**

There are no other Payments or Deductions, verify your Payroll Items list

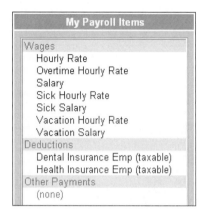

Click **Continue**

Click **Enter Vendors for Payroll Liabilities**

Click the Paid-to drop-down list arrow for federal taxes, click **CA State Bank**

Click the Paid-to drop-down list arrow for CA taxes, click **Employment Development Department**

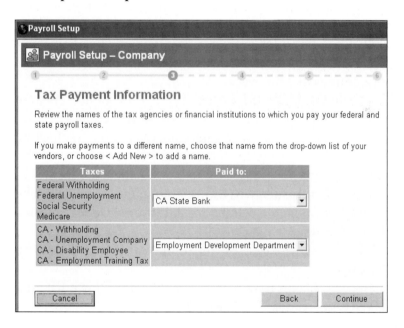

Click **Continue**

Click the Payable to Vendor drop-down list arrow, click **Medical and Dental Ins., Inc.** for both the Dental Insurance and the Health Insurance vendor

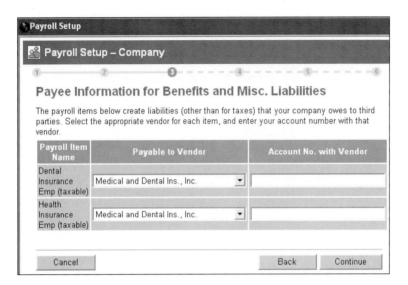

Click **Continue**

Click **Enter default payroll settings for new employees**

Click **Edit**

Click the drop-down list arrow for **Pay Period**, click **Semimonthly**

Do not click any of the items shown in the list of payroll items to indicate the type of Earnings of employees

- The template is created so that information common to *all* employees may be entered. Because some of Movies & More's employees are paid on an hourly basis and others are paid a salary, there are no payroll earnings items common to *all* or even most of the employees.

Because *all* employees may elect to participate in the **Dental Insurance (Emp)** and **Medical Insurance (Emp)**, both items are added to the template

Click in the **Item Name** column for **Additions, Deductions and Company Contributions**

Click the drop-down list arrow for **Item Name**, click **Dental Insurance Emp Taxable**

Click the next line in **Item Name**, click the drop-down list arrow, and click **Health Insurance Emp Taxable**

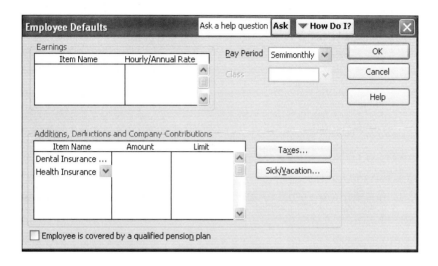

Click the **Taxes** button
- Since all employees are subject to federal withholding, Social Security, FUTA, and Medicare, accept the information shown on the Federal tab.

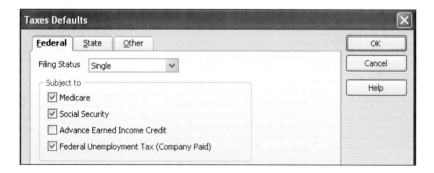

Click the **State** tab
Click the drop-down list arrow for **State Worked**, click **CA**,
SUI (Company Paid) and **SDI** should be checked
If not, click **SUI (Company Paid)** and **SDI** to check
Click the drop-down list arrow for **State Subject to Withholding**, click **CA**,

Click the **Other** tab

Click the drop-down list arrow for Item Name, click **CA-Employment Training Tax**

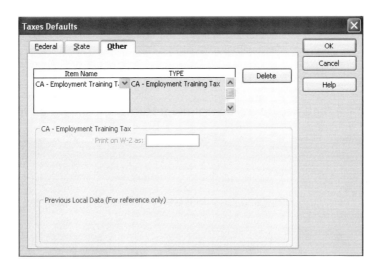

Click **OK**

Click **Sick/Vacation** button

- If the majority of employees are given the same number of sick and/or vacation hours for an accrual period, complete this section. If you use different accrual periods for employees or if employees earn different amounts of sick and/or vacation hours, do not complete this section of the Employee Defaults.

Select **Beginning of year** as the accrual periods for both Sick and Vacation

- Since the employees accumulate different amounts of hours for sick and vacation time, leave these fields blank. There is no maximum number of hours nor do we reset hours each new year, so leave these fields blank.

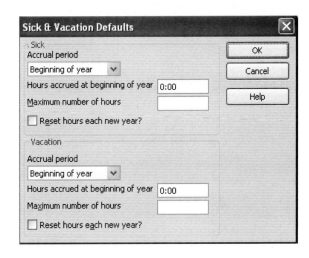

Click **OK** for Sick/Vacation Defaults

This completes the Employee Defaults for the Employee Template, click **OK**

Click **Continue** for Default Payroll Settings

Click **Done** for Company Setup Tasks

ADD EMPLOYEES USING EMPLOYEE TEMPLATE

Once the Company Setup is complete, the Employees Setup portion of the Payroll Setup is completed. Employees are added at this time.

MEMO

DATE: July 1, 2005

Add individual employee information (only the information that needs to be entered is given below; if information is not provided, it is 0):

Mr. Morris Carter: Social Security No. 100-55-2525; Male; Birthday 12/28/1949;1077 Columbia Street, San Diego, CA 92101; 760-555-1232; Foreign Languages Spanish; Salary $35,000; Dental $35; Medical $75; Federal: Head of Household, 4 Allowances; State: Head of Household, 4 Allowances; Hours Available: Sick 40; Vacation 40; Sick/Vacation Accrual Period: Beginning of year; Sick/Vacation Hours at beginning of year: 40; Sick/Vacation Maximum Hours 120; Regular Employee, Hired 03/17/1995;

Ms. Carrie Benson: Social Security No. 100-55-3274; Female; Birthday 05/23/1957; 751 7th Street, San Diego, CA 92101; 760-555-3654; Foreign Languages None; Salary $26,000; Dental $25; Medical $50; Federal: Single, 0 Allowances; State: Single, 0 Allowances; Available: Sick 20; Vacation 20; Sick/Vacation Accrual Period: Beginning of year; Sick/Vacation Hours at beginning of year: 40; Sick/Vacation Maximum Hours 120; Regular Employee, Hired 04/23/1996

Mr. James Hansen, Social Security No. 100-55-6961; Male; Birthday 04/23/1973; 2985 A Street, San Diego, CA 92101; 760-555-9874; Foreign Languages None; Hourly Regular Rate $22.50; Dental $20; Medical $40; Federal: Married, 2 Allowances; State: Married (2 incomes), 2 Allowances; Available: Sick 50; Vacation 40; Sick/Vacation Accrual Period: Beginning of year; Sick/Vacation Hours at beginning of year: 40; Sick/Vacation Maximum Hours 120; Regular Employee, Hired 06/30/1996;

Ms. Sandra Roberts, Social Security No. 100-55-8723; Female; Birthday 07/27/1975; 159 Kettner Street, San Diego, CA 92101; 760-555-8591; Foreign Languages Spanish; Hourly Regular Rate $10; Federal: Married, 1 Allowance; State: Married (1 income), 1 Allowance; Hours Available: Sick 0; Vacation 0; Sick/Vacation Accrual Period: Beginning of year; Sick/Vacation Hours at beginning of year: 40; Sick/Vacation Maximum Hours 120; Regular Employee, Hired 05/02/1996;

DO: Add the employees and the information listed above

Click **Set up employees**

Click the **Add Employee** button

Use the information in the Memo to complete the **Personal tab,** the **Address and Contact** tab, and the **Additional Info** tab for Morris Carter

Enter the Personal information about Morris on the Personal tab

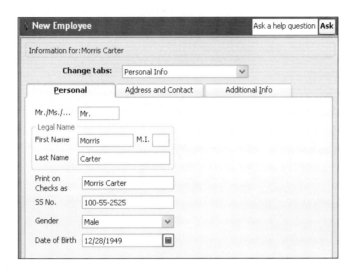

Click the **Address and Contact** tab and enter the appropriate information

Click the **Additional Info** tab
- This tab allows custom fields to be created. Custom fields contain information such as a foreign languages, name of spouse, and so on. Custom fields may be created and used for additional information for employees, customers, and vendors.

Click **Define Fields** button

Enter **Foreign Languages** as the first label, click the check box under **Employees** to use for employees

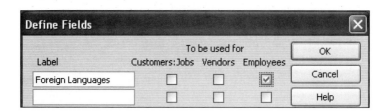

Click **OK**

Enter **Spanish** as Morris's Foreign Language

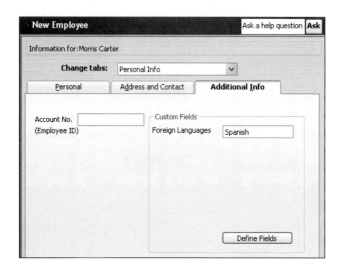

Click the drop-down list arrow for **Change tabs**

Click **Payroll and Compensation Info**

Click in the **Item Name** column

Click the drop-down list arrow for **Item Name**, click **Salary**

Tab to or click **Hour/Annual Rate**, enter **35000**

- Pay Period should be Semimonthly; if it is not, click the drop-down list arrow, click **Semimonthly**.

Click in the **Amount** column next to Dental Insurance, enter **35**

Tab to or click the **Amount** column next to Medical Insurance, enter **75**

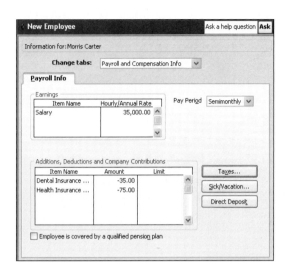

Click the **Taxes** button

Complete the federal tax information:

Click the drop-down list for **Filing Status**, click **Head of Household**

Tab to or click **Allowances**, enter **4**

Extra Withholding is **0.00**

Morris is subject to Medicare, Social Security, and Federal Unemployment Tax (Company Paid); if necessary, click to select

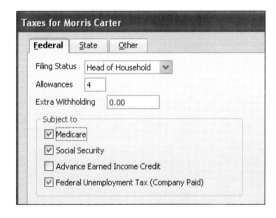

Click the **State** tab

- The **State Worked** is CA, **SUI** and **SDI** should be selected
- The **State Subject to Withholding** is **CA**

Tab to or click **Filing Status**, click the drop-down list arrow, click **Head of Household**

Tab to or click **Allowances**, enter **4**

- Extra Withholding is **0.00** and Estimated Deductions are **0**.
- There are no local taxes.

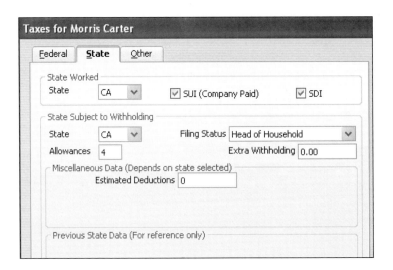

Click **Other** tab
Click **OK**

Click the **Sick/Vacation** button
Enter **40** as the Sick Hours available as of 07/01/05

- Unless you change the date of the computer, you may show the current date rather than 07/01/05. If this is the case, continue with the setup and enter the 40 hours.
- Accrual period should be Beginning of year

Hours accrued at beginning of year enter **40.00**
Maximum number of hours enter **120.00**

- Reset hours each new year? should *not* be selected.

Tab to or click **Vacation Hours available as of 07/01/2005**, enter **40**

- Unless you change the date of the computer, you may show the current date rather than 07/01/05. If this is the case, continue with the setup and enter the 40 hours.
- Accrual period should be Beginning of year,

Hours accrued at beginning of year enter **40.00**
Maximum number of hours enter **120.00**

- Reset hours each new year? should *not* be selected.

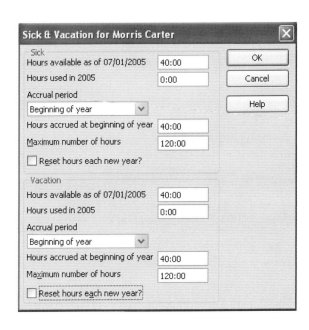

Click **OK**
Click the drop-down list arrow for **Change tabs**
Click **Employment Info**
Enter his Hire Date of **03/17/1995**
Employment Details should be **Regular**
- If not, click the drop-down list arrow and click Regular

Click **OK** to add Morris Carter
Click Continue
Click **Add Employee**
Repeat the above procedures to add the other employees listed in the Memo
When all the employees have been added, click **Continue**, click **Employee List**
- When complete, the Employee List will show all four employees.

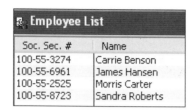

- Because the employee names were not entered last name then first name, the employee names are alphabetized by the first name.

Close the Employee List

Click **Continue** to return to Employee Setup

Click **Continue**

ADD YEAR-TO-DATE AMOUNTS

The year-to-date amounts are summaries of employee paychecks, the liabilities, and the deductions for the year to date. Year-to-date amounts may be entered as an amount for each quarter to date or, if information is being entered for the current quarter, pay period by pay period. Entering the amounts for the year is the fastest way to enter this historical information. Entering the amounts by the quarter allows each quarter to be summarized and allows quarterly reports to be created.

Memo

DATE: July 1, 2005

Enter the payroll summaries for each employee for 1/1/05 through 3/31/05 and 4/1/05 through 6/30/05. Use the information provided in the following Employee Summary Table. The information in the table shows the amounts for one quarter. Repeat the same figures for the second quarter.

 DO: Enter the year-to-date summary information for each employee by quarter

EMPLOYEE SUMMARY TABLE AMOUNTS PER QUARTER FOR JAN-MAR 2005 AND APR-JUN 2005				
	Colleen Benson	**James Hansen**	**Morris Carter**	**Sandra Roberts**
Item Name	Salary	Hourly Regular Rate	Salary	Hourly Regular Rate
Period Amount	6,499.98	10,800.00	8,749.98	4,800.00
Hours for Period	480	480	480	480

Dental Insurance Employee	150.00	120.00	210.00	0
Medical Insurance Employee	300.00	240.00	450.00	0
Federal Withholding	876.00	1,182.00	816.00	378.00
Social Security Company	403.02	669.60	542.52	292.60
Social Security Employee	403.02	669.60	542.52	292.60
Medicare Company	94.26	156.60	126.90	69.60
Medicare Employee	94.26	156.60	126.90	69.60
Federal Unemployment	28.00	28.00	28.00	28.00
CA Withholding	189.90	517.86	91.62	42.06
CA Disability Employee	32.52	54.00	43.74	24.00
CA Unemployment Company	140.00	140.00	140.00	140.00
CA Employment Training Tax	140.00	140.00	140.00	140.00

Click **Setup year-to-date amounts** on the Payroll Setup Steps screen
Click **Setup YTD amounts**

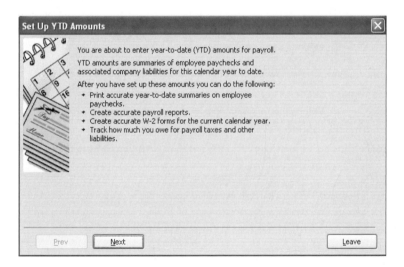

Click **Next**
The YTD summaries should affect accounts as of **07/01/2005**

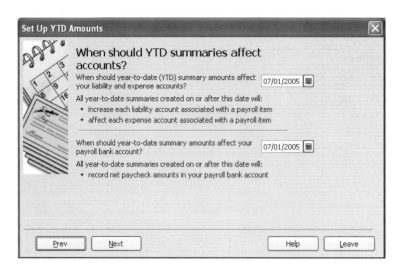

Make sure both dates are **07/01/2005**, click **Next**
The Earliest QuickBooks payroll date is **07/01/2005**

Make sure the date is **07/01/2005**, click **Next**
To enter the YTD summary for Colleen Benson, click **Enter Summary**

Employee summary information

To enter a YTD summary for an employee, select the employee's name and then click Enter Summary.

Employee	Jan-Mar	Apr-Jun
Carrie Benson	--	--
James Hansen	--	--
Morris Carter	--	--
Sandra Roberts	--	--

Enter Summary

Enter the information from the Employee Summary for Colleen Benson for the
Jan-Mar quarter

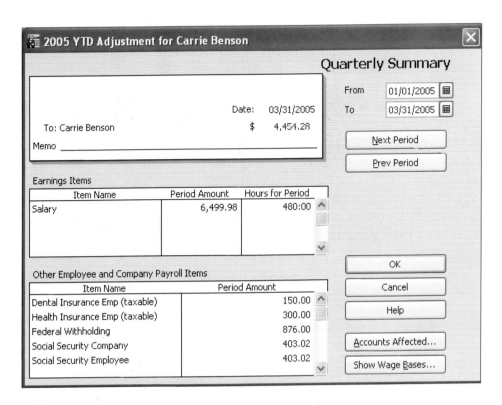

Click **Next Period** and enter the same figures for the Apr-Jun quarter

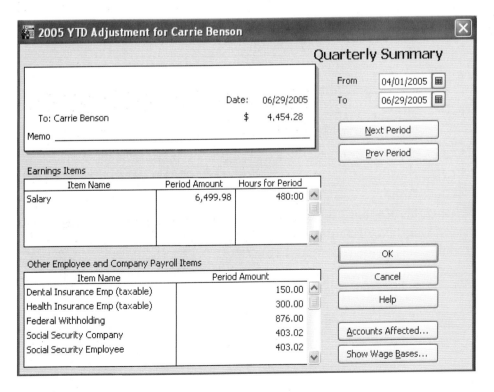

Click **OK**

Employee summary information

To enter a YTD summary for an employee, select the employee's name and then click Enter Summary.

Employee	Jan-Mar	Apr-Jun
Carrie Benson	4,454.28	4,454.28
James Hansen	--	--
Morris Carter	--	--
Sandra Roberts	--	--

Enter Summary

- The YTD information appears for Colleen Benson.
- Repeat the above steps and add the YTD information for the other employees. Remember to repeat the exact same figures for the Apr-Jun quarter as you entered for the Jan-Mar quarter.

Employee summary information

To enter a YTD summary for an employee, select the employee's name and then click Enter Summary.

Employee	Jan-Mar	Apr-Jun
Carrie Benson	4,454.28	4,454.28
James Hansen	7,859.94	7,859.94
Morris Carter	6,469.20	6,469.20
Sandra Roberts	3,993.74	3,993.74

Enter Summary

When all employees have amounts for both quarters, click **Leave**

Click **Continue**

Click **Done**

Click the **Report Finder** on any Navigator, click **Employees & Payroll**, click **Employee Earnings Summary**

The dates of the report are **From 01/01/05 To 06/30/05**

Adjust the column widths, do not print the date prepared, time prepared, or report basis in the header, print the report in landscape orientation

Movies & More--Student's Name
Employee Earnings Summary
January through June 2005

	Dental Insurance Emp (taxable)	Health Insurance Emp (taxable)	TOTAL
Carrie Benson	-300.00	-600.00	10,519.12
James Hansen	-240.00	-480.00	17,988.28
Morris Carter	-420.00	-900.00	14,893.24
Sandra Roberts	0.00	0.00	9,327.88
TOTAL	-960.00	-1,980.00	52,728.52

Partial Report

Close the report

Print the **Payroll Item Listing** for July 1, 2005

Adjust the column widths, do not print the date prepared, time prepared, or report basis in the header, print the report in landscape orientation

Close the report and Report Finder

Click **Lists** on the menu bar

Click **Employee List**

Click **Employee** button, click **Print List**

Click **OK** on the List Reports screen

Print the **Employee List** in portrait orientation, close the **Employee List**

ADJUSTING ENTRIES

When the EasyStep Interview is completed, all existing balances are placed into the Uncategorized Income and Uncategorized Expenses accounts so that the amounts listed will not be interpreted as income or expenses for the current period. This adjustment transfers the amount of income and expenses recorded prior to the current period into the owner's capital account. In actual practice this adjustment would be made at the completion of the EasyStep Interview.

MEMO

DATE: July 1, 2005

Colleen: Make the adjusting entry to transfer Uncategorized Income and Uncategorized Expenses to David Watson's capital account.

DO: Transfer the Uncategorized Income and Expenses as indicated above

Open the Chart of Accounts, double-click on the account **Uncategorized Income**, enter the to and from dates as **07/01/05**, tab to generate the report, note the amount of Uncategorized Income **$1,025.00**, close the report

Movies & More--Student's Name
Account QuickReport
July 1, 2005

◇ Type ◇	Date ◇	Num ◇	Name ◇	Memo ◇	Split ◇	Amount
Uncategorized Income						
Invoice	07/01/2005		Goldin, Bernard	Opening balance	Accounts Receivable	50.00
Invoice	07/01/2005		Morales, Raul	Opening balance	Accounts Receivable	550.00
Invoice	07/01/2005		Reese, Yvonne	Opening balance	Accounts Receivable	350.00
Invoice	07/01/2005		Thompsen, Rick	Opening balance	Accounts Receivable	75.00
Total Uncategorized Income						1,025.00
TOTAL						**1,025.00**

Repeat to determine the balance of the Uncategorized Expenses account

Movies & More--Student's Name
Account QuickReport
July 1, 2005

◇ Type ◇	Date ◇	Num ◇	Name	Memo	◇ Split	◇ Amount
Uncategorized Expenses						
Bill	07/01/2005		DVD and Video Supplies	Opening balance	Accounts Payable	3,000.00
Bill	07/01/2005		Films & Disks Galore	Opening balance	Accounts Payable	4,000.00
Total Uncategorized Expenses						7,000.00
TOTAL						**7,000.00**

Click the **Activities** button at the bottom of the Chart of Accounts, click **Make General Journal Entries**

Enter the date **07/01/05**

Tab to or click **Account**, click the drop-down list arrow, click **Uncategorized Income**, tab to or click **Debit** enter **1025**, tab to or click **Account**, click the drop-down list arrow, click **David Watson, Capital**

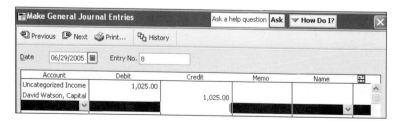

Click **Save & New**

Enter the adjustment to transfer the amount of **Uncategorized Expenses** to **David Watson, Capital**

• Remember, you will debit the Capital account and credit the Uncategorized Expenses account.

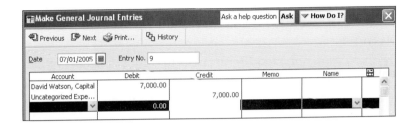

Click **Save & Close**

Close the Chart of Accounts

SPECIFYING A COMPANY LOGO

If you have a special symbol or logo for your company, QuickBooks Pro allows this logo to be printed on checks, paychecks, sales, and purchase forms. The logo must be a bitmap file (the filename has an extension of .bmp) and is added to the desired forms and checks via the printer setup or by customizing a business form.

MEMO

DATE: July 1, 2005

Add Movies & More's name, address, and logo to checks, paychecks, invoice and purchase order.

 DO: Add the Movies & More logo to the above items

- Before completing this portion of the chapter, you should have a copy of the file **MM_Logo.bmp** on the data disk you are using to create the company. The **MM_Logo.bmp** file is located on the CD-ROM that accompanies this text. Instructions for copying the file in Windows using the Explorer are: The disk containing **Movies & More–Student's Name.qbw** is in **A:**, insert the CD-ROM from your text in **D:**, open Windows Explorer by right-clicking the Start button and clicking Explorer, click **(D:)** on the left side of the window, click **MM_Logo.bmp** on the right side of the window, right-click

MM_Logo.bmp, click **Send To**, click **3½ Floppy (A:)**, close Explorer. If you do not have a CD-ROM or you have a different configuration in your classroom, check with your instructor for specific instructions to copy the logo file.

Click the **File** menu, click **Printer Setup**, click **Check/Paycheck**,

- Print company name and address should have a check; if not, click **Print company name and address**, click **Use Logo**

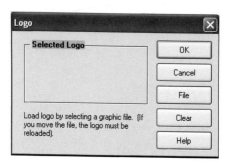

Click **File** button on **Select Logo** screen

Look in should be **3 ½ Floppy (A:)** for the drive location; if not or if you have a different file location, click the correct location for Look in

Click **MM_Logo.bmp**

Click **Open**

If you get a message regarding copying the logo to an images folder, click **Yes**

- When you return to the Logo screen, the logo will be displayed as Selected Logo.

Click **OK** on the Logo screen

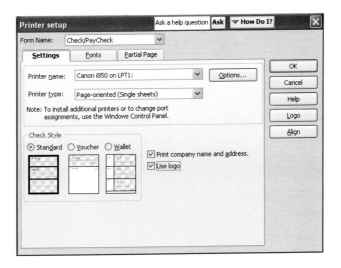

Click **OK** on Printer Setup
Add the Logo to an Invoice
Click **Customers** on the menu bar, click **Create Invoices**
Click **No** on the screen offering help selecting the correct sales form
Click the **Customize** button
Click **Intuit Product Invoice**

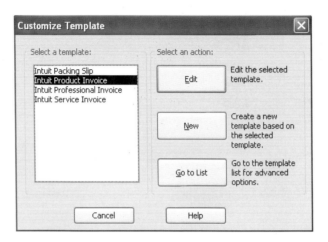

Click **Edit**, click the **Company** tab
- If necessary, click **Print Company Name**, click **Print Company Address** to select.

Click **Use Logo**

Click **File** and repeat the procedures used to add the logo to the checks/paychecks to select MM_Logo.bmp for the logo

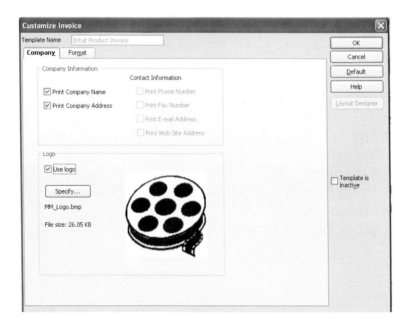

Click **OK**,

Click the drop-down list arrow for **Print**, click **Preview** to view the invoice with the logo, click **Zoom In** to get a close-up view of the logo, click **Close** to close the preview, click the **Close** button to close the invoice

Follow the procedures used for the invoice to add the name, address, and logo to a purchase order

- If your name makes the company name longer than one line, use only your last name as part of the company name.

CUSTOMIZE FORMS

In addition to adding a logo, forms used by QuickBooks Pro may be customized to change the fields (information areas) used, heading information, column arrangement, footer information (something appearing at the bottom of the form), and the print size and style (font). The Layout Designer allows the placement, size, and style of items on the printed form to be changed and customized.

QuickBooks Pro allows you to design your own forms for use by creating a custom form template for your business.

MEMO
DATE: July 1, 2005

Customize the Purchase Order by changing the words Purchase Order in the header to **PURCHASE ORDER**, change the font for the company name to Arial 16. Use Layout Designer to change the width of the Company Name column on the printed Purchase Order form.

 DO: Customize the Purchase Order as indicated above

Open a Purchase Order, click the drop-down list arrow next to **Customized Purchase Order**, click **Customize...**, Custom Purchase Order should be selected (click to select if necessary), click **Edit** button

Delete the title **Purchase Order** on the **Header** tab, enter **PURCHASE ORDER** as the title

Click the **Format** tab, click **Company Name** in Change Font For, click the **Change** button

Use the scroll bar and scroll to **Arial**, click **Arial** as the font
- *Note*: The font governs the shape and form of the letter. The default print style is Times New Roman. Not all printers will support all print styles. If your printer does not have Times New Roman or Arial, select a different font for the company name.

Look at the **Sample** box to see the change in the letter shape and form as you change from Times Roman to Arial

Click **16** as the **Size** of the font

Click **OK** on **Example**

Click **Layout Designer** button

Scroll through the Purchase Order, click in the PURCHASE ORDER column

Position the cursor on the line on the left side of the column, hold down the primary mouse button (the cursor will turn into a large line with arrows on the left and right side), drag the column line to the right until the area for PURCHASE ORDER is smaller

Click in the **Company Name** column

Position the cursor on the line on the right side of the column, hold down the primary mouse button (the cursor will turn into a large line with arrows on the left and right side), drag the column line to the right until it reaches the area for PURCHASE ORDER, release the mouse

Click **OK** on Layout Designer

Click **OK** on Customize Purchase Order
- Notice the change in PURCHASE ORDER on the Create Purchase Order screen.

Click **Preview** to view the Purchase Order, click **Zoom In** to enlarge the Invoice
- Notice the larger size print and the different print style on the company name.

Movies & More–Student's Name	**PURCHASE ORDER**	
8795 Mission Bay Drive	Date	P.O. No.
San Diego, CA 92109	7/1/2005	1

Click **Close** to close the preview, click **Print** to print a blank custom purchase order

- If you find that the company name prints on more than one line, just use your last name. You will need to change the company name via Company Info.
- Note: As illustrated in previous chapters, before an invoice can be customized using Layout Designer, it must be duplicated. Other template forms, such as the purchase order, do not need to be duplicated before using the Layout Designer.

CUSTOMIZING REPORTS

As with the business forms, reports may also be customized to better reflect the information or a format required by a business. In earlier chapters, report formats were customized when the date prepared, time prepared, and report basis were no longer printed as part of the header.

MEMO

DATE: July 1, 2005

Customize Report formats by deselecting the Date Prepared, Time Prepared, and Report Basis from the header and by enlarging the Company Name to Arial 16. Also, change My Preferences to have reports Refresh automatically.

 DO: Make the changes indicated in the memo

Select Report & Graph Preferences as instructed previously; if necessary, click **Company Preferences** tab

Verify the reporting preference of **Accrual**

Click **Format** button

Click the **Fonts & Numbers** tab

Click **Company Name** in the **Change Font For** list , click **Change Font** button

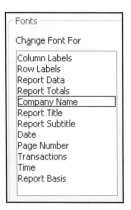

Font should be **Arial** (if not, scroll through fonts, click Arial), click **16** for **Size**

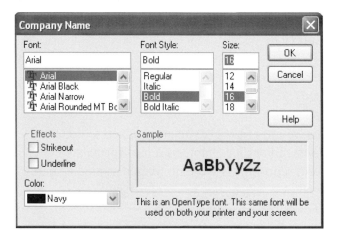

- Notice the TT symbol next to some of the Arial fonts in the Font selections. The TT stands for a TrueType font. This means that the font will appear the same on the printed copy as it does on the computer screen.

Click **OK**

Click **Yes** to Change all related fonts

Click the **Header/Footer** tab on Report Format Preferences, click **Date Prepared**, **Time Prepared**, and **Report Basis** to deselect, click **OK** on Format Header/Footer, click **OK** on Report Format Preferences,

Click the **My Preferences** tab, click **Refresh automatically**

Click **OK** on **Preferences**

Prepare a Standard Balance Sheet for **07/01/05** as previously instructed

Movies & More--Student's Name
Balance Sheet
As of July 1, 2005

	Jul 1, 05
Total Current Liabilities	7,500.00
Long Term Liabilities	
Store Equipment Loan	3,000.00
Store Fixtures Loan	35,000.00
Total Long Term Liabilities	38,000.00
Total Liabilities	45,500.00
Equity	
David Watson, Capital	
David Watson, Investment	5,000.00
David Watson, Capital - Other	24,861.00
Total David Watson, Capital	29,861.00
Retained Earnings	-1,025.00
Net Income	1,025.00
Total Equity	29,861.00
TOTAL LIABILITIES & EQUITY	**75,361.00**

Print the report in Portrait orientation, close the report

BACKUP

As in previous chapters, a backup of the data file for Movies & More should be made.

 DO: Back up the company file to **Movies & More.qbb** as instructed in earlier chapters and make a duplicate disk as instructed in Appendix A.

SUMMARY

In this chapter a company was created using the EasyStep Interview provided by QuickBooks Pro. Once the interview was complete, the Chart of Accounts/General Ledger was customized. Detailed information was given for customers and vendors. An Employee Template was created, and employees were added using the Payroll Setup. Employee year-to-date payroll and earnings figures were entered. Adjusting entries were made. A logo was added to forms. A Purchase Order was customized, and reports were customized.

END-OF-CHAPTER QUESTIONS

TRUE/FALSE

ANSWER THE FOLLOWING QUESTIONS IN THE SPACE PROVIDED BEFORE THE QUESTION NUMBER.

_____ 1. You must return to the EasyStep Interview to add additional customers, and vendors.

_____ 2. The EasyStep Interview is used to add employees and year-to-date earnings.

_____ 3. The TT symbol next to a font means that the font will appear the same on the printed copy as it does on the computer screen.

_____ 4. A company logo is a group of alphabetic symbols representing the company name.

_____ 5. The start date is the date you select to give QuickBooks Pro the financial information for your company.

_____ 6. The EasyStep Interview allows you to include the balances for all asset accounts.

_____ 7. When selecting company preferences from the Preferences menu, select Sales & Customers Preferences to indicate whether or not you charge sales tax.

_____ 8. When using the EasyStep Interview to set up income and expenses, you must type in the name of every income and expense account you use.

_____ 9. The Additional Info tab for an employee is where custom fields may be created and is used for information such as an employee's foreign languages.

_____ 10. Customer addresses, credit terms, and credit limits are entered during the EasyStep Interview.

MULTIPLE CHOICE

WRITE THE LETTER OF THE CORRECT ANSWER IN THE SPACE PROVIDED BEFORE THE QUESTION NUMBER.

_____ 1. To use account numbers, select ___ Preferences from the list of preferences.
  A. General
  B. Accounting
  C. Menus
  D. Tracking

_____ 2. The Start Date is provided in the ___ section of the EasyStep Interview.
  A. Preferences
  B. Menu
  C. General
  D. Details

_____ 3. When adding a new employee, you use the ___created in the payroll set up.
  A. Employee Template
  B. Employee File
  C. Employee Roster
  D. Employee Menu

_____ 4. The EasyStep Interview is accessed on the ___.
  A. File menu
  B. QuickBooks Company Navigator Preferences screen
  C. Activities menu
  D. all of the above

_____ 5. The use of the payroll feature is indicated in the ___ of the EasyStep Interview.
  A. Payroll section
  B. Preferences section
  C. Documents section
  D. Menu Items topic

_____ 6. In the EasyStep Interview, section tabs are located on the ___ of the screen and topic tabs are located on the ___ of the screen.
  A. left side, bottom
  B. bottom, right side
  C. left side, top
  D. right side, top

_____ 7. Select the use of a(n) ___ to keep track of all transactions—including those that have been deleted.
   A. General Journal
   B. Summary Report
   C. audit trail
   D. unedited transaction list

_____ 8. A company logo for checks and paychecks is selected on the ___.
   A. File menu, Printer Setup
   B. Customized check form, Customize button
   C. both of the above
   D. none of the above

_____ 9. Items for the Employee Template may be selected ___.
   A. during the EasyStep Interview
   B. during the Payroll set up
   C. by clicking the Reports button at the bottom of the employee list
   D. all of the above

_____ 10. Accounts that are listed individually but are grouped together under a main account are called ___.
   A. dependent accounts
   B. secondary accounts
   C. mini-accounts
   D. subaccounts

FILL-IN

IN THE SPACE PROVIDED, WRITE THE ANSWER THAT MOST APPROPRIATELY COMPLETES THE SENTENCE.

1. When the EasyStep Interview is completed, all existing balances for receivables and payables are placed into the _____ and the _____ accounts.

2. Year-to-date payroll summaries may be added by the _____, or by the _____.

3. When you complete the Opening Balances section of the EasyStep Interview, opening balances are given for _____, _____, and _____ accounts.

4. Payroll items used for the majority of employees are identified as _____ on the Employee Template.

5. Another name for the Chart of Accounts is the _____.

SHORT ESSAY

List the five sections in the EasyStep Interview. Describe the portion of the company setup completed in each section.

_____

_____

_____

_____

_____

NAME_____

TRANSMITTAL

CHAPTER 9: MOVIES & MORE

Attach the following documents and reports:

Chart of Accounts
Customer:Job List
Vendor List
Employee Earnings Summary
Payroll Item Listing
Employee List
Customized Blank Purchase Order with Logo
Balance Sheet, July 1, 2005

END-OF-CHAPTER PROBLEM

PAM'S

Pam's is a fictitious company that sells candy, pastries, and coffee. Pam's is located in San Francisco, California, and is a sole proprietorship owned by Pam Sloan. Ms. Sloan is involved in all aspects of the business. Pam's has a full-time employee who is paid a salary—Mr. Alex Taylor, who manages the store, is responsible for the all the employees, and keeps the books. There is one full-time hourly employee, who works in the shop, Marie Lopez.

CREATE A NEW COMPANY

Use the EasyStep Interview to create a new company.

Pam's—Your Name is used for both the Company Name and the Legal Name
Address: 550 Geary Street, San Francisco, CA 94102. Tax ID 456-22-1346, tax year and fiscal year both begin in July, Other/None is the tax form used.

The following includes information that will help you answer some of the EasyStep Interview questions: You will also need to refer to various lists provided in the problem.

Pam's is a general retail business. It does have an inventory. The file for the company should be **Pam's—Your Name.qbw**. Use the disk in **A:**. Have QuickBooks Pro create the chart of accounts. Only the owner will have access to QuickBooks Pro. Do not assign passwords. It does collect sales tax for California at the rate of 7.25%. The California sales tax is payable to the State Board of Equalization. Pam's uses a Custom invoice. As previously stated, there are two employees. QuickBooks Pro payroll feature will be used. No estimates, time tracking, or classes will be given or used. Bills will be entered first and paid later. The Reminders List should show when I ask for it. Use accrual-based reporting. The company start date is 07/01/05.

You will enter new income and expense accounts during the EasyStep Interview. Pam's does not have any service items, non-inventory part items, or other charge items. There are no lines of credit. Pam's will not charge finance charges and does not want to use statements. You do want to set up inventory items.

CHART OF ACCOUNTS

Use the following Chart of Accounts and balances as you answer the EasyStep Interview questions and edit the accounts after the interview. (Abbreviations used: C.A. = Current Asset, F.A. = Fixed Asset, C.L. = Current Liability, COGS = Cost of Goods Sold. ***Balance is generated by QuickBooks Pro. Only Balance Sheet accounts have balances. Accounts that are indented are subaccounts of the preceding account that is not indented—for example, Loan Interest is a subaccount of Interest Expense. This chart will appear on two pages. You will need to look at the end of the first column on the second page of the chart before using the second column

PAM'S CHART OF ACCOUNTS				
ACCOUNT	**TYPE**	**BALANCE**	**ACCOUNT**	**TYPE**
Checking (6/30/05)	Bank	25,875.15	Interest Expense	Expense
Accounts Receivable	Accts. Rec.	***	Licenses and Permits	Expense
Inventory Asset	Other C.A	***	Miscellaneous	Expense
Office Supplies	Other C.A.	500.00	Office Expenses	Expense
Prepaid Insurance	Other C.A.	600.00	Postage and Delivery	Expense
Sales Supplies	Other C.A.	1,000.00	Printing and Reproduction	Expense
Store Equipment	F.A.	6,000.00	Payroll Expenses	Expense
Store Equipment: Depreciation	F.A.	0.00	Professional Fees	Expense
Store Equipment: Original Cost	F.A.	6,000.00	Accounting	Expense
Store Fixtures	F.A.	10,000.00	Legal Fees	Expense
Store Fixtures: Depreciation	F.A.	0.00	Rent	Expense
Store Fixtures: Original Cost	F.A.	10,000.00	Repairs	Expense
Accounts Payable	Acct. Pay.	***	Building Repairs	Expense
MasterCard (6/30/05)	Credit Card	250.00	Computer Repairs	Expense
Payroll Liabilities	Other C.L.	0.00	Equipment Repairs	Expense
Sales Tax Payable	Other C.L.	0.00	Supplies	Expense
Store Equipment Loan	Long Term L.	1,000.00	Taxes	Expense
Store Fixtures Loan	Long Term L.	4,000.00	Telephone	Expense
Pam Sloan, Capital	Equity	***	Uncategorized Expenses	Expense
Pam Sloan, Drawing	Equity	0.00	Utilities	Expense

Pam Sloan, Investment	Equity	5,000.00	Interest Income	Other Income
Retained Earnings	Equity	***	Other Income	Other Income
Candy Sales	Income		Other Expenses	Other Expense
Coffee Sales	Income			
Pastry Sales	Income			
Uncategorized Income	Income			
Cost of Goods Sold	COGS			
Purchases Discounts	COGS			
Bank Service Charges	Expense			
Depreciation Expense	Expense			
Dues and Subscriptions	Expense			
Equipment Rental	Expense			
Insurance	Expense			
Disability Insurance	Expense			
Fire Insurance	Expense			
Liability Insurance	Expense			

ITEMS LIST

Use the following Inventory Items List and balances as you answer the EasyStep Interview questions.

INVENTORY ITEMS			
Item Name	**Candy**	**Coffee**	**Pastry**
Sales Description	Candy Sales	Coffee Sales	Pastry Sales
Sales Price	0.00	0.00	0.00
Taxable Item	Yes	Yes	Yes
Income Account	Candy Sales	Coffee Sales	Pastry Sales
Purchase Description	Candy	Coffee	Pastry
Cost	5.00	5.00	0.50
Reorder Point	100	100	100
Quantity on Hand	2,000	2,000	500
Value	10,000	10,000	250

CUSTOMER LIST

Use the following Customer List and balances as you answer the EasyStep Interview questions and as you edit customers after the interview. Pam's does not track projects.

Ridgeway Training, Inc., 785 Harvard Street, San Francisco, CA 94102, Contact Susan Jones, 916-555-8762, Fax 916-555-2678, Net 30, Credit Limit $1,500, Balance $1,450, Taxable

Maurice Walker, 253 Mason Street, San Francisco, CA 94102, Phone 415-555-2264, Net 30, Credit Limit $350, Balance $350, Taxable. (Enter his last name, first name for Customer:Job. Enter his first name then last name for Bill To address.)

VENDOR LIST

Use the following Vendor List and balances as you answer the EasyStep Interview questions and edit vendors after the interview.

Confections, Inc., 559 7th Street, San Francisco, CA 94104, Contact Alexis Sams, Phone 415-555-2788, Fax 415-555-8872, 2% 10 Net 30, Credit Limit $15,000, Balance $800

Custom Coffee Importers, 785 Market Street, San Francisco, CA 94103, Contact Colleen Jones, Phone 415-555-3184, Fax 415-555-4813, 2% 10 Net 30, Credit Limit $5,000, Balance $1000

Pastry Perfection 1095 8th Street, San Francisco, CA 94104, Contact Ron Raymond, Phone 415-555-5759, Fax 415-555-9575, 2% 10 Net 30, Credit Limit $15,000, Balance $500

Employment Development Department; 10327 Washington Street, San Francisco, CA 94107; Phone 415-555-8877 (Used for California Taxes and Withholding)

State Bank; 302 Second Street, San Francisco, CA 94104; Phone 415-555-9889 (Used for all Federal Taxes and Withholding)

Medical and Dental Ins., Inc.; 20865 Oak Street, San Francisco, CA 94101; Phone 415-555-4646 (Used for Medical and Dental Insurance deductions)

State Board of Equalization, 7829 West 17th Street, Sacramento, CA 94267; Phone 916-555-1000

EMPLOYEE LIST

Use the following information, Employee List, and year-to-date balances as you create the Employee Template and add employees. The YTD information is provided for the Jan-Mar and

Apr-Jun quarters. The chart contains the amounts for one quarter. Both quarters have the same amounts.

Only the information that needs to be entered is given below. If information is not provided, it is zero (0).

Select Manual Calculation as the payroll option. Filing State is California, the EDD number is 999-9999-9, State Unemployment Tax Rate is 4%, Employees are paid hourly and salary. Pam's does want to track Salary-Regular, Salary-Sick, and Salary-Vacation, Hourly Wage-Regular, Hourly Wage-Overtime , Hourly Wage-Sick, Hourly Wage-Vacation. There is employee paid health insurance taxable, not all employees pay the same amount, and there are no limits on the amount of premiums. All federal taxes are paid to State Bank and state taxes are paid to Employment Development Department. Health insurance premiums are paid to Medical and Dental Ins., Inc. Employees are paid semimonthly and have a deduction for Health Insurance.. Federal Taxes: all except Advance Earned Income Credit, State Taxes: CA is the state worked and subject to withholding and SUI and SDI are withheld, Other Taxes: CA Employment Training Tax. Track vacation and sick time. Hours are given at the beginning of the year, 40 hours per year may be accrued, maximum number of hours are 80. Hours are not reset at the beginning of the year.

Mr. Alex Taylor; Social Security No. 100-55-5259; Male; Birthday 11/28/1949; 177 Post Street, San Francisco, CA 94101; Phone 415-555-1222; Foreign Languages: None Salary $24,000; Medical $30; Federal: Single, 1 Allowance; State: Single, 1 Allowance; Available Sick 40 hrs; Available Vacation 40 hrs; Regular Employee; Hired 02/17/1995

Mrs. Marie Lopez, Social Security No. 100-55-6456; Female; Birthday 12/07/1970; 833 Pine Street, San Francisco, CA 94102; Phone 415-555-7862; Foreign Languages: Spanish; Hourly Regular Rate $10 per hour; Medical $20; Federal: Married, 3 Allowances; State: Married (two incomes), 3 Allowances Regular Employee; Hired 04/03/1996

EMPLOYEE SUMMARY TABLE FOR THE QUARTERS OF JAN-MAR AND APR-JUN		
	Alex Taylor	**Marie Lopez**
Item Name	Salary Regular	Hourly Regular Rate
Period Amount	6,000.00	4,800.00
Hours for Period	480	480
Medical Insurance Employee	180.00	120.00
Federal Withholding	702.00	180.00

Social Security Company	372.00	297.60
Social Security Employee	372.00	297.60
Medicare Company	87.00	69.60
Medicare Employee	87.00	69.60
Federal Unemployment	28.00	28.00
CA Withholding	143.16	46.08
CA Disability Employee	30.00	24.00
CA Unemployment Company	140.00	140.00
CA Employment Training Tax	140.00	140.00

MAKE ADJUSTMENTS

Customize the report format so that reports refresh automatically, the Date Prepared, Time Prepared, and Report Basis do not print as part of the header, and the Company Name will print in Arial Bold 16-point font on all reports. Change all related fonts.

Change the accounts for Pam's as necessary so they are identical to the Chart of Accounts provided. Print a Chart of Accounts. Use the Reports menu, Lists, Account Listing to print the Chart of Accounts in Portrait orientation.

Add customer and vendor information. Print a Customer List and a Vendor List as instructed in the chapter.

Complete the Payroll Set Up: Indicate a manual calculation. Associate Payroll Items with Vendors as indicated in the vendor table. Create an Employee Template by identifying Employee Defaults. Add employees and YTD information. Go to the Report Finder and print an Employee Earnings Summary in landscape for January through June 2005 and a Payroll Item Listing in landscape. Print an Employee List as directed in the chapter.

Transfer the Uncategorized Income and Uncategorized Expenses to the owner's Capital account on July 1, 2005. Print a Balance Sheet as of July 1, 2005.

Customize a Purchase Order. Change the Default Title to PURCHASE ORDER. Change the font for the Company Name to Times New Roman 16 point. Print the Company Name and Address. Add a logo to a purchase order (use the PAM_Logo.bmp contained on the CD-ROM that accompanies this text. Copy this file to the disk containing your Pam's.qbw file). Change the width of the Company Name and the Purchase Order fields so the entire company name displays on one line. Print a blank purchase order with lines around each field.

NAME_____

TRANSMITTAL

CHAPTER 9: PAM'S

Attach the following documents and reports:

Account Listing
Customer List
Vendor List
Employee Earnings Summary, January through June 2005
Payroll Item Listing
Employee List
Standard Balance Sheet, July 1, 2005
Customized Blank Purchase Order with Logo

CAPITAL BOOKS PRACTICE SET: COMPREHENSIVE PROBLEM

The following is a comprehensive practice set combining all the elements of QuickBooks studied throughout the text. In this practice set you will set up a company and keep the books for April 2005. You will use the EasyStep Interview to create Capital Books. Once the company has been created, detailed information will be provided for customers, vendors, and employees. Adjustments will be made to accounts and various items, and transactions will be recorded.

During the month, new customers, vendors, and employees will be added. When entering transactions, you are responsible for any memos you wish to include in transactions. Unless otherwise specified, the terms for each sale or bill will be the term specified on the Customer or Vendor List. The Customer Message is usually *Thank you for your business*. However, any other message that is appropriate may be used. If a customer's order exceeds the established credit limit, accept the order and process it. If the terms allow a discount for a customer, make sure to apply the discount if payment is received in time for the customer to take the discount. Remember, the discount period starts with the date of the invoice. If an invoice or bill date is not provided, use the transaction date to begin the discount period. Use Sales Discounts as the discount account. If a customer has a credit and has a balance on the account, apply the credit to payments received for the customer. If there is no balance for a customer and a return is made, issue a credit memo and a refund check. Always pay bills in time to take advantage of purchase discounts.

Invoices, purchase orders, and other similar items should be printed <u>without lines</u> around each field. Most reports will be printed in Portrait orientation; however, if the report (such as the Journal) will fit across the page using Landscape orientation, use Landscape. Whenever possible, adjust the column widths so that reports fit on one-page wide without selecting Fit report to one page wide.

<u>CAPITAL BOOKS</u>

Capital Books is a fictitious company that provides a typing service and sells books and educational supplies. Capital Books is located in Sacramento, California, and is a sole proprietorship owned by Raymond Childers. Mr. Childers does all the purchasing and is involved in all aspects of the business. Capital Books has a full-time employee who is paid a salary, Ms. Elise Nelson, who manages the store, is responsible for the all the employees, and keeps the books. Laura Ellis is a full-time hourly employee who works in the shop. The store is currently advertising for a part-time employee who will provide word processing/typing services.

CREATE A NEW COMPANY

Use the EasyStep Interview to create a new company.

Capital Books--Your Name is used for both the Company Name and the Legal Name. Address: 1055 Front Street, Sacramento, CA 95814. Telephone 916-555-9876, Fax 916-555-6789, Email CapitalBooks@reader.com, Web Site www.CapitalBooks.com. Tax ID 466-52-1446, tax year and fiscal year both begin in April, Other/None is the tax form used.

The following includes information that will help you answer some of the EasyStep Interview questions: Capital Books is a Retail:General business. It does have an inventory. The file for the company should be **Capital Books–Your Name.qbw**. Use the disk in **A:** (or wherever your instructor directs you to store your company file). Initially, allow QuickBooks to generate the chart of accounts for a Retail: General company. As you continue with the EasyStep Interview, refer to the Chart of Accounts provided for Capital Books to find account names and balances for the accounts. Even though Elise Nelson will help keep the books, indicate that there are 0 people other than the owner who have access to QuickBooks. Do not assign passwords. The company does collect sales tax for California at the rate of 7.25%. The California sales tax is payable to the State Board of Equalization. Capital Books uses a Custom invoice. As previously stated, there are two employees. QuickBooks' payroll feature will be used. No estimates, time tracking, or classes will be given or used. Bills will be entered first and paid later. The Reminders List should show *When I ask for it*. Use accrual-based reporting. The company start date is 04/01/05. Capital Books does have service items; it does not have any non-inventory part items or other charge items. There are no lines of credit. In the company setup, indicate that the To Do list will be used often. Capital Books will not charge finance charges and does not want to use QuickBooks for budgeting.

CHART OF ACCOUNTS

Use the following chart of accounts and balances as you answer the EasyStep Interview questions. (Chart abbreviations: C.A. = Current Asset, F.A. = Fixed Asset, C.L. = Current Liability, COGS = Cost of Goods Sold. ***Balance is generated by QuickBooks. Only Balance Sheet accounts have balances. (Accounts that are indented are subaccounts of the preceding account that is not indented—for example, Disability Insurance is a subaccount of Insurance Expense.) When finalizing the chart of accounts, be sure to look at the end of the column on the left before adding accounts at the top of the column on the right.

CAPITAL BOOKS
CHART OF ACCOUNTS

ACCOUNT	TYPE	BALANCE	ACCOUNT	TYPE
Checking (03/31/05)	Bank	35,870.25	Health Insurance	Expense
Accounts Receivable	Accts. Rec.	***	Liability Insurance	Expense
Inventory Asset	Other C.A	***	Interest Expense	Expense
Office Supplies	Other C.A.	450.00	Marketing and Advertising	Expense
Prepaid Insurance	Other C.A.	1,200.00	Miscellaneous	Expense
Sales Supplies	Other C.A.	900.00	Office Expenses	Expense
Store Equipment	F.A.	6,000.00	Postage and Delivery	Expense
Store Equipment: Depreciation	F.A.	0.00	Printing and Reproduction	Expense
Store Equipment: Original Cost	F.A.	6,000.00	Payroll Expenses	Expense
Store Fixtures	F.A.	10,000.00	Professional Fees	Expense
Store Fixtures: Depreciation	F.A.	0.00	Accounting	Expense
Store Fixtures: Original Cost	F.A.	10,000.00	Legal Fees	Expense
Accounts Payable	Acct. Pay.	***	Rent	Expense
MasterCard (03/31/05)	Credit Card	50.00	Repairs	Expense
Payroll Liabilities	Other C.L.	0.00	Building Repairs	Expense
Sales Tax Payable	Other C.L.	0.00	Computer Repairs	Expense
Store Equipment Loan	Long Term L.	1,500.00	Equipment Repairs	Expense
Store Fixtures Loan	Long Term L.	4,500.00	Sales Discounts	Expense
Raymond Childers, Capital	Equity	***	Supplies	Expense
Raymond Childers, Drawing	Equity	0.00	Office	Expense
Raymond Childers, Investment	Equity	10,000.00	Sales	Expense
Retained Earnings	Equity	***	Taxes	Expense
Purchases Discounts	Income		Federal	Expense
Sales and Services	Income		Local	Expense
Book Sales	Income		State	Expense
Supplies Sales	Income		Telephone	Expense
Word Processing/Typing Service	Income		Uncategorized Expenses	Expense
Uncategorized Income	Income		Utilities	Expense
Cost of Goods Sold	COGS		Gas and Electric	Expense
Purchases Discounts	COGS		Water	Expense
Bank Service Charges	Expense		Interest Income	Other Income
Depreciation Expense	Expense		Other Income	Other Income
Dues and Subscriptions	Expense		Other Expenses	Other Expense
Equipment Rental	Expense			
Insurance	Expense			
Disability Insurance	Expense			
Fire Insurance	Expense			

ITEMS LIST

As you progress through the EasyStep Interview, you will want to answer *Sometimes* for the receipt of payment. You will not be issuing statement charges.

There is only one service item for Capital Books—Item Name: WP/Typing, Sales Description: Word Processing/Typing Service, Price: 0.00, not Taxable, Income Account: Word Processing/Typing Service Income

There are no subcontracted items, non-inventory parts, or other charges.

Use the following Inventory Items List and balances as you answer the EasyStep Interview questions to add inventory items.

INVENTORY ITEMS					
Item Name	**Textbooks**	**Paperback Books**	**Paper**	**Stationery**	**Pens, etc.**
Sales Description	Textbooks	Paperback Books	Paper Supplies	Stationery	Pens, etc.
Sales Price	0.00	0.00	0.00	0.00	0.00
Tax Code	Tax	Tax	Tax	Tax	Tax
Income Account	Book Sales	Book Sales	Supplies Sales	Supplies Sales	Supplies Sales
Purchase Description	Textbooks	Paperback Books	Paper Supplies	Stationery	Pens, etc.
Cost	0.00	0.00	0.00	0.00	0.00
Preferred Vendor	Book Suppliers	Book Suppliers	Supply City	Supply City	Pens of the World
COGS Account	Cost of Goods Sold	Cost of Goods Sold	Cost of Goods Sold	Cost of Goods Sold	Cost of Goods Sold
Asset Account	Inventory Asset	Inventory Asset	Inventory Asset	Inventory Asset	Inventory Asset
Reorder Point	100	30	100	25	50
Quantity on Hand	2,000	45	200	30	50
Value	10,000	180	3,000	150	100

CUSTOMER LIST

Use the following Customer List and balances as you answer the EasyStep Interview questions. During the Interview, enter customers who are individuals last name first for Customer:Job but first name then last name on the Bill to address. You do not do job tracking. *Note:* Remember that the only time an opening balance may be entered is when the customer is created. An opening balance is not eligible for a discount. The terms given are for future sales to a customer.

Complete Training, Inc., Balance $1,450, 785 Harvard Street, Sacramento, CA 95814, Contact Sharon Jackson, 916-555-8762, Fax 916-555-2678, Net 30, Taxable, Credit Limit $1,500
Morgan Waverly, Balance $350, 253 Mason Street, Sacramento, CA 95814, 916-555-2264, Net 30, Taxable, Credit Limit $350
Lorraine Norris, Balance $100, 8025 Richmond Avenue, Sacramento, CA 95814, 916-555-8961, 2% 10 Net 30, Taxable, Credit Limit $500
Sacramento School, Balance $1,000, 1085 2nd Street, Sacramento, CA 95814, Contact Alicia Vincent, 916-555-1235, 2% 10 Net 30, Taxable, Credit Limit $5,000
Dr. Geoffrey Silverman, Balance $0.00, 158 16th Street, Sacramento, CA 95814, 916-555-3693, Net 30, Taxable, Credit Limit $100
Vivian Newton, Balance $0.00, 6784 Front Street, Sacramento, CA 95814, 916-555-6487, Net 30, Taxable, Credit Limit $100

VENDOR LIST

Use the following Vendor List and balances as you answer the EasyStep Interview questions. . *Note:* Remember that the only time an opening balance may be entered is when the customer is created. An opening balance is not eligible for a discount. The terms given are for future purchases from a vendor.

Book Suppliers, Balance $1,000, 559 4th Street, Sacramento, CA 95814, Contact Al Daruty, 916-555-2788, Fax 916-555-8872, 2% 10 Net 30, Credit Limit $15,000
Pens of the World, Balance $500, 2785 Market Street, San Francisco, CA 94103, Contact Dennis Johnson, 415-555-3224, Fax 415-555-4223, 2% 10 Net 30, Credit Limit $5,000
Supply City, Balance $800, 95 8th Street, Sacramento, CA 95814, Contact Raymond Ahrens, 916-555-5759, Fax 916-555-9575, 2% 10 Net 30, Credit Limit $15,000
Employment Development Department; 1037 California Street, Sacramento, CA 95814; 916-555-8877 (Used for California Taxes and Withholding)
State Bank; 102 8th Street, Sacramento, CA 95814; 916-555-9889 (used for all Federal Taxes and Withholding)
Medical Ins., Inc.; 20865 Oak Street, San Francisco, CA 94101; 415-555-4646 (used for Medical Insurance deductions)
State Board of Equalization, 7829 West 17th Street, Sacramento, CA 94267; 916-555-1000

EMPLOYEE LIST

Complete the Payroll Setup. Use the following information, Employee List, and year-to-date balances as you complete the payroll setup, employee template, add employees and year-to-date amounts.

The Payroll Option is Manual Calculation
The Company Payroll State is CA
Accept the Federal Payroll Tax information shown
California EDD Account number is 999-9999-9
CA-State Unemployment Tax is 4% for each quarter
Payroll list items for wages, tips, and taxable fringe benefits are:
    Salary Regular, Salary Sick, Salary Vacation
    Hourly Wage Regular, Hourly Wage Overtime, Hourly Wage Sick, Hourly Wage Vacation
Insurance Benefits are:
    Health Insurance (Taxable)
Retirement Benefits: None
Other Payments and Deductions: None

Vendors for Payroll Liabilities:
    Federal Withholding, Federal Unemployment, Social Security, Medicare: <u>State Bank</u>
    CA Withholding, CA Unemployment Company, CA Disability Employee, CA Employment
        Training Tax: <u>Employment Development Department</u>
    Health Insurance: <u>Medical Ins., Inc.</u>

Employee Defaults:
    Pay Period: Semimonthly
    Additions, Deductions and Company Contributions: Health Insurance Emp Taxable
    Federal Taxes: Medicare, Social Security, Federal Unemployment Tax (Company Paid)
    State Taxes: State Worked and Subject to Withholding: CA, SUI (Company Paid), SDI
    Other: CA-Employment Training Tax
    Sick/Vacation: Beginning of year accrual period

Ms. Elise Nelson, Social Security No. 100-55-5244; Gender Female; Birthday 11/28/49; 1777 Watt Avenue, Sacramento, CA 95814; 916-555-1222; Name of Spouse: None, Type Regular; Hired 02/17/95; Salary $26,000; Health Ins. $30; Federal and State: Single, 0 Allowance; Sick Available and Accrued 40 hrs; Vacation Available and Accrued 40 hrs; Maximum Sick and Vacation Hours 80.

Mrs. Laura Ellis, Social Security No. 100-55-6886; Gender Female; Birthday 12/07/70; 833 Oak Avenue, Sacramento, CA 95814; 916-555-7862; Name of Spouse: Jim, Type Regular; Hired 04/03/96; Hourly Regular Rate $10 per hour; Overtime Hourly Rate $15 per hour; Health Ins. $20; Federal and State: Married (one income), 1 Allowance; Sick Available and Accrued 40 hrs; Vacation Available and Accrued 40 hrs; Maximum Sick and Vacation Hours 80.

EMPLOYEE YEAR-TO-DATE SUMMARY TABLE AS OF 3/31/2005		
	Elise Nelson	Laura Ellis
Item Name	Officer Salary Regular	Hourly Regular Rate
Period Amount	6,500.00	4,800.00
Hours for Period	480	480
Health Insurance Employee	90.00	60.00
Federal Withholding	876.00	378.00
Social Security Company	403.02	292.59
Social Security Employee	403.02	292.59
Medicare Company	94.26	69.60
Medicare Employee	94.26	69.60
Federal Unemployment	27.99	27.99
CA Withholding	189.90	42.06
CA Disability Employee	30.00	24.00
CA Unemployment Company	140.00	140.00
CA Employment Training Tax	140.00	140.00

MAKE ADJUSTMENTS

Customize the report format so the date prepared, time prepared, and report basis do not print as part of the header and the Company Name will print in Arial 16 point font on all reports. Have reports refresh automatically.

Add, delete, and change the accounts for Capital Books as necessary so they are identical to the Chart of Accounts provided. Print a Chart of Accounts in Portrait using Report menu, List,

Account Listing. (Fit to one-page wide by adjusting the column widths and remove the column for Tax Line.)

Add customer and vendor information. Print a Customer List and a Vendor List from Print List on the File menu.

Associate Sales Items with Vendors. Print an Item Listing from the Reports menu for List. Use landscape orientation.

Complete the Payroll Setup.

Add a new part-time hourly employee: Kelli King, Social Security No. 100-55-3699; Gender Female; Birthday 1/3/76; 1177 Florin Road, Sacramento, CA 95814; 916-555-7766; Name of Spouse: None, Type Regular; Hired 04/01/05; Hourly Regular Rate $6.50; Federal and State: Single, 1 Allowance. Sick and Vacation Hours Available 0; Sick and Vacation Hours Accrued 20; Maximum Sick and Vacation Hours 40. Print an Employee List.

Transfer the Uncategorized Income and Uncategorized Expenses to the owner's capital account. Print a Balance Sheet as of April 1, 2005.

Customize the Invoice: Use a duplicate of a Product Invoice. Select Print the Company Name and Print Company Address. Add a logo to an invoice (copy the Books_Logo.bmp to your data disk and use for the logo). Change the title of the invoice to INVOICE. Change the font for the Company Name to Arial Narrow, bold, 12 point. Use Layout Designer to make the area for the company name wide enough for your name and to position the address so that it is not overlapping the logo. Do not print lines around each field. Print a blank Invoice. Customize Credit Memos, Sales Receipts, and Purchase Orders so they have the same format as the invoice. Add the logo to checks. Do not print these additional forms.

ENTER TRANSACTIONS

Print invoices, sales receipts, purchase orders, checks, and other items as they are entered in the transactions. Use the product invoice for all invoices, voucher checks for payroll, and standard checks for all other checks. Create new items, accounts, customers, vendors, etc., as necessary. Refer to information given at the beginning of the problem for additional transaction details and information.

Prepare an Inventory Stock Status by Item Report every five days as the last transaction of the day to see if anything needs to be ordered. If anything is indicated, order enough so you will have 10 more than the minimum number of items. (For example, if you needed to order textbooks and the minimum number on hand is 100, you would order enough books to have 110 on hand.) For this problem, the price per book ordered is $15 per textbook and $5 per paperback; pens are $2.50 each, paper is $2.00 per ream, and stationery is $4.00 per box.

Full-time employees usually work 80 hours during a payroll period. Hourly employees working in excess of 80 hours in a pay period are paid overtime. Normally, there is a separate Payroll

Checking account used when paying employees; however, this problem uses the regular checking account to pay employees.

Check every five days to see if any bills are due and eligible for a discount. If any bills can be paid and a discount received, pay the bills; otherwise, wait for instructions to pay bills. Remember that an opening balance is not eligible for a discount.

April 1:

Cash sale of one $40 textbook.

Complete Training purchased 30 copies of *QuickBooks Pro ® 2004: A Complete Course* on account for $40 each.

Sold three paperback books at $6.99 each to a cash customer.

Received Check No. 1096 from Lorraine Norris for $100 as payment in full on her account.

Sold 25 pens on account at $8.99 each to Sacramento School for awards to students.

Sold five textbooks at $39.99 each for the new quarter to a student using a Visa.

Prepare and print an Inventory Stock Status by Item report to see if anything needs to be ordered.

Prepare and print Purchase Orders for any merchandise that needs to be ordered.

Check bills for discount eligibility between April 1-4. Pay any bills that qualify for a discount. (Opening balances do not qualify for an early payment discount.)

April 3:

Received Check No. 915 for $350 from Morgan Waverly for the full amount due on his account.

Sold five pens at $12.99 each to Lorraine Norris.

Received payment of $1,450 from Complete Training, Inc., Check No. 7824.

April 4:

Kelli typed a five-page paper for a student at the rate of $5 per page. Received Check No. 2951 for $25 as full payment.

Sold two textbooks at $40 each to a new customer: Brian Sauer, 478 Front Street, Sacramento, CA 95814, Phone: 916-555-6841, E-mail: bsauer@email.com, Terms Net 10, Credit Limit $100, Taxable.

April 5:

Received the pens ordered from Pens of the World with the bill.

Sold five boxes of stationery at $10.99 per box to Vivian Newton.

Sold five reams of paper at $4.99 per ream to Sacramento School.

Prepare and print Stock Status by Item Inventory Report. Order any items indicated.

Check bills for discount eligibility. Pay any bills that qualify for a discount between April 5-9.

Deposit all cash, checks, and credit card payments received.

April 7:

The nonprofit organization, State Schools, bought a classroom set of 30 computer training textbooks for $40.00 each. Add the new customer: State Schools, 451 State Street, Sacramento, CA 95814, Contact Allison Hernandez, 916-555-8787, Fax 916-555-7878, Terms Net 30, Taxable, Credit Limit $2000. Include a subtotal for the sale and apply a 10% sales discount for a nonprofit organization. (Create any new sales items necessary.)

Add a new sales item for Gift Ware, Purchase Description: Gift Ware, Cost: 0.00, COGS Account: Cost of Goods Sold, Preferred Vendor: Deluxe Gift Gallery (125 Oak Street, Sacramento, CA 95814, Contact: Mary Ellen Morrison, 916-555-5384, Fax 916-555-4835, E-mail gifts@abc.com, Terms Net 30, Credit Limit $500) Sales Description: Gift Ware, Sales Price: 0.00, Taxable: Yes, Income Account: Supplies Sales, Asset Account: Inventory Asset, Reorder Point: 15, Quantity on Hand: 0, Value: 0.00,

Order 15 gift items at $5.00 each from the Deluxe Gift Gallery.

April 8:

Sold ten reams of paper to Geoffrey Silverman at $3.99 per ream.

Received Check No. 10525 from Complete Training, Inc., $1,000 as partial payment on account.

Lorraine Norris returned two pens purchased on April 3. She did not like the color.

Paid Book Suppliers full amount owed on account. Print using Standard Checks.

April 10:

Sold three pens at $14.95 each, two sets of stationery at $9.99 each, and three paperback books at $6.99 each to a cash customer.

Kelli typed a 15-page report at $5.00 per page for Vivian Newton.

Sold eight additional computer textbooks to Sacramento School at $40 each.

Received Check No. 825 as payment from Sacramento School for the 4/1 transaction for $236.22, the full amount due, less discount.

Deposit all cash, checks, and credit card receipts.

Prepare Stock Status by Item Inventory Report. Order any items indicated.

Check bills for discount eligibility. Pay any bills that qualify for a discount between April 10-14.

April 11:

Sold ten paperback books at $6.99 each and two pens at $5.99 each to a customer using a Visa.

Sold ten reams of paper to a cash customer at $4.99 each. Received Check No. 8106.

April 12:

Received gift ware ordered from Deluxe Gift Gallery. A bill was not included with the order.

Sold one pen at $8.99 and a box of stationery at $9.99 to a cash customer.

Kelli typed a one-page letter with an envelope for Morgan Waverly, $8.00. (Qty is 1.)

April 13:

Received Check No. 1265 from Lorraine Norris in payment for full amount due, $40.41. (Be sure to apply any credits to her account first, then check for and apply any discounts. If you apply a discount, use the amount QuickBooks provides as the discount.)

Received a notice from the bank that Check No. 915 from Morgan Waverly was marked NSF and returned. Record the NSF check and charge Morgan the bank's $25 fee for the bad check plus Capital Books's fee of $15. Payment is due on receipt. Add any necessary items and/or accounts. Record charges for returned checks in an account called Returned Check Service Charges.

April 14:

Received Check No. 870 from Sacramento School for $26.22 as payment in full for Invoice No. 6.

Received Check No. 10-283 for $85.80 from Brian Sauer in payment of Invoice No. 4.

April 15:

Received all but three boxes of stationery ordered. The bill was included with the stationery and the three missing boxes are on back order. (Did you order 10 boxes?)

Received Morgan Waverly's new Check No. 304 for payment in full of his account including all NSF charges.

Sold five paperback books to a customer using a Visa. The books were $6.99 each.

Deposit all cash, checks, and credit card receipts.

Check to see if any bills qualify for a discount between April 15 and 19. If any qualify, pay them.

Prepare and print a Stock Status by Item Inventory Report for April 1-15 in Landscape orientation. Prepare Purchase Orders for all items marked Order on the Stock Status by Item Inventory Report. Place all orders with preferred vendors.

Pay the payroll using the regular checking account: Elise worked 80 hours, Laura worked 64 hours and took 16 hours of vacation time, and Kelli worked 40 hours during the pay period. Print using Voucher Checks.

PAYROLL TABLE: APRIL 15, 2005			
	Elise Nelson	**Laura Ellis**	**Kelli King**
HOURS			
Regular	80	64	40
Overtime			
Sick			
Vacation		16	

PAYROLL TABLE: APRIL 15, 2005			
	Elise Nelson	**Laura Ellis**	**Kelli King**
DEDUCTIONS OTHER PAYROLL ITEMS: EMPLOYEE			
Medical Ins.	30.00	20.00	
DEDUCTIONS: COMPANY			
CA Employment Training Tax	30.00	26.52	3.47
Social Security	67.17	49.60	16.12
Medicare	15.71	11.60	3.77
Federal Unemployment	6.00	5.30	1.26
CA-Unemployment	30.00	26.52	3.47
DEDUCTIONS: EMPLOYEE			
Federal Withholding	146.00	63.00	6.00
Social Security	67.17	49.60	16.12
Medicare	15.71	11.60	3.77
CA-Withholding	31.65	7.01	0.00
CA-Disability	5.42	4.00	1.30

April 17:

Sold eight textbooks at $50 each to State Schools, which is a nonprofit organization.

Brian Sauer returned one textbook he had purchased for $40.

Received Credit Memo No. 721 from Supply City for the return of ten reams of paper. (Be sure to apply the credit when you pay your bill.)

April 18:

Print a Stock Status by Item Report after recording the return of the paper. Print in Landscape.

Sold three paperback books to Morgan Waverly at $8.99 each.

April 20:

Received the bill and the three boxes of stationery that were on back order with Supply City.

A cash customer purchased four textbooks at $59.99 each using Check No. 289.

Received Check No. 891 from Sacramento School for $336.34 in payment of Invoice No. 11.

Prepare Stock Status by Item Inventory Report. Order any items indicated.

Check to see if any bills qualify for a discount between April 20 and 24. If any qualify, pay them.

April 21:

Sold one textbook for $89.95. Customer used a VISA card to pay for the purchase.

Kelli typed an eight-page exam for a professor at $5 per page. Add Professor John Smith, 1052 Florin Avenue, Sacramento, CA 95814, 916-555-8741, Terms Net 30, Taxable, Credit Limit $100.

Received the bill from Deluxe Gift Gallery for the gift ware ordered and received April 12. Date the bill April 21.

Deposit all cash, checks , and credit card receipts.

April 22:

Sold one gift ware item at $15.99 to a cash customer. Received Check No. 105.

Sold five gift ware items at $9.99 each to Lorraine Norris.

April 24:

Sold three pens at $8.99 each to Brian Sauer.

Received Check No. 127 for $42.79 as payment in full from Geoffrey Silverman.

April 25:

Prepare Stock Status by Item Inventory Report. Order any items indicated.

Check to see if any bills qualify for a discount between April 25 and 29. If any qualify, accept the discount offered by QuickBooks, and pay them. If there any credits to apply to any bill payments, be sure to use them. (Print a voucher-style check so you can see the discounts and credits used.)

Deposit all cash, checks, and credit card receipts.

April 27:

Received the bill and all of the paperback books ordered from Book Suppliers.

April 29:

Received Check No. 4325 for $133.93 from Vivian Newton.

Received Bill No. 1092-5 and pens on order from Pens of the World.

Sold 60 textbooks to Complete Training, Inc., for $59.95 each.

Sold 45 textbooks to Sacramento School for $49.99 each.

April 30:

Prepare Stock Status by Item Inventory Report. Order any items indicated.

Deposit all checks, cash, and credit card receipts.

Pay balance due to Supply City as well as any bills eligible for a discount between April 30 and May 4. Print using a standard style check.

Pay $900 rent for May to the State Rental Agency, 1234 Front Street, Sacramento, CA 95814, Contact: Gail Ruiz, 916-555-1234, Fax 916-555-4321, Terms Net 30.

Pay gas and electricity bill of $257 to California Utilities, 8905 Richmond, Sacramento, CA 95814, 916-555-8523, Terms Net 30.

Pay the telephone bill of $189 to Sacramento Telephone Company, 3899 Oak Avenue, Sacramento, CA 95814, 916-555-8741, Terms Net 30.

Pay the payroll: Elise took 2 hours sick time during the pay period, Laura worked 3 hours overtime, and Kelli worked a total of 40 hours during the pay period. Use the information in the following table and print the paychecks using a voucher-style check.

PAYROLL TABLE: APRIL 30, 2005			
	Elise Nelson	**Laura Ellis**	**Kelli King**
HOURS			
Regular	78	80	40
Overtime		3	
Sick	2		
Vacation			
DEDUCTIONS OTHER PAYROLL ITEMS: EMPLOYEE			
Medical Ins.	30.00	20.00	
DEDUCTIONS: COMPANY			
CA Employment Training Tax	43.33	33.80	10.40
Social Security	67.17	52.39	16.12
Medicare	15.71	12.25	3.77
Federal Unemployment	8.67	6.76	2.08
CA-Unemployment	43.33	33.80	10.40
DEDUCTIONS: EMPLOYEE			
Federal Withholding	146.00	70.00	6.00
Social Security	67.17	52.39	16.12
Medicare	15.71	12.25	3.77
CA-Withholding	31.65	7.91	0.00
CA-Disability	5.42	4.23	1.30

Prepare and print the Payroll Summary Report for April in Landscape orientation. (Adjust column widths to print the report on one page.)

Prepare and print the Payroll Liabilities Balances Report for April in Portrait orientation.

Pay all the payroll taxes and other payroll liabilities for April. Print the checks.

Prepare and print Forms 941 and 940. (Use 06/30/2005 as the date the quarter ended. There are three employees employed. Assume there are no adjustments to be made to either report. Any overpayments will be applied to the next return. Deposits are made monthly. When preparing Form 940, the year is 2005. Answer Yes to Questions A, B, and C.)

Prepare Sales Tax Liability Report for April 1-30, 2005. Print in Landscape orientation. Adjust column widths so the report fits on one page, maintains the same font, and has column headings shown in full.

Pay Sales Tax and print the check.

Print a Sales by Item Summary Report for April in Landscape orientation. Adjust column widths so report fits on one-page wide.

Print a Trial Balance for April 1-30 in Portrait orientation.

Transfer amount of purchases discounts from Income: Purchases Discounts to Cost of Goods Sold: Purchases Discounts.

Enter adjusting entries: Depreciation—Store Equipment $100, Store Fixtures $166.66. Supplies used—Office Supplies $150, Sales Supplies $250. Insurance a total of $100—$50 Fire Insurance, $50 Liability Insurance. (Use a compound entry to record insurance adjustment.)

Record the owner withdrawal for the month $1,500.

Prepare a bank reconciliation and record any adjustments. Use the bank statement on the next page. Print a Reconciliation Detail Report.

CONTINUE WITH PROBLEM

Print a Standard Profit and Loss Statement.

Transfer the Net Income/Retained Earnings into the capital account.

Print the following for April or as of April 30: Trial Balance After Adjustments, Standard Balance Sheet After Adjustments.

Print Statement of Cash Flows for April

Journal (Landscape, adjust column width to fit to one-page wide with the standard font)

STATE BANK
102 8th Street
Sacramento, CA 95814
(916) 555-9889

BANK STATEMENT FOR:

Capital Books
1055 Front Street
Sacramento, CA 95814   Acct. # 97-1132-07922   April 2005

Beginning Balance, April 1, 2005			$35,870.25
4/5/2005, Deposit	2,204.84		38,075.09
4/9/2005, Check 1		1,000.00	37,075.09
4/10/2005, Deposit	1,328.24		38,403.33
4/13/2005, NSF Check		350.00	38,053.33
4/15/2005, Deposit	749.61		38,802.94
4/16/2005, Check 2		85.75	38,717.19
4/16/2005, Check 3		787.38	37,929.81
4/17/2005, Check 4		232.81	37,697.00
4/17/2005, Check 5		644.79	37,052.21
4/18/2005, Check 6		42.90	37,009.31
4/21/2005, Deposit	690.17		37,699.48
4/25/2005, Check 7		7.44	37,692.04
4/25/2005, Deposit	59.94		37,751.98
4/30/2005, Service Charge, $15, and NSF Charge, $25		40.00	37,711.98
4/30/2005, Store Fixtures Loan Pmt.: $80.12 Interest, $15.49 Principal		95.61	37,616.37
4/30/2005, Store Equipment Loan Pmt.: $26.71 Interest, $5.16 Principal		31.87	37,584.50
4/30/2005, Interest	94.03		37,678.53
Ending Balance, 4/30/2005			$37,678.53

(*Reminder*: Print the Detail Reconciliation Report. Return to previous page to complete the problem.)

NAME_____

TRANSMITTAL

END OF SECTION 3: CAPITAL BOOKS

Attach the following documents and reports:

Account Listing
Customer:Job List
Vendor List
Item Listing
Employee List
Standard Balance Sheet, April 1, 2005
Blank Invoice with Logo
Sales Receipt No. 1: Cash Customer
Invoice No. 1: Complete Training, Inc.
Sales Receipt No. 2: Cash Customer
Invoice No. 2: Sacramento School
Sales Receipt No. 3: Cash Customer
Inventory Stock Status by Item, April 1, 2005
Purchase Order No. 1: Pens of the World
Invoice No. 3: Lorraine Norris
Sales Receipt No. 4: Cash Customer
Invoice No. 4: Brian Sauer
Invoice No. 5: Vivian Newton
Invoice No. 6: Sacramento School
Inventory Stock Status by Item, April 1-5, 2005
Purchase Order No. 2: Supply City
Deposit Summary, April 5, 2005
Invoice No. 7: State Schools
Purchase Order No. 3: Deluxe Gift Gallery
Invoice No. 8: Geoffrey Silverman
Credit Memo No. 9: Lorraine Norris
Check No. 1: Book Suppliers
Sales Receipt No. 5: Cash Customer
Invoice No. 10: Vivian Newton
Invoice No. 11: Sacramento School

Deposit Summary, April 10, 2005
Inventory Stock Status by Item, April 1-10, 2005
Sales Receipt No. 6: Cash Customer
Sales Receipt No. 7: Cash Customer
Sales Receipt No. 8: Cash Customer
Invoice No. 12: Morgan Waverly
Invoice No. 13: Morgan Waverly
Sales Receipt No. 9: Cash Customer
Deposit Summary, April 15, 2005
Check No. 2: Pens of the World
Inventory Stock Status by Item, April 1-15, 2005
Purchase Order No. 4: Deluxe Gift Gallery
Purchase Order No. 5: Book Suppliers
Check No. 3: Elise Nelson
Check No. 4: Kelli King
Check No. 5: Laura Ellis
Invoice No. 14: State Schools
Check No. 6: Brian Sauer
Credit Memo No. 15: Brian Sauer,
Inventory Stock Status by Item, April 1-18, 2005
Invoice No. 16: Morgan Waverly
Sales Receipt No. 10: Cash Customer
Inventory Stock Status by Item, April 1-20, 2005
Sales Receipt No. 11: Cash Customer
Invoice No. 17: John Smith
Deposit Summary, April 21, 2005
Sales Receipt No. 12: Cash Customer
Invoice No. 18: Lorraine Norris
Invoice No. 19: Brian Sauer
Inventory Stock Status by Item, April 1-25, 2005
Purchase Order No. 6: Pens of the World
Check No. 7: Supply City
Deposit Summary, April 25, 2005
Invoice No. 20: Complete Training, Inc.
Invoice No. 21: Sacramento School
Inventory Stock Status by Item, April 1-30, 2005
Deposit Summary, April 30, 2005
Check No. 8: Supply City
Check No. 9: State Rental Agency
Check No. 10: California Utilities
Check No. 11: Sacramento Telephone Company

Check No. 12: Elise Nelson
Check No. 13: Kelli King
Check No. 14: Laura Ellis
Payroll Summary, April 2005
Payroll Liability Balances, April 30, 2005
Check No. 15: Employment Development Department
Check No. 16: Medical Ins., Inc.
Check No. 17: State Bank
Employer's Quarterly Federal Tax Return, Form 941
Employer's Annual Federal Unemployment (FUTA) Tax Return
Sales Tax Liability Report, April 2005
Check No. 18: State Board of Equalization
Sales by Item Summary, April 2005
Trial Balance, April 30, 2005
Check No. 19: Raymond Childers,
Bank Reconciliation Report
Standard Profit and Loss, April 2005
Trial Balance After Adjustments, April 30, 2005
Balance Sheet After Adjustments, April 30, 2005
Statement of Cash Flows, April 2005
Journal, April 2005

INTRODUCTION TO WINDOWS®— SCREENS, TERMINOLOGY, AND DISK DUPLICATION

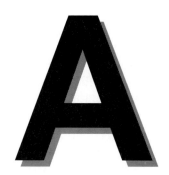

INTRODUCTION TO WINDOWS®

When you turn on the computer, Windows will automatically be in use and icons will be visible on the desktop. (Some computer laboratories require the use of passwords in order to access Windows and the various application programs available. Check with your instructor regarding the configuration of your classroom computers.) Currently, there are several versions of Windows in use. Most things will work in a similar manner so only one set of screen shots will be displayed in this appendix. These screen shots are from Windows® XP.

    DO: If needed, turn on your computer and monitor
Windows will begin running, and the desktop will be displayed on the screen

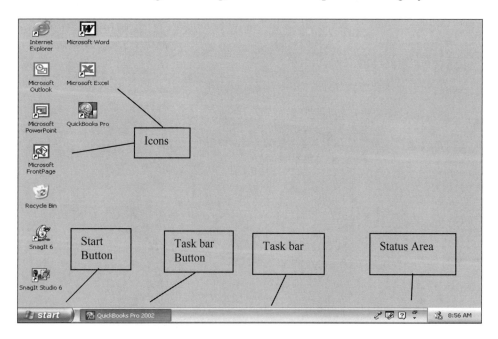

In order to use Windows effectively, it is helpful to understand the terminology used in describing the various Windows elements.

Desktop is the primary work area and covers the entire screen.

Icons are pictorial representations of objects. Some icons on the desktop are "shortcuts" used to access programs and/or documents. Other icons are used to access information regarding your computer or to delete files/programs from the computer.

Taskbar is the major focal point of Windows. It usually appears at the bottom of your screen. The taskbar contains the Start button, which is used to launch (open) programs, access documents, alter the appearance of the desktop, and shut down the computer when you are finished working.

Taskbar buttons indicate the names of any programs/files that are currently open.

Status area is on the taskbar. Programs can place information or notification of events in the status area. Windows places information in the status area: the time and (if available on your computer) a sound icon, which is used to control the volume of the computer's sound system.

ToolTip is a definition, instruction, or information that pops up when you point to something. For example, pointing to the time in the status area of the taskbar gives you a ToolTip that displays the full date; pointing to the Start button gives you the ToolTip "Click here to begin."

Start button is used to access the primary menu in Windows. This menu lists the main functions available.

All Programs is a menu listing the application programs available on your system. Frequently, you must make selections from several menus to access a program. For example, to access Calculator, which is a Windows Accessory Program, you point to the **All Programs** menu, then point to the **Accessories** menu, and finally point to and click on **Calculator**.

My Documents lists the names of documents stored on the hard disk of the computer. (In a classroom environment, documents may be stored on an external floppy disk or on a network. Always check with your instructor prior to saving any work.)

My Pictures lists the names of pictures stored on the hard disk of the computer.

My Music lists the names of music files stored on the hard disk of the computer.

My Computer provides access to and gives information about disk drives and other hardware connected to your computer.

My Network Places gives access to and provides information about files and folders on other computers.

Control Panel provides options for computer customization, adding or removing programs, and setting up network connections and adding user accounts.

Connect To is used for Internet connection.

Help and Support opens a central location for Help topics.

Search opens a window in which you can select search options and work with search results.

Run Opens a program, folder, document, or Web site. Run also allows you to execute a program by name.

Turn Off Computer is *always* used to exit Windows or restart the computer.

Once you have opened a program and are ready to work, Windows will provide several items that are similar to those shown in the following QuickBooks Pro window.

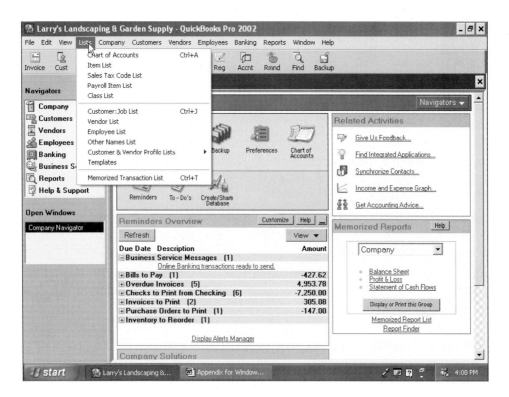

Control menu icon is always in the upper left corner of every window. Clicking on this allows you to access a drop-down menu, which is used for resizing, moving, maximizing, minimizing, closing, or switching a window.

Title bar indicates the name of the program and the file in use.

Minimize button is located on the upper right side of the screen. It appears as a button with a minus sign. Clicking on this allows you to shrink or minimize a window into a button, which appears on the taskbar. When a window is minimized, the program/document is still open and usable; it is just placed on the taskbar as a button so it is out of the way.

Maximize button is a button with a single window as the icon. This is the middle button on the right side of the title bar. Clicking on this allows you to fill the entire screen with the contents of the window. (This is not shown on the QuickBooks window above.)

Restore button appears when a window is maximized, the maximize button changes into a button with two windows. (This is shown on the QuickBooks window above). Clicking on this restores the window to its previous size.

Close button is on the far right side of the title bar. This button has an **X** on it. Clicking on this button closes both the document and the program. (The document window may also have its own minimize, maximize, and close buttons to be used only with the document. If so, these buttons will usually appear below the program minimize, maximize, and close buttons.)

Windows borders are the borders around the outside of open windows. You may point to a border, get a double arrow, then hold down the primary mouse button and drag the border to resize a window.

Menu bar will drop down a menu when clicked. These different menus allow you to access most of the commands within a program.

Dialog box is a box that appears in the middle of your screen and presents information to you or requests information from you.

Message box is a type of dialog box that informs you of a condition—a question, information, or a critical error. Most message boxes require you to confirm, cancel, or retry an action by clicking on a command button.

Command button is a button used to answer the questions within a dialog box.

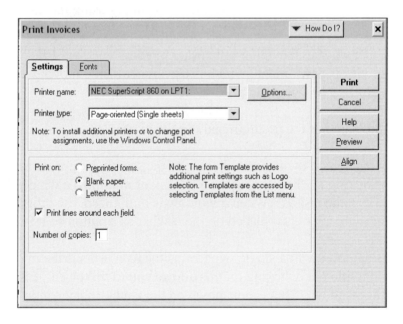

Other items in dialog boxes are:

Drop-down list or box contains the default choice. If you wish to make another selection, click the arrow next to the drop-down list box. If your choice is displayed, simply click on the desired item. (Look at the arrow next to the text box for "Printer name" in the "Print One Invoice" dialog box above.)

Option buttons present more than one choice; however, only one item may be chosen. The selected option contains a black dot. Options that are unavailable are dimmed. (Look at the section for "Print On" in the "Print One Invoice" dialog box.)

Text box allows you to key in information. (Look at the box next to "Printer name.")

Check box provides a choice that may be enabled or disabled. More than one item may be selected. If an option is unavailable, it is dimmed. (Look at the check box for "Do not print lines around each field.")

Spin box allows you to key in a number or to click on up or down arrows to increase or decrease a number. (This is not shown on the illustration.)

HOW TO USE A MOUSE

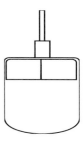

A mouse is an input device that is primarily used to issue commands within a software program. When working in a graphical user interface environment such as Windows, the user sends instructions to programs by simply using the mouse to position the mouse pointer and clicking either the right or left mouse button. A mouse pointer is an arrow that can be used to point to an icon. When you are in a document or a dialog box that requires typing, the mouse pointer turns into an I-beam so it may be positioned more easily.

MOUSE TERMINOLOGY

When using a mouse, terms such as "click," "double-click," "right-click," "drag," and "drag and drop" will be used.

Mouse pointer is the arrow used when pointing to icons.

I-beam is the shape of the mouse pointer when being positioned within a document or a dialog box requiring typing.

Click means pressing the primary (usually left) mouse button one time.

Right-click means pressing the secondary (usually right) mouse button one time.

Double-click means to press the primary (usually left) mouse button two times very quickly.

Drag means to hold down the primary mouse button while dragging the mouse pointer through something (usually text) to highlight.

Right drag means to hold down the secondary mouse button while dragging the mouse pointer through something. Releasing the secondary mouse button will frequently cause Windows to display a popup menu.

Drag and drop means to reposition something. This is achieved by pointing to an object or highlighted text with the mouse pointer, holding down the primary mouse button, and moving the mouse pointer/object by moving the mouse. When the item is repositioned, release the mouse button to "drop" the item into the new position.

Right drag and drop means to reposition something. This is achieved by pointing to an object or highlighted text with the mouse pointer, holding down the secondary mouse button, and moving the mouse pointer/object by moving the mouse. When the item is repositioned, release the mouse button to "drop" the item into the new position. Releasing the secondary mouse button will frequently cause Windows to display a popup menu.

DUPLICATING A DISK

When working with any computer program, it is essential to make a backup disk of your work. In QuickBooks Pro you regularly make a backup file of the company on the same disk as your work. This is not a backup disk; it is a backup of company data that must be restored to a company file before it can be used. A backup file has an extension of .qbb and as indicated it must be restored to a company file with an extension of .qbw.

A backup or duplicate disk is extremely important to have available for use. If something happens to your company disk, you no longer have any of your work. Thus, it is a good practice to make a complete copy of all the files on your company disk to a separate disk. This is usually called a backup disk. For the sake of clarity, this text calls this a duplicate disk.

        DO: Turn on the computer and monitor, if not already on
                    You should see the taskbar at the bottom of the screen and several icons on the
                        desktop
                    Insert the disk containing your company file in the A: drive
                    Point to the **Start** button
                    Right-click on the **Start** button

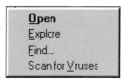

            Click **Explore**

Right-click **3½ Floppy (A:)**

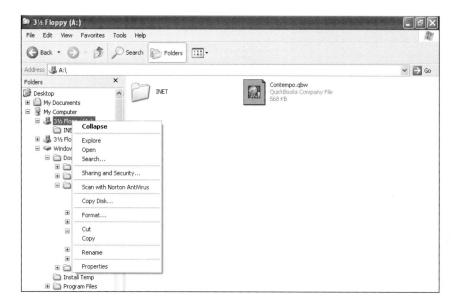

Click **Copy Disk**

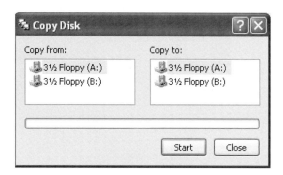

Click **Start**
If you have not already inserted your company disk into the A: drive, do so when
 prompted
Click **OK**

When the computer has finished with the original company disk, remove your
disk from A: and insert a new disk into A:

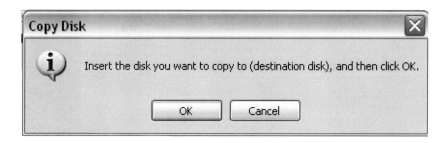

- The disks must be the same storage size. For example if your original disk is a
high-density disk, the disk you copy to must also be a high-density disk.

Click **OK**

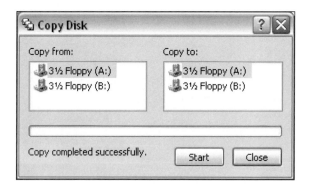

Once the disk has been copied successfully, click **Close**

Label this disk as **Duplicate Company Disk**

- It is important to reduplicate your disk at the end of each chapter. It is a better
practice to duplicate your disk at the end of each computer work session. If
your original disk is lost or becomes damaged, you have the duplicate disk
that you can use.

HOW TO CREATE A QUICKBOOKS® PRO BACKUP FILE

As you work with a company and record transactions, it is important to back up your work. This allows you to keep the information for a particular period separate from current information. A backup also allows you to restore information in case your data disk becomes damaged. There are two different ways in which you can make a backup of your data. If you use Windows Explorer you can make a duplicate disk. In Windows, this is called making a backup. If you use QuickBooks Pro to make a backup, you are actually asking QuickBooks Pro to create a condensed file that contains the essential transaction and account information. This file has a **.qbb** extension and is not usable unless it is restored to a working company file that has a **.qbw** extension. Before entering transactions for Contempo Computer Consulting (CCC) in Chapter 2, make a QuickBooks Pro backup of the company data from the Contempo disk created above.

If you use a floppy disk when working in QuickBooks, the disk will contain the company file. When you place your QuickBooks backup files on the same disk, you may have difficulty when using the company file. This may occur because QuickBooks accesses the same disk used for the company file when it needs to temporarily store information for processing. Thus, even though the disk is not full, it does not have enough room to store the company file, backup files, and temporary files. Should this occur, you may want to duplicate your disk as previously shown and delete the backup files on the disk used for working.

DO: Insert the disk containing the .qbw company file in **A:** (Check with your instructor regarding the storage location you should use for your company and backup files. This example uses **Contempo.qbw** in the A: drive.)
Launch (open) **QuickBooks Pro**
Click **File**
Click **Open Company**
Click the drop-down list arrow for **Look in**
Click **3½ Floppy [A:]**
Click **Contempo.qbw** in the center of the dialog box
Click the **Open** button

Once Contempo Computer Consulting is open, click **File** on the menu bar
Click **Back Up...**

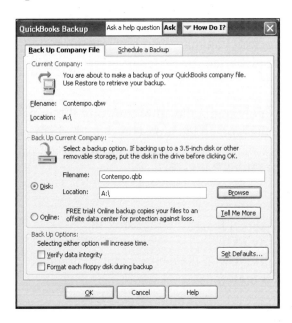

Verify the Current Company information
    Filename is Contempo.qbw
    Location is A:\
Backup Current Company should be to Disk
    The circle in front of Disk should have a black dot in it
    Filename should be Contempo.qbb
        If it is not, click in the text box and enter Contempo.qbb
    Location should be A:\
        If it is not, click in the text box and enter A:\

OR
Click the **Browse** button
The **Back Up Company To...** dialog box appears
Click the drop-down list arrow next to **Save in**, click **3½ Floppy [A:]**.
Click **OK**

Click **Back Up**

- If you get a dialog box asking if you would like to find out about Remote Backup services, click the **No** button.
- QuickBooks Pro will back up the information for Contempo Computer Consultants on the **Contempo** data disk in the A: drive.
- QuickBooks Pro displays a dialog box stating that the backup was successful.

Click **OK** on the message regarding your successful backup
Click **File**
Click **Close Company**

HOW TO RESTORE A QUICKBOOKS® PRO BACKUP FILE

If you make an error in your training, you may find it beneficial to restore your .qbb backup file. The only way in which a .qbb backup file may be used is by restoring it to a .qbw company file. Using QuickBooks' Restore command on the File menu restores a backup file. A restored backup file replaces the current data in your company file with the data in the backup file.

When restoring QuickBooks backup files to a company file, it is important to note that if you are using a floppy disk containing the company file and your backup file, you may get a message that you cannot restore the file. This may occur because QuickBooks accesses the same disk used for the company file and backup file when it needs to store information temporarily while restoring the data contained in the backup file. Thus, even though the disk is not full, it does not have enough room to store the company file, backup files, and temporary files. Should this occur, you may want to ask your instructor about access to an alternate storage location

DO: Insert the disk containing the .qbw company file in **A:** (Use the storage location containing your company and backup files. This example uses **Contempo.qbw** in the A: drive.)
Open the company as previously instructed
Once Contempo Computer Consulting is open, click **File** on the menu bar
Click **Restore...**
Complete the **Get Company Backup From:** area of the screen
Insert **Contempo.qbb** for the Filename
Insert the Location as **A:** (or the location you are using for your files)
OR

Click the Browse button and click on **Contempo.qbb**; and, if necessary, click
the drop-down list arrow for Look in, and click **A:** (or the location you are
using for your files)
Complete the **Restore Company Backup To:** area of the screen
Insert **Contempo.qbw** for the Filename
Insert the Location as **A:** (or the location you are using for your files)
    OR
Click the Browse button and click on **Contempo.qbw**; and, if necessary, click
the drop-down list arrow for Save in, and click **A:** (or the location you are
using for your files)

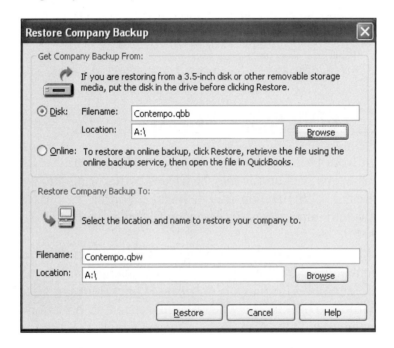

Click the **Restore** button
You will get a warning that you are choosing to overwrite an existing company
    file

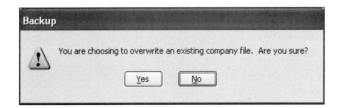

Click **Yes**
You will get a screen telling you how much space you have available on the disk

- *Note:* QuickBooks needs a minimum of over 525 K available on a disk so it can open the company file and use the disk for temporary storage when processing transactions. If QuickBooks cannot restore your file on the disk in A: because there is not enough room, ask your instructor about the procedures you should follow.

Click **OK**

You will get a **Delete Entire File** warning screen

Enter the word **Yes** and click **OK**

- When you restore a file to an existing company file, all the data contained in the company file will be replaced with the information in the backup file.

When the file has been restored, you will get the following

Press Enter or click **OK**

HOW TO CLOSE OR SHUT DOWN WINDOWS®

When you have exited your application program and are ready to close Windows, you need to follow proper exit/closing procedures. Simply turning off the machine is *not* the method to follow when exiting Windows. This might corrupt files that are needed to make the program work properly. When you close or shut down, Windows must close certain files and write information to disk so it will be ready for use the next time the computer is needed. Always be sure to follow the appropriate steps for closing/shutting down Windows.

    DO: Remove the company disk from drive A:
Click **Start**
Click **Turn Off Computer** or **Shut Down**

Click **Turn Off** or **Shut down**
- Follow the above procedures unless you are instructed to use a different procedure by your instructor.

QUICKBOOKS PROGRAM INTEGRATION WITH MICROSOFT® WORD AND EXCEL

QuickBooks Pro and QuickBooks Premier are integrated to work in conjunction with Microsoft Word and Excel to prepare many different types of letters or send QuickBooks reports directly to an Excel workbook. QuickBooks Basic does not have this feature. In order to use the integration features of the program, you must have Microsoft Word 97 (or higher) and Microsoft Excel 97 (or higher) installed on your computer

QUICKBOOKS LETTERS

There are many times in business when you need to write a letter of one type or another to your customers. This is an important feature because QuickBooks will insert information, such as the amount a customer owes, from your customer files directly into a letter. In order to create a letter using QuickBooks, you must have access to the QuickBooks Letters folder. Since there is not enough room on a 3½-inch floppy disk to store a company file and the QuickBooks Letters folder, we will use the sample company, Larry's Landscaping, to work with QuickBooks Letters and prepare a collection letter for David Hughes.

  DO: Prepare a Collection Letter for David Hughes
Open the Sample Company file for a Service Business
Click **File** menu, click **Open Company**
Click **sample_service-based business.qbw**
      You may need to ask your instructor for help in locating the sample company

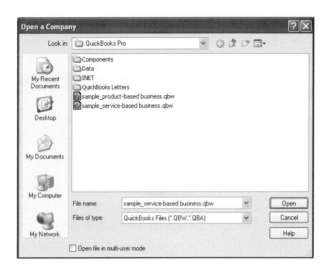

Click **Open**

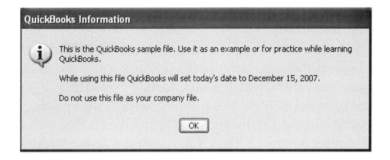

Click **OK** on the QuickBooks Information screen
Click **Customers** on the Navigator bar
Click **Write Letters** on the Customers Navigator

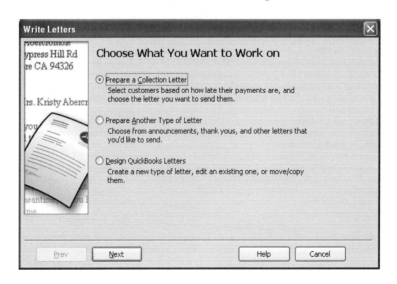

- If it is not already selected, click **Prepare a Collection Letter**

Click **Next**

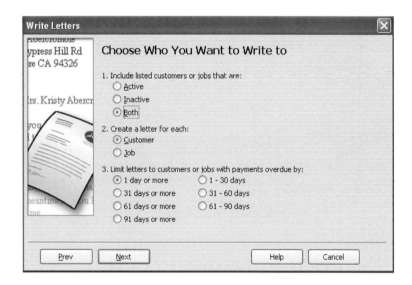

Make the following selections:

1. Include listed customers or jobs that are: **Both**
2. Create a letter for each: **Customer**
3. Limit letters to customers or jobs with payments overdue by: **1 Day or More**

Click **Next**

Click **Clear All** button, then click in the check column to select David Hughes

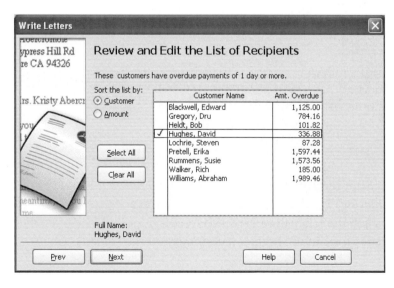

Click **Next**

Click **Friendly Collection** as the type of letter

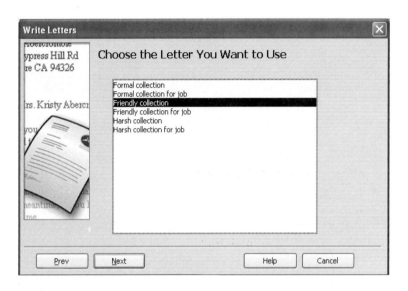

Click **Next**

Enter **Your Name** (your actual name not the words your name) for the name at the end of the letter

Enter your title as **President**

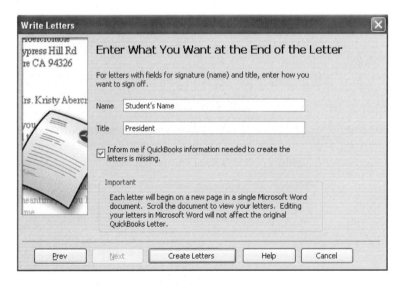

Make sure *Inform me if QuickBooks information needed to create the letters is missing.* is selected, click **Create Letters**

- When the letter is created, Microsoft Word will be opened and the collection letter for David Hughes will appear on the screen.

Larry's Landscaping & Garden Supply
1045 Main Street
Bayshore, CA 94326
(415) 555-4567

December 15, 2007

David Hughes
95 Amber Street
Bayshore, CA 94326

Dear David,

Just a friendly reminder that you have 1 overdue invoice(s), with an overdue balance of $336.88. If you have any questions about the amount you owe, please give us a call and we'll be happy to discuss it. If you've already sent your payment, please disregard this reminder.

We appreciate your continuing business, and we look forward to hearing from you shortly.

Sincerely,

Student's Name
President
Larry's Landscaping & Garden Supply

To make the short letter appear more balanced:
Press **Ctrl+A** to select the entire document
Click **File** menu, **Page Setup**
Change the Left and Right margins to **2"**

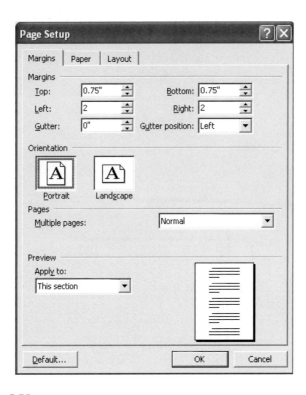

Click **OK**

Position the cursor between the date and the letter address

Press the **Enter** key **5** times so there are 8 blank lines between the date and the letter address

Delete one of the blank lines between the letter address and the salutation

Larry's Landscaping & Garden Supply
1045 Main Street
Bayshore, CA 94326
(415) 555-4567

December 15, 2007

David Hughes
95 Amber Street
Bayshore, CA 94326

Dear David,

Just a friendly reminder that you have 1 overdue invoice(s), with
an overdue balance of $336.88. If you have any questions about
the amount you owe, please give us a call and we'll be happy to
discuss it. If you've already sent your payment, please disregard
this reminder.

We appreciate your continuing business, and we look forward to
hearing from you shortly

Sincerely,

Student's Name
President
Larry's Landscaping & Garden Supply

- Your letter should look like the one above.
  Close Word without saving the letter

EXPORTING REPORTS TO EXCEL

Many of the reports prepared in QuickBooks Pro can be exported to Microsoft® Excel. This allows you to take advantage of extensive filtering options available in Excel, hide detail for some but not all groups of data, combine information from two different reports, change titles of columns, add comments, change the order of columns, and experiment with *what if* scenarios. In order to use this feature of QuickBooks Pro you must also have Microsoft Excel 97 or higher.

DO: Continue to use the sample company: Larry's Landscaping
Click **Report Finder** on the Company Navigator
With Report Finder on the screen, click **Company and Financial**
Click **Balance Sheet Standard**
Enter the **From** date as **10/01/07** and the **To** date as **12/15/07**
Click **Display**

Click the **Export** button

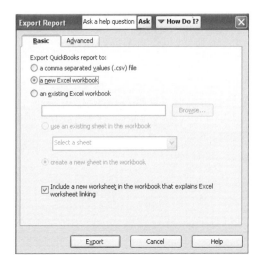

Make sure the Export QuickBooks Report to has **a new Excel workbook** selected
as the File option

Click **Export**

- The Balance Sheet will be displayed in Excel.

					F	G
1						Dec 15, 07
2	ASSETS					
3		Current Assets				
4			Checking/Savings			
5				Checking		32,622.80
6				Cash Expenditures		225.23
7				Savings		5,887.50
8			Total Checking/Savings			38,735.53
9			Accounts Receivable			
10				Accounts Receivable		35,730.02
11			Total Accounts Receivable			35,730.02
12			Other Current Assets			
13				Prepaid Insurance		500.00
14				Inventory Asset		6,937.08
15			Total Other Current Assets			7,437.08
16		Total Current Assets				81,902.63

Partial Report

Scroll through the report and click in Cell A60

Type **BALANCE SHEET IMPORTED TO EXCEL**

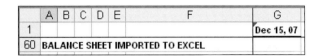

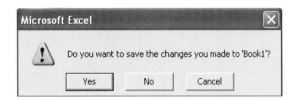

Click the **Close** button in the upper right corner of the Excel title bar to close **Excel**

Click **No** to close **Book1** without saving

IMPORTING DATA FROM EXCEL

A new feature of QuickBooks is the ability to import data from Excel into QuickBooks. You may have Excel or .csv (comma separated value) files that contain important business information about customers, vendors, and sales that are not contained in your QuickBooks Company File. That information can now be imported directly into QuickBooks and customized as desired. An import file must conform to a specific structure for QuickBooks to interpret the data in the file correctly.

It is recommended that you set up your import file correctly in order to transfer the data properly and avoid errors. This includes preparing the file for import into QuickBooks, mapping the data from your file to QuickBooks, and previewing the imported data. QuickBooks has a built-in Reference Guide for Importing Files that may be accessed and printed through Help.

Before you import your file, you should prepare it for import into QuickBooks.

- From the File menu, choose Import, then choose Excel Files.
- At the Set up Import tab, choose the file you want to import.
- If there are multiple sheets, select the sheet. If there is only one sheet, select "Sheet 1."
- Specify whether the file you are importing has header rows.
- From the drop-down list, choose a mapping. You can choose an existing mapping or create a new mapping.
- At the Preferences tab, set your preferences.
- Click Preview to see how the data will be imported into QuickBooks, then click Import if it looks okay or click Import without previewing.

QUICKBOOKS® FEATURES: NOTES, TIME TRACKING, JOB COSTING AND TRACKING, MAILING SERVICES, SHIPPING, AND PRICE LEVELS

The QuickBooks Program contains many areas that were not explored during the training chapters of the text. Some of these areas are time tracking, job costing and tracking, price levels, and notes. To Do Notes, customer notes, vendor notes, employee notes, other names notes, and customer:job classifications are available in all versions of QuickBooks while the other features listed are available only in QuickBooks Pro and QuickBooks Premier. This appendix will use the sample company. Rock Castle Construction, to provide information regarding the features mentioned in the appendix title. Since saving the demonstration transactions will make permanent changes to the sample company and the company file will not fit on a separate floppy disk, you will not need to do the demonstration transactions unless they are assigned by your instructor.

QUICKBOOKS NOTES

QuickBooks allows you to use several types of notes. These are To Do notes, Customer notes, Vendor notes, and Time Tracking notes.

To Do Notes

To Do notes are available in all the versions of QuickBooks. To Do's are accessed by clicking the To Do's icon on the Company Navigator. To Do's are QuickBooks version of a tickler file, which is used to remind you to do something on a particular date.

Steps to Create a To Do Note:

Click **To Do's** icon on the Company Navigator
Click **To Do** button, click **New**
Enter the text of the note
Enter the **Remind me on date**

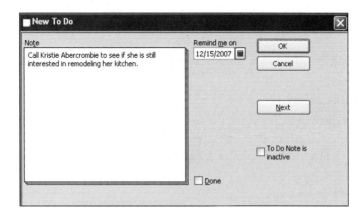

Click **OK**

- The note will be added to the list of To Do notes

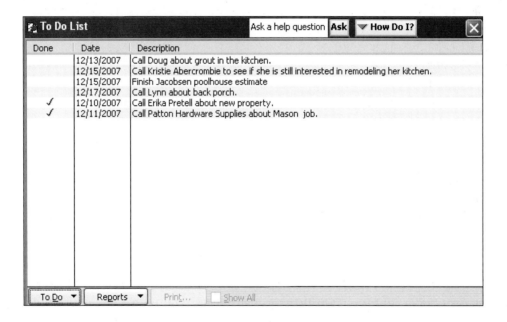

Customer Notes

The customer list contains information about each customer and/or job. One of the columns available is the Notes column. QuickBooks provides a notepad for recording notes about a customer or job. Approximately ten windows worth of text can be displayed on each customer's notepad. You can also write on the customer notepad when viewing a customer's record or when entering a transaction. When using the customer notepad, an entry may be date stamped, To Do notes may be accessed, and the note may be printed.

Steps to Create Customer or Job Notes

Click **Lists** on the menu bar
Click **Customer/Job List**
Double-click in the **Notes** column
- If a notepad icon is showing, there are notes that have been recorded for the customer. You may add to these notes. If there is no notepad showing, there are no notes for the customer.

Click the **Date Stamp** button and QuickBooks will enter the date of the note, then type the note

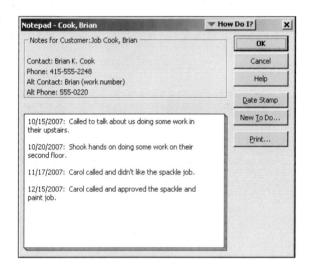

Click **OK** to save and exit the notepad

Vendor, Employee, and Other Names Notes

Vendor notes are recorded on the vendor notepad. As with customer notes, this is where important conversations and product information would be recorded. The vendor notepad can be accessed for the Edit Vendor window, from the Vendor List, or any time you are viewing a transaction related to the vendor. When using the vendor notepad, an entry may be date stamped, To Do notes may be accessed, and the note may be printed. Each entry on your Vendor, Employee, and Other Names lists has its own notepad where you can keep miscellaneous notes to yourself about that vendor, employee, or name. The procedures followed for employee or other names are the same as illustrated for customers and vendors and will not be demonstrated.

Steps to Create Vendor Notes

Click **Lists** on the menu bar
Click **Vendor List**

Double-click in the **Notes** column
- If a notepad icon is showing, there are notes that have been recorded for the customer. You may add to these notes. If there is no notepad showing, there are no notes for the customer.

Click the **Date Stamp** button and QuickBooks will enter the date of the note

Type the note in the vendor notepad

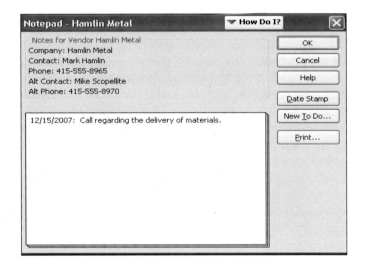

Click **OK** to save and exit the notepad

Notes for Time Tracking

The Timer is a separate program that is installed and works in conjunction with QuickBooks Pro and Premier. Time Tracking will be discussed separately later in this appendix. Notes regarding the time spent working on a task are entered when using the stopwatch.

Steps to Create Notes for Time Tracking

Click the **Employees Navigator**

Click **Time/Enter Single Activity** icon

Click the drop-down list arrow for **Name** and select the employee

Click the drop-down list arrow for **Customer:Job** and select the customer

Click in the **Notes** section of the window

Enter the note

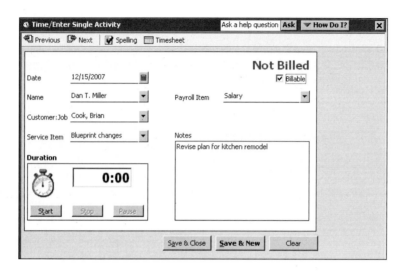

Click **Save & Close**

TRACKING TIME

Many businesses bill their customers or clients for the actual amount of time they spend working for them. In this case you would be tracking billable time. When you complete the invoice to the customer, you can add the billable time to the invoice with a few clicks. In other situations, you may not want to bill for the time; but you may want to track it. For example, you may want to find out how much time you spend working on a job that was negotiated at a fixed price. This will help you determine whether or not you estimated the job correctly. Also, you may want to track the amount of time employees spend on various jobs, whether or not you bill for the time.

Both QuickBooks Pro and Premier come with a separate Timer program. Timer can be run on any computer whether or not it has QuickBooks. You have a choice between tracking time via the Timer and then transferring the time data to QuickBooks, using the Stopwatch on the Time/Enter Single Activity window, or entering time directly into QuickBooks manually on the Weekly Timesheet window or the Time/Enter Single Activity window.

Steps to Track Time as a Single Activity

Click **Employees** on the **Navigator List**
Click the icon for **Time/Enter Single Activity**
Enter the date or accept the date the computer provides
Click the drop-down list arrow for **Name**
Click the name of the employee doing the work
Click the drop-down list arrow for **Customer:Job**
Click the name of the customer or the job for which time is being recorded
Click the drop-down list arrow for **Service Item**

Click the appropriate service item

Indicate whether or not the time recorded is billable

- A check in the billable box means that this is recorded as billable time. No check means that the time is being tracked but not billed.

Click the drop-down list arrow for **Payroll Item**

Indicate the payroll item for the time

Enter any notes regarding the work being performed

Click **Start** on the timer

When finished with the work, click **Stop** on the timer

- If work is stopped at any time, you may click Pause when stopping and click Start when resuming work.

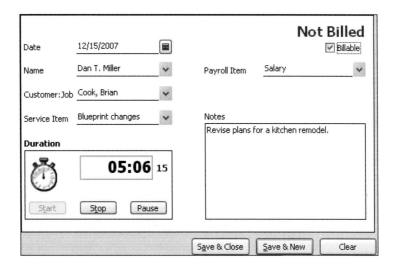

When finished, click **Stop** and **Save & Close**

Steps to Track Time on a Timesheet

Click **Employees** on the **Navigator List**

Click the icon for **Use Weekly Timesheet**

Click the drop-down list arrow for **Name**

Click the name of the employee doing the work

Enter the date, accept the date the computer provides, or click the **Set Date** button

- Any work completed as a Single Activity will appear on the time sheet

If the information is the same as the previous timesheet, click Copy Last Sheet

- The information for the previous timesheet will be entered for this time period.

If you need to enter the information for the time period, click the drop-down list arrow for Customer:Job

Click the name of the customer for whom work is being performed

Click the drop-down list arrow for **Service Item**

Click the name of the service item

If necessary, click the drop-down list arrow for **Payroll Item**

Click the name of the payroll item

Enter any notes regarding the work

Enter the number of hours worked in the appropriate columns for the days of the week

Indicate whether or not the hours are billable

- QuickBooks Timer records all hours as billable unless otherwise indicated. The icons in the last column indicate whether or not the items are billable, have been billed on a previous invoice, or are not billable.

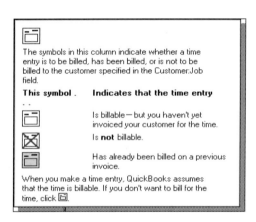

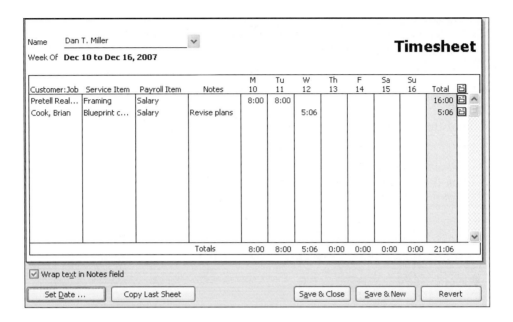

When the timesheet is complete, click **Save & Close**

Prepare an Invoice Using Billable Hours

Click the **Invoice** icon on the Customer Navigator

Enter the name of the **Customer:Job**

- QuickBooks will search for any estimates to be billed to the Customer:Job. If necessary, select the estimate to be billed. Indicate whether the estimate should be billed in full or in part. Complete this section of the invoice.

Since we do not want to bill for estimates, click **Cancel** to go directly to the invoice and not bill for the estimates.

Click **Time/Costs** on the top of the Create Invoices screen

Click the **Time** tab

Scroll through the list of Time and Costs for the customer

Click the time you wish to bill

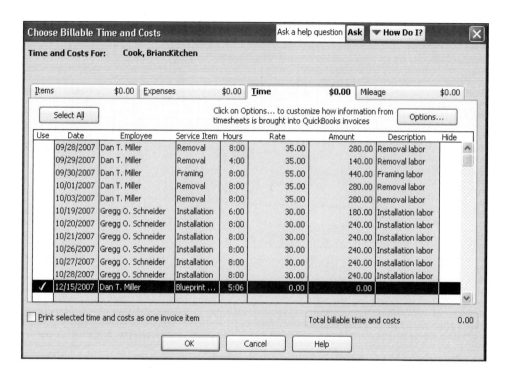

Click **OK**

* The time will be entered on the invoice.

Complete the invoice as previously instructed

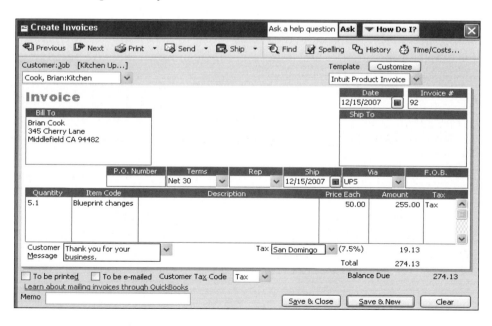

* The time clock keeps time in minutes but enters time on the invoice in tenths of an hour.

Click **Save & Close**

JOB COSTING AND TRACKING

Many companies complete work based on a job for a customer rather than just the customer. In QuickBooks, a job is a project done for a particular customer. You must always associate a job with a customer. However, if you are only doing one job for the customer, you do not have to add a new job to the Customer:Job list. Instead, you can use the Job Info tab to track the status of the job. This tab is available in the New Customer (or Edit Customer) window when you have not set up any jobs for the customer. You may also track several jobs for one customer.

When tracking jobs, there are several reports that may be prepared. These reports use the information provided when tracking the jobs and display information. These reports answer questions about how well you estimate jobs and how much time you spend on jobs. Some of the reports available are:

Job profitability summary: This report summarizes how much money your company has made to date from each customer. If your company did multiple jobs for a customer, the report shows subtotals for each job.

Job profitability detail: This report shows how much money your company has made to date on the customer or job whose name you entered. The report lists costs and revenues for each item you billed to the customer so you can see which parts of the job were profitable and which parts were not.

Job estimates vs. actuals summary: This report summarizes how accurately your company estimated job-related costs and revenues. The report compares estimated cost to actual cost and estimated revenue to actual revenue for all customers. If your company did multiple jobs for a customer, the report shows subtotals for each job.

Job estimates vs. actuals detail: This report shows how accurately your company estimated costs and revenues for the customer or job whose name you entered. The report compares estimated and actual costs and estimated and actual revenues for each item that you billed. That way, you can see which parts of the job you estimated accurately and which parts you did not.

Job progress invoices vs. estimates: This report compares each estimate with progress invoices based on the estimate. For each customer or job, this report shows whether or not the estimate is active, the estimate total, the total invoiced from the estimate on progress invoices, and the percentage of the estimate already invoiced on progress invoices. The report includes progress invoices marked as pending.

Time by job summary: This report shows how much time your company spent on various jobs. For each customer or job, the report lists the type of work performed (service items). Initially, the report covers all dates from your QuickBooks records, but you can restrict the period covered by choosing a different date range from the Dates list.

Time by job detail: This report lists each time activity (that is, work done by one person for a particular customer or job on a specific date) and shows whether the work is billed, unbilled, or not billable. The report groups and subtotals the activities first by customer and job and then by service item.

Steps to Create a Job for a Customer

From the Lists menu, choose **Customer:Job List**
Select the customer for whom you want to add a job
Choose **Add Job** from the Customer:Job menu button
In the New Job window, enter a name for this job
On the **Job Info** tab, choose a job status (Pending, Awarded, etc.) from the drop-down list.
(Optional) Enter a start date and an end date (projected or actual) for the job
(Optional) Enter a job description and a job type

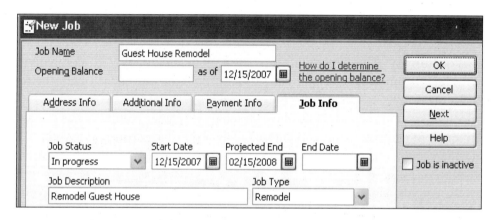

Click **OK** to record the new job.
The job is added to the customer or the Customer List

Steps to Create a Bill Received for Expenses Incurred on a Job and Items Purchased for a Job

Enter the bill information as instructed in Chapter 6
Click the drop-down list arrow for Customer:Job
Click the appropriate Customer:Job
Enter the date and amount of the bill
Enter the expense on the Expenses tab

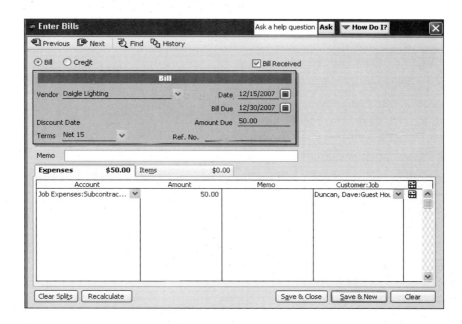

To prepare a bill for both expenses and items, click the Items tab and enter the appropriate information.

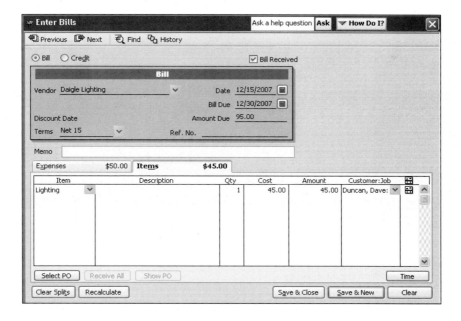

Click **Save & Close**

Steps to Create an Invoice for Items and/or Expenses Billed for a Job

Open an Invoice as previously instructed
Indicate the Customer:Job as previously instructed
Click **Time/Costs** at the top of the Create Invoices window

Click the **Items** tab
Select the Item by clicking in the **Use** column

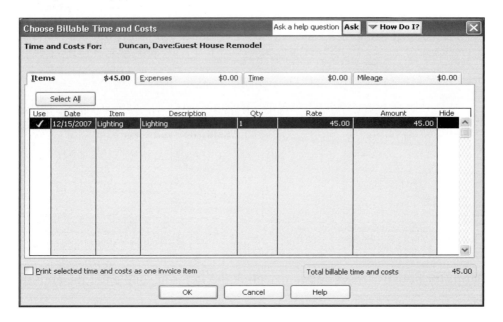

Indicate whether or not you have a markup percentage and the account associated with markups
Click the **Expenses** tab
Click the Expense in the Use column to select

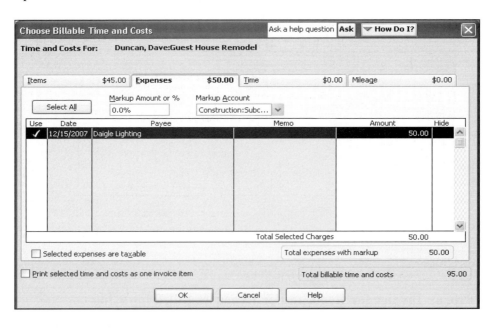

Click **OK**
Complete the Invoice

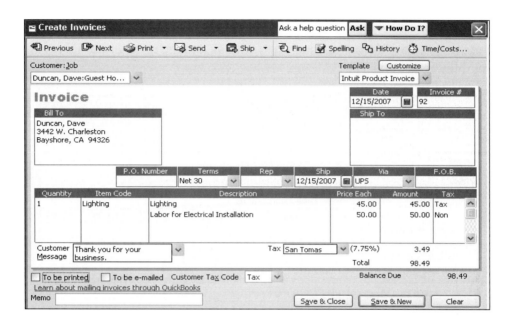

Click **Save & Close**

Creating Reports Using Jobs and Time

Use **Report Finder** or the Reports Menu
Click **Jobs & Time**
Click the report you wish to prepare

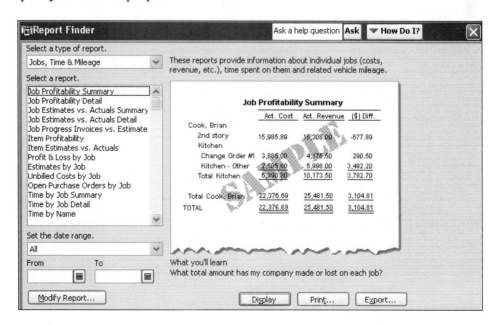

If using Report Finder, set the date range or enter the **From** and **To** dates, click **Display**

OR

If preparing the report from the menu, enter the Dates as a range or enter the **From** and **To** dates at the top of the report and Tab

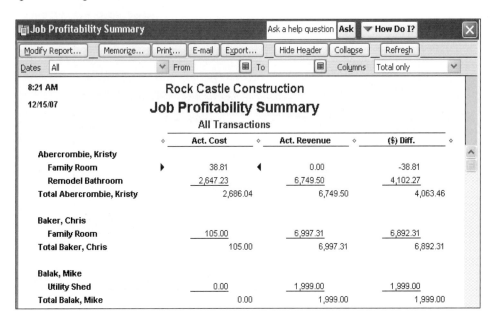

Scroll through the report to evaluate the information

SENDING INVOICES THROUGH QUICKBOOKS' MAILING SERVICE

QuickBooks Pro offers a mailing service that is available for a fee. This mailing service will provide a folded invoice with a tear-off remittance slip, and a return envelope. A copy of the Send Invoice screen is shown below. We will not be using this service in the text.

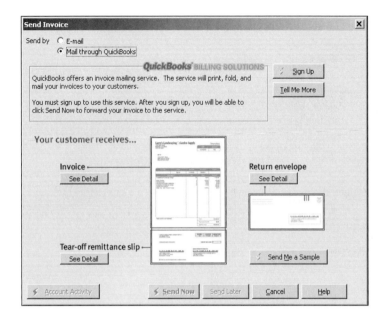

SENDING MERCHANDISE USING QUICKBOOKS SHIPPING MANAGER

QuickBooks has a shipping manager that works in conjunction with FedEx. In order to send merchandise to a customer, you must set up the shipping manager and have an account with FedEx. Since we are working for a fictitious company we will not do this. The steps listed below will illustrate the setup of the Shipping Manager but will not complete the shipping procedure.

> To set up the Shipping Manager, you would click the **Ship** button at the top of an invoice
>
> Click **Ship a Package**
>
> Complete the information on the QuickBooks Shipping Manager Setup Wizard
>
> * *Note:* The address information is available in the Company Info and may be accessed by clicking the Company menu.
> * Be sure to insert a name in the text box for Name.

Click **Next**

Click **Next**

You would enter your FedEx Account number on this screen and click Next
Since we do not have a FedEx account and do not want to create one, you would
click **Cancel**

PRICE LEVELS

In QuickBooks Pro and Premier you can create price levels. Price levels are created to increase
or decrease inventory, non-inventory, and service item prices. For each price level you create,
you assign a name and percentage of increase or decrease. You can use price levels on invoices,
sales receipts, or credit memos. When you apply a price level to an item on a sales form, the
adjusted price appears in the Rate column. You can assign price levels to customers and jobs.
Then, whenever you use that customer and job on a sales form, the associated price level is
automatically used to calculate the item price.

Create a Price Level List

From the Lists menu, choose **Price Level List**

From the Price Level menu, choose **New**

In the New Price Level window, enter the name of the new price level

Select Increase sales price by or Reduce sales price by

In the Percentage % field, enter the percent number by which the item price will be increased or reduced.

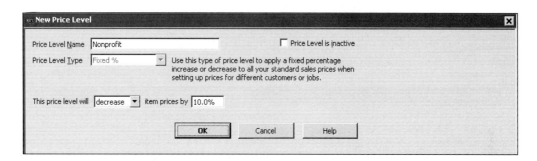

Click **OK** to go back to the Price Levels list.

Apply a Price Level on an Invoice

Fill out the invoice as previously instructed

In the Rate column, click the drop-down button

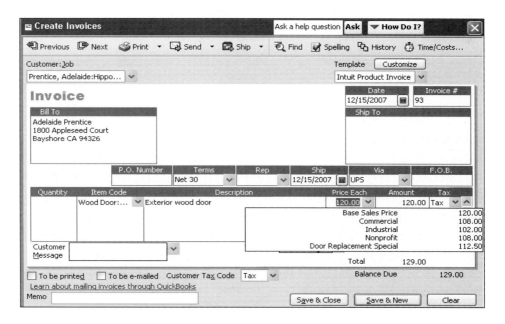

Choose a price level to apply to the item

• The amount shown next to each price level is the adjusted amount of the item

Save the invoice

Associate a Price Level with a Customer

From the Customers menu, choose **Customer:Job** list
Select the **Customer**
Click the **Customer:Job** button
Click **Edit**
Click the **Additional Info** tab
From the Price Level drop-down list, select the price level you want to associate with the
    customer

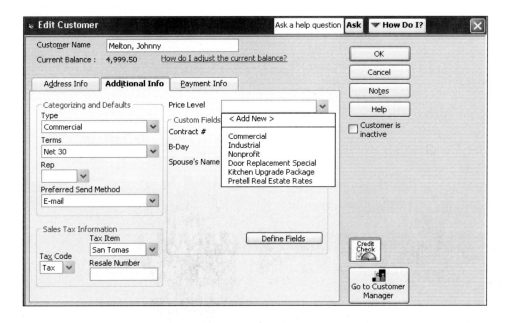

Click **OK**
When preparing an invoice, items will automatically appear at the price level selected for the
    customer
To verify this, click the drop-down list arrow for Price Each and notice that the price for the
    Exterior wood door has been entered at the commercial rate (the price level selected for the
    customer).

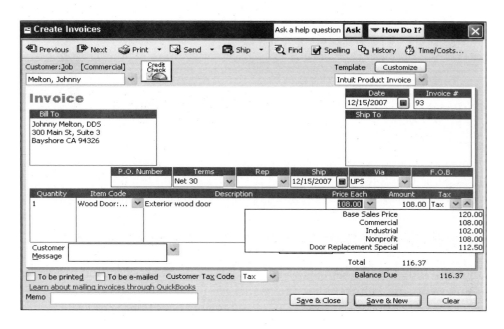

Click **Save & Close**

QUICKBOOKS® PRO
ONLINE FEATURES

QuickBooks Pro is up-to-date in its online capabilities. It has integrated Internet access built into the program and Internet Explorer is included on the QuickBooks Pro CD-ROM. It performs online updates to the program, subscribers to the Basic Payroll Services can receive online updates to tax tables, Trial Versions of the program can be downloaded, and online banking can be performed within the program. In addition, through QuickBooks.com you can obtain product support, access training resources, find a professional advisor in your area, access user-to-user forums, obtain information about business resources, access Intuit's Home Page, and order checks and business forms online.

In addition to the included online items, there are several online subscription programs that may be used in conjunction with QuickBooks. These include processing credit card payments, credit check services, a QuickBooks credit card, a shipping manager, bill pay, and others. Intuit also offers the QuickBooks Solutions Marketplace that brings together over 100 companies that have integrated their software products with QuickBooks Pro, Premier and QuickBooks Enterprise Solutions.

This Appendix will explore some of the online options listed above.

INTUIT AND THE INTERNET

At Intuit's Web site you may get up-to-date information about QuickBooks Pro and other products by Intuit. You can access the Intuit Web site at www.Intuit.com through your browser.

When you access Intuit's Web site, you can download a Trial Version of the software. There is no cost for this version of the software; however, it may be used only 15 times. To continue using the program after that, you should purchase the program and register it.

DOWNLOADING A TRIAL VERSION OF QUICKBOOKS® PRO

Intuit offers a free Trial Version of the software. To download a trial version of QuickBooks Pro, you need to connect to the Internet, access your browser, and enter www.Shopintuit.com as the Web address.

Open your Internet Connection and Web Browser
Enter www.Shopintuit.com as the URL
When you get to Shop Intuit, click the **QuickBooks** tab and follow the procedures listed to obtain the trial version of the software

OR
Call **888-729-1996**

QUICKBOOKS® PRO UPDATES

Intuit has a service that is free of charge and allows you to check the Web site to download messages and updates for QuickBooks Pro. You may have QuickBooks Pro do this automatically, or it will remind you to update periodically. QuickBooks Pro provides two methods for updating—automatic and immediate. Both methods require an Internet connect and may be used concurrently.

Update QuickBooks Pro Automatically

With this method, updates of your choice are automatically downloaded from the Intuit server to your computer. QuickBooks Pro periodically checks the Intuit server for new updates, and proceeds to download information gradually at times when your open Internet connection is not being used by another process or application.

The advantages of updating QuickBooks Pro automatically are:

- Updates are downloaded to your computer unobtrusively, without interrupting a QuickBooks Pro session or other tasks that you perform with your computer.
- Updating occurs whether or not QuickBooks Pro is running.
- You can disconnect from the Internet anytime and not worry about updating. When you reconnect to the Internet, QuickBooks Pro resumes downloading updates at the point where it was previously halted.

QuickBooks Pro continues to download updates automatically until you turn off the Automatic Update option. Even with the Automatic Update option turned on, you can still download all available updates immediately whenever you choose to do so.

If you have several different copies of QuickBooks Pro running and you share data, it is essential that computers be updated at the same time so they all have the same exact version of the program in operation. If you update QuickBooks Pro on one computer and not another, QuickBooks Pro may not be able to read the company file on the computer that did not receive the update.

Update QuickBooks Pro Immediately

With this method, updates of your choice are downloaded immediately from the Intuit server to your computer. You can use this method at any time—even when your computer is configured to download updates automatically.

To download immediately, click the **File** menu, click **Update Update QuickBooks**, click **Update Now** tab

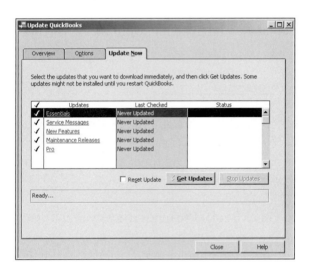

Click **Get Updates**

Select or Deselect Automatic Updates

To select or deselect automatic updates, click the **File** menu, click **Update QuickBooks**, click the **Options** tab

To select Automatic Update, click **Yes**, click **Select All** to choose updates of New Features and Maintenance Releases

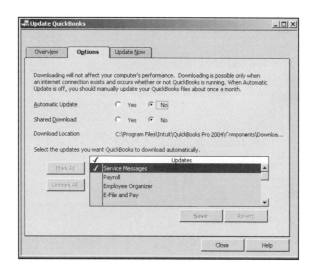

To deselect automatic update, click **Off** and **Save**

CONNECTING TO INTUIT INTERNET IN QUICKBOOKS® PRO

Before connecting to Intuit's Web page, you must have the QuickBooks Pro program and a company open. In addition, you must have a modem for your computer, and the modem must be connected to a telephone line or cable. Once the modem is connected and QuickBooks Pro and a company are open, you may establish your Internet connection.

QuickBooks Pro has a step-by-step tutorial that will help you do this. Pointing to Internet Setup allows you to click on Internet Connection Setup and complete the tutorial. The first screen you see informs QuickBooks Pro of your choice for your Internet connection. You may tell QuickBooks Pro that you have an existing dial-up Internet connection, that you plan to use a direct connection through a network at school or work, or that you want to sign up for an Intuit Internet account with limited access. Because every computer may be different, go through the steps for connection when you have an established Internet provider. As in earlier chapters, you will need to click **Next** to go from one screen to another. Check with your instructor to see if you will be completing the Internet connection or simply reading this appendix.

Click the **Help** menu, click **Internet Connection Setup**

To Use an Established Internet Connection

Click **Use the following connection**, click the connection, click **Next**

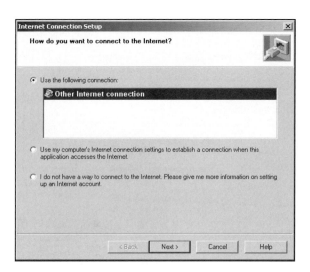

Verify the information provided, click **Done**

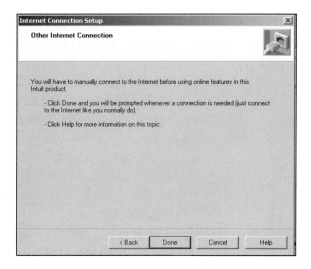

To Use a Computer's Internet Connection

If you have a direct Internet connection, select **Use my computer's Internet connection settings to establish a connection when this application accesses the Internet**, click **Next**

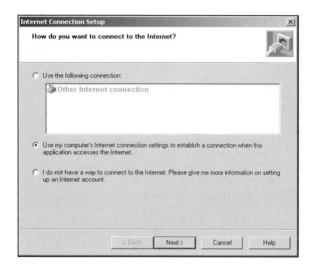

Verify the information, click **Done**

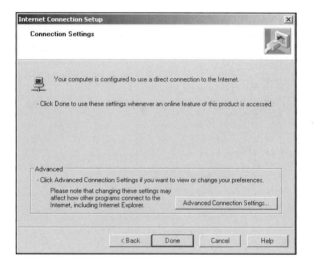

To Establish an Internet Provider and Connection

If you do not have an Internet provider, click **I do not have a way to connect to the Internet. Please give me more information on setting up an Internet account**

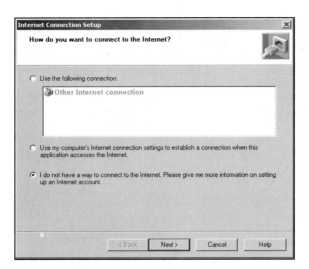

Click **Next**

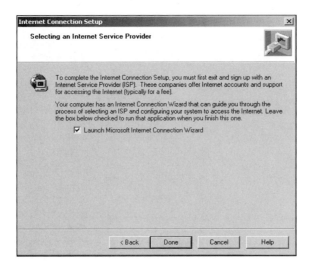

Click **Done** and complete the steps listed in the Microsoft Internet Connection Wizard

ACCESS QUICKBOOKS' ONLINE FEATURES

Anytime you see a lightning bolt, this denotes information or services that require an Internet connection. Click on the lightning bolt.

If you have a direct Internet connection, you will go directly to the QuickBooks Web site
If you use a dial-up service to connect to the Internet, you may get the following screen.

If necessary, click **Connect**

When you are connected, you will go to the areas requested. For example, on the Company Navigator, I clicked

If you position the cursor on the any of the tabs at the top of the screen, the cursor will turn into a hand. This means you can click on any of these items and get item descriptions and ordering information.

ONLINE BANKING AND PAYMENTS

Online banking and payment services are offered through QuickBooks Pro in conjunction with a variety of financial institutions. You must apply for this service through your financial institution. If you bank with or make payments to more than one institution, you must sign up with each institution separately. Most banks will charge a fee for online services and may not offer both online banking and online payment services. Many financial institutions provide online services.

Online Banking

Online account access allows you to download transactions from a checking, savings, money market, or credit or charge account. You can also transfer money online and send e-mail to your financial institution.

To use the online banking services for account access or payment, you need access to the Internet and an account at a participating financial institution. You must also apply for the service through QuickBooks or through a participating financial service. To see a list of participating financial institutions, click the Banking menu, point to *Set Up Online Financial Services,* and click **Online List of Available Financial Institutions**

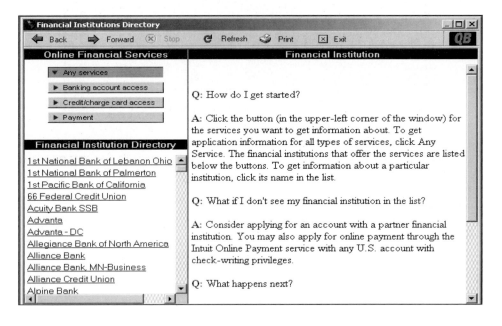

In order to provide security and confidentiality in online services, QuickBooks uses state-of-the-art encryption and authentication security features. All of your online communications with your financial institution require a Personal Identification Number (PIN) or password, which only you possess. You may also use passwords within QuickBooks Pro.

For this appendix, we will use Larry's Landscaping as our business and use ANYTIME Financial services as our financial institution

Set Up Online Banking

To apply for an online account, click the **Banking** menu bar
Point to Setup Online Financial Services
Click **Setup Account for Online Banking Access**
Complete the Online Setup Interview

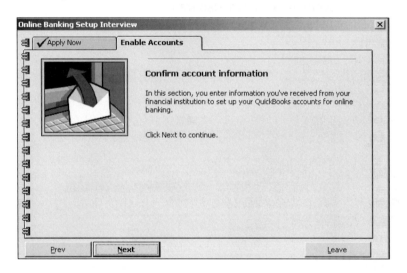

Click **Next**
Click the drop-down list arrow for **I would like to enter information for my accounts at:**
Click **ANYTIME Financial**

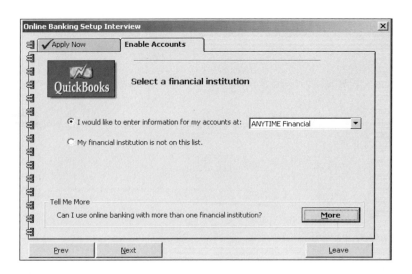

Click **Next**
Review the account information provided
Make any necessary changes

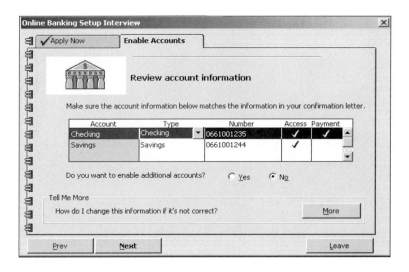

Click **Next**
Read the Service Agreement Information screen

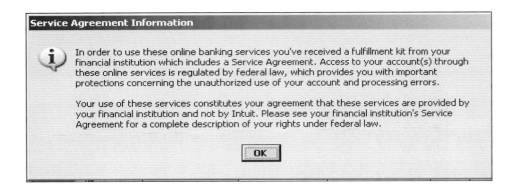

Click **OK**

You do not wish to enable accounts at another institution

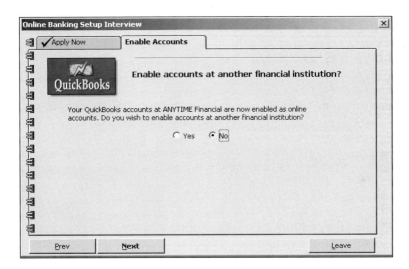

Click **Next**

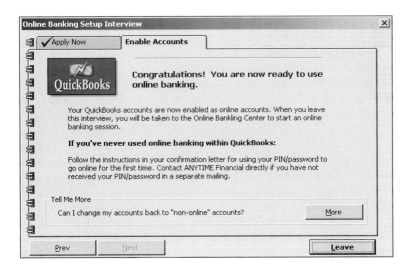

The Online Setup Interview is complete, click **Leave**

Using Online Banking

Online banking allows you to download current information from and send messages to your financial institution. This can include transactions, balances, online messages, and transfer of funds. To use online banking, click **Banking** on the Navigator bar, click **Online Banking Center**.

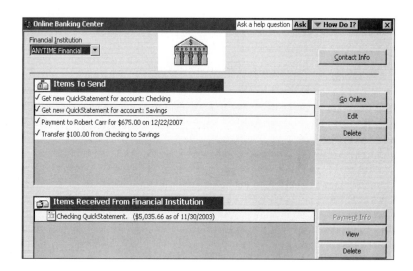

You can automatically compare the downloaded transactions with those in your register. QuickBooks Pro will match downloaded transactions to those in your register and note any unmatched transactions so that they may be entered into your register.

- *Note:* Even though the date used in the sample company is 2007, in several instances, as in the above screen shot, you will see the date of 2003.

Click the **View** button

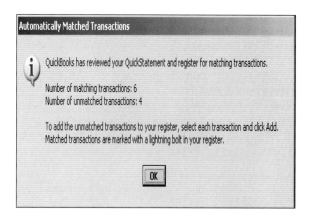

Click **OK**

The QuickStatement shown lists the transactions that occurred since your last download and any transactions that were not matched from previous downloads. The QuickStatement does not replace your paper statement. You will receive your usual paper statement by mail from your financial institution listing your monthly account transactions.

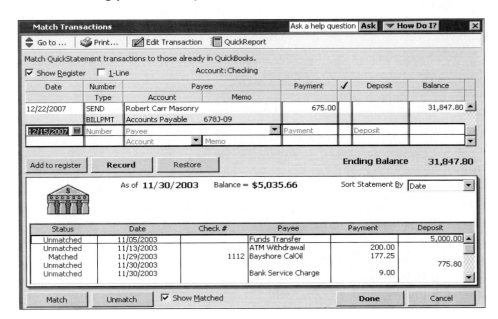

To match the ATM Withdrawal to the QuickStatement, you must add the transaction to the register.

Click the **Unmatched ATM Withdrawal** transaction in the lower portion of the screen, click the **Add to Register** button.

Click **Add To Register** on the Unmatched Transaction screen

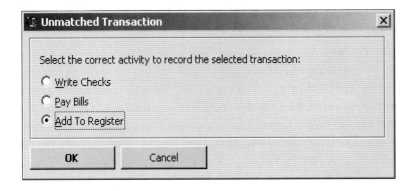

Click **OK**

Click the drop-down list arrow for Account, click **Owner's Draw** from the list of accounts.

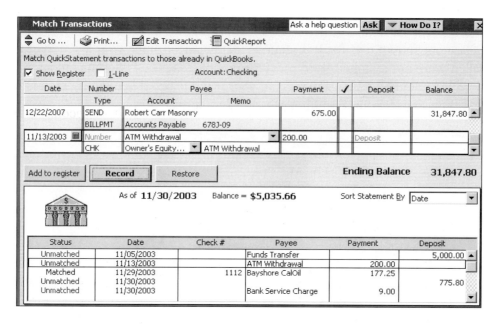

Click **Record**

The transaction status is Matched

Click **Done**, if you get a message that not all transactions are matched, click **Yes**

Online Payments

You may use the online payment services to create online payment instructions for one or more payments, then send the instructions via your modem. You may schedule a payment to arrive on a certain date, inquire about online payments, and cancel them if need be. You can record and pay your bills at the same time, all from within QuickBooks.

With online payment you can:

- Pay bills without writing checks or going to the post office.
- Attach additional information to the payment (such as invoice number and invoice date) so your vendor knows which bill to apply it to.

- Schedule a payment in advance, to be delivered on or before the date you specify.
- Apply for online payment services online.

Online banking through QuickBooks uses state-of-the-art encryption technology and requires a PIN to send transactions. You can use online payment with any U.S. bank account with check-writing privileges.

There are three ways to send an online payment:

- From the Pay Bills window
- From the Write Checks window
- From an online account register

You use these methods the same way you always do, except that you designate the transaction as an online transaction and send the payment instructions to your financial institution.

To use online payments, you need to set up a payee. Once the payee is set up, you may either send an electronic funds transfer (EFT) to the payee's institution or have your financial institution print a check and send it to the payee. An electronic funds transfer deducts money from your account and transfers it into the payee's account electronically. This usually takes one or two business days. This is called lead time and must be considered when sending online payments. If you have your institution mail checks to payees, you should allow four days lead time.

A check used to send an online payment will use Send as the No. and will have a checkmark for Online Bank Payment.

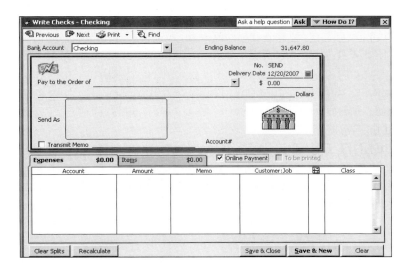

PERSONALIZED WEB SITE AND DOMAIN NAME

QuickBooks Pro enables your company to create a Web site. In order to qualify for this service, you must have a registered copy of QuickBooks Pro. Information about the Web site service can be obtained from the QuickBooks screen online.

Your Web address is an important element of your online identity. It sets the tone for your online brand and provides a name your customers will remember to find your Web site on the Internet. And since no two parties can ever hold the same Web Address simultaneously, your Web Address is totally unique.

Without a Web address, people can't find you on the Web. Your Web address is the first step to being online. Your Web address is what is typed into computers to find your Web site. A Web address is also known as a domain name or a URL. Technically, a Web Address is a naming convention used for identifying and locating computers on the Internet. Computers use Internet Protocol (IP) numbers to locate each other on the Internet, but IP addresses are difficult to remember. Therefore, Web addresses were developed so that easily remembered words and phrases could be used to identify Internet addresses.

Every Web site you find on the Internet has a Web host. The Web host is responsible for storing the Web site and making it available on the Internet 24 hours a day. To do Web hosting yourself is complicated and involves expensive hardware and software, not to mention technical expertise to maintain it.

Web site designs are professional-quality templates that include complex features such as intricate page layouts (versus basic headers and wallpapers), custom interactive buttons (versus hyperlink navigation), unique font and color schemes (versus basic HTML text styles), and the use of dynamic button rollovers.

To create or view your Web site, click the **Company** menu, click **Company Web Site**, and go online to QuickBooks and follow the instructions provided to register for business services. Since we are not working with an actual company, we will not be creating a company Web site.

QUICKBOOKS CREDIT CHECK SERVICES

QuickBooks has teamed with Dun and Bradstreet to provide credit checks of potential customers to companies. There are three programs available with various fees and numbers of reports included. This service can be valuable when it comes to making decisions regarding extending credit to customers.

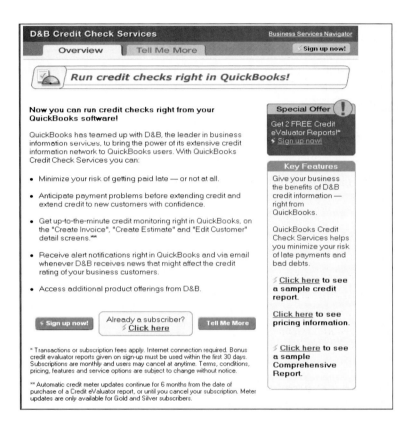

There are three plans available and the some of the pricing at the time of publication is shown on the following chart

Features	Gold Package	Silver Package	Basic Package
Credit eValuator Reports in QuickBooks Gold and Silver subscribers access reports right from QuickBooks, including automatic updates for 6 months. **	4 reports per month included in package	2 reports per month included in package	$24.99 each
Additional Credit eValuator Reports Incremental credit reports beyond those included in your package.	$12.99 each	$12.99 each	$24.99 each
Bonus Credit eValuator Reports* Free reports, just for signing up!	2 FREE reports when you sign up!	2 FREE reports when you sign up!	None
Comprehensive Reports D&B's most detailed business credit report including analyses of credit scores, financial stress indicators and payment habits and trends.	$99.00 each	$117.00 each	$117.00 each
Industry Reports A national market overview of your industry with a listing of competitors and their locations.	$16.99 each	$19.99 each	$24.99 each

A sample credit report and other information appear as follows:

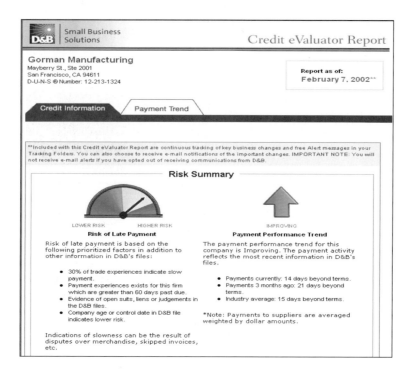

QUICKBOOKS BILLING SOLUTIONS

QuickBooks offers an invoice e-mail service that will instantly e-mail easy-to-read PDF files of invoices, statements and estimates from QuickBooks. It also has a mailing service that will print, fold, and mail invoices to customers. In addition, payment reminders, online e-mail tracking, and online payment options are also included. This requires signing up for the optional QuickBooks Billing Solutions.

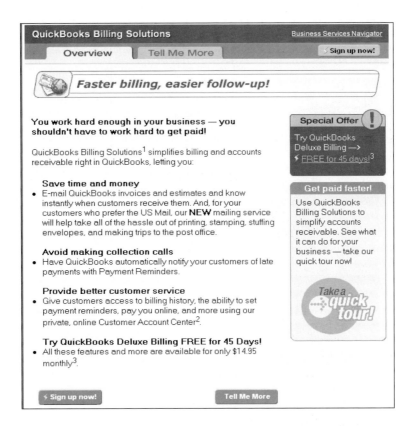

The three types of Billing Solutions accounts, their features, and fees are illustrated in the following table:

Features Available	Basic Billing	Billing Plus	Deluxe Billing
E-mail professional forms as a PDF[1]	YES	YES	YES
Automatic historical record of all invoices sent	YES	YES	YES
Accept credit card payments online[4]	YES	YES	YES
Send invoices via US Mail from QuickBooks[3]	NO	YES	YES
Automatically send payment reminders	NO	NO	YES
Know if your e-mailed invoice was received	NO	NO	YES
Auto alerts when payments are late	NO	NO	YES
Give customers access to their own online payment center	NO	NO	YES
Display billing information directly in your e-mails	NO	NO	YES
How to Sign Up	Comes built in to QuickBooks	Sign-up through QuickBooks	Sign-up through QuickBooks
Monthly fee	FREE	$4.95	$14.95
Per transaction fee for mailed invoices	Not Available	0-50 invoices: $.99 51-200 invoices: $.89 201+ invoices: $.79	0-50 invoices: $.99 51-200 invoices: $.89 201+ invoices: $.79

QuickBooks Billing Solutions include:

E-mail Options: Instantly e-mail easy-to-read PDF files of invoices, statements and estimates from QuickBooks.

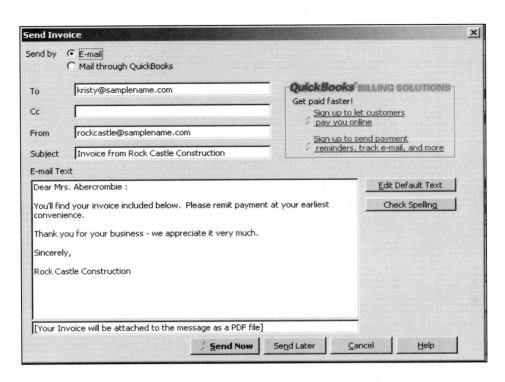

Invoice Mailing Service: Send fully customized, professional looking invoices and statements by US Mail directly from QuickBooks. This mailing service includes a remittance tear-off and return envelope.

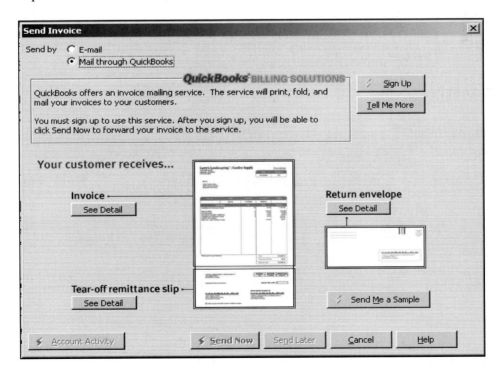

Payment Reminders: Reduce collection calls by sending payment reminders to customers with outstanding or overdue invoices.

Customer Account Center: Improve customer service by offering your customers access to a private, customized Web page where they can view billing history, print invoices, submit inquiries, set payment reminders and more.

E-mailed Forms Tracking: Know when invoices have been received and viewed by your customers.

Online Payment Options: Allow customers to pay you online by credit card (optional feature).

QUICKBOOKS MERCHANT SERVICES

QuickBooks Merchant Services allows your business to accept credit cards from customers. As a subscriber to QuickBooks Merchant Services, credit card charges are processed and deposited into your designated bank account. Funds will be generally deposited into your account within two to three business days depending on your financial institution and your Demand Deposit Account. Everything needed to process credit cards is built right into QuickBooks. This enables you to offer customers more payment options, process credit cards in QuickBooks or remotely. Credit card payments may be entered manually into QuickBooks or by swiping the credit card by using a card reader purchased separately. You can also process recurring charges and bill customers online.

Additional features are

Feature	Benefits
Card Acceptance	Offer customers better payment options by accepting all major credit cards, plus corporate cards.
Card Swiped Rates	Get better rates when you swipe credit cards using our card reader (card reader sold separately).
Automatic Credit Card Billing	Easily set up recurring charges to bill customers regularly for services, such as membership fees.
Online Billing	Use our FREE Online Billing service to e-mail invoices and get paid online.

The costs associated with QuickBooks Merchant Services, at the time the textbook was written, are:

Fees	Innovative Merchant Solutions
Discount rate for Visa and MasterCard	Card-swiped: 1.69% * Key-entered: 2.39% †
Monthly fee	$17.95
Per-authorization fee	$0.23
One-time set-up fee	$59.95
Monthly minimum transaction fee	Variable from $0 - $20
Cancellation fee	None
Time to funding**	Two to three business days

Enter credit card transactions

When a transaction is processed for a credit card payment, sales receipt or customer payment is recorded as usual. The checkbox for Process Credit Card Payment should be selected.

On the Process Credit Card Payment screen, enter any additional credit card information and click **Submit.**

The QuickBooks Merchant Account Service will run a quick check on the card to help you protect yourself and your customers against fraud.

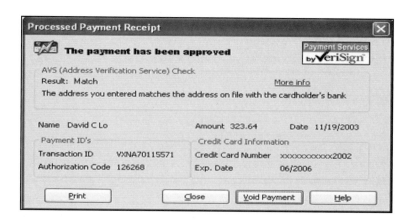

After the payment is authorized, the funds will be automatically transferred into a business account at the bank of your choice. Print the payment receipt for your records.

Credit card activity can be monitored with transaction reports. QuickBooks will show you the total number of transactions processed per card type (Visa, MasterCard, American Express and so on), as well as minimum, maximum and average dollar amounts.

Automatic Credit Card Billing

QuickBooks Merchant Account Services has an Automatic Credit Card Billing feature that allows you to bill a customer's credit card a fixed amount at regular intervals for recurring services, such as membership fees, insurance premiums, or subscriptions. Prior to setting up a recurring charge, you must have written authorization from your customer.

A Recurring Charge is set up using the Customers menu, click **Accept Credit Card Payments**, click **Manage Automatic Credit Card Billing** to access the Recurring Charges page.

1. Print the Automatic Credit Card Billing Authorization Form. Visa and MasterCard require that you and your customer complete this form in order to use Automatic Credit Card Billing. After completing the merchant sections, deliver the form to your customer to complete and sign.

2. On the Recurring Charges page, click **Set Up Recurring Charge**, complete all fields

3. Click **Next** to review and then save the charge information.

Billing begins on the start date you specify. You can stop the automatic billing at any time. Your customer's credit card is billed automatically each billing period for the amount specified. After payment is authorized, funds are transferred to the account used for the QuickBooks Merchant Account Service, and an e-mail is sent to you informing you of the payment.

To record each recurring charge transaction in QuickBooks, choose **Record Payments** from the **Recurring Charges** options.

ONLINE BACKUP SERVICES

In addition to having a backup stored in the office, having an offsite backup copy of your company data files is extremely important. This is necessary in case something happens to your computer or your office.

QuickBooks provides an offsite backup service for its users and uses data encryption to protect the confidentiality of your data. QuickBooks Online Backup Service encrypts your data using triple DES encryption (112-bit)—the same standard used by many banks and the United States government. Data is compressed and encrypted before leaving the PC and stored at dual data centers in its compressed and encrypted state. All information is stored using identical data centers in two geographically separate locations to help promote the highest levels of data protection and availability. Only you can read your files with an encryption key you create.

There are three different options available

Select a Service Plan	Storage Space	Price after Your Free 30-day Trial*
Small Business File Backup Protect your most important data. Select only your most valuable data for backup, including your QuickBooks data files	Up to 200MB	$99.95 per year Try Now
Premium Data Backup Protect ALL your data. Automatically selects ALL the data files on your entire PC for backup.**	Up to 4GB	$189.95 per year--Save 10% compared to monthly fees. Try Now $17.95 per month. Try now.
Premium Plus System Backup The most comprehensive protection you can get. Backs up all files on your PC including data*, applications, and operating systems. Includes PC Heal to help you easily recover your data from any computer disaster.	Up to 10GB	$269.95 per year--Save 10% compared to monthly fee. Try Now $24.95 per month. Try now.

When backing up data files online, the same procedure is followed as instructed in Appendix A. The only change is that you click Online rather than Disk.

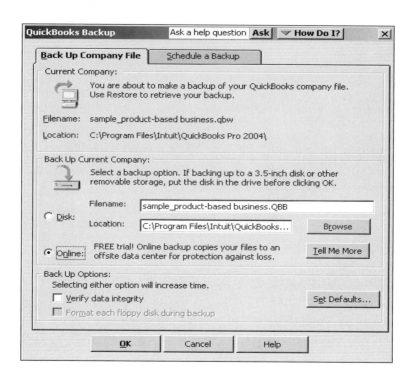

DIRECT DEPOSIT

Rather than mail or give paychecks to your employees, you may sign up for Direct Deposit if you are using the QuickBooks Basic Payroll plan. When you sign up for the Basic Payroll service, you can add the Direct Deposit option. You will fill out and print Welcome Packet forms and mail or fax them to the payroll service using the information provided with the forms. Some of the information you need to do this is your federal employer identification number, the company's principal name, the company's legal name and address, your financial institution routing and account numbers, and your QuickBooks registration number.

You also need to set up those employees who wish to receive their checks by direct deposit. This is done by:

Clicking **Employee List** on the Employee menu
Select the employee you want to set up for direct deposit
Click **Edit** on the Employee button
Select the **Payroll & Compensation Info** tab
Click the **Direct Deposit** button
Select the checkbox to use direct deposit for this employee
Select whether to deposit the paycheck into one or two accounts
Enter the employee's financial institution information

Index

A

Accessories (Windows®), 674
Account names, 577
Account Not Found dialog box, 289
Account numbers, 577
Account register, 266
Accountant's Copy of business files, 189–90
Accounting, 132, 189, 196-97, 429-34
  accrual-basis, 132, 189, 423
  cash-basis, 197, 429
  depreciation, 200–201, 432-34
  manual vs. computerized, 5
  for payables and purchases, 120-21
  prepaid expenses, 197–99, 430-32
  for sales and receivables, 40
  See also Accounts payable;
    Accounts receivable; General
    accounting; Sales
Accounting preferences, 600
Accounts
  asset, 596–98
  Balance Sheet, 592
  bank, 595-97
  changing names of, 191-94, 424-25
  effect on subaccounts, 193-94
  Chart of Accounts
    adding new to, 74-76, 288
    deleting existing from, 195-96, 426-27
    petty cash, 154-57
  credit card, 593-94
  drawing, 207
  equity, 598-99
  inactivating, 194-95, 425-26
  income, 267, 578-79
  loans, 594-95
  See also specific accounts
Accounts payable
  accounting for, 120-21, 358-59
  graphing by aging period, 103-4, 178-79, 411
  petty cash account, 154–57
    adding to Chart of Accounts, 154-55
    establishing petty cash fund, 155-56
    recording payment of expense, 156-57
  QuickReport on, 139-40
    for a vendor, 177
  Vendor Balance Summary, 176-77
Accounts Payable Aging Summary, 174-75
Accounts Payable Graph, 178-79
Accounts Payable Ledger, 121
Accounts Payable Register
  bills entered using, 134-37, 393-94
  credit in, 148
  editing transactions in, 137-138, 394-95

QuickReport from, 139-40, 395-99
Accounts Payable Subsidiary Ledger.
  See Vendor List
Accounts receivable, 40-41
  correcting invoices, 286-88, 292-94
  created in EasyStep Interview, 582
  credit memos, 338-40
  Customer Center, 342-43
  depositing checks, 98-100
  graphing, 102–4, 267, 344-45
  nonsufficient funds (NSF) checks, 334-37
  payments on account, 93-97, 324-25
  reports, 267, 284-88
    Customer Balance Detail, 73-74, 285
    Customer Balance Summary, 332
    printing, 57-59
    Transaction List by Customer, 331
  See also Invoice(s)
Accounts Receivable by Aging Period, 344-46
Accounts Receivable Ledger (Customer:Job List), 46
  modifying customer records, 81-82
Accounts Receivable Register, 25, 40, 266, 286
Accounts Receivable Subsidiary Ledger. *See* Customer List
Accounts topic (EasyStep Interview), 592-99
Accrual-basis accounting, 132, 189, 423
  adjustments for, 196-99, 429-34
    depreciation, 200-201, 432-34
    prepaid expenses, 197-99, 430-32
Accrual-basis reports, 223, 466-67
Additional Info file tab, 283
Adjusting entries, 197, 429-34
  for accrual-basis accounting, 196-97
  in computerizing manual systems, 629-31
  for depreciation, 200-201, 432-34
  during reconciliation, 213-17, 451-53
  inventory adjustments, 482-83
  for Net Income/Retained Earnings, 229-31, 470-72, 483-84
  for prepaid expenses, 197-99, 430-32
  for purchase discounts, 434
Administrator, 236, 478
Advanced Find feature, 304
Aging period, accounts payable graph by, 103-4, 178-79, 411
Aging of transactions, 102-4

All Programs (Windows®), 674
Alt key, 17
American Express credit cards, 314
Analysis
  of QuickReports, 64, 90-91
  of sales, 91-93
Application software, 4
Arithmetic/Logic Unit (ALU), 2
Asset accounts, 596-98
Assets, purchased with company check, 170-72
Assisted Payroll service plan, 514-15
Audit trail feature, 165

B

Back-ordered items, 380-81
Backup, end-of-period backup, 235-36, 477-78
Backup file, 32-34, 108-9, 180, 681-83
  restore QuickBooks file, 683-85
Backup services online, 741-42
Balance Sheet, 26-27, 441-42, 468-69
  accounts topic (EasyStep Interview), 592-99
  capital accounts, 442-46
    Net Income/Retained Earnings transfer to, 470-72
  Post-Closing, 242-44, 486-88
  preparing, 441-42
  printing, 231-32, 472-73
  Standard, 228-29, 468-69
  viewing, 207-8
Balance Sheet report, 267
Bank accounts, 595-97
Bank collections, 423
Bank reconciliation,208-218, 446-63
  adjusting/correcting entries, 213-217, 451-53, 457-63
  bank statement information, 210-212, 447-49
  begin reconciliation, 209, 447-49
  Locate Discrepancies screen, 459
  mark cleared transactions, 213, 449-50
  print reconciliation report, 218, 454
  Undo Reconciliation feature, 459-63
Bank statements, 189, 423
Banking menu, 13
Banking navigator, 11
Banking online, 724-31
  set up, 725-28
  using, 728-30
Bar charts, 27-28
Billing, online, 739-41
Billing solutions, 734-348
Bills, 358, 388-94
  checks to pay, 158-61, 402-4
    Check Detail Report, 167-69
  deleting, 163-65

editing, 161-62
Missing Check Report, 169-70
printing, 152-53, 165-67
voiding, 162-63
credit from vendor, 146-48
viewing, 148
deleting, 141-43, 409
detail section of, 123, 388
editing and correcting errors,
125-26, 137-38
entering, 123-24, 388-91
using Accounts Payable
Register, 134-37, 393-94
items already received, 376-78
items not accompanied by bill,
373-75
for job expenses, 706-7
paying, 149-52, 398-400
applying credits/ discounts,
400-402
with credit card, 404-5
printing checks for, 402-4
preparing
detail section of, 128-29
more than one expense account,
127-29
vendor-related section of, 127-28
without step-by-step instructions,
132-34, 392-93
printing by vendor report, 129-31
QuickZoom in, 131-32
received with items, 378-79
reviewing paid, 153
unpaid, 397-98
Unpaid Bills Detail Report, 175-76
vendor-related section of, 123-24,
388
changing existing vendors'
terms, 391
new vendor added while
recording bill, 143-45
verify that marked paid, 402
voiding, 409
See also Accounts payable;
Purchases
Bits (binary digit), 2
Business forms, customizing, 272-74
Business Services navigator, 11
Business vehicles insurance expense,
198-99
Buttons on forms, 22-23
By Class Profit and Loss Statement,
227, 467
By Job Profit and Loss Statement,
227, 467
Bytes, 2-3

C
Calculations
QuickMath, 30
with Windows® calculator, 30-31,
674
Capital accounts, 442-46
for each owner/partner, 442-46

Net Income/Retained Earnings to,
229-31, 470-72
noncash investment by owner in,
206
Cash-basis accounting, 197, 429
Cash-basis reports, 223, 466
Cash control, 165
Cash customer, 73, 321-23
Cash flow, 224-26
Cash Flow Forecast, 224-26
Cash Flows Statement, 225-26
Cash investment by owner, 205
Cash purchases, 358
Cash receipt transactions, 266
Cash sales, 40, 266, 311-13, 321-23
depositing checks, 98-100, 332-34
depositing credit card receipts for,
332-34
QuickReport on, 321-23
recording, 82–84, 311-13
sales tax and, 311-13
transactions without step-by-step
instructions, 85-86, 316-17
Central processing unit (CPU), 2, 4
Charges (bank), 189
Chart of Accounts, 121, 562
adding new account to, 74-76, 288
changing name of accounts in,
191-94, 424-25
deleting existing account, 195-96,
426-27
EasyStep Interview to set up,
565-71, 604-5
petty cash account added to, 154-55
Check(s)
asset with, 170-72
bills paid by, 158-72, 311
Check Detail Report, 167-69
deleting, 163-65
editing, 161-62
Missing Check Report, 169-70
printing, 152–53, 165-67
voiding, 162-63
creating, 516-23
deleting, 409
depositing, 98-100, 332-34
duplicate, 161
online payment, 730-31
paychecks, 515-24
correcting, 531-32
deleting, 532-34
for next pay period, 529-31
printing, 523–24, 531-32
viewing, 531-32
voiding, 532-34
printing, 402-4
refund, 338-40
returned for nonsufficient funds,
334-37
sales paid by, 315-16
voiding, 409
writing, 152-53
Check box (Windows®), 677
Check Detail Report, 167-69
Check face/check detail, 158

Check numbers, 167
Checking account, bank
reconciliation, 208-18, 446-55
adjusting/correcting entries, 213-17,
451-53
bank statement information,
210-12, 447-49
begin reconciliation, 447-49
cleared transactions, 212-13,
219-20, 449-50
print reconciliation report, 218
Reconcile-Checking window,
209-10
viewing Checking Account
Register, 218-19, 454-55
Checking Account Register, 218-19,
454-55
Checking preferences, 600
Checking Register, petty cash funding
through, 155-56
Clear button, 22
Clicking, mouse, 2, 4, 677
Close button (Windows®), 675-76
Closing
a company, 31-32, 108-9, 180
Windows®, 685-86
Closing date, 189, 237, 478-79
Command button (Windows®), 676
Commands, menu, 12-13
Company Info topic (EasyStep
Interview), 565-71
Company logo, 631-35
Company menu, 12
Company name, personalizing, 44-45,
268
Company navigator, 10-11
Company preferences, 363-64
Company web site, 732
Company(ies)
closing a, 31-32, 108-9, 180
opening a, 7-9, 43-44
verifying, 9, 44
Comparison Balance Sheet, 469
Complete Payroll service plan, 514-15
Computer hardware, 1-3
input devices, 2
output devices, 3
processing devices, 2
QuickBooks Pro® system
requirements, 6
storage devices, 3
Computerizing a manual system,
560-639
adjusting entries, 629-31
Chart of Accounts, 604-5
company logo, 631-35
create a new company, 561-62
customer information, 606-7
customizing forms, 635-37
customizing reports, 637-39
EasyStep Interview for, 560,
562-63
General section, 563
Income & Expenses section,
577–81

Income Details section, 582-88
Opening Balances section, 589
What's Next section, 599
employees, 609
Payroll Setup Interview, 609-17
    Company Setup, 609-17
    Employees Setup, 617-24
    year-to-date amounts, 624-29
Preferences section, 600-604
    Accounting, 600
    Checking, 600
    Desktop View, 601
    Finance Charge, 601
    General, 601
    Integrated Applications, 601
    Jobs & Estimates, 601
    Payroll & Employees, 601
    Purchases & Vendors, 602
    Reminders, 602
    Reports & Graphs, 602
    Sales & Customers, 602
    Sales Tax, 603
    Send Forms, 603
    Service Connection, 603
    Spelling, 603
    Tax: 1099 form, 603
    Time Tracking, 604
vendor information, 607-9
Computers, 1-4
    hardware, 1-3
    input devices, 2
    introduction to, 1-3
    output devices, 3
    processing devices, 2
    software, 4
    storage devices, 3
    as way of life, 1
Connect To (Windows®), 674
Control menu icon (Windows®), 675
Control Panel (Windows®), 674
Copy command, 126
Copying files, 32
Correcting
    bills, 125-26
    during bank reconciliation, 213-17,
        451-53
    invoices, 50-51, 61-64, 286-88
        to include sales discount, 292-94
    paychecks, 531-32
    sales receipt, 88-90, 319-21
    sales transactions, 267, 276-77
    See also Editing
Cost of goods sold, 434-36
CPA, 423
CPU (central processing unit), 2
Credit
    in Accounts Payable Register, 148
    applying, 325-27, 400-402
    from vendor, 146-48, 382-84
    lines of, 594
Credit card accounts, 593-94
Credit Card Charges, 385-86
Credit card receipts, depositing,
    332-34

Credit card reconciliation, 423,
    455-57
Credit card transactions
    automatic billing, 740-41
    bill payments, 404-5
    business purchases, 384-86
        inventory items, 386-88
    online services, 738-41
    sales, 311, 314-15
    voiding, 409
Credit check services online, 732-34
Credit checks, 11
Credit customer, 73
Credit limit, transaction exceeding,
    283-84
Credit memos, 71-73, 146-48, 307-9,
    325, 338-40, 382-84
Customer(s)
    adding new, 77-80
    cash, 73, 321-23
    credit, 73
    credit limit of, 283-84
    information on, 606-7
    modifying records, 81-82, 302-3
    new
        adding, 295-97
        sale to, 297-302
    overdue balances, 342
    price level associated with, 714-15
    QuickZoom of item/customer,
        107-8
    viewing transactions by, 97-98
Customer Account Center, 738
Customer Balance Detail Report,
    73-74, 267, 285
Customer Balance Summary, 57-61,
    267, 332
Customer Center, 342-43
Customer Contact Information, 343
Customer Detail Center, 343-45
Customer:Job List, 24, 46
    modifying customer records, 81-82
Customer List, 266, 283, 295, 606-7
    modifying records in, 302-3
Customer menu, 13
Customer message, 50
Customer navigator, 11
Customer notes, 697-98
Customer Tax Code, 279
Customer topic (EasyStep Interview),
    589-90
Customizing report format, 172-74

D

Data encryption, 741
Date
    closing, 189, 237, 478-79
    keyboard shortcuts, 15
    start, 563, 576-77
Delete Accounts dialog box, 196
Delete Transaction dialog box, 164,
    306
Deleting
    accounts, 195-96
    bills, 141-43, 409

checks, 163-65, 409
credit card payments, 409
existing account from Chart of
    Accounts, 195-96
invoices, 65, 67-71
paychecks, 532-34
purchase orders, 409
sales forms, 65-71
Deposits
    for cash sales and payments on
        account, 98-100
    of checks and credit card receipts,
        332-34
Depreciation, 197, 200-201, 423, 429,
    432-34
    adjusting entries for, 200-201
DES encryption, 741
Desktop, 673
    QuickBooks® Pro, 9-10
    Windows®, 653-54, 672-77
Desktop View Preferences, 601
Detail Balance Sheet, 228, 468
Detail Profit and Loss Statement, 227,
    467
Dialog box
    Delete Accounts, 196
    Delete Transaction, 164, 306
    Did check(s) print OK?, 167
    Make Payment, 448
    New Account, 290
    QuickBooks Message, 171-72
    Resize Columns, 319
    Vendor Not Found, 143-44
    Windows®, 676
Dictionary, spelling, 283-84
Direct deposit, 742
Discounts, 267, 288-94
    adjusting entries for, 434-36
    applying to bills, 400-402
    correcting invoices to include,
        292-94
    Cost of Goods Sold and, 434-36
    early-payment, 267, 327-29, 359
Discover cards, 314
Disks, 3
    duplicate, 35, 678-80
Do-It-Yourself Payroll, 514
Domain name, Internet, 732
Double-click, 677
Drag and drop, 678
Dragging mouse, 677
Drawing account, 207
Drop-down list arrow, 21
Drop-down list or box (Windows®),
    676
Dun and Bradstreet, 732
Duplicate checks, 161
Duplicate disks, 35, 678-80

E

E-mail
    billing solutions, 736
    Forms Tracking, 738
    invoices, 280

Early-payment discount, 267, 327-29, 359
Earnings
  adjustments for, 483-84
  retained, 229-30
  transferring to capital accounts, 470-72
EasyStep Interview, 560
  General Section, 563-76
    Company Info topic, 565-71
    Preferences topic, 572-76
    start date, 576-77
  Income & Expenses section, 577-81
    Expense Accounts topic, 579-81
    Income Accounts topic, 578-79
  Income Detail section, 582-88
    Introduction topic, 582
    Inventory topic, 586-88
    Items topic, 582–85
  Opening Balances section, 589
    Accounts topic, 592-99
    Customers topic, 589-90
    Vendors topic, 591-92
Edit menu, 12
Editing
  bills, 125-26
    using Accounts Payable Register, 137-38, 394-95
  checks, 161-62
  cleared transactions, 219-20
  Customer:Job List, 81-82
  invoices, 50–51
  keyboard shortcuts, 15
  purchase orders, 379-80
  sales transactions, 276-77
  transactions from previous period, 238-39, 480-81
Electronic funds transfer (EFT), 731
Employee(s)
  adding new, 525-29, 609, 617-24
  changing information about, 524-25
  W-2 forms, 546-47
Employee Defaults, 609
Employee Earnings Summary Report, 535
Employee menu, 13
Employee navigator, 11
Employee notes, 698
Employee template, 609
  adding employees using, 617-24
End-of-period procedures, 189-90, 208-44, 421-22
  accrual-basis reporting, 466-67
  backup, 235–36, 477-78
  Balance Sheet, 468-69
    Post-Closing, 242-44, 486-88
    Standard, 228-29, 231-32, 468-69
  bank reconciliation, 208-18, 436-63
    adjusting/correcting entries, 213-17, 451-53
    bank statement information, 210-12, 447-49
    begin reconciliation, 447-49

cleared transactions, 212-13, 219-20, 449-50
  print reconciliation report, 218, 454
  Reconcile-Checking window, 209-10, 447-48
  reconciliation adjustment, 457-63
  viewing Checking account register, 218-19, 454-55
Cash Flow Forecast, 224-26
close drawing/transfer to owners' capital account, 473-74
closing date for period, 237, 478-79
credit card reconciliation, 455-57
exporting reports to Excel, 475-76
inventory adjustments, 482-83
Journal, printing, 233
Net Income/Retained Earnings adjustments, 229-31, 483-84
Profit and Loss Statement, 227-28, 467-68
  Post-Closing, 241-42, 485-86
reporting preference, 223
Statement of Cash Flows, 225-26
transactions from previous period, 479-80
  accessing, 237-38
  editing, 238-39
Trial Balance, 221-23, 464-65
  Post-Closing, 240-41, 484-85
  preparing, 221-23
  printing, 222-23
  QuickZoom in, 222
Enter Bills feature, 120, 358, 383-84
Equity, owners', 442-46, 473-74
Equity accounts, 598-99
Esc key, 17
Excel
  exporting reports to, 233-34, 475-76, 693–95
  importing data from, 476-77, 695
Exiting QuickBooks Pro®, 35
Expense(s)
  business vehicle insurance, 198-99
  insurance, 197-99
  office supplies, 197-99, 423, 481-82
  petty cash payments for, 154-57
  prepaid, 197-99, 430-32
Expense Accounts topic (EasyStep Interview), 579-81
Expenses tab, 388
Exporting reports to Excel, 233-34, 475-76, 693-95

F
Field(s), 21
File menu, 12
File(s)
  backup, 32-34
  copying, 32
  master, 32
Finance Charge preferences, 601
Financing activities, 225

Find icon, 22
Fixed asset management, 427-29
Flash drive, 3
Floppy disks, 3
Form 940 Employer's Annual Federal Unemployment Tax Return (FUTA), 11, 538, 543-46
Form 941 Employer's Federal Quarterly Tax Return, 11, 538-39
Form 1099s, 11
Forms, 20-23
  customizing, 635-37
  sales
    deleting, 306-7
    deleting an invoice, 67-71
    voiding, 303-7
    voiding an invoice, 65-67

G
General accounting, 189-209, 421-22
  adjusting entries, 196-201, 429-34
    depreciation, 197, 200-201, 432-34
    prepaid expenses, 197-99, 430-32
  Balance Sheet, 207-8, 441-42
  changing name of accounts, 191-94, 424-25
    effect on subaccounts, 193-94
  deleting accounts, 195-96, 426-27
  General Journal, viewing, 201-2, 220-21, 437-38
  inactivating accounts, 194-95, 425-26
  owner cash investments, 205
  owner noncash investments, 206
  owner withdrawals, 202-5, 439-41
  partnerships, 438-41
  Profit and Loss Statement, 434-37
General Journal, 11, 40
  cash investment by owner, 205
  depreciation in, 200-201
  prepaid expenses in, 197-99
  printing, 340-41
  viewing, 201-2, 437-38, 463-64
  See also Journal
General Ledger, 604.
  See also Chart of Accounts
General preferences, 601
General section of EasyStep Interview, 563-76
  Company Info topic, 565-71
  Preferences topic, 572-76
  start date, 576-77
  Welcome topic, 563-65
Gigabyte (GB), 3
Graph(s), 27-29, 102, 344-46
  Accounts Payable by aging period, 103-4, 178-79, 411
  Accounts Receivable, 102-4
  sales graphs, 106-7, 267, 345-46
  setting preferences for, 602
Graphical user interface (GUI), 4

H

Hard disk, 3, 7
Hardware. *See* Computer hardware
Help
    keyboard shortcuts, 14
    on-screen, 18–20
    Windows®, 674
Help & Support navigator, 11
Help menu, 13
History icon, 22

I

I-beam, 677
Icon bar, 9, 18
Icons, Windows®, 4, 11-12, 673
Importing Data from Excel, 476-77, 695
Inactivating accounts, 194-95, 425–26
Income
    in accrual-basis accounting, 429-30
    in cash-basis accounting, 429
    net, 229–30
    Net Income, 423
        adjustments for, 483–84
        transferring into capital accounts, 470–72
Income accounts, 267, 578–79
Income Accounts topic (EasyStep Interview), 578-79
Income Details section of EasyStep Interview, 582-88
    Introduction topic, 582
    Inventory topic, 586–88
    Items topic, 582–85
Income & Expenses section of EasyStep Interview, 577–81
    Expense Accounts topic, 579–81
    Income Accounts topic, 578–79
Income Statement, 227–28
Input devices, 2
Insurance, 423
    prepaid, 197–99
Insurance Benefits, 612–13
Integrated Applications preferences, 601
Internet, 716
    connecting to, 719–22
    domain name, 732
    personalized web site, 732
    See also Online features
Internet protocol (IP) addresses, 732
Introduction topic (EasyStep Interview), 582
Intuit Web site, 716
Inventory, 266–67, 359
    adjustments to, 482–83
    credit card payment for items on order, 386–88
    item report, 371–72
    receipt of items without bill, 373–75
    See also Purchases
Inventory Stock Status by Item report, 371–72
Inventory topic (EasyStep Interview), 586–88

Investing activities, 225
Investments by owner
    cash, 205
    noncash, 206
Invoice(s), 40
    adding new customers while creating, 77–80, 295–97
    billable hours, 703–4
    correcting, 50–51, 61–64, 286–88
        to include sales discount, 292–94
    deleting, 67–71, 306–7
    e-mailing, 280
    editing, 50–51
    for job items and expenses, 706–7
    more than one sales item, 278–80
    nonsufficient funds (NSF) check recorded in, 334–37
    price level applied on, 713
    printing, 52–55, 61–64, 277-78, 286–88
        by customer report, 309–11
    sales tax, 278–80
    for two sales items, 53–54
    voiding, 65–67, 304–5
    without step-by-step instructions, 55–56, 281–82
Invoice form, 21–23
Invoice icon, 48
Invoice mailing service, 737
Item List, 46–47, 74–77, 269
    adding new items to, 288-91
Items topic (EasyStep Interview), 582–85

J

Job costing and tracking, 705-10
    bill for expenses, 706–7
    creating job for customer, 706
    invoicing, 707–9
    reports on, 705, 709–10
Job estimates vs. actuals detail, 705
Job estimates vs. actuals summary, 705
Job notes, 698
Job Profitability Detail, 705
Job Profitability Summary, 705
Job progress invoices vs. estimates, 705
Jobs & estimates preferences, 601
Journal, 5
    printing, 100–101, 233, 477
    viewing, 201–2, 220–21
Jump drive, 3

K

Keyboard, 2
Keyboard conventions, 16-17
    Alt key, 17
    Esc key, 17
    Shift+Tab, 17
    Tab key, 17
Keyboard shortcuts, 14–16
    activity, 16
    dates, 15
    editing, 15

    general, 14
    help window, 14
    moving around a window, 15-16
Kilobyte (K), 3

L

Layout Designer, 272–73
Lead time, 731
Ledger, 5
Liabilities
    graphing, 27–28
    taxes and other liabilities, 536–38
Lines of credit, 594
List(s), 23–24, 46
    adding new items to, 74-77, 288–91
    Customer:Job, 46
    Customer, 266, 283–84, 295, 606-7
        modifying customer records, 302–3
    Item, 74–77
    maximum number of entries, 23
    Price Level, 712–15
    Purchase Order, 368–69, 379
    Receive Items, 376–78
    Reminders, 360–62, 370-71
    Sales Item, 46
    Vendor List, 121–22, 359-60, 607-9
Lists menu, 12, 24
Loan accounts, 594–96
Loan Manager, 11
Logo, company, 631–35

M

Mailing service, 710–11
Make Payment dialog box, 462
Manual accounting, 5.
    See also Computerizing a manual system
Master file, 32
MasterCard, 314
Maximize button (Windows®), 675
Megabyte (MB), 2
Memory, random access memory (RAM), 2
Memos
    credit, 71–73, 146–48, 307–9, 338-40, 382–84
    transactions, 270, 360
Menu
    Alt key access to, 17
    lists, 24
    reports, 26–27
Menu bar
    in QuickBooks® Pro, 9
    in Windows®, 676
Menu commands, 12–13
Merchandising business
    accounts payable in, 358-59
        graphing by aging period, 411
    accounts receivables in, 266-67, 284–88
    credit memos, 338–40
    Customer Balance Summary, 332

Customer Center, 342–44
  graphs for, 267, 344–46
  nonsufficient funds (NSF)
    checks, 334–37
  payments on account, 324-25
  reports, 267, 284–88
  sales discount, 292–94
  Transaction List by Customer,
    331
end-of-period procedures in,
  421–22
  accrual-basis reporting, 466–67
  backup, 477–78
  Balance Sheet, 468–69
  bank reconciliation, 446–63
  close drawing/transfer into
    owners' capital account, 473–
    74
  closing date for period, 478–79
  credit card reconciliation, 455–
    57
  exporting reports to Excel,
    475-76
  inventory adjustments, 482-83
  modifying transactions for
    previous period, 479–80
  Net Income/Retained Earning
    adjustments, 483-84
  post-closing profit and loss
    statement, 485–86
  post-closing trial balance, 484-85
  printing journal, 477
  profit and loss statement, 467–68
  reconciliation adjustment,
    457-63
  trial balance, 464–65
general accounting in, 421–22
  adjusting entries, 429–34
  Balance Sheet, 441–42
  changing name of existing
    accounts, 424-25
  deleting accounts, 426–27
  General Journal viewing, 437–38
  inactivating an account, 425–26
  owner withdrawals, 438–41
  partnership, 438–41
  Profit and Loss Statement,
    434-37
practice set (comprehensive
  example), 500–511
  business description, 500
  documents and reports, 512–13
  instructions, 500–502
  recording transactions, 502-11
purchases in, 358–59
  credit card, 384–86
  recording receipt of items, 373–
    79
sales in, 266–67
  cash, 266, 311–13, 321–23, 332–
    34
  check payment for, 311, 315–16
  correcting errors, 267, 276-77
  correcting receipts, 319–21
  credit card, 311, 314–15

deleting an invoice, 306–7
discounts, 288–94
editing, 276–77
entering, 274–76
exceeding customer's credit
  limit, 283–84
graphing, 267
graphs of, 344–46
income accounts, 269
invoices, 277–78
multiple items and sales tax,
  278–80
new customer, 297–302
printing Sales by Item Summary
  Report, 318–19
printing sales receipt, 313
recording, 297–302
report format for, 270–71
reports, 267
sales on account, 274–76
terms of, 270
trial balance, printing, 341-42
voiding, 303–7
sales tax and, 311–13, 323, 406–9
shipping manager, 711–12
Merchant services, online, 739-41
  Automatic Credit Card Billing,
    740–41
  credit card transactions, 738-41
  Online Billing, 739–41
Message box (Windows®), 676
Microsoft Word, integration with,
  687–93
Minimize button (Windows®), 675
Missing Check Report, 169–70
Monitor, 3
Mouse, 2, 4
Mouse pointer, 677
My Computer (Windows®), 674
My Documents (Windows®), 674
My Music (Windows®), 674
My Network Places (Windows®), 674
My Pictures (Windows®), 674

N

Navigator(s), 10–12, 45
  examining lists with, 24
  Reports, 26
Net Income, 423
  adjust Journal entry, 483–84
  transferring to capital accounts,
    229–30, 470–72
Net Income account, 207
Net Worth, graph of, 27–29
New Account dialog box, 290
Next icon, 22
Non-inventory parts, 585
Nonsufficient funds (NSF), 334-37
Notes, 696–700
  customer or job, 697–98
  time tracking, 699
  To Do notes, 696–97
  vendor, employee, and other names,
    698–99

O

Object linking and embedding (OLE),
  4
Office supplies expense, 197-99, 423,
  481–82
OLE (object linking and embedding),
  4
On-screen help, 18–20
Online features, 716–42
  accessing, 722–23
  backup services, 741–42
  banking, 724–31
  connecting to Internet, 719–22
  credit check services, 732–34
  direct deposit service, 742
  merchant services, 738–41
    Automatic Credit Card billing,
      740–41
    credit card transactions, 738–41
    Online Billing, 739–41
  payments, 730–31
  personalized Web site and domain
    name, 732
  Trial Version of QuickBooks® Pro,
    716–17
  updates, 717–19
Online Payment options, 738
Open Invoices report, 309–11
Opening
  a company, 7–9, 43–44
    verifying, 9, 44
  QuickBooks® Pro, 7, 42–43
Opening Balances section of EasyStep
  Interview, 589
  Accounts topic, 592–99
  Customers topic, 589–90
  Vendors topic, 591–92
Operating activities, 225
Operating system software, 4, 6
Option buttons (Windows®), 677
Ordering merchandise, 359–61
  preparing purchase order for,
    364-65
Other Names notepad, 698–99
Output devices, 3
Outstanding Items on Order, 343
Owner(s)
  cash investment by, 205
  noncash investments by, 206
  withdrawals by, 202–5, 423,
    438-41
Owners' equity, 442–46, 473–74

P

Partial receipt of merchandise ordered,
  380–81
Partnerships, 438–41
  capital account for each owner,
    442–46
  definition of, 438
  owner withdrawals, 439–41
Passwords, 236, 478
Paste command, 126
Pay Bills command, 359, 386, 398
Pay Bills features, 120, 149–52

Pay period, 614
Payables. *See* Accounts payable
Payee, 731
Payment reminders, 738
Payments
  of bills, 398–400
  applying credit/discounts, 325-27,
    400–402
    with credit card, 404–5
    printing checks for, 402–4
    verifying marked paid, 402
  depositing checks and credit card
    receipts, 98–100, 332–34
  online, 730–31
  recording, 93–95
    applying credit and, 325–27
    customer with early-payment
      discount, 327–29
    payments on account, 324-25
    without step-by-step instructions,
      95–97, 329–30
  sales tax, 408–9
Payroll, 514–47
  creating, 516–23
  employee information
    adding new employee, 525-29
    changing, 524–25
  paychecks, 515–24
    correcting, 531–32
    deleting, 532–34
    for next pay period, 529–31
    printing, 523-24, 531–32
    viewing, 531–32
    voiding, 532–34
  reports, 534–35
  Schedule B (Employer's Record of
    Federal Tax Liability), 538–43
  selecting a payroll option, 516
  tax forms, 538–47
    Form 940, 543–46
    Form 941 and Schedule B,
      538-43
    W-2 forms, 546–47
    W-3 forms, 546
  taxes and other liabilities, 536–38
Payroll & Employees preferences, 601
Payroll Liabilities Balances Report,
  535–36
Payroll option, 516
Payroll service plans, 514
Payroll Setup Interview, 609–17
  Company Setup, 611–17
  Employees Setup, 617–24
  year-to-date amounts, 624–29
Payroll Summary Report, 534–35
Personalizing company name, 44–45,
  268
Petty cash account, 154–57
  adding to Chart of Accounts,
    154-55
  establishing fund, 155–56
  recording payment using, 156–57
Petty Cash Register, 156
Petty Cash Voucher, 154
Pie charts, 27–28

Post-Closing Balance Sheet, 242–44,
  486–88
Post-Closing Profit and Loss
  Statement, 241–42, 485–86
Post-Closing Trial Balance, 240–41,
  484–85
Practice sets
  comprehensive problem, 652-71
    adjustments, 659–60
    business description, 652-53
    Chart of Accounts, 653–54
    creating new company, 653
    Customer List, 656
    Employee List, 658–59
    Items List, 655
    recording transactions, 660-68
    Vendor List, 656–57
  for merchandising business, 500–
    511
    business description, 500
    documents and reports, 512–13
    instructions, 500–502
    recording transactions, 502-11
  for service business, 255–65
    business description, 255
    instructions, 255–256
    transactions,257–263
Preference topic (EasyStep Interview),
  572–76
Preferences settings, 600–604
Prepaid expenses, 197–99, 430-32
Prev Year Comparison Profit and Loss
  Statement, 227, 467
Previewing, QuickReport from
  Accounts Payable Register, 139–40
Previous icon, 22
Price levels, 712–15
Print icon, 22
Printers, 3
Printing
  Accounts Payable Aging Summary,
    174–75
  accounts receivable (A/R) reports,
    57–59
  Balance Sheet, 228–29, 231–32,
    472–73
  Cash Flow Forecast, 224–26
  checks, 152–53, 165–67, 402-4
  Customer Balance Summary, 332
  Deposit Summary, 334
  General Journal, 340–41
  invoices, 52–55, 277–78
    by customer report, 309–11
    corrected, 286–88
  Journal, 100–101, 233, 477
  payroll checks, 531–32
  Post-Closing Balance Sheet,
    242-44, 486–88
  Profit and Lost Statement, 227–28,
    467–68
    Post-Closing, 241–42, 485-86
  QuickReports
    from Accounts Payable Register,
      139–40, 395–99
    for Purchase Orders, 372-73

Reconciliation Report, 218, 454
Reminders List, 362
Sales by Customer Detail report,
  86–87
Sales by Item Summary Report,
  318–19
sales receipt, 84, 88–90, 313,
  319–21
transactions by vendor report,
  129–31
Trial Balance, 101–2, 221–23, 341–
  42, 466
  Post-Closing, 240–41, 484-85
Unpaid Bills Detail Report, 175-76,
  397–98
Vendor Balance Summary, 176–77
Processing devices, 2
Profit and Loss Statement, 227-28,
  267, 434–37
  Post-Closing, 241–42, 485–86
  preparing, 436–37
  Prev Year Comparison, 227, 467
  printing, 227–28, 467–68
  purchase discounts, need for
    adjustment, 434–35
  Standard, 227–28, 467–68
  YTD Comparison, 227, 467
Purchase Order List, 368–69, 379
Purchase orders, 359, 362–69
  closing manually, 381–82
  customizing, 362, 635–37
  deleting, 409
  editing, 379–80
  marked *Received in Full*, verifying,
    375–76
  for more than one item, 365-67
  preparing to order merchandise,
    364–65
  printing QuickReport for, 372–73
  verifying, 363–64
  viewing list of, 368–69
  voiding, 409
  without step-by-step instructions,
    367–68
Purchases, 120–21, 358–59
  assets with company check, 170–72
  credit card, 384–86
  recording receipt of, 373–79
    items already received, 376–78
    items with a bill, 378–79
    partial receipt of order, 380–81
    verifying marked in full, 375–76
    without a bill, 373–75
Purchases & vendor preferences, 602

Q
.Qbb files, 32, 108
.Qbw files, 32
Quick Add method, 77–78, 295
QuickBooks alerts, 342–43
QuickBooks Letters folder, 687
QuickBooks Merchant Services,
  738-41
QuickBooks Notes, 696–700
QuickBooks Pro® 2004

automatic updates to, 717–19
backup file, 32–34, 681–83
billing solutions, 734–38
desktop features of, 9–10
Excel and, 693–95
exiting, 35
forms in, 20–23
graphs in, 27–29, 102, 344
Internet connection, 719–22
job costing and tracking, 705-10
keyboard conventions/ shortcuts,
    14–17
lists in, 23–24
mailing service, 710–11
menu commands, 12–13
navigators in, 10–12, 45
notes, 696–700
online features, 716–42
on-screen help, 18–20
opening in Windows®, 7, 42-43
price levels, 712–15
QuickMath, 30
QuickReport, 29
registers in, 25–26
reports in, 26–27
restoring backup file, 683–85
shipping manager, 711–12
spelling check, 283
system requirements for, 6
Tracking Time, 699–704
Trial Version of, 716–17
updates/online updates, 717-19
versions of, 6
Windows® calculator, 30–31
Word and, 687–93
QuickBooks Spell Check, 283
QuickMath with Windows®
    calculator, 30–31
QuickReport(s), 29
    analyzing, 64, 294–95
    on cash sales, 321–23
    from Accounts Payable Register,
        139–40
    for Purchase Order, 372–73
    for sales transactions, 90–91
    for vendor, 177
    viewing, 64, 321–22
QuickZoom, 27
    in Accounts Payable graph details,
        179–80
    in bills, 131–32
    in Customer Balance Summary
        Report, 59–61
    individual customer details, 105
    individual item/customer, 107–8
    in reports, 286
    in Trial Balance, 222, 465–66

R

Random access memory (RAM), 2
Receipts, sales
    adding new customers while
        ⁻ting, 77–80, 295
        ⁻yments, 315–16
        g, 88–90, 319–21

credit card, depositing, 332-34
deleting an invoice, 306–7
printing, 84, 88–90, 313, 319-21
voiding, 303–5
Receivables. *See* Accounts receivable
Received in Full, 363, 375–76
Received Items List, 376–78
Reconcile-Checking window, 209–10,
    447–48
Reconciliation. *See* Bank
    reconciliation; Credit card
    reconciliation
Reconciliation report, 218, 454
Record
    modifying customer, 81–82
    of vendors, 146
Recording payments on account,
    93-95, 324–25
    applying credit, 325–27
    customer with early-payment
        discount, 327–29
    without step-by-step instructions,
        95–97, 329–30
Refund check, 338–40
Registers, 25–26
    Accounts Receivable, 40, 286
    Checking Account, 454–55
    Petty Cash, 156
    Sales Tax Payable, 323
    Undeposited Funds, 40
Reminders List, 360–62, 370–71
Reminders preferences, 602
Reorder limits, 369
Reorder point, 370–71
Report(s), 5, 26–27
    Accounts Receivable, 57–59, 267,
        284–88
    accrual-basis, 223, 466–67
    Balance Sheet report, 267
    cash-balance, 466
    cash-basis, 223
    Check Detail Report, 167–69
    Customer Balance Detail, 73-74,
        267, 285
    Customer Balance Summary,
        57-59, 267, 332
    customizing, 172–74, 270–71, 637–
        39
    Employee Earnings Summary
        Report, 535
    exporting to Excel, 233–35, 475–76,
        693–85
    Inventory Stock Status by Item,
        371–72
    job-tracking, 705
    Liabilities, Payroll Liability
        Balances Report, 535–36
    Missing Check Report, 169–70
    Open Invoices, 309–11
    Payroll Liabilities Balances Report,
        535–36
    Payroll Summary, 534–35
    Post-Closing Balance Sheet, 242-44
    Post-Closing Profit and Loss
        Statement, 241–42

Post-Closing Trial Balance, 240–41
Profit and Lost, 267
QuickZoom for, 286
Reconciliation, 218
sales, 267
Sales by Item Summary, 318-19
Sales Tax Liability, 406–7
Transaction List by Customer, 331
Transaction Reports by Customer,
    97–98, 267
Trial Balance, 267
Unpaid Bills, 140–41, 397–98
See also QuickReport(s)
Reports & graphs preferences, 602
Reports Finder, 11, 26
Reports menu, 13, 26
Reports navigator, 11, 26
Resize Columns dialog box, 319
Restore backup file, 683–85
Restore button (Windows®), 675
Retail business, 266–67
Retained Earnings, 229–30
    adjustments for, 483–84
    transferring into capital accounts,
        470–72
Retained Earnings account, 189
Revenue
    in accrual-basis accounting, 429
    in cash-basis accounting, 429
Right-click, 677
Right drag, 678
Right drag and drop, 678
Run (Windows®), 674

S

Sales, 40, 266–67
    analysis, 91–93
    cash, 40, 311–13
        depositing checks received from,
            332–34
        QuickReport on, 321–23
        recording, 311–13
        sales tax and, 311–13
        transactions without step-by-step
            instructions, 316–17
    check payment for, 309–11, 315-16
    correcting errors, 267, 276–77
    credit card, 311, 314–15
    credit memos, 71–73
    deleting, 65–71, 306–7
    depositing checks received from,
        98–100
    depositing credit card receipts,
        332–34
    discounts, 288–94
    editing, 275–77
    entering in account, 274–76
        multiple sales item and sales tax,
            278–80
    entering sales on account, 47–50
    exceeding customer's credit limit,
        283–84
    graphs of, 106–7, 267, 344–46
    income accounts, 269
    invoices, 277–78

new account, 74–76
new customer, 77–80, 297-302
printing Sales by Item Summary
 Report, 318–19
QuickReport, 90–91
QuickZoom of item/customer,
 107-8
receipts
 correcting, 88–90, 319–21
 creating, 82–84
 printing, 84, 88–90, 313, 319–21
 recording, 82–84, 297–302
 report format for, 270–71
 reports, 267
 sales tax, 278–80, 311, 323, 406
 terms of, 270
 transactions using two sales items,
  53–54
 transactions without step-by-step
  instructions, 85–86
 Trial Balance, 101–2, 341–42
 voiding, 65–67, 303–5
 See also Invoice(s)
Sales & Customers preferences, 602
Sales on account, 47–50
Sales by Customer Detail report,
 printing, 86–87
Sales by Item Summary Report,
 318-19
Sales Item List, 46–47, 74–77, 269
Sales receipt, 266, 312–13
Sales supplies, 481–82
Sales Tax Liability Report, 407
Sales Tax Payable Register, 323
Sales Tax Preferences, 603
Save & Close button, 22
Save & New button, 22
Scanner, 2
Search (Windows®), 674
Send Forms preferences, 603
Send icon, 22
Service business
 accounts payable in, 120–21
  graphing by aging period, 178–79
  petty cash account, 154–57
  QuickReport, 139–40, 177
  Vendor Balance Summary,
   176-77
 accounts receivables in, 40
  Customer Balance Detail Report,
   73–74
  depositing checks, 98–100
  graphs for, 102–4
  payments on account, 93–97
  printing A/R reports, 57–59
 end-of-period procedures in,
  189–236
  backup, 235–36
  bank reconciliation, 208–18
  Cash Flow Forecast, 224-26
  closing date for period, 237
  Journal, printing, 233
  Net Income transfer to proprietor
   capital, 229–31

Post-Closing Balance Sheet,
 242–44
Post-Closing Profit and Loss
 Statement, 241–42
Post-Closing Trial Balance,
 240-41
 reporting preference, 223
 Standard Balance Sheet, printing,
  228–29, 231–32
 Standard Profit and Loss
  Statement, 227–28
 Statement of Cash Flows, 225-26
 transactions for previous period,
  237–39
 Trial Balance, 221–23
general accounting in, 189–209
 accrual-basis adjustments,
  196-97
 Balance Sheet, 207–8
 changing name of accounts,
  191–94
 deleting accounts, 195–96
 General Journal, 201–2, 220–21
 inactivating accounts, 194-95
 owner cash investments, 205
 owner noncash investments, 206
 owner withdrawals, 202–5
purchases in, 120–21
sales in, 40
 analysis, 91–93
 cash, 40, 82–84, 98–100
 credit memos, 71–73
 deleting forms, 65–71
 entering sales on account, 47–50
 graphs of, 106–7
 new account, 74–76
 new customer, 77–80
 QuickReport, 90–91
 QuickZoom of item/ customer,
  107–8
 receipts, 82–84, 88–90
 transactions using two sales
  items, 53–54
 Trial Balance, 101–2
 voiding an invoice, 65–67
 training tutorial/procedures, 41
Service Connection preferences, 603
Service Items, 583–85
Session, ending, 35
Set Credits button, 150–51
Set Up method, 77–80, 295
Shift+Tab key combination, 17
Ship icon, 22
Shipping manager, 711–12
Shortcuts, keyboard, 14–16
Sick/vacation hours, 616–17
Software, 4
 application software, 4
 operating system software, 4
Sole proprietorship, 202
Sort Bills text box, 149–50
Spelling check feature, 283
Spelling icon, 22
Spelling preferences, 603
Spin box (Windows®), 677

Standard Balance Sheet, 228-29,
 231-32, 468–69, 472–73
Standard Profit and Loss Statement,
 227–28, 467–68
Start button (Windows®), 673
Start date, 563, 576–77
Statement of Cash Flows, 225-26
Statement Charges, 582
Status area (Windows®), 673
Stopwatch, 700
Storage devices, 3
Summary Balance Sheet, 228, 468
Supplies, 429
System requirements, 6
System software. See Operating
 system software

T
Tab key, 17, 21
Taskbar (Windows®), 673
Taskbar buttons (Windows®), 673
Tax(es), 536–38
 paying sales tax, 408–9
 payroll, 609–11, 615
 sales, 278–80, 311–13, 323, 406–9
Tax forms, 538–437
 Form 940, 543–46
 Form 941 and Schedule B, 538–43
 W-2 and W-3 forms, 546–47
Tax tables, 514
Tax: 1099 preferences, 603
Text box, 21, 677
Time by Job Detail, 705
Time by Job Summary, 705
Time tracking, 700–704
 billable hours, 703–4
 notes for, 699–700
 steps to, 700–703
 timesheets, 701–3
Time Tracking preferences, 604
Time/Cost icon, 22
Timer program, 700
Timesheets, 701–3
Title bar, 9
 in forms, 21
 in Windows®, 675
To Do notes, 696–97
Toolbar, in forms, 22
ToolTip (Windows®), 673
Tracking. See Job cost and tracking;
 Time tracking
Transaction date, 47, 270
Transaction List by Customer, 331
Transaction Reports by Customer, 267
Transactions
 aging of, 102–4
 cleared, 212–13, 219–20
 description of, 162
 editing in Accounts Payable
  Register, 394–95
 entering, 20–21
 from pervious period, 479–80
  accessing, 237–38, 479–80
  editing, 238–39, 480–81
  verifying corrections, 481-82

graphing, 102–4
QuickZoom in, 27
viewing by customer, 97–98
See also Accounts receivables;
   Purchases; Sales
Trial balance, 221–23, 464–66
preparing, 221
printing, 101–2, 222–23, 341-42,
   466
   post-closing, 240–41, 484-85
QuickZoom in, 222
Trial Balance report, 267
Trial version of QuickBooks®,
   716-17
Turn Off Computer, 674

U
Unbilled job-related expenses, 342
Undeposited Funds account, 93, 98,
   266, 311, 324, 332
Undeposited Funds Register, 40
Undo Reconciliation feature, 459–63
Unpaid Bills Detail Report, 397–98
printing, 175–76, 397–98
Unpaid Bills Report, 140–41
Unused credits, 326–27
URL, 732
USB storage, 3

V
Vacation hours, 616–17

Vendor(s)
adding new while recording bill,
   143–45
changing terms for, 381
credit from, 146–48, 382–84
information on, 607–9
modifying records of, 146
QuickReport for, 177
Vendor Balance Reports, printing,
   176–77
Vendor Detail Center, 409–10
Vendor List, 121–22, 358, 360, 607–9
Vendor menu, 13
Vendor navigator, 11
Vendor Not Found dialog box, 143–
   44
Vendor notes, 698–99
Vendor Report, transactions by, 129–
   31
Vendors topic (EasyStep Interview),
   591–92
Verifying an open company, 9, 44
View menu, 12
Visa credit cards, 405–6
Voiding
bills, 409
checks, 162–63, 409
credit card payments, 409
invoices, 65–67
paychecks, 532–34
purchase orders, 409

W
W-2 forms, 11, 515, 546–47
W-3 forms, 515, 546
Web address, 732
Web hosting, 732
Web sites, personalized, 732
Welcome topic (EasyStep Interview),
   563–65
Window menu, 13
Windows®, 4, 672–77
calculator, 30–31
closing or shutting down, 685–86
disk duplication in, 677–80
keyboard shortcuts, 15–16
mouse use in, 677–78
terminology used by, 672–77
Windows® borders, 676
Withdrawals, by owner, 202–5, 423,
   438–41
Withholding, payroll, 609, 611

Y
Year-to-date amounts, adding, 624–29
YTD Comparison Profit and Loss
   Statement, 227, 467

Z
Zip disks, 3
Zoom. *See* QuickZoom

DATA DISK LICENSE AGREEMENT AND LIMITED WARRANTY

READ THIS LICENSE CAREFULLY BEFORE USING THIS PACKAGE. BY USING THIS PACKAGE, YOU ARE AGREEING TO THE TERMS AND CONDITIONS OF THIS LICENSE. IF YOU DO NOT AGREE, DO NOT USE THE PACKAGE. PROMPTLY RETURN THE UNUSED PACKAGE AND ALL ACCOMPANYING ITEMS TO THE PLACE YOU OBTAINED THEM. *THESE TERMS APPLY TO ALL LICENSED SOFTWARE ON THE DISK EXCEPT THAT THE TERMS F.OR USE OF ANY SHAREWARE OR FREEWARE ON THE DISKETTES ARE AS SET FORTH IN THE ELECTRONIC LICENSE LOCATED ON THE DISK:*

1. GRANT OF LICENSE and OWNERSHIP: The enclosed data disk ("Software") is licensed, not sold, to you by Pearson Education, Inc. publishing as Prentice Hall ("We" or the "Company") for academic purposes and in consideration of your purchase or adoption of the accompanying Company textbooks and/or other materials, and your agreement to these terms. This license allows instructors and students enrolled in the course using the Company textbook that accompanies this Software (the "Course") to use, display and manipulate the data for academic use only, so long as you comply with the terms of this Agreement. We reserve any rights not granted to you. You own only the disk(s) but we and our licensors own the Software itself

2. RESTRICTIONS ON USE AND TRANSFER: You may <u>not</u> transfer, distribute or make available the Software or the Documentation, except to instructors and students in your school in connection with the Course. You may <u>not</u> reverse engineer, disassemble, decompile, modify, adapt, translate or create derivative works based on the Software or the Documentation. You may be held legally responsible for any copying or copyright infringement that is caused by your failure to abide by the terms of these restrictions.

3. TERMINATION: This license is effective until terminated. This license will terminate automatically without notice from the Company if you fail to comply with any provisions or limitations of this license. Upon termination, you shall destroy the Documentation and all copies of the Software. All provisions of this Agreement as to limitation and disclaimer of warranties, limitation of liability, remedies or damages, and our ownership rights shall survive termination.

4. DISCLAIMER OF WARRANTY: THE COMPANY AND ITS LICENSORS MAKE NO WARRANTIES ABOUT THE SOFTWARE, WHICH IS PROVIDED "AS-IS." IF THE DISK IS DEFECTIVE IN MATERIALS OR WORKMANSHIP, YOUR ONLY REMEDY IS TO RETURN IT TO THE COMPANY WITHIN 30 DAYS FOR REPLACEMENT UNLESS THE COMPANY DETERMINES IN GOOD FAITH THAT THE DISK HAS BEEN MISUSED OR IMPROPERLY INSTALLED, REPAIRED, ALTERED OR DAMAGED. THE COMPANY DISCLAIMS ALL WARRANTIES, EXPRESS OR IMPLIED, INCLUDING WITHOUT LIMITATION, THE IMPLIED WARRANTIES OF MERCHANTABILITY AND FITNESS FOR A PARTICULAR PURPOSE. THE COMPANY DOES NOT WARRANT, GUARANTEE OR MAKE ANY REPRESENTATION REGARDING THE ACCURACY, RELIABILITY, CURRENTNESS, USE, OR RESULTS OF USE, OF THE SOFTWARE.

5. LIMITATION OF REMEDIES AND DAMAGES: IN NO EVENT, SHALL THE COMPANY OR ITS EMPLOYEES, AGENTS, LICENSORS OR CONTRACTORS BE LIABLE FOR ANY INCIDENTAL, INDIRECT, SPECIAL OR CONSEQUENTIAL DAMAGES ARISING OUT OF OR IN CONNECTION WITH THIS LICENSE OR THE SOFTWARE, INCLUDING, WITHOUT LIMITATION, LOSS OF USE, LOSS OF DATA, LOSS OF INCOME OR PROFIT, OR OTHER LOSSES SUSTAINED AS A RESULT OF INJURY TO ANY PERSON, OR LOSS OF OR DAMAGE TO PROPERTY, OR CLAIMS OF THIRD PARTIES, EVEN IF THE COMPANY OR AN AUTHORIZED REPRESENTATIVE OF THE COMPANY HAS BEEN ADVISED OF THE POSSIBILITY OF SUCH DAMAGES. SOME JURISDICTIONS DO NOT ALLOW THE LIMITATION OF DAMAGES IN CERTAIN CIRCUMSTANCES, SO THE ABOVE LIMITATIONS MAY NOT ALWAYS APPLY.

6. GENERAL: THIS AGREEMENT SHALL BE CONSTRUED IN ACCORDANCE WITH THE LAWS OF THE UNITED STATES OF AMERICA AND THE STATE OF NEW YORK, APPLICABLE TO CONTRACTS MADE IN NEW YORK, AND SHALL BENEFIT THE COMPANY, ITS AFFILIATES AND ASSIGNEES. This Agreement is the complete and exclusive statement of the agreement between you and the Company and supersedes all proposals, prior agreements, oral or written, and any other communications between you and the company or any of its representatives relating to the subject matter. If you are a U.S. Government user, this Software is licensed with "restricted rights" as set forth in subparagraphs (a)-(d) of the Commercial Computer-Restricted Rights clause at FAR 52.227-19 or in subparagraphs (c)(1)(ii) of the Rights in Technical Data and Computer Software clause at DFARS 252.227-7013, and similar clauses, as applicable.

Should you have any questions concerning this agreement or if you wish to contact the Company for any reason, please contact in writing: Director, Media Production
Pearson Education/Prentice Hall
1 Lake Street
Upper Saddle River, New Jersey 07458